DOING SOCIOLOGY

Also by Lee Harvey

Critical Social Research
Myths of the Chicago School

DOING SOCIOLOGY

A practical introduction

Lee Harvey and

Morag MacDonald

MACMILLAN

First published 1993 by
MACMILLAN PRESS LTD
Houndmills, Basingstoke, Hampshire RG21 6XS
and London
Companies and representatives
throughout the world

ISBN 0–333–55082–X

A catalogue record for this book is available
from the British Library.

11   10   9   8   7   6   5   4
03   02   01   00   99   98   97   96

Printed in Hong Kong

CONTENTS

PREFACE

This book is a practical introduction to sociology. It provides an introduction to the discipline through a student-oriented activity approach. It relates sociological theorising to research practice and draws out the interrelationship between method, theory and social philosophy. It is designed to draw the user into the complexities of sociology through an approach which locates sociological theorising in everyday activities.

Doing Sociology is also unique among introductory sociology books in taking a clear 'race', class and gender perspective. It also identifies *three* alternative philosophical perspectives: positivist, phenomenological and critical.

Doing Sociology is a resource for sociology students who intend to undertake practical project work or small scale social research. Practical work serves two broad purposes on sociology courses. First, it is used to consolidate theoretical aspects of a course and as a vehicle for teaching and learning methodology. In this case the project tends to come near the end of the course. This is currently the main approach in most A level courses and most traditional undergraduate degrees. Second, practical work is integral to courses that adopt a student-centred approach. In such courses, from the outset, learning is by doing. Methodology is thus the pivot around which students develop an understanding of sociology. This approach is more popular on Access courses and introductory undergraduate courses. It is also being slowly adopted at A level in the wake of similar innovations in GCSE.

Doing Sociology is principally aimed at A level and Access students. However, each chapter takes the subject matter and level of analysis just a little further than current A level. This is done for three reasons. First, the shift towards projects and a more central role for methodology means, inevitably, that A level students will need to become more informed about methodological issues to an extent greater than required by current A level syllabuses. Second, A levels are likely to change in emphasis soon. In the light of the proposed shift to a mixture of A and AS level study, A levels will focus more on understanding than content. Third, courses for Access students have traditionally had more emphasis on project work and tend to be more methodologically sophisticated than standard A level sociology.

Pushing the limits, then, makes this book also suitable for introductory year degree students especially where old 'chalk and talk' methods courses are being replaced by student-centred project-based methodology courses. The high level of student activity in the book and the suggestions for project work make this book applicable to a wide variety of students because the suggested activities can be developed to a level that reflects the student's abilities and meets the criteria of whatever course they are on. Indeed, the material in the book has also been used successfully with second and final year degree students and students on taught post-graduate courses. Clearly, the way that the material is adapted, the degree of theoretical sophistication and the exhaustiveness of the analysis will vary considerably depending on the level at which the student is operating. It is, for example, just as reasonable, in principle, to ask an A level student to explore changes in inequalities in health as it is a postgraduate student.

Finally, because of its emphasis on doing small-scale research, *Doing Sociology* will also be of use for the growing number of people whose work in areas such as health, social services, local authorities, education, community work and business is increasingly involving them in social research.

ACKNOWLEDGEMENTS

The authors and publishers wish to thank the following who have kindly given of copyright material: Association for Education in Journalism and Mass Communication for material from 'TV Beauty Ads and Role Expectations of Adolescent Female Viewers', *Journalism Quarterly*, vol. 56, no. 2, pp. 283–88; Birmingham Evening Mail for material from their 11 January 1990 issue; British Sociological Association for material from BSA Guidelines on Anti-Sexist Language and their Statement of Ethical Practice, 1991; The Controller of Her Majesty's Stationery Office for Crown copyright material from *Social Trends 12*, *19* and *20*; International Thomson Business Publishing for material from *Broadcast*, 12 October 1990; IPC Magazines Ltd for a picture from *Oh Boy Monthly*, February, 1990; John Libbey & Company Ltd for material from *Violence in Television: What the Viewers Think* by Gunther and Wober, 1988; Marvel Comics Ltd for strip cartoon, 'The Sylvanian Families'; Unemployment Unit for material from *Unemployment Bulletin*, 32, Spring 1990, p. 3; Michael Filby for material from his betting shop research field notes; Anne Devany for material from her interviews with young Asian women; and David Cooper for the cartoons.

Every effort has been made to trace all the copyright holders but if any have been inadvertently overlooked the publishers will be pleased to make the necessary arrangement at the first opportunity.

The authors would like to take this opportunity to thank the following for their help, encouragement or support: Michael Filby, Jane O'Brien, Jenny O'Connor, David Lea, Michael Little, Brian Poultney and Nick Stanley. Thanks especially to Sue Niebrzydowski, Martin Huggins, Pat McNeill, Martin Marcus and several anonymous reviewers for reading and commenting on earlier drafts. Thanks too, to the editorial and production team at Macmillan who have been involved with the making of this book: Steven Kennedy, Dilys Jones, Tom Ruppel, Stephen Rutt, Frances Arnold, Tim Fox; and Keith Povey for proof reading the final drafts.

CHAPTER 1
INTRODUCTION

This book is called *Doing Sociology* because it shows you how to use project work to develop your sociological understanding. It is organised around the main approaches to data collection: social surveys, observation, in-depth interviews, secondary data analysis and experimentation. *Doing Sociology* is thus about how to do sociological research. It takes a realistic view about what can be achieved in an introductory sociology project.

Although showing you how to do research, *Doing Sociology* is unlike other methods books. *Doing Sociology* not only explores methods of data collection but also sees your project as a whole, linking theory to data.

Doing Sociology is a *methodology* book, not just a 'methods' book. It shows you, through examples, how to relate theory to practice. It also goes further and examines the philosophy underlying different approaches to sociological research. The book emphasises student activity. Each chapter contains a number of suggested activities and ends with a list of possible research topics. The student activities are designed to help you get to grips with different aspects of doing sociology. Some of them could be expanded into full projects. In all, there are over one hundred suggested student activities throughout the book. It is unlikely that you will have the time to attempt them all. The way you tackle them will depend on how you are using the book.

How to use the book

If you are doing project work in the later stages of a course you may have decided on the method or methods that you are going to use. You may thus be using *Doing Sociology* as a guide to carrying out the research. If this is the case, it would be an idea to work through the relevant chapters and do as many suggested activities as you can. On the other hand, you may not be sure what doing a project involves, or may not have much idea about research methodology. In which case, you should work through the book trying some of the different research activities that occur early in each chapter and gradually getting a feel for practical sociological enquiry. You can focus on a particular method once you have decided what sort of project you want to do.

Alternatively, you may be using *Doing Sociology* as part of a student-centred learning approach. In this case you should read the book chapter by chapter and attempt as many of the activities as are feasible in the time you have available. (Those activities that are time-consuming and which you may want to omit are indicated in the text.) You should also follow up the theoretical issues that are identified in the theory boxes.

Either way, we suggest that after this introduction you start by reading Chapter 2, whether or not you intend to do any media research. Chapter 2 uses the media, which we all know something about, to provide a general introduction to *doing* sociology.

Method and methodology

We use media research to illustrate the difference between method and methodology. Method refers to the techniques of *empirical data* collection and we show how mass media researchers have used a variety of techniques. These are then examined in detail in the following chapters. Methodology refers to the research approach and includes the philosophical and theoretical perspectives of the researcher. We identify and use three distinct methodological approaches throughout the book. These are the *positivist*, which focuses on causes; the *phenomenological* or interpretive, which focuses on meanings; and the *critical*, which focuses on oppressive structures. The differences are explored in detail in Chapter 2.

Theory and method

In Chapter 2 we also consider the problem of relating theory to method. We suggest that this problem arises when researchers start by collecting empirical material and then try to relate it to theory. This so-called *method-led* research tends to be descriptive and non-theoretical. What we suggest is a *methodological* approach that asks theoretical questions, relates these to a broad approach (positivist, phenomenological or critical) and then works out which are the most appropriate ways of collecting and analysing empirical data. As you will see, the same method can be adopted by different approaches. We use the example of the way that gender is portrayed in the media to illustrate the methodological approach. We do this by relating the way women and girls are shown on television and in newspapers and comics (the media content) to sociological theories of patriarchy and socialisation.

The intention of the book is to enable you to undertake your own research. So we do not just report research that has been done and published by other sociologists but also use original material to show how you can do your own research.

Although we see methodology as the coming together of method and theory, *Doing Sociology* is not a comprehensive guide to theory. However, to ensure the book is self-contained we have provided explanations of all the key concepts and theories to which we refer. We look at theoretical issues as they arise in our examples. When presenting and interpreting research evidence we do not usually offer an exhaustive variety of interpretations or address a number of theoretical alternatives. To do so would make the text overly long and shift the emphasis away from the practice of empirical sociological enquiry. Usually our findings are interpreted from a single point of view. However, we make it clear that this is just one approach and not the only approach to the data or theoretical issue. We invite you to develop alternative interpretations and suggest different emphases you might pursue. We signpost some major theoretical issues but leave you to explore them in more detail.

Each chapter has suggested further reading, with the emphasis being on recent texts. Some older methods books and some 'classic' studies are suggested. There are a lot of suggested further readings. These are for reference purposes; we do not expect that you will have the time to consult many texts. We provide several suggestions under each heading with the

EMPIRICAL DATA is based on observation of the world. It refers to things that can be seen (or heard, touched, smelt or tasted). In relation to the social world this may be objects or actions. Empirical data is thus all those things that are going on in the world that we are directly aware of or we accept that someone else has experienced.

We make sense of empirical data through our theories about the social world. Conversely, empirical data is also used in order to make theories more concrete. Empirical data is also used to assess the appropriateness of theory.

NOTE All the concepts used in this book can be found on an electronic text data base of DEFINITIONS available from Lee Harvey. Details can be found on page 268

hope that you may be able to locate one of them. The full set of references in alphabetical order is at the end of the book.

Information technology

New computerised technology plays an increasing part in our everyday lives. These days all of us come into contact with applications of new technology including computerised check-outs in supermarkets, bank cash withdrawal machines, computerised bills, and so on. We have therefore included occasional references and information about using computers in sociology and would urge you to make use of information technology while doing sociology. There are a number of reasons for this. First, if you obtain information technology skills it will enhance your future employment or further education prospects. Second, being able to use information technology increases the amount of knowledge and information you will be able to access. Third, for a variety of reasons, women are disproportionately excluded from access to information technology. Sociology, as a discipline that attracts large numbers of women, should aim to redress this imbalance. Doing sociology gives you the opportunity of making use of new technology. Fourth, information technology makes doing sociology so much easier. You can use a microcomputer to prepare questionnaires, store quantitative or qualitative data, analyse data, prepare charts and graphs, write up the research, and produce well laid out printed reports. Being able to use a microcomputer is not essential for doing sociology but it saves a lot of time and effort.

There are software packages specifically designed for the analysis of both quantitative and qualitative data. These will be referred to in Chapters 4 and 6. Word-processing, computerised graphics and desk-top publishing packages are getting increasingly sophisticated while also becoming cheaper and easier to use. As there are many different packages and different makes of personal computer we will not usually discuss specific software or hardware. Instead you should make use of your own computer or those provided by your school or college.

The research process

The book is designed to give you specific help in developing research practice and each chapter deals with specific approaches in detail. There are, however, some general things about doing sociological research that you need to bear in mind whatever technique you are using.

Feasibility
It is important when doing a research project that you do not attempt to do too much. There is tendency to overestimate how much you can do in the available time.

New researchers also tend to think that they will be able to gain access to more or less any area that they want to research. This is not so. You might, for example, think it would be interesting to do research into youth custody centres. No doubt it would, but you are extremely unlikely to obtain clearance from the Home Office to get access to a detention centre to do the research. Even if you got clearance it would take a long time, involve a

Extract 1.1

ETHICAL GUIDELINES

The guidelines point to a set of obligations to which members should normally adhere as principles for guiding conduct. Any departure from the principles should be the result of deliberation, not ignorance. The guidelines are meant to inform members' ethical judgements rather than to impose a set of external standards on them.

Professional integrity
Members have a responsibility to
1. *safeguard* the proper interests of those people affected by their work.
2. report their findings *accurately* and *truthfully*.
3. consider the *effects* of their involvement and the consequences of their work or its misuse for those they study and other interested parties.
4. recognize the boundaries of their professional *competence* and not accept work they are not qualified to carry out.
5. avoid claiming *expertise* where they have none.
6. ensure they have regard for *reputation* of the discipline when dealing with the media.
7. satisfy themselves that the research they undertake is *worthwhile*.
8. use *appropriate techniques*.

Relations with and responsibilities towards research participants
Sociologists, when they do research, enter into personal and moral relationships with those they study, be they individuals, households or corporate entities. Although committed to the advancement of knowledge, sociologists should be aware that that goal, in itself, does not provide an entitlement to override the rights of others. Members should, therefore,
1. satisfy themselves that a study is *necessary* for the furtherance of knowledge.
2. be aware that they have some *responsibility* for the use to which their research may be put.
3. avoid actions which may have deleterious consequences for sociologists who come after them or which might undermine the reputation of sociology as a discipline.

Relationships with research participants
Sociologists should strive to:
1. ensure that the physical, social and psychological *well-being* of research participants is not adversely affected by research.
2. protect the *rights* of those they study (including their interests, sensitivities and privacy).
3. *balance* conflicting interests.
4. ensure a relationship of *trust* (with powerless as well as more powerful research subjects).
5. obtain the *consent* of those studied.
6. explain as fully as possible what the research is *about*.
7. explain who is *financing* the research.
8. explain *why* it is being undertaken.
9. explain how the results will be *disseminated*.
10. ensure that participants are aware of their *right to refuse* to participate.
11. indicate to what extent participants will be afforded *anonymity* and *confidentiality*.
12. ensure that respondents can reject the use of data-gathering devices such as *tape-recorders* and *video cameras*.
13. ensure that films or recordings are *not shown* to people other than those to whom the participants have agreed.
14. *renegotiate* consent during the course of the research (especially in long-term fieldwork studies).
15. be careful not to *jeopardise* the relationship between *gate-keepers* and *participants*.
16. *anticipate any harmful effects* on the participants as a consequence of the research and take steps to guard against them (having consent does not absolve researchers from responsibility).
17. *minimise the disturbance* on the participants that results from the research process.
18. be particularly careful where research participants are *vulnerable* because of their age, social status or powerlessness.
19. avoid *intruding* on the personal space of the ill, very young or elderly and frail (and where suitable use informants or intermediaries to provide the data).

Covert research
There are serious ethical dangers in the use of covert (or secret) research but in some circumstances covert methods may avoid certain problems. Covert methods violate the principles of informed consent and may invade the privacy of those being studied. Participant or non-participant observation in non-public spaces or experimental manipulation of participants without their knowledge should be resorted to only where it is impossible to use other methods to obtain *essential* data. Inexperienced researchers are *strongly advised* to avoid covert research.
Covert researchers should:
1. *safeguard* the anonymity of research participants;
2. ideally *obtain consent* to the research after it has been concluded (prior to publication).

Anonymity, privacy and confidentiality
Social researchers should:
1. *respect* the *anonymity* and privacy of research participants.
2. keep *personal* information concerning research participants *confidential*.
3. decide whether it is necessary or appropriate to *record* personal data.
4. *anticipate threats* to confidentiality and anonymity.
5. store data in a *secure* manner.
6. be aware of obligations under the *Data Protection Act*.
7. use *pseudonyms* or other technical means to break the link between identifiable individuals and the data
8. *advise* participants who may be identifiable from a combination of factors that are unique to them that it may not be possible to completely conceal their identity.
9. ensure that research *colleagues* also respect guarantees of confidentiality and anonymity.
10. be aware that research data given in confidence do not enjoy *legal privilege* (i.e., they may be liable to subpoena by a court).
11. honour guarantees unless there are *clear and compelling* grounds not to do so.

Adapted from British Sociological Association 'Statement of Ethical Practice' (1991). The full document and the associated 'Guidelines for Good Professional Practice' (1991) are available from the BSA.

considerable amount of bureaucratic paperwork and, on top of that, you would be expected to sign the Official Secrets Act, which would limit what you could report. In short, you need to be realistic about what you can research. If you do not have much time (less than a year) you should stick to areas to which you already have some access or where access is easily gained.

Ethics

There are also ethical considerations to be borne in mind when undertaking research. Ethical issues are complicated and there are few hard and fast rules. However, we would suggest that, as someone new to research, you always consider the well-being of the people you are researching and never abuse their trust. You should consult the ethical guidelines produced by the British Sociological Association, before setting out on your research, for detailed suggestions of what might or might not be considered acceptable practice. The main points are summarised in Extract 1.1.

You should always discuss your research project with your tutor before you start. Your tutor will provide you with guidance on whom and what to consult, the feasibility of your proposal and the likely problems you will meet when collecting data. Under no circumstances should you send out questionnaires, interview people, do participant observation or conduct experiments before you have discussed with your tutor what you intend to do.

Background

Students new to research sometimes have big ideas about how they can change social theory as a result of their research. You are unlikely to do this but your research project should greatly improve your own theoretical understanding. New researchers also tend to underestimate how much research and theoretical writing already exists in the areas in which they are interested. You should, thus, spend time tracking down and getting acquainted with the theoretical and empirical research that has already been done.

Referencing

Keep a card or electronic database reference of every thing you read. Ensure that the reference is complete (see Extract 1.2). Get into the habit of keeping references in this format and make notes as you go along as it is very time-consuming to have to go back to sources afterwards. When making notes on reading ensure that you put the reference on the front page of the notes and when writing out quotes, ensure that you note the page number. Also, make sure that you date everything. Put a date on completed interview schedules, the date you got a mailed questionnaire back, put the date on every page of field notes you write, date video and tape recordings and newspaper cuttings. This will help when you are sorting things out at the analysis stage.

Planning and timing

It is important that you plan the research carefully. You should have a specific focus to the research, especially if you have a limited time in which to do it. As far as possible, have a clearly stated aim and make sure that the data collection, analysis and reporting of your research relate to it. Timing is crucial and we suggest that you should think of a research project as made

---

Extract 1.2

REFERENCING

It is important that you record and report references systematically and consistently. The following is an example based on the method used in this book. Slight variations occur from publication to publication, for example, some authors underline or use italics rather than bold type for the title of the publication.

A reference to a book should include the author(s), including initials, the date of publication, the book title in full, place of publication and publisher. For example,

> Abel-Smith, B. and Townsend, P., 1965, **The Poor and the Poorest**. London, Bell.

A reference to an edited book (sometimes called 'A Reader') should include the editor(s)' name(s), including initials, the abbreviation 'ed.' (or 'eds.') the date of publication, the book title in full, place of publication and publisher. For example,

> Clarke, J., Critcher, C. and Johnson, R., eds., 1980, **Working Class Culture: Studies in History and Theory**. London, Hutchinson.

(**Note** some authors place 'ed.' in brackets.)

A reference to an article in a journal should list the author(s), date of publication, title of the article, the name of the journal, and the pages on which the article appears. For example,

> Atkinson, J. M., 1968, 'On the sociology of suicide', **Sociological Review**, 16, pp. 83–92.

A reference to an article in an edited book requires the names of the author(s), the date, the title of the article, the editor(s) of the book, the title of the book, the page numbers on which it occurs in the book, the place of publication and the publisher. For example,

> Cartwright, A. and O'Brien, M., 1976, 'Social class variations in health care and in general practitioner consultations', in Stacey, M. (ed.), 1976, **The Sociology of the NHS**, Sociological Review Monograph no. 22, University of Keele.

(**Note** that only the first word, and any proper noun, in an article title begins with an upper case letter.)

up of three, approximately equal, time periods:
1. planning (including preparation and background);
2. data collection;
3. analysis and write-up.

So, for example, if you have six-months to do a project you should spend the first two months planning the research, the next two collecting data and the last two analysing the data and writing up.

It is very tempting, if you are doing a six month project, to think that you only need a couple of weeks to plan what you are going to do and then you can get on with the data collection. Researchers also underestimate how long it takes to analyse data and write up a report. New researchers tend to think that it will only take a couple of weeks to write the report and are thus tempted to carry on with the data collection for far too long. It is important that you decide in advance what your data collection deadline is and then stick to it. Do not be tempted to collect just a little more data, or wait for a few more questionnaires to come back, or just go and talk to a couple of other informants. You will need every day of the analysis and write-up time.

In Chapter 8 we provide a detailed breakdown of these stages. You may want to familiarise yourself with different methodological approaches before considering the step by step details. In practice, of course, very few professional research projects make a thorough job of every stage of the research process, so you are not likely to as a student doing a project. There is a big gap between knowing what you ought to do and having the time and resources to be able to do it. This is why we have put the detailed breakdown in the concluding chapter, rather than overwhelm you with it at this stage. When doing a project the important thing is to do what you can and make the most of it.

Disasters

Never forget that the 'best laid plans' can backfire. This book describes how to do research but there is no way that it can possibly document all the ways in which things can go wrong. No research project goes smoothly from start to finish, as the various accounts of the research process testify (Hammond, 1964; Bell and Newby, 1977; Bell and Encel, 1978; Roberts, 1981).

So do not get disheartened when your questionnaire gets printed with the pages in the wrong order, you get no answer to your letters, your respondent isn't in when you call, the meeting you have gone to observe is cancelled, the video recorder is set to the wrong channel, or the tape recorder jams after five minutes of an hour-long in-depth interview. Don't despair when you can't find the books and articles that are 'vital' for your background research, or there are never any computers free when you have time to use one. Don't scream with frustration when you realise that you have incorrectly coded half your data or you get in a muddle when you try to work out the statistics you need. Don't get suicidal when you accidentally erase the floppy disk on which you have just saved the final version of your report.

Make the best of what you have been able to do. Write up a report, however little data you end up with. Document the problems and limitations as well as the successes. Keep a research diary to record the research process. Make a note of your ideas as the research proceeds and record the ups and downs of your work. A research project is a learning experience. No one expects you to come up with stunning new revelations. So, when writing up your research show what you have learned. In particular, show how what you have found out relates to social theory.

Epistemology

EPISTEMOLOGY means the theory of the nature of knowledge. Epistemology is thus about *knowing*. Epistemological statements are statements about what we accept as knowledge.

We have defined three epistemological positions that can be found in sociological research. These are *positivism, phenomenology* and *critical* approaches.

For example, suppose you were researching domestic violence. As a *positivist* you would want to identify the *causes* of domestic violence (such as money problems, drunkenness, unemployment, and so on). The presumption is that appropriate knowledge in such circumstances would be an *explanation* that would allow you to *predict* the likely occurrence of domestic violence and thus be able to intervene to stop it.

As a *phenomenologist* you might want to try and get some idea of what the people involved in domestic violence make of it. Do they regard it as normal? Do they think of it as wrong but cannot get out of violent situations? In short, you may want to try and grasp the *meaning* that domestic violence has for the people involved. Only then can you begin to understand how and why people get mixed up in it. You are not interested in causes that fail to take account of what people think.

As a *critical* sociologist you want to understand domestic violence as part of a wider process of oppression. A *feminist* approach to critical social research would see domestic violence as part of *patriarchal control of women* and would thus look at how 'wife battering' is a rarely reported crime, with even fewer convictions. Such an approach might look at how the police avoid being involved in 'domestic' incidents that involve violence. How patriarchal ideology condones the dominance of men over women. How women's primary role is seen as being within the home caring for the family, and so on. In short, a feminist critical approach would set domestic violence within a broader framework in which men have power over women.

For critical social researchers, specific *causes* of domestic violence such as 'poverty' or 'drugs' only conceal the real *structural* processes by which women are oppressed by men. Similarly, trying to understand the *meanings* of domestic violence only partly deals with the issue. Why is it, for example, that women feel that *they* are the problem if they are attacked violently by their husbands. For critical social researchers, it is only when these feelings are related to the wider ideology that supports male dominance that they make sense.

Doing sociology involves three interrelated aspects. First, you need to look at the *theoretical* issues surrounding your particular area of enquiry. Second, you need to consider different *techniques* for data collection. Third, you need to think about the *kind of knowledge* you are producing. This last aspect is known as *epistemology*. As this is a slightly complex idea we will say a little more about it.

Epistemology means the theory of the nature of knowledge. Put another way, epistemology is concerned with what does and does not count as knowledge. Without going into a detailed philosophical discussion we will outline the epistemological *perspectives* that underlie the three main approaches to social research.

Positivism

Our taken-for-granted view of scientific knowledge is that science should be able to *explain* the world in terms of what *causes* the things and events that we observe. In other words, this view of knowledge assumes that we only know about something if we can explain what caused it. This epistemological perspective is usually known as *positivism*. The notion of cause and effect is thus at the heart of positivist methodology.

Phenomenology

However, this is not the only way of knowing. There are other views of what constitutes knowledge in the social world. Another epistemological perspective is that we know social processes if we can *interpret* what they *mean*. People are not things, they think and reflect on what they do. The social world has meaning for social actors. Thus, to know the social world, it is necessary to discover these meanings. This epistemological perspective is usually known as phenomenology. Phenomenological methodology is thus more concerned with interpreting the world than explaining it.

Critical

A third epistemological perspective argues that while it is important to see the social world as made up of reflective people it is also important to remember that they are constrained in what they do and how they think. To know the world we must look at how people are limited in what they do and think by the nature of the social world in which they live. To know the world we thus have to relate observable social phenomena to the wider *social context*. We can only know what something means if we understand how it has come about historically or how it relates to social structures.

For example, to understand a strike, it is necessary to do more than look for the cause of the strike or to explore the meanings of those on strike. It is necessary to relate the strike to the history of industrial relations, employment prospects, government policy, legal constraints, media campaigns and so on.

Marxists, for example, see the constraints on people as a result of class oppression which results from the capitalist process of production. The majority of people under capitalism are exploited as workers and the social structure, through the courts, school, media and so on, ensure that this system is maintained and seen as natural. The resulting capitalist knowledge is thus a distorted view of reality. To really know about the world we have to *dig beneath the surface* and reveal what is really going on. Real knowledge for Marxists is that which reveals how people are oppressed by the processes of class-based social production.

Feminists adopt a similar approach, arguing that positivist 'scientific' knowledge is essentially male knowledge and it is used to oppress women. Anti-racists similarly see 'scientific' knowledge as white knowledge that serves to oppress black people.

Marxists, feminists and anti-racists are all *critical* of existing knowledge, arguing that it supports oppression of one sort or another. To know the world it is necessary to break down taken-for-granted knowledge of the social world to see how it really works, then to build an alternative understanding.

The examination of media research in Chapter 2 outlines what is involved in the three different methodological approaches (positivist, phenomenological and critical) and provides examples of them.

Identifying approaches

We have identified three broad *epistemological approaches*, positivist, phenomenological and critical. Within each of these it is possible to identify a variety of *sociological perspectives* (or general sociological orientations as they are also known). Each of these involves a general theory of society or of social processes. Each sociological perspective develops particular *theories* about specific areas of sociology. These theories are investigated using particular *methods*. For example, in Chapter 2, we show that *reinforcement theory* of the media depends on the general *perspective* known as behaviourism which involves a *positivist approach* that assumes the media reinforces behaviour and that experiments provide a *method* for investigating this.

> **Student Activity 1.1**
> **From the following list of nine items, identify the three sociological perspectives, the three sociological theories and the three social research methods:**
> **functionalism, labelling theory, feminism, in-depth interviewing, participant observation, race relations cycle, sociobiology, experiments, patriarchy.**

However, it is important to note that sociological theories cannot be fitted neatly into a set of pigeon holes. Sociology is far too varied and dynamic for any way of classifying it to be universally agreed or to have long-term validity. What we offer here is a way of organising sociology that works for us from the point of view of *doing sociology*.

We take the central epistemological feature (cause, meaning or critique) as the basis for organising our overview of sociology. Into this, various perspectives and particular theories can be located, depending on whether they are primarily concerned with *causal explanations* or *subjects' meanings* or *structural analysis*.

The *positivist* approach, looking for causal explanations, is widely used in sociology. It takes various forms. These range from attempts to provide causal laws, through identifying possible causal factors, to testing theoretical

NOTE ON TERMINOLOGY The terms phenomenology and interactionism can lead to a great deal of confusion because they are used in different ways.

Phenomenology is a philosophical perspective that basically argues that we cannot take appearances for granted. Phenomenology covers the work of a wide range of philosophers and it is argued that there is very little in common between them other than a sceptical view of positivism.

A *phenomenological approach* to sociology concentrates on social meanings rather than causes. It is concerned with what sense people make of the world rather than what the world appears to be.

Phenomenological sociology is a term given to a social perspective within the broad phenomenological approach. This view focuses on the everyday activities and routines that people adopt in making sense of the world. It is very similar to *ethnomethodology* (see page 42 for more details). There is also a variant of phenomenological sociology called *reflexive sociology*.

Interactionism is a sociological perspective, developed in the early years of sociology, that attempts to combine social psychology with social theory. It attempts to take account of individual actions and attitudes when constructing causal explanations at a *social level* (see page 165 for more details). We call this *traditional interactionism*. It is similar to Weber's *Verstehen sociology*. They both attempt to link meanings with causes. In our classification they appear to be both positivist and phenomenological. Throughout the book we tend to refer to both of them as phenomenological because of their concern with meaning. However, you should not forget their attempt to fit this into a more conventional 'scientific' approach that seeks out causes.

Interactionism is also used in a different sense to refer to any approach that analyses the details of social interaction. Interactionism has thus been applied to all theories of face-to-face and small group interaction irrespective of whether there is any attempt to develop causal explanations. This usage follows from the development of *symbolic interactionism* in the mid 1930s. Interactionism, in this sense, also usually includes *phenomenological sociology* and *ethnomethodology* as well as the various different approaches to *symbolic interactionism*.

Table 1.1 Summary of the three epistemological approaches

	Positivism	Phenomenology	Critical
Knowledge via	Explanation	Interpretation	Understanding
Seeking out	Causes	Meanings	Structural relationships
Type of 'data'	Social facts	Social interactions	Historical, structural, ideological
Analytic approach	Scientific method	Direct involvement	Dialectical

statements against observable evidence. The approach is usually regarded as based on the work of Emile Durkheim (1897). It can be found in sociological perspectives such as *functionalism, behaviourism, sociobiology* and *social ecology.* (We will explore the different sociological perspectives in relation to particular issues throughout the book.) Positivist methodology is considered in detail in Chapter 4 when we look at social surveys. This is the preferred, but by no means the only, method used by positivists.

The *phenomenological* approach, investigating meanings, also takes a wide variety of forms. There are two broad strands. First, the *interpretive*, which draws on the work of Max Weber (1947, 1963, 1969) and usually takes a wide social or historical view (this also referred to as Weberian or *Verstehen* sociology). Second is the *interactionist*, which focuses on social interaction, particularly face-to-face or small group interaction. This strand includes *symbolic interactionism, reflexive sociology, ethnomethodology* and *phenomenological sociology.*

The *critical* approach, critiquing the oppressive nature of social structures, includes *Marxist, feminist* and *anti-racist* perspectives. There are a number of variations within each of these, often with major disagreements over theory.

The three approaches are summarised in Table 1.1. It must be remembered that this is not a definitive model, but one that we use to help address methodological questions. Nor should practitioners be seen to fall neatly into one of the three approaches. It is individual research studies rather than the entire work of an individual that can be categorised in terms of research approach. For example, Durkheim is often regarded as the 'founder' of positivist sociology. His account of the *Rules of Sociological Method* and his work on *Suicide* and the *Division of Labour* reflect positivist concerns with identifying causes. However, there is an argument that Durkheim's work is far more critical than anyone has given him credit for (Pearce, 1989). Furthermore, in his later work on religion, *Elements of Religious Life*, he abandons cause and effect and adopts a phenomenological approach.

Class, 'race' and gender

We attempt to integrate aspects of class, 'race' and gender into the discussions of sociological concepts and theory throughout the book. Sometimes one or other area will be highlighted but we intend to show how class, 'race' and gender are all integral to the analysis of society.

However, it seems appropriate, from the outset, to outline the main approaches to class, gender and 'race' so as to avoid undue repetition later in the book. You may want to read the rest of this chapter at this point to get a basic theoretical appreciation of class, 'race' and gender. Or you may want to go on to Chapter 2 and subsequent chapters and refer back to this theoretical outline as and when the issues are raised. We have use cross-referencing throughout the book to help you refer back at appropriate points.

Class

Most sociological analyses of class derive from the idea of class developed by Karl Marx in his analysis of capitalism (Marx and Engels, 1887). Marx argued that industrial society was characterised by two classes: the *bourgeoisie*, who owned the *means of production* (factories, machinery and so on); and the *proletariat*, the workers who worked for a wage. The bourgeoisie exploit the working class and the two are in constant conflict. The exploitation and oppression of the working class leads to the development of *class consciousness* and eventually a revolution in which the working class overthrow capitalism and take control of the means of production. We shall look at Marx's theory in more detail after we have considered positivist and phenomenological approaches to class.

Positivist approaches to class

Positivists tend to have an ambiguous view of class. The two main positivist approaches to class are to be found in *Durkheim's theory of society* and in *functionalism*. They see society as a unified whole. Conflict is seen as a temporary aberration disrupting the social consensus. Social class is not seen as divisive, as Marx suggests, but as a way of organising different kinds of social *role*. For example, the middle classes include managers, administrators and intellectuals while the lower classes include service and production workers.

Although positivists have attempted to define and measure class (for example, Hollingshead, 1957; Hollingshead and Redlich, 1958; Duncan, 1961) the predominant approach is to use occupational classification (such as the Registrar General's Classification of Occupation) as an indicator of a social class. This approach ignores all the other aspects of social class and reduces class to *occupational role*. Such an approach derives from Durkheim's work (Durkheim, 1895, 1897, 1947).

Durkheim's analysis of industrial society

Durkheim argued that the key difference between pre-industrialised and industrialised societies was the *division of labour*. He argued that pre-industrial society was characterised by social solidarity and by shared beliefs and values because people, on the whole, shared the same roles. There was

---

THE MEANS OF PRODUCTION refers to the way commodities are produced. In capitalism, the bourgeoisie own the factories and machinery. Workers sell their labour and the product of their labour belongs to the capitalist. The bourgeoisie accumulate capital by appropriating the *surplus value* of labour (see page 72).

CLASS CONSCIOUSNESS is an awareness of the class system and an appreciation of the position that an individual has within it. Marx distinguished between a 'class in itself' and a 'class for itself'. A 'class in itself' refers to a social group who have the same relation to *the means of production*, for example, are all waged workers. A 'class for itself' is fully aware of the nature of capitalist exploitation, recognises its shared interests and attempts to act in solidarity. The working class only has revolutionary potential once it develops class consciousness and becomes a 'class for itself'.

DIVISION OF LABOUR refers to the specialisation of work tasks that characterises modern society. Virtually all societies have some form of division of labour, usually on gender lines. Modern industrial society has a very complex division of labour that often extends beyond national boundaries. For example, in the multinational car manufacturing corporations, parts may be made in several countries and the cars are assembled in a different one.

NORMS are prescriptions for carrying out everyday activity. They provide guidelines for social action. Norms embody expectations that govern 'correct' social behaviour.

Norms imply consent and legitimacy, that is, norms are what everybody agrees are the proper ways of conducting social interaction.

ANOMIE occurs when *norms* governing social interaction breakdown. It refers to the failure of the social system to regulate expectations. This leads to individuals feeling dissatisfied, unhappy, meaningless or even suicidal. Societies normally restrict the boundless desires of humans by imposing attainable norms that restrict what members of society can expect to achieve. When these norms do not change rapidly enough to changing social situations then anomie occurs.

Durkheim saw the high rates of marital break-up, suicide and industrial conflict at the end of the nineteenth century as indicators of anomie.

little specialisation and this uniformity bound people together into a tight community. This unity he referred to as *mechanical solidarity*.

Industrial society, with the specialisation that comes from the division of labour, is characterised by *organic solidarity*. He equates society to a living organism with its different parts all working together, in their different ways, to maintain the system. As, for example, each part of the body (the brain, heart, lungs and so on) each have a function in the working of the body, so Durkheim argued different occupational roles each had a *function* in the working of industrial society. Solidarity came from the organic interrelationship between the different roles. Each occupational group needed the others for the social system to work. Although specialisation requires co-operation, this is unlikely to happen spontaneously. Rules and a moral code are required to regulate behaviour for the good of the system overall. There are, in short, a set of social *norms*.

The rapid development of industrial society at the end of the nineteenth century showed that there were limits to this notion of organic solidarity. Durkheim saw two basic problems with organic solidarity. First, the division of labour leads to individualism and self-interest. There is an erosion in the sense of duty towards others that Durkheim regarded as essential to solidarity. Second, rapid expansion provides the potential for increased prosperity. This leads people to have increased expectations and desires. The result is that previous moral obligations and social control become strained. In short, the old norms and values cannot cope. This leads to a *normless* situation which Durkheim called *anomie*. A new moral consensus and new structures of social control are needed to overcome anomie and restore *equilibrium*.

Durkheim thus understates the impact on society of class differences. Differentiation is seen in terms of the roles people play within the division of labour. Conflict is seen in individual rather than class terms.

Functionalist theories of class

Functionalists tend not to talk of class as such but of *stratification*. By this they mean any system of ordering by which society is broken down into layers (or strata). This may be in terms of fairly rigid 'class', 'caste', 'gender' or 'racial' differences, or it may be in terms of an occupational hierarchy. Talcott Parsons (1951), for example, argues that it is the commonly held values within a society that guides the way people are ranked into different strata (Kohn, 1959). So those people who perform well in terms of society's criteria will be ranked highly. This assumes that there is a set of shared values and that the inevitable ranking and differences in material reward that result from them is reasonable and just.

Functionalists adopt the Durkheimian view of a unified social system with various elements having a function within it (see page 82 for a summary of functionalism). They assume that there are certain basic needs or functional prerequisites that must be met if society is to survive. They see stratification within society as having a function in maintaining equilibrium. People have a role and everyone is aware of its value. A society will operate only if the necessary roles are filled and performed efficiently. Social stratification is the mechanism that ensures this happens.

Some roles are functionally very important and it is vital that the most able people fill them. Thus high rewards are attached to these roles to attract the best talent and compensate for the sacrifices involved in the training required to fill the role. Stratification thus ensures that the most important positions are filled by the most qualified people (Davis and Moore, 1945). This leads to an inevitable inequality and in terms of material reward, prestige and power. Differences in power are seen as legitimate because they too are based on shared values. Differences in power are functional because they integrate the diverse elements of the social system. Furthermore, differences in power ensure social control through the exercise of authority. Authority is accepted by society as a whole because it is assumed to be used for the shared benefit of all members of the society.

Needless to say, there has been criticism of functionalism as an idealistic system that takes no account of social reality (Bendix and Lipset, 1972; Lopreato and Lewis, 1974; Tumin, 1967; Young, 1961). Societies are not unified, power and authority do not rest on shared values, and the powerful are self-serving and do not benefit society as a whole. In short, stratification leads to divisions not solidarity.

> **Student Activity 1.2**
> **What other criticisms of the functionalist view of stratification can you think of?**

Overall, positivists see class in terms of social strata. The differences between the strata are explained by the division of labour and the function and rewards of different roles. Class, defined in terms of occupational category, is used to explain other social phenomena. This can be seen, for example, in the discussion of the explanations of inequalities in health in Chapter 3.

Phenomenological approaches to class

Phenomenological approaches to class focus on the *meaning* that class has for people rather than in terms of 'objective' measures of class.

The symbolic interactionist approach

The symbolic interactionist approach is mainly concerned, as its name suggests, with interaction between people (see page 183 for a summary of symbolic interactionism). This might be interpersonal interaction, group interaction, or interaction within an organisation. The focus is very much on how people make sense of their immediate world. Attention is usually directed at one of the following: first, verbal and non-verbal communication in face-to-face interaction; second, the impact of group actions and attitudes on the individual group member; third, the way people develop informal practices within the formal structure of an organisation. For symbolic interactionists, class is not a major analytical tool. Symbolic interactionists tend not to be particularly concerned with issues of class or social structure (Meltzer *et al.*, 1975). Class is only important when it inhibits interaction. The concepts of power and oppression are addressed in interpersonal rather than class terms (for example, the power structure in a group or organisation, or the power relationships within face-to-face interaction).

Interpretive approach

Interpretive approaches rely on Weber's notion of *status*. Weber argues that class divisions derive from economic divisions. However, these are not just based on ownership of the means of production, as Marx argued (see page 13, below). They also reflect differences in income from different kinds of jobs. Thus Weber sees class as ranging from upper class through various

> **STATUS** is the social worth, honour or prestige that a person has within a social group. This is usually based on the economically active role that a person plays, that is, the person's occupation, or the public office that a person may have through inheritance, appointment or election. Weber used the notion of *status group* as an alternative to class as a means to stratify society. Status is socially defined, whereas class (in a Marxist sense) is based on the relation of the group to the means of production (see page 10).

middle class groups (managerial, clerical and so on) to various levels of skilled and unskilled working class. For him, class differentiation is based on skill and education. Rewards, in the form of income and wealth, reflect the market demand for the different groups. Whereas Marx argued for distinct and conflicting classes, Weber argues that social classes are not polarised (not least because the middle class is expanding) and that people in the same class do not necessarily share a common consciousness (which reduces the revolutionary potential of the working class).

While class is important, Weber argued that differentiation also takes place along *status* lines. Status and class do not necessarily coincide. Status refers to the honour and prestige that social groups are accorded by others. He argues that some social groups have positive prestige and are accorded high status in the social order. Other groups are accorded negative status and seen as *pariah groups*, that is, they are discriminated against and often restricted. Status often matches wealth, although not all wealthy people are afforded high status nor are all poor people given low status.

> **Student Activity 1.3**
> **Write down two occupations:**
> 1. **one that has high income and low status;**
> 2. **one that has low income and high status.**

Whereas class is based on 'objective' differences (property and earnings), status is based on 'subjective' evaluations of social difference, usually linked to life-style. There is, Weber argues, a common feeling of belonging to a status group. Often status groups place barriers on membership and restrictions on the way outsiders may interact with them. Weber saw the caste system of traditional Hindu society as the ultimate status system.

Weber argues that *power* is not necessarily linked to class. Status groups also provide a basis for power, as do political *parties*. A party may be a religious or nationalist grouping, an informal pressure group, trade union, or association as well as the more familiar parliamentary parties. Weber defines parties as groups that are specifically concerned with influencing policies or gaining political power. Thus, for Weber, conflict and power need to be seen in terms of status and party as well as class.

Critical approaches to class

Critical approaches to class are dominated by the work of Karl Marx and subsequent Marxists' revisions. Class is not just about strata differentiation and reward, but relates to the organisation of capitalism. Class is seen as an *integral* part of the process of capitalist exploitation and oppression. Marxist class analysis attempts to show how class works as an *oppressive* mechanism.

We briefly outline Marx's view at the beginning of this section to give a context in which other views of social stratification have been developed. We will now say a little more about Marx's approach, and that of subsequent Marxists.

Marxism

Marx saw capitalism as one way of organising production. He set out to reveal how capitalism worked. How was it that the bourgeoisie who owned the means of production were able to accumulate wealth and thus power? The short answer was that they exploited the workers by paying them less for their labour than the value of the goods they produced were worth (see page 71 for a summary of surplus value). The capitalists took the difference and accumulated wealth without doing any productive work.

Marx argued, then, that what distinguished people under capitalism was their *relation* to the *means of production*, that is, did they own the means of production (the bourgeoisie) or did they sell their labour (the proletariat). No other ways of differentiating people were relevant for understanding capitalism. In the last resort, social position was defined by economic position and the nature of society was dependent on who controlled the means of production. A class society would persist while the bourgeoisie continued to exploit the workers.

To increase profits the capitalist needs to make and sell more. But there is a limit to the market and so capitalists begin to compete with each other. This leads to an increased investment in labour-saving machinery and a reduction in the numbers of people employed. There are two long-term problems with this. First, if the capitalists accumulate all the wealth there will be fewer people with incomes sufficient to buy the goods. Second, the greater investment in labour- saving machinery the fewer workers there will be left in the factories to exploit. The capitalists will squeeze the remaining workers ever harder. Conflict will result as the bourgeoisie increase the exploitation in order to make more and more profit as they compete amongst themselves. Eventually, the system will break down. Marx argued that capitalism is not viable in the long run. The workers will resist and ultimately unite in a common cause to get rid of the capitalists. Marx assumed that the socialist revolution would take place in advanced capitalist societies because they would be the ones where the system reached breaking point.

Student Activity 1.4
Write down the countries that you can think of in which a revolution has taken place during the twentieth century. How many of these were in advanced capitalist countries? How many of them were Marxist or communist revolutions?

Marxist analyses of Marx's class theory

Marxism is characterised by ongoing debate and Marx's views have been amended and developed by Marxists over the last 100 years. Both the accuracy of Marx's own analysis of capital and its applicability to changed circumstances have been questioned. The greatest impact on world history has come from revolutionary leaders such as Lenin and Mao-Tse Tung (Mao Zedong) who saw Marx's analysis as essentially correct. They both adapted Marxism for use in predominantly rural societies and developed a vanguard party of professional revolutionaries to activate the workers. However, the basic principles of Marxism underlay both the Russian and Chinese Revolutions.

Criticisms, by Marxists, of Marx's analysis of capitalism and the role of the working class take three forms.

First, Marx was mistaken in expecting capitalism to continue the polarisation of classes with capitalism forcing wage earners into ever greater poverty. Capitalism creates wealth and increases the standard of living for everyone, although this is uneven. Thus the working class is neutralised as a revolutionary force. This view, often referred to as *revisionism*, takes a reformist approach and argues for extending parliamentary democracy.

Second, Marx assumed that political power was embedded in economic

HEGEMONY refers to the process and structures by which a dominant social group maintains and *legitimates* its privileged position. Hegemonic theorists argue that the privileged position is safeguarded through the mechanisms of the state. It is important to ensure that people accept the role and power of the state as natural (rather than as an oppressive force to be opposed). So all new dominant economic classes create what is known as an 'organic intelligentsia' to undertake social and governmental functions on behalf of the dominant group in order to ensure consensus. These functions include ensuring that the philosophy of the dominant group (which allows them to retain their privileges) is 'spontaneously' accepted by the mass of the population. The media, along with the education system, religion, the family, and so on, all play a part in this 'spontaneous' acceptance. The other main function of the organic intelligentsia is to ensure that, if necessary, the power of the state can be brought to bear to ensure consensus.

Hegemony is a concept developed in the work of the Italian Marxist writer Antonio Gramsci. Hegemonic theorists are traditionally Marxists but the approach has been adopted and developed by feminists and anti-racists. Instead of focusing on class dominance, feminist see dominant ideology in terms of gender oppression and anti-racists focus on ethnic oppression.

LEGITIMATION is the process by which the actions of a group or class are made legitimate or acceptable. The dominant group (or ruling class) use state apparatuses to legitimate their actions. The law is used to legitimate government policy. The media are used to convince people of the acceptability of events or restrictions on their lives. The education system is used to tell people what the world is like and what they should expect from it, and so on. In general, a dominant view of the world (the dominant *ideology*) is built up which gives validity to the existing social structure. The privileges of the powerful are made acceptable to the powerless, oppressed majority.

Ideology is central to the process of legitimation as it conceals the real nature of oppression and exploitation.

Non-dominant groups legitimate their actions through non-dominant ideology and culture. This is reflected in specific sets of group values.

IDEOLOGY refers to the sets of taken-for-granted ideas and presuppositions that exist in a given social structure. The prevailing ideology is known as the dominant ideology and it serves to legitimate and preserve the existing social structure by making the order of things appear natural and unchallengeable and conceals the extent of social divisions. Ideology is sometimes equated with 'false consciousness', which hides the real nature of oppression and exploitation. This view presupposes that non-dominant ideologies are able to 'raise consciousness' and effect changes in the social structure. An alternative view suggests that ideology cannot be detached from the economic, social and political structure in which it is located. Ideology is everywhere and can only be changed when the social structure is itself changed.

Originally, ideology was analysed in terms of class but more recently gender, race and sexuality have also been used as the basis for analysing ideology.

An overview of ideology can be found in Haralambos, 1990, chapters 1 and 3.

SUPERSTRUCTURE is a term used in Marxist analysis to refer to institutions such as the family, school, church, mass media, courts, police, and armed forces. These are sometimes referred to as the apparatuses of the state and split into two groups. *Repressive* state apparatuses (courts, police, army) use force to maintain the capitalist system of production. *Ideological* state apparatuses (media, school, religion and so on) ensure consensus by reproducing dominant ideology (Althusser, 1971).

The superstructure thus *legitimates* and preserves the nature of the economic base (or infrastructure). The base refers to the relations of production, that is, capitalism, which consists of the bourgeoisie, who own the *means of production* (see page 10), and the workers.

relations. He ignored the role of the state which has played an important and independent role in limiting the powers of the wealthy and in providing civil, political and social rights to all.

Third, Marx exaggerated the importance of property ownership as a source of social division and conflict. Income, occupation and education have all proved to be important bases of stratification within capitalist society. Status differences have reduced the importance of class divisions. Conflict between employers and employees has been accommodated and institutionalised. In short, Marx gave *superstructural* aspects of social formations inadequate consideration.

Hegemony

An alternative Marxist tradition, heavily influenced by Gramsci (1971) argues for a major overhaul of Marxism with far more emphasis placed on the superstructure. Central to Gramsci's analysis is his notion of *hegemony*. The approach argues that class power does not just depend on economic class relations and repression. The dominant classes utilise *ideology* to win consent from subordinate groups. Hegemony thus shifts attention from repression to consensus when analysing class domination.

Consent is rooted historically in the prestige and power that the dominant group has as a result of its control over the means of production. Repression only occurs in moments of crisis. The apparatus of 'legal' state coercive power is brought to bear on those groups who do not 'consent' either actively or passively.

Although the dominant group control 'The State', it is not seen as simply reflecting class interest. The state is not just repressive, it also has a positive educative force. It actively promotes new forms of organisation of capitalist production, and ensures some basic forms of justice or even welfare. Intellectuals (such as teachers, writers, television producers) are used to encourage consent. They justify the dominant ideology and get people to believe that capitalism is natural and in every one's best interest. In short, they ensure consent by reproducing *false consciousness* among the oppressed groups.

Changes in the nature of the state can only occur, Gramsci (1971) argued, through a revolutionary party that provides a new conception of the world. A Marxist strategy for the West would have to be very different from that adopted by Lenin in Russia since, in capitalist societies, the bourgeoisie exercise a hegemony that would have to be undermined before a frontal assault on state power could be successful.

The hegemonic view has led to a growing interest in *culture* (Williams, 1965; Thompson, 1968; Berger, 1972). Cultural Marxists argue that it is necessary to see class in terms of distinct class cultures and not just in terms of relations to the means of production (Hall *et al.*, 1980; Willis, 1977) (see page 171 for a summary of Cultural Marxism).

Structuralist Marxism

Althusser (1971) argued that these developments of Gramsci's hegemonic view were placing too much emphasis on the individual and detaching the superstructure from the economic base. In the last resort, he argued, the superstructure was dependent on the economic base. Capitalism is intent on *reproducing* its economic base (that is, the process of production and consequent class relations) and the superstructure operates to assure this.

Althusser saw the superstructure in terms of *state apparatuses*. The *ideological state apparatuses* (such as the schools, church and media) legitimated the capitalist system of production and inequality and it manufactured consensus. The *repressive state apparatuses* (such as the police, army and law courts) enforced the system when consensus broke down.

For him, the superstructure is *relatively autonomous*, that is, it is not just a reflection of the economic base. So, for example, the education system does not simply indoctrinate people to accept the capitalist process of production. Some education is highly critical of capitalism. Overall, though, the education system is designed to produce adequately trained people to ensure the reproduction of the capitalist system. Thus the superstructure is only *relatively* autonomous. Conversely, changing the economic base (the way production is organised) will not necessarily result in a thoroughgoing revolution. It is also necessary to change dominant ideology (which is part of the superstructure).

Ideology thus has a central influence in both the Cultural Marxist and Structuralist Marxist approaches. The emphasis, in the hegemonic analysis, has shifted away from the productive base of class analysis and given more prominence to the superstructure.

'Race'

'Race', racism, racialism and ethnicity are complex phenomena that have been analysed from many perspectives. Although they are interrelated concepts they should, however, be clearly differentiated.

'Race' refers to the *apparent* racial group into which a person can be categorised. In one sense 'race' is a meaningless concept for sociology as there are no inherent biological characteristics or traits attributable to racial origin.

Biologists have attempted to classify humans into different races by suggesting that groups of physical characteristics combine to determine particular racial categories. For example, the broad categories of 'Mongoloid', 'Negroid' and 'Caucasoid' based on eyes, face shape, hair and skin colour. Nevertheless no schema, however many subdivisions it includes has, resulted in acceptable and scientifically useful groupings.

Similarly, geneticists have shown that there are no genetic groupings that conform to 'racial' groups, that is, there is no such thing as a 'pure' 'race'. Within any subgroup there is a considerable diversity as members do not share exactly the same genes. More importantly, there is considerable overlap between groups.

> Scientifically speaking, *'race'* (in the sense of gene pools) refers to clusters of biological characteristics which are changeable rather than unalterably fixed and which relate to gradually altering gene frequencies among diverse human groups rather than to clearly identifiable basic human types. (Richardson and Lambert, 1985, p. 15)

For this reason, we use the current convention of writing 'race' in inverted commas to indicate that it a socially constructed rather than a biological category.

'RACE' TERMINOLOGY The terms 'race', 'racism', 'black', 'Black', 'Afro-Caribbean', 'Asian' are all politically charged and dynamic concepts. There are no terms that do not have overtones of repression (Bulmer, 1986). This means that the selection of terminology is both transitory and to some extent arbitrary. Throughout the book we will refer to white and black or non-white (to include all non-whites, sometimes split into Asian and Afro-Caribbean). This is not to imply any phenotypical characteristics or hierarchy. On the contrary, the terms used merely represent socially constructed notions of 'race'.

Racism and racialism

Racism refers to a cluster of cultural *ideas*, beliefs and arguments that transmit mistaken notions about the attributes and capabilities of 'racial' groups, usually relating to moral, cultural and intellectual inferiority.

INSTITUTIONAL RACISM There is a certain amount of confusion over the terms institutional *racism*, institutional *racialism* and *structural* racism in the literature. All three have been used to refer to *institutional* policies that lead to discrimination. This we refer to as *institutional racialism*.

Structural racism refers to the view that capitalist society is racist (Sivanandan, 1982). Racism serves to support capitalism and to legitimate exploitation. This is discussed in more detail below, in the section on critical approaches to 'race'.

For example, the allocation of rented housing may lead to institutional racialism if councils or housing associations have a policy of housing ethnic minorities in certain areas. Housing is also an area in which structural racism is evident, as ethnic minorities have been systematically disadvantaged in the housing market. The kinds of jobs traditionally open to ethnic minorities has made it difficult for them to obtain standard mortgages. Thus ethnic minorities have often become victims of slum landlords, overcrowding and so on.

BIOLOGICAL THEORIES OF 'RACE' There are a variety of biological theories of racial conflict. They tend to see conflict in terms of prejudice and regard prejudice as a natural instinct. *Sociobiology*, probably the most sophisticated of the biological theories (see page 82), sees prejudice in terms of reproduction and survival. It argues that genes are 'selfish' and that humans are biologically driven to maximise the potential reproduction of their genes. Racial prejudice thus results because of the supposed threat to the racial gene pool. However, this, along with other versions of biological theories have no credibility because, as we have seen, there are no genetic, or other biologically distinct races.

Biological theories have also attempted to explain differences in intelligence and culture in terms of biological properties of different races. Ethnic minorities or 'racial' groups are usually seen as innately inferior. However, there is no credible evidence whatsoever that biology has any bearing on intelligence or culture. The biological argument is a convenient fiction that is used to provide an excuse for colonial oppression, slavery and genocide.

Racialism refers to *actions* (behaviour, policies or types of treatment) that are informed by racism. These may be individual or institutional. (Racist motivated actions have also been referred to as *racist actions* or as *racial discrimination*. However the preferred terminology these days is to call such actions racialist.)

Institutional racialism occurs when major institutions operate in a way that results in racialism (Mason, 1982). In other words, institutional racism occurs when the procedures and rules (whether official or unofficial) of an institution are such that groups (socially defined as 'races') are systematically disadvantaged in respect of social rewards, capacities or opportunities, for example when firms do not interview people from ethnic minorities for job vacancies (McIntosh and Smith, 1974).

Student Activity 1.5
Write down two other examples of institutional racism.

Ethnicity

Ethnicity has been defined in a number of ways (Schermerhorn, 1970; Yinger, 1981; Bulmer, 1986). Broadly, an ethnic group is a collectivity within a larger society that has a shared *culture*. The culture is dynamic and transmitted from generation to generation. The central features of the culture are usually a *common language*; a sense of *historical past* or ancestry; a *geographic* point of reference; a *political* background; regular social *interaction* in which the common origin and culture are significant ingredients; a sense of *belonging*; and a set of identifiable cultural *symbols*. These symbols may be rooted in a sense of nationhood, clan membership, religion, lifestyle, forms of dress, artistic expression and so on. 'Race' may also be seen as an intrinsic element of the ethnic culture (for example, black culture).

To sum up, an ethnic group is defined culturally and a 'racial' group is defined physiologically. An ethnic label does not necessarily imply 'racial' characteristics as well as cultural. A 'racial' category, however, usually implies ethnic (that is, cultural) characteristics as well as physiological ones.

Positivist approaches to 'race'

The positive approach is to attempt to provide *explanations* of 'race' or to use 'race' to explain social phenomena. Positivist approaches attempt 'objective' categorisations of racial groups. They link racism to prejudice and see racialism as an expression of individual or group attitudes and values. Functionalism is the main positivist sociological approach to 'race'.

Functionalist theory of 'race'

Functionalism depicts society as essentially an integrated and cohesive system. There is a common set of norms and values that leads to consensus. Each element in the system performs some function that keeps the system in equilibrium. Racial tension disrupts the equilibrium. The functionalist view has it that this disruption is temporary and a process of 'healing' will take place. The theory thus approaches 'race' from the point of view of *'race relations'*. Harmony must be promoted by removing unnecessary obstacles placed in the path of ethnic minorities. This approach is best exemplified in the *'race relations cycle'* theory.

The 'race relations cycle'

The 'race relations cycle' was developed at Chicago University in the 1920s. It has taken various forms but is basically a model of the sequence that accounts for the integration of immigrants into a host community. The classic cycle is of competition, conflict, accommodation and assimilation. The immigrant group provides competition for economic resources. This eventually leads to conflict, which is subsequently resolved by each side accommodating the other until finally the immigrant group becomes part of the dominant culture. The immigrant group is *assimilated* into the dominant culture. Assimilation is often taken to imply the adoption of the 'host' culture by the 'migrant'. In fact, it was originally more flexible, suggesting that the host culture would also evolve as a result of drawing on migrant culture. None the less the result would be a relatively homogeneous culture with the migrants being absorbed. Normally, this would require some help through state policies and anti-discrimination laws (Patterson, 1963).

This functionalist, equilibrium model ignores conflicts within culture such as those of class and gender, and ignores institutional and structural racism. It is criticised for being vague about the stages, for assuming assimilation is the correct outcome or policy and for underestimating the extent of prejudice and discrimination.

More recently the assimilation view has been replaced by an *integration* model that shifts the emphasis from absorption into a homogeneous culture to the harmonious and tolerant integration of different groups with distinct cultures. The integration model implies dialogue and sharing, with a resulting overlap and merging of cultures, rather than tolerant but rigid segregation.

> **Student Activity 1.6**
> **What stereotypes can you think of that are used to distinguish different ethnic cultures?**

'New right' racism or cultural absolutism

'New right' racism is another positivist approach to 'race'. It reworks biological approaches and asserts that 'race' and ethnicity are *cultural absolutes*. Rather than different 'races' being biologically distinct it argues that they are *culturally* distinct and incompatible. Prejudice is caused by this cultural incompatibility, which leads to racial conflict. The argument has been used in the United States and now in South Africa to support separate development. In Britain 'new right' racism appeared initially in the views of Enoch Powell who predicted that the (white) British people would not tolerate alternative cultures in their midst. Thatcherism embodied a trivial version of Powellist racism in its call for an end to immigration in 1978 in order to 'avoid being swamped by alien cultures' (Barker, 1981). The new right relies heavily on cultural stereotypes (see Chapter 2) to support its racist theory.

Phenomenological approaches to 'race'

Phenomenological approaches focus on the social meanings of 'race'. Phenomenological approaches argue that people have *subjective* notions of racial groups that affect how they act towards them. The two main approaches have been *interactionist* and *Weberian*.

Interactionist approach

The interactionist approach also focuses on 'race relations'. It sees 'race' in terms of prejudice. It thus argues that to solve problems of 'race relations' it is necessary to investigate the nature of prejudice (Blumer, 1958). Prejudice tends to be seen as the result of individual personality defects. Prejudiced people are 'sick', 'depraved', have 'hang-ups' or have 'a chip on their shoulder'. This is often seen as the result of childhood socialisation (see page 50 for a summary of socialisation). Attention is thus focused on the anxieties, insecurities and fears of the prejudiced personality (Zanden, 1973).

Alternatively, prejudice is seen as a group attitude that serves to shift the frustration of living and working in a capitalist society on to some 'out group', that is, finding a scapegoat. Prejudiced people thus act in ways that disadvantage the 'out group' who in turn have low self esteem as a result of their victimisation.

Both approaches tend to rely on psychological theories, and whilst pointing to aspects of racial prejudice, have little to say about the social processes that lead to racialism.

Weberian approach

The Weberian approach sees 'race' in terms of *status*. John Rex (1970) has been one of the most consistent advocates of a Weberian approach. He argues that although the social meanings of 'race' contain falsehoods and errors it is the actors' point of view that matters. 'Subjective' perspectives about race are translated into 'objective' consequences. However, perspectives on 'race' are not simply the result of individual mistaken ideas or false consciousness. The underlying social structure helps sustain racial beliefs and tensions. Racial categories become translated into status categories. The ethnic minority has a low status and forms an *underclass*.

Underclass

The concept of underclass was first developed in the United States where it was used to refer to the part of the population that was permanently locked in a situation of poverty and unemployment. Although this was not restricted to ethnic minorities, the term has tended to be equated with the urban ghettos in the United States (Glasgow, 1971; Tabb, 1971; Weis, 1985) where many of the ethnic minority residents are in low-status, insecure, casual employment (that is, are part of the *secondary labour market*, see page 78).

Rex and Tomlinson (1979) used the term 'underclass' to signify a disadvantaged group which does not share the same experiences or privileges as the white working class. They argued that it does not make sense to describe ethnic minorities as part of the working class despite their characteristic working-class employment profile. In their study of Handsworth, they found a 'structural break' between the white working class and the non-white underclass in respect of employment, housing and education. Add to this racial discrimination and the exclusion of ethnic minorities from traditional working-class organisations, such as trade unions and the Labour Party, and the underclass lead a marginalised existence.

Rex and Tomlinson argue that underclass does not necessarily imply unemployment, although ethnic minorities suffer higher unemployment rates. Even for those employed, the expectation is that the underclass are highly concentrated in the secondary labour market. This results in a vicious

UNDERCLASS comes from the Weberian analysis of stratification. An underclass is a group at the bottom of the stratification system below other classes. It is economically deprived. An underclass has a weak market situation. Members of this group do not have the skills which are in demand that would enable them to earn high wages. The underclass also lacks status because of the way that society evaluates them.

circle. The stigmatised racial minority can only get jobs in the secondary market and their overrepresentation serves to reinforce the view of their inferiority.

However, ethnic minorities are not exclusively concentrated in the secondary market and this raises questions about the underclass theory.

The concept of underclass is about status and discrimination rather than class relations. Underclass theorists are not convinced of the revolutionary potential of the working class nor the coincidence of interests of the blacks and whites. Rex and Tomlinson think that separate ethnic organisation and political activities are a fruitful means of furthering the special interests of ethnic groups until they gain full entry into the dominant political and social institutions. They see *reform* in the form of multicultural education, employment and housing policies as the way to help the underclass.

> **Student Activity 1.7**
> **Do you think the underclass theory characterises the situation of ethnic minorities in Britain in the 1990s?**

Critical approaches to 'race'

Critical approaches see society as oppressive, characterised by division and conflict rather than equilibrium and consensus. Marxists and anti-racists have provided a number of perspectives on 'race'. At the heart of all these though is a fundamental questioning of the significance that ought to be given to the concept of 'race'. For most critical analysts, 'race' is an *ideological* concept. It does not refer to biological or social reality but involves a number of preconceptions about 'racialised' subgroups that 'legitimate real positions of social domination or subordination' (Cohen and Bains, 1988, p. 23). Thus critical analyses tend to concentrate on *racism* and *racialism* rather than 'race'.

Critical approaches see racialism as *structural*. Institutional racialism, for example, should not be seen as the result of rules and procedures within a given institution (such as a housing department) but as something that is the consequence of wider structural inequality (Carmichael and Hamilton, 1969). This is not just a matter of racialist government policy. The organisation of production, distribution of wealth, the forms of social control, the culture and ideology are all structural factors that provide a racist *legitimation* for institutionally-based discrimination. In short, capitalism is characterised by a racist *hegemony* (see page 14).

Marxist approaches

The key aspect of Marxist approaches to 'race' and racism is that they see racism as a form of oppression. Marxists do not see racism in individual terms (biological, psychological or moral) nor in terms of group norms or values. 'Race' is not a causal factor. Nor are the issues around 'race' about integration or status. Rather, racism is an *integral* part of the capitalist process of exploitation and oppression. Racism is not an attitude of mind but is 'a set of economic, political and ideological practices' (Hall *et al.*, 1980).

The nature and organisation of capitalist production shapes intergroup conflicts, including 'race' conflicts. Issues around 'race' and racism are rooted in class conflict and derive from the exploited role of migrant labour. Thus racism does not exist in isolation; it is not an external 'problem' but is part and parcel of capitalism.

Capitalism utilises racism in order to reproduce itself. Racism provides a legitimation for exploitation and oppression. It does so via notions of 'racial superiority'. Both indigenous populations of colonies and minority groups at home are viewed as 'racially inferior'. Racism is useful to capitalism because it divides and thus weakens the working class. It is preferable for capitalists if workers blame one another for their exploitation rather than the capitalist. Racism provides convenient scapegoats.

Marxists are thus critical of a 'race relations' approach because it represents class conflict in terms of 'race relations' and directs attention away from capitalism (Hall *et al.*, 1978). Marxist analyses therefore tend to approach 'race' within more general class analyses of society and argue that whites and blacks should join forces in the class struggle. Marxists adopt either a *unitary*, *divided*, or *fractional* approach to the working class.

Unitary working class

Westergaard and Resler (1976) adopt the Marxist distinction between bourgeoisie and proletariat and argue that the majority (non-ethnic) working class and minority (ethnic) groups are both oppressed by their *relation* to the means of production. To focus on 'colour' prejudice, they argue, is to deflect attention from the basic oppression of all workers that occurs under capitalism. They thus see 'class' rather than 'race' as the basic issue for a Marxist analysis. The predominant view amongst Marxists, however, is that the working class is not unified.

Divided working class

Other Marxists have argued that the working class is divided, not unitary. The simplest view is that the working class is divided, with ethnic minorities forming a sub-group within it. Castles and Kosack (1973), for example, undertook an extensive study of migrant workers in Europe and showed that although immigrant workers are members of the working class they form a bottom stratum because of the subordinate status of the jobs they do. This analysis is similar to the Weberian 'underclass' view but sees the bottom stratum in economic rather than status terms and argues that ethnic minorities form a *reserve army of labour* (see page 73) that capitalism uses during boom periods.

An alternative view suggests that the working class is divided, but into a number of *fractions* not just into two groups based on 'colour' (Edwards *et al.*, 1975; Miles, 1982). The working class is divided on the basis of gender, skill and age as well as ethnicity (Cockburn, 1983). For Miles, people from ethnic minorities appear at different class levels (mainly within the working class, but also in middle-class groups) but always as a distinctive fraction that has been 'racialised', that is, endowed with overtones of racial inferiority.

Miles criticises the Weberian *underclass* thesis for exaggerating the disadvantage suffered by black groups and placing too much emphasis on racial discrimination rather than on the dynamics of class conflict. Whatever the actual social and economic conditions faced, for example, by Black or Jewish people they do not constitute, for all time, an 'underclass'. The privations and abuse they suffer is a function of *hegemonic* racism (see page 14). To see ethnic minorities as an 'underclass' denies the historical process and gives credibility to the negative stereotypes (Cohen and Bains, 1988, p. 27).

Anti-racist approaches

Radical black approaches

There are a number of radical black perspectives that vary from the consciousness raising approach of 'black is beautiful', through the 'black power' movements that demanded more political and economic power for black people, to black separatist movements who saw no hope of black liberation within white-dominated society (Ramdin, 1987).

Although these were basically political movements they had an impact on sociological theorising. The work of Joyce Ladner (1971) was influenced by the 'black power' movement and she argued that 'race' is a much more powerful variable in American society than social class. She also challenged the dominant positivist view that black people were 'a problem' that society and sociology needed to deal with. On the contrary, it was society and sociology that were the problem for not recognising 'institutionalised racism' and the impact it had on people's lives and for not examining the positive aspects of black culture.

Multiculturalism

Multiculturalists sees 'race' and class as fundamentally separate spheres. They argue that issues around racism and racialism have no contact with class politics.

This approach tends to be concerned with social policy and has also been referred to as the *social policy approach* (Gilroy, 1987). The policy approach supposes that radical theorists of 'race' and racism should produce critiques of official 'race' policy and formulate alternative policies (Gabriel and Ben-Tovim, 1979; Ben-Tovim *et al.*, 1981, 1986).

The policy approach depends on a view that racism is a 'populist' democratic form divorced from class. Multiculturalism is also optimistic about the potential and capacity of state institutions to be able to confront racism. The favoured vehicle of the approach is to involve 'black para-professionals' in the development of 'race relations' legislation, multicultural education policies and racism awareness training.

> **Student Activity 1.8**
> **To what extent does multiculturalism reflect the views of underclass theorists?**

Some Marxists are sceptical of the multiculturalism of social policy initiatives (Gilroy, 1987, Cohen and Bains, 1988, Duffield, 1988). They see picemeal, institutionalised approaches to anti-racism as part of the cultural *hegemony* that sustains racist oppression. The problem, they argue, is that multiculturalist approaches confuse 'race' with ethnicity. This confusion leads to ethnicity being seen as a set of traits. Ethnicity becomes 'Jewishness', 'Irishness', 'Blackness'. These are abstract expressions devoid of historical relevance. Cultural identity becomes naturalised. These trans-historical traits can be used successfully in anti-racist work, for example, positive images of 'Blackness'. However, there is the danger that the identification of ethnic traits leads to the construction of stereotypes and to the notion of cultural uniqueness. In short, multiculturalism is very close to the *cultural absolutism* of the new right racism.

Black Marxism

Black Marxism offers an alternative to conventional Marxist approaches.

Black Marxism argues that 'race' and class are interrelated but distinct. It is necessary to see racism as a *process* that is not detachable from issues of class but neither is it subsumed under it.

The processes of 'race' and class formation are not identical. Class analysis can help to illuminate the historical development of racism provided it is not just applied in old-fashioned ways. It requires the asking of questions about the potential of a unified working class and the adequacy of the distinction between capital and labour. Class struggle is not just about the organisation of production in capitalism, but also involves gender, racial, and generational divisions of labour.

The issue for Black Marxists is one of how, at any point in history, 'race' relates to class. 'Race' is potentially a feature of class consciousness and class formation and is likely to be 'a more potent means to organize and focus the grievances of certain inner-city populations than the languages of class politics' (Gilroy, 1987, p. 27). The disturbances in Brixton, Handsworth and elsewhere during the 1980s were about class concerns such as poverty and housing but were crystallised around racist oppression.

Thus it is argued that 'race' has real radical potential and therefore must be retained as an analytic category. 'Race' does not corresponds to any biological or cultural absolutes, but it directs attention to collectivities which 'are the most volatile political forces in Britain today' (Gilroy, 1987, p. 247).

Gender

There has been a notable absence of sociological theories of gender until recently. Traditional sociological theories such as Marxism, Weberianism, functionalism and interactionism have had very little to say about the situation of women. Indeed, they assume that what applies to men applies equally to women. Feminism has attempted to correct the 'sex-blindness' of sociology and to promote sociological awareness of gender issues.

Positivist approaches to gender

Positivist sociological approaches have tended to see gender in terms of roles within the family. *Functionalists*, for example, see the family as providing a number of functions for the maintenance of the social system (Murdock, 1949). First, the family, in most societies, is the unit within which male sexual activity, *reproduction* and child-rearing take place. Clearly these are important functions for society if it is to continue. The biology of women means that they play a central role in reproduction. By extension they are expected to play a major role in nurturing children. It is assumed that this nurturing role is natural.

Functionalists draw on biological notions to support this. For example, one view suggests that as males are stronger they are best suited to do heavy work while the weaker females who, having given birth, are better suited to rearing children. This is an assumption that feminists deny, pointing to the heavy work *and* child rearing that many women in 'Third World' countries have always done.

A sociobiological view suggests that men are genetically more aggressive and dominant than women. Historically men have done the hunting and fighting to protect the group. They thus monopolise positions of power.

Women on the other hand are supposedly genetically programmed to care for children (Tiger and Fox, 1972). This view argues that as genetic roles change much more slowly than cultural roles, attempts to change traditional male and female roles goes against nature. Critics argue that these genetic predispositions cannot be proven and that they are a convenient fiction to justify the continuing dominant roles of males in society. (See Chapter 3 for an example of the functionalist and sociobiologist theories applied to gender differences in the take-up of higher education.)

The second function of the family is *economic*. The family is the basic unit that sustains life, for example, through the provision and preparation of food. Traditionally, in Western societies, women play a major role in the preparation of food while males 'provide' it through the income they obtain from their paid employment. They are literally the 'breadwinners'. This is a convenient arrangement for the family unit as it leaves the women free to care for the family while nurturing the children.

Feminists have pointed out that this arrangement works far more conveniently for men than women. The extension of the nurturing role to a caring role means that women are also required to care for men through domestic labour.

The third function of the family is *socialisation* (see Chapter 2). This too, is very important for maintenance of society. The family is the context in which children first learn how to behave, what is acceptable, and so on. Again, women have a major role in this initial (or primary) socialisation because they raise the children and thus spend a lot of time with them. Women are also assumed to have a close and strong relationship with the children because they bear them. Consequently women are expected to play a major role in socialisation of the children. This function of the family reproduces male and female roles.

Each of these functions of the family imply a set of gendered roles. It is these roles that provide the basis of functionalist assumptions about gender.

Liberal feminism

Liberal feminists have objected to these role expectations and consequent career opportunities for women. They argue that women are artificially restricted to domestic roles because they are disadvantaged by unfair discrimination. In short, the *cause* of women's relative powerlessness is discrimination against women, not women's biology. The barriers to women's wider career development must be removed. This can be done through equal opportunities policies applied rigorously and fairly (such as the Sex Discrimination Act and the Equal Pay Act); through positive discrimination for women where they are underrepresented; by providing work-place child-care facilities; by having women-only seats on committees and so on. The aim is to reform society to provide women with the opportunity to compete, overall, on equal terms with men.

This approach has been advocated for a long time and was at the root of the suffragette movement in the early twentieth century. In essence it involves a call for equality for women within the *existing* social system. A modern version of this can be found in *post-feminism*, which claims that women now have equality of opportunity and that women must grasp it.

Once women have equality of opportunity, it is argued, then it will only be a matter of time before men's dominance of women disintegrates.

TYPES OF FEMINISM Many prefixes have been added in various combinations to feminism: socialist, Marxist, bourgeois, radical, materialist, positivist, idealist. Unfortunately, these labels have not always been used to mean the same thing in every case, nor are they mutually exclusive. More profoundly, the theoretical positions embodied in different perspectives are not entirely distinct.

So no set of definitions will be entirely satisfactory and it could be argued that any subdivision, even the long-standing socialist/radical feminist division, is misleading. The very factors that have led to the confused distinctions within feminism are themselves indicative of the blurred epistemological underpinnings of different feminist perspectives.

Recent new alliances and reworkings of feminist theoretical and political concerns have further blurred old distinctions.

PATRIARCHY refers to a view of the world in which men dominate and oppress women for their own benefit. For some people, patriarchy simply refers to male power over women. For others, patriarchy refers to an ideology which legitimates male domination.

For Marxist and socialist feminists, patriarchy is related to the economic structure. They argue that patriarchy cannot be analysed in isolation from capitalism.

Radical feminists see patriarchy as the male hierarchical ordering of society. They define patriarchy as a sexual system of power in which the male possesses superior power and economic privilege. The sexual division of society produces structural limits on the activities, work, and aspirations of women. Often, radical feminists argue that patriarchy is at root biological rather than economic or historic.

Student Activity 1.8
Write down any examples you can think of that support the post-feminist view that women now have the opportunity to compete equally with men. Write down any examples which show that this is not the case.

Phenomenological approaches to gender

Phenomenology offers very little in the way of theories of gender. Weberian analysis tends to see women as reflecting the status of their fathers or husbands. Interactionism pays little attention to broad theories of gender in its analysis of face-to-face and small-group interaction. The focus tends to be on the exercise of power or influence within the setting, given a general social context. For example, Fred Strodtbeck (1951) studied husband and wife discussions to see who won most decisions. Amongst Mormons, where women are seen as mothers and as having the status of their husbands, the man won significantly more decisions. In Navaho society, where women have a more active, independent role, women won more decisions than men.

Interactionist studies of organisations either adopt taken-for-granted functionalist theories of gender related roles (see, for example, William Foote Whyte's study in Chapter 6, Extract 6.12) or relate the analysis to feminists critiques of patriarchy, discussed below. (For an example see Michael Filby's study of betting shops in Chapter 6.)

Psychoanalytic feminism

Psychoanalytic feminism provides a rare example of a phenomenological theory of gender. Psychoanalytic feminism concentrates on what it means to be a woman. It argues that women, from childhood, are not allowed to develop as women. Indeed, it is argued that women have never existed because they have had to use male points of reference. In short, this approach is concerned with the masculinity in women's heads that results from them being in a patriarchal society (Mitchell, 1974; Marks and Courtivron, 1980; Coward, 1984).

Psychoanalytic feminism argues that women must therefore re-evaluate their own worth, celebrate their own bodies and generally learn to appreciate and nurture their 'womanness'. Strategies to do this include psychoanalysis, women-only spaces, redefinition of sexuality, breaking with dependence on men, and developing new concepts and language. This approach has been criticised for making social constructed gender distinctions into a rigid cognitive distinction (Benhabib and Cornell, 1987).

Critical approaches to gender

Feminism provides the basis for critical approaches to gender. Feminists argue it is a disgrace that sociologists have made little attempt to address the interests of women. Men and women are different and sociology can no longer continue to ignore women and presume that whatever theories apply to men must also apply to women. However, biological differences cannot be used to legitimate male *oppression* of females. There is nothing natural about the roles that women are expected to play. Nor should women be assumed to have the same status as their husbands or fathers. Feminists distinguish clearly between sex and gender. *Sex* is a biological property to do with reproduction. *Gender* is a socially constructed (or cultural) concept that implies various expectations and roles. There is no necessary link between biological sex and socially constructed gender. On the contrary, for many feminists, biological sex has been the excuse used by men to ensure that they control and oppress women.

The shift from liberal feminism to more critical approaches occurred around 1970, reflecting the Women's Movement of the 1960s. There was an emphasis on 'sisterhood' which redefined women's relations to one another. The 'personal' realms of women's experience were also taken seriously in sociology for the first time (Gavron, 1966; Ladner, 1971; Oakley, 1974) Feminism began to directly engage *oppression* of women rather than their social disadvantage. Reformism, to provide equality of opportunity for women in a man's world, was rejected. Instead, feminists argued that the position of women cannot be changed within male dominated social structures. Only a fundamental change in social relations will provide women with equality.

There are several critical views about the nature of, and mechanisms for, the oppression of women. Historically, the most important difference amongst critical feminists has been between socialist and radical feminists.

Socialist feminism

Socialist feminism argues that the position of women cannot be divorced from a Marxist analysis of capitalism. There are two basic versions of this approach.

First, a view which suggests that *productive relations* within capitalism underpin the oppression of women (Seccombe, 1974; Zaretsky, 1976). This is similar to the view of Marxists who argue (as we saw on page 21) that 'race' is basically a class conflict problem.

The version of socialist feminism that sees gender issues as basically a by-product of a class issue might be better referred to as 'a socialist class analysis of the oppression of women'. The approach is based on Frederick Engels' (1884) analysis of gender oppression in *The Origin of the Family, Private Property, and the State*. This is virtually the only account within nineteeth-century Marxism of relations between the sexes. Engels argued that emancipation of women depends on their full integration into social production. For him, private property is at the root of class conflict. Class distinctions are based on the ownership of private property. He argued that the origin of the monogamous family and its attendant domination of women by men results from the emergence of private property. The oppression of women is thus linked to the emergence of socioeconomic classes. At the extreme women are the property of men. At the least women are expected to maintain and add to male-controlled property through their work in the home and through reproduction. The only hope for female emancipation is through class conflict that changes the way people relate to both the means of production and reproduction (Sayers *et al.*, 1987). This approach has been attacked for ignoring the benefits to all men, regardless of class, of *patriarchal* oppression (Cockburn, 1983).

The second approach of socialist feminists gives as much weight to feminist as to socialist concerns (Eisenstein, 1979). There are a number of variants of this position. In general, though, socialist feminists argue that women are oppressed by both *capitalism* and *patriarchy*. This approach requires that social structures and practices are viewed both in terms of gender oppression and class oppression (Hartmann, 1979; Cockburn, 1983). This view is similar to the argument of Black Marxists who see class and

---

CAPITALISM AND PATRIARCHY

Socialist feminists vary in how they see the relationship between capitalism and patriarchy. First, the view that capitalism and patriarchy are fused into a single oppressive mechanism. The capitalist patriarchy view argues that women are exploited as labourers in class terms and also as women in patriarchal terms. Men and women are separated into their respective hierarchical sex roles with their related duties in the family domain and within the economy. The sexual division has evolved from ideological and political interpretations of biological difference that men have chosen to interpret and make political use of.

The view argues that capitalism 'needs' patriarchy in the sense that patriarchy provides the necessary order and control. Male supremacy involves a system of cultural, social, economic and political control. The capitalist concern with profit and patriarchal concern with sexual hierarchy are inextricably connected (but cannot be reduced to each other), patriarchy and capitalism become an integral process; specific elements of each system are necessitated by the other (Eisenstein, 1979). This approach has been criticised for linking patriarchy so closely with capitalism. Patriarchy pre-dates capitalism and operates in non-capitalist societies.

Second, there is a dualist approach which sees capitalism and patriarchy as separate but interrelated oppressive structures. The dual approach requires that social structures and practices are viewed in terms of both gender and class oppression (Hartmann, 1979; Cockburn, 1983). This reverses the intention of socialist feminism to dissolve the distinction between the radical feminist gender-oriented perspective and the socialist or Marxist class-oriented perspective. Dualist approaches have been criticised for proposing a mysterious coexistence of unrelated explanations of social development. Each of the dual realms remain relatively autonomous and the unsatisfactory analysis of patriarchy that derives from radical feminism and the gender-blind analysis of class that derives from Marxism remain more or less intact (Young, 1981; Vogel, 1984).

MARXIST FEMINISM Radical materialist feminists sometimes refer to themselves as *Marxist feminists* as opposed to socialist feminists because they prefer to take on board Marx's analytic framework and dialectical *methodology* rather than his socialist or class theory (for example, Christine Delphy, 1985).

'race' as separate but related forms of oppression (see page 22).

The view that women are oppressed by both patriarchy and capitalism has been the dominant approach of socialist feminism. However, it tends to be biased towards white Western women and pays only lip service to racial oppression (Vogel, 1984).

Radical feminism

Radical feminism argues that at root, women are oppressed by men. Radical feminists see it as a mistake to subsume the oppression of women under class oppression. There are two basic forms of radical feminism, the idealist and the materialist approaches.

Idealist radical feminism

Idealist radical feminists make up the bulk of what is usually referred to as radical feminism. In the early 1970s they were often referred to simply as feminists. More recently they have been referred to (rather inappropriately) as cultural feminists. They adopt a view that the biological differences between men and women make them distinct in how they perceive and know the world. (For this reason idealist radical feminists are also sometimes referred to as biological feminists.) In effect, idealist radical feminists adopt a separatist approach which ascribes sex specific characteristics to men and women (Arcana, 1983; Daly, 1979, 1984; Griffin, 1984a, 1984b; Morgan, 1978, 1982; Orbach, 1981; Rich, 1977; Spender, 1980, 1982, 1984). They suggest that women are biologically different and, as a consequence, are psychologically different. Therefore they have a view of the world that men cannot grasp. Men are usually projected in negative ways, emphasising aggressiveness, insensitivity and egocentrism. Women are seen in positive ways, emphasising togetherness, caring and sensitivity. It is this innate difference that excludes men from female perspectives and that has led men, in the past, to dominate and oppress women.

Materialist radical feminism

Materialist radical feminism also sees the oppression of women as primarily an oppression by men. However, it is opposed to idealist radical feminism because it argues that such oppression is rooted in *social* relations and not biology. Materialist radical feminism therefore does not advocate 'cultural separatism'. Materialist radical feminism proposes radical changes in social relationships between men and women, and thus of radical changes in society, as the only long-term solution to the oppression of women.

In the main, materialist radical feminism accepts that women are oppressed by capitalism as well as patriarchy but gives precedence to gender over class oppression (Delphy, 1985). Gender is related but somehow prior to, and distinct from, class oppression.

Overview of feminism

Socialist feminism differs from *idealist radical feminism* because it does not accept that gender is the sole or primary determinant of women's oppression. Socialist feminism differs from *materialist radical feminism* in more subtle ways, but primarily socialist feminism argues that sexual oppression within classes is (at least in part) a structural effect of capitalist relations. Patriarchy and capitalism are separate but interrelated. Materialist radical feminism argues that patriarchy and capitalism are separate forms of oppression and that, chronologically, patriarchy precedes capitalism. Although capitalism and partriarchy may be linked it is a mistake to apply old-fashioned class theory to the position of women. The first job is to understand women's oppression before trying to link it to class oppression.

So, feminists are divided over the operation of gender oppression. For some, it is fundamentally due to the dominance exercised by men. For others, it is intertwined with class-based oppression, or at the very least cannot be seen in isolation from the structural organisation of society. Women have been systematically denied access to resources and thus to power.

There is also considerable disagreement among feminists about suitable political tactics. A liberal democratic view asks no more than equal opportunity and access to resources. Socialist feminism broadly requires an economic and gender transformation. Radical feminism argues the transformation must be directed to a new politics of gender, possibly achievable only through separatism (see Segal, 1987).

Feminist debate has been dominated by class and gender issues but more recently 'race' and sexuality have become important issues. These have provided a basis for redirecting feminist analyses away from approaches that emphasise a unitary perspective to those which suggest the need for a multifaceted analysis. For example, it is increasingly clear that the absence of black women in feminist discourses cannot be resolved by simply adding them to existing theory (Joseph, 1981; Moraga and Anzaldua, 1981; Carby, 1982; Davis, 1982; Jones, 1982; Parmar, 1982; Bourne, 1983; Dill, 1983).

> **NOTE** The introductions to the work of Marx, Weber and Durkheim presented here in no way reflect the subtlety and depth of their writing. These are necessarily very crude overviews and you should endeavour to look more closely at the work of these authors as you become more familiar with sociology. There are thousands of commentaries on the writings of Marx, Weber and Durkheim. They are useful summaries but are, of course, the points of view of the people who write them. If you really want to understand the views of Marx, Weber and Durkheim you should try to read some of their own work for yourself.

Class, 'race' and gender: overview

Positivists approach class, 'race' and gender as variables. They may be dependent variables that can be explained in terms of role or expectations. More usually they are used as independent variables to explain other social phenomena. All surveys these days ask people to indicate their class (usually via occupation), 'race' (usually via ethnic group) and sex. These are 'key variables' for positivist sociological analysis. The results of the survey are compared for each of these groups. Differences are then attributed, at least in part, to the effect of class, 'race' or gender. For example, in Chapter 3, we show how inequalities in health are explained by class, sex and ethnic group.

Phenomenology has very little interest in general theories of class, race or gender. Indeed, it is surprising how little reference there is to class, 'race', ethnicity, sex or gender in sociological writing that falls within the broad area of phenomenology. For example, a sample of 84 symbolic interactionists were asked to indicate the most important concepts in sociology. Between 35% and 45% mentioned 'self', 'interaction', 'culture' and 'norm'. Only 7% mentioned 'conflict' and just 2% mentioned 'social class'. None of the respondents mentioned 'race' or 'gender' (Reynolds, 1969).

Critical approaches see class, 'race' and gender as means by which people are oppressed. Much critical sociology is based on Marxism. However, there is a growing body of research and theorising that shifts the emphasis away from the overwhelming insistence on class that has characterised Marxist analysis. Increasingly, critical sociology sees oppression as involving a number of interlinked structures of which class 'race' and gender are the main ones, although sexuality, disability and age can also be oppressive.

> **Further Reading**
>
> *Class and stratification*: Giddens, 1989, chapter 7; Haralambos, 1990, chapter 2; Marshall, Rose and Newby, 1989; Saunders, 1989.
>
> *'Race' and ethnicity*: Braham *et al.*, 1992; Giddens, 1989, chapter 8; Miles, 1989; Richardson and Lambert, 1985; Sherman and Wood, 1982, chapter 6.
>
> *Gender and sexuality*: Bilton *et al.*, 1981, chapter 6; Garrett, 1987; Giddens, 1989, chapter 6; Haralambos, 1990, chapter 9; Weeks, 1986.
>
> *Ideology*: Abercrombie, Hill and Turner, 1990; Thompson, 1986.
>
> *Hegemony*: Bocock, 1986.
>
> *Doing a sociology project*: Barrat and Cole, 1991; Bell, 1989.

CHAPTER 2
MEDIA ANALYSIS

Introduction

In this chapter we will be looking at some of the ways in which the mass media can be examined. The study of the mass media, as we suggested in Chapter 1, provides a useful starting point for doing sociology, for three reasons. First, the mass media are something we all know about and make use of. Just about everybody watches television, listens to the radio, reads newspapers, magazines or comics and is bombarded by advertising messages. In short, the mass media provide us with a readily accessible source of material for research purposes. Second, the study of the mass media involves a wide range of research techniques from social surveys, through observation to analysis of media content. Third, there are many different views about the mass media and about how they should be researched. Some social researchers think that it is important to study the *effects* of the mass media on the audience. An alternative approach considers the way that the audience makes *use* of the mass media. Some researchers consider how media messages are *produced,* while others look at the *content* of the messages.

The study of the media involves several different perspectives and aims. It thus provides an accessible example of the different methodologies that social researchers can adopt.

Although we show the full range of media research in this chapter, we do not attempt to go into the details of all the different *techniques*. We explore techniques such as observation, interviewing and secondary data analysis in the following chapters. We concentrate, in this chapter, on techniques for the analysis of media *content* as this is the one area that is more-or-less unique to media research. Thus, most of the practical examples focus on ways of analysing media messages.

When we talk of the mass media we refer to the means by which messages are conveyed to very large, widely dispersed and socially mixed audiences. These include television, radio, cinema, video, newspapers, magazines, comics, popular books, and advertisements. Indeed, it is any form of communication that is intended to inform, educate, entertain or persuade a large, diverse audience.

A major area of research into the media involves finding out who watches which television programmes and what the readership is for different newspapers and magazines.

Newspaper readership

Readership patterns are monitored in the *National Readership Survey* conducted by the Joint Industry Committee for National Readership Surveys (JICNARS). They publish their findings and the results are summarised in *Social Trends* (see Chapter 3 for more detail on official statistics and *Social Trends*). The readership figures for 1988 are shown in Table 2.1.

> **NOTE** We do not discuss *ownership* and *control* of the media. For details of the history of broadcasting, ownership, accountability, censorship and future trend, see Gration *et al*., 1988, chapters 8, 9 and 11; and Haralambos, M., ed., 1985, pp. 418–28.

Table 2.1 Reading of national newspapers and most popular magazines by sex and by age, 1988

	% of adults reading each publication in 1988			% of each age group reading each publication in 1988				Readership (millions)	
	All	*Males*	*Females*	*15–24*	*25–44*	*45–64*	*65+*	*1971*	*1988*
Daily newspapers									
Sun	25	23	27	34	25	24	17	8.5	11.3
Daily Mirror	19	22	17	21	19	21	17	13.8	8.7
Daily Mail	10	10	9	8	9	11	10	4.8	4.3
Daily Express	10	10	9	8	8	12	12	9.7	4.3
Daily Star	7	9	6	10	8	6	4		3.3
Daily Telegraph	6	7	5	4	5	8	7	3.6	2.7
Guardian	3	4	2	3	4	3	1	3.6	2.7
Today	3	4	3	4	4	3	1		1.5
The Times	2	3	2	2	3	3	2	1.1	1.1
Independent	2	3	2	3	3	2	1		1.1
Financial Times	2	2	1	2	2	2	0	0.7	0.8
Any daily newspaper	67	70	64	68	65	71	64		
Sunday newspapers									
News of the World	29	30	28	38	30	27	21	15.8	13.2
Sunday Mirror	20	21	18	22	20	20	16	13.5	8.9
People	17	18	16	16	17	19	17	14.4	7.8
Sunday Express	13	13	12	9	10	16	17	10.4	5.7
Mail on Sunday	12	12	12	3	14	12	6		5.3
The Sunday Times	8	9	8	9	10	9	4	3.7	3.8
Sunday Telegraph	5	6	5	4	5	6	6	2.1	2.3
Observer	5	5	4	5	6	5	2	2.4	2.1
Any Sunday newspaper	73	74	71	73	72	76	69		
General magazines									
TV Times	20	19	21	22	22	19	18	9.9	9.1
Radio Times	20	19	21	21	21	19	18	9.5	9.0
Reader's Digest	14	14	14	9	15	17	14	9.2	6.4
Smash Hits	4	3	4	14	2	0	0		1.7
Exchange and Mart	3	5	2	5	5	3	1		1.6
What Car?	3	6	1	6	4	2	1		1.6
Women's Magazines									
Woman's Own	10	3	17	11	11	10	8	7.2	4.6
Woman	7	2	13	7	9	7	5	8.0	3.3
Woman's Weekly	7	2	12	4	6	8	10	4.7	3.1
Best	6	2	9	8	7	5	3		2.6
Prima	5	1	9	7	8	4	2		2.5
Family Circle	5	2	9	4	7	6	3	4.4	2.4

Adapted from *Social Trends* 20. Original source: *National Readership Surveys*, 1971 and 1988.

Student Activity 2.1

1. Which was the most widely read daily newspaper in 1971 and which was the most widely read in 1988?
2. Which Sunday newspapers have increased their readership since 1971?
3. Do more people read daily or Sunday newspapers?
4. Which publication has the highest number of readers per copy?
5. Which women's magazine has the highest percentage readership among the oldest age group?
6. Which was the most popular magazine with women readers in 1988?
7. Which was the most read women's magazine in 1988?

Table 2.2 Top 50 TV Programmes, week ending 23 September 1990

	Channel	Day	Millions
1 Eastenders	BBC1	Th Su	17.7[a]
2 Coronation St.	ITV	W Sa	17.1[b]
3 Coronation St.	ITV	F Sa	16.5[c]
4 Coronation St.	ITV	M W	16.4[d]
5 Eastenders	BBC1	Tu Su	16.3[e]
6 Neighbours	BBC1	M–F	15.2[f]
7 The Bill	ITV	Th	11.9
8 Beadle's About	ITV	Sa	11.8
9 Casualty	BBC1	F	11.2
10 Best of Blind Date	ITV	Sa	11.2
11 Bread	BBC1	Su	11.0
12 Generation Game	BBC1	F	11.0
13 Star Trek IV	ITV	Sa	10.9
14 Taggart	ITV	Tu	10.7
15 Birds of a Feather	BBC1	Th	10.5
16 Home and Away	ITV	M–F	10.5[g]
17 Family Fortunes	ITV	F	10.2
18 The Bill	ITV	Tu	10.2
19 On The Up	BBC1	Tu	10.1
20 Emmerdale	ITV	Th	10.1
21 News	BBC1	Su	10.0
22 Last of the S. W.	BBC1	Su	10.0
23 Krypton Factor	ITV	M	9.6
24 Never the Twain	ITV	W	9.5
25 King Solomon's..	ITV	M	9.5
26 Stay Lucky	ITV	Su	9.4
27 Emmerdale	ITV	Tu	9.4
28 News	ITV	Su	9.2
29 All Creatures...	BBC1	Sa	9.0
30 News	ITV	Sa	9.0
31 Howard's Way	BBC1	Su	8.9
32 Carrot's Comm...	BBC1	Th	8.9
33 'Allo 'Allo	BBC1	M	8.5
34 In Sickness...	BBC	Sa	8.4
35 48 Hours	ITV	Sa	8.4
36 News, Sport	BBC1	Sa	8.3
37 May to December	BBC1	Tu	8.1
38 9 O'Clock News	BBC1	M–F	7.9
39 6 O'Clock News	BBC1	M–F	7.8
40 Columbo	ITV	F	7.7
41 Bergerac	BBC1	W	7.7
42 Tomorrow's W'ld	BBC1	Th	7.6
43 Top of the Pops	BBC1	Th	7.6
44 Tales of the Un...	ITV	Su	7.5
45 Runaway	BBC1	Tu	7.4
46 Every Second ...	BBC1	Sa	7.3
47 Russ Abbot	BBC1	Sa	7.3
48 Catchphrase	ITV	Sa	7.3
49 Everybody's Equal	ITV	Tu	7.1
50 The Match	ITV	W	7.0

The viewing figures for programmes shown twice in a week broke down as follows: a. 13.4/4.3 b.14.9/2.2   c.13.7/2.8   d.14.6/1.8   e.13.1/3.2 f. 5.7/9.5   g 3.5/7.0

Source: BARB. Adapted from *Broadcast*, week ending 12 October 1990. Original list compiled by Laing Henry Hill Holliday.

Television viewing

British television viewing is constantly monitored by the Broadcasters' Audience Research Board (BARB) and the results are published each week in the magazine *Broadcast*. Table 2.2 shows the top 50 programmes for the week ending 23 September 1990.

Student Activity 2.2

1. **Which single broadcast programme during the week of 23 September 1990 had the highest viewing figures? On which channel and which day was it broadcast?**
2. **Which was the most popular news programme?**
3. **What were the total viewing figures for each of the following soap operas during the week ending 23 September 1990: *Coronation Street, Eastenders, Neighbours*?**
4. **How many BBC2 and C4 programmes appear in the Top 50?**
5. **Which was the most watched sports programme?**
6. **Which was the most watched music programme?**

These viewing figures show how many people are watching each programme. But how does BARB work out how many of us are watching each programme? Clearly it is not possible to ask everybody each day which programmes they watched. So instead, a sample of people is used. BARB use a volunteer panel of around 3000 viewers. The panel is selected so that it represents the different types of household in the population. Each household in the panel has a remote detection meter attached to the back of the television. This monitors when the television is on and to which channel it is tuned. This information is transmitted through the mains electrical supply to a meter that records the information. The meter is linked to the telephone system and the data in the meter is sent to a central computer, via the telephone system, each night. Each member of the family is allocated a number. When they are in the room when the television is on they press their number on a remote control device and this lights up the corresponding number on a small display unit on top of the television. Currently, Audits of Great Britain (AGB) are the company who administer the system and provide detailed viewing figures. They work out the percentages of their panel who are watching each programme and use them to estimate the numbers of the population who would be watching the programme.

Student Activity 2.3

How accurate do you think the method used to collect viewing figures is? What problems can you see arising from this method? Do you think that the average viewing figures reported in *Broadcast* are a valid measure of how many people watch each programme?

Accuracy, reliability and validity

The aim of much social research is to collect data that is accurate, reliable and valid. *Accuracy* refers to the collection of data without making mistakes. So using a detection unit to record when the television is on and which viewer buttons are pressed is extremely accurate (assuming the electronics are working properly).

Reliability refers to the extent to which a method of data collection is consistent and repeatable and is not distorted by the researcher. As there is no researcher involved in collecting the data the reliability depends on the viewers ensuring that they indicate when they are watching the television. There is another problem that arises when guests visit. Although there are buttons on the remote control for guests (the unit has eight buttons in all), visitors are often not used to the system and may not reliably indicate what they view. In some circumstances there may be more guests watching a programme than there are available buttons on the remote. It is estimated that audiences for the World Cup were higher than the panel viewing figures indicated because watching matches was often done in large groups, which the panel system was unable to cope with. Thus, although it is an accurate system of recording what programme is on, the system is not necessarily reliable when it comes to monitoring who is watching the programme. However, the system is much more reliable than, for example, interviews that would require people recalling what they had watched the day before.

Validity refers to whether or not the data collected actually reflects the concept being measured. When we refer to television viewing do we mean those people who are in the room when the programme is on, whether or not they are paying full attention to the programme, or do we only mean those people who are sitting and closely watching the programme? If the panel members are left to decide whether or not they are 'watching' then there might be a problem over the validity of the data. For example, someone reading a newspaper in a room with a television on might or might not regard themselves as 'watching'. To overcome this problem AGB give the following instruction to their panel members:

> When any members of the family aged 4 and over, and/or Guests are present in a room with a TV set on then they should operate their individual button on the Handset for that TV set. This should be done regardless of whether full attention is actually being given to the television. (AGB, undated)

Thus AGB provide all their respondents with a single definition of what constitutes watching. However, while this may lead to consistency within the sample, there are questions about the validity of the concept. AGB's notion of what constitutes 'watching' may differ from what a sociologist or media analyst might regard as 'watching' (see Extract 2.1).

> **Student Activity 2.4**
> Undertake a study of viewing habits of people in your class or group. Arrange for the group members to record which programmes they watch over the weekend. Make sure that everyone records what they watch in the same way so that data is accurate, reliable and valid. Assess how successful you have been in achieving accuracy, reliability and validity.

Attitudes to the media

Research is also undertaken on people's opinions about what they read, listen to and view on television. For example, the Independent Broadcasting Authority (IBA) undertook an annual survey of *Attitudes to Broadcasting* every year from 1970 to 1990 (except 1978). BARB also supervises a national *Television Opinion Panel* (TOP). This panel consists of a weekly sample of 3000 respondents aged 12 years and over. The TOP is administered by post. Each week the panel member receives a booklet to cover 7 days' programmes. It is designed to get viewers' appreciation for each programme seen, more detailed reactions about particular aspects of

---

TYPES OF AUDIENCE Not everybody who watches a programme watches all of it and so the system used by AGB provides information on how many people in the panel are watching each minute of each programme. This allows them to work out the number of people who have watched any part of a particular programme (this is called the 'reach' of the programme); the number of people who watch all of the programme (this is called the 'core' audience); and the average number of people who watch each minute of the programme (this is called the 'average' audience and is less than the 'reach' and more than the 'core'). Average viewing figures are usually the ones used in published viewing figures.

Extract 2.1

WATCHING TELEVISION

Peter Collett, a research psychologist, hid video cameras inside television sets to see what people did while the television was on. His tapes show people talking, reading, sleeping, practising their golf putting and making love, amongst other things, while the television was on. Often no one is actually watching the television set at all.

The commercial breaks are a cue for people to leave the room to go to the toilet, make tea, use the remote control to 'zap' to other channels, and so on.

Source: *Guardian* 12 November 1991.

Table 2.3 Attitudes towards British-made crime series

Percentages of viewers who agree with the statement:	Bergerac	Juliet Bravo	Cats Eyes	The Bill	Dempsey and Makepeace
There are many more violent programmes than – on TV	93	95	87	84	84
From what I have seen, the violence in – is often necessary to the story	66	74	62	74	60
– features too many extreme forms of violence for my liking	6	4	10	10	18
I think the use of violence by the police in – is nearly always justified	53	70	49	58	40
The police in real life would never behave like – does	28	17	31	18	51
The police in – are often far more violent than they need to be	10	5	16	15	35
– portrays the behaviour of criminals unrealistically	19	13	25	14	28
– is suitable for children to watch	47	72	41	33	44
– is not likely to be taken seriously by children	40	23	47	27	42
– is not suitable for family viewing	12	10	13	26	22
I would be glad to see – taken off the screen	7	5	14	12	8

Adapted from Gunter and Wober (1988).

Example answer to Student Activity 2.5 Part 3

The following is a paraphrase of Gunter and Wober's summary of viewers' attitudes to these British crime series.

Violence is perpetrated by different types of characters on TV, who, within the context of different story lines, have different motives or reasons for their aggressive actions. An important element likely to affect viewers' judgement about TV violence is the nature of the aggressor. Overall, a large proportion of the sample perceived the use of violence by fictional police to be nearly always justified. However, the opinion varied over series and was not always a majority opinion. Only in a few cases, however, were fictional police viewed as more violent than necessary.

With one exception, there were reservations about the suitability of the programmes for children. Many respondents felt that children were likely to take these programmes seriously. This seems to relate to the possibility of children watching these programmes without an adult present as most respondents indicated that they thought the series were suitable for family viewing. General evaluations of UK crime series were, on the whole, positive and few respondents said they would be glad to see any of these series taken off the screen. This opinion prevailed despite earlier reservations about the suitability of these programmes for young viewers.

programmes, and detailed opinions about more general topics related to television viewing. The panel is designed to be nationally representative.

The issue of violence on television is one about which there is considerable public concern. In opinion surveys most people tend to say that there is too much violence on television. For example, Gallup Polls in November 1985 and September 1987 showed that 60% and 56% respectively thought that there was 'too much violence in television entertainment shows' (Gunter and Wober, 1988, p. 5). The problem with this kind of opinion survey is that the question is rather vague. So, as part of their research into audience perceptions of television violence, Gunter and Wober (1988) sought viewers' attitudes about specific television series. The main results for a selection of British-made crime series are shown in Table 2.3.

Student Activity 2.5
1. **Referring to Table 2.3, do the respondents think that**
   a. these series are particularly violent?
   b. the violence in each of these series is an acceptable part of the story?
   c. these programmes should be taken off the screen?
   d. the use of violence, by fictional police, is justified?
   e. these crime series programmes are suitable viewing for children?
   f. the programmes are suitable family viewing?
2. **How do you explain the apparent contradiction between answers e and f?**
3. **Gunter and Wober make two contradictory statements:**
   'The perceived realism of the police varied across series too, but in general relatively few respondents accepted that these series gave unrealistic portrayals of police behaviour' (p. 36); and
   'Fictional portrayals of the police were generally not perceived by the majority to reflect the behaviour of real life police' (p. 38).
   Which of these two statements would you say the data in Table 2.3 supports?

The social impact of the media

Measuring audience viewing or newspaper readership and asking for audience reaction to programmes are important areas of research for the producers of television programmes and for newspaper editors and owners. They also provide essential information for advertisers, who can select where and when to place advertisements to reach the kind of people the product is being aimed at. However, for the social researcher, this descriptive information, while interesting, only scratches the surface of social enquiry. Social researchers are not just concerned, for example, with who watches what but also want to find out what social impact the media have.

There are three sorts of questions that media researchers are concerned with. First, what effect does the mass media have on the audience? Second, how are media messages produced and interpreted? Third, what role does the media play in reproducing the social structure?

These three types of question represent three very different methodological concerns. Effects research is essentially positivist; interpretation research is, broadly speaking, phenomenological; and structural research is critical (see Chapter 1). We will look at examples of these types of research to illustrate the principles of different social research methodologies, and sum up the three approaches in the conclusion to this chapter.

Effects of the media

A large amount of research has analysed the effects that the mass media have on their audience. There is a widespread public belief that the media do affect the audience in various ways.

Behaviourist theories of media effects

A spectacular example of media effect occurred in the 1930s when Orson Welles' adaptation of *War of the Worlds* was broadcast on American radio. The programme began with a mock news broadcast of an alien invasion. It caused considerable panic, about 6 million listeners believed what they heard, and many people who lived in the vicinity of the supposed invasion got in their cars and fled.

An area of public concern, as we have seen, is the relationship between violence on television and violence in society. 'Over the years, more funding and research effort has been invested in the study of television violence than in any other aspect of television output. It is one of the most researched areas in the social sciences' (Gunter and Wober, 1988, p. 1).

In particular, it is assumed that children are susceptible to violent media images and are liable to act in a violent or aggressive way as a result of watching violent television. In one study children were shown a video of adults acting aggressively towards larger-than-life dolls. When subsequently given the opportunity to play with the dolls the children imitated the aggressive behaviour of the adults on the video (Bandura and Walters, 1964). Similarly, children exposed to violent programmes were shown to be slower in seeking adult help when they witnessed violence among children than were children who had not been exposed to violent programmes (Drabman and Thomas, 1975).

Similar effects research has examined the impact of the media on sex-role

BEHAVIOURISM is an approach that sees action as a mechanical response to external stimuli. Behaviourists argue that what we do is determined entirely by the environment. They argue for a stimulus–response model of behaviour. Behaviourists argue that we cannot know what is going on in someone's mind therefore we cannot attempt to show what effect this has on behaviour. Some behaviourists, notably Skinner, argue that the mind does not exist as a separate entity affecting behaviour. Our mental states, they argue, are just conditioned behaviour. Behaviourists thus argue that all mental states, including values, beliefs, motives and reasons, can only be defined in terms of *observable behaviour*. Behaviourists are thus not at all interested in the mental processes, intentions or meanings that lead to behaviour.

Behaviourism is a positivist approach and behaviourists see it as part of natural science. Behaviourists only accept 'scientific measurement' and most prefer experimental data. They all reject any data that refers to intentions.

MAGIC BULLET theory of the effects of the media is a crude view that suggests that the media transmit simple direct messages to which the audience react in direct, predictable and uniform ways. In short, media messages are like magic bullets. They provide a straightforward stimulus to which the audience respond. This approach, although popular following the Orson Welles incident, no longer has much credibility among media sociologists.

CULTIVATION THEORY of the media argues that media effects are indirect, gradual, generalised and symbolic. That is, the media does not have a direct effect on people's behaviour but it does affect how people perceive the world and their attitudes towards it. This effect is gradual. People slowly build up a view of the world which reflects what they see on television or read in newspapers rather than what they encounter in real life.

Gerbner *et al.* (1986) argue that heavy viewers of television have a more distorted view of the world than light viewers. This has been criticised for not taking into account control variables. For example, the relationship between fear of crime and heavy viewing is explained by the neighbourhood in which viewers live. People who live in high crime areas have a higher fear of being a victim of crime but also stay at home and watch more television (Hirsch, 1980).

A major problem with cultivation theory, from a positivist point of view, is that it cannot make causal statements as it provides no controlled environment. Cultivation theory is only able to show correlations.

stereotyping. For example, young girls, aged 5 and 6 years old, were shown to hold less gender-stereotyped attitudes after watching a low-stereotyped cartoon, compared to those who saw neutral or high-stereotyped cartoons (Davidson *et al.*, 1979). This kind of research supports the notion that the media have a direct (and often harmful) effect. It is based on a behaviourist view that sees social action in terms of a stimulus-response model. The media provide a *stimulus*, to which the reader, listener or viewer *directly responds*.

Cultivation theory of the media

An alternative perspective on the effects of the media is cultivation theory. The assumption is that viewers' behaviour and attitudes are not directly and immediately effected by the media, rather people's general views of reality are gradually affected by exposure to the media. Alexis Tan's (1979) study of the effect of advertisements is an example of the cultivation approach. She examined the impact that advertisements, which relied on sex appeal and beauty to sell their products, had on the attitudes of young women. She argues that television cultivates certain perceptions of reality through a selective representation of particular themes rather than causes direct responses in individuals, as the behaviourist model suggests. In this case, what is being cultivated by the media is the desirability of various beauty characteristics. The study is summarised in Extract 2.2 on page 36.

> **Student Activity 2.6**
> 1. **What sort of research is Alexis Tan using in this study and what is she trying to show?**
> 2. **What do the results suggest to you about the effect of watching a heavy concentration of beauty advertisements?**
> 3. **What do you think are the limitations of this type of research?**

Tan asserts that the experiment supported the causal relationship between media exposure and attitude.

Although Tan used experiments, cultivation theorists, on the whole, are more likely to undertake surveys of people to find out what they watch and to relate this to questions about attitude or behaviour. For example, surveys have shown that people who watch a lot of television are more likely to have a view of the world that corresponds to how television portrays the world than are people who do not watch much television. In particular, older people are underrepresented on television, and heavy viewers tend to underestimate the numbers of elderly people in society. Similarly, there is a lot of violence on television and heavy viewers tend to think there is a lot more violent crime in society than do light viewers (Gerbner and Gross, 1976; Gerbner *et al.*, 1986). We look in more detail at how to carry out a social survey in Chapter 4.

It has been argued that surveys and experiments do not provide an accurate picture of the way people respond to television because they involve contrived settings in which people's reactions and views are obtained. A standard objection to experimental approaches is that they are such artificial situations that people are likely to react in a way that is different from the way they would react in everyday circumstances (see Chapter 5).

A more *naturalistic* approach to the analysis of effects is to examine the relationship between events that have happened in the real world.

For example, one study looked at the suicide rate in America following the highly publicised 'suicide' of well-known fictional characters on television (Phillips, 1986). Seasonal variations and some other factors were taken into

NATURALISTIC is a term applied to social research that attempts to grasp the 'natural' processes of social action and interaction. Naturalistic approaches attempt to collect information from social settings without creating artificial situations. Naturalistic approaches avoid asking direct questions or setting up experimental situations. Naturalistic research usually applies to research that uses direct observation of an existing social setting. Sometimes, as in Phillips' research, the term is used to refer to research that uses available data about the social world. This is more often referred to as *secondary data analysis* (see Chapter 3). In either case, the aim is to avoid creating artificial situations as a basis for collecting data.

Extract 2.2

AN EXPERIMENTAL STUDY

The study focuses on television advertisements which use sex appeal, beauty and/or youth as selling points. These Tan refers to as 'beauty commercials'. An example of one she used was an advertisement which suggested that using a particular toothpaste increased 'sex appeal'.

The main concern was to determine whether exposure to TV beauty commercials affected a viewer's perception of the importance of beauty, sex appeal and youth in various 'real life' roles. The 56 subjects in the study were all female high school students aged between 16 and 18. Four roles were tested: success in a career or job; success as a wife; to be popular with (or liked by) men; and 'for you personally to be desirable as a woman'. The general hypothesis tested was 'that all subjects exposed to the TV beauty commercials will rate sex appeal, youth and beauty characteristics more important in the four defined role relationships than subjects not exposed to the beauty commercials'.

The subjects were divided into two groups at random. The first group (called the experimental group) were shown 15 network TV 'beauty commercials' (called the treatment). The second group (called the control group) were shown 15 network commercials, such as Alpo dog food, all devoid of these 'beauty' features. In other respects the time and place in which the commercials were viewed and the length of the sequence of 15 commercials were identical.

To measure how important the two groups rated sex appeal, beauty and youth the subjects were asked to identify what they thought were the five most important characteristics, ranked in order, to be successful in the four different roles mentioned above. The subjects had to choose their five most important characteristics from the following list which contained five beauty traits and five non-beauty traits:

a pretty face	intelligence
sex appeal	hard-working
a youthful appearance	articulate (good) talker
a healthy, slim body	a good education
glamour	competence

In coding the data the mostly highly rated trait was scored 5 and the least highly (of the five selected) scored 1, Each respondent's score was added up for the five beauty traits (those in the first list). The resultant score ranged from 0 to 15. A person whose selection included all beauty traits scored 15 (i.e., 5 + 4 + 3 + 2 + 1) while a respondent who did not include any scored 0. The average for the two groups for each role were as follows:

	Experimental Group (n=23)	Control Group (n=33)
To be successful in career	2.91	2.21
To be a successful wife	3.47	4.00
To be popular with men	12.87	9.96
Personally desirable characteristic	4.13	2.81

Adapted from Tan (1979).

account and Phillips showed a link between these 'famous' suicides and suicide rates in general. The study has been heavily criticised for not taking into account sufficient other factors that may have effected the suicide rate and for Phillips' reliance on national suicide statistics. In Chapter 3 we look in detail at the problems of using official statistics, and in particular the problems of suicide statistics.

Content analysis

If assertions are made about the *effects* of the media on viewers then it is necessary to find out something about the *content* of the media. This is known as content analysis and it usually takes the form of counting or measuring specified features of media content. For example, counting the

---

Example answer to Student Activity 2.6

1. Tan's study was an experiment involving a control group and an experimental group. A single independent variable, beauty commercials, was manipulated. It was assumed that the independent variable would effect the subsequent attitudes of the subjects. The experimental group were exposed to a treatment in which the independent variable was present. The control group were used for comparison purposes and were given a treatment in which the independent variable was not present. Any difference in attitude would be assumed to be caused by the independent variable.

2. Beauty characteristics were not rated particularly highly in real life by the subjects except when it came to being popular with men. Furthermore, there was very little difference between the average scores for the two groups for the 'career' and 'wife' roles. However, the difference in the average score when it came to 'being popular with men' was more marked and this suggests that the perceptions about the group that had been heavily exposed to beauty advertisements thought beauty to be more important in relationships with men than the group who had not seen the beauty advertisements. Similarly, although to a lesser degree, there is a difference between the two groups as to the personal desirability of beauty characteristics. Tan concludes:

> The effects shown in this study, although short term, support the general theoretical model of television's 'cultivator' role in society. These effects since they were elicited in a laboratory setting with rigid controls and where time-order of variables was pre-determined, support the cause (media exposure) and effect (social reality perceptions) inferences which are usually drawn in media cultivation research. If such an effect can be attained from a single, saturated exposure to TV contents, it is very likely that long-term, repeated exposures (as those occurring in the real world) will yield stronger and lasting effects on viewers. (Tan, 1979, p. 288)

3. The limitations of experimental studies are discussed in detail in Chapter 5.

STEREOTYPES are inflexible categories which are used to ascribe particular characteristics to other groups of people. The British have a stereotype of Australian men as unsophisticated, macho beer drinkers. Such stereotypes may be facile but are not necessarily dangerous. However, when stereotypes are used as a basis for prejudice or as a *legitimation* for oppression then they are dangerous. In such circumstances stereotypes are often linked to hatred, abuse or violence.

Example findings – Student Activity 2.7

Product 1: *Ariel* washing powder
The advertisement consists of a sequence of eight well-dressed, attractive, white women in their twenties telling an unseen male interviewer what they would like from a washing powder. The women are shown washing, ironing or doing the shopping. We are told by a male voice-over that the women are the experts who have designed a new powder that 'we' (the unseen male) have made for them.

Product 2: *Birds Eye: Menu Master, Healthy Options*
The advertisement starts with a young white male holding a tray with two meals on it. He tells us that he has invited his friend's girlfriend to dinner. He has just taken the meal out of the microwave. A young, attractive, white woman in a leotard enters the room and sits on the sofa. Her boyfriend runs into the room and tells us that he has been working out in the gym. He too sits down on the sofa. The first man, carrying the tray, says that his game is squash, and squeezes between the two on the sofa. A male voice-over tells us that 'you don't have to be health mad to take the healthy option'. The advertisement finishes with a close-up of the product.

Product 3: *Walker's* crisps
An owl hoots and flies out of the dark towards the camera. Three boys are in a shed in the woods telling ghost stories about Walker's crisps, which they are eating. Outside, an unseen figure moves towards the shed through the wood. The boys hear a noise, the one who has taken up telling the ghost story is scared. The door bursts open. It is one of their friends. The newcomer and the other boys laugh at the their scared, but relieved, friend. All the boys are white.

number of aged people represented on 'prime time' television programmes and comparing them to real life; analysing the percentage of radio phone-in calls that criticise state agencies on different radio stations (Verwey, 1990); comparing the numbers and roles of males and females in soap operas (Pingree, 1983); analysing the portrayal of gender roles in pre-school books (Weitzman, 1974) and so on.

Media stereotyping

The media have been accused of reproducing a wide range of stereotypes, particularly around class, 'race', gender, age, disability and sexuality. Content analysis research has been widely used to examine the nature and extent of sexist stereotypes. Sexist portrayals of males and females appear to be widespread throughout all aspects of the media from advertisements to news broadcasts, from comics through trade journals to newspapers and popular fiction.

Women in advertisements and on other television programmes are, it is claimed, usually shown as wives and mothers and often seen to be in a panic, needing a male to sort out their problems, or as excited by the latest brand of washing powder, and so on. Alternatively, they are depicted as sex objects advertising products aimed at men, usually things like cars or cigars. Even when a product is aimed at women the voice-over is usually male, the idea is that women will respond to the voice of authority and buy the product! Men are more likely to be shown at work, having a drink in the pub or being active in some way. When a man is shown in the home he is often shown as being waited on by a woman or depicted as unable to use simple domestic equipment like a washing machine or cooker.

Student Activity 2.7
Undertake a content analysis of a selection of five television advertisements in which people appear. Look at how different people are portrayed. Write a paragraph describing what happens in the advertisement. Make sure you include the following:
1. the product being advertised;
2. the number, ages and ethnic groups of the men and women who appear;
3. the setting in which the action takes place.
4. what the males and females are doing; and
5. whether there is a voice-over and whether it is male or female.
SUGGESTION You will find a video recorder invaluable when analysing television output.

Our example findings suggest that this gender stereotyping is prevalent. Advertisements do not reflect the real world where women go out to work, drive cars and where men live alone, wash their clothes, shop and clean their homes. As a group you will have many such descriptions and you will probably find that the same advertisement is described in different ways by different people. What can we do with such a mass of data? How can we use the material systematically to analyse media output?

Constructing a content analysis grid
One way of analysing the data is to construct a grid in which to enter the findings in a systematic fashion. We are interested in gender stereotyping and so we designed a grid that would allow us to consider the descriptive data

Table 2.4 Summary of sample advertisements

Product	Setting	Participants		Activities		Active		Passive		Voice-over	Comments
		Male	*Female*	*Male*	*Female*	M	F	M	F		
Ariel	Domestic	0	8YW		Washing, ironing, shopping	0	8	0	0	Male	Powder developed scientifically by men
Birds Eye	Living room	2YW	1YW	Cooking, running	Sitting	2	0	0	1	Male	Only heating up a meal
Walker's Crisps	Playing in a den in a dark wood	4CW	0	Telling ghost stories		4	0	0	0	None	Boys having an adventure

KEY A Asian B Black C Children M Middle-aged N None O Older adult T Teenager VO Voice-over W White Y Young adult

in terms of gender stereotypes (Table 2.4).

This structured approach to content analysis provides us with a way of making some general statements about what we observe in our sample of advertisements. First, we note that all fifteen actors in the advertisements were white. Clearly this is not a 'representative' sample of advertisements but, even so, ethnic minorities seem underrepresented. Similarly, there were no old people in the advertisements, which again is unrepresentative of the population.

Analysing the data in the grid

Let us now consider the extent of the sex-role stereotyping in the advertisements. We can draw up a few simple statistics.

Total number of men in the advertisements	9
Total number of women in the advertisements	6
Number of male voice-overs	2
Number of female voice-overs	0
Number of men in domestic settings	2
Number of women in domestic settings	9
Number of men in active roles	6
Number of women in active roles	8

These show that in our sample more men than women were used in advertisements; voice-overs are male; and more women than men are shown in domestic settings. This confirms the view that advertisements represent gender stereotypes. However, Table 2.4 shows that more women than men are shown in active roles. This runs counter to expectations of gender stereotyping. However, if we take this analysis one stage further and analyse

CROSSTABULATION is a useful device in social science for showing the extent to which two or more groups differ in terms of a particular variable. It allows you to *break down* data to make comparisons. So, for example, opinion polls report the percentages of the sample who support Labour, Conservative, Liberal Democrat, and so on. This can be broken down to show the support for each party amongst men and women, or the support in different social classes, and so on.

REINFORCEMENT THEORY argues that the media *confirm* audience beliefs and attitudes rather than create new ones (Schramm and Roberts, 1971). The media only change opinions if the audience are predisposed to change. For example, the media are unable to change political and religious beliefs but their influence on fashion and popular music is considerable (McQuail, 1983). In a study of voting habits, Lazarsfeld *et al.* (1944) showed that the media strengthened political opinion rather than changed it.

USES AND GRATIFICATIONS THEORY has been mainly developed in relation to television. Uses and gratifications researchers argue that viewers makes use of the media for their own ends (or gratifications). They make more (or less) of the message than the broadcaster intended. Classic uses and gratifications theory sees four main types of gratification. First, television is a form of *escapism*. Second, it is a means of *social integration* (for example, having something to talk about at work). Third, it is an aid to *self-awareness* (comparing oneself to broadcast personalities). Fourth, it is a means of getting *information*.

Most uses and gratifications theory suggests that broadcasters have little influence over their audience. The audience is in control, makes use of the media, and is able to resist media effects.

the nature of the active roles we find:

Active roles	Domestic	Non-domestic
Males	1	5
Females	8	0

This crosstabulation shows that although there were more active females than males in our sample, they are much more likely to be doing domestic tasks than are males.

Clearly we have only a very small sample and would not want to make any definitive statements about the extent of gender stereotyping from this data. Does your own data bear out our tentative findings?

Student Activity 2.8
As a more extensive study, watch the advertisements on a television channel over a period of a week. Decide on the days and times when you will view. Justify your choice. Record the number of advertisements that represent females in stereotypical roles and those that show women in non-stereotypical roles. Do your results support the view that women are represented in sexist, stereotypical ways?

Content analysis is a way of quantifying the output of the mass media. It deals with the obvious, surface messages of the media (that is, the words, phrases or images that are produced). Content analysis requires that specific words, or images are defined in advance. The number of times they occur in an article, story or programme are counted as indicators of the extent of a particular phenomenon, such as gender stereotyping.

Content and effect

Content analysis studies often assume a relationship between content and effect. This rests on a common-sense notion that media content (at least some kinds of it, such as 'violence') must have some effect. Often, however, the media are not seen as causing new behaviour or attitudes but as *reinforcing* existing attitudes. In *The People's Choice*, for example, Paul Lazarsfeld *et al.* (1944) argued against the idea of the media as a stimulus and showed that the media seemed to act to reinforce people's preconceptions and prejudices rather than to change them (Klapper, 1960). Similarly, we have seen that cultivation theorists see the media as having a gradual effect. However, there is always the problem when analysing content of whether the content affects the viewers or whether the content reflects the society in which the viewers already live. In other words, does the media effect society or are the media effected by society (McQuail, 1983)?

Most studies of media *effects* tend to adopt quantitative approaches of one sort or another in attempts to show how the media are linked to social phenomena or attitudes. For example, Tan constructed scores for an experimental and control group based on how the subjects *rated* a list of characteristics, which she then compared statistically. Phillips used suicide *statistics* in his study of the effects of fictional suicides. Pingree *counted* the numbers and roles of males and females in soap operas, and so on.

Interpreting the media

Not all media research of the audience is concerned with the effects on the audience. An alternative approach has looked at what the audience get out of the media. *Uses and gratifications research*, for example, undertook surveys to analyse how the audience use the media to satisfy particular desires or needs (Blumler and Katz 1974; Blumler and McQuail, 1968). This is an early example of research that gave priority to the audience.

Market theory of the media

Uses and gratifications research has been used by so-called *market theorists* who argue that the media simply provide what the public wants. Sex and violence predominate because that is what the public finds interesting. The media are not potentially harmful, they simply cater for the market. Market theorists argue that research has shown that people do not usually accurately recall what they saw on television or read in the newspapers the previous day. So the media cannot be seen to have long-term effects (Whale, 1977). This approach is the opposite of *cultivation theory* (see page 35), which suggests that long-term exposure to the media does not result in immediate effects but gradually results in a particular set of views of society.

Agenda setting

An alternative interpretive framework is provided by the *agenda setting* theory of the media. It differs from the *uses and gratifications approach* and *market theory* by suggesting that individuals are not free to make use of, and interpret, the media as they want. *Behaviourist* theories (especially the cruder ones such as the *magic bullet* model (see page 35)) suppose that the media tell us what to think. The agenda setting view argues that although the media do not tell us what to think they *do* tell us what to think about (Noelle-Neumann, 1974; Tichenor *et al.*, 1970). The media provide the framework within which we approach issues. The media *define the situation* for us. This approach is most effective where readers and viewers have little or no other source of information, such as the media campaign around AIDS in the late 1980s (McCombs and Gilbert, 1986).

Reception theory

A more recent approach to understanding the audience is *reception theory*. This focuses, in detail, on the way that the audience receives and *interprets* media messages, rather than trying to identify the general needs of the audience. Reception theory focuses on what the audience makes of the programmes it watches. This is different from the content approach, which tends to ignore the idea that media content can be received in various alternative ways by audience members.

For example, Ien Ang (1985) undertook a study of audience reception of *Dallas*. She argued that the popularity of the series is associated with the pleasure viewers got from watching *Dallas*. Therefore it was important to find out from viewers what happens in the process of watching. Her empirical data came from 42 letters she received in reply to an advertisement in a Dutch magazine. She showed that fans do not see the plot of *Dallas* as being realistic but do find the programme *emotionally* realistic. She concluded that the pleasure of *Dallas* consists in the recognition of ideas that fit in with the viewers' imaginative world. The short-lived happiness and

MARKET THEORY OF THE MEDIA accepts that there is bias in the mass media. Most British newspapers, for example, support the Conservative party, show women as sex objects, and are racist. Market theorists use notions of profitability and consumer demand to suggest that readers and viewers get what they want. Most people want to read or hear conservative views, indulge in trivia, and so on. There are small-scale circulation alternative newspapers and magazines for people who want a different perspective. Market theorists thus adopt the *reinforcement* view and argue that the media does not influence our views and attitudes; rather it reinforces the ones we already have. They claim, like *uses and gratifications* theorists, that the public make use of the media for different reasons and there is no cause for concern about the harmful effects of the media. The market view ignores the obvious fact that the major organs of the mass media are controlled by the state or are in the hands of a few large companies, hence real consumer choice is restricted.

AGENDA SETTING argues that the media operate in the interests of the dominant, powerful groups or classes and transmit messages which reinforce dominant ideology. They limit the audience's ability to see issues in alternative ways by setting a limited agenda. The media thus acts to exclude some things from public debate whilst ensuring the limits within which other things are discussed.

DEFINITION OF THE SITUATION refers to the idea, first proposed by W. I. Thomas in the early 1900s, that people act in given circumstances on the basis of the way that they define the situation they are in. The definition of a situation will depend on experience. Where individuals do not have the appropriate experience, or where that experience is called into question, then they have to work out anew what the situation means. This process of defining the situation, in complex circumstances, can be aided by having someone else provide a definition. This is precisely the role that some media analysts say that the mass media play in mass society.

RECEPTION THEORY of the media attempts to show how people actively make sense of popular culture. Media messages are constructed in a particular way to have a specific meaning, However, reception theorists argue that media messages do not make sense independently of an interpreting reader. The interpreting reader may not get the same meaning from a message as was intended.

The reception analyst thus has to do three things. First, to make clear what the expected receiver of the message (or 'model reader' of the 'text') is presumed to be. Second, to determine at what points and in what ways the model reader is required to contribute so that the text makes sense (in the way it was intended). Third, to discover how the people who receive the message actually do make sense of it.

Not all reception theorists do the last stage. Ang (1985), Morley (1980) and Hobson (1982) all attempted the final stage. Other reception theorists such as Eco (1979), Jauss (1982) and Iser (1980) have been more concerned with the first two stages, in particular with developing the idea of the model reader.

constant recurrence of crisis in *Dallas* reflect, in melodramatic ways, the lives of viewers. 'They can "lose" themselves in *Dallas* because the programme symbolizes a structure of feeling which connects up with one of the ways in which they encounter life' (Ang, 1985, pp. 82–3).

Another analysis of how viewers interpret programmes was undertaken by David Morley (1980) who showed an edition of *Nationwide* (the BBC's long running, early evening, national and local news magazine) to different groups. The research, which used group discussions, indicated how different people 'read' the same programme in different ways.

In her study of the soap opera *Crossroads* (which ran on ITV from 1964 until the early 1980s) Dorothy Hobson (1982) attempted to link the production process of specific episodes with audience reception and understanding. She observed what went on in the ATV studios where the programme was made and had lengthy conversations with the producer, director and some of the actors. While this gave her some insight into the production process, she needed to undertake separate research on how the audience received the programme. This is illustrated in Extract 2.3.

Student Activity 2.9
1. **What method does Hobson use to find out how viewers receive *Crossroads*?**
2. **How is she able to recall and examine what happens during her research?**
3. **Would you say that Diane, in Extract 2.2, paid attention to *Crossroads* or just watched it automatically because it was on?**

The emphasis in reception studies is on the media experiences of viewers and the focus is usually on 'fans' rather than one-off viewers. Thus much reception research concentrates on serials, especially soap operas.

Most reception studies adopt what are known as *qualitative* approaches. They use in-depth interviewing, group discussions, direct observation, and

---

Extract 2.3

WATCHING *CROSSROADS*

I watched the programme sitting in Diane's kitchen/dining area in her modern house. I should point out that although I was sitting, Diane, with whom I had gone to watch the programme, was serving the evening meal, feeding her five- and three-year-old daughters and attempting to watch the programme on the black and white television situated on top of the freezer opposite to the kitchen table. Although I was sitting watching the programme, young children have no respect for the sanctity of media researchers and their need to be undisturbed in the research situation! To them I was as much a target for their attentions as was their mother. I became a part of the shared experience of viewing in that situation and struggled to concentrate against the same odds as their mother. The three-year-old invited me to help her eat her tea, the five-year-old to look at drawings from play school and talk about new shoes in the same manner they talked to their mother. Mercifully, the tape-recorder remains undistracted by everyday life and in the transcription of the interviews afterwards the whole situation was recaptured for me. Reliving the experience was not purely nostalgic, for it revealed that points of the story which had been missed by Diane coincided with points on the tape when the children had been at their most demanding, and showed that repetition is necessary in programmes to allow for any points missed by the viewers. However, women with young children do have ways of coping with them and half-watching/half-listening to television pro-

grammes at the same time. Listening is the operative word. In this sense the story line has to be carried by the verbal level and cannot always rely on the visuals augmenting the story. Diane explained her way of watching *Crosssroads*.

D   I don't sit and watch it. I'm usually pithering about, but I listen to it. I know what's going on. I think I prefer to listen rather than watch.

DH   So you rarely actually go in the front room and watch it on the colour television?

D   No. I never watch it in there. Just an odd time if somebody looks as if they've got something interesting on, I go to see what colour it is. Or if there was something like a wedding I suppose, a sort of occasion, when it would be a bit out of the ordinary, then I'd probably go and see what they were all wearing and ... but normally I just pither about in here.

DH   So, I assume as you watch it then you quite like it, or is it that that's what you have on?

D   Yes I do really, because Monday and Friday I have *Nationwide* on, but the rest of the time I put that on, and I quite often turn over afterwards.

Adapted from Hobson (1982, pp. 112–13).

the analysis of personal documents such as letters or diaries (see Chapters 6 and 7). The main aim of data collection in such cases is to explore the meanings that the media message has for the receiver rather than to attempt quantification of effects.

Interpreting media production

The interpretive approach has also been applied in studies of the *production* of media messages. A classic example is Philip Elliott's (1972) *The Making of a Television Series*. It provided a detailed account of the making of *The Nature of Prejudice*, a seven-part documentary series made in autumn 1967 for ATV and transmitted in spring 1968. The study, which used direct observation, traced the evolution of the programmes through all the processes of selection from the emergence of an idea, through the recruitment of the production team and the collection of a wide range of material, to their final realisation in the studio. Elliott shows how haphazard the process of programme production is and how much it is constrained by the social and organisational framework in which it takes place.

Ethnomethodological studies of media production

A different emphasis on the way media output is produced comes from ethnomethodology. For example, ethnomethodological studies of the construction of the news emphasise the *routine* way in which news is produced (Tuchman, 1973). Molotch and Lester (1974) argue that the news is a 'constructed reality' and not the reporting of an 'objective' world. The news is not just a selection from a set of events that have 'really happened out there'. On the contrary, what is 'really happening' is identical to what people attend to and it is this that determines the news. Rather than significant social occurrences becoming news, the news is made up of 'public events' that have been manufactured by the various agencies of news production. These agencies are the news promoters, assemblers and consumers. The news assemblers take note of what the promoters and consumers of news will make out of the event.

News promoters, assemblers and consumers all have various needs that do not necessarily coincide. The needs of the assemblers, for example, may relate to the formal organisation of the media such as the routines for getting work done, the career mobility patterns of a group of professionals, or the profitability of the organisation. Such routines and practices may not fit with the needs of news promoters. This view suggests that one approach to the mass media is to look not for reality, but for *purposes* which underlie the strategies of creating one reality instead of another. Ethnomethodological studies of the news thus undertake a close analysis of the routines and practices of news-making in terms of 'event needs' and event construction in order to see how the content of the news is constrained.

The interpretive studies discussed above thus provide insights into the way that media messages are produced and received. Most interpretive studies use qualitative techniques of data collection. Ang analysed the content of letters written to her. Morley used discussion groups to see how different people 'read' *Nationwide*. Hobson visited people in their homes and watched television with them and discussed the way they viewed *Crossroads*. Elliott used direct observation in his study of how a programme was put together, and Moloch and Lester adopted a similar technique in their ethnomethodological analysis of news production.

ETHNOMETHODOLOGY is concerned with taken-for-granted aspects of the social world. It concentrates on how people make *sense* of everyday aspects of their world. People adopt different roles and different sets of meanings in different situations and in so doing construct a variety of rationalities. They argue that we operate with a number of different *accounts* of the world and we apply the appropriate one in different situations. Thus, rather than see people as having a single rationality, ethnomethodologists see people as culturally very complex. Indeed, they criticise social scientists for seeing people as *cultural dopes*.

Ethnomethodologists argue that, to understand the actor's point of view, the social scientist must examine the *routine*, practical activities of everyday life.

Ethnomethodology is a development from symbolic interactionism, particularly Ervin Goffman. It attempts to bring together the phenomenology of Alfred Schutz and the sociology of Talcott Parsons.

Ethnomethodology began in the mid-1960s in a series of seminars at the University of California, Berkeley, under the direction of Harold Garfinkel. Garfinkel introduced the term ethnomethodology and published his first book *Studies in Ethnomethodology* in 1967.

Ethnomethodologists use a variety of *ethnographic* techniques (see Chapters 5, 6 and 7).

Conversation analysis is a branch of ethnomethodology that has developed its own techniques (see Chapter 7).

Some of these interpretive studies also point to, although do not concentrate on, the wider social and ideological context in which the media operate. It is this ideological and structural framework that is at the core of critical analyses of the role of the media.

Critical analyses of the media

Critical analyses of the media are concerned with the relationship between the mass media and the existing social structure. They examine what media messages contain, how they are 'read' and how they are produced. The aim is not to look at cause and effect relationships nor to interpret the processes of production and reception of the media. Critical studies see the media as part of the wider processes of control and as reproducing the *status quo* through the constant reassertion of dominant *ideology* (see page 15 for a summary of ideology).

Manipulative theory of the media

Early versions of the critical approach tended to see the media as being very powerful and manipulative. The *manipulative* theory derived from the experience in Germany in the inter-war years. The effective use of the mass media by Nazi propagandists led to a pessimistic view of the manipulative power of the media. At its simplest, the manipulative view is summed up in the *hypodermic* model. The media 'injected' ideas and the audience responded to them. In this approach, which parallels the *magic bullet* theory of the effects of the media (see page 34), the audience is seen as atomised and completely powerless in the face of unscrupulous propaganda.

A second, more sophisticated, version of manipulation theory can be found in the work of the *Frankfurt School*. They argued that the second half of the twentieth century was an era of mass society that had resulted in the loosening of traditional social ties. People lived in a bewildering world where they were bombarded by mass culture. The mass media provided a simple view of the complexities of mass society. The problem was that mass society was one-dimensional, it offered no alternative conceptualisations. The media were thus manipulative because they reproduced this one-dimensional world.

The one-dimensional view of the manipulative media is similar to the *agenda-setting* approach (see page 40). The agenda-setting view disagrees with other interpretive approaches that suggest media users are free to make what they like of the content. Agenda setting, as we have seen, argues that the situation is defined for us. The one-dimensional approach argues not only that the situation is defined for us, but the definition is also part of a much broader process of social control within mass society.

A third version of the manipulative theory is the *control-of-the-media* view. The argument is that ownership and control of the major elements of the mass media is in the hands of conservative white men and that their views are reproduced by the media, most noticeably in the case of newspapers. These owners are committed capitalists and, although giving journalists and editors a degree of independence, expect to see their views expressed in the newspapers they own. This is achieved through the appointment of like-minded editors, or by making it clear that certain conservative principles cannot be contravened. For example, editors should ensure that they do not attack the idea of free enterprise; they should see trade unionists as the

MANIPULATIVE THEORY of the media argues that the powerful and wealthy own the media and use them to maintain the existing social structure. Where the media are publicly owned they are part of the state apparatus. In which case the media provide a point of view that shows the importance of a powerful central state. The media concentrate on conservative ideas and ridicule radical or revolutionary ones. They deflect attention from important matters by providing a steady diet of trivia, such as quiz shows, chat shows on television and titillating and banal stories in newspapers. Manipulative theory suggests that audiences are powerless and easily influenced.

problem in industrial relations rather than employers; they should not support left-wing or revolutionary political movements; and so on. A second way in which the media are controlled by bourgeois interests is through advertising revenue. The main advertisers are the multinational corporations and they tend to direct their large advertising budgets to newspapers and magazines that are sympathetic to them. A third form of bourgeois control comes through the government. Rarely does this involve direct censorship. However, government ministries and other official agencies provide the media with prepared explanations of official policy and these are often uncritically included in newspapers (Miliband, 1973).

Hegemonic theory of the media

The more recent critical approach to media analysis adopts Gramsci's notion of *hegemony* and links the media to *ideology* (see pages 14 and 15). The hegemonic view argues that the media do not attempt deliberately to manipulate the audience. Rather the media reassert a dominant view of the world and *legitimate* existing forms of social oppression, ownership of wealth, civil liberties and so on. The media are thus not seen as important in themselves, they are one element in the production and reproduction of dominant ideology.

The earliest versions of this approach saw the audience as incidental to the study of the way the media produced ideological meanings. Audiences were seen as powerless recipients of dominant ideological messages. Having received the messages the audience simply recirculated them, thus contributing to the taken-for-granted nature of the dominant ideology (Fejes, 1984). The role of critical media analysis was thus to uncover the hidden meanings of media texts (Newcomb, 1982; Rowland and Watkins, 1984).

A more recent development of the hegemonic approach has argued that the audience is not completely powerless and that recipients of the media are able to 'read' them in a variety of ways, including critical readings. However, the media operate in a hegemonic framework within which there are *preferred readings* (Hall, 1973). The preferred meanings are those of the dominant groups. They are ideological and derive from the social structure, particularly from class, 'race' and gender relations. The preferred meanings serve to reproduce the social structure by making dominant views appear as normal. For example, television news takes for granted the idea that the royal family is an admirable institution of which all Britons are proud. This does not mean that it is not possible to read something other than the preferred meaning in a media message. (You might, for example, read a news report about the royal family as the actions of a decadent and parasitic elite.) However, it requires a good deal of critical work to do this, whereas the taken-for-granted views are much easier to read because they appear obvious.

Critical studies of content thus see media messages not as having direct effects, nor as open to any interpretation the receiver might put on them, but as containing a preferred meaning.

Critical studies of media production

Philip Schlesinger's (1978) study of BBC News is an example of a critical analysis of the *production* of media messages. He observed how the *News* was produced at the BBC but also linked his observations to a study of the structure, history and ideology of the BBC that led him to the wider issue of how *BBC News* reproduces dominant ideology.

MASS SOCIETY AND MASS CULTURE *Mass society* refers to the view that we live in a world dominated by mass production. Mass production involves large units of production and distribution, and national (or international) scale marketing. Changes in technology, transport and communications has made mass production and mass marketing possible. In so doing it has broken down traditional communities and values. People in mass society have become a mass of consumers. In the process of developing mass consumption, old cultural distinctions have also been eroded and a new, extensively marketed and profitable, *mass culture* has emerged. Mass culture tends to be undemanding, diverting and uncritical. It includes soap operas, pop music, fashion, Hollywood films, quiz shows, comics, mainstream glossy magazines, pulp fiction, advertisements, package holidays and adventure parks.

Schlesinger asks, how is the news actually put together in the BBC newsrooms? How does the way it is assembled result in a specific version of reality? In particular, what are the *practices* and ideology that lie behind BBC news? He used direct observation, formal and informal interviews with BBC news staff. Schlesinger looked at the history of BBC news and the routines that news producers adopted. He examined myths about news production, such as the reporters' belief that they are free to do the job as they think appropriate, and the notion that news is somehow produced out of chaos without any noticeable organisational structure. Schlesinger, like the *ethnomethodologists*, shows, on the contrary, that news is produced in routine ways (see page 42). Furthermore, a system of controls operates, such as the process by which stories are allocated to reporters. These particular constraints reinforce a commitment to the BBC's world view. Central to this world view is the concept of impartiality.

Officially, the BBC's news output is value-free. The myth of value-freedom is essential for public consumption, and is believed by those who propagate it. To have individuals with identifiable political positions opens up the BBC to criticisms of bias. So there is a 'desired identity' for news workers to which all, in different ways, conform. At its most basic, Schlesinger argues, this is 'a condition of employment'; at its most developed it becomes a 'vocation'.

This 'desired' identity of BBC employees was subsequently shown to be 'required' when, in 1985, it was revealed that the government's internal security department (MI5) had an office in the BBC and were actively involved in vetting the selection of journalists and production staff.

However, the reporting of Northern Ireland stretches the credibility of the notion of impartiality. Coverage of Northern Ireland consists mainly of reports of violence, taken out of context, which fail to analyse the historical roots of the Irish conflict. The treatment of Ireland shows that while the BBC is not a simple tool of the ruling group (government, army and so on) it is constrained by them and is not entirely independent. Occasionally, government control of the BBC comes into the open. For example, *Real Lives*, a programme about those involved with terrorism in Northern Ireland was banned by the Home Secretary in 1985. A modified version was subsequently shown following a public outcry and a strike by television journalists.

Schlesinger examines the news production process and links it to the role of the BBC as a reproducer of the *status quo*. His study does more than examine the routine practices and organisational constraints. It also links the process of news production to wider social factors, such as government policy and the need for the BBC to retain the myth of collective neutrality.

Critical analyses of media content

Critical analyses also focus on media *content* although without using a statistical approach. For example, the Glasgow Media Group (1977, 1982) have used content analysis to look at the bias in news programmes. In particular, they have assessed how industrial disputes have been portrayed. They use case studies to show how the pro-establishment bias is constructed as much by what is not shown as by what is reported. Studies which expose the jingoist and racist content of the British press use case studies to indicate the presence of racist messages (Murray, 1986; Searle, 1987; Gordon and Rosenberg, 1989). Similarly, Angela Barry (1988) has shown how images of black people on television reproduce racist mythologies by portraying black people as either trouble makers, dependants or entertainers. Black people are usually treated as 'a problem' by the press and much reporting has focused on incidents of racial conflict or portrayed cultural difference in negative terms (Hartmann and Husband, 1974; Troyna, 1981; Braham *et al.*, 1982).

Extract 2.4 is a *critical* content analysis that looks at the portrayal of terrorism on television, both in news and in fiction programmes. It illustrates how critical content analysis differs from conventional, quantitative, content analysis. First, critical content analysis makes no attempt to quantify content. Second, it links the content to the production and marketing of the programmes and to ideology.

> **Student Activity 2.10**
> **Undertake a study of a fictional television programme about terrorism, such as a one-off play or a serial. If possible, select a fictional form other than an action-adventure series. Use the same approach as in Extract 2.3. Is the programme you examine open or closed, tight or loose?**
> **WARNING   Student Activity 2.10 may not be possible if fictional accounts of terrorism are not scheduled for broadcast. You will need to video the programme to do the analysis as you will need to review the content several times. This is likely to be a very time-consuming activity.**

Unlike traditional content analysis, which deals with surface appearances, the critical approach attempts to show what *underlies* the apparent content.

Semiological analysis

Another way of getting beneath the surface of the apparent content is to use an approach called semiology. For example, Fiske and Hartley (1978) undertook a semiotic analysis of *News at Ten*, *Come Dancing* and various television police series. Similarly, Hodge and Tripp (1986) examined children's semiological decoding of a cartoon series called *Fangface*. What each of these studies attempted to show was that beneath the obvious content of media messages there was a second level of meaning that related to a set of taken-for-granted myths about the social world.

If we reconsider the analysis of advertisements (Student Activity 2.7) there is only so much that the quantitative approach can tell us. It tends to deal with surface appearances. There is a lot more implicit in these advertisements than is apparent from content analysis. The advertisements embody a set of underlying assumptions and a set of taken-for-granted codes of representation. We have hints of these in the 'comments' column in the grid. Semiological analysis is concerned with examining these underlying aspects. This is not something unique to advertisements but is found in all forms of communication.

Denotation and connotation

Semiology is the science of signs. Semiologists argue that any sign, be it a word, a picture, a flag or a piece of fashion clothing, communicates a meaning to us. However, this meaning is not fixed or straightforward. Each

---

SEMIOLOGY applies to all sign systems including direct communication (such as semaphore and language), ambiguous communication (such as literature) and conventions (such as ritual, etiquette and fashion). Semiologists argue that signs get their meaning from the system in which they are located. All signs are made up of a *signifier* (that is, the sound or visible object, such as the letters DOG) and a *signified* (that is, what is represented by the signifier, such as 'a hairy animal that barks'). The sign is the coming together of the signifier and the signified. Signs thus *denote* something, the word 'dog' denotes an animal.

However, a sign may *connote* something else, for example in a discussion about controlling dogs, such as pit bull terriers, the word 'dog' connotes 'danger' or 'viciousness'.

Social semiologists thus argue that the meaning of a sign is dependent on its context. Signs do not have a single straightforward meaning. In some contexts, for example, the sign 'rose' means a flower, in others it means passion and in others it means the British Labour Party. Signs often connote something other than their obvious meaning and this depends on the taken-for-granted view of the sign reader. So when looking at the media, social semiologists attempt to reveal the taken-for-granteds that are implied by the use of certain language and to expose the ideology underlying media content.

Extract 2.4

TERRORISM ON TELEVISION

Philip Elliott, Graham Murdock and Philip Schlesinger undertook a study of television portrayal of terrorism. They refer to statements by leading politicians to outline the 'official' perspective on terrorism. The official view is that terrorism is not legitimate political activity but illegitimate criminal activity which involves unwarranted violence and is associated with left-wing groups outside British society. Elliott *et al.* also identify alternative approaches which see terrorism as a necessary or legitimate last-resort response to state terrorism.

They examine various journalistic and fictional programme formats to see how terrorism is dealt with. They found that the presentation of terrorism on British television was a good deal more diverse and complex than simpler assumptions about television's relation to the state and to dominant ideology predict. However, some types of programme, such as the news and adventure series are 'closed', that is, *they operate mainly or wholly within the terms of reference set by the official perspective*. These programmes also tend towards a 'tight' format, that is, *one in which the images, arguments and evidence offered by the programme are organised to converge upon a single preferred interpretation and where other possible conclusions are marginalised or closed-off.* (The opposite of 'closed' and 'tight' are 'open' and 'loose', respectively.)

For example, they consider the action-adventure series *The Professionals*. Such series are at the forefront of the battle for mass audience ratings and tend to work with images and ideological themes that are most familiar and endorsed by the widest range of potential viewers. *The Professionals* is one of the most successful action-adventure series produced in Britain in recent years. Almost all the episodes have featured in the top ten most popular programmes and the series has been sold in most of the major overseas markets. The action centres around Bodie and Doyle, the two top agents of CI5, a crack Criminal Intelligence unit which bears more than a passing resemblance to the SAS. According to the publicity blurb for the series:

> Anarchy, acts of terror, crimes of violence – it's all grist to the mill of the formidable force who make up CI5 (TV Times Extra, 1979: 11).
> CI5 breaks all the rules: no uniforms, no ranks and no conscience – just results. Formed to combat the vicious tide of violence that threatens law and order, its brief is to counter-attack. And when there's a hijack, a bomb threat, a kidnap or a sniper, men from CI5 storm into action.

This highlights two key elements of the official view. Firstly, it places terrorism firmly within a criminal rather than a political frame and defines it exclusively in terms of the violence it entails. Secondly, it legitimates the state's use of violent counter-measures by arguing that exceptional threats to the social order require exceptional responses in which consideration of civil liberties, democratic accountability and due process are held in abeyance in the interests of efficiency. In practice, Bodie and Doyle can use the same dirty tricks as their opponents. However, they must be aware of the potential outcry from the public and the democratically elected representatives.

Hence, while it operates firmly within the terms of the official discourse, the programme must also work *actively* to head off dissent and enlist the audience's support for powerful counter-measures by underlining the exceptional nature of the terrorist threat and pointing up the irrelevance of alternative perspectives on state violence. This process of ideological mobilisation is well illustrated in the episode entitled *Close Quarters*.

The episode opens with the assassination of a British politician at a check-in desk at London airport. He is killed by the leader of the Meyer-Helmut terrorist group using a syringe of poison. This opening incident introduces four central themes: the essential criminality of terrorism; its identification with the Left; its characterisation as an alien incursion originating outside Britain; and the absolute contrast between the legitimate pursuit of parliamentary democracy and the illegitimacy of direct action. The assassination is a direct attack on the 'British way of life'.

The audience have already been invited to see Meyer's act as essentially criminal rather than political by the very fact that it is going to be tackled by CI5, a *criminal* intelligence unit. This point is reinforced by the briefing that Cowley, the group commander, gives his men.

Meanwhile, Bodie, who has been excused the briefing because of an injured gun hand, spots Meyer, follows him to a 'safe house' and arrests him. But the other members of the group arrive and give chase. Bodie eludes them and eventually barricades himself in a country vicarage that the terrorist group, heavily armed, surround.

The group's utter ruthlessness is confirmed when they shoot the vicar in cold blood as he is climbing out of a window in an effort to reason with them. This incident clinches the central ideological theme of the narrative; that you cannot bargain with terrorists and that faced with their arbitrary violence, the state is justified in using similar tactics. Popular support for this response is mobilised through the common-sense response of the vicarage housekeeper and Bodie's girlfriend, Julie, who was with him when he originally spotted Meyer and is caught up in the plot. The audience is invited to see its real-life position as analogous to the women's situation within the narrative. They are innocent bystanders who are caught up in the events they do not fully understand but who can recognise the state's moral right to combat terrorism with all the weapons at its command.

> Meyer : How does this concern you? You have no conception of what this fight is about. Its not your fight.
> Julie: You're right. I have no idea what you're fighting about. I just know it means violence and killing and someone's got to stop you.

Despite these protestations Julie still has reservations about the legitimacy of Bodie's use of violence (after he has shot two members of the group as they attempt to enter the vicarage). However, at the climax of the plot, when the chips are down, Julie overcomes her qualms. As the last member of the gang storms the room where they are hiding, Bodie is disarmed by Meyer and it is Julie who picks up the gun and shoots. The ideological circle is finally closed, around the official discourse. *The Professionals*, then, endorses the official view (that is, it is 'closed') and it is unambiguous with a well-rounded conclusion that does not leave the viewer with job of interpretation (that is, it is 'tight').

Adapted from Schlesinger, P., Murdock, G. and Elliott, P. (1983) and Elliott, P., Murdock G. and Schlesinger, P. (1986).

sign has a surface meaning, which is what the sign is supposed to denote. This first-level meaning is called the *denotative* level.

For example, the sign in the margin denotes a light bulb. However, in some contexts it might stand for 'a bright idea'. This second level is called the *connotative* level. The mass media, like all communication systems, operate at both the denotative level and the connotative level. Social semiology is concerned with analysing not just the surface appearance operating at the denotative level but also what is implicit in any communication at the connotative level.

Student Activity 2.11
The following words are a set of signs. Fill in the gaps showing the denotative and connotative meanings and the context in which the connotations operate.
(We have filled in the first one to give you the idea.)

Sign	Denotative level	Connotative level	Context
Pig	A farm animal	Male chauvinist	Women's Liberation
Rose	Thorny stemmed flower	Passion	
Bottle	Glass container		Football match
Beast			Sex attack
Grass			Police station

The semiological approach can also be applied to the analysis of advertisements. Television advertisements are a series of signs. Take, for example, the *Bird's Eye* advertisement (see Example findings on page 37). The description tells us what is going on in the scene at a denotative level. However, there is a lot more going on beneath the surface. Our comment in the grid and the voice-over message provide initial clues to the underlying connotations. The advertisement opens with the man holding a tray of two already-cooked meals, and there is a microwave oven in the background. The viewer is invited to fill in what is missing, that is, that he has opened the packet, put it in the microwave and, minutes later, taken out two delightfully cooked dinners. The simple connotation is that it takes no effort to cook the 'healthy' food. This is contrasted with the other man who runs into the room and flops on to the sofa. His attempts to be healthy have clearly involved a lot of effort.

There is a clear implication that the man who has cooked the food is cleverer than the man who has worked-out in the gym. The story goes on to reaffirm this. The first man has invited the second man's girlfriend to dinner. Her physical appearance and clothing connotes her concern with 'healthy living' and the first man has been clever enough to cook her a meal of which she would approve. He has only cooked two meals and further excludes the other man by making a witticism and squeezing between him and his girlfriend on the sofa. Cleverness is clearly associated with effortlessness and the voice-over confirms this by telling us that 'you do not have to be health *mad* to choose the healthy option'.

Social myths

This connotative level operates within the context of the scenario of the advertisement. However, it does not just get its meaning from the advertisement. It draws on the taken-for-granted notions of the viewer. These operate at a deeper, 'mythical' level. By myth, we do not mean ancient myths (in the sense of creation myths); rather we mean those everyday common-sense notions that are taken for granted. Regarding the roles of women, the myths are that women are nurturers and carers. Women's primary work is domestic work; additional work is for 'pin-money'. Women are weak, indecisive and manipulable (whereas men are strong, decisive and determined) and so on. Myths, in this sense, then, are broader social presumptions and the connotations in media messages draw on these. In the *Healthy Options* advertise-

MYTH originally referred to historical legends about the origins of humanity. More recently, myth has been used to refer to taken-for-granted notions about aspects of the social world. For example, it is a myth that all Northerners in Britain have poor diets or wear cloth caps and go to football matches. Not all myths are so obviously false, indeed, many myths are taken for granted by at least a portion of the population. There are myths about the work women do that sexists choose to believe. Similarly, there are racial myths about ethnic minorities that racists choose to perpetuate. Some myths are much less obvious and tend to be generally taken for granted and are reproduced in the media, such as myths about democracy, freedom, the fairness of the market economy and so on. Social myths are part of the process of *legitimation* and are linked to *ideology* (see pages 14 and 15).

TRANSFERENCE refers to the process by which the viewer of an advertisement transfers the qualities of the setting or events in the advertisement to the product being advertised. A well-known television lager advertisement shows exceptional circumstances and uses the punch line 'I bet he drinks Carling Black Label' in order to lead the viewer to make the transference of the qualities of the events depicted (usually, witty, clever and unusual) to the drink. Some advertisements are more obvious about the transference. An older advertisement for menthol cigarettes described the product as 'cool as a mountain stream' and so the viewer was directed to transfer the properties of the stream (cool, refreshing, healthy) to the cigarette. All modern advertisements work in this way.

Williamson (1978) argues that there are three frames of reference that advertisers use to ensure we make the transference: these are nature, science and history. We have taken-for-granted views about the desirability of nature, of the benefits of science and the tradition of history. When a product is set in any of these contexts we transfer these desirable or beneficial quali-

ment, several myths are drawn upon to make the connotation effective. First, there is the idea that healthiness is associated with attractiveness. More heightened awareness of the nature of the food we eat and the activity we engage in has led to a reconceptualisation of being healthy. (This has not always been the case; vegetarianism, for example, used to be depicted as the pursuit of spotty, emaciated, bearded cranks.)

Second, and specific to our analysis of gender stereotyping, is the myth of domestic labour. The presumption is that women do domestic labour. So showing a man cooking surely contradicts a basic myth? However, if we reconsider the advertisement we see that the man is not shown cooking. Rather, he has already cooked. We are not even shown him opening the packet. Indeed, he is not even seen in the kitchen. The microwave is in the lounge. This appears to be a flat without a kitchen. The man is dissociated from domestic labour completely. The overt connotation embodied in the voice-over message that it takes no effort to prepare healthy food if you use this product is confirmed by the implication that it is so simple a man can do it. This implication draws on and reconfirms the myth of domestic labour being a female occupation. Finally, the advertisement draws on the myth of male strength, determination, intelligence and decisiveness, and female weakness. The woman in the advertisement takes a completely passive role, takes no part in the manoeuvring between the two men, and is effectively manipulated by the 'clever' man.

Student Activity 2.12
Undertake semiological analysis of one (or more) of the advertisements you have seen and made notes on in Student Activity 2.7, drawing out the overt connotations and the underlying social myths that the advertisement draws on.

Advertisements deliberately manipulate connotations. They do so to create a *transference of meaning* from the action or surroundings in an advertisement to the product. Various techniques are used. In the *Healthy Options* advertisement the clever male is always associated with the food; he never puts the tray down. The not-so-clever male is clearly excluded from the food. The viewer is invited to make the transference subconsciously (Judith Williamson, 1978, in *Decoding Advertisements*, explores this process in great detail using over 100 advertisements).

Theory and method

In this section we consider further examples of the analysis of media messages to show how a more developed sociological analysis of an aspect of the media might be undertaken.

When undertaking empirical research projects there is always a problem of relating data or 'findings' to social theory. This problem usually arises, especially for people new to research, because they start with a *method*. They collect some descriptive data about a particular phenomenon, such as the different roles played by men and women on television, the most popular newspapers with different social classes, the difference in alcohol use between different ethnic groups, the extent of take-up of social service provision, and so on. The problem with this approach is that there is no explicit theory guiding the enquiry. This means that it is difficult to make other than superficial links to social theory. A better way is to start by asking *theoretical* questions and then use whatever methods are appropriate to examine these questions in practice.

A good deal of media research in the past has been of the method-led type. It tends to be 'social problem'-based. For example, as we have seen, public concern has been expressed about the negative effects of television, notably in relation to violence. Studies are set up to show what these effects are. Unfortunately, a lot of this research takes for granted that effects will follow from the content of television programmes. There is often little or no concern with the social environment nor even any examination of the psychological processes involved in watching and assessing television programmes. Thus, you might examine media content and show that there is a lot of violence on television, or that traditional sex roles are reproduced. But what does that tell you about society? Without an explicit theoretical enquiry to start with you are faced with common-sense conclusions such as 'all the violence on television must bear some relation to violence in society'.

From the point of view of *doing sociology* this approach does not get us very far. It does not investigate the social world but just represents existing common-sense or popular notions. It certainly does not provide us with an understanding of the relation, say, between television and society. What is needed is to frame your enquiry in terms of social theory in the first place. We will consider two examples of media portrayal of gender. First, sex-role stereotyping in children's comics and, second, rape reporting in the press.

The role of comics in pre-school socialisation

Socialisation is often defined as the process by which individuals learn to conform to social norms and learn appropriate ways to behave. The individual internalises these social norms and becomes committed to them and thus internalises social rules of behaviour. People do this because they wish to enhance their self-image by gaining acceptance and status from other people. In other words, individuals become socialised as they learn to act in a way that is in keeping with the expectations of others. In short, socialisation is the transmission of culture.

The major agencies within society that are involved in the socialisation process are the family, the school and the media. It is important not to focus on just one of these, as they all affect our socialisation.

Grabrucker (1988) suggests that the process of socialisation starts early. For example, she describes a situation where she is with her baby girl, talking with her friend and her new baby boy. The doctor comes up to them and congratulates her friend on bringing a new man into the world while completely ignoring Grabrucker and her female child. This incident, she suggests, starts the process of how a mother may view her child and thus how she may treat her. The family plays an important role in this socialisation process, where male and female babies are dressed in different colours (Chafetz, 1974), given different toys to play with (Belotti, 1975) and treated differently. Boys are expected not to cry, girls are praised for their appearance and so on. This process is continued in outside institutions during primary socialisation. In nurseries, for example, the language used to describe the behaviour of girls and of boys is different, as can be seen in Table 2.5.

The school is a major agency of socialisation (Byrne, 1983). It has both a formal curriculum and an informal, hidden curriculum, which among other

SOCIALISATION There are a number of different *general* theories of the socialisation process. Talcott Parsons *et al.* (1955), for example, propose a three-stage process. In the primary stage the child is socialised in the family. In the secondary stage the child is socialised by the school. In the tertiary stage individuals are socialised to take other roles, such as employee or parent, for which they have not previously been prepared. This view has been criticised for overstating the effectiveness of the socialisation process.

George Herbert Mead (1934) views the process as much more tentative. He argues that the individual's actions may be influenced rather than determined by beliefs and actions. Infants and young children become social beings by imitating other people around them. They gradually become aware of themselves as separate individuals by seeing how others behave towards them. As the individual takes a more active part in society, learning the rules of play and general social values, he or she becomes aware of the cultural rules of the society.

Sigmund Freud sees the socialisation process from a different perspective. He argues that young children learn to be individuals only as they learn to balance their unconscious desires with the demands of the environment. The child's ability to be self-aware is founded on its ability to repress its unconscious drives (Sulloway, 1980).

Jean Piaget's theory involves several stages in which the child is gradually able to make sense of the world. Each of these stages involves learning new cognitive skills. To progress to the next stage involves completing the previous stage successfully. These stages of cognitive development are seen by Piaget as universal features of the socialisation process (Boden, 1978; Silverman, 1981).

An overview of socialisation can be found in Bilton *et al.*, 1981, chapter 1; Giddens, 1989, chapter 3; Haralambos, 1990, chapters 1, 5, 8 and 9.

Table 2.5 Description of girls' and boys' behaviour

	Description	
Quality or behaviour	**Girls**	**Boys**
Quiet, withdrawn	Shy	Strong silent type
Noisy, rushing about	Disturbed, disruptive	Boisterous, active, lively
Showing emotion freely	Over-sensitive	wet, cry-baby, softie
Organising others, initiating activities	Bossy	Born leader
Physical characteristics		
Slim, slender, below average weight	Delicate	Skinny, weedy
Above average weight	Fat, plump	Stocky, solid, well-built
Attractive	Beautiful, pretty	Handsome, good-looking

Adapted from Stanworth (1980).

things reproduces gender differences. It encourages boys and girls to take different subjects, not overtly but, for example, by clashes on the timetable (Stanworth, 1980). Even if there appears to be open choice it takes considerable determination for a boy or girl to choose a subject that is not considered suitable for their gender. Boys and girls are expected to behave in different ways.

The media arguably enhance these differences and play an important role in *reinforcing* socially acceptable norms and values and ways of behaving. Indeed, the analysis of sex-role stereotyping has been a major concern of media researchers because it is assumed that such stereotypes have an impact on the socialisation process. Studies of the portrayal of women on television show that women are underrepresented in action drama programmes and when they do appear they tend to be portrayed in a very narrow range of roles (Butler and Paisley, 1980; Cathey-Calvert, 1983; Durkin, 1985). Women on television are more often in the home than at work and are usually shown as incompetent in anything other than domestic roles. Women, far more often than men, are the helpless victims of violence, especially on American-made television programmes. Even when taking a leading role outside the home, women are surrounded and rescued by men (Gerbner, 1972; Gerbner and Gross, 1976; Tuchman, 1978; Signorielli, 1984).

This reinforcement of sex-role socialisation is seen as important because of its potential impact on young children at the stage when they are learning appropriate sex-role behaviour and attitudes. Several studies have shown that heavy viewing of television by young children is associated with exaggerated stereotyping of sex-role beliefs among both boys and girls (Beuf, 1974; Frueh and McGhee, 1975; McGhee and Frueh, 1980; Morgan, 1982). For a review and assessment of this literature, see Gunter (1986).

Sex-role stereotyping occurs in other media besides television, notably in reading material directed at young children. In her study of pre-school books Weitzman (1974) showed that men were more prominent and outnumbered women in the ratio of 11 to 1. Girls were shown as passive and housebound where they spent their time waiting or cleaning for males. Boys, on the other hand, were seen outdoors being involved in various adventures showing how strong and independent they were. The adults portrayed in the stories also conformed to stereotypical gender roles. Women were either wives and mothers or were mythical creatures such as witches or fairy godmothers. The men however were seen in a variety of work roles, all of which were active. Not one non-mythical female role was portrayed as being outside the home.

Comics aimed at pre-school children also play a part in the socialisation process. These comics also raise issues of stereotyping. There are a variety of comics aimed specifically at pre-school children. Many of them are linked to a particular product or television programme. Some pre-school comics are marketed in a gender-neutral way, but increasingly comics for this age group appear to be targeted at either boys or girls.

Student Activity 2.13
1. **Visit your local newsagent and record the titles of pre-school comics that are: (a) gender-neutral; (b) aimed at boys; and (c) aimed at girls. Are there more gender-specific pre-school comics than gender-neutral ones?**
2. **Obtain a copy of a current pre-school comic aimed at both boys and girls. Using content analysis techniques draw up a grid to look at the following areas story by story: (a) numbers of males and females; (b) the characters playing the leading roles; (c) which**

characters are active and which are passive; (d) what activities are they involved in?

3. Select one story and look at the underlying assumptions using semiological techniques.

SUGGESTION Use Illustration 2.1 if you do not have one of your own.

We have analysed a page from one story of the *Sylvanian Family* (see Illustration 2.1). In the example findings we have not only drawn out the gender stereotypes operating at a connotative level but also suggested how they link to an established social theory.

Thus, in this example, the comic can be said to be an empirical confirmation of John Berger's theory about how socialisation turns women into objects.

The media production of gender stereotypes

It is important, however, that you also consider how the mass media come to reproduce gender stereotypes. It would be simple to imply that the mass

Illustration 2.1 Sylvanian Family: Duck Lake

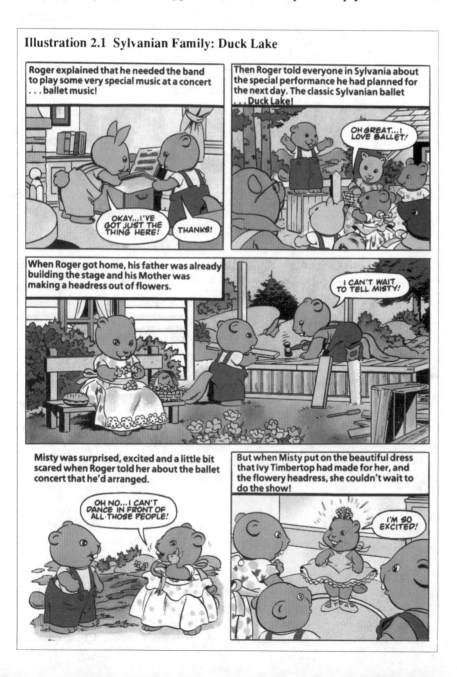

media operate like one big conspiracy to reproduce sexist imagery. To do so ignores the reality of media message production. Television producers, newspaper editors and so on are not engaged in an overt process of gender socialisation designed to oppress women. The mass media reproduce gender stereotypes (and other forms of socialisation) because the people involved in producing the media are as much subject to the process of socialisation as the people who read newspapers, watch television and so on. Indeed, it is difficult for the mass media to produce alternatives to dominant, taken-for-granted notions. For example, Marvel Comics, a large comic publishing house who produce *Sylvanian Family*, have attempted consciously to combat sexism in their comics. Just wanting to make the changes does not result in a different product over night. It is a difficult and slow process to change the entrenched ways of working of writers, cartoonists and editors. Illustration 2.2 is from a later edition of *Sylvanian Family* and is a direct response to the story in Illustration 2.1.

> **Student Activity 2.14**
> **Look at Illustration 2.2 (on page 54). Undertake a semiological analysis of the excerpt from a story called *The Big Match*. Compare your analysis with our analysis of Illustration 2.1 and discuss to what extent Illustration 2.2 overcomes gender stereotypes.**

As we have seen, pre-school children's comics have traditionally reinforced stereotypical gender roles. The aims and ambitions of girls and boys are portrayed in a gender-specific way.

This difference is, arguably, accentuated in comics for the older age group as they are more likely to be aimed specifically at either males or females. There are significant differences between the two types of comic. Most stories in boys' comics (such as *Sleeze Brothers*) are action-packed adven-

---

Example findings: Student Activity 2.13, part 2

The excerpt from *Sylvanian Family* reproduces some familiar stereotypes. Males are shown as active and a male character plays a leading and decisive role. The story tells us that Roger needed the band to play ballet music. Roger told everyone about the performance he had planned. Roger's father was building the stage. Roger told Misty about the ballet he'd arranged. Meanwhile the females are passive or undertake very sedate or domestic tasks. Mother was making a headdress out of flowers. Misty was surprised, excited and a little bit scared when told about the concert. Ivy Timbertop had made the beautiful dress. Roger is shown taking the music, standing on a box addressing a crowd, carrying a piece of wood. Misty is seen carrying a doll and then posing in her ballet dress. The presentation of the active, decisive, pragmatic male is contrasted to the inactive, indecisive, but fundamentally ornamental female.

John Berger (1972) looked at a specific aspect of socialisation in *Ways of Seeing*. He argued that sexism within society has meant that the social presence of women is different from that of men. He argues that a man's presence is dependent upon the promise of power which he embodies, and thus of what he is capable of doing to you or for you. By contrast, a woman's presence expresses her own attitude to herself, and

defines what can and cannot be done to her. Her gestures, voice, opinions, expressions and clothes among other things are indicative of her presence. Thus a woman learns to continually watch herself.

> One might simplify this by saying: men act and women appear. Men look at women. Women watch themselves being looked at. This determines not only most relations between men and women but also the relation of women to themselves.... Thus she turns herself into an object – and most particularly an object of vision: a sight. (Berger, 1972, p. 47)

The extract from *Sylvanian Family* confirms the active, powerful male and the ornamental function of females. This is reproduced through other signs, notably the clothes they wear. The males all wear plain dungarees while the women wear long, frilly, patterned dresses. Mother also wears a pretty apron (to reinforce her domestic role). The only exception is the ballet dress worn by Misty in the last frame. However, this serves to reinforce the ornamental connotation as Misty changes from 'surprised and scared' to 'excited and expectant' once she puts on the dress and feels that she looks right.

Illustration 2.2 Sylvanian Family: The Big Match

Soon it was half time, and Buster tired to encourage his team so that they would play better in the second half.

Scarlett asked if she could play in the second half, but Buster said no, because she was a girl, and girls are no good at football.

Please let me play, Buster! I'm the Captain and I said no!

With the Rovers' star player injured there was only one thing Buster could do to save the day. He had to let Scarlett come on and play.

Scarlett soon took control of the ball and using all her skill and determination, she tackled one player . . .

Roger Waters had heard what Buster had said and he didn't think it was fair. He knew Scarlett was a good player and that Buster was being mean. But Roger was clever and knew what to do.

The second half was a fierce battle for control of the pitch and the score remained the same, one goal all. Roger decided it was time to put his plan into action.

. . . then another, and another and then, just as the whistle was about to blow to end the match . . .

. . . she scored the winning goal. The final score was Rovers 2, Rangers 1. The whole team rejoiced. This time she'd really shown Buster!

Three cheers for Scarlett!

As he went to kick the ball, Roger pretended to twist his ankle. Then he fell to the ground and rolled around as if he was in agony!

Oh! Oh! My ankle. I've hurt it!

It's no good. He can't play on.

They had won the S.A. cup and all thanks to Scarlett. From that day on, the Rovers had a new captain for their team. Can you guess who it was? Yes! It was Scarlett!

NEXT ISSUE: FREE SYLVANIAN FIGURE!

tures. Physical feats are performed against all odds; contests and conflicts, battles, tests of skill and ingenuity pour continually out of every page. The heroes are usually adults, for example, soldiers or footballers who lead active and often dangerous lives. On the other hand, comics aimed at girls are saturated with romantic love, with girls dreaming of wealth and fortune. Examples of this can be seen in such comics as *Jackie* (McRobbie, 1981, 1983) or *Oh Boy*. Finding the right man is the only road to true happiness. Articles give advice on fashion and make-up to help girls achieve this end. The 'heroines' in girls' comics, if not portrayed as in love, are usually teenage schoolgirls involved in sorting out family problems, who occasionally gain a place in the school's gymnastic team or win the final of the netball competition.

Student Activity 2.15
Select one boys' and one girls' comic aimed at the 7–15 age group. Carry out a content analysis and a semiological analysis of one story in each.

Although the media do reproduce gender stereotypes, and this can also be seen in comics, readers and viewers are not passive recipients of media messages. It is a mistake to think that people simply absorb media messages uncritically and reproduce what they are told. For example, *Sleeze Brothers* is a comic directly aimed at males, but there is a small but growing female readership. Similarly, not all girls who read *Jackie* passively absorb the idea

Illustration from *Oh Boy* comic

that their one aim in life is to 'catch a man'. Although comics have a *preferred reading* some people read them critically. Media messages are simply part of a wider process of socialisation. The media are just one of several institutions that reproduce ideology.

Rape reporting in the press

Our second example looks at the way rape is reported in the press, using a feminist view of *hegemonic* control (see page 14). It is widely argued by feminist theorists that rape is a form of *patriarchal* social control (see page 25). Rape, and the threat of rape, serves to reinforce women's dependence on men and to restrict women's movements, activities and presentation of self. Far more women than is usually acknowledged suffer physical sexual assault. In 1980, for example, the Birmingham Rape Crisis Centre dealt with calls from 500 women, six times the number reported to the police in that period. Other studies have shown that 75% or more of rape victims do not report the attack to the police (Bains, 1989). However, the social control function of rape does not come about through individual acts but through the taken-for-granted social notions of the nature of rape and its ever-threatening presence. There is a dominant notion of rape that conjures up an image:

> of a brutal attack by a male sexual psychopath unable to control his desires. The victim is an innocent woman, naive or foolish enough to leave herself vulnerable to attack by being in an isolated space (socially or geographically) usually after dark or 'curfew'. (Smart and Smart, 1978)

It has been repeatedly argued that this image of the rapist, although widespread, is inaccurate and misleading (London Rape Crisis Centre, 1984; Toner, 1982). None the less, the image persists and is reproduced in the way the British press reports rape (Walby *et al.*, 1983; Britten and Fry, 1979). In effect, the media emphasise particular aspects of rape and thus reproduce a stereotype of rape. The aspects that are singled out are those which endorse a patriarchal myth. We saw above (when looking at advertisements on page 48) that connotations, while specific to a context at one level, rely upon taken-for-granted presuppositions at a deeper level. Maria Camargo Heck (1980) argues that myth is *universalised connotation*. Meanings specific to certain contexts become generalised and taken for granted. They become 'naturalised'.

In short, then, the dominant image or stereotype relating to rape serves to act as a means of social control on women by being presented in male terms. The way in which the issue of rape is addressed is in terms of dominant, *patriarchal ideology*. For example, women are warned that it is dangerous to go out alone at night. Rape reports appear to confirm this warning. If women ignore this warning they are putting themselves at risk. If they comply with it they are perpetuating patriarchal ideology, for they are not questioning why half the population have to restrict their movements to avoid being raped.

Patriarchy works so well as a system of socialisation that it becomes transparent. General assent and agreement to patriarchal ideology is so complete that, on the surface, it does not appear to exist. Patriarchal notions appear to be just simple common sense. However, they are a male 'common sense'. Patriarchy invokes a form of socialisation that compromises women to the benefit of men. This is no clearer than for rape. It is women who have to take steps to avoid being raped rather than men ensuring that they do not

---

MYTHS ABOUT RAPE IN THE PRESS
The following are the main assumptions, or myths, that have been shown to recur in the reporting of rape.

1. *Loss of control*. The rapist is portrayed as having uncontrollable urges. These may be the result of permanent psychological factors (including bestiality, being oversexed or mentally ill) or of temporary psychological factors (such as sex starvation, lust or frustration, exaggerated by drink, drugs or pornography).
2. *Sexual provocation*. The victim is seen to have been somehow provocative, either because of the clothes she wore, her previous sexual experiences (including those with the rapist), or her physical state (drunkenness).
3. *Spatial provocation*. Again the victim is portrayed as provocative because of where she goes. This includes being in 'male' space (for example, a bar); a public space (especially at night); an open space (where she is 'unprotected'); or hitch-hiking.
4. *Brutal attack*. Rape is neither seen as newsworthy, nor even regarded as rape, unless it is accompanied by other signs of brutal physical violence.
5. *Spontaneous event*. The rape act is portrayed as a spontaneous event arising out of irrational or unexpected circumstances rather than as a planned rational process. The one exception to this is the planned revenge attack, although this is planning of a 'deranged' mind.
6. *Attack by a stranger*. Rape is seen as an attack by an unknown stranger who usually surprises the unwary victim in an isolated outdoor location.

Illustration 2.3 Rape report

If you heard it, or saw it, don't ignore it.

CRIMESTOPPERS NEEDS YOU!

phone free
0800 555 111

Just between you and me.

The Community, Police and Media — standing against crime.

Shopping time !

TURN IN VILLAINS - FOR £500

PEOPLE who shop robbers, rapists and violent criminals to police in Birmingham can now earn cash rewards of up to £500.

The *Evening Mail* is helping the West Midlands force launch a Crimestoppers scheme in the city in a bid to bring offenders to book.

A free hotline opened today — 0800 555 111 — for vital information to be passed on to detectives about unsolved crimes.

And if the tip-off leads detectives to a charge and an arrest,

a reward will be paid.

The scheme respects the right of the callers to remain anonymous.

Sex attack

When they phone the round-the-clock line they will be given a codeword or nickname and told to ring back.

If their tip proves successful

they will pick up a cash bounty, the size of which will be determined by a panel of crime prevention experts.

Each week a selected crime will be publicised in the *Mail*. It will be a serious offence like murder, armed hold-up, sex attack or brutal mugging.

It will be paid regardless of whether there is a conviction.

The public will be urged to leave information on the hotline so officers can follow it up to track down the offenders.

Mr Tom Meffen, Assistant Chief Constable (Crime), said: "We are asking for help on violent unsolved crimes and hope the rewards on offer will provide an incentive to people to give us information."

He added: "Some crooks get off on legal technicalities so we do not think it is fair to insist on them being found guilty."

Nick's king of the pint sales

CHEERS! That's the message from Nick Oliver — the landlord who sells more pints than any other pub tenant in the Midlands.

Nick, who runs The Station at Sutton Coldfield with his wife Joy, sold 2,200 barrels of booze last year.

That is 79,200 gallons or 633,600 pints — equivalent to 12,185 pints a week.

It is the first time in his 11 years as a Bass Mitchells & Butlers tenant that Nick has sold so much.

Magic

Although 24 M&B tenants sold more than 1,000 barrels last year he was the only one to break the magic 2,000 barrel barrier.

And he edged out Ansells superstar John Rose, who runs The Varsity Tavern in Selly Oak and sold 2,132 barrels last year.

So what is the key to Nick's amazing success, achieved against a national trend of falling beer sales?

"All-day opening has certainly given us a huge boost," said Nick who was given a weekend in Paris as a reward by the brewery.

"But the tremendous summer also played an very important part."

Another key was Nick's association with Sutton Coldfield Rugby Club. The 6ft 4in publican is a member of the 1st XV squad and The Station is often an extension of the rugby clubhouse on Saturdays.

Music

Nick, newly elected chairman of Birmingham Amalgamated LVA, has a few other tricks up his sleeve including regular live music.

He has a loyal team of full and part-time staff and has arranged their pension schemes.

Nick's father Derek runs the Wilson's Arms at Knowle, Solihull.

RAPE TERROR OF GIRL, 17

THIS pock-marked Rastafarian pounced on a teenage girl, frogmarched her through the streets, and subjected her to a terrifying sex attack in a Birmingham school playground.

During a 1½-hour ordeal, the 6ft tall fiend — who is believed to have been high on drink or drugs — raped the 17-year-old and subjected her to degrading bodily abuse after threatening to stab her.

Police described it as a particularly horrific attack which

By PHIL BANNER
Mail Crime Correspondent

shocked the girl so badly that she has since quit her job.

The man, who had yellow bloodshot eyes and long dreadlocks that fell to the middle of his back, stalked the pretty hairdresser through Newtown.

He called out to her when she strolled across a grassy area in Wheeler Street and then suddenly leapt from the shadows. He ordered her to give him her leather jacket. When she refused, he grabbed

the teenager and overpowered her in a frenzied struggle.

The muscular attacker then marched the girl about 600 yards to William Cowper School in Summer Lane.

In an isolated spot in the playground, he raped her.

The girl said:"I hope he can be caught before he has the chance to do it again.

The man detectives are hunting is black, believed West Indian, and aged about 28. He had a very bad skin which was heavily pockmarked on the cheeks and chin and his complexion was noticeably dark.

One of his front teeth had a

partial gold cap and his breath smelled strongly of tobacco.

He wore a black leather zip-up jacket with a waistband that had leather belt hoops. He had on black baggy trousers and white trainers with blue stripes.

He also wore a lot of gold jewellery, including four rings on his left hand — some of which appeared to be sovereigns — and two square-faced rings on his right hand.

Police, who are appealing for information, said that anyone who knew him would be certain to recognise him from the picture.

Band is set for takeoff to US

A SANDWELL youth orchestra is a step nearer an American tour — thanks to backing from councillors.

The Sandwell Youth Band, made up of pupils from 19 high schools, is due to jet away in March for a tour of America's east coast.

However, the cost of the two-week tour has been put at £46,000, with the 46-member band and seven staff have been able to raise only £31,000 from contributions, concerts, LPs and fund-raising events.

Ambassadors

Members of Sandwell education committee have now agreed to provide the remaining £15,000, which should enable the trip to go ahead.

Mr Gerald Brinsdon, director of education, said the band members were "excellent ambassadors" for the borough.

They were now "ideally prepared musically" for a tour of the United States, he added.

The band has already earned an international reputation after winning a prize at the 1988 International Festival of Music for Youth in Vienna.

Splash hit exercises

WOMEN in Birmingham are taking the plunge and signing up for the latest in exercise classes — Splashdance.

Among them are (foreground, from left) Mrs Susan Clarke, Mrs Jane Cunningham and Mrs Jennie Matthewman, pictured with classmates at Perry Common School, Perry Barr.

The idea of underwater aerobics has been catching on in the South for more than a year.

Now the trend has reached the Midlands, with three new classes starting in Birmingham this week, and Tamworth-based

teachers Mr and Mrs Bob and Lesley Sterman riding the crest of a wave.

Mr Sterman said: "It is really popular. We have a class somewhere every night of the week.

"Because it's done in water, there is less danger of injury than with aerobics on dry land, and it tones the muscles up with the resistance of the water.

"We do it in the shallow end, so people don't have to be able to swim. It's good fun, especially when it comes to dancing."

Details of Birmingham classes are available on 0827 895915.

SET FOR WEDDING REPLAY

COUPLES married at a Smethwick church could be returning for an "action replay" — to celebrate its diamond jubilee.

A reunion with former members who have moved away is being planned by officials of Akrill Memorial Methodist Church in The Uplands, Smethwick — and couples wishing to renew their marriage vows are among those being sought.

Mrs Audrey Carpenter is helping to plan events.

Father in pay-out after row

A MIDLAND father-of-five has been ordered to pay his neighbour £100 compensation after admitting attacking him in a parking row.

Anthony Jacomb, (29) of Wychbury Road, Pedmore, admitted assaulting Mr Alfred Timmins causing actual bodily harm.

He also admitted damaging a front door belong to Dudley housing department.

Stourbridge magistrates ordered Jacomb to pay Mr Timmins compensation and fined him a total of £125. He was also ordered to costs of £20.

Mr Stuart Rose, prosecuting, said Mr Timmins, his son John and Jacomb were involved in an argument just before Christmas.

Blocked

Jacomb claimed Mr Timmins had blocked his driveway with his car and during the row which followed he elbowed Mr Timmins in the face, causing bruising and swelling.

Five minutes later Mr Timmins and his son were in their house when they heard the sound of breaking glass and found Jacomb wielding a piece of exhaust pipe which he had used to smash a pane of glass in their front door.

Example results of Student Activity 2.16

Feminist analysis of an extract from the Birmingham *Evening Mail*, 11 January 1990, p. 17 (Illustration 2.3)

Under the headline RAPE TERROR OF GIRL, 17 the story of a rape is unfurled in dramatic terms. We are told that the victim was terrorised by a 6ft tall fiend who subjected her to a terrifying attack. The rapist stalked the victim, pounced on her, overpowered her in a frenzied struggle, then frogmarched her to the spot where she was raped. This was a long ordeal in which the victim was abused and threatened with a knife. To endorse the brutality the police are reported as confirming that this was a particularly horrific attack. Indeed, the victim was so shocked by the attack that she has given up her job.

Without doubt this was a horrendous attack. But the important thing is that the woman was raped. Not that she was threatened with a knife. All rape is violent. Rape is a violation of a woman's body by a man against her will. As such it is an act of violence. What the newspaper report is doing is reproducing the myth of rape as an overtly vicious or brutal attack. Many rapes, however, are not accompanied by direct physical violence. Threats or other forms of coercion may be used by the rapist. Such coercion might arise simply out of the position of authority that the rapist has over the victim, be it an employer, father or husband. Such rapes are rarely reported nor do they even get drawn to the attention of the police. It is clear that the *Evening Mail* would not have given such prominence to rape if it had not been a terror attack. The article is literally framed within a new feature called 'Crimestoppers'. It is a sales gimmick using a cash reward (£500) and echoing popular television programmes. The column will feature serious offences such as murder, armed hold-up, sex attack or brutal mugging. Not rape as such. Only crimes where overt violence is in evidence. Indeed, almost half the article is devoted to a description of the rapist with a view to inviting readers to identify him and claim the reward.

Part of the reason for the lack of detection of so-called 'non-violent' rape, then, is because such incidents do not correspond to the myth of rape as a brutal and violent attack. This leads the victim to acknowledge that her attack was not a 'real' rape. Even to the extent of redefining it in terms of her own unconscious provocation.

This view of rape as essentially violent reflects the patriarchal ideology of the property rights of men over women (Brownmiller, 1976; Carter, 1985). A violent attack constitutes damage to 'male property' and is unacceptable. 'Non-violent' rape, particularly perpetuated within the bounds of the family, is disregarded on the same grounds, that the women 'belongs' to the man and is there to serve him.

The rapist in the *Evening Mail* article was, it is implied, temporarily out of control. He was believed to be high on drink or drugs, had yellow bloodshot eyes and smelled strongly of tobacco. While his action was inexcusable, it is implied that the use of drugs had been a major contributory factor. The first mention of rape in the text of the article is prefaced by the information that the rapist was believed to be using drugs. The structure of the sentence provides the excuse: '...the 6ft tall fiend – who is believed to have been high on drink or drugs – raped the 17-year old.' There is a further implication that the rapist's problem goes deeper to a more permanent psychological state that might cause him to lose control. Clearly, he was unattractive (in conventional terms), the opening words of the article tell us that he was a pock-marked Rastafarian. We are later told that he had very bad skin and was heavily pock-marked on the cheeks and chin, as well as being 'noticeably dark'. Apart from the racist implications, what is being connoted was that the rapist was doubtless frustrated because of his unattractiveness. The apparent dual reason for his loss of control reflects an ambiguity in the article concerning the spontaneity of the rape. On the one hand we are told that initially he ordered the victim to give him her leather jacket. Only after she refused did the

frenzied struggle ensue. The implication is that the sexual assault was an uncontrolled corollary of the robbery once he realised he had overpowered her. On the other hand, he is supposed to have stalked the victim, which connotes a planned attack on his 'prey'. Further, the victim is quoted as saying that she hopes he is caught before he can do it again. Implying something more than mere spontaneity.

Whether the rape was a drug-induced assault following a mugging which went wrong, or a animalistic attack by a frustrated male, it is clear that the rapist is portrayed as acting as a deviant. This was the action of a 'sick man' at least partially unable to control what he was doing. Patriarchal ideology constantly reaffirms the strong sexual needs of men. Most men use legitimate means to satisfy them. The rapist is deviant because of the illegitimate way in which these needs have been satisfied. It is not that the expectation of fulfilment of sexual desires itself is considered in any way oppressive to women, it is only because of the overt violence used in gratification that the rapist is condemned.

We are also confronted by the role of the victim. She is not described as a young woman, or child, but as a girl of 17. Irrespective of what she actually looked like this description has connotations of youthful, nubile attractiveness. These are partially confirmed by the description of her as a 'pretty hairdresser'. Inadvertently, the report implies, she was provocative because of what she looked like. Further, she was provocative because of where she was. The rapist called out to the victim whilst she was crossing a grassy area and then leapt from the shadows. We are not told the time of day. Readers are left to fill in the details of the events from their own taken-for-granted notions. What is conjured up, then, is an image of an unaccompanied woman in an exposed location which was clearly unsafe. This view is reinforced by the information that he was able to force her to an isolated spot in a school playground.

This all serves to reinforce not only the unconscious complicity of the woman in the rape but also the myth that rape is an attack by a stranger that takes place outside (normally in dark, lonely places). Researchers have shown that this view is unfounded (Amir, 1971). London Rape Crisis Centre (1984) reported that 60% of rapes occurred in buildings, 30% in the victim's home and that in over 50% of cases the rapist and victim had had some previous contact. This was echoed by the cases handled by the Birmingham Rape Crisis Centre in 1980/81. They found that 59% of rapes occurred indoors (30% in the woman's home) and that in most cases the rapist was known to the victim. The myth therefore serves to warn women not to go out alone and to avoid strangers. As such, it perpetrates taken-for-granted notions about restrictions on the movements and actions of women. Men are not restricted because they may rape, women are restricted because they may be victims.

This myth, apart from being used as a form of control by declaring the only really safe place for women is at home with their men to protect them, reflects a wider ideology of women's legitimate place in society. They are defined in terms of their domestic function in society, that is, mother, wife or sexual object. In short, women are not taken seriously as people (outside the domestic setting) and rape is not taken as a serious offence in male-dominated society.

This lack of seriousness is reflected in the reporting. Directly beneath the account of the rape is a picture of eight women in swimming costumes standing in a pool with legs astride and arms waving in the air. They are members of 'Splashdance' exercise classes (underwater aerobics).They look as though they are volunteering for something. Other stories bordering the article on rape include an account of a man who had to pay £100 fine for attacking a neighbour, and a report on the pub that sells more beer than any other in Birmingham. These other stories range from the trivial to the banal and devalue the seriousness of the rape. There is also an inference that physical attack is cheap (£100) and that it is laudable to sell lots of beer (despite it possibly being a major factor in the horrendous rape).

rape women. However, patriarchal oppression is not seen for what it is but is represented as the deviant act of a pathological individual.

Student Activity 2.16

1. **Locate some examples of rape reporting in newspapers. Select both 'quality' and 'popular' national newspapers (or local newspapers). (Use Illustration 2.3 if you cannot find any.)**
2. **Undertake a content analysis to identify the percentage of reports in each type of newspaper that identify each of the elements above. (It is helpful to draw up a grid with each element as a column and each report as a row.)**
3. **See if there is any difference in the way various types of newspaper use these elements.**
4. **Undertake a detailed semiological analysis of some of the reports to see how they reproduce myths about rape and thus legitimate patriarchal ideology.**
5. **Analyse the rape report (Illustration 2.3), using a semiotic approach, from an anti-racist perspective.**

Supplementary research activity 2.1

Through a review of literature and official statistics, see if you can answer the following questions. Are there any particular sorts of people who are likely to be rape victims? What sorts of people are likely to be attackers? Where does the majority of rape take place? What proportion of attacks get reported to the police and, of these, what proportion result in convictions? Compare 'official' and 'non-official' figures for rape. See Chapter 3 on secondary statistics.

Positivist, phenomenological and critical perspectives

In this chapter we have looked at a wide range of research into the mass media. In so doing we have pointed to several research techniques and identified and illustrated the three main methodological approaches.

Positivism

Tan's experimental study, Gerbner's surveys designed to examine the cultivation thesis, and Phillips' correlation research based on official statistics are all, in their different ways, interested in trying to assess the effects that the media had on the audience. In each of these studies the researchers concentrate on observable events (or phenomenal forms) that they can identify and measure. They assume that these measurements are objective and that they do not depend on the views or actions of any particular researcher. The aim is to see the extent to which the identified *cause* (the media) leads to a consistent *effect*. This general approach thus attempts to provide causal explanations and is usually called the *positivist* approach.

Positivism takes a variety of forms (Halfpenny, 1982) but it does have some general characteristics. Positivists in the social sciences attempt to discover the factors that cause observed phenomena in the same way that natural scientists construct theories to explain the behaviour of matter. If events are observed that differ from that predicted by a theory, then the theory is either modified or changed. Thus by reference to observable and measurable data, the positivist is able to develop and refine theories that predict and *explain* phenomena.

Positivism maintains that knowledge should be based on 'positive' real facts, not on abstract deductions. In other words, knowledge should be based on observation and experiment and no attempt should be made to understand the inner meaning or essence of things.

POSITIVISM

The three central tenets of positivism are:

1. *Phenomenalism* (not to be confused with phenomenology): science uses only data that can be directly observed and recorded or measured in some way. (Note that in this case 'observation' can involve any of the senses, not just sight.)
2. *Causality*: phenomena are interrelated via causal propositions and thus the aim of science is the discovery of cause and effect laws.
3. *Objectivism*: scientific enquiry should be objective and value-free; its methods should be independent of the researcher, repeatable and reliable.

Phenomenology

In Dorothy Hobson's study of *Crossroads* and other reception studies, the focus was not on cause and effect but on what sense the audience made of the programmes. This research is concerned with meanings and interpretations, and does not presuppose that the media affect the audience, rather that the audience uses and interprets the media for its own ends. Similarly, in examining the making of a television series, Philip Elliott also undertook a detailed study of the way that the meanings held by the production team effected what was finally produced. His research thus analysed the process of negotiation and interpretation. Similarly, ethnomethodologists concentrate on the routines used in the process of, for example, news production. None of these approaches attempts to measure directly observable phenomenal forms, rather they try to grasp people's underlying perceptions and *meanings*. This approach is influenced by *phenomenology*.

Phenomenologists argue that there is a fundamental difference between the subject matter of the natural world and the social sciences. Phenomenology is a term used in social science to refer to the philosophical underpinnings of a variety of approaches that tend to concentrate on the essential nature of the social world. It is a term that is applied to diverse approaches to social enquiry. However, some features are common to all of them.

In practice, phenomenological approaches see sociological knowledge as being fundamentally dependent upon an interpretation of the meanings of social actors or a close analysis of interactive processes.

Critical

Schlesinger's (1978) study of the production of BBC News, Barry's (1988) study of racist stereotypes on television, Elliott *et al.*'s (1986) study of the portrayal of terrorism, Walby *et al.*'s (1983) feminist analysis of rape reporting in the press, and Fiske and Hartley's (1978) semiotic analysis of television police series all adopt a critical approach to the media. What they show is how media production and output are linked to wider social structures and ideology.

The critical perspective, which covers a variety of approaches, attempts to *dig beneath the surface* of oppressive social structures. This approach is found in Marxism, structuralism and in most feminism and black perspectives. At the heart of this approach is the idea that knowledge is structured by existing sets of social relations. What we 'know' is dependent on the social structure we live in. Most knowledge reaffirms the oppression in that social structure, be it class oppression, gender oppression, racial oppression, sexual oppression and so on. The critical approach, in getting beneath the surface, is not just interested in meanings or in establishing the essence of social relations or practices. The critical approach sees societies as specific to a particular time and place and not as having any eternal aspects. The aim is to reveal the underlying nature of social structures and to show how oppression operates and is sustained.

So the critical perspective, in practice, is concerned with revealing underlying social relations, in their broad social and historical context, showing the impact of social structure and ideology (Harvey, 1990).

PHENOMENOLOGY

The tenets of phenomenology are:

1. *Anti-phenomenalism*: the social world is not grasped simply by looking at its surface appearances.
2. *Interpretation*: people are conscious beings and are able to act to construct their own social reality. Causal laws do not, therefore, operate in the social world.
3. *Meaning*: the world makes sense only because of the meanings that actors bring to it and impose upon it. Sociological enquiry must analyse these meanings.

CRITICAL

The tenets of the critical approach are:

1. *Anti-phenomenalist*: understanding the social world cannot be done on the basis of surface appearances.
2. *Totalistic*: aspects of the social world cannot be understood independently of the wider social and historical context in which they exist.
3. *Dialectical analysis*: it is necessary to break down (deconstruct) existing social relationships in order to fully understand what is often taken for granted in order to build up (reconstruct) an alternative view of the oppressive mechanisms that operate in society.
4. *Ideology*: mechanisms of oppression are legitimated and concealed by ideology.

Summary and conclusion

In this chapter we have drawn attention to several different research techniques. These are examined in the following chapters, except for content analysis and semiology which we have discussed in some detail using the issue of gender stereotyping for illustrative purposes.

Content analysis is a systematic way of describing the substance of television programmes, advertisements, newspaper reports, comics and so on. While content analysis explores the denotative level, semiological analysis examines the connotative level to reveal the underlying messages. There are problems with each of these approaches. Content analysis has been criticised for expressing qualitative aspects in quantitative terms. Semiological analysis is criticised for being unsystematic. Furthermore, the identification of the connotations is sometimes regarded as a matter for the researcher's own interpretation. However, as you have seen, undertaking research is not just about the methods used but also about the way in which the data is linked to wider theoretical concerns. For example, in our analysis of rape we related the content of the newspaper report to the feminist critique of patriarchy. This is not the only approach and you could, for example, analyse rape reporting using market theory. Whatever you decide to study you must ensure that the theory you use is an integral part of your research methodology.

Project ideas

The techniques for analysing media content discussed in this chapter lend themselves to a variety of research topics. The following suggestions for topics are just an indication of the large range of possibilities for student projects. It is important that you do not try to do too much. Focus on specific events or forms of media rather than try to cover everything. Make sure you relate your analysis of media content to theory. You could look at the content in relation to theories of the media discussed in this chapter. Or you could consider content in relation to theories around the subject matter as we did when looking at children's comics and theories of socialisation.

1. Compare the reporting of industrial relations disputes in television news broadcasts on different channels.
2. Analyse the way different ethnic groups are presented in advertisements.
3. Compare the political bias of different national newspapers.
4. Analyse the racial stereotypes in children's television programmes.
5. Compare British and Australian (or American) social class stereotypes in soap operas.
6. Analyse the reporting of sport in the popular national press.
7. Undertake a historical analysis of the way ethnic groups have been shown in British or American feature films.
8. Analyse the way that disability is treated in newspapers or on television.
9. Assess the nature of the 'moral panic' around AIDS in the tabloid press.
10. Assess whether disc-jockey talk on Radio 1 (or a local music radio station) is 'agenda setting'.

Further Reading

Content analysis: Berelson, 1952; Greenberg, 1981; Holsti, 1969; Krippendorf, 1982; Lasswell and Leites, 1965; Mayntz *et al.*, 1976.

Semiology: Blonsky, 1985; Culler, 1983; Eco, 1981; Hawkes, 1977; Hodge and Kress, 1988; Innis, 1986; Snead and West, 1988.

Topics

Gender socialisation: Deem, 1978; Grabrucker, 1988; Johnson, 1992; McRobbie and McCabe, 1981; Stanworth, 1980; The National Lesbian and Gay Survey, 1992; Weiner, 1985; Weitzman, 1974.

General socialisation theory: Boden, 1978; Mead, 1934; Parsons *et al.*, 1955; Silverman, 1981; Sulloway, 1980.

Mass media theory: Glover, 1985; Hall, 1973; Livingstone, 1990; McQuail, 1983; Richards *et al.*, 1986; Trowler, 1988.

Mass media studies: Ang, 1985; Barrat, 1986; Elliott, 1972; Fiske and Hartley, 1978; Gerbner *et al.*, 1986; Glasgow Media Group, 1982; Goldman, 1992; Gunter and Wober, 1988; Gunter and McAleer, 1990; Hobson, 1982; Hodge and Tripp, 1986; Jensen and Jankowski, 1991; Lull, 1990; Molotch and Lester, 1974; Moore-Gilbert and Seed, 1992; Morley, 1980; Schlesinger, 1978; Troyna, 1981; Twitchin, 1990; Van Dijk, 1991; Wartella *et al.*, 1983; Weitzman, 1974; Williamson, 1978.

Stereotyping, myth and ideology: Barthes, 1974; Hall *et al.*, 1980.

Violence against women: Dunhill, 1989; London RCC, 1984; Radford and Russell, 1992; Smart and Smart, 1978; Soothill and Walby, 1991; Toner 1982; Walby *et al.*, 1983.

CHAPTER 3
SECONDARY
STATISTICAL DATA

Introduction

There are a lot of published statistics available in Great Britain compiled by both government and non-government organisations. These statistics are wide-ranging and cover most of the general topic areas of interest to social scientists. They are therefore a useful resource that the social researcher should not ignore.

It is important to draw a distinction between *looking up* available statistics and undertaking *further analysis* of statistical sources. Further analysis is called *secondary data analysis*. The first part of this chapter will focus on consulting available sources and presenting findings derived from them. Towards the end we will consider the possibilities of secondary data analysis.

Table 3.1 Destination of YTS leavers – GB and Greater London, by sex and ethnic background between July 1987 and June 1990, as recalculated by Unemployment Unit/Youthaid.*

	Total	Early	Male	Female	Disabled	White	Black	Asian	Other	PNS**
Total leavers										
GB	692226	495484	385942	306284	22494	657471	12596	13176	3578	5045
London	34077	24245	19309	14768	1845	24373	5473	2194	931	1106
Questionnaires sent	32628	23210	18491	14137	1711	23406	5191	2111	878	1042
Response rate	46.7%	42.8%	40.0%	50.9%	42.5%	46.8%	35.2%	48.5%	42.4%	40.3%
Usable sample	13584	8940	6902	6682	642	10282	1646	921	340	395
In work										
Same employer	30.0%	15.0%	35.9%	24.0%	14.3%	33.1%	18.0%	23.2%	24.1%	20.8%
Different employer	40.0%	48.1%	36.7%	43.5%	32.6%	42.3%	31.4%	35.5%	29.1%	37.7%
Self-employed	2.2%	2.2%	3.5%	0.9%	2.2%	2.4%	1.6%	1.7%	0.6%	2.3%
Part-time	2.4%	2.7%	1.8%	3.1%	3.6%	2.1%	3.5%	2.5%	3.8%	3.8%
Total in work	74.7%	67.9%	77.8%	71.4%	52.6%	79.9%	54.6%	63.0%	57.6%	64.6%
Unemployed	16.3%	20.7%	15.0%	17.6%	32.6%	13.5%	28.6%	20.4%	22.9%	23.5%
Full-time course	4.6%	5.9%	3.6%	5.7%	6.1%	2.9%	10.7%	10.7%	10.0%	6.3%
Something else	3.5%	4.5%	6.6%	4.4%	6.7%	2.9%	5.0%	5.1%	7.4%	5.1%

*The figures have been recalculated because the Training Agency's method of data collection includes young people who move between schemes and thus obscures the real outcome of those actually leaving YTS.

**Preferred not to say.

Source: *Unemployment Bulletin*, 32, Spring 1990, p. 3.

Looking up statistics

Most statistics that are available for you to use come in the form of tables or charts. Table 3.1 is an example of the kind of table of statistics that you are likely to find.

This table shows where young people on YTS schemes go once they leave the scheme. For example, the table shows that in Great Britain as a whole 692,226 young people left YTS schemes between July 1987 and June 1989. Of these 495,484 left early (that is, 495,484/692,266 x 100 = 71.6%).

Student Activity 3.1
Using Table 3.1, what percentage of disabled leavers are in work after they leave the scheme? Compare the unemployment rates of 'White', 'Black' and 'Asian' leavers. Are males or females more likely to be employed by the same employer after they leave the scheme? Do a larger percentage leave early in London than in Great Britain as a whole?

Graphical representation of data

Data in tabular form can sometimes be a little daunting and it is often easier to make sense of the figures when they are presented in pictorial form. There are several ways that parts of the data in Table 3.1 can be represented.

For example, Figure 3.1 is a pie chart showing the destinations of the total sample. Figure 3.2 is a bar chart showing the unemployment rates for the different ethnic groups.

Student Activity 3.2
Represent the data on destinations for the males and females in three different diagrammatic forms (using bar charts, line charts and stacked bar charts). In each diagram show what percentage are (a) employed by the same employer; (b) employed by a different employer; (c) self employed; (d) part-time; (e) on a full-time course; (f) unemployed and (g) 'something else'. Which representation do you think is best and why?
HINT Find out if your college or school computer has a graphics pack or a graphics facility on spreadsheet or database software and use this to draw the graphs or charts. We used *Excel* to produce the two diagrams on the right.

Figure 3.1 Destinations of YTS leavers: 1987–89

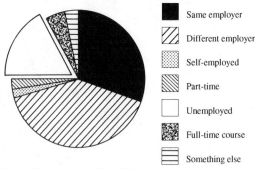

- Same employer
- Different employer
- Self-employed
- Part-time
- Unemployed
- Full-time course
- Something else

Source: *Unemployment Bulletin*, 32.

Figure 3.2 YTS leavers: unemployment rates

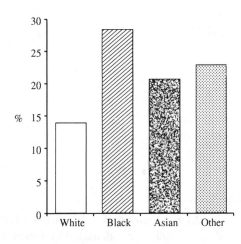

Source: *Unemployment Bulletin*, 32.

Sources of statistics

Statistics produced by the government to help it in the day-to-day running of the country are often called 'official statistics'. For convenience, we will refer to any other statistical sources as 'unofficial'. There are a variety of such sources. These include statistics produced by independent organisations such as opinion pollsters; media monitoring organisations; pressure groups such as Friends of the Earth and the automobile organisations; trade unions; polytechnics and universities; independent research units; and so on.

This should not be taken to mean that 'unofficial' are any less correct than official statistics. The distinction is simply that official statistics are the ones that 'officially' the government agencies collect and use.

There are many sources of statistical data and it would take several books to document them all. We outline the main sources that would provide the

---

LOCAL 'OFFICIAL' STATISTICS
Official statistics' are also produced by local government, health authorities, educational establishments and so on. It is useful, however, to distinguish between government statistics as produced by the Government Statistical Service, which are directed towards the management of the nation state, and non-government 'official' statistics that are of concern at the local level. Some of the locally produced statistics are reported to the appropriate government departments and become incorporated into national statistics. Some statistics, however, are used (and published) only at the local level.

basis for any project work you might undertake and refer you to other publications for more detailed sources should you need them.

Government official statistics

The British government produces a vast array of statistical data, and much of it is published on a regular basis. The data produced by the central government is a unique source, as no other body has the resources or the need to produce the data. Government official statistics are widely referred to and the scale of the available material makes them worth looking at in more detail.

Each government department prepares and publishes its own statistics (either directly or via Her Majesty's Stationery Office (HMSO)). The statistics divisions of all major departments plus the Business Statistics Office (BSO) and the Office of Population Censuses and Surveys (OPCS) makes up the Government Statistical Service (GSS). The Central Statistical Office (CSO) co-ordinates the system.

The GSS is the largest single provider of statistics in the country and has the greatest concentration of statistical expertise. It exists to service the needs of government and produces economic and social statistics, including data on population and households, education, the workforce, earnings and retail prices, taxation, standard of living, home affairs, justice and law, health, personal social services, safety, social security, defence, the environment and transport.

For initial research purposes the data collected in the general abstracts are satisfactory. The main general publications are described in Table 3.2.

Social Trends

Of all the general digests produced by the Government Statistical Service the most accessible, readable and widely used publication by sc.. al scientists is *Social Trends*. It is published by HMSO, was established in 1970 and has been produced annually ever since. It has become the major source of information about the social life of the country, drawing on a vast array of official statistics. It is packed with information presented in a readable form. For many students this will be the only source immediately available. Most of the student activities in this chapter that invite you to look up statistics can be attempted by just using *Social Trends*.

> **Student Activity 3.3**
> **Using *Social Trends* look up the following statistics for the most recent year available. In each case also note the original source of the statistics and which parts of Great Britain are included in the total figures.**
> **1. The number of divorces.**
> **2. The number of people working in the manufacturing sector.**
> **3. The average gross weekly earnings for men and for women.**
> **4. The number of male and female prisoners.**
> **5. The number of people who died of Acquired Immune Deficiency Syndrome (AIDS).**
> **6. The number of people who went to Spain on holiday.**
> **7. The percentage of the population who were full-time students.**

Although *Social Trends* is a useful summary source you may sometimes want to take your analysis further. In which case it is often necessary to refer to the original source that is used in *Social Trends*, or to consult a special

---

Table 3.2 Government summary statistics publications

Monthly Digest of Statistics
A collection of the main series of statistics from all government departments.

Annual Abstract of Statistics
Contains many more series than the *Monthly Digest* and provides a longer run of years.

Key Data
Contains over 130 tables, maps and coloured charts and covers a wide range of social and economic data. Each table and chart is accompanied by a reference to sources. This is a recent addition to the general digests and the most recent issue is for the preceding year.

Social Trends
Brings together key social and demographic series in colour charts and tables, including population, households, education, health, housing, environment and leisure. It is published in February each year.

Regional Trends
Provides a selection of the main statistics that are available on a regional basis. It is published around May or June each year. In addition there are Abstracts of Statistics for Scotland, Wales and Northern Ireland as well as *Welsh Social Trends*. In general, these tend to be issues for the previous year.

Table 3.3 Major surveys used in *Social Trends*

	Frequency	Sampling Frame*	Type of respondent	Location	Sample	Response %
Census of Population	10 years	All households	Head of household	UK	All	100
General Household Survey	Continuous	Electoral register	All adults in household	GB	15000	82
Family Expenditure Survey	Continuous	Electoral register	Households	UK	11000	67
National Food Survey	Continuous	Electoral register	Housewife	GB	14500	55
International Passenger Survey	Continuous	Passengers at airports	Individual traveller	UK	255000	89
National Readership Survey	Continuous	Electoral register	Individual adult	GB	30000	74
Survey of Personal Incomes	Annual	Inland Revenue records	Tax units	UK	118000	94
New Earnings Survey	Annual	National Insurance No.	PAYE Employees	GB	170000	—
EC Labour Force Survey	Biennial	Valuation List	Adults in households	UK	105000	84
National Travel Survey	3 years	Electoral register	Households	GB	15000	55

*See Chapter 4 for an explanation of sampling frame.

Adapted from *Social Trends*.

government department publication or even request a special tabulation from the department (which you will have to pay for). The main surveys used in *Social Trends* are summarised in Table 3.3.

The government produces far more statistics than this brief outline can adequately describe; detailed information about government statistical publications can be found in the *Guide to Official Statistics* (HMSO) that is published annually. You will find the main official statistics in public libraries. In addition, the library at OPCS holds a wealth of national and international data on social subjects. If you have trouble finding the statistics you want, telephone or write to the Information Services Division (address at the end of the chapter).

Unofficial statistics

Unofficial statistics are even more wide-ranging than government statistics and we cannot possibly list all the available statistics from non-government sources in this brief overview. Some unofficial statistics are produced on a regular basis, such as the media viewing figures (see Chapter 2) while others are one-off surveys for a specific purpose. Unofficial statistics appear within publications and reports of various bodies such as monitoring bodies (like the Low Pay Unit), trade unions, charities and so on. Increasingly, unofficial statistics are being made available through the Economic and Social Science Research Council Data Archive at Essex University. There is a catalogue (Taylor, 1986) and a bulletin published three times a year by the archive that is available on request.

In the main, locating published unofficial statistics involves detective work in the library. You will probably need to ask your teacher or lecturer for help in getting started. Once you have one unofficial source this often leads on to others. However, this can be time-consuming and often frustrating when your available libraries do not have what you are looking for. This may mean that if you want to make use of unofficial statistics then you have to make a trip to a major reference, university or polytechnic library. This may not be possible, of course, in the time you have available. The important thing in using published statistics is not to try to locate all the possible sources but to make sense of the ones that you do find.

Administrative records and social surveys

Secondary statistical data comes from two types of activities. First, *administrative records*, such as monthly unemployment figures that are compiled by the Department of Employment from returns made by local benefit offices. Second, *social surveys* such as the *General Household Survey*, the monthly National Opinion Poll political attitude surveys, and one-off surveys undertaken by government and academic researchers.

Administrative records

Data generated by administrative procedures have been the least attractive to sociologists because they are almost always based on standard definitions and classifications of, for example, unemployment, crimes, strikes, and so on. These do not necessarily correspond to the categories that sociologists would apply and thus are not designed to address sociological questions. This clearly raises issues of *validity* (see page 32). Nor are they necessarily *reliable* measures of the social phenomena they are supposed to represent (see page 32). Often data collection may be a small part of an official's job and it is also often given to the most inexperienced officers. This, as well as the numbers of people involved, makes checking back difficult (Government Statisticians' Collective, 1979).

Survey statistics

Although administrative records tend to be unreliable and insensitive to the concerns of sociologists, the same does not apply to surveys and censuses. Survey data is collected independently of administrative processes and provides a different perspective on 'official' administrative statistics.

The Office of Population Censuses and Surveys (OPCS) is responsible for the main multipurpose surveys including the *Census*, the *General Household Survey*, the *Family Expenditure Survey* and the *Labour Force Survey*. The OPCS is the major source of government survey data. It is scrupulous in the administration of surveys and the reporting of methods and definitions used. Their interviewers are trained in the 'official' style, which attempts to ensure that, as far as possible, all interviewees receive the same set of questions in the same way without any intervening bias from the interviewer. This 'official' style, in its attempt to ensure the neutrality of the interviewer, tends to be rather formal and rigid. However, this is a problem of surveys in general (see Chapter 4) and is not specific to OPCS.

The OPCS is not limited to administrative definitions of concepts and is able to ask questions that relate more closely to sociological concepts. Government surveys are thus more valid for sociological analysis than most administrative statistics. However, some standardised definitions and classifications are used that are not necessarily suitable for sociological analysis. For example, the Socio-Economic Group (SEG) classification is commonly used in OPCS surveys as the only indicator of social class. Some surveys also have a restrictive scope. For example, the *New Earnings Survey* excludes part-timers and the self-employed.

The following discussion of unemployment statistics illustrates differences between administrative and survey statistics and shows how statistics might be used to address sociological issues.

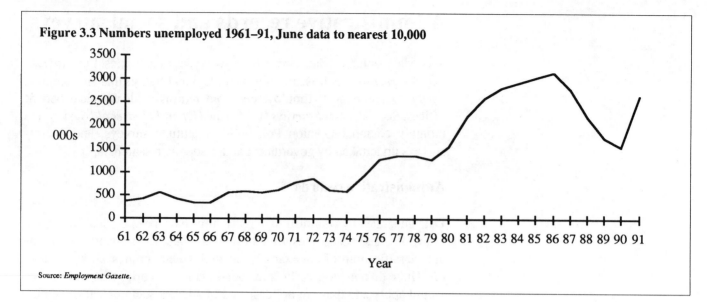

Figure 3.3 Numbers unemployed 1961–91, June data to nearest 10,000

Source: *Employment Gazette.*

Unemployment

Unemployment is important socially, economically and politically. It has been a major problem in Britain since the late 1970s when unemployment exceeded a million people for the first time since the 'Great Depression' of the 1930s.

Student Activity 3.4
Figure 3.3 shows the numbers of people in Britain unemployed in June of each year from 1961 to 1991 according to the Department of Employment.
1. Approximately how many people were unemployed in June 1961, 1971, 1981 and 1991?
2. In which year was unemployment at its highest?
3. Where do you think these figures come from and how do you think they are they collected?

Unemployment statistics

The government collects and publishes unemployment statistics each month. A seasonal adjustment is made to the statistics to take account of variations in the labour market in particular months. The published statistics thus show the underlying trend in unemployment.

Unemployment data are collected by each local unemployment benefit office and the Department of Employment releases a monthly press notice of total figures. These are then published in the *Employment Gazette.* Recent figures can also be obtained by telephoning Department of Employment Enquiries (071–273 6969).

Who is included?
The figures for unemployment compiled by the Department of Employment include only some categories of those people who are registered as unemployed. The official registered unemployed figure has traditionally only included people who sign on as unemployed at unemployment offices or job centres. Thus government statistics on unemployment do not measure all those not in paid work. There are many people who are not in paid work but

who do not actively sign on as unemployed because they are not entitled to state benefit payments. Thus the official figure for unemployment underestimates the number of unemployed people.

Student Activity 3.5
Why do the official figures not attempt to show the full numbers of people out of paid work?

The official unemployment count is thus based on an administrative procedure and does not correspond to a social scientific definition of unemployment. This problem of definition is made worse by changes in the administrative definition of unemployment.

DEFINITIONS OF UNEMPLOYMENT

Department of Employment:
People claiming benefit (that is unemployment benefit, supplementary benefits, or national insurance credits) at Unemployment Benefit offices on the day of the monthly count who, on that day, are unemployed and able and willing to do any suitable work. (Students claiming benefit during a vacation and who intend to return to full-time education are excluded.)

The *rate* of unemployment expresses the numbers unemployed as a percentage of the latest available mid-year estimates of the working population (including the self employed and the armed forces) plus the unemployed. Prior to 1986 the self-employed and armed forces were not included. (Note: The change has meant that the unemployment rate has been reduced about 1% because the base population has now increased with the inclusion of the self-employed.) (*Social Trends*, 1988, p. 202)

General Household Survey:
Unemployed persons consist of those who, in the week of interview, were looking for work, would have looked for work if they had not been temporarily sick, or were waiting to take up a job they had already obtained. In this context temporary sickness refers to illness lasting 28 days or less. These definitions of unemployment apply whether or not the person was registered as unemployed.

Full-time students who reported themselves as unemployed during the reference week are counted as unemployed in 1986. In previous years all full-time students have been counted as economically inactive. (*General Household Survey*, 1986, p. 252)

Labour Force Survey:
Everyone without work who has undertaken no work for pay or profit during the previous week, is free to begin a job within two weeks, and has actively sought work within the previous four weeks (Taylor, 1990).

Changing definitions of unemployment

The administrative definition of unemployment is constantly changing. Indeed, it has been changed *thirty* times between 1979 and December 1989 (Unemployment Unit, 1989). For example, in 1982, 170,000 people were removed from the figures when only those claiming unemployment *benefit* were counted as unemployed rather than those registered unemployed. Among other groups, the Department of Employment figure now excludes married women with working husbands, early retired people looking for part-time work, males over 60 (since 1983) and unemployed 16-17 year olds (since 1988). In addition, since the early 1980s, various training schemes (including the Youth Training Scheme, Restart and so on) have also artificially reduced the numbers of people on the unemployment register by up to half a million. Alan Gordon (1988) noted that:

> In September 1986 the 'official' unemployment count was given as 3,332,897, an unemployment rate of 13.5 percent of the labour force. If we still calculated unemployment in the way acceptable in 1980, the figure would have been 3,858,500, or 15.6 percent.

The constant redefinition has meant that the Government underestimated the rise in unemployment in the 1980s and the early 1990s and overestimated the decrease in between.

Alternative sources of data on unemployment

Official surveys

Government surveys such as the *General Household Survey*, the *Family Expenditure Survey* and the *Labour Force Survey* provide ongoing estimates of unemployment. The *Census* provides a comprehensive figure every ten years. They are more reliable and valid as they tend to use a consistent definition of unemployment that more closely reflects numbers of people out of work.

The difference between the official administrative figure of unemployed people and the number of people who regard themselves as out of work can be seen by comparing *Census* data with Department of Employment figures. For example, while the Department of Employment was showing an unemployment total of only 773,800 in 1971, those who described themselves as unemployed in the census numbered 1,365,775 (Miles and Irvine, 1979, p. 121).

The *General Household Survey* also provides larger estimates of unemployment. For example, in 1977, it was estimated that the registered unemployed accounted for about 90% of all unemployed men, 75% of all unemployed non-married women and 50% of all unemployed married women (*Social Trends*, 1980). In 1979 the *General Household Survey* found that the official figure would be increased by 25% if all those who were shown to be unemployed by the definitions used in the survey were included in the unemployment figure.

An alternative annual unemployment figure is also available via the *Labour Force Survey* based on the numbers of people out of, but actively seeking, work rather than the numbers drawing benefit.

> **Student Activity 3.6**
> **Compare the percentage of the work force unemployed according to the Department of Employment (as published in *Employment Gazette*) with**
> 1. **the numbers who describe themselves as unemployed in the most recent *Census* data;**
> 2. **the numbers defined as unemployed in the *General Household Survey*;**
> 3. **the numbers defined as unemployed in the *Labour Force Survey*.**
> **Make sure that you compare the same years and the same national statistics (GB or UK).**
> **WARNING   You will need access to a library with good official statistics reference section to do this activity. It may therefore not be possible in the time you have available.**

Unofficial sources

Unofficial sources suggest that even these survey statistics underrepresent the numbers of unemployed because of the way they define and collect the data. The Trades Union Congress (TUC), for example, estimated that in October 1985 there were at least 4,500,000 people out of work compared to the Department of Employment's claim of 3,276, 861 people unemployed.

In its monthly *Working Brief* the Unemployment Unit publishes Department of Employment figures, which are based on claimants, plus an adjusted figure that is based on actual numbers of unemployed. For example, in January 1990 the Department of Employment's count for the UK was 1,687,000 (6%) while the UU Index was 2,445,000 (8.3%) (Unemployment Unit, 1990).

Types of unemployment

Social scientists distinguish between different types of unemployment, the main ones being frictional, structural, cyclical and technological.

Frictional unemployment occurs when workers change employment but there is some delay between ending one job and starting a new job. This short-term unemployment is regarded as inevitable in a dynamic economy and is not usually viewed as a problem.

Structural unemployment occurs when the people unemployed do not match the jobs that are available. This may be because the unemployed people do not live in areas where jobs are available. This form of structural unemployment is known as *regional unemployment*. Alternatively, the unemployed people may lack the qualifications or skills required to fill the vacancies. For example, when traditional industries decline, such as shipbuilding and iron and steel manufacture, the unemployed workers may find that their skills have become obsolete. This is known as *sectoral unemployment*.

Cyclical unemployment occurs when the supply of labour outweighs the

---

> **Example answer to Student Activity 3.5**
>
> There are, arguably, three reasons why official statistics do not show the full numbers of people out of paid work.
>
> First, the monthly returns for unemployment come from the unemployment register. It would be far too costly to carry out an ongoing national census of people out of work other than those making use of the register.
>
> Second, from a policy point of view, priority is given to counting how many people are claiming unemployment benefit, and thus the cost of unemployment to the state. There is little concern with the social cost of unemployment, thus no need to monitor actual numbers of people out of work if they are not claiming. This disregard for the social cost has become more and more marked over the decade of the 1980s.
>
> Third, the numbers claiming will always be less than the total out of work and unemployment is a politically sensitive issue which all governments want to minimise.

demand. It is a feature of all Western capitalist economies that they experience fluctuations in economic activity with alternate periods of depression and boom. These are known as economic *cycles*. They may be short-term (around five years from boom to depression) or longer term (up to twenty years) for example when the slump of the early 1930s in Britain was followed by a boom in the 1950s.

Technological unemployment occurs as a result of new technology reducing the demand for labour. Car making and painting robots mean that fewer assembly line workers are required. Computerised stock control means that fewer warehouse staff are needed. Word-processors and other electronic office equipment mean that fewer clerical staff are required. Computerised printing plants require far fewer people than did old fashioned 'hot metal' printing presses. These are just a few of the areas where technology has reduced, and will continue to reduce, the demand for labour (Gill, 1985).

Student Activity 3.7
1. **Look at Figure 3.3. Does this suggest that unemployment between 1961 and 1991 was (i) cyclical (ii) technological?**
2. **Using *Social Trends*, find out whether there are differences in levels of unemployment in different regions of Britain. Do your results suggest that Britain has suffered from structural unemployment?**
3. **Using *Social Trends*, see whether age has an effect on the length of time a person is unemployed? If so, what type of unemployment would you say this is?**

There are various ways in which we can estimate the numbers of people unemployed. This provides us with a description of unemployment but as sociologists we want to look at implications of unemployment. For example, we may want to investigate the causes of unemployment, consider its consequences, assess what it means to be unemployed, or relate unemployment to the way the capitalist system operates. In short, we need to look at theories of unemployment.

Positivist approaches to unemployment

Positivist social scientists focus on the *causes* of unemployment and the *effects* on the economy.

Liberal theory of unemployment: Keynesian model

Liberal theories essentially see unemployment as undesirable, wasteful and harmful. From the 'Great Depression' of the 1930s until the 1970s the British government and economists adopted the liberal view and directed policies at ensuring full employment. John Maynard was the leading liberal economist of the 1930s and 1940s. He argued that unemployment in the 1930s was caused by *lack of demand* in the economy. An increased demand for goods and services would lead to an increase in employment. Governments should thus attempt to manage demand. An increase in government expenditure would increase employment. The notion of a mixed economy, with government control of key industries, would allow the government to manipulate the economy and thus avoid mass unemployment.

In the late 1970s, however, unemployment began to rise and once it exceeded one million people out of work the Conservatives launched a vigorous political campaign attacking the Labour Government's record on unemployment.

Inflation also began to rise sharply in the 1970s and the liberal view of unemployment came under attack from *neo-classical* economists. It was argued that policies aimed at maintaining demand were *not* able to ensure full employment but were contributing to increased inflation.

Monetarism

The *monetarist* approach to neo-classical theory was adopted by the Conservative Government of the 1980s. Monetarists argued that controlling inflation was more important than maintaining full employment. It was argued that inflation undermined the wealth of people who were on fixed incomes (such as pensioners or people who lived on investment income). More importantly, inflation was seen as destroying Britain's competitiveness in international trade. The assumption was that if inflation could be controlled, Britain would be competitive, there would be more demand for British goods and full employment would follow.

Milton Friedman, a leading exponent of monetarist economic theory, argued that inflation was caused by 'too much money chasing too few goods'. This came about because wages were too high and productivity too low. Monetarists argued that the government could reduce inflation by cutting the money supply, that is, to allow less money to circulate in the economy. The easiest way to do this was to *reduce* government spending. Cutting public expenditure would not only reduce the amount of money circulating in the economy, it would also increase unemployment (as the government is a major employer). Increased unemployment would put pressure on workers to take lower wages.

Friedman argued that there was a 'natural' rate of unemployment that was affected by such things as the level of unemployment benefit and wages. Monetarists argued that the unemployed would work for less if employment benefit was cut and if wage rates were more flexible and could be driven down by employers (Minford, 1985). To do this the unions, whom monetarists argued kept wage rates 'artificially' high, would need to be restricted.

Government policy of the 1980s

These approaches were adopted by the Conservative Government of the 1980s. They made cuts in public expenditure (notably in health and education); reduced income tax (notably tax on the rich); increased the burden of taxes from direct to indirect (that is, from the ability to pay to flat rate payments); made changes in labour laws that reduced the effectiveness of the unions to safeguard workers' rights; and reduced benefits for the unemployed and the poor. The role of the state in economic affairs was reduced by selling off nationalised assets to private investors. Free market forces were supposedly to increase the competitiveness, efficiency and profitability of British industry.

Two successive slumps resulted in the destruction of traditional industries and record numbers of bankruptcies of small businesses.

> **Student Activity 3.8**
> **Look at Figure 3.3 (and any other statistics that you can find on unemployment). Have the British government's monetarist policies managed to reduce unemployment?**

Monetarist policy has resulted in an increase in unemployment, not a reduction. Although unemployment may have increased as a result of technological changes and the 'world recession' during the 1980s, Britain

---

NEO-CLASSICAL THEORY OF UNEMPLOYMENT Neo-classical economists see the role of government simply as ensuring the smooth working of the market, both for goods and for labour. They are thus rooted in nineteenth century classical free market view of economists such as Adam Smith. That is, 'market forces' should be allowed to regulate the economy and governments should not interfere in the operation of the market economy.

Neo-classical economists see unemployment as an indication that the supply of labour exceeds the demand. Thus on the basis of supply-and-demand economics, if the supply exceeds demand then the price should fall. Applied to labour, this means that wages should be reduced. If employers could offer lower wage rates they would make more profit and would be more willing to take on workers. In this way, unemployment would be reduced because there would be more demand for workers and people would be more prepared to take poorly paid jobs as they would have little alternative.

Thus, if unemployment persists then there must be various factors that get in the way of the operation of the labour market. Much of the research of these neo-classical theorists has been attempting to identify what these factors are (Gordon, 1988).

has a worse record of unemployment than the United States and Europe. Between 1980 and 1986, *employment* in the United States rose by 10%, but fell in the European Community by 2%. In Britain it fell by 3%. Most of the increase in employment that occurred during the brief boom of 1983 to 1986 was due to an increase in *part-time* jobs (MacInnes, 1987). What is more, the real increase in unemployment has been concealed by changes in the way it is officially measured. This has reduced the actual numbers of unemployed by around a million people.

Neo-Keynsian economists Richard Layard and Stephen Nickell (1986) have used statistical data to show that unemployment in the 1980s in Britain and in many other countries was caused by a chronic shortage of demand. They looked at several factors that might explain the rise in unemployment, such as the aggregate level of demand in the economy, unemployment benefits, employer's taxes (such as national insurance contributions), trade union power, import prices, and the mismatch of skill between the unemployed and job vacancies. Of these factors, the one that explained around 80% of the increase in unemployment was the lack of demand in the economy. So, they argue, the Conservative Government's policies to reduce inflation by dampening demand have been the main cause of unprecedentedly high unemployment.

Phenomenological approaches to unemployment

Phenomenological analyses of unemployment focus on what it *means* to be unemployed. In Chapter 1 we saw that a Weberian approach focuses on *status* rather than class, and that Rex and Tomlinson (1979) used this in their analysis of Handsworth. They showed that ethnic minority groups were systematically at a disadvantage compared to working-class whites. The ethnic minorities formed their own organisations instead of identifying with working-class culture, community and politics. In effect they became a separate underprivileged group, or *underclass* (see page 19).

The underclass suffers from a combination of prejudice, low status and a lack of marketable skills. They are thus overrepresented in the *secondary* labour market, which is less skilled and where there is less job security (see page 78). The underclass is thus more likely to experience high levels of unemployment.

An alternative phenomenological approach can be found in the work of Paul Jackson and Susan Walsh (1987) who looked at the impact of unemployment on family life. For example one woman (Jane) described how she felt that her unemployed husband's presence at home during the day was an intrusion into her life:

> I had this friend; for two to three years we saw each other every day – we were extremely close. And then, I don't know I've seen very little of her these past two years. I think it's more since he's been at home all of the time. With Paul being at home she doesn't come round so I don't see her. (Jackson and Walsh, 1987, p. 205)

Jackson and Walsh showed that the families they studied managed to cope in the face of overwhelming difficulty although they did so in different ways. Some families faced with long-term unemployment resisted change while others attempted to build new lives.

Adrian Sinfield (1981) used available statistics from a variety of official and unofficial sources to document the extent and unevenness of unemployment. However, he also used published studies to assess what unemploy-

Supplementary research activity 3.1

It is argued that unemployment statistics are unable to give any sense of the meaning that unemployment has for people. Undertake an in-depth interview with an unemployed person to find out what it means to him or her to be unemployed (see Chapter 7, on in-depth interviews).

ment meant for different people including redundant skilled workers, school-leavers waiting for their first job and older workers facing early retirement. For example, he notes that nearly every study of unemployment suggests that the most common reaction to being out of work is surprise. The unemployed lack awareness about the problems of being out of work. As one apprenticed tradesman in his early twenties commented in 1979:

> It's changed my attitude to the unemployed. I used to think they were just skivers and was quite a lot against them, but now I've experienced it, it's no joke man. (Newcastle upon Tyne City Council, 1980, p. 35)

Traditionally, studies of unemployment have been concerned with the economic impact of unemployment on individuals and families and the effect of levels of benefit on the search for work. Sinfield argued that it is also necessary to assess how unemployment affects the lives of those who remain *in work* and other members of society. He shows that those in work feel less secure and have their standard of living threatened because of reduced bargaining power. The fear of unemployment results in workers being less mobile, more frustrated and more *alienated* (see Chapter 6). Divisions in society are likely to grow as the unemployed and those employed in unsatisfactory jobs blame other groups. Male workers may blame women for taking their jobs by entering the labour market, or racists may use ethnic minorities as scapegoats, thus increasing sexual and racial tensions. Similarly, equal opportunity policies will suffer in practice when there is an abundance of unemployed labour.

Critical approaches to unemployment

Critical approaches explore unemployment in terms of the operation of capitalism. Marxists see unemployment as an element of capitalist oppression of workers. Feminists see unemployment as a way of restricting and exploiting women. Anti-racists see unemployment as part of the process of racist oppression of ethnic minorities.

Marxist theories of unemployment

Marx saw unemployment as an inevitable result of the capitalist system. He argued that capitalism has varying levels of unemployment because capitalist economies go through cycles of expansion and contraction. According to Marx, capitalists accumulate wealth (or capital) by appropriating *surplus value*. Put simply, surplus value is the difference between what workers are paid for their labour and the market value of the products they produce. By pocketing the difference capitalists accumulate capital.

The more a capitalist firm produces, the more surplus value the capitalist accumulates. According to Marx, capitalists aim to maximise surplus value. Attempts to maximise surplus value leads to competition amongst capitalists. To be successful the capitalist has to invest in machinery so that more can be produced. The accumulated capital is thus turned into machinery. This increases a firm's capacity. This leads to increased production, more surplus value, more accumulation, more machinery and yet more production. While the market expands this process of expansion of capital is likely to continue. These periods of expansion are known as periods of growth (or booms).

Periods of profitable growth produce full employment and so strengthen the working class. Workers have a choice of jobs, and unions can demand higher wages and better working conditions. This begins to reduce the

---

COMMODITY EXCHANGE AND SURPLUS VALUE   Marx argued that positivist economics, with its emphasis on supply and demand, free markets and profit, concealed the real way the economy worked. At the root of capitalism was the process of *commodity exchange*. Commodities are things that are produced for the market.

Commodities have an *exchange value* that is the amount the capitalists are able to get for the commodities that are produced for them by their workers. Commodities also have a *use value*, that is, a value that cannot be easily measured, which is the *use* the commodity has for the purchaser. Marx argued that the only way to measure the use value was by the amount of *labour power* (or labour time) that went into making the commodity.

For example, a capitalist has a labourer producing chairs. It takes the labourer two hours to produce a chair. The chair has a *use value* of 2 labour hours. The capitalist sells the chairs for £50 each. The chairs have an *exchange value* of £50 each.

Capitalists buy labour power (by paying workers wages) and thus have the right to the commodities produced. In the example above, the labourer is paid £10 per hour. So the *exchange value* of *labour power* is £10 per hour.

Capitalists accumulate wealth by setting the exchange value of the commodity *higher* than the use value. This is only possible by *exploiting* labour. That is, by setting the exchange value of labour (wages) at less than the exchange value of the products of that labour (for example, chairs). In the example, the *exchange value* of the chair is £50, the *exchange value of the labour* that produced it is £20 (2 hours at £10 per hour). The *surplus value* that is accumulated by the capitalist is £30 per chair.

The idea that profit is the income *earned* by capitalists for the work they did and the risks they took, ignores the fact that *labour* is paid less for the work than its *use value* (that is, what it is worth in terms of the products it produces). The capitalists pocket the difference without having *produced* anything.

surplus value. Firms thus attempt to reduce their wage bill to remain competitive.

As more and more capital is used, production tends to outstrip consumption and goods do not sell. Workers are laid off and the demand for goods falls further. Capitalists cut back on investment as the rate of profit falls (the declining surplus value per worker is no longer compensated by high volumes of sales). The boom is broken, there is a crisis. Weak firms go bankrupt. The economy contracts, workers are laid off, unemployment rises. There is a recession. The weakened working class is unable to resist the depression of wages and the increased control and authoritarianism of capitalists and capitalist governments. The units of capital that survive do so by investing in new areas where labour is cheaper, such as the 'Third World' or by developing new technology that cuts the reliance on costly workers (Cockburn, 1983). Gradually, business confidence and profitability increase and the economy starts to expand again.

This cyclical process depends on there being a *reserve army of labour* that capitalists can draw on in times of expansion. The size of the reserve army also leads to competition among workers for jobs and this results in depressed wages and higher rates of exploitation.

Reserve army of labour

Traditionally, the reserve army of labour was made up of agricultural workers who migrated to cities and towns as industrial societies became more urbanised. Women formed another major reserve army. As more and more women became employed the reserve began to dry up and ethnic minority immigrants provided a further cheap labour supply that could be exploited.

Stephen Castles and Godula Kosack (1973) studied immigrant workers in France, Germany, Switzerland and Britain. They too showed that immigrants worked in poorly paid, low skilled jobs with poor working conditions and high rates of unemployment. They argued that this is primarily due to discrimination in Britain. In France, Germany and Switzerland the migrant workers are foreigners in the country in which they are working and subject to restrictive laws and regulations that prevent them from gaining employment in more desirable jobs. Discrimination and restrictive regulations are, however, only the superficial reasons why immigrants are unemployed. The real problem is capitalism's need for a reserve army.

The ethnic minority reserve army is not an underclass but part of the working class, which, according to Castles and Kosack, is divided in two on ethnic lines (white and non-white). There is nothing new about this, as Marx pointed out more than a century ago. 'England now possesses a working class *divided* into two *hostile* camps, English proletarians and Irish proletarians' (Marx, 1870).

The lack of unity in the working class benefits the capitalists because the working class is unable to develop a class consciousness opposed to ruling class ideology. Ethnic minorities, rather than the capitalist system, are blamed for housing and job shortages, as the Irish were in the nineteenth century. The myth that ethnic minorities take white people's jobs is perpetuated to ensure a divided working class.

Class fractions

Annie Phizacklea and Robert Miles (1980) studied South Brent in London (in the mid-1970s) and agree with Castles and Kosack that the ethnic

---

RESERVE ARMY OF LABOUR Marx argues that capitalism requires workers who can be hired during booms and fired during slumps. The part of the work force used in this way is the *reserve army of labour*. Every worker who is unemployed or partially employed makes up the reserve army.

There are three groups within the reserve army. First, the *floating* category, who are attracted to areas of high employment. Second, the *stagnant* category, who are irregularly employed. Third, the *latent* category, mainly agricultural workers, who are absorbed into the proletariat as industrialisation proceeds. The unemployed (reserve army) are victims of the *cyclical* way in which capitalist economies work.

minorities form distinctive strata *within* the working class. However, they deny that immigration alone has led to a split in an otherwise unified working class. They argue that the working class is also divided by gender and levels of skill. The working class is thus split into several *class fractions* based on gender, skill and ethnicity. Immigration added another dimension to an already divided working class.

Phizacklea (1982, 1983a) argued, further, that the situation of immigrant and migrant women workers could not be explained by the reserve army theory. West Indian women workers in Britain and migrant women workers in Europe represent a further fractionalisation of the working class.

> Having become wage-labourers in rapidly increasing numbers, the occupa-
> tional distribution, the sectoral mobility, the rate of 'de-skilling', the
> unemployment and re-employment of women to warrant the description of
> a sexually and racially categorised class fraction (Phizacklea, 1983, p. 109).
> Patterns of migrant women workers provide evidence of their subordinate
> position in economic relations. Combined with their subordinate position in
> politico-legal and ideological relations I believe that their objective position
> within the working class is sufficiently distinct from that occupied by their
> male counterparts or indigenous men and women to warrant the description
> of a sexually and racially categorised class fraction (Phizacklea, 1983, p.
> 109).

Contradictions of capitalism

There are, however, two *contradictions* in this process that make it unlikely that cycles of boom and slump will go on indefinitely. First, capitalism needs wealthy consumers in order to sell its expanded output and to make more profit. However, each firm (or nation) needs poorly paid workers if it is to remain competitive in the long run. Second, so-called profit is in fact *surplus value* and thus capitalist accumulation is dependent on the exploitation of waged labour. Investment in machinery increases the *surplus value per worker*, but if it results in *fewer* workers then, eventually, the level of profit will fall. In Marxist terms it is impossible to have surplus value if no workers are employed, as surplus value arises from the exploitation of *labour power*.

Capitalism, some Marxists argue, has within it the seeds of its own destruction. Booms and slumps will become increasingly frequent and more and more pronounced. The exploitation of labour and technological devel-opment mean that full employment is impossible in the long term. Cyclical, technological and structural unemployment will get worse. In the end, the whole process will fall apart. For Marx, the end of capitalism will come about because the process of increased exploitation cannot go on for ever as workers will realise what is happening and will act together to overthrow the system of capitalist exploitation.

Student Activity 3.9
1. Look at Figure 3.3 (page 66). Does this suggest that booms and slumps are becoming more pronounced and more frequent?
2. What other evidence would you need apart from unemployment statistics to make claims about the increasing instability of capital-ism?
3. Use *Social Trends* to see which socioeconomic groups are most likely to be unemployed. How might you interpret the data from a Marxist perspective?

Feminist views of unemployment

It is claimed that as official figures include only those people who are registered as unemployed they disguise the extent of female unemployment.

> **Student Activity 3.10**
> 1. Use *Social Trends* to find out the numbers and proportions of men and women unemployed in Britain over the last decade (or for whatever years you have data available).
> 2. Compare the percentages of men and women who are unemployed according to Department of Employment statistics for the most recent year you are able to obtain data with the percentages of men and women defined as unemployed in the *General Household Survey* or the *Labour Force Survey* for the same year.
> **WARNING You may not be able to attempt this part of the activity if you do not have access to a good statistics library.**

Official figures show that men's unemployment is much higher than women's (Allim and Hunt, 1982; Joseph, 1983). Although female employment has grown more rapidly than male employment since the 1950s, fewer women are in work than men. Unemployment statistics only refer to 'economically active' people, that is, those employed or registered as actively looking for work. Large numbers of married women or single women with children do not register because they are defined as 'ineligible' for benefit. They are categorised as 'housewives'.

> The acceptance of a sexual division of labour which sees men as the breadwinners (expected to do paid work or, if unable to secure employment, to register as unemployed and claim benefit) and women as the carers (expected to perform a disproportionate share of unpaid domestic work and be financially dependent on men) is, thus, embodied in social policies and reflected in the official unemployment figures (Henwood and Miles, 1987, p. 95).

This underpins the sexist view of the right of males to available jobs. Rather than women's unemployment being seen as a problem it is female *employment* that is often seen as the problem because women are 'taking men's jobs'. Work is a source of identity for men but is seen as being less important for women (Sinfield, 1981). Thus there is an assumption that unemployment is a particular problem for men. Felicity Henwood and Ian Miles (1987) jointly reported studies that showed women were as deprived as men by being unemployed. (See Henwood (1983) and Miles (1983) for full details of the surveys.) They argued that unemployment is at least as potentially damaging for women as it is for men and that 'housewives' suffer some of the problems associated with unemployment.

Angela Coyle (1984) exploded the myth that unemployed women are simply absorbed back into the family. From her study of the effect of closure of a clothing factory in Harrogate on the lives of the women made redundant she concludes that women have a strong attachment to their paid employment. This is not simply a matter of financial need. Women derive satisfaction and status from their work.

> This should not be surprising but it is. Familial ideology has been very successful in marginalising women's work, even to women themselves, and, paradoxically, it is often only on the occasion of the loss of that work that its full significance becomes apparent. (Coyle, 1984, p. 121)

Table 3.4 Employment of mothers with children, 1983 and 1989

	Percent. employed		Percent. full-time		Percent part-time	
Age of youngest child	1983	1989	1983	1989	1983	1989
Under 5	24	41	5	12	18	29
Between 5 and 9	54	69	13	19	41	50
10 or older	66	75	25	31	42	43

Some women are able to use the domestic role as a way of making sense of job loss and thus do not suffer a crisis of identity as some men do. However, unemployment for women still leads to financial hardship, isolation, depression and, most importantly, a crisis of autonomy. The resort to a domestic role is no compensation for a loss of independence.

Many women in Britain are employed in part-time work. Figure 3.4 shows the percentages of the total female work-force employed in part-time work in 1988 for twelve European countries. Britain has the second highest proportion of part-time female workers. What the table does not show is that many part-timers work less than 10 hours a week in Britain. Although female employment has been increasing, much of it has not been on a full-time basis. Part-time work is the main mode of employment for mothers with children (see Table 3.4).

Student Activity 3.11
Look at the data in Table 3.4 and in Figures 3.4 and 3.5.
1. **Were more mothers with dependent children working in 1989 than 1983?**
2. **Was there a larger proportionate increase in part-time or full-time employment for mothers after 1983?**
3. **Does the data support the view that women are seen as the primary child-carers?**
4. **Does the data suggest that the government ought to increase child-care provision?**

Some feminists use the notion of a *reserve army of labour* (see page 73) in an attempt to explain the particular situation of women (Dex, 1985). Beechey (1977, 1978) argues that women occupy any of Marx's categories of reserve army but also constitute a separate category. Married women are uniquely flexible and disposable workers because they are 'supported' by males and are not thus seen as primary earners; their main task is seen as being their domestic role within the family. Furthermore, married women in Britain tend to be employed in part-time work and thus are not strongly unionised, are unlikely to receive redundancy pay and do not qualify for benefits. These structural factors add to the disposability of married women as workers. Beechey argues that unless this unique position of women in the reserve army is considered one cannot begin to answer the question of why the demand for labour, which drew women into the twentieth-century work-force, was a demand for women's labour.

Power (1983) argues that women are part of the *latent* reserve army. Housework has changed from 'production' to 'maintenance' or 'domestic reproduction tasks'. Increasingly, capitalism has taken over home-based production activities and women are released to join the reserve army (much as agricultural workers were in the nineteenth century). The expanding demand for industrial labour through the twentieth century has resulted in the development of 'female' jobs. As housework is no longer so demanding women are likely to remain part of the paid work-force.

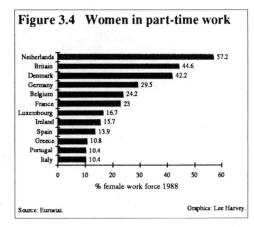

Figure 3.4   Women in part-time work

% female work force 1988

Source: Eurostat.   Graphics: Lee Harvey.

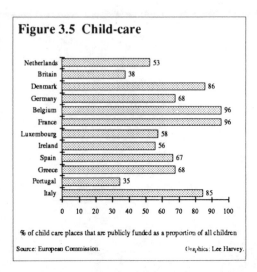

Figure 3.5 Child-care

% of child care places that are publicly funded as a proportion of all children

Source: European Commission.   Graphics: Lee Harvey.

Some feminists are sceptical of the adequacy of the reserve army theory (Bruegel, 1979), arguing that the notion of a reserve army cannot explain *why* particular racial or sexual groups fill categories of the reserve army. Anthias (1980) argues that women, like children, have always been part of the latent reserve army. Women are not underemployed as domestic labourers in the same way that agricultural labourers are, because domestic labour cannot be treated as a mode of production in the same sense. More importantly, to conceptualise women as a reserve army marginalises women's employment. Instead, Anthias wants to develop a framework which integrates women and takes their position seriously.

Student Activity 3.12
1. **What statistical data would you consider necessary to assess whether women constitute a reserve army of labour?**
2. **Is this data available in *Social Trends*?**

Anti-racist approaches to unemployment

Unemployment amongst blacks in the United Kingdom has exceeded the national rate since the 1970s (Runnymede Trust, 1980, pp. 55, 64–8). The Third Policy Studies Institute Survey of 1982 (Brown, 1984) showed that both males and females from ethnic minorities were disproportionately represented in the lower levels of the occupational hierarchy and suffer higher rates of unemployment. Researchers have found that this situation is accentuated in areas of the country with large ethnic minority populations (Fevre, 1984; Harvey, Wells and Place, 1990).

Student Activity 3.13
1. **Use *Social Trends* to find out what differences there are in unemployment rates between different ethnic groups.**
2. **See if you can find out, using the latest available data, if there are any regional variations in ethnic minority unemployment.**

There are several of theories about the disadvantages suffered by ethnic minorities in the labour market.

Racial discrimination

The *racial discrimination* theory argues that racist employers discriminate against ethnic minority groups by refusing to employ them, employing them in poorly paid jobs or failing to promote members of ethnic minorities. Ralph Fevre (1984) used statistical data and case studies of two major employers in Bradford to show that, in the job market, racial discrimination is even more severe than sex discrimination:

> As employment declines it becomes clear that employers prefer to employ white workers, of *whatever sex*, to Black workers.... With mass unemployment Blacks increasingly find that they are denied access to *any* jobs, even the most menial. (Fevre, 1984, p. 166)

Various studies using matched white and non-white applicants for jobs have also shown the extent of employer discrimination (McIntosh and Smith, 1974; Brown and Gay, 1985).

Dual labour market

An alternative view makes use of *dual labour market* theory. New Commonwealth immigrants were encouraged to come to Britain in the 1950s and

---

Example answer to Student Activity 3.12, part 1

You might look up the extent of 'economic activity' of women, the 'occupational structure' of women's work and the extent of female unemployment.

1960s to fill vacancies in the less skilled and less attractive jobs in manufacturing and service industries. West Indian and Asian immigrants were thus recruited to jobs in the *secondary* labour market, where they became trapped.

The dual labour market appears to describe the position of both blacks and women according to empirical studies in America. It has also been used in British research (Barron and Norris, 1976; Bosanquet and Doeringer, 1973). However, it has its drawbacks, not least because it presents a vague and static view of labour markets (Dex, 1979, 1983).

Student Activity 3.14

What statistical data would you need to assess the theory that immigrant workers (a) are overrepresented in the secondary labour market; (b) constituted a class fraction? Is this data available in *Social Trends*?

Crime

While unemployment statistics are unrealistic about the numbers out of waged work, this is primarily a function of the official definition of unemployment and the deliberate minimisation of unemployment figures by successive governments because of the politically sensitive nature of the issue. Crime statistics are somewhat more complicated.

The Home Office produces annual statistics on crime rates. Crime figures are compiled from police records. Each police force sends details of reported crime to the Home Office in London. Crime rates are used to show trends in different types of crime from one year to the next. They are then used for policy decisions. For example, policing is targeted on some sorts of crimes and in specific areas of high crime. Social scientists, especially criminologists, use these figures in their explanations of crime. The figures are also published by the media, in a suitably modified form, to 'inform' the public about crime rates and the likelihood of being a victim.

However, there is considerable scepticism as to the validity and reliability of these statistics. Crime figures do not show the full extent of crime because a lot of crime goes unnoticed. For example, fraud and forgery are crimes that often involve very large sums of money, yet they are rarely uncovered because they are so complicated and well hidden. A rare success was the conviction, in August 1990, of Ernest Saunders, former chairman of Guinness, for the theft of over £8 million, false accounting and conspiracy (Pilkington, 1990, p. 2).

Definitions of crime

As with employment statistics, there are problems over definition. However, these are more complex problems than for unemployment. Crime statistics are based on legal definitions and these are problematic because the same forms of social behaviour can be *classified* differently. When upper class Oxbridge undergraduates cause a disturbance in a public place they are often labelled as 'high spirited'; when working-class football supporters do it they are labelled as 'hooligans'.

Furthermore, *legal definitions* change and this can make comparisons over time very difficult. For example, a change occurred with the 1968 *Theft Act*, which redefined 'theft' to include the former categories of 'larceny', 'breaking and entering' and 'robbery'.

DUAL LABOUR MARKET THEORY is a particular case of general *segmented labour market* theories that emerged in the 1960s as an alternative to the *neo-classical* labour market models that treated the labour market as a whole. Segmented labour market theories claimed to provide a better understanding of occupational segregation, wage differentials and discrimination by showing how they were interrelated. There are a variety of segmented labour market models (Loveridge and Mok, 1979).

The *dual labour market* theory, which suggests primary and secondary labour market, is the simplest of the segmented labour market theories.

The *primary* labour market consists of jobs with high wages, good working conditions and job security. There are opportunities for on-the-job training and promotion. These are usually 'skilled' jobs. They are seen as crucial to a company's success.

The *secondary* labour market consists of jobs with low wages, poor working conditions, little job security and few opportunities for on-the-job training and promotion. These are usually 'semi-skilled' or 'unskilled' jobs (Piore, 1975).

Reported crime

More importantly, crime statistics do not measure the number and extent of crimes *committed*. They measure the number of crimes *reported* by the public and subsequently collated into criminal statistics via the police and the courts. The police do not always *record* crimes even when they are reported. The police may think the reported crime is not important enough or that there is not sufficient evidence to investigate it. The police thus decide which reports of crimes are included in their figures and thus, from their point of view, what is and what is not a crime.

For example, we saw in Chapter 2 that rape is an under-reported crime (Hall, 1985). Rape Crisis Centres tend to receive about six times as many calls per year from victims than are reported to the police and they estimate that they probably only receive calls from one in three victims. Rape Crisis Line estimate that two out of three women who have been raped do not report it to the police because they feel embarrassed or fear that the police will not take them seriously. Of those that are reported to the police, only a fraction ever results in a conviction because of the problems of proof. Thus very few actual rapes ever get officially defined as crimes. So the official statistics on rape convictions in no way reveal the extent of the crime. This under-reporting also applies to domestic violence and the police do not always record incidents of domestic violence even when they are reported. Conversely, OutRage, a group representing lesbians and gay men argues that 'the recent rise in the number of "sexual" crimes is due to the police arresting more men who meet in public places' (Pilkington, 1990, p. 2).

The high level of reporting of car theft and burglary and the very large increase in these crimes over the last twenty years is almost certainly due to the insistence by insurance companies that a report is made to the police before they will make payments against household contents or car insurance.

Racial attacks

Statistics on racial attacks are also very hazy. There are no standard official statistics other than a Home Office survey in 1981 that, based on reports to the police, estimated that 0.4% of Asians and 0.3% of Afro-Caribbeans could expect to be the victims of racial attacks in a one year period. This figure is well below figures more recently available from unofficial sources according to the Racial Attack Group (1989). For example, the Leeds Community Relations Council found 305 cases of harassment over an eighteen-month period in a population of 4,000, an annual rate of 5.1%, over ten times the Home Office estimate. Similarly, a Harris Opinion Poll in Newham (East London) in 1987 found that 25% of the borough's 'black' residents had been the victim of an attack in the previous year. These widely different findings are due to several features including defining what counts as a racially motivated attack; the willingness of victims to report incidents; and the ability of agencies to recognise attacks as being racially motivated.

Inconsistencies in reporting and recording of this type means that figures are difficult to interpret. For example, there were 2179 'racial incidents' reported to the Metropolitan Police in 1987, an increase of 446 (or 25%) over the previous year. However, there is no real way of knowing whether this figure is greater than the overall increase in violent crime (running at about 12% per annum, according to Home Office figures). It may actually hide a stabilising of racial attacks and represent a greater willingness of victims to report such crimes. On the other hand there may be less inclination to report such crimes, because of the perception that they are treated unsympathetically, and the increase may, in reality, be much higher.

> **Student Activity 3.15**
> Using your local library, local authority, courts or police find out which categories of crimes vary from one part of your local area (county, city or town) to another. What reasons can you think of to explain these differences?
> **HINT** Link your explanations to social theory. You may find the discussion of deviance theory in Chapter 6 useful.

Self-report surveys

The difference between the amount of crime committed and the amount finally recorded by the police has been revealed by The *British Crime Surveys* of 1981 and 1983 (Hough and Mayhew, 1983,1985). The survey interviewed 11,000 people over the age of 16, from different households in Britain. It asked people if they had been the victim of any crimes in the last year, whether they had reported them to the police and whether the police had recorded the crime. The survey showed, for example, that only 22% of acts of vandalism were reported and only 8% of such acts were recorded (see Figure 3.6).

Virtually all cases of thefts of motor vehicles were, on the other hand, reported and recorded. The survey showed a massive under-recording and under-reporting of crime, although white-collar crime, tax evasion and corporate crime were not included, nor were crimes related to drugs and prostitution.

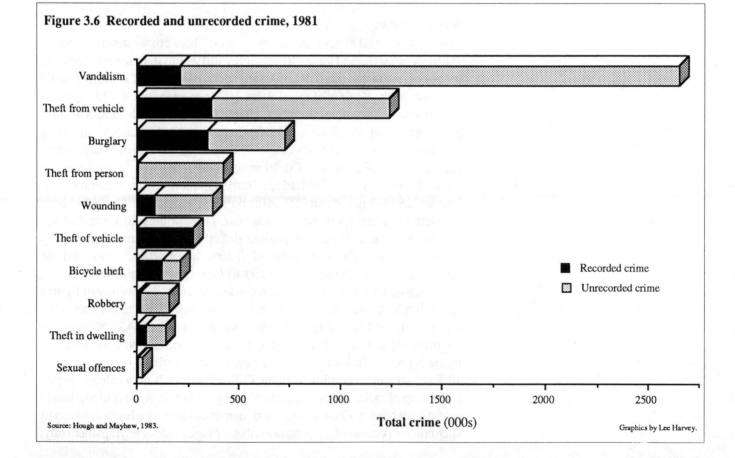

Figure 3.6 Recorded and unrecorded crime, 1981

Total crime (000s)

■ Recorded crime
▨ Unrecorded crime

Source: Hough and Mayhew, 1983.

Graphics by Lee Harvey.

Supplementary research activity 3.2

Do your own self-report study of members of your lecture group or class or some other convenient group. Either devise the questions yourself (we explain how to do a survey in Chapter 4) or adapt the set of crime self-report questions in Campbell (1981). You will find some example questions in Chapter 4 in the section on Religion and Delinquency.

Student Activity 3.16
If possible, obtain a copy of *The 1988 British Crime Survey* (Home Office Research Study, 111, London, HMSO).
1. **What proportion of all crime does the survey suggest is reported?**
2. **What kinds of crime are most likely to be reported?**
3. **What kinds of crime are least likely to be reported?**
4. **In what areas of the country is serious crime most under-reported?**

Self-report surveys have a number of problems (Kinsey, Lea and Young, 1986). For example, even within the confidentiality of the survey, women still under-reported sexual offences committed against them compared to data available from other sources (London Rape Crisis Centre, 1984). Self-report surveys also rely on the respondent's memory of events that have taken place over a long period. Minor events are often forgotten or not seen as important and so do not get mentioned. Self-report surveys also rely on the ability of respondent's to classify crimes. None the less, the surveys, while not necessarily being an accurate quantification of crime, do show, with other research, that official figures substantially underestimate most categories of crime.

In general, then, emphasis in crime statistics is placed on street crime rather than 'white collar crime' (Lea and Young, 1984). Self report-studies (which need to be approached cautiously as well) clearly indicate a far smaller difference between middle and working-class deviance, and of female and male rates, than that revealed in official statistics.

It must be remembered that changes in specific categories of crime statistics may reflect factors other than a change in the numbers of crimes supposedly measured. An increased willingness to report crimes, increased sensitivity and tolerance by officials, changing policy on dealing with crimes, changes in recording of crime reports, or changes in the categorisation of crime may all lead to changes in numbers in official categories without there being any significant change in the numbers of actual crimes committed. The 32% increase in the official figures for rape between 1988 and 1990 was, the police argue, to do with their efforts to gain women's confidence rather than to any growth in the crime itself. Such reservations, added to the bias of class, race and gender built into the statistics, mean that using official crime statistics must be done with great care.

Student Activity 3.17
There is widespread fear of crime, especially among elderly women. Do the statistics indicate that the fear of crime is reasonable? You can use *Social Trends* or any other crime data you can locate for this activity.

The problems associated with crime statistics make it difficult to use them in addressing sociological questions. The credibility of theories of deviance that rest entirely on official crime statistics must be suspect.

We might be interested in why the crime rate has increased, but first we need to establish that it really *has* rather than that more crimes are being reported. Homicide rates (that is, murder and manslaughter) are probably the best indicators of *serious* crime rates because nearly all cases get reported. A comparison of British homicide rates for 1890 and 1990 shows that the rate is the same at 1.3 for every 100,000 people (Gatrell, quoted in Pilkington, 1990). This suggests that serious crime has not increased. On the other hand, it has been argued that there has been a real increase in non-serious crime, although there is disagreement about the causes, see Extract 3.1.

Extract 3.1

REASONS FOR THE INCREASE IN CRIME

The rise in crime is seen as:

1. part of a long-term upward trend in crime that began in the 1950s and that has occurred as society has become more affluent. Crime has increased because there is now more property to steal.
2. due to an increase in unemployment and poverty. Recent Home Office research has shown that rising crime is directly related to a fall in people's spending power.
3. the result of the rise in unemployment and the breakdown of moral control over young people due to the 'climate of individualism created by government policy'.
4. the result of allowing too many criminal suspects to go free on bail while awaiting trial.
5. due to prison sentences being too short.
6. the result of too little discipline at home and at school.
7. due to drugs causing more petty crime.

Adapted from Pilkington, 1990.

Student Activity 3.18
Using *Social Trends* or any other sources of official or unofficial statistics, which, if any, of the explanations in Extract 3.1 do you think the data supports?

Interpretation of statistical data

A further issue that arises when using published statistics, as with any other data, is that the statistics do not speak for themselves. They have to be interpreted. Any set of figures can be interpreted in a number of ways. A study by the National Children's Home (1991) showed that one poor family in five is going hungry, and the report regarded this as scandalous. On the other hand, Ann Widdecombe, a Conservative Government minister welcomed the report, saying that it showed that four out of five adults had not gone hungry.

We will look at some education statistics to illustrate how the same data can be interpreted sociologically in different ways. Tables 3.5 to 3.7 show the educational qualifications attempted, qualifications gained, and post-school destinations of school leavers (for 1986–7). We will offer two alternative interpretations of the data from different theoretical positions; first, a view based on sociobiology, and second a functionalist view.

A possible sociobiology interpretation

Sociobiology (Wilson, 1975) argues that the genetic make-up of humans is an important, if not indispensable, element in many aspects of social life. Genetic factors explain, for example, why men tend to be dominant and women passive. Such views are controversial and resurrect the nature–nurture debate in sociology. The moderate sociobiological view of the importance of biological factors suggests that while our behaviour is genetically influenced it only affects the limits of what we might do rather than determining specific actions. The following interpretation of the tables makes use of the sociobiological view.

Table 3.5 shows that over 80% of both boys and girls attempt mathematics and English GCSE/CSE. This reflects the priority placed on these subjects at school. While as many boys as girls attempt science, it is noticeable that boys are almost three times as likely as girls to attempt technology. On the other hand, girls are much more likely to attempt foreign languages and creative arts. These differences reflect the differing aptitudes of boys and girls.

If we consider Table 3.6, then, we can see that there are more girls (18.9%) with A-levels than boys (16.1%). Overall, 59.9% of girls get O or A level qualifications compared to 53.5% of boys. This indicates that girls tend to develop earlier than boys. However, although girls develop faster they reach a peak and tend not to go on to develop academic careers to the same extent as do the later-developing boys.

Table 3.7 shows that more boys than girls go into employment and this probably reflects their bent towards technology and the availability of jobs in such areas. Although 33.2% of girls go into further and higher education compared to only 25.4% of boys, a larger percentage of boys (8.3%) than girls (6.6%) take degrees. Furthermore, if we only consider those who go into further and higher education this difference is accentuated. Only 19.9% of girls who stay in education (6.6% of 33.2%) go on to degree courses while

SOCIOBIOLOGY is an approach to explaining the social world based on Darwinian evolutionist analyses of the natural world. A key aspect of sociobiology is reproduction. Sociobiologists postulate that species want to reproduce, or more specifically that they want to transmit their genes. It is this need to continue the species that is at the root of the disparity in sexual roles in the animal world, and by extension, in the social world. Females want their young to be healthy if their genes are to continue to be transferred through generations. Thus it is important to attract a robust, healthy male. However, it is also important to keep him to help with raising the young. The male also wants to transfer his genes, so the more females he reproduces with the more likely it is that his genes will survive. So the female must develop a strategy to keep the male as provider for the offspring. The strategy she adopts is one that involves a high degree of investment by the male, for example, nest building. This discourages the male from leaving and taking up with another female because he would have to make the investment all over again.

FUNCTIONALISM, as its name suggests, examines the function that social phenomena play in society. Social phenomena come into being and continue to exist because they are useful for a given society. To establish the usefulness of a social phenomenon it is necessary to refer to the wider society in which it occurs. Functionalists assume that society requires a certain level of consensus about values, harmony and solidarity and integration between its various parts.

Functionalists see society as an organic whole in which the phenomenon plays a part in regulating and maintaining the 'health' of the society. Functionalism has its roots in the early ethnographic work of anthropologists such as Bronislaw Malinowski and A. R. Radcliffe-Brown. In sociology, functionalism has taken a number of forms. It can be seen in Herbert Spencer's early work and is developed by Emile Durkheim. It was also very influential in the 1950s with Talcott Parsons' development of structural functionalism.

Table 3.5 Percentage of leavers who attempted GCE/CSE in the following subjects, 1970–1 and 1986–7

| | 1970–1 | | 1986–7 | |
	Boys	Girls	Boys	Girls
English	55	54	83	88
Mathematics	53	45	80	82
Science	40	36	64	66
Technology	36	8	57	20
Modern Languages	26	32	32	49
History/Geography	44	42	63	58
Creative Arts	18	22	30	38
Total numbers (000s)	315.3	298.1	387.7	372.2

Source: Department of Education.

Table 3.6 Highest qualifications achieved on leaving school, 1986–7 (percentages)

	Boys	Girls
2 A levels/3 S.Highers	12.1	14.7
1 A level/1 or 2 SH	4.0	4.2
5 or more O-levels*	9.4	11.8
1–4 O levels*	27.0	29.2
Other CSE passes	28.4	31.0
No GCEs or CSEs**	19.1	9.1
Total numbers	365,240	350,750

* Or equivalent CSE grades.
** Grade D or less and/or equivalent CSE grades.
Source: Department of Education.

Table 3.7 Destination of school leavers 1986–7 (percentages)

	Boys	Girls
Degree	8.3	6.6
Teacher training	0.1	0.5
Further education	17.0	26.0
Employment	61.0	53.0
Not known	14.0	13.0
Total numbers	365,240	350,750

Source: Department of Education.

32.7% of the boys who stay in education (8.3% of 25.4%) take degree courses. This shows that girls are probably less academically inclined than boys and that they are naturally more drawn to practical, caring and nurturing occupations, which tend to be taught on further education courses, rather than to academic degrees.

A possible functionalist interpretation

Functionalist approaches to education would see it as providing pupils with the training, knowledge and skills necessary for their effective participation in the labour force. A functionalist analysis might therefore argue that the overall increase in the number of pupils taking examinations, and the dramatic increase for girls, is simply a response to the changing demands of the labour market (Table 3.7). If modern industrial economies need an increasingly skilled work force then it is the role of education to meet this need. Other developments in education such as the introduction of a National Curriculum and the growth of vocationalism provide further evidence of the functional relationship between the education system and the labour force.

The functionalist perspective also sees the education system as being important in reproducing the 'social consensus' by transmitting society's norms and values. They may suggest that part of this consensus relates to the different roles men and women perform in society. Parsons (1951), for example, argued that a gender-based division of labour was the most efficient way of organising society. Within the modern nuclear family the male performs an instrumental role as the main family 'breadwinner' and this is complemented by the supportive or 'expressive' role performed by his partner. This view might suggest that, although more girls than boys are taking examinations and are more successful in terms of grades, they are less likely to have a serious commitment to a career and thus to higher education, because this would conflict with their future primary function within the domestic sphere. This would account for the fact that although more girls get A levels (18.9%) than boys (16.1%), fewer girls go on to degree level (6.6%) than boys (8.3%).

Student Activity 3.19
Reinterpret the tables from a feminist perspective.

Political pressure on published statistics

It must be remembered that statistics are collected and published for a purpose. They may be instruments of policy-making, such as those produced by central or local government. Or they may be collected or manipulated to give weight to the cases of pressure groups such as Shelter who use information to lobby MPs. In other words, the collection and reporting of statistics is not done neutrally.

Central government exerts a considerable amount of pressure on the production of social and economic statistics, especially when they relate closely to party policy. Inflation, employment, inequality and crime rates were key issues in the 1980s and the Conservative Government ensured several changes were made to the way in which statistics relating to these areas were compiled and published. As we have seen, the method of counting unemployment was constantly changed to minimise the 'official' numbers of people out of work. Similarly, moves were made to recalculate the rate of inflation, with suggestions that the real rate should exclude mortgage repayments and the poll tax. Similarly, as the party of 'law and order', the Conservative Government tended to recognise only the 'official' crime statistics, although, as we saw above, they greatly under-represented the extent of crime as revealed by numerous unofficial surveys.

Furthermore, statistics may well not be published, or may be delayed if they are politically embarrassing. Figures on low-income families were published annually until 1979. Then the Department of Social Security began to publish the figures less regularly and by 1991 the latest figures available were for 1988. This reluctance to provide up-to-date information on poverty coincides with research that shows that in Britain the poor got poorer throughout the 1980s (Bradshaw, 1990; EC Commission, 1991; Oppenheim, 1990; Townsend, 1991).

The report of the National Foundation for Educational Research (a government-funded research body for the National Audit Office) on the dangerous and unhealthy state of Britain's schools was blocked for five months by two senior civil servants. The report detailed accidents to teachers and pupils caused by neglect to buildings that became hazardous. Both Sir John Caines (Permanent Secretary at the Department of Education) and Sir Terry Heiser (Permanent Secretary at the Department of the Environment) halted publication by refusing to accept its findings. The report was embarrassing for the government at a time when education was high on the political agenda because essentially it blamed the Department of Education for inadequately financing maintenance of schools. Similarly, the *Registrar General's Decennial Supplement on Occupational Mortality for 1979–83* was published in 1986 with the minimum statistics and no commentary (overturning a tradition dating from 1850). This concealed the continuing widening differences in death rates between social classes that otherwise would have embarrassed the Conservative Government.

Changes in *Social Trends*

Despite its widespread use and the large range of surveys it draws on, *Social Trends* must not be treated as a neutral or 'objective' publication. Indeed, it provides a good example of political manipulation and presentation of statistical data. The original purpose of *Social Trends*, as set out in its first editorial in 1970, was to make readily accessible to Parliament, the media and the population at large, statistics that could be used to measure both social and economic progress. The first editions were very much about people, but following cuts in the Government Statistical Service in the early 1980s *Social Trends* became limited to work needed for government. Although its readership still goes far beyond Whitehall there are now subtle differences in presentation. Rather than revealing the problems and plight of specific groups as it used to, *Social Trends* now concentrates on broad social changes on a wide range of topics.

For example, *Social Trends* (1990) openly reproduces the Conservative Government's philosophy by suggesting that on average we are getting richer, enjoying more education and longer holidays, and living in better-equipped houses. There is little detailed analysis by income group, social class, family type or region. This effectively conceals major divisions that have arisen in Britain in the 1980s such as the North–South divide (Fothergill and Vincent, 1985; Smith, 1989) and the growing gap between rich and poor

Questions for Student Activity 3.21

A. Compare the number of legal abortions carried out in different regions in 1970 with the most recent figures. To what extent are marital status and age of the mother associated with abortion rates?

B. Outline the changes in the number of children adopted since 1970. Has the age pattern of the adoptees changed over this period?

C. Compare the survival rates of males and females in different age groups and social classes for all types of cancer since 1970. What are the major differences in survival rates for different types of cancer?

D. What, currently, are the principal causes of death of males and females in different age groups? Have there been any significant changes in causes in these groups since 1970?

E. What changes have there been in the total number of divorces since 1970? Is there any tendency for marriages to be shorter now compared with 1970? Are there any changes in the ages of divorcees since 1970?

F. What changes have there been in average household size and type since 1970? What changes have there been in the population of one-parent families over this period?

G. Highlight the trends in major forms of housing tenure by gender of the head of household since 1970.

H. Analyse changes in smoking habits since 1970 in terms of age, sex and socio-economic group.

I. What changes have there been over the last two decades in respect of the extent of tooth decay among children? To what extent are there regional variations in this change?

HINT: You may find it easier to work in pairs on this activity. If you are unable to locate statistics that go back to 1970 use whatever statistics you can find to answer the question.

(Lilley, 1990). Similarly, the first page of the section on education picks out only the figures that show how things are getting better. The chart which shows Britain bottom of the international ratings for education of 16 to 18-year-olds, and the tables of teacher vacancies are not highlighted. Nor are there any regional breakdowns of expenditure per pupil. The appalling difficulties faced in some areas are simply covered up by omission. These statistics do exist, but they have to be unearthed from CSO publications such as *Regional Trends*. The point is that such regional variations used to be published in the most accessible of government statistical publications, but slowly *Social Trends* is being manipulated to reproduce government ideology.

Student Activity 3.20
Look at the crime section of a recent edition of *Social Trends*. To what extent do you think the reporting of crime statistics reflects government policy and ideology?

A critical attitude to published statistics

So while published statistics are a resource for researchers they need to be approached cautiously. It is necessary to consider carefully how they were collected, why they were collected and exactly what is being measured. Published statistics, from whatever source, are dependent on the definitions used and are affected by the way in which they are collected. As the Government Statisticians' Collective (1979, p. 149) so aptly pointed out, 'statistics do not, in some mysterious way, emanate directly from the social conditions they appear to describe'. They are not self-evident but rely on the assumptions, conceptions and priorities of the agencies that collect them. Furthermore, the actual statistics are compiled by people, usually within imperfectly functioning bureaucracies, and the result is not a perfect measure but the best that time, money, and the pressures of the job allow.

Published statistics, then, should be seen not as 'facts' but as evidence for the social researcher. In the end, published statistics are data like any other data and they cannot be detached from the theoretical context within which they were generated. It is important to read statistics, and the commentaries on them, as critically as any other forms of evidence.

Student Activity 3.21
Select one of the questions listed in the box opposite. Locate the appropriate official statistics to answer it. Prepare a brief report that:
1. **Fully and clearly documents sources (also indicate sources that proved unfruitful when consulted).**
2. **Answers the question (making sure that tables and diagrams are specific to the answer).**
3. **Comments on the results and analysis, suggesting reasons for trends or differences.**
4. **Relates the discussion to sociological theory.**
5. **Assesses the adequacy of the statistical sources used.**

To recap, published statistics raise the following issues:

- Using available statistics greatly reduces the *time* and effort required to collect information.

- There are a *variety* of published statistics ranging from regularly produced government official statistics through to one-off unofficial statistics. Seeking out appropriate data often requires a considerable amount of work. *Social Trends*, however, brings together many official and semi-official sources and is a useful first reference.

- There are problems of *validity* when using statistics that have been collected for other purposes. Your theoretical concerns may not be the same as the ones that guided the original data collection. There are often problems of definition of basic concepts.

- There are problems over the *reliability* of some published statistics. Government administrative statistics are often regarded as unreliable. Government survey statistics are usually much more reliable. The survey division of GSS is scrupulous in its methods of data collection. Unofficial statistics vary enormously and it is often difficult to judge the reliability of the data collection process.

- Published statistics are often affected by *political* pressures both in terms of collection and presentation. Using a variety of sources helps to reveal some of the ways that statistics have been manipulated.

- *Comparisons* over time can be a problem when using government statistics because of the numerous inconsistencies in collection, analysis and presentation.

- Published statistics do not 'speak for themselves' but must be *interpreted;* different sociological perspectives can lead to very different interpretations of the same data.

Epistemological issues

Besides these practical and conceptual issues, the use of published statistics also raises epistemological issues for sociologists.

Positivism and published statistics

The positivist approach, as we have seen in Chapters 1 and 2, is to adopt a natural scientific model and attempt theoretical explanations of apparent social phenomena. This, positivists do, in the main, by processes that allow the identification and measurement of social 'facts', with the intention of building cause-and-effect relations.

Thus positivists find no fundamental epistemological objection to using government statistics. Positivists are concerned that all statistics are collected in systematic ways that make them 'valid' and 'reliable' (see Chapters 2 and 4). They are, therefore, critical of definitions and collection procedures. In this respect, while official statistics may not be based on sociological definitions, the Government Statistical Service is as scrupulous as it can be in documenting changes in definitional categories, difficulties in collection procedures, sample sizes and sampling frames. It thus provides users with clear information by which to judge the statistics collected. Positivists thus see official statistics as a useful source, which provide a much wider coverage than any independent enquiry could.

Phenomenological critique of published statistics

Phenomenology is an approach that is primarily concerned with looking at the way people interpret the world. It concentrates on the meanings that people have rather than on any attempt to construct causal theories about the world. Thus phenomenologists argue that statistics do not represent the world but represent the way that the people who construct the statistics see the world.

For example, statistics generated from administrative records, such as official statistics on deviance, while bearing some relationship to actual rates of deviance, are, more accurately, indicators of the official processes that differentiate between individuals as being deviant or non-deviant (Kitsuse and Cicourel, 1963). Categories of crime are constructions of meaning placed on certain individuals and actions that are seen to be of a certain kind.

In short, the phenomenological critique raises a fundamental epistemological issue that goes far beyond the adequacy of government statistics. Phenomenologists question the possibility of measuring social phenomena at all because they *deny* the notion of social facts.

Thus, for example, researchers who treat official statistics on crime as facts and then explain their causes may simply reveal the assumptions of police and probation officers to categorise what they see as crime. Thus the appropriate question for phenomenologists is 'how do some actions become categorised as criminal?'

Similarly, statistics on some topics reflect fashion and current thinking rather than any underlying phenomena. For example, the number of reported tonsils operations reveals more about fashions in treatment and good practice than they do about childhood illness (Radical Statistics Health Group, 1980).

> **Student Activity 3.22**
> **Compare the positivist and phenomenological view of Durkheim's study of suicide. To what extent does Durkheim consider the reliability and validity of national suicide statistics? Does Durkheim consider how deaths come to be classified as suicides?**

Critical analysis of published statistics

Critical sociologists argue that elements of the social world cannot be separated from the broader social structures in which they are located. Published statistics need to be seen in a wider historical and social context. Government statistics come in for particular criticism. Marxists, for example, argue that government statistics are collected to facilitate the day-to-day running of the state. Far from being a neutral observer, the state plays a political and economic role in sustaining and reproducing the *status quo* and it is argued that the collection and presentation of statistics reflects this (Miles and Irvine, 1979).

Critical sociologists, as we saw in Chapter 1, argue that social structures act as oppressive mechanisms by which one group or class holds power over another. Government statistics thus reflect the concerns of the state in *legitimating* the existing sets of power relations (see page 14). They do not provide a picture of what really exists, but reflect the priorities of the state. Thus government statistics are subject to political manipulation through selective redefinition of social phenomena in ways that support the prevailing social structure. The state reflects ruling class *ideology* and interests, and

Example answer to Student Activity 3.22

In *Rules of Sociological Method*, Durkheim argued that human behaviour constituted 'social facts' and were thus observable and measurable and had causes in other social facts. In *Suicide* he argued that his research demonstrated that real laws are discoverable and that social phenomena obey laws in the same way as natural phenomena.

Durkheim's study has been taken as a major example of *positivist* methodology (Selvin, 1958) because he treats suicide as a *social fact* and attempts to relate it to other social facts, such as religion. Positivists have criticised Durkheim for being rather naive because he appears not to have checked on the validity and reliability of the statistics he used. In theory, they argue, there is a finite and absolute suicide rate for a given population but official statistics do not provide an accurate record of this rate as they do not represent the actual extent of suicide.

For example, there was no systematic medical examination for the cause of death in Europe until the last half of the nineteenth century and the extent of examinations differed in rural and urban areas. Family and friends of the deceased go to great lengths to disguise a suicide. Suicide was more disapproved of by the Catholic church, so Catholics make more effort to hide suicide (see Taylor, 1989).

Phenomenologists, however, go one stage further and argue that the whole basis of Durkheim's approach is incorrect. To see official statistics on crime and suicide as referring to activities that have an objective reality of their own, is to misunderstand their nature. Statistics are not social facts. Such statistics are simply the *meaning* given by social actors to events that they have perceived and interpreted as crime and suicide.

Certain events become defined as suicide by coroners, medical practitioners, newspaper reporters, the family and friends of the deceased and so on. Definitions depend on their interpretation of the event, thus suicide is not an objective fact and the appropriate question for sociologists to ask is, how do deaths get categorised as suicide? Answering this question involves investigating the meanings employed by those concerned with interpreting the cause of what is seen as unnatural death. This approach is less likely to distort the social world as it seeks to explore and understand the procedure used by its members to construct their social reality.

Atkinson (1968) argues that you can not uncover the 'real' facts and then scientifically study suicide. More to the point, if researchers adopt Durkheim's positive approach they will 'ride roughshod over the very social reality they are trying to comprehend'. Thus Atkinson's research focuses on the methods used by coroners and their officers to categorise death. He argues that coroners' common-sense theories contain explanations of the causes of suicide, that is, if information about the deceased's background fits these explanations, then a verdict of suicide is likely. For example, when the millionaire publisher Robert Maxwell died in 1991 it was first thought inconceivable that such a man would commit suicide. When the extent of his debt and misappropriation of funds came to light, far more credibility was given to the possibility that he had committed suicide.

---

these influence the statistics it produces (see page 15 for a summary of ideology). Official statistics are then indicators of the state's role and priorities.

> It is extremely difficult, if not impossible, to make a really radical criticism
> of society using available statistical sources, which imprison us in the
> concepts and concerns that dominate official politics and economic life.
> (Government Statisticians' Collective, 1979, p. 138)

Feminists argue that published statistics, especially official statistics, are sexist. This sexism does not arise out of any deliberate attempt by government statisticians to oppress women, but because the conceptual schemes used in government statistics embody a particular sexist mode of thinking (Oakley and Oakley, 1979).

Women are rendered invisible in many official statistics such as employment and unemployment statistics (as we saw above). This is not because the data cannot be collected but because dominant *patriarchal* ideology (see page 25) allocates women to specific roles and activities and the official statistics reproduces this ideology. For example, the *New Earnings Survey* looked at part-time employment among women, but not men. The *Family Intentions Survey* is based on a survey of women only, although it refers to intended family size. Marital status is often included in the analysis of statistics for women but not for men (as in employment figures). Housework, an area of work in which women are overrepresented, is not included in official statistics on work because it is not paid employment. Men, rather than women, are usually defined as 'head of household' and the socio-economic characteristics of many women are defined in terms of their husband or father. Women's own occupational identities are deemed irrelevant where they are not seen as head of the household. Such statistics reproduce the idea of women working for 'pin money' and as the primary carers and nurturers within families.

We saw above that administrative crime statistics appear to under-represent the real level of crime. This distortion is even more acute for women than for men. The picture from crime statistics is that women are far less likely than men to commit violent or aggressive crimes but far more likely to commit crimes like shoplifting or prostitution. This reflects the patterns of *socialisation* to which the sexes are exposed (see page 50) and the different social roles that they play as adults (Oakley, 1972). However, such statistics also reflect sexist bias at the level of data collection because the processes by which a person becomes a criminal are particularly vulnerable to the influence of sexist attitudes (see Chapter 6).

Much of the sexism in published statistics is a reflection of sexist social reality. This applies particularly to official statistics but also can be found in unofficial statistics and, indeed, is prevalent in much social research (Eichler, 1988). Not all the problems with government statistics, however, can be explained in terms of the general sexism within society. Official statistics impose specific sexist models and attitudes on the data. Thus, Oakley and Oakley (1979) argue that sexism limits the usefulness of official statistics since it is impossible to subtract the influence of sexism from the data available. It is often difficult for the social scientist to establish just what the position of women is from the official statistical data. However, as official statistics are collected to satisfy the needs of government and these needs are intimately bound up with the preservation of a sexist social order, the presence of sexism in official statistics serves to reproduce patriarchal ideology.

> **Student Activity 3.23**
> **Assess the adequacy of official statistics from a anti-racist point of view. For example, how adequate are official definitions of ethnic minority groups? To what extent are official statistics available for ethnic minority groups? Do official statistics take account of cultural differences?**

Secondary data analysis

Although this chapter has concentrated on the presentation and interpretation of available published statistics, there have been occasions when some further analysis of the data has occurred. For example, the data in Table 3.1 was the result of a reworking of government statistics by the Unemployment Unit. Data from the Training Agency were recalculated to omit people who moved between schemes and thus provide a clearer indication of the destinations of those actually leaving YTS.

In the example of the interpretation of education statistics it was shown how it is possible to represent data by calculating new percentage figures. Then the difference between boys and girls going on to degree courses was shown to be much greater than suggested in Table 3.7 when only the students who went into further and higher education were taken into account. In Student Activity 3.11 you were asked to use data from three different sources to discuss government expenditure on nursery places.

The reworking of statistical data sources in this way is known as secondary data analysis. Hakim (1982) defines secondary data analysis as 'any further analysis of an existing *data set* which presents interpretations, conclusions, or knowledge additional to, or different from, those presented in the first report on the inquiry as a whole and its main results'.

Secondary analyses thus include:

- studies reporting more condensed data;
- studies reporting more detailed data;
- studies focusing on a specific sub-topic or social group;
- studies angled towards a specific policy issue;
- analyses based on an alternative conceptual framework or theory;
- analyses using more sophisticated analytic techniques.

The extent to which you can undertake secondary data analysis depends on three things: the rigidity of the data; the nature of the enquiry; and the ingenuity of the sociologist.

Rigidity of the data

The form in which the original data is available restricts what you can do with it. If the data is only available in already-published tables, then the researcher can only undertake secondary analysis within the framework set up by the table. For example, in Table 3.1, while we can compare employment rates for males and females on YTS schemes, and we are also provided with data for Asians, we cannot compare the employment rates for Asian males and Asian females. To do that we would need to have data on the individual cases and construct our own table from scratch.

Individual case data is available in data archives. Obtaining such data allows researchers the freedom to reanalyse it any way that they think suitable, as they might if they had collected the data themselves. In Britain, as noted above, the largest and most accessible data archive is the Economic and Social Science Research Data Archive (ESRCDA). It was established in the late 1960s and more and more data sets, deriving from academic research, and independent research as well as government surveys, are becoming available from the ESRCDA. These include the key surveys carried out by the Office of Population Censuses and Surveys: the *Labour Force Survey*, the *General Household Survey* and the *Family Expenditure Survey*. These government surveys are designed for secondary analysis (see, for example, Payne, 1987) and are widely reanalysed by government departments, academics, local government, quangos, trade unions, pressure groups, market researchers and so on.

The nature of the enquiry

The scope for secondary analysis depends on the *nature* of the sociological enquiry. It may be that the specific hypotheses under consideration cannot be addressed through secondary analysis as there is no available survey that has collected data on all aspects of the hypothesis. Or the definition of the theoretical concept used in available studies in no way matches the theoretical concerns of the researcher (such as the use of SEG to stand for class). However, although government definitions may be different from those of sociologists, there is scope to overcome these problems according to Catherine Hakim (1982, p. 141), who suggests that many official surveys could 'yield new or additional results if re-analysed within the framework of social science theory'.

> **A DATA SET** is the answers to the questions asked by survey researchers. The data is usually coded and the data set consists of an array of numerical codes. Each line of the data set refers to each respondent. See Chapter 4 for more details. Appendix 1 is an example of a data set.

The ingenuity of the sociologist

This takes us to the third factor that influences secondary data analysis: the *ingenuity* of the sociologist. Secondary data analysis depends on the researcher's imagination. This can be summed up as 'looking for a different angle on the data'. While this is most easily undertaken when data sets of individual cases is available from archives, it can also be done using composites of already-published tables. For example, in *State of the Nation*, Fothergill and Vincent (1985) bring together a large number of official statistics to demonstrate how the North–South divide has widened over the decade up to 1984. Similarly, in their study of poverty, Abel-Smith and Townsend (1965) developed procedures to overcome data discontinuities such as changes in income banding, pattern of household composition and changes in definitions in the 20-year span of *Family Expenditure Survey* data used in their study.

Reworking data to produce new findings requires some data analytic skills. Although we say a little more about data analysis in Chapter 4, an extensive account of statistical procedures is beyond the scope of this book. However, a lot can be done with some simple and straightforward reworking and comparison of available data, as can be seen in the following discussion of inequalities in health. This discussion also further highlights the problems of definition and measurement, limitations in available statistics, political influences on statistics and the relation of data to theory.

Inequalities in health

Inequalities in health have been a cause of concern for politicians and sociologists since the 1970s.

The Black Report

In 1979 the Report of the Royal Commission on the National Health Service argued that the service should 'provide equality of entitlement and access to health services'. The subsequent Working Group on Inequalities in Health chaired by Sir Douglas Black investigated apparent inequalities in health provision and submitted a report to the Secretary of State in April 1980. It became known as the *Black Report* (Townsend and Davidson, 1982).

The Black Report revealed substantial inequalities in health. As this was politically embarrassing, the Conservative Government delayed the publication of the report by one year and restricted its circulation to 250 copies. Permission to hold a press conference was refused. The subsequent publication of an edition by Penguin rapidly sold out.

The *Black Report* summarised its findings on inequalities in health in Britain as follows:

1. Most recent data show marked differences in mortality rates between the occupational classes, for both sexes and at all ages....
2. The lack of improvement, and in some cases deterioration, of the health experience of the unskilled and semi-skilled manual classes (class V and IV), relative to class I, throughout the 1960s and 1970s is striking....
3. Inequalities exist also in the utilization of health services, particularly and most worryingly of the preventive services. Here, severe under-utilization by the working classes is a complex result of under-provision in working-class areas and of costs (financial and psychological) of attendance which are not, in this case, outweighed by disruption of normal activities by sickness.... (Townsend and Davidson, 1982)

Defining and measuring health

Looking at inequality in health raised problems of defining and measuring both 'health' and 'inequality'. The *Black Report* noted that there were many indicators of health including mortality rates, morbidity (illness) rates, sickness-absence rates and restricted activity rates. These are all measures obtainable from government statistics. However, mainly for practical purposes, the report focused on *mortality* rates. Similarly, the main means of assessing inequality was to compare statistics between different occupational status groups, noting also differences between males and females. The Registrar General's classification was thus employed as an indicator of social class.

> **Student Activity 3.24**
> 1. **What are the limitations in defining health in terms of mortality rates and class in terms of the Registrar General's classification of occupation?**
> 2. **How else might health be defined?**

The emphasis on mortality rates and the problem of definition has led to some commentators arguing that there are no real inequalities in health, only artificial ones that result from inadequate statistics. This is known as the *artefact* view of inequalities in health. Recent research has, however, shown that the degree of economic inequality not only effects inequalities in health but is directly related to it. 'The relationship is not a statistical freak. It has now been found on four different data sets using different countries, different dates and different measures of income distribution' (Wilkinson, 1991).

Health statistics

There are surprisingly few statistics about ill health and disability. The administrative morbidity statistics (collected and published regularly in *OPCS Monitors* before being included in DHSS publications such as *On the State of the Public Health* and other HMSO summary publications) include figures on cancer survival rates, notifications of infectious diseases, congenital malformations, and hospital in-patients. These are limited and a lot of analyses are based on mortality statistics (Townsend and Davidson, 1982; Radical Statistics Health Group, 1980, 1987). However, the *General Household Survey* includes questions on health.

> **Student Activity 3.25**
> Using the *General Household Survey*, locate data that shows differences in illness by socioeconomic group since 1979.
> 1. **Is the level of reported illness increasing or decreasing for all groups?**
> 2. **Is the difference in reported illness by socioeconomic group getting larger or smaller?**
> 3. **Are there any differences in reported illness for men and for women?**
> 4. **How adequate is reported illness as an indicator of health?**
> **WARNING You may not be able to attempt this activity if you do not have access to a good statistics library.**

ARTEFACT VIEW OF INEQUALITIES IN HEALTH There is a view that there are no real inequalities in health. The so-called *artefact* view (Hart, 1985) suggests that apparent differences between social groups are simply the result of the inability to measure a complex phenomenon such as health. Constant changes in classification, the multidimensional nature of health, the inadequacy of health statistics (especially the concentration on mortality) and the changes in occupational structure make it impossible, some statisticians argue, to measure inequality. A major plank in this argument is that the lowest socioeconomic group has a disproportionate number of older people (because of the upward mobility of younger people) and this skews statistics on mortality. However, Nicky Hart (1985, p. 583) argues that 'it is amongst younger people that inequality is most pronounced and moreover increasing. This means that the evidence of inequality in mortality risk is not an artefact, but a real phenomenon of class advantage and disadvantage which must be explained in other ways'.

This sceptical view of the ability to measure complex phenomena can, of course, be applied to any social phenomena. It is difficult to refute because it hinges on the adequacy of theoretical definitions and the ability of social scientists to translate them into measurable variables. This process is known as *operationalisation* and is discussed in detail in Chapter 4.

ETHNIC INEQUALITIES IN HEALTH The *Black Report* made very little attempt to assess ethnic differences in health care, mainly because there are very few official statistics that cover ethnicity or 'race'. The first comprehensive study of ethnic differences in mortality rates was *Immigrant Mortality in England and Wales 1970–78* (Marmot *et al.*, 1984), which is based on place of birth as recorded on death registrations since 1969. See also *Health, Race and Ethnicity* (Rathwell and Phillips, 1986) and *Facing the Figures* (Radical Statistics Health Group, 1987).

Example answer to Student Activity 3.25

The following analysis is not exhaustive, but provides an *indication* of how you might make use of survey data to explore differences in reported illness.

Data from the *General Household Survey* for the 1980s on three questions related to illness are summarised in Tables 3.8 to 3.10.

1. The *General Household Survey* data suggest that for all socioeconomic groups sickness is on the increase. There has been a steady increase in the percentage of people reporting *chronic* sickness over the period 1979 to 1986 (Table 3.8). Similarly, the average number of days of restricted activity due to *acute* sickness is increasing, as are the percentages of people who *consulted* a National Health GP in the two weeks prior to the interview.

Table 3.8 Chronic sickness: prevalence of reported long-standing illness by sex and socioeconomic group, Great Britain (percentages)

	Males			Females		
Socioeconomic group	*1979*	*1983*	*1986*	*1979*	*1983*	*1986*
Professional	19	25	25	18	25	25
Employers, managers	23	28	30	22	26	28
Other non-manual	25	31	29	27	30	34
Skilled manual	27	32	33	25	31	32
Semi-skilled manual	30	34	34	33	39	39
Unskilled	34	34	40	39	45	47
All	27	31	32	28	33	34

Table compiled by Lee Harvey from *General Household Survey*, 1979–86.

2 and 3. The increase in ill health varies according to socioeconomic group and sex.

The prevalence of reported long-standing illness has increased for all socioeconomic groups and for men and women (27% up 32% for males and 28% to 34% for females). However, there is less *chronic* illness in professional and managerial groups than in the manual groups. The differential for men has not improved since 1979 and for women it has got even greater. In the top two socioeconomic groups women had a marginally lower incidence of chronic illness than men in 1986, but in the lower two classes women have a markedly higher illness rate.

There is a steady rise in restricted activity days due to *acute* illness for everyone, although the lower socioeconomic groups suffer more restricted activity days on average (Table 3.9). However, the differential is closing for men,

Table 3.9 Acute sickness: average number of restricted activity days per person per year, by sex and socioeconomic group, Great Britain

	Males			Females		
Socioeconomic group	*1979*	*1983*	*1986*	*1979*	*1983*	*1986*
Professional	19	25	25	18	25	25
Employers, managers	23	28	30	22	26	28
Other non-manual	25	31	29	27	30	34
Skilled manual	27	32	33	25	31	32
Semi-skilled manual	30	34	34	33	39	39
Unskilled	34	34	40	39	45	47
All	27	31	32	28	33	34

Table compiled by Lee Harvey from *General Household Survey*, 1979–86.

due to relatively large increases in restricted days for higher socioeconomic groups (12 to 17 for professionals and 15 to 22 for managers, compared to 25 to 29 for semi-skilled and 29 to 30 for unskilled). One could speculate that, due to increases in income, top socioeconomic groups can afford to allow illness to restrict work activity while lower income groups cannot afford time off work. Possibly, the competitive individualism of the market economy in the 1980s is taking a heavy toll on the health of mangers and professionals. For females, the situation is slightly different. In 1979 professional women lost 13 days on average compared to 35 for unskilled manual women (a difference of 22 days). This differences increased to 26 days in 1983 (18 compared to 44 days) and then reduced to 24 days in 1986 (19 compared to 43). However, the most recent figure shows a differential above the 1979 figure.

The percentages *consulting* a doctor have remained fairly stable since 1979, again with a larger percentage of the lower socioeconomic groups reporting visits (Table 3.10).

Table 3.10 NHS GP consultations, percentage who had consulted a doctor in the 14 days before interview, by sex and socioeconomic group, Great Britain

	Males			Females		
Socioeconomic group	*1979*	*1983*	*1986*	*1979*	*1983*	*1986*
Professional	10	9	8	9	12	14
Employers, managers	9	10	11	13	14	14
Other non-manual	11	11	11	14	15	16
Skilled manual	11	12	11	15	16	15
Semi-skilled manual	12	13	13	15	17	18
Unskilled manual	13	13	15	15	18	19
All	11	12	11	14	16	16

Table compiled by Lee Harvey from *General Household Survey*, 1979–86.

The data from the General Household Survey thus shows that illness increased generally in the 1980s and that there has been no reduction in the inequalities in health noted in the *Black Report*, indeed, the most notable changes have been a widening of the class differential for women.

4. Reported illness is only one aspect of health. Macintyre (1986) suggests four different approaches to health. First, the *medical* model in which health is seen as the absence of disease. The problem with this is the difficulty of adequately defining and identifying disease and the failure to take into account positive health or psychiatric health. Second, the *sociological* model in which health is seen as the absence of illness. This depends on the reactions of people and tends to a definition of health *post hoc* (that is, retrospectively, in the sense of recalling whether one was ill or not). The sociological model also tends to see illness in relative terms and is thus of limited use for comparative purposes. Third, the *ideal* model, like the one used by the World Health Organisation, defines health as 'a state of complete physical, mental and social well-being, not merely the absence of disease or infirmity' (Macintyre, 1986, p. 83). This definition is rather too broad and difficult to measure. Fourth, the *pragmatic* model sees health as defined in terms of particular characteristics, such as pain, functional capacity, emotional state and so on, suitable to a given purpose or study.

Theories of inequality in health

The *Black Report* expressly avoided any simple causal analysis but did suggest that work accidents, overcrowding and smoking, all prevalent among the working class, were major causes of illness. The working class tends not to use available preventative health care. Apart from these specific class-related factors, the more general features of the class structure such as poverty, deprivation and work conditions have consequences for health.

The theoretical debate around inequalities in health has been intense. There are a variety of theories; however, the main ones fall into four camps.

Individualist theory

First, the *individualist* theory, which sees people's own actions as the principal cause of health inequalities. The individualist theory essentially blames the victim, arguing that people have to take responsibility for their health and that it is people's own fault if they eat the wrong food, smoke and drink, and adopt reckless practices at work. Edwina Currie, then Junior Minister of Health, adopted this view when in 1986 she stated that the real cause of the poorer health of people living in the North of England was their poor diet. She also subsequently suggested that old people who suffered from a lack of adequate heating should wear woolly hats! The individualist theory thus suggests that the 'lower' social classes have poorer health because, through choice or ignorance, they adopt unhealthy behaviour. They tend to smoke and drink more, take less exercise and thus suffer from more heart problems. Low-income families tend to go for processed meat and fried foods, fewer fresh vegetables and less fibre-rich food. They have larger families, despite fewer resources, with more chance of infection spreading. In this view the higher level of fatal accidents in the lower classes is explained by lower level of parental supervision. It is not income but attitude that is at fault.

Natural selection theory

Second, the *natural selection* approach (Stern, 1981) suggests that people with better health move up the social hierarchy and those with poor health move down. It is a reworking of the notion of the 'survival of the fittest'. This presupposes class mobility and assumes that healthy people are better able to hold on to their wealth than are unhealthy people. The natural selection theory of inequalities in health suggests that it is not social class that affects health but health that affects social class.

> **Student Activity 3.26**
> **What statistical data would you need to test out Stern's theory of natural selection in relation to inequalities in health?**

Structural theory

Third, the *structural* theory sees inequalities in health in terms of the general inequalities within British society. (This is also referred to as the *material deprivation* theory). The structural theory thus accepts that the working classes probably do not 'look after themselves' and do not make the most of preventative opportunities, but this is not an individual decision nor can it be overcome by any individual action. The problem lies in the inequalities in resources (economic, psychological, intellectual) available to the working classes. Working-class people are unhealthy because they have low in-

---

Example answer to Student Activity 3.26

Stern argues that his theory raises a methodological issue. If healthy people are indeed upwardly mobile, then it is necessary to look at inequalities in health in terms of the class of *origin* of people and not their achieved class. Nicky Hart (1985, p. 584) notes:

> to prove or disprove this thesis would require data which trace the progress of individuals throughout the course of their lives. Since most sociological and statistical data lack the biographical dimension, it is impossible to settle the claims of this thesis one way or the other. Its plausibility depends on the extent to which people can insulate their health from material disadvantage during the course of their lifetimes. This leads to a consideration of the importance of material deprivation in shaping health and survival prospects.

Of course it's curable – but you're only working class!

comes, which leads to poor diet; poor housing with consequent dampness and cold; overcrowding with increased risk of infection; hazardous and debilitating work conditions; strenuous and dangerous work; poor education, which affects knowledge about health care and provision, ability to communicate with medical professionals, and consequent non-optimum usage (Cartwright and O'Brien, 1976). All this leads to greater stress and consequently greater use of alcohol and tobacco. Furthermore, areas where working-class people are more numerous tend to be provided with fewest and worst health facilities. Unless there are structural changes, reducing inequality, then inequalities in health will not diminish. Working-class culture does not 'cause' these problems but is a response to the structural inequalities.

Student Activity 3.27
Using *Social Trends* or any other suitable statistics that you have available compare the level of income and death rates for different socioeconomic groups. Do the results support the structural view of inequalities in health? What are the limitations of using death rates, socioeconomic groups and levels of income in assessing the structural view of class inequalities in health? What other indicators of structural inequality might you use?

Cultural theory

Fourth, is the *cultural* theory, which sees the poorer health of the working class as a function of aspects of working-class culture. Cultural theorists argue that individuals are affected by the culture within which they are

---

Example answer to Student Activity 3.27

Statistics from *Occupational Mortality 1970–72* (OPCS, 1978) show that average weekly income tends to be higher for higher socio-economic groups and mortality rates tend to be lower (see Figure 3.7, page 96). This suggests that there are structural inequalities in health.

Socioeconomic group provides us with only a limited notion of social class. It ranks people by occupation and ignores other aspects of social class, such as accumulated wealth, housing, lifestyle and so on.

Similarly, income is only one aspect of material well-being related to occupation. Work conditions, security of employment and job satisfaction are also important aspects of deprivation (see Chapter 4 for a fuller discussion of the concept of deprivation).

Mortality is, as we have seen in the example answer to Student Activity 3.25, only one way of measuring health.

The structural view would suggest that worsening of health and widening of the inequality gap parallels increasing structural inequalities. To assess this view we could consider some other statistics that reflect structural factors.

Unemployment, which hits lower socioeconomic groups hardest, increased from 1.4 million in 1979 to 3.3 million in 1986 (Department of Employment). In the same period the numbers of people on supplementary benefit also increased (Department of Social Security) as did the proportion of households with below half the average income (Depart-

ment of Social Security).

These structural indicators suggested a growing number of poor people and the distribution of wealth has changed, with the top quarter of tax payers receiving 50% of the income in 1989–90 compared to 45% in 1978–9 (Lilley, 1990). Differentials in gross weekly earnings have also increased during the 1980s, as Table 3.11 shows.

Table 3.11 Mean gross weekly earnings of full-time employees

	Males		Females	
	1981	*1986*	*1981*	*1986*
Non manual	£161	£250	£98	£157
Manual	£120	£174	£75	£108
Difference	£41	£76	£23	£49

Compiled by Lee Harvey from *Social Trends*.

These are just a sample of the structural statistics that could be used. They do not prove the structural theory but they certainly give it considerable credibility. They show that structural inequality has increased and this reflects inequalities in health and a continuing or even widening of the differential between socioeconomic groups despite efforts to redress the inequalities pointed to by the *Black Report*.

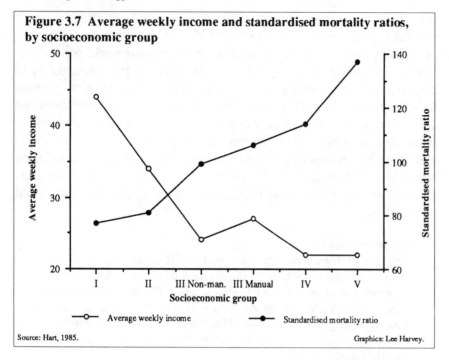

Figure 3.7 Average weekly income and standardised mortality ratios, by socioeconomic group

Source: Hart, 1985.

Graphics: Lee Harvey.

located, and working-class culture is influential in determining what working-class people eat and drink, what leisure pursuits they enjoy, their general distrust of medical professionals, their stoicism about illness, and their machismo that leads to more fatal accidents. At one extreme this view simply provides a rationale for the individualist theory. At the other extreme this view shades over into the structural argument as it sees features of working-class culture as being dependent on structural factors such as poverty, overcrowding, poor education, lack of knowledge about health issues (Brotherston, 1976) and bad working conditions (see Extract 3.2).

Student Activity 3.28
Look up statistics on the extent of smoking, alcohol consumption, deaths from lung cancer and from heart disease since 1960 (*Social Trends* is a useful first source).

1. What trends are there in the incidence of smoking overall and how do these differ for men and women and for different socioeconomic groups? What changes have there been since the data used by Nicky Hart shown in Extract 3.2?
2. What trends are there in the incidence of alcohol consumption overall and how do these differ for men and women and for different socioeconomic groups?
3. What trends are there in deaths caused by lung cancer overall and how do these differ for men and women and for different socioeconomic groups?
4. What trends are there in deaths caused by heart disease overall and how do these differ for men and women and for different socioeconomic groups?
5. Does the data support the cultural theory of inequalities in health?
6. What are the limitations of using this data in assessing the cultural theory?

This section on inequalities in health has illustrated how rearrangement and comparison of available statistical data allows you to begin to investigate competing sociological theories. It also further illustrates the problem of

Extract 3.2

SMOKING

In 1960, there was little difference between the social classes in the consumption of cigarettes. Since then, consumption in the middle class has fallen off substantially, leaving a class gradient in tobacco consumption which closely reflects the gradient for lung cancer mortality (see Figure 3.8).

The general correspondence between these gradients implies that higher death rates are largely due to heavy smoking. This leads to the question of why the people most at risk of premature death have failed to take heed of the message that 'smoking is bad for your health'. Could it be ignorance? Is it possible that manual workers have not understood the warning on each deadly packet? Since this is hardly likely to be the reason, we must look elsewhere for an explanation of this apparently dangerous class-related behaviour.

Remember that the behaviour in question is not a series of random individual acts. It is a group phenomenon, a cultural norm rather than a personal habit. In the past, smoking was a socially valued behaviour that was encouraged and associated with independence and adulthood. Giving up therefore involves more than giving up an addictive habit. Why should giving up be more culturally difficult in the working class than in the middle class?

One reason might be that manual workers make the transition from school to work earlier and smoking is a clear symbol of the status change. The middle classes have a less uniform and less abrupt transition to work, often involving further education and training, and the symbolic value of smoking is less.

What of the physical needs that smoking satisfies? Here we must ask whether the seeming reluctance of manual workers to take the health warning seriously is because of the narcotic value as a means of reducing the sheer physical stress of manual work. If so, the problem is one of material and not cultural deprivation. On the other hand, if smoking is not a pacifying drug but is really just a pleasurable activity, then giving up may simply denote the availability of a wider range of other sources of enjoyment.

Another possibility is that middle-class men and women have responded more rapidly to the idea that smoking is bad for the health because their socialisation leaves them better equipped to adapt to the shifting character of modern culture. Group solidarity is less important in their lives because they experience more social and geographical mobility. For them, individualism is not merely an ideological banner, they have direct experience of it in their personal lives in the absence of any lasting attachment to particular groups or communities. Consequently the redefinition of a cultural norm, in terms of everyday behaviour, may gather momentum more rapidly in the middle class because it depends more on individual initiative. Furthermore, behavioural innovation, in this more privatised world, is less subject to negative group sanctions.

Adapted from Hart (1985) pp. 591–3.

defining and measuring sociological concepts, and the limitations and political pressures on published statistics.

Student Activity 3.29
We identified four theories of inequality in health. Which of these would you say were (a) positivist; (b) phenomenological; and (c) critical?

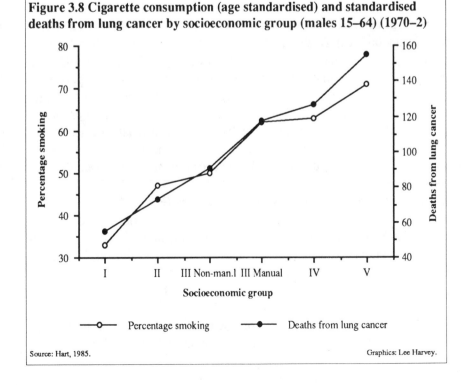

Figure 3.8 Cigarette consumption (age standardised) and standardised deaths from lung cancer by socioeconomic group (males 15–64) (1970–2)

Source: Hart, 1985.

Graphics: Lee Harvey.

Summary and conclusion

In this chapter we have looked at the different ways sociologists can make use of existing statistical information for their research. It has been stressed that secondary data should be approached cautiously. Like all data, they rely upon the assumptions, conceptions and priorities of those who collect them and should not, therefore, be treated as neutral or 'objective' facts. However, this does not render secondary statistics unsuitable for further examination and analysis, indeed they can constitute a useful, highly accessible and comprehensive resource if approached critically.

Clearly, the theoretical position adopted by the user will shape the interpretation of any statistical data, which are themselves subject to a multitude of influences during their production. Are secondary statistics then of any value for sociological enquiry? This leads us to the more fundamental questions about the possibility of measuring social phenomena at all, that is, to questions of epistemology.

We have seen how positivist, phenomenological and critical perspectives approach statistical data in different ways. The positivist and phenomenological standpoints are illustrated in the debate surrounding Durkheim's *Suicide* while the critical approach is suggested in the structural analysis of inequalities in health.

When examining the health issue we also undertook secondary data analysis, reanalysing and comparing existing statistical data. While there is substantial tradition within social science of survey work, most social scientists think of collecting new data rather than re-analysing existing data sets. Researchers like to collect data in a way that explores their particular concerns and tend to think that data already collected will be inadequate, for three reasons. First, it was collected with another aim in mind and therefore does not fit the research *hypotheses* closely enough. Second, the researcher lacks *control* over the collection process and so does not really know how 'good' the data is. Third, the data is '*old*' data; it has already been used and is 'out of date'.

However, secondary analysis can be a useful addition to new research in initial stages of development, such as using demographic statistics to define sample quotas. It may also complement data collected in other ways by providing a comparison or a national framework (see Townsend, 1979). In addition, secondary analysis offers economies of time, money and personnel as well as limiting the 'reporting burden placed on the public'. Furthermore, some research can only be done through secondary research. Those using census data are an obvious example. The sociology of labour, health and poverty rely heavily on secondary data. Demographic research is necessarily based on secondary data derived from censuses, surveys and administrative records.

Although secondary analysis has a long history (Booth, 1889; Durkheim, 1897) the establishment of data archives and the development and accessibility of information technology has provided the impetus for the development of secondary data analysis. This has also been helped by the increasing use of social surveys, rather than administrative records, by the Government Statistical Service and the availability of these via the ESRCDA. Secondary statistical analysis is now used within all the social scientific disciplines: sociology, politics, economics, history, demography, education, geography, planning, social psychology, social medicine and labour force studies.

Further Reading

Using official statistics: Slattery, 1986 provides an easy introduction; Irvine *et al.*, 1979 is a useful reference for a critique of official statistics. Kitsuse and Cicourel, 1963, provides a phenomenological critique. Fothergill and Vincent, 1985, shows how official statistics can be used in a critical way.

Secondary data analysis: Key reading for British sources are Dale *et al.*, 1988 and Hakim, 1982. Stewart, 1984 is useful for an American perspective.

Topics

Crime: Campbell, 1981; Hough and Mayhew, 1983, 1985; Kinsey *et al.*, 1986; Lea and Young, 1984; LRCC, 1984; Moore, 1988; Scraton *et al.*, 1991.

Unemployment: Brown, 1984; Coyle, 1984; Gordon, 1988; MacInnes, 1987; Payne, 1987; Phizacklea, 1983; Taylor, 1990; Unemployment Unit, 1989.

Health: Cartwright and O'Brien, 1976; Hart, 1985; Le Grand, 1987; Marmot *et al.*, 1984; Radical Statistics Health Group, 1980, 1987; Rathwell and Phillips, 1986; Townsend and Davidson, 1982; Whitehead; 1987; Wilkinson, 1991.

Suicide: Atkinson, 1968, 1978; Douglas, 1967; Durkheim, 1952; Moore, 1988; Taylor, 1989.

General: Denscombe, 1991; *Social Trends*.

Useful addresses:

Information Services Division,
Room 58/G,
Cabinet Office,
Great George Street,
London
SW1P 3AL
(Tel. 071-270 6363/6364).

Business Statistics Office,
Cardiff Road,
Newport
Gwent
NP9 1XG
(Tel. 0633 812973).

ESRC Data Archive,
University of Essex,
Wivenhoe Park,
Colchester,
Essex
CO4 3SQ.

Unemployment Unit and Youthaid,
9 Poland Street,
London
W1V 3DG
(Tel. 071-439 8523).

Indeed the same data set is often analysed from different perspectives by more than one discipline. This contributes to a multidisciplinary understanding of social issues. In the end, however, despite the availability of the data and the technology to analyse it, secondary data analysis only occurs if the data is worth reanalysing.

Project ideas

There are available statistical data on most areas of interest to sociologists and they can be used as a basis for project work. The following suggestions for topics are just an indication of the large range of possibilities for student projects. It is important that you do not try to find all the available statistics as this could be a monumental task. On the other hand, you may well want to look at sources other than *Social Trends*. A useful, cheap, first source is *Sociology Update* (Denscombe, 1991). It is important that you analyse what statistics you do find and link the data to theory. It is not satisfactory simply to provide lots of statistics and hope that they 'speak for themselves'. Your analysis and interpretation is vital and you need to show it in your project.

1. An analysis of alcohol consumption by age in view of the moral panic surrounding 'lager louts'.
2. An explanation of changes in occupation and class structure since 1975 and the implications for sociological models of class.
3. An examination of the 'take-up' of state benefits; for example, the social fund.
4. A critical analysis of football attendance figures over the last 20 years and an explanation of the changes.
5. A study of the extent to which theories of the inequalities in health are able to account for regional differences in health.
6. Compare and account for the variation in incidence of strikes in different European countries.
7. Assess the influence of race, class and gender on voting behaviour.
8. Examine the rate of change of population growth over the last 10 years world-wide and relate them to arguments for population control.
9. Consider the case for increasing Britain's major road network using figures provided by environmental groups (such as Friends of the Earth) and the transport lobby (for example, British Road Transport Federation).
10. An examination of suicide patterns to determine the relevance of Durkheim's theory.

CHAPTER 4
SOCIAL SURVEYS

Introduction

Surveys of one sort or another are not only an important aspect of sociological enquiry, they are part of everyday life. 'Eight out of ten cat owners prefer Whiskas'; 'Labour has a 4% lead'; 'More women than men now smoke cigarettes'. These are all examples of surveying of one kind or another. They all involve asking people questions and summarising the answers in quantitative terms. Market researchers spend enormous amounts of time and money finding out who buys what products. Opinion pollsters try to keep track of which political party is most popular and which issues cause most concern to electors. Social policy surveys focus on the extent and nature of social problems and so on. In Chapter 2 we saw that surveys are used to find out who reads which newspapers and what people thought of different television programmes.

Extract 4.1 is an example of an opinion survey. It provides descriptive data on attitudes towards the proposed changes in the European Community. The answers are given for the sample as a whole and are broken down to show variations in views for males and females and for people in different socioeconomic groups.

Student Activity 4.1
1. How many people were there in the sample used in Extract 4.1?
2. What percentage of the sample disapproved of the pound being used as a new European currency?
3. Which socioeconomic group most disapproved of the pound being used as a new European currency?
4. What percentage of women thought that a European federation to deal with foreign policy would be a good idea?
5. How many people in the sample thought that a European federation to deal with defence and social policy was a good idea?

In general, social surveys involve selecting a group of people and asking them a set of questions that you have designed in advance. You collect the information either by using interviewers or by asking the respondents to write down their answers on a form provided.

Student Activity 4.2
To get the feel of doing a social survey, carry out a small-scale survey of classmates or another suitable group to find out one of the following:
1. Which television programmes are most popular with the group? How much time on average do they spend watching television per week? Are there differences between the viewing habits of males and females, different classes or ethnic groups?
2. What newspapers does your group read or buy? Is there a difference by class, ethnicity or sex?
3. Does the college/school canteen provide meals that meet the needs of all ethnic groups? Are the results the same for each sex and class?

Extract 4.1

WE'LL TAKE THE SLOW ROAD

British voters are predominantly unwilling to accept a single European currency if that means losing the pound. A majority favour a limited degree of co-operation across the community rather than a single community with common laws and institutions. More oppose than support a system of majority decision-making on economic policy. But there is more support than rejection for common decisions on issues of foreign policy and defence.

ICM interviewed a tightly controlled sample of 1,376 adults over 18 in 103 randomly selected constituencies nationwide on 7–8 December 1990.

Would you approve or disapprove of the pound being used as a new Europe-wide currency?

Percentage	All	Men	Women	AB	C1	C2	DE
Approve	29	34	24	38	33	26	23
Disapprove	49	47	51	45	43	52	54
Neither	10	11	10	11	11	9	11
Don't know	11	8	15	6	12	13	13

If a federation of the 12 countries of the European Community is created then major decisions would no longer be taken by each individual government but by a majority agreement between the 12 countries. In your opinion would this be a good idea with regard to:

Percentage	All	Men	Women	AB	C1	C2	DE
Economic policy							
Good idea	35	42	28	41	36	34	32
Bad idea	40	42	38	46	39	40	38
Don't know	25	16	33	13	26	26	30
Foreign policy							
Good idea	41	46	36	53	41	40	34
Bad idea	34	38	30	33	34	32	36
Don't know	26	17	34	14	26	28	29
Defence and security							
Good idea	43	47	38	57	41	44	35
Bad idea	33	37	29	27	33	34	35
Don't know	24	16	32	16	26	22	30

Adapted from *Guardian* 14/12/90.

Example answer to Student Activity 4.1e

43% of the total sample thought a European federation to deal with defence and security policy was a good idea. That is 43% of the sample of 1,376. To work out how many people that is, multiply the sample size by the percentage and divide by 100.

Thus:

number of people = (1376 x 43) / 100
                  = 59168 / 100
                  = 591.68
                  = 592

to the nearest whole number.

So 592 of the sample of 1,376 thought that it would be a good idea to have a European federation to deal with defence and security policy.

You will have found from this that doing a survey is not as simple as it seems. Apart from problems of designing and asking questions that cover all the possible options in something as apparently straightforward as television viewing, newspaper readership or canteen provision there are also particular problems in defining what you mean by social class and ethnicity.

These kinds of surveys are useful for asking questions such as: How many people watched *Coronation Street* last Wednesday? Which is the most widely read daily newspaper? Is there a demand for a bigger variety of vegetarian food in college canteens? What percentage of the electorate would vote Labour if there was a general election tomorrow? How many people go to work by car? Has there been an increase in crime? This is known as *descriptive* data.

Sociological surveys

Although this descriptive data is informative, sociologists usually want to take things further. Instead of just collecting 'facts' about the social world, many sociologists want to provide *explanations* for social phenomena. For example, sociologists might ask:

Why are women more likely to watch soap operas than men?
What effect will certain policies have on voting intentions?
Why do people choose to drive to work rather than use public transport?
Why has there been an increase in violent crime?

Such attempts at explanation usually involve investigating the relationship *between* social phenomena. This requires that we *measure* social phenomena in some way so that we can show relationships. For example, to answer the first of the questions above, we could measure the amount of time men and women spend watching soap operas. This would be one way of finding out if there is any difference in soap opera viewing but it wouldn't tell us *why* there is a difference. We would need to look at other things that might give us some clues, such as the time soap operas are broadcast, the sorts of things that happen in soap operas, the number of males and females in central roles, what kind of audience soap operas are aimed at, why viewers are attracted to soaps, and so on (see Chapter 2). In short, to get an idea of why more women than men watch soap operas we would need to collect information on several related *factors*.

Quantitative approach

This approach, which involves measuring social phenomena and drawing some conclusions about relationships between them, is often called the 'quantitative approach'. However, this does not mean that you need to be a mathematical or statistical expert to use the approach, as the examples in this chapter will show.

Quantitative sociologists usually prefer to use surveys to collect data. They argue that if you are going to analyse relationships then you need a large amount of data. If you are going to generalise the results, then the data has to be *representative* of the population. If you are measuring social phenomena then you need a measuring instrument that is *reliable* and *valid* (see pages 31–2). The only method that can do this, quantitative sociologists argue, is the survey.

Figure 4.1 Stages of quantitative research

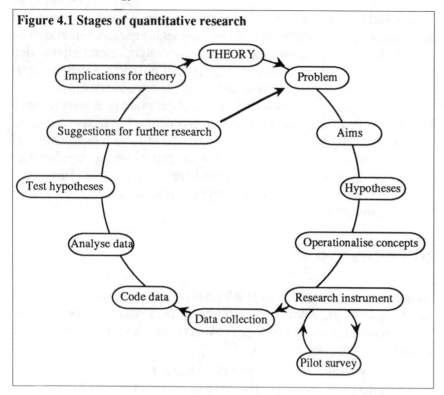

Stages of quantitative research

Sociological research using the survey method involves several stages. These are summarised in Figure 4.1. This is an idealised view of the quantitative approach that is often difficult to keep to in practice. However, it does provide a model to guide you through quantitative research. We will now take you through the model and explain how to carry out each stage. You should realise that in your project you will not always have time to deal with each stage in as much detail as we do in what follows. It is important, though, that you understand what is involved and try to do as much as you can.

The model shows that undertaking a sociological survey is not just about asking a few questions. It is part of an integrated approach to sociological enquiry that begins and ends with sociological theory. You design questions to collect data about the theoretical issues that interest you.

This is important and you should avoid doing surveys the other way round. Inexperienced social surveyors often start with a few 'interesting' questions and then struggle to fit the data they get to a meaningful sociological theory. In other words, don't start with the social survey, start with the substantive *problem*. The survey is just the means by which you collect the data, it is part of a larger *methodology*. At the core of this methodology is the idea that it is possible to answer questions about *why* social phenomena occur. You do this by defining and measuring social phenomena and showing relationships between them.

Aims

So, before undertaking a sociological survey, you need to have a clear idea of what you are trying to explain. You may well have a general area of interest in mind for your project, such as poverty, women and work, ethnic differences

**Example answer to Student
Activity 4.3**

To illustrate how to undertake a survey we will use an adapted version of a student project as an example (Todd *et al.*, 1990).

The aim of the survey was to see why gays and lesbians were subject to hostile public attitudes. In particular, to see if:

(a) there was any link between dislike and distrust of gays and media labelling of AIDS as the 'gay plague'; and

(b) if government treatment and condemnation of gays had an impact on attitudes.

NOTE At this stage you may find that the kind of research question you are asking is not suitable for a social survey. In which case you should consider another method. For example, you might have asked: What are the everyday strategies that women, working in a mixed-sex office environment, adopt in order to deal with sexual harassment? While you could still construct a questionnaire in order to get some information on this you would find it difficult to know what things to ask and would only be likely to get some superficial information. You would be better observing what goes on in offices (see Chapter 6) or talking in depth to women office workers about their experiences (see Chapter 7).

---

in educational achievement, attitudes to gays and lesbians, and so on. The first task is to narrow down your proposed research area and formulate your research topic in a way that asks a 'why' question. This research question will be the *aim* of the research.

You should try to make your aim as specific as possible. For example, why do women put up with sexual harassment at work? Why do Asian children do better at A-level than children from other ethnic groups?

Student Activity 4.3
Draw up a research aim for a sociological survey of any area of enquiry that interests you.
NOTE If you do not have a particular area in mind think of a research aim that deals with attitudes to gays and lesbians as this is the topic we will use in the example answers.

Your first attempt at an aim will probably be less specific than the one given in example answer 4.3. Do not be surprised by this. Initial aims are often based on common sense and you will probably have only a slight familiarity with sociological literature in the area. You should, however, attempt to define the aim of the research more precisely. This will take time and effort. The research aim is part of the general planning stage that, as we suggested in Chapter 1, will take up about a third of your research time.

Background

What you decide upon as your research aim will relate closely to the work you do on the 'background' to your project. Working on the background is important because as your background knowledge develops then your aim is likely to become more specific and thus more manageable. It also provides you with a context within which to locate and report your research.

Background knowledge comes from a review of the sociological literature (see Chapter 1), an examination of the relevant theoretical and political issues, and from talking to people. Indeed, getting advice from a wide range of people about what to focus on in your research is a useful strategy. For example, in their study of poverty, Peter Townsend *et al.* (1987) took advice from and involved a range of interested organisations, such as the Disability Resources Group and various ethnic minorities groups. The combined knowledge and experience of these groups ultimately went into the design of the question schedule. The study was thus enriched by involving these community organisations in the design team.

Student Activity 4.4
Outline the 'background' to the research aim you produced in student activity 4.3.
NOTE Initially your 'background' may be very hazy but over time you should fill it out and provide a sound context for your research.

Feasibility

Once you have decided on your broad aim you have to further focus your project into something that is manageable, given your time and resources. Researchers, especially those new to research, are often overambitious and try to cover everything that they find interesting. It is much better to complete a small-scale, specific study than to abandon a large-scale, unfocused study.

Example answer to Student Activity 4.4

Homosexuality in Britain has been subject to various laws. In 1533 an Act of Parliament was passed making homosexuality illegal and anyone proven guilty liable to be executed. The last execution was in 1836 and in 1861 the Offences Against the Person Act changed the maximum penalty to life imprisonment. In 1885 legal sanction was extended against homosexuals when the Criminal Law Amendment Act also made 'gross indecency' punishable by two years imprisonment with hard labour. One of the first people convicted for gross indecency was Oscar Wilde, who spent two years in Reading Gaol. An attempt was made in 1921 to extend gross indecency to women but, although passed in the Commons, it was thrown out by the Lords.

Parliamentary opinion changed decisively following the 1966 election. The Sexual Offences Act was passed in 1967, which decriminalised homosexual activities in private by no more than two consenting adults over the age of 21 (Cook, 1990a). By 1990 homosexuality had become legal in all of Europe with the exception of Guernsey.

However, despite being legal, homosexuality has continued to be a taboo issue. Homosexuality has been the of subject derogatory attacks and is the butt of crass humour. More seriously, the 1980s has seen an 'official' backlash against gay and lesbian rights. During the 1980s the Conservative Government attacked left-wing councils who spent 'ratepayers money' on things which appeared to promote gay and lesbian activity. Projects such as Haringey Council's initiative on positive images of homosexuality was widely attacked inside and outside Parliament. For example,

> My Lords I beg leave to ask...Her Majesty's Government whether they approve of Haringey Borough Council's plans for compulsory lessons intended to promote 'positive images' of homosexuality in nursery, primary and secondary schools in the borough? (House of Lords, 28 July 1986, cited in Jones and Mahony, 1989)

This official attack shifted emphasis away from the more radical aspects of local authority policy. Promoting homosexuality was also counter to the Conservative Government's attempt to promote family values. The culmination of the attack on homosexuality came in the Local Government Act of 1988 in which a Clause (number 28) was included which prohibited local authorities from actively promoting homosexuality. Clause 28 has thus been at the centre of recent controversies surrounding personal rights and freedom.

The media played a leading role in condemning any extension of tolerance towards homosexuality. An article in *Today* (2 September 1986) is illustrative.

> There was a time in the dawn of the permissive society when enlightened liberals campaigned for an end to the laws which made homosexuality illegal – on the ground that they were a vicious discrimination against a minority. But by a law of human nature, once this reasonable concession was granted, some homosexuals could not stop there. Next they wanted homosexuality to be regarded as socially quite acceptable. Then they wanted actually to crusade for it, by having it taught in schools and written about in books for children as something quite admirable.

The issues surrounding Clause 28 have also been compounded by concerns about AIDS (Acquired Immune Deficiency Syndrome). AIDS is not a single disease, it is a 'syndrome', that is, a group of specific infections and cancers that occur because the body's immune system, which fights off disease, is not working properly. The immune deficiency arises as a result of infection by a Human Immunodeficiency Virus (HIV) (Terrence Higgins Trust, 1990). There has been considerable media portrayal of AIDS as a condition closely associated with homosexuals since it was first reported in the USA. Between June and November of 1981 there were 159 reports of AIDS, 75% were in three major American cities and 95% were gay men. The first report of AIDS in Britain was in London in December 1981. Although AIDS did exist before 1981 it was exceedingly rare before the mid-1970s anywhere in the world, although recent research suggests it dates back to the 1950s. Most people, worldwide, with AIDS are heterosexual men and women but this has not diminished the view that AIDS is a 'gay plague'. The statistics for the United Kingdom reinforced this view (see below).

Table 4.1 Cumulative totals of UK reports of AIDS to 31st March 1990

	Males	Females	Total	Deaths
Homo/Bisexual	2530	0	2530	1421
Intravenous drugabuser (IVDA)	78	21	99	44
Homo/Bi & IVDA	43	0	43	21
Haemophiliac	186	2	188	123
Recipient of blood	25	23	48	17
Heterosexual contact *	8	16	24	14
Others:				
exposure abroad	89	42	131	63
no exposure abroad	10	7	17	7
child of infected parent	10	14	24	14
undetermined	47	6	53	30
Totals	3026	131	3157	1773

*With partners with above risk factors
Source: Terrence Higgins Trust, 1990, p. 5 (adapted by Lee Harvey).

In Britain, the majority of new cases of AIDS are now among heterosexuals. None the less, some elements of the mass media have used the link between AIDS and homosexuality as an excuse for further stigmatising gays and lesbians. The backlash against the gay community has reached its most extreme forms among those who see AIDS as the retribution of God against those who practice 'sexual perversion'. The popular press represent this view. The *Daily Star* editor, for example, described AIDS as 'a gift from God – a stick to beat gays with' (Blackie & Taylor, 1987).

An opinion poll of MPs conducted for the television programme *Out on Tuesday* (6 March 1990) showed that 43.6% of a sample of 245 MPs favoured reducing the age of consent for male homosexual acts. Only 6% of MPs in the sample thought that homosexuality for men should be made illegal and this dropped to 5% for women. Reflecting the Conservative Government policy against homosexuality, 90.8% of Conservative MPs were against repealing Section 28 of the Local Government Act 1988 whereas only 11.5% of Labour MPs were against repeal (Cook, 1990b).

**Example answer to Student
Activity 4.5**

The example study focused on the attitudes of *further* education students aged between 16 and 20. There are three reasons for this. First, the researchers wanted a population of young people who had 'grown up' in an era of overt hostility to gays and lesbians. Second, they wanted a population of young people who were exposed to influences outside their immediate social circle and their workplace. Third, they did not want *higher* education students because there is a more established anti-racist, anti-sexist and anti-homophobic culture in higher educational institutions. In short, further education students would be articulate without being overly informed about gay and lesbian issues.

The kinds of things the researchers wanted to find out were:

1. how hostile the students were to gays and lesbians;
2. to what extent they supported government policies that affected gays and lesbians;
3. how influenced they were by the media portrayal of gays and lesbians;
4. what other factors might have a bearing on peoples' attitudes, in particular personal acquaintance with gays and/ or lesbians.

Student activity 4.5
Outline a feasible research project based on your aim (Student Activity 4.3). Indicate who you intend to ask, and state why. Outline what kinds of things you are trying to find out.

Although you are gradually narrowing the research down into something you could manage, it is still likely to be too vague. The next two stages, constructing research *hypotheses* and *operationalising concepts*, closely define the kinds of relationships that are being investigated and the way in which concepts are to be measured. They are the crucial stages in defining the exact nature of the research because it is through them that the research aim gets put into practice. The *validity* of the survey depends on these stages.

Hypotheses

A hypothesis is a specific statement about the research area that can be tested using *empirical* data (see page 2). When constructing hypotheses, you will probably find it easier to have a general hypothesis that sums up the aim of the research plus a few sub-hypotheses. Through the background research, you will usually have an 'informed notion' about the relationships you expect to find. This informed notion guides the construction of hypotheses.

The *general hypothesis* is normally more specific than the research aim and outlines precisely the nature of the main relationship you are investigating. The sub-hypotheses break down the general hypothesis into more manageable chunks. Hypotheses are normally expressed in terms that ask *the extent to which one factor is dependent upon one or more independent factors*. An example of a general hypothesis about soap-opera viewing might be as follows:

> The amount of time people spend watching soap operas depends on the time soap operas are broadcast and the extent to which viewers identify with the characters.

The dependent factor in this hypothesis is 'the amount of time people spend watching soap operas'. There are two independent factors, first, 'the time soap operas are broadcast' and, second, 'identification with characters'.

Student Activity 4.6
Write down a general hypothesis that takes account of the research aim in Student Activity 4.3. Suggest some sub-hypotheses that break down this general hypothesis.
NOTE Hypotheses are normally expressed in terms of operationalised concepts (see below) and so you may want to return to this activity after you have attempted Student Activity 4.8.

Operationalisation

Operationalisation is the process of transforming a theoretical *concept* into something that you can define and *measure* in practice. Your survey is a measuring instrument so it is necessary to define clearly what it is that you are measuring. Operationalising concepts involves the following:

1. *define* the theoretical concept;
2. think of the different aspects of the concept and break it down into the *dimensions* that cover the meaning of the concept;
3. think of several possible *indicators* for each dimension;

4. *select* one or more indicators for each dimension; and
5. design *questions* to collect information for each indicator. These are the *variables* in your study.

We will illustrate what is involved using poverty as an example.

Poverty

Poverty has been a major concern of social scientists, and research into poverty dates back more than a century to the early days of sociology. We have a notion that poverty means that some people are disadvantaged compared to others and that poor people do not have enough to maintain a decent standard of living. However, this 'theoretical' notion is rather vague. What do we mean by a 'decent standard of living'? What don't poor people have enough of? In short what precisely do we mean by poverty?

To do research on poverty the notion we have in our head must be *defined* more clearly. The first problem, then, is to find some agreement about what is meant by poverty in *theory* before trying to measure it in *practice*.

Defining poverty

The meaning of the notion of poverty is constantly under debate. Different definitions of poverty reflect different ideologies. Townsend (1979) in his major study of poverty in Britain discusses at length the concepts of poverty and deprivation. He concludes that different definitions of poverty are used for different purposes and that the most commonly discussed difference is that of *absolute* and *relative* poverty.

Absolute poverty
Early research into poverty, for example the work done by Booth (1889–97) and Rowntree (1901), used an *absolute* definition of poverty based on subsistence, that is, the things people need in order to keep alive. This definition is problematic because it defines human needs in terms of food, shelter and clothing, and no account is taken of social needs, that is, the funds required to go out and mix with others. Similarly, an absolute measure does not account for different dietary needs of people working in different occupations and so on.

Relative poverty
Social scientists have discussed means of overcoming the inflexibility of the absolute measure of poverty and the changing expectations of minimum standards. As a result, the concept of *relative* poverty was devised. It defines people as being 'in poverty' if they are unable to meet the standard of living of their particular society. People in Britain would thus be in poverty if they were unable to heat their home adequately in winter, or were unable to afford items such as a washing machine, refrigerator or television that are taken for granted by most of the population. Thus the relative concept of poverty differs from the absolute because the standards used to measure poverty are not taken from a calculation of minimum needs but from comparisons with the acceptable levels of affluence of a particular society.

Example answer to Student Activity 4.6

General hypothesis

The extent to which the population is hostile to gays and lesbians and supportive of government actions will depend on their age, sex and the extent to which they rely on media images of homosexuality.

Sub-hypotheses

1. The population are hostile towards gays and lesbians. Specifically they:
a. think homosexuality should be illegal;
b. think the age limit for consenting adults should be raised;
c. do not support the idea of gay or lesbian families;
d. think that affectionate acts between gays and between lesbians should be confined to their own home.

2. The population supports recent government action. Specifically they:
a. support Clause 28;
b. do not think that homosexuality should be part of school sex education;
c. are not prepared to discuss homosexuality with children.

3. The age and the sex of the respondent will affect attitudes towards homosexuality.

4. Those who have friends or family who are gay or lesbian will have more positive views of homosexuality than those who have not.

5. Those who heard about homosexuality through the media are more supportive of the idea of a 'gay plague' than those who did not.

ABSOLUTE POVERTY is based on the idea that there is a subsistence level of income necessary to sustain life. It is usually measured by calculating the price of the absolute necessities of life. Anyone whose income is insufficient to provide the necessities of life is said to be in poverty. The necessities are assumed to include nutrition, shelter and health. Nutrition, for example, is measured by working out diet sheets that cover minimum protein and calorie intake (Drewnowski and Scott, 1966; Townsend *et al.*, 1987).

Measuring poverty

Using the relative concept of poverty it then becomes important to decide how to measure it. One way to do this is to measure the level of assistance benefits provided by the state (Abel-Smith and Townsend, 1965). This shows that, in comparison to nationally fixed standards, many people still live in poverty despite increasing levels of affluence in society.

Mack and Lansley (1985) revealed that 7.5 million people were living in relative poverty. Their study involved asking respondents what they consider necessary items of expenditure to maintain a minimum standard of life. The authors defined respondents who could not afford these necessary items as living in poverty.

The notion of a *poverty line* is often used as a base measure of poverty. Some poverty line measures are based on absolute measures of poverty, such as the poverty index used officially by the United States government (US DHEW, 1976). It is based on the minimum cost of an adequate diet multiplied by three as it is estimated that a typical poor family spends about one third of its income on food. In Britain, there is no official poverty line, but various measures have been adopted as indicators of the extent of poverty. The term was first used by Rowntree (1901) in an absolute sense and was based on the cost of bare essentials. More recently (since 1987) the government has defined the poverty line in terms of supplementary benefit or income support. Groups such as the Child Poverty Action Group prefer to see the poverty line in terms of average income. Anyone living on or below 50% of average income is regarded as in poverty (Pilkington, 1991). Using income support and average income provide approximations to a relative measure of poverty. The use of a 'poverty line' is clearly open to political manipulation, as the government will tend to want to make it as low as possible because the number of people defined as impoverished is an indicator of the effectiveness and fairness of government policy to alleviate economic hardship.

Deprivation

Townsend (1974, 1979) used the concept of relative *deprivation* to define poverty. He felt that it was not enough just to use monetary wealth because this excluded such additional things as perks at work, (for example, company cars, cheap holidays), ownership of capital assets such as houses that not only increase wealth but also give power to control one's own life. Further, not all social groups have equal access to services and benefits due to racist divisions in Britain that result in black people being relatively further deprived of state support. This makes full participation in British society more difficult. People are relatively deprived if they are unable to obtain the diets, amenities, standards and services that allow them to play the roles, and follow customary behaviour, that are expected of them by their membership of society (Townsend *et al.*, 1987).

Thus it is not enough simply to see poverty as one of simple needs or even the relative levels of cash income but as also to do with the structure and distribution of society's resources and of the power to control and use these, that is, it is also to do with inequality and power in British society.

RELATIVE POVERTY defines poverty in terms of the standards of living in a particular society at a given time. It does not start from an absolute minimum subsistence level. What constitutes poverty in relative terms changes over time. Lack of a refrigerator might be seen as an indicator of impoverishment in Western societies in the 1990s but would certainly not have been in the 1940s. So relative poverty is measured in terms of the level of affluence of the society at a given point in time.

DEPRIVATION is an alternative perception of poverty. It sees impoverishment in terms of life-styles. People are not poor just because they do not have a certain level of material wealth but because they are deprived of a particular way of life due to their poverty.

For example, although nutritionally worthless, tea drinking in Britain is part of a way of life and if someone is unable to afford to offer a visitor a cup of tea then that person is deprived (Townsend, 1979). Deprivation thus includes lack of access to normal social activities as well as insufficient income or capital assets.

Operationalising deprivation

Townsend *et al.* (1987) developed this idea of deprivation and used the term rather than poverty in their study of *Poverty and Labour in London*. They argued that deprivation has several *dimensions*, and thus used the concept of *multiple deprivation* as the basis for measuring poverty. They identified 13 dimensions, which they grouped into two broad areas, *material* and *social* deprivation (see Table 4.2).

For each of the dimensions they drew up a list of *indicators*. For example, they suggested five indicators of dietary deprivation:

Dietary deprivation
1. At least one day in the last fortnight with insufficient to eat.
2. No fresh meat or fish most days of the week (alternative formulation for vegetarians).
3. No special meat or roast most weeks.
4. No fresh fruit most days.
5. Short of food on at least one occasion in last 12 months to meet needs of family.

He then designed *questions* for each indicator, for example:

Do you eat a piece of fresh fruit every day as part of your normal diet?

The same process was done with all indicators for all the 13 dimensions. In all, Townsend constructed 94 questions or *variables* for deprivation covering the different dimensions.

Student Activity 4.7
Townsend *et al.* (1987) suggest the following indicators for 'Deprivation of Family Activity'. Write 6 questions that cover these indicators.
1 Difficulties indoors for child to play.
2. Child has not had holiday away from home in the last 12 months.
3. Child has not had outing during the last 12 months.
4. Child has no days staying with other family or friends in previous 12 months.
5. Problem of the health of someone in family.
6. Respondent has care of disabled or elderly relative.

Variables

Operationalising a concept is the process of turning a theoretical notion into a variable. It is the process through which *abstract concepts* such as poverty are *defined in theory*, their different *dimensions* are specified, *indicators* are drawn up for each dimension, and through designing questions, these are converted into *variables*. So operationalising concepts is a crucial part of a sociological survey and has a profound effect on the results. Different definitions of poverty, for example, will result in different variables. This will have far-reaching effects on the findings of any survey to do with poverty.

If we are trying to measure poverty, then our definition of poverty will actually produce the amount of it that we find. If we decide that poor people are those whose income falls below a certain specified level, then we will have to count all those who are in that category. But if we lower our 'poverty line', we will at the same time reduce the number of poor people, and if we raise it, we will increase the number. (McNeil, 1990, p. 25)

In short, the *validity* of the survey depends upon the operationalisation. If the *operationalised* concepts do not reflect the *theoretical* concepts then, no

Table 4.2 Townsend's (1987) dimensions of deprivation.

Material deprivation	Social deprivation
Dietary	Rights to employment
Clothing	Family activities
Housing	Integration into community
Home facilities	Work (paid and unpaid)
Environment	Recreation
Location	Education
	Formal participation in social institutions

NOTE In their study Townsend *et al.* (1987) were also concerned not to use indicators which would be discriminatory. This can happen, for example, if more of the selected items in the measure of deprivation apply to men than to women, or cover the situation of whites better than blacks.

Supplementary research activity 4.1

1. Choose two of the following dimensions of deprivation that Townsend *et al.* also used and design suitable questions for them:
clothing;
housing;
home facilities;
environment;
location;
work (paid and unpaid);
rights to employment;
integration into community;
formal participation in social institutions;
recreation;
education.

2. When you have finished get Townsend *et al.* (1987) *Poverty and Labour in London* from the library and compare your indicators with Townsend's (Appendix 1). Do you think any of yours would have been better indicators than Townsend's?

Example answer to Student Activity 4.8

The operationalisation of one of the concepts in the example study is shown below. The complete questionnaire can be found in Extract 4.3 on page 115. The coding frame with the variable numbers is in Extract 4.7 on page 128.

Operationalising 'hostility towards gays'

Concept:	Hostility towards gays.
Definition:	Expression of dislike of male homosexuality and the desire to curb activities of gay men.
Dimensions:	a. Legal restrictions. b. Family life. c. Public display.
Indicators:	a. Illegalisation of homosexuality. b. Raising age limit for consenting adults. c. Opposition to gay families. d. Affectionate acts between gays to be restricted.
Variables:	a 'Do you think homosexuality should be made illegal?' (Question 14, variable 23).
	b. 'What is the age at which homosexuality is legal?' 'What do you think the consenting age limit should be?' (Questions 12b & 13b, variables 20 and 22).
	c. 'Do you agree with two gay men, or two lesbian women, rearing children in a family situation?' (Question 18a, variable 25).
	d. 'Do you think that acts of an effectionate nature, between homosexuals (male and female) should be confined to their home?' (Question 15b, variable 28).

matter how *reliably* and *accurately* you collect and record data, the result will have little to do with the research aim (see pages 31–2).

Student Activity 4.8
Operationalise the concepts that occur in your hypotheses (Student Activity 4.6).

The research instrument

Social surveys usually involve either formal interviews or questionnaires. *Formal interviews* are a structured dialogue between two people, the interviewer and the respondent. The interviewer reads questions from an *interview schedule* in a predetermined order and records the respondent's answers. *Questionnaires* do not involve interviewers; respondents are asked to complete questions by themselves.

Designing the questionnaire or interview schedule

Whether a questionnaire or schedule is used, the basic principles for designing the set of questions are much the same. It is important to ask questions in a logical sequence so that the respondent is led easily from one point to the next. It is also a good idea to start with questions that are easy to answer and generally interesting, leaving the more difficult ones until later. It is usually advisable to leave until the last 'personal' questions (usually called classificatory questions) such as age, occupation, marital status, education, income, ethnicity and so on.

When designing questions you need to consider both the *content* and the *style*.

Question content
Content of questions involves your imagination, but they are determined by three things. First, the *hypotheses* you are testing. Make sure your questions relate to your hypotheses and are such that you are able to test your hypotheses on the basis of the answers you receive. Avoid including 'interesting' questions that do not relate to your hypotheses.

Second, you will have a set of questions as a result of the operationalisation of the concepts you have undertaken. Decide how many questions you are going to use for each of the indicators of the concepts you have operationalised. You may have a large number of indicators for each dimension and this, potentially, may lead to a very large questionnaire. You might decide to cut back the number of indicators, and thus questions. For example, Townsend *et al.* (1987) had 94 variables for deprivation. This is rather a lot and would be far too many for a student project. Perhaps, instead of five indicators for dietary deprivation (see page 108) you could select just one to represent them all. Of course, reducing the number of indicators should not be done in an arbitrary way, but should be the result of careful *theoretical* consideration.

Third, you will probably need additional 'lead-in' questions to help the *flow* of the questionnaire or schedule. You should not overload your questionnaire with lead-in questions, just include those that help the questionnaire move from one subject to another.

Question style

The *style* of the questions also depends on circumstances, but some general guide-lines can help you avoid the most obvious traps.

The questions should make sense to the informant and be possible for the informant to answer. This can be done by using words that will be *familiar* to the sampled population. Do not use technical terms or slang if they are not familiar to the respondents. For example:

Do you think that your socialisation has affected your gender role?

The terms 'gender role' and 'socialisation' are well known to sociologists but not necessarily to the public at large. On the other hand, do not be afraid of using technical terms if they are appropriate, such as medical jargon when surveying a sample of doctors.

Ambiguity should also be avoided. For example:

When did you leave school?

is a very vague question and could be interpreted differently by different respondents. It would be much better to ask something like:

At what age did you complete your school education?

If different informants read the meaning of the questions differently then you will be unable to compare their answers.

Make sure that each question asks only *one thing* at a time. Do not combine two questions in one. For example:

Did you know that it is possible to work part-time up to 10 hours and to claim an attendance allowance?
Yes / No

Respondents could quite easily answer 'yes' to the first part of the question and 'no' to the second part but be unable to indicate their different answers.

Questions should be *short and clear* rather than complex. This can sometimes be done by using a series of questions, for example:

Has it happened to you that over a long time, when you neither practised abstinence, nor used birth control, you did not conceive?
Yes / No   (from *The Family Limitation Survey*, 1949)

This question asks so much at once and contains so many negatives, that it is initially impossible to know whether to answer 'yes' or 'no'. The information that this question is trying to find out could be collected by using a sequence of questions such as:

Have you conceived in the last 'x' months?	*Yes / No*
Did you practice abstinence?	*Yes / No*
Did you use birth control methods?	*Yes / No*

If the informant can make a wide range of possible responses to a question it may be easier for the respondent to ignore the question altogether rather than try to sort it out.

A common error in questionnaire design is the use of *leading* questions which may direct the informant to a response that they would not normally have given. This can bias the results. Leading questions arise in several ways. First, by providing a *restricted set of answers* to choose from which exclude other possible answers. Second, by using a *leading structure* to the question, such as 'You don't think do you...?' (which leads to a negative answer) or 'Shouldn't something be done about...?' (which leads to a positive answer). Great care must be taken with your question design to avoid this. Third, a *leading sequence* of questions can also lead the respondent to answer in an inaccurate way, for example:

Question design:
Criticise these example questions
NOTE These questions are in no way connected with each other, that is, they do not form a complete questionnaire.

1. How old are you?
Under 20
18–21
21–33
33–50
50–65
65 and over

2. How much do you earn?

3. How much do you drink per day?
Less than 1 unit
5–10 units
More than 10 units

4. Have you committed a crime in the last 12 months?
Yes   No

5. Do you spend a lot of time watching television?
Yes   No

6. Do you feel influenced by your peer group?
Yes   No

7. Do you find your job satisfying?
Yes   No

8. 'Everybody knows that equality for women is unnatural nonsense'.
Agree   Disagree

9. 'Britain should scrap nuclear weapons.'
Very strongly agree
Strongly agree
Agree
Disagree

Did you know that privatisation of water cost millions of pounds to the tax payer? Yes / No
Should the privatisation of water be stopped?
Yes / No

Care must also be taken when attempting to design questions that involve the respondents *recalling* information from their past as this can often be inaccurate.

Some respondents will agree with what they perceive as the researcher's opinion, especially if they have not got much interest in the survey. Try to avoid giving *clues*, in questions, that might enable the respondent to do this.

Student Activity 4.9
Look at the sample questions in the box on page 110. Decide what is wrong with each question and write a suitable alternative.
SUGGESTION You may find it easier to work in groups for this exercise.

Suggested answers to Student Activity 4.9

Question 1
a. The categories are not even. For example, there are 3 years between 18–21, 12 between 21–33. The categories must reflect what you are trying to find out.
b. The categories overlap, thus a person could be in two categories. For example, if you were 21 years old you could tick either the 18–21 box or the 21–33 box.

Question 2
a. People find this a sensitive issue and do not usually like to say how much they earn. It is better to provide categories which offer a range, for example, £20–£30, £31–£50 etc.
b. It is also ambiguous as it is not clear whether hourly, weekly, monthly or annual income is required; whether gross or net after tax, or whether from all work or just primary employment.

Question 3
a Categories are too restrictive as they do not allow for people to answer that they do not drink. Therefore, a 'none' category is required.
b. The categories are too large. There is a lot of difference between drinking 5 units and 10 units per day.
c. Using technical terms like units can cause confusion as not everybody knows what they mean.

Question 4
a. What is meant by the word 'crime'? This can cause confusion.
b. Even if respondents had committed a crime would they admit it?
c. A better way to get this information would be to use a sequence of questions or a self-report study (see page 80).

Question 5
a. This question is too vague. The term 'a lot' needs to be defined. For example *Do you spend 1 hour per day? Do you spend 2–4 hours per day?* and so on.

Question 6
a. Using technical or specialised terms can cause problems. Respondents may not know what you mean by 'peer group'.
b. People may not agree about what is meant by the term 'influenced'.

Question 7
a. The categories provided are too restrictive as they do not provide a category for people who sometimes enjoy their job.
b. It is a presumptuous question as it implies that the respondent has a job.

Question 8
a. This is a statement which assumes the writer is correct and could influence the respondent into agreeing. It also uses emotive language to bias the respondent, for example *'everybody knows'*, *'unnatural nonsense'*. This kind of approach is only suitable in an attitude survey where all the items are of this statement type and are expressed in a mixture of positive and negative ways.

Question 9
a. This is a leading question because, although respondents are able to agree or disagree, there are three agreement categories and only one disagreement category. This implies that 'agreement' is the suitable answer.
b. How much difference is there between *'very strongly'* and *'strongly'* agree? This may ne an unnecessary set of distinctions. When analysing this question, what benefit is there in distinguishing between these different forms of agreement?
c. The term *'scrap'* also has connotations of 'rubbish' and this may further influence uncommited respondents to agree with the proposition.

In summary, the problems associated with question design are as follows:

1. Using technical and undefined terms.
2. Leading questions and sequences.
3. Ambiguous or vague questions.
4. Presumptuous questions.
5. Complex questions.
6. Multiple questions.
7. Uneven and overlapping categories in pre-coded answers.
8. Restricted range of categories in pre-coded answers.

Self-completion questionnaires

The points already discussed apply to both self-completion questionnaires and to interviewer schedules. However, for self-completion questionnaires there are special problems resulting from the absence of an interviewer. The first few questions on the questionnaire must capture the interest of the respondent to motivate her or him to participate in the survey.

The researcher must provide clear guidance and instructions to respondents about how to record their answers. For example, should they write out their answers in full, or tick a suitable box? Should only one box be ticked per question or can the respondent tick as many as are relevant? Researchers must accept that without an interviewer to probe or follow up leads, the information gleaned will be in less depth or detail than an interview schedule and will also be more suited to closed questions.

In the case of self-completion questionnaires it is not possible to guarantee the order in which the respondent will read the questions. This can be overcome to some extent by taking great care in the design so that the answers to a question are not influenced by questions that come later but which the respondent may read in advance.

Closed and open questions

Questions on schedules and questionnaires may be either *closed* or *open*. Extract 4.2, from the Sandwell Skills Audit (Harvey, Wells and Place, 1990), illustrates the different types of closed and open questions.

Closed questions are designed with a set of alternative answers. These are known as *pre-coded* answers. Recording pre-coded answers is easy. Where they occur on questionnaires the respondent normally just has to tick an appropriate box. When they occur on an interview schedule the interviewer just has to indicate the correct code. Sometimes pre-coded questions permit only one answer (for example, questions 11, 13, 14 and 17 in Extract 4.2). Sometimes the respondent can indicate more than one answer (for example, questions 10, 12 and 15). The list of alternative answers may have to be read out by the interviewer (as in question 10) or they may be typed on to a card and handed to the respondent to read (question 12). If the pre-coded categories are not known to the respondent (that is, are just on the interviewer's schedule) then the interviewer has to fit the response given by the interviewee to one of the pre-coded categories (question 15). Pre-coding questions in advance enables the data to be put easily on the computer for analysis. The problem with pre-coded questions is that the list of alternatives is restricted to the researcher's preconceived ideas about what is important.

Open questions do not have any pre-coded answers. Thus the respondent's answer has to be written down in full, either by the respondent on a

Extract 4.2

INTERVIEW SCHEDULE LAYOUT

1. The questions are grouped under broad headings ('Skills' and 'New Job').

2. There are two vertical lines down the page. To the left of the first line are the variable numbers. Between the two lines are the question number, the question, the pre-coded answers and the interviewer instructions. To the right of the second line are the answer codes and the appropriate next question.

3. Question numbers, variables and values are clearly differentiated. Questions are numbered in order (in the example we have questions 9 to 17). Each question has one or more variables, depending on the type of question (in the example the questions cover variables v11 to v44). Question 9 has a single variable (v11), but each coded answer in question 10 is itself a variable (v12 to v17). The values for pre-coded questions are on the right of the schedule, for example question 17 (variable v44) has 4 possible values (coded 1 to 4), most of the other variables have just two values (1 or 2).

4. Questions are in bold print and start on the left of the page. They are easily distinguished from answers and interviewer instructions, which are underlined.

5. Precoded answers are aligned to the right-hand line and there is a code immediately opposite, on the other side of the vertical line.
In question 12 the pre-coded answers are not read out, instead the respondent is handed a card with the alternatives on it. The interviewer circles the 1 on the schedule next to each of the skill areas that the respondent mentions. The 2 is circled against the ones that are not mentioned.
Where the pre-coded answers are to be read to the respondent they are in bold type, as in question 14, and the interviewer is instructed to read out the alternative answers.
In question 15 the list is neither read nor shown to the respondent and the interviewer circles the 1 next to any of the reasons indicated by the respondent in response to the question.

6. The next question is asked unless an answer redirects the interviewer to another question. For example, if the respondent answers 'No' to question 11 the interviewer circles the 2 and goes on to question 13.

var	no.	question	Code	
		SKILLS		
11	9.	**What skills have you acquired in your present employment?** (If none go to **Q.11**)		
	10.	**Were these skills acquired through?**	Yes	No
12		READ LIST AND WAIT **on the job experience**	1	2
13		FOR ANSWER TO EACH **employer sponsorship: day release**	1	2
14		**employer sponsorship: short course**	1	2
15		**trade apprenticeship**	1	2
16		**formal training in the workplace**	1	2
17		other (*specify below*)	1	2
18	11.	**Are you interested in acquiring new skills?**		
		Yes	1 Q12	
		No	2 Q13	
	12.	**What type of skills would you be interested in gaining?**	Yes	No
19		SHOW CARD 1 basic education	1	2
20		building	1	2
21		business/enterprise	1	2
22		catering	1	2
23		computing	1	2
24		driving	1	2
25		engineering	1	2
26		health/caring	1	2
27		secretarial	1	2
28		teaching	1	2
29		languages	1	2
31		other (*please specify*)	1	2
		NEW JOB		
32	13.	**Are you looking for a different or additional job at the moment?**		
		Yes	1 Q14	
		No	2 Q19	
33	14.	**Are you looking for**		
		a new job to replace your old one	1	
		or an additional job	2	
	15.	**Why are you looking for another job?**	Yes	No
		(Circle 1 for those indicated by respondent, DO NOT READ OUT LIST)		
34		present job may come to an end	1	2
35		present job is just to fill in time	1	2
36		pay is unsatisfactory in present job	1	2
37		journey to work is unsatisfactory	1	2
38		want to work longer hours	1	2
39		want to work shorter hours	1	2
40		unable to make use of current skills	1	2
42		other reasons (specify)	1	2
43	16.	**What kind of job are you looking for?** Enter job type		
44	17.	**How far are you prepared to travel for another job?**		
		stay in immediate area	1	
		anywhere in Sandwell	2	
		as far as Birmingham/Wolverhampton/Dudley/Walsall	3	
		further afield	4	

Source: Harvey, Wells and Place (1990).

questionnaire or by an interviewer recording the reply verbatim on a schedule (for example, questions 9 and 16 in Extract 4.2). Open questions thus require more work from the respondent or interviewer than closed questions. In practice, in an interview situation the interviewer may not be able to record every word because she or he cannot ask the respondent to slow down as this may upset the flow of the interview.

The researcher also has to decide how to deal with open questions. There are two options. To 'post-code' the answers or to treat the data qualitatively. Post-coding involves reading through the answers and deciding on a set of categories into which the answers can be put. This might be a simple set of categories such as 'broadly in favour' and 'broadly opposed', or a more detailed list of alternatives that arise from the answers given. The alternative is to deal with the responses in a qualitative way, similar to in-depth interview answers (see Chapter 7). This option is used when the answers cannot be fitted into convenient categories or when more detailed case material is needed than can be provided from statistical summaries.

Student Activity 4.10
Design a set of questions, which will form the basis of an interview schedule, to test your hypotheses (from Student Activity 4.6).

Layout

Designing the questions is only part of the process of constructing a schedule or questionnaire. You then have to put them in the right order and lay them out on the paper to make a usable questionnaire or schedule. Taking time preparing a proper layout is important for several reasons. First, it makes it easier to extract the data for analysis later. Second, it makes it easier for respondents or interviewers to use. Third, a good layout makes your research look more 'professional' and thus it gets taken more seriously.

Where possible, questionnaires and schedules should be typed without any errors. A word-processor is by far the best way of doing this, not least because you can easily make changes after the pilot stage (see below). If you produce hand-written questionnaires make sure they are neat and legible.

It is also important to make a clear distinction between the questions, the variables and the values used to denote the answers. Number each question in order; this is the *question number*. A question may refer to one or more *variables* depending on the type of question. Each variable should also be clearly numbered (see Extract 4.2). It is important, as you will see from the discussion that follows, that you think in terms of variables rather than questions. For each variable, there are at least two possible answers, these are known as the *values* for each variable. So a question such as:

Do you have a current driving licence? Yes/No

consists of a variable 'driving licence' and two values, 'yes' and 'no'.

When coding questions it is advisable to use numbers to represent the answers. So, for example, use '1' to represent 'yes' and '2' to represent 'no', in the question above. It is advisable to use '0' only to represent a 'not applicable' or 'missing' answer. There is a tendency to code 'no' answers as '0' but this can lead to confusion as missing answers and 'no' answers end up being coded in the same way. So, use non-zero numbers to code actual answers, including 'don't know' answers.

Extract 4.2 provides a useful illustration of layout. This layout makes the schedule easy for the interviewer to use. All the codes are on the same part

Extract 4.3

QUESTIONS FROM THE SURVEY OF ATTITUDES TOWARDS HOMOSEXUALITY AMONGST 16–20-YEAR-OLD FURTHER EDUCATION STUDENTS IN BIRMINGHAM.

Clause 28 of the Local Government Bill came into force on 27 May 1988. This law prevents local councils from 'intentionally promoting homosexuality'. Nor may they 'promote the teaching... of the acceptability of homosexuality as a pretended family relationship' in schools.

(Circle the answers you think are applicable)

1) Had you previously heard of Clause 28?

    yes   no

2) Do you understand the clause?

    yes   no

3) Do you agree with the clause?

    yes   no

4) Do you feel that Clause 28 affects only gay and lesbian people in society?

    yes   no

5) Do you think that the clause will make any difference to general opinion on homosexuality?

    yes   no

6) Do you agree with homosexuality being included in sex education at school?

    yes   no

7) Do you think the inclusion of homosexuality, as part of sex education in schools, intentionally promotes homosexuality?

    yes   no

8) Do you consider that the timing of Clause 28 is in any way a response to the AIDS media scare?

    yes   no

9) How did you become aware of homosexuality?
    (Tick the appropriate answer(s)) :

    a) Friends
    b) Parents
    c) School
    d) Media (i.e., newspapers, television, etc.).

10) Which groups in society, do you consider, to be most at risk from AIDS?

a) Gays	yes	no
b) Heterosexuals	yes	no
c) Intravenous drug users	yes	no
d) Lesbians	yes	no
e) Prostitutes	yes	no

11) Do you consider there to be any truth in the term 'The gay plague', in connection with the problem of AIDS?

    yes   no

12) What is the age at which homosexuality is legal?
    (Circle your answer).

    a) Females:16 18 20 21 25 other (please state)
    b) Males: 16 18 20 21 25 other (please state)

13) What do you think the consenting age limit should be?

    a) Females   ....
    b) Males   ....

14) Do you think homosexuality should be made illegal?

    yes   no

15) Do you think acts of an affectionate nature, between homosexuals (male and female), should be confined to their home?

    a) Female   yes   no
    b) Male   yes   no

16) Is there anyone in your family or social circle, either male or female, whom you know to be homosexual?

    yes   no

17) If you had, or have a child, would you be, or are you prepared to discuss homosexuality with them?

    yes   no

18) Do you agree with two gay men, or two lesbian women, rearing children in a family situation?

    a) Gay men   yes   no
    b) Lesbian women   yes   no

This questionnaire is anonymous and confidential, however it would help us if you would provide some general details about yourself

Age   ....

Sex   Male   Female

Religion   ....

Would you describe yourself as being: (please tick one)
    African
    Afro/Asian
    African Caribbean
    Asian
    European
    Oriental
    Other (please specify)

If you have any general comments on this issue, or the questionnaire overall please write them on the back.

Thank you very much for your time and co-operation.

> **NOTE: the original questionnaire was printed on separate pages rather than in this column format.**

Adapted from Todd *et al.*, 1990.

of the questionnaire, that is, down the right-hand side. The words the interviewer has to read out are clearly identifiable and it is easy to see what question to ask next. It is also easy for the researcher to enter the data on the computer for analysis later because the appropriate code for each pre-coded variable can be read easily off from the completed questionnaire (see the section *Coding your data* on page 127).

When constructing a questionnaire, the same design could be used, although one that is more 'user-friendly' for the respondent is often preferred. Extract 4.3 (on page 115) is the questionnaire used in the example survey of attitudes to gays and lesbians. Note it has neither variable numbers on the page nor codes to circle; instead there are just boxes to tick or spaces to write in. If you produce this type of questionnaire you also need to produce a coding frame to facilitate analysis later (see Extract 4.7 on page 129).

> **Student Activity 4.11**
> **Prepare an interview schedule like the one in Extract 4.2 for the questions you devised in Student Activity 4.10.**

Sampling

It is not possible for sociologists to study everybody in the population due to the constraints of time and cost. Thus researchers need to select a sample to represent the population. Population in this sense does not necessarily mean everyone in a country but can refer to subgroups, for example, women, students, shop stewards and so on. Thus we can talk about the population of women in Great Britain or the population of shop stewards working for British Leyland. Sociologists may not therefore talk to all women but take a *representative* sample from the population of women. Using a representative sample allows us, in theory, to make *generalisations* about the population from the information gleaned from the sample.

For example, in their study of poverty, Townsend *et al.* (1987) took a sample of 2,700 adults from the population of London. The addresses were chosen at random from 30 wards selected from the total of 755 wards. They thus had a representative sample of households and were able to generalise about poverty in London from their findings.

Sampling is essential to make social scientific analysis possible. A small representative sample can provide 'accurate' data on large populations. Fifteen hundred people in an opinion poll can give a good indicator of how twenty million will vote at a general election.

In the following sections we outline how to select a sample and the different kinds of samples that can be used. It is important that you are aware of different sampling procedures and understand the notion of a representative sample. In practice, however, you will be unlikely to obtain a representative sample for your project. Selecting a representative sample can be a complex and time-consuming process, as you will see, and you may not have the resources to be able do it. You need to bear in mind that if you do not have a representative sample then your results are likely to be biased. Therefore you should be wary of making generalisations about the population from which the sample was taken. On the other hand, as a learning experience, it is more important to complete a project with an unrepresentative sample (provided that you show you are aware of it) than to abandon the project because you cannot get a representative sample.

Sampling frame

To draw a representative sample it is necessary to find a sampling frame that provides a list of everyone in the population from which the sample is to be drawn. The sampling frame to use is dependent upon the type of study being carried out. For example, the electoral roll, which contains the names and addresses of all people eligible to vote in Great Britain, would be an appropriate frame from which to select a sample for a study of voting patterns in Great Britain. However, if the study was about political attitudes of bus drivers in London a much better sampling frame would be the personnel lists of London Transport.

It is important that the frame selected includes every member of the survey population because if it does not you will get sampling bias. This can lead to some groups of the population being overrepresented and others underrepresented and some not represented at all. For example, if you wanted a sample of children under ten years old it would be no use using school registers as children too young to go to school would be excluded.

> **Student Activity: 4.12**
> **How would you compile a sampling frame to undertake the following research:**
> 1. **An analysis of church attendance in Great Britain.**
> 2. **Child-care problems of single parents with children under five years of age?**

There are two broad types of sampling procedure, random and non-random.

Random samples

Random samples are designed to give everybody in the population an equal (or known) probability of being in the sample. In this way the sample will not be biased towards any particular group within the population. This is important if you want a representative sample. To get a random sample it is necessary to have a complete and up-to-date sampling frame. Random sampling, despite its name, is therefore a systematic form of sampling and is sometimes known as probability or scientific sampling. There are several ways of drawing a random sample.

Simple random sample
Simple random sampling is equivalent to putting all the names of the population being sampled in a container and then drawing out the required number for the sample. In practice, simple random sampling is done by selecting from a list using random numbers. Computers are often used for this task.

Systematic random sample
Systematic random samples are like simple random samples. Instead of the sample being selected from a list by using randomly generated numbers, a random start point is selected and then every nth item on the list is included in the sample. For example, if the sample frame contains 1000 names and a sample of 100 is required, then a random start point is selected by generating a random number between 1 and 10 and every tenth item is taken from the list. There is a possibility that this process might give an unrepresentative

sample if the list is ordered in a particular way. For example, if the list was an address list in house number order then every tenth house might generate only even numbers that would (in Britain) lead to the houses selected all being on one side of a street. It is possible that this might generate a sample with an unrepresentative housing class.

> **Student activity 4.13**
> **How might you select a systematic random sample of 200 businesses listed in your local area telephone book?**

Random cluster sample

In random *cluster* sampling the population is viewed as divided into groups (for example, school children into school classes, bank workers into bank branches) and these groups are then sampled. For example, to get a sample of first-year secondary school children in Brighton you could select a random sample from all the first-year class registers in the area. This is a time-consuming job. Alternatively, you could select one first-year class at random from each school in the area and survey all the pupils in the class. This is a much quicker way to compile the sample. Cluster sampling may often save time and money but it can lead to a biased sample. In the example above, some schools will be a lot larger than others, and so some schools will have five or six first-year classes while other much smaller schools might have just one or two. If one class is taken from each school, irrespective of school size, then some students will have a much greater chance of being in the sample than others. Where there is only one first-year class the students in that school will have a hundred per cent chance of being in the sample but where there are five first-year classes they will only have a twenty per cent chance. Cluster sampling might be single-stage, where everyone in the cluster is in the sample (that is, everybody in the class selected is part of the sample). Or it might be multi-stage, where further subsamples may be selected from within the cluster. For example, we may only want one in three students from the randomly selected first-year class.

Multi-stage random sample

Multi-stage random sampling is a means of selecting a sample covering a large and dispersed population without having to interview one or two people in a lot of widely scattered locations. This is important when you have limited resources. It is much less costly and much quicker to interview people in a small area than it is to interview people spread thinly over a large area. Multi-stage random sampling works by selecting in stages. For example, a sample of 1,000 voters in Britain might be chosen by first selecting 20 constituencies at random from the list of all British constituencies, then choosing 2 wards at random within each constituency, and then selecting 25 voters from the electoral register of each ward. The sample will be selected at random but the location of the interviewees would be more concentrated than if a sample of 1,000 people had been selected by simple random sampling techniques from the whole electoral register for Great Britain. In practice, multi-stage random sampling tends to bring in an element of bias as it is rare that the different probabilities of selection for individuals are taken into account. Usually it is assumed that each member has an equal chance of being in the sample. In the above example this would not be the case if, for example, a constituency of 100,000 voters and one of 50,000 were selected at stage one. The probability of any individual from the first constituency being in the sample would be half that of a voter in the second constituency.

Stratified random sample

Stratified random sampling occurs when the population is split into different groups (or strata) before the random selection is made. The selection of the strata depends on the purpose of the investigation. If a gender comparison is being undertaken, the population under investigation would be split into male and female and the sample selected so that the population proportions of men and women are reflected in the sample. For example, if the population consisted of doctors and the sampling frame showed that twice as many doctors were males than females then, if a sample of three hundred was required, a hundred females would be selected from the female doctor list and two hundred males from the male doctor list.

Student Activity 4.14
Using Table 4.3, determine the percentage within each of the following strata that you would need for a sample of the population of Britain aged 20 or more.

Strata:	Males	Females
20–39	19.9%	_____
40–59	_____	_____
60 or more	_____	_____

We have worked out the first one for you. There are 7.88 million males between 20 and 39 out of a total population of 39.63 million adults aged 20 or more: 7.88 ÷ 39.63 = .199 = 19.9%.

Stratified random sampling is often combined in practice with multi-stage sampling. For example, when selecting a sample of voters, opinion pollsters rank order British constituencies according to the percentage Conservative vote at the last general election. They thus stratify the population in terms of political opinion at the constituency level. Then they use systematic random sampling to choose the constituencies and, finally, random sampling to select voters.

Area sampling

Area sampling is an attempt at random sampling when a sampling frame is not available. A geographic area is selected for the study, sometimes at random, but more often the study is directed to a particular area. Then the dwellings in it are selected in some random fashion, such as calling at every nth house in each street in the area. The residents may then make up the sample or there may be a further screening if the research is only interested in certain categories of respondents (for example, people over 75 years of age).

Non-random samples

A non-random (or non-probability) sample is any sample where it is not possible to say that all the members of the relevant population had a known probability of being selected at the outset. Convenience samples, volunteer samples, snowball samples and quota samples are all types of non-random samples. Non-random sampling does away with the need for a sampling frame but also usually results in biased samples.

Table 4.3 Age structure of the population of Great Britain, 1980, millions.

	Males	Females
Under 9	3.77	3.57
10–19	4.68	4.45
20–29	4.08	3.90
30–39	3.80	3.75
40–49	3.19	3.04
50–59	3.20	3.36
60–69	2.59	3.08
70–79	1.58	2.46
80 or more	0.41	1.09
Totals	27.30	28.70

Source: *Annual Abstracts.*

Convenience sample

Convenience sampling is the crudest form of sampling, in which anyone who is convenient becomes part of the sample. Samples of this sort might be used in the pre-pilot stage of a research project to test out some initial wording of questions but are of little use otherwise. They can lead to enormous distortions, for example an opinion poll survey carried out by a local newspaper in the Midlands in 1974 showed that the Conservatives had a 20% lead in the area. Days later, Labour narrowly won the election. The inaccuracy supposedly arose because the paper's interviewer stood at the main entrance to one of the most prestigious and expensive department stores in the region and asked the opinions of people who went to shop there. This highly biased convenience sample led to the serious distortion in the results.

Volunteer sample

A *volunteer* sample is one that uses volunteers. They are often recruited through advertisements. We saw in Chapter 2 (page 40) that Ien Ang's (1985) study of viewers' attitudes to *Dallas* was based on a volunteer sample of people who responded to her advertisement in a Dutch magazine. Volunteer samples are thus self-selecting and usually biased as they are a subgroup of a population who are prepared to be involved in the research. Sometimes researchers have to resort to volunteer samples as there is no other way of reaching sufficient numbers of people to build up a sample. A researcher may want to locate a sample of people who have given up smoking for the whole of the last month. It would be very time-consuming to locate potential sample members through random sampling and so advertising and inviting people to participate in the research may be the only feasible way forward. The results, however, would have to be treated with care as the sample will inevitably be biased. The problem of volunteer samples is also discussed in Chapter 7 when we look at personal document analysis.

Snowball sample

Snowball samples occur when the researcher makes contact with a suitable subject and is then directed to, or makes contact with, other members in a network of contacts. Participant observers often build up their sample in this way (see Chapter 6). It is a useful technique for locating sample subjects when you are looking for a narrow range of people (such as career criminals) where no sampling frame exists. However, this does tend to mean that the research is focused on a set of interlinking networks. For participant observers who are trying to understand the nature of a particular social phenomenon without necessarily attempting to generalise the results, this is an acceptable approach to broadening their investigation.

Quota sample

Non-random sampling is therefore almost always biased. One possible exception, in practice, is the use of *quota* sampling. This method does not give every member of the population an equal (or known) chance of being in the sample. However, it attempts representativeness by selecting respondents, from those available, in proportion to a predetermined quota that reflects data already known about the population (usually demographic data such as age, gender and so on). Quota sampling works by dividing the population into subgroups and then giving interviewers a quota of people from each subgroup that they have to locate. For example, a quota of 40 interviewees might be made up of 20 females and 20 males, of whom 10 of

Table 4.4 Types of sample

Type	Advantages	Disadvantages
Random		
Simple	Gives a true random sample	Requires complete sampling frame Selecting sample is time consuming Widely dispersed sample
Systematic	Quick to select sample	Requires complete sampling frame Widely dispersed sample
Cluster	Concentrated sample	May not be truly random Only need sampling frame for cluster
Multi-stage	Random selection of concentrated sample Complete sampling frame for selected areas only	May not be truly random Need sampling frame at each stage
Stratified	Ensures that relevant independent variables match population	Requires knowledge of components of strata
Area	Useful when no sampling frame available	Unlikely to be truly random
Non-random		
Convenience	No selection procedure necessary	Will not be representative Unreliable
Volunteer	Overcomes some problems of selection when sampling frame impossible	Self-selecting thus not representative
Snowball	Useful technique to build up a sample	Not representative
Quota	Alternative way of getting a representative sample No need for sampling frame	Need to construct representative quotas Unlikely to be a random sample

each must be under forty and 10 over forty. When one quota is full, for example, the interviewer has questioned 10 women under forty, then she or he must not ask any more young women, but must continue until the rest of the quotas are completed.

Quotas are designed, as far as possible, so that the subgroups are in the same proportion in the sample as they are in the population being investigated. Sometimes, however, quotas are decided arbitrarily without a full knowledge of the population demographic data. The difference between quota and stratified random sampling is that the interviewer is free to ask anybody, within the geographic area they have been allocated, who falls into their quotas. With stratified random sampling, although the population is divided into strata, the individuals are still selected at random by name from a sampling frame.

Student Activity 4.15
Design a quota for a sample of 50 students, aged over 16 in your school or college. The quota should be selected so that it provides a good cross-section of students assuming that you were going to do some research to assess student attitudes to the amount of coursework they have.

Table 4.4 summarises the main advantages and disadvantages of the different types of sample. Random samples are more *representative* but, as we said at the beginning of this section, you are unlikely to have the resources to get a random sample for your project. You should try to get one that is as representative as possible and be aware of its limitations. Extract 4.4 describes the sample used in the example survey.

Student Activity 4.16
Does Extract 4.4 provide you with enough information to be able to identify what sampling procedure was adopted in the example survey? If so what would you say it was? What else would you need to know to be able to judge the adequacy of the sampling procedure used?

Extract 4.4

EXAMPLE SURVEY SAMPLE

The sample consisted of 151 students from 3 further education colleges in Birmingham. The subjects taken by the students included printing, design, art, hairdressing, catering, hotel management, tourism, language, sociology and government. The questionnaires were handed out to the respondents by lecturers teaching selected classes and the completed forms were returned to the researchers.

Adapted from Todd *et al.* (1990).

Interviewing

The interviewer's job is to locate the respondent, obtain an interview, ask the questions and record the answers as accurately as possible. This is not always as easy as it seems.

Locating the respondent

Interviewers need to be given clear instructions about who to ask, how many times they should try to locate particular respondents and who, if anybody, they may substitute for missing respondents. Whether you are doing the interviewing yourself or you have other people to help you should still produce a set of interviewer instructions so that the same procedures are used throughout the interview stage (see Extract 4.5 taken from the *Sandwell Skills Audit*). The exact nature of these instructions will depend on the nature of the sample and the adequacy of the sampling frame. If, for example, your sample consists of names drawn from the electoral register, you must decide whether to allow the interviewer to substitute new occupants of houses for people in the sample who have moved out of the area.

Obtaining an interview

Having located a potential respondent, you have to persuade that person to answer your questions. It helps if you are pleasant and the interview seems to be about something relevant and interesting to the respondent. If respondents find the topic threatening or are suspicious of your motives or the organisation you represent then you are unlikely to get an interview. You must assure the respondent that the information they give you is confidential, anonymous and will not be passed on to anyone else. For example, in the *Sandwell Skills Audit Survey*, which included questions on employment, the interviewers had to make it clear that they were from Sandwell College and not from the Department of Employment nor, given that the poll tax had just been announced, from the local authority. Further, assurances were given that no personal information would be passed on to either of these organisations.

Your opening statement when approaching someone for an interview is therefore important. It should summarise these points very briefly and seek to reassure the respondent and gain their co-operation (see Extract 4.6)

Asking the questions

The interview should resemble as closely as possible a structured conversation in which the interviewer leads the dialogue. Interviewers need to be familiar with the interview schedule, both the content and sequence of the questions, so that the interview flows without artificial breaks caused by the interviewer stumbling over questions or not being sure which question to ask next. A well-designed schedule that clearly indicates which question to ask next and that has clear instructions to the interviewer makes the process of asking the questions much easier than one that is poorly designed.

The interviewer should attempt to establish 'rapport' so that the respondent feels at ease in answering the questions. Conventionally, it is argued that the best way of doing this is for the interviewer to talk to people in their homes with the respondent seated facing the interviewer (so that the respondent cannot read the schedule) (Atkinson, 1967; Moser and Kalton, 1971). However, it is not always possible or desirable to conduct interviews in the respondent's home. As a student doing a project you may prefer not to go into people's homes if you do not know them. Although, as an interviewer, you

---

Extract 4.5

LOCATING AND INTERVIEWING RE-SPONDENTS

1. You will be given a set of names and addresses on file cards and a map of the area.

2. The sample should only consist of people between **18 and 65** years of age, **not** in full time education and **not** chronically sick.

3. On the first visit to the address please attempt to interview the named person. If the named person is over 65 or in full time education or is chronically ill please substitute another suitable member of the household.

4. If possible make sure the substitute is the same sex as the named person.

5. If you get a reply from the address but the named person is not available on the first visit (and falls into the 18-65 category etc.) but is available at another time, please call back and interview the named person.

6. If you get a reply from the address but the named person is not available on the first visit and will not be available at another time then substitute another member of the household. If the named person no longer lives at the address then substitute a person currently at the address (preferably of the same sex as the named person).

7. If no reply is obtained on the first visit call back one time only. Attempt to obtain an interview with the named person (if applicable). If this is not possible substitute another member of the household.

8. If no suitable member of the household is available for interview or if no reply is obtained on the second visit please go to the next nearest house/flat until you get a reply. At the new address try to substitute someone of the same gender as the named respondent.

9. Write the name and address of the respondent interviewed on the file card that contains the original name.

10. Please do not lead the respondent and ensure that ambiguous replies are clarified. Use standard prompts like 'anything else' but do not suggest answers to the respondent. If, for any reason, you feel uncomfortable or threatened in an interview situation feel free to terminate the interview. Try at all times to be polite and pleasant.

Adapted from Harvey, Wells and Place, 1990.

Extract 4.6

INTERVIEWER'S INTRODUCT-ION: SANDWELL SKILLS AUDIT

Hello, is Mr./Mrs./Ms. ... at home?

I am from Sandwell College.

We are doing a study of Sandwell to see what skills people have to offer and what educational, training, and other activi-ties they want.

Would you be prepared to help us in our survey of the needs of Sandwell resi-dents?

The interview will take about twenty min-utes.

The interview will be in the strictest con-fidence. Nothing you tell us will be passed on to anyone else.

If necessary, assure the respondent that all published material will be anonymous and that there is no way that anything they tell you can be traced back to them.

If the respondent is reluctant ask if there is a more convenient time to call back. (Indi-cate how important it is we have a random sample so that it is representative of the people of Sandwell.)

If the respondent wants to know why she or he has been selected say :

Your address has been selected at ran-dom from the electoral register in the local library.

(Go on to explain further if necessary.)

Adapted from Harvey, Wells and Place, 1990.

---

are unlikely to encounter any hostile or aggressive behaviour, you should always take care. Make sure, if you are doing house-to-house interviews that you let someone else know where you are going. You may also prefer to work in pairs rather than alone in some circumstances. This might involve two people doing the interview together (although the respondent might feel threatened by this) or it might mean two people working together in the same street, keeping an eye on the movements of each other.

Never be afraid of terminating an interview and leaving whenever you feel uncomfortable or threatened. This also applies to situations where respond-ent are clearly wasting your time by not taking the interview seriously.

Recording the answers

The point of the interview is to get the *respondent's* answers. The interviewer must try to record these as accurately as possible and should seek clarifica-tion of ambiguous answers rather than simply presuppose or guess what they mean. Similarly, the interviewer should avoid leading the respondent by suggesting answers. The interviewer must be honest and under no circum-stances write in answers that were not provided by the respondent.

Interview bias

There is no doubt that however good the interviewer is, bias still does creep in. An artificial situation such as an interview will have an impact on the information respondents are prepared to provide about their attitudes and opinions (see Oakley, 1981). Despite attempts at rapport, interviews will result in selective information, the part that the respondent is prepared to make available and that she or he thinks will be of interest to the researcher. This is known as *interview effect*.

Interviewing on a large scale that involves employing interviewers, who may be less committed to the enquiry than the researcher, leads to problems called the '*hired-hand effect*'. This includes the accidental mis-checking of an item on a schedule; the failure of adequately recording open answers; deliberately questioning the wrong people out of convenience; and even outright fraudulent completion of schedules by the interviewer without interviewing anyone. Hired-hand effect, especially the minor accidental mistakes, is often difficult to spot.

It has been established for a long time that the 'race', class and gender of an interviewer can affect the answers given by respondents (Schuman and Converse, 1971; Hatchett and Schuman, 1975; Sudman and Bradburn, 1974). Deming (1944) noted that *interviewer bias* was a well-established source of error in surveys. He looked at a study by Stuart Rice that showed the response of an interviewee can be highly influenced by the interviewer. Two thousand 'destitute men' were interviewed and their destitution was attributed to the 'evils of alcohol' by those interviewed by a teetotaller and to 'industrialisation' by those interviewed by a socialist. Deming suggests that the educational, economic status, environmental background, political, religious and social beliefs of interviewers will all affect the interview situation and thus the results. A further study in America (Williams, 1964) showed that, in a survey where all the respondents were black and interview-ers were black or white, the largest potential source of bias occurred when questions were 'threatening', that is, they challenged accepted social norms. In particular, middle-class white interviewers obtained a significantly higher percentage of conservative responses from lower-class blacks than did middle-class black interviewers on these highly threatening questions.

Pilot survey

It doesn't matter how experienced you are, problems will always arise when carrying out a survey. To minimise the potential problems you should undertake a pilot survey. The pilot survey will bring to light problems that you can put right before doing the full scale survey. A *pilot* survey usually consists of two stages: the pre-pilot and the complete pilot.

Pre-pilot

The *pre-pilot* usually just tests the adequacy of the schedule or questionnaire. By asking a small number of people, the pre-pilot indicates whether any of the questions cause problems for respondent or interviewer and whether they flow from one to the next in a logical and meaningful sequence. It helps if the respondents at this stage are as similar as possible to the people in the final sample.

> **Student Activity 4.17**
> **Pre-pilot the schedule you prepared in Student Activity 4.11. Make a note of any questions that are a problem.**

Complete pilot

A *complete* pilot of a survey involves a small-scale trial run-through of the entire survey from data collection to analysis to see if it works and whether the right kind of information is being collected.

When undertaking a survey as part of a student project you are unlikely to go further than the pilot stage, that is, you are unlikely to have the time or resources to do a large-scale survey. In practice, the report you produce will be the report of a pilot survey and you should indicate that you are aware of this.

The pilot survey provides you with an opportunity to assess the *reliability* and *validity* of the survey (see pages 31–2).

Survey reliability

Social surveys are presumed to be reliable, because they use a schedule of questions to measure the same thing in the same way each time the schedule is applied. If you use a tape-measure to measure someone's height you would expect it to be consistent. If you had a tape-measure that stretched you would regard it as unreliable and probably unusable. Checking a questionnaire or interview schedule for reliability, however, is not as easy as checking to see whether your tape-measure has stretched.

There is no sure way of testing the reliability of a survey. The problem is that the subject matter of a social survey is both complex and changing.

External reliability

One method of testing the reliability of a questionnaire over time (so-called *external* reliability) is by administering it to the same sample again and checking to see if you get the same results. The problem with this *test–retest* method is that the sample itself will have changed from the first to the second testing. So you will not know whether any difference in answers is due to an unreliable survey or a change in attitude and knowledge of the respondents.

Internal reliability

However, there are various ways of assessing the *internal* consistency of the survey. By far the best way to do this is to divide the responses on the questionnaire into two groups at random and compare the answers on each half for the sample. A high degree of agreement between the two sets of results suggests, although by no means confirms, a reliable set of questions, that is, a set that is measuring the same thing at any given point in time. This reliability test is known as the *split-half* technique. Split-half thus gives some idea of the reliability of the questions at one point in time but does not tell us whether the measurement is reliable over time.

Reliability is not enough in itself though. A questionnaire, for example, may be consistent, but it may be consistently measuring the wrong thing.

Validity

The major concern of operationalisation is the problem of *validity*. How can you be sure that the operational measurement still measures the theoretical concept? For example, do Townsend's questions about deprivation actually measure poverty?

There is no way in which the validity of a set of questions can be 'tested'. The choice of questions is ultimately a subjective decision of the researcher based on theoretical consideration, personal preference and prior experience. The pilot survey can show whether a question 'works' but even so there is no guarantee that it means the same thing to all the respondents. Different age groups or different ethnic groups may understand different things by similar questions. The connotation of a word can be quite different for different respondents (see the section on *denotation and conotation* on page 46). Assessing the answers to questions in the pilot will give you some clue as to when very different interpretations are being put on questions (this usually shows up in 'open' questions). Subtle differences of meaning in closed questions are often very difficult to detect because fitting answers into pre-codings may conceal different meanings. So, in short, there is no simple check on question validity. There is always a problem of whether or not the questions represent the concept the researcher is trying to find out about from the point of view of both the researcher and the respondent.

Pilot sample

There is no fixed size for a pilot sample. It depends on the complexity of the interview schedule and the nature of the population being sampled. If it is to be at all meaningful, then each interviewer should do a minimum of five pilot interviews and the total should not be less than about twenty-five.

Piloting a questionnaire or schedule interview is an extremely important part of the research process. There is a tendency for researchers to skip this part and to get on with the research proper. They subsequently regret having missed the pilot survey out! The final data collection is a time-consuming and expensive process that you only do once so it is important to get it right. Piloting the research is invaluable in identifying problems such as the wording or ordering of the questions, ambiguities in instructions to interviewers, the adequacy of the introductory statement, the suitability of the coding frame and difficulties in the analysis of the data.

Student Activity 4.18
Pilot the schedule you pre-piloted in student activity 4.10.
1. Are there any remaining problems with the schedule?
2. What problems arise in locating respondents?
3. See whether the schedule gives you the sort of data you want and in a way that you maybe able to analyse.
4. Assess the interviews to see whether any form of interview bias arises when carrying out your pilot. If so, consider how you would overcome it.
NOTE We will look at how to analyse the data you collected below.

As we have said, when undertaking a project you may not be able to do much more than pilot your survey. This is not unusual and you should not be overly concerned about it. It is important that you undertake a complete pilot, including analysis. When writing up the report indicate what changes you would make to your hypotheses, research instrument, sample and so on, if you were to undertake a larger survey.

Response rate

A major problem with surveys is ensuring a sufficient response rate, that is, the number of people in your sample who agree to participate in your survey. The response rate for postal questionnaires is often very low, between 10% and 40%. For schedules administered by interviewers the response rate is usually higher, between 40% and 80%. A sample is chosen to represent a population and if only 30% return their questionnaires then the research becomes problematic. You have to ask whether the group of people who returned questionnaires differ from those who did not? In short, the problem with non-response is that you are unlikely to know whether the people who responded are a biased subgroup. The bigger the non-response the bigger the potential distortion will be.

Response rates to mailed questionnaires can be improved by various techniques. Researchers should enclose stamped reply envelopes, and some pre-contact is likely to be advantageous. Follow-up procedures, such as sending reminders, will usually lead to increased response rates. Economic incentives also seem certain to raise response rates but may increase costs to unacceptable levels. The questionnaire should be constructed in a way that is likely to appeal to the respondent. It should direct itself to arousing, rather than assuming, the interest of the respondent (Harvey, 1987a).

Analysis

Having spent considerable time and effort operationalising concepts, devising questions, constructing a schedule or questionnaire, interviewing respondents or distributing and following-up questionnaires it is important to make a good job of the analysis. Otherwise all the work will have been for nothing. There are some standard practices that you can follow to analyse sociological surveys. We will outline some basic ones below. A more detailed exploration of data analysis is provided in Appendix 2.

In the end, the analysis is guided by the hypotheses you are exploring and relies on your ingenuity and imagination as a sociologist in relating the data

COMPUTER ANALYSIS SOFTWARE PACKAGES It is impossible for a single chapter on survey data analysis to refer to all the different software packages. For the purposes of illustration, only SPSS-PC+ will be referred to directly. SPSS is the most established survey analysis package and has been around in various mainframe versions since the 1960s. It is extremely comprehensive even in its micro version. It is, unfortunately, expensive and so your school or college is not likely to have many copies of it. A lot of cheaper, less comprehensive, packages approximate the SPSS approach so it is a useful reference. If you have access to SPSS then you will find Bryman and Cramer (1990) useful for a detailed account of using SPSS for data analysis.

to sociological theory. We will explore this further later in the chapter when we look at a study of religion and delinquency.

Coding your data

Completed interview schedules or questionnaires provide a wealth of material but they have to be approached systematically if you are to make sense of the data. The first job is to extract the data from the questionnaires and put it into a form that is easier to refer to and to manipulate. There is nothing more confusing when analysing survey data than to be constantly shuffling piles of questionnaires whilst trying to show the relationship between different variables.

The job of analysis is made much easier if you use a computer. You do not need to use a large mainframe computer, a personal microcomputer is usually adequate and preferable as it gives you direct control over the process. Given the right software, you can use the microcomputer to write the schedule, to store the data, to undertake the analysis and to write the final report.

Coding frame

The first steps in analysis is to code the data and create a data file. The easiest way to do this is to draw up a coding frame. The *coding frame* lists all the alternative values for a given variable and allocates a number for each possible answer. The coding frame for *closed* questions can be taken directly from an interview schedule (see Extract 4.2). Additional coding for *open* questions needs to be devised. To make questionnaires easier to use and less cluttered for the respondent, it is usual not to include codings (see Extract 4.3). The coding frame should then be drawn up for the questionnaire before attempting to code data (see Extract 4.7).

Data file

What you then need to do is to produce a grid on which to record the appropriate codes for each respondent. Normally, each *row* of the grid represents a *respondent* and each *column* represents a *variable*. Sometimes a variable has more than 9 values and takes up more than one column of figures. For example, question 30 in the survey asks for age and values range from 18 upwards. This takes up two columns.

To produce the *data file* you have to fill in the grid. Start with the first questionnaire or schedule. Write an identity number on the schedule (if there is not one already there) and then enter the identity number in the first column of the grid. You then go through the schedule inserting the correct code for each variable in the appropriate column. Be very careful about how you do this as errors can easily creep in at this stage and they are very hard to detect later. One way to reduce errors is for two people (or teams) to code the data independently and then to compare the two data files. This is very effective but increases the work load. The data file for the answers to the example questionnaire can be found in Appendix 1 at the back of the book.

Student Activity 4.19
1. **Look at Appendix 1. What answer did respondent number 3 give to the question *Do you agree with homosexuality being included in sex education at school?* What age did respondent 150 think the consenting age limit for males should be?**
2. **Code the data you got from your pilot survey, Student Activity 4.18.**

CODING DATA There are only two circumstances when coding your questionnaire and transferring the data to a data file might not be worth doing. The first is when you have less than twenty questionnaires or schedules. The second is when your questionnaire or schedule is made up of predominantly open, uncoded questions which have resulted in a wealth of qualitative data. In the first case you are unlikely to do much explanatory analysis and will probably only be able to report numbers in various categories in a simple descriptive manner. In the second case you probably should have adopted a different technique from the outset, such as in-depth interviewing, because the bulk of the analysis will be of an ethnographic type (see Chapter 7). Other than in these unlikely circumstances always create a datafile. It may seem like hard work to start with but will make life much easier later, even if you do the analysis by hand rather than use a computer.

NOTE Apple and IBM–PC compatible versions of the example data file and SPSS–PC+ 'include file' program to generate tables and crosstabulations are available, on floppy disk, from Lee Harvey (see details on page 268).

Answer to Student Activity 4.19, part 1

Respondent 3's answers are in row 3 of the datafile (Appendix 1). The inclusion of homosexuality in sex education at school is variable 7. The first column of the data file consists of 3 digits (the identity number). The variables begin in the next column (that is, the second column of figures is variable 2). So, variable 7 is in the eighth column. The code in column 8 for row 3 is 2. The coding sheet (Extract 4.7) shows that code 2 for variable 7 means 'No'.

Extract 4.7

CODING FRAME: ATTITUDES TOWARDS HOMOSEXUALITY

Var	Qu.	Question	Values	Code
1	1	Had you previously heard of Clause 28?	yes	1
			no	2
			missing	9
2	2	Do you understand the clause?	yes	1
			no	2
			missing	9
3	3	Do you agree with the clause?	yes	1
			no	2
			missing	9
4	4	Do you feel that Clause 28 affects only ...	yes	1
			no	2
			missing	9
5	5	Do you think that the clause will make...	yes	1
			no	2
			missing	9
6	6	Do you agree with homosexuality being...	yes	1
			no	2
			missing	9
7	7	Do you think the inclusion of...	yes	1
			no	2
			missing	9
8	8	Do you consider that the timing of ...	yes	1
			no	2
			missing	9
9	9a	...aware through friends	yes	1
			missing	9
10	9b	...through parents	yes	1
			missing	9
11	9c	...through school	yes	1
			missing	9
12	9d	...through media	yes	1
			missing	9
13	10a	are gays most at risk from AIDS?	yes	1
			no	2
			missing	9
14	10b	Are heterosexuals most at risk?	yes	1
			no	2
			missing	9
15	10c	Are intravenous drug users most at risk?	yes	1
			no	2
			missing	9
16	10d	Are lesbians most at risk from AIDS?	yes	1
			no	2
			missing	9
17	10e	Are prostitutes most at risk from AIDS?	yes	1
			no	2
			missing	9
18	11	Any truth in the term 'the gay plague'	yes	1
			no	2
			missing	9

Var	Qu.	Question	Values	Code
19	12a	Legal age for females?	years	*
20	12b	Legal age for males?	years	*
21	13a	Age limit be for females?	years	*
22	13b	Age limit be for males?	years	*
23	14	Should homosexuality be made illegal?	yes	1
			no	2
			missing	9
24	15a	Do you think lesbian acts of affection...	yes	1
			no	2
			missing	9
25	15b	Do you think gay acts of affection...	yes	1
			no	2
			missing	9
26	16	Anyone in your family or social circle..	yes	1
			no	2
			missing	9
27	17	...discuss homosexuality with children?	yes	1
			no	2
			missing	9
28	18a	Do you agree with gay men rearing...	yes	1
			no	2
			missing	9
29	18b	... lesbians rearing children?	yes	1
			no	2
			missing	9
30		Age	years	*
31		Sex	male	1
			female	2
32		Religion	Atheist	1
			Other	2
			'Christian' & Protestant (exc C/E & RC)	3
			Church of England	4
			Roman Catholic	5
			Muslim	7
			Sikh	8
			Missing	9
33		Would you describe yourself as		
			African/African-Caribbean	1
			Asian	2
			European	3
			Other	4
34		Type of college course		
			Design and printing	1
			Government and sociology	2
			Catering and tourism	3

* code is the number provided by the respondent

NOTE: variable 1 begins in column 2 of the data file. The first column (3 digits) is the respondent identity number.

Frequency tables

Once you have constructed your data file you can start the analysis. We will use the example sample survey to illustrate some analytic techniques for testing hypotheses. The questionnaire, coding frame and data file are provided so you could check the analysis we have done and develop your own analysis. Inevitably, when dealing with survey data, you are confronted by having to deal with quantitative material. Not everybody is comfortable with numerical data, and manipulating figures is more of a problem for some people than others. What we have suggested, however, is that you can come up with interesting results without being swamped by statistical procedures.

The first thing is to produce *frequency tables* for each variable. This provides both actual numbers and percentages. It involves counting the numbers of times each code occurs in a column. Consider variable 1, 'Had you previously heard of Clause 28?'. Look at the data file in Appendix 1. Reading down the column there are fifty '1's, ninety-nine '2's and two '9's. This can be presented as a frequency table as in Table 4.5. This can, of course, be done quickly if you use a computer software package that is designed for this purpose. Packages like SPSS-PC+, MINITAB and others are able to provide frequency tables from a data file like the one in Appendix 1.

Table 4.5 provides a model that you would be advised to follow when creating frequency tables. (SPSS, for example, produces a table very similar to this.) Note that the table has a heading with the variable number and name, and the value labels are on the left followed by the codes used to represent them in the data file. The third column is the *actual frequencies* (the number of time each code appears). The fourth column gives the *percentage* that each frequency is of the *whole sample*. The fifth column is the percentage *adjusted* for missing values, this is called the *valid* percentage.

So, in the example, 50 people said 'Yes' they had previously heard of Clause 28, 99 said 'No', and there were 2 missing cases. In percentage terms 33.1% said 'Yes', (that is, (50/151) x 100 = .331 x 100 = 33.1%) 65.6% said 'No' and there was no information on 1.3% of the sample. If the missing values are excluded then the 'valid percentage' (that is, calculated on a reduced sample of 149) is 33.6% 'Yes' and 66.4% 'No'.

You should construct the frequency tables for each of the variables. This can be a time-consuming process if you do not have a computer but you usually need this basic data for two reasons. First, it provides a detailed summary of the responses so that you have a complete description of the sample. Second, it acts as another check on the data file. If you come across a code that is not possible (for example, if there was a 7 in the column for variable 3) then you must go back to the original schedule and find out what the proper value should be. You do this by finding the questionnaire with the same identification number as the one recorded at the start of the row that contains the incorrect code. Look up the appropriate variable on the original questionnaire or schedule and then change the incorrect code in the data file, inserting the correct one. You will then need to correct your frequency table if it has already been compiled.

Table 4.5
V1. Had you previously heard of Clause 28?

Value label	Value	Frequency	Percentage	Valid percentage
Yes	1	50	33.1	33.6
No	2	99	65.6	66.4
Missing	9	2	1.3	
TOTAL		151	100.0	100.0

Student Activity 4.20
Using the data set in Appendix 1,
1. Compile a frequency table for variable 3 similar to Table 4.5. What percentage of the sample agree with Clause 28? Does this suggest that the population being surveyed support government initiatives?
2. Refer to the hypotheses in the example answer to Student Activity 4.6. What other frequency tables would you need to assess all parts of hypothesis 2? Compile the frequency tables necessary. Is hypothesis 2 confirmed? What do you conclude from the results?
3. Compare the support for Clause 28 among males and females. What do you conclude from this comparison?

Example answer to Student Activity 4.20, part 3

To compare the support for Clause 28 for males and females you need to split the answers to variable 3 (Question 3 'Do you agree with the clause?') into two groups, those for males and those for females. The easiest way to do this by hand is to draw a 2 by 3 grid . Write 'males' and 'females' on top of the two columns and 'yes' (1), 'no' (2) and 'missing' (9) on the rows (see below). Go down columns for variables 3 and variables 31 (sex) simultaneously. Put a mark in the appropriate square of the grid for each person in the sample, then total the number of marks in each square. The grid below shows the results. Check these using the data in Appendix 1.

	Male	Female
Yes (1)	41	26
No (2)	35	39
Missing (9)	5	5

This is known as a *crosstabulation*. In this case it is the crosstabulation of variable 3 ('Do you agree with the clause?') by variable 31 (sex). You normally exclude all missing value categories and add in the totals for the rows and columns. So the crosstabulation ends up as follows:

	Male	Female	Totals
Yes (1)	41	26	67
No (2)	35	39	74
Totals	76	65	141

Missing values 10

This shows that more males (41) than females (26) supported Clause 28. However, there were more males than females who answered the question. So, it would be useful to record what *percentage* of males and females supported the clause. The table below shows the raw numbers and the % of males and females in each cell (the column percentages). This shows that 47.5% of the sample as a whole supported the clause. There was a difference in male and female support; 53.9% of males supported the clause compared to 40% of females.

	Male	Female	Totals
Yes (1)	41	26	67
	53.9%	40.0%	47.5%
No (2)	35	39	74
	46.1%	60.0%	52.5%
Totals	76	65	141
	53.9%	46.1%	100%

Missing values 10

A more extensive account of data analysis using the example data can be found in Appendix 2. For many readers, though, the use of frequency tables and percentages will be all that you will need.

Student Activity 4.21
Using the analytic techniques described above test the hypotheses you drew up in Student Activity 4.6.

In the following section, we will look at an example of the way in which survey research, using fairly simple statistical analysis, has been used to test social theory.

Religion and delinquency

Travis Hirschi and Rodney Stark (1969) undertook a study of the effect of religion on delinquency. They argued that relations between religiousness and delinquency offer a critical test of the relevance of religion. If religion is immaterial in an area where it has concentrated its efforts then its failure seems to be acute.

Background
Despite the assumptions of law enforcers, the judiciary and the clergy in the United States that religion has a beneficial effect on delinquency, empirical studies are less conclusive. Unfortunately, there is a

relation between the findings and the religiosity of the researcher. While most studies conducted by criminologists suggest that religion has little or no effect, research by religionists tends to indicate that religion is just what it has always been thought to be, a powerful "aid to the sword" in the maintenance of conformity, a factor in delinquency at least equal to

NOTE ON HIRSCHI AND STARK'S STUDY In reviewing this study we report some of the questions used. These adopt American phraseology and slang which may seem dated and alien. We have also numbered the questions sequentially, although this does not correspond to the original numbering on Hirschi and Stark's lengthy questionnaire.

As a check, on the self-report data the police records of reported delinquency for the boys were also made available to the researchers. Hirschi and Stark did a separate analysis using them as the operationalisation of delinquency. There were considerable differences in self-reported and official data on delinquency (as one would expect, see page 80). However, the overall results for self-report and official records were very similar. Therefore we will not report the results based on the official data.

FUNCTIONALIST ANALYSES OF RELIGION focus on the contribution of religion to social solidarity, consensus and values. Emile Durkheim (1912) saw all societies as divided into the *sacred* and the *profane*. Using the example of Australian aborigines, Durkheim showed how religion was a reification of society. That is, religion, with its sacred objects, is used a channel for the veneration of society. Hierarchies of gods and religious beliefs reflect the organisation of society, the power structures and the norms and values that operate in society. Religion thus has a function of a providing a simplified version of society that people can relate to. Apart from anything else, it is easier for a person to direct feelings of awe towards a symbol than towards something as complex as society.

Religion thus served a function of promoting social consensus. Religious worship is the exaltation of society. Through religion, people recognise the importance of the social group and their dependence upon it. Religion provides social solidarity, that is, it strengthens the unity of the group.

Ritual is important in this respect. It strengthens the social group as its members come together in religious rituals to express their faith in common values and beliefs. In so doing members communicate and understand the moral bonds that unite them.

Bronislaw Malinowski (1954) and Talcott Parsons (1951) agree that religion reinforces social values and promotes solidarity. However, they see religion not so much as reflecting society as a whole but as being focused around specific areas of *strain*. These include critical life events, such as birth, death, puberty and marriage, and unpredictable and uncontrollable forces such as the weather and its impact on agriculture.

The functionalist perspective emphasises the positive contributions of religion to society and tends to ignore its dysfunctional aspects. Functionalism's preoccupation with integration, harmony and solidarity leads it to ignore religious divisions within communities. Such divisions are between religions (for example, Christian versus Muslim in Lebanon) and within religions (for example, Catholic versus Protestant in Northern Ireland).

the variables traditionally considered important by criminologists. (Hirschi and Stark, 1969, p. 203)

Aim

The *aim* of the study was to see if religious belief and affiliation had any effect on delinquency.

Theory

Hirschi and Stark assess functionalist analyses of religion. Functionalists argue that religion functions to maintain social control. Religious sanctioning systems play an important role in ensuring conformity to social norms (Durkheim, 1912; Davis, 1948). The Durkheimian view is that religion plays this role:

1. By legitimating social and individual values.
2. Through rituals that reinforce commitment to these values.
3. Through a system of eternal reward and punishment that helps to ensure the embodiment of these values in actual behaviour.

Religious ritual has a central place in functionalist analyses. According to Hirschi and Stark, involvement in ritual promotes:

1. The internalisation or acceptance of moral values including the belief that people deserve fair and just treatment.
2. Aceptance of the legitimacy of legal authority.
3. Belief in the literal existence of a supernatural world and therefore the belief that one may be punished in the world to come for violations in this world.

Belief in supernatural sanctions is presumed by sociologists to promote and maintain conformity. For example, Edward Ross (1920) has argued that Christianity has made the doctrine of future life a strong deterrent influence.

Hirschi and Stark accept that people probably do have internal values and ethics that sometimes govern their actions. What they questioned was whether religion has anything to do with sustaining these personal values. Does belief in hell-fire and heavenly glory deter people from unlawful acts?

Hypotheses

They had three main *hypotheses*:

1. Religious training prevents delinquency by promoting the development of moral values.
2. Religious training prevents delinquency by promoting the acceptance of conventional authority.
3. Religious training prevents delinquency because it promotes belief in the existence of supernatural sanctions.

Concepts

These hypotheses involve five concepts: delinquency, morality, conventional authority, belief in supernatural sanctions, and religiosity.

Operationalisation

Delinquency was operationalised using the following self-report questions:

1. *Have you ever taken little things (worth less than $2) that did not belong to you?*
2. *Have you ever taken things of some value (between $2 and $50) that did not belong to you?*

3. *Have you ever taken things of large value (worth over $50) that did not belong to you?*
4. *Have you ever taken a car for a ride without the owner's permission?*
5. *Have you ever banged up* [destroyed] *something that did not belong to you on purpose?*
6. *Not counting fights that you may have had with a brother or sister, have you ever beaten up on* [sic] *anyone or hurt anyone on purpose?*

These represented operationalisations of petty larceny [theft], grand larceny, auto theft, vandalism and assault. Respondents were asked to date any acts that fell into these categories. Those who admitted to two or more offences in the year prior to the survey are referred to below as the 'delinquent' group.

Morality was operationalised through two statements that the respondents were asked to agree or disagree with:

7. *To get ahead, you have to do some things that are not right.*
8. *Suckers deserve to be taken advantage of.*

Wordly authority was operationalised using the following two statements:

9. *It is alright to get around the law if you can get away with it.*
10. *I have a lot of respect for the local police.*

Belief in supernatural sanctions was operationalised through the following two statements:

11. *There is life beyond death.*
12. *The devil actually exists.*

'High believers' were those people who agreed with both statements.

Religiosity was operationalised through church attendance. This was in accord with the theoretical view about involvement in religious ritual.

There were five categories of church attendance:

A. Once a week
B. 2–3 times a month
C. Once a month and/or religious holidays
D. Hardly ever
E. Never.

Student Activity 4.22
Do you think that these operationalisations are adequate for the study? If not what would be appropriate changes? If you were to do a study in Britain today, how might you operationalise these concepts?

Sample
The sample was drawn from all students entering the public junior and senior high schools in Western Contra Costa County, California, in the autumn of 1964. The original sample was 5,545 students, 4,077 (74%) completed the questionnaire. This total sample consisted of 1,588 white boys, 1,001 black boys, 675 white girls and 813 black girls.

Controls
Hirschi and Stark controlled for gender and 'race' in their study and presented data separately for black and white, boys and girls. For illustrative purposes we shall just use the data for the white boys.

Analysis
Table 4.5 shows the percentages of 'delinquents' (white boys who admitted

THEORIES OF RELIGION There are other theories of religion that we do not have space to pursue here. See, for example, Max Weber's (1904) classic work *The Protestant Ethic and the Spirit of Capitalism*, in which he argues that religion can lead to social change. For a phenomenological perspective see Peter Berger and Thomas Luckmann (1963). Bryan Turner (1983) provides a materialist view of religion. The *secularization thesis*, which suggests the inevitable decline of religion, is discussed in Acquaviva (1979), Bruce (1990), Glock and Stark (1965) and Wilson (1966). Bynum *et al.* (1986) looks at gender and religion. Cashmore (1979) and Mortimer (1982) provide analyses of Rastafarianism and Islam respectively.

committing two or more delinquent acts) who agree with various statements. It shows that delinquents were more likely to agree than disagree with amoral statements (No. 6 and No. 7). It also showed that they were more likely to feel it was 'all right to break the law if they could get away with it' (44% of delinquents agreed with this compared to 13% who disagreed). Delinquents were also three times more likely to disagree than agree that they had respect for the local police.

For each of these four statements the *gamma* coefficient is reasonably high. The gamma coefficient is a measure of association. The nearer gamma is to 1 the higher the relationship between delinquency and attitude. The nearer gamma is to 0 the lower the relationship.

These results suggest that delinquency is fairly strongly related to attitudes about morality and authority. This is what you might expect. The question is, to what extent does religion effect this relationship?

Hypothesis 1 suggests that religion prevents delinquency by promoting the development of moral values. Table 4.7 shows that high church attenders are virtually no different from low church attenders in agreeing with the statements about morality (Nos. 7 and 8).

Hypothesis 2 suggests that religious training prevents delinquency by promoting the acceptance of conventional authority. Table 4.7 shows that high church attenders are not much different from low attenders in their attitude towards law and the police.

So church attendance does not seem to have any effect on attitudes and hypotheses 1 and 2 are rejected.

Hypothesis 3 suggests that religious training prevents delinquency because it promotes belief in the existence of supernatural sanctions. Table 4.7 does suggest that church attendance is related to belief in supernatural sanctions (49% of high attenders are high believers while only 12% of low attenders are high believers). However, the final row of Table 4.6 shows that there is no relationship between delinquency and belief in supernatural sanctions. So hypothesis 3 is also rejected.

Overall, then, it appears that religiosity has no effect on delinquency. The

---

GAMMA is a measure of association between variables. It provides an indication of the extent to which one variable is related to another. If, for example, all the boys who committed two or more delinquent acts (the delinquents) agreed with statement 7 and all the non-delinquents disagreed then gamma would be equal to 1. If, as in Table 4.6, some delinquents agree and some disagree then the value of gamma will be less than 1. The nearer it is to zero the weaker the relationship between the two variables. In practice, in social situations, a gamma value of more than 0.2 can be regarded as indicating some degree of relationship.

Table 4.6 Percentage of white boys committing two or more delinquent acts, by attitude

Statement	Agree	Undecided	Disagree	Gamma
No. 7	30	22	12	–0.27
No. 8	27	26	13	–0.26
No. 9	44	29	13	–0.41
No. 10	13	23	39	+0.34
High believers	19	20	16	–0.03

Table 4.8 Percentage of black boys committing two or more delinquent acts, by attitude

Statement	Agree	Undecided	Disagree	Gamma
No. 7	26	28	17	–0.12
No. 8	26	28	17	–0.12
No. 9	33	27	16	–0.18
No. 10	15	32	33	+0.26
High believers	19	21	25	+0.09

Table 4.7 Percentage of white boys accepting amoral statements, by church attendance

| Statement | Church attendance | | | | | Gamma |
	A	B	C	D	E	
No. 7	25	29	30	27	32	–0.04
No. 8	26	30	35	28	35	–0.08
No. 9	10	8	18	9	17	–0.13
No. 10	65	63	62	60	49	+0.09
High believers	49	28	23	19	12	–0.40
Delinquent	17	21	23	20	22	+0.02

Table 4.9 Percentage of black boys accepting amoral statements, by church attendance

| Statement | Church attendance | | | | | Gamma |
	A	B	C	D	E	
No. 7	43	41	43	53	40	–0.03
No. 8	49	48	60	50	52	–0.04
No. 9	21	20	28	32	28	–0.10
No. 10	62	65	56	49	37	+0.09
High believers	50	34	30	21	32	–0.30
Delinquent	22	24	21	25	40	+0.10

final line of Table 4.7 would further confirm this, as the percentage of delinquents (those admitting two or more offences) varies only slightly for different church attendance groups.

Student Activity 4.23

1. **Are you convinced by the logic of the analysis? If not, what do you think is wrong with it?**
2. **Do you think that it is reasonable to do the analysis using as delinquents those who have admitted two or more offences in the last year?**
3. **Would it have been preferable to have simply compared church attenders with church non-attenders?**

Hirschi and Stark argued that the data for all four groups supported the findings that religiosity had no effect on delinquency. This raises doubts about the functionalist view of religion. As religion appears to have no impact on delinquency, the idea that religion serves to maintain social control is undermined. This is reinforced by the apparent lack of effect that belief in religious sanctions has on ensuring conformity to social norms.

Functionalists provide only one view of the role of religion. Marxists argue that religion has traditionally been used to oppress people. It has been used as a direct instrument of social control (for example, the inquisition in Spain, fundamentalist religious courts in Iran and so on). Religion also provides legitimacy for unequal and oppressive social structures. It thus has an *ideological* role (see page 15). However, it has been argued that, in Western capitalist societies, the once-dominant role of religion as an ideological tool has been replaced by education (Althusser, 1971).

Student Activity 4.24

1. **Do the data in Tables 4.8 and 4.9 (which show the results for the black boys in the sample) confirm the conclusions based on the white boys?**
2. **How might the research above be developed to take account of the Marxist view, especially the idea that education is a more important ideological tool than religion.**

Falsificationism

Social surveys are a major tool of quantitative social research. Quantitative methodology attempts to provide *explanations* of the social world. The social survey is the means by which data is collected. The data is analysed to test hypotheses about the relationships between variables. These relationships are suggested by sociological theory and the variables are the result of operationalising theoretical concepts.

This positivist explanatory approach *implies* causal relationships (as we discussed in Chapters 1 and 2). Establishing cause and effect in the social world is extremely difficult. The quantitative survey approach implies cause but rarely *proves* a causal relationship. Social phenomena are generally too complex for it to be possible to establish causes. Quantitative sociologists tend to talk about 'likely factors' that lead to a particular phenomenon, rather than their specific causes. The aim of most quantitative research is to identify the independent factors that have an effect upon a given dependent factor.

The process by which this is done is summarised in Figure 4.1 (see page 102) and is based upon Robert Merton's notion of *middle range theory*. Middle range theory lies between grand, sweeping, but untestable specula-

---

MARXIST ANALYSES OF RELIGION

In his analysis of religion, which predated Durkheim's by half a century, Marx also argued that religion reflected society. However, he went further and argued that religion *reifies* the social structure (McLellan, 1977). That is, religious systems represent an idealised version of the existing social order. For example, Christianity referred to 'the rich man in his castle and the poor man at his gate' as the natural order of things. Through the notion of the Virgin Mary, it controlled women's sexuality and promoted the idea of women as nurturers. Christianity has also been used to excuse racial abuse such as the slave trade.

Marx thus argued that, rather than contributing to social solidarity, religion was used to *oppress* people. Religion is an *instrument* of oppression and is also used to *legitimate* class, gender and racial oppression. Marx described religion as the 'opium of the people'. By this he meant that religion operates to dull people's awareness of their oppressed position and to provide them with a rationale for accepting their lot. Religion is thus an instrument of the ruling class who use it to maintain their own power and status.

The Marxist view of religion has been applied to religions other than Christianity. For example, Muslim and Hindu religions are used to control and subordinate women, and the caste system in India is based on Hindu religious doctrine.

tion about the social world, on the one hand, and microscopic 'proven' statements about an insignificant aspect of the social world on the other. Middle range theories are statements about aspects of the social world that can be tested by reference to data. Epistemologically, this is directly linked to a form of positivism called *falsificationism*.

Falsificationism asserts that it is impossible to *prove* scientific statements on the basis of observable data because there may always be a future instance that will reverse any proof. What it is possible to do, they claim, is to *disprove* statements on the basis of empirical evidence. Proper scientific theories, then, are ones that involve statements that are testable and are capable of being refuted. These are what Karl Popper, the best known falsificationist, calls 'bold conjectures'. At any point in time scientific theories, consisting of conjectures that have been tested and not refuted, are the best theories we have. Science progresses through a constant process of testing and refuting bold conjectures.

Hirschi and Stark (1969), as we explored above, drew up three hypotheses that suggested a relationship between delinquency and religion and then collected data to test them out. For example, their third hypothesis suggested that religious training prevents delinquency because it promotes belief in the existence of supernatural sanctions. As we saw, there is no relationship between delinquency and belief in supernatural sanctions. This leads us to reject the hypothesis. Having tested all three hypotheses we conclude that, contrary to the original theory, religion does not have an effect on delinquency.

In this way quantitative sociologists attempt to uncover causal-type factors. By testing hypotheses derived from theory, quantitative sociologists are able either to confirm that a theory appears to be adequate or to suggest that the theory is inadequate and needs to be modified.

The middle range theory approach is cumulative. It suggests that testing one set of hypotheses derived from theory will lead to modifications in the theory. A new set of hypotheses will then emerge by which the new theory can be further tested, and so on round the circle. Each circuit, it is assumed, will lead to an ever better theory.

In practice, few sociologists are likely to go round the circuit more than once. The usual approach, when writing a report, is to put forward how suggested changes in theory can be further tested and to leave this up to other people to pursue. A single circuit would be the most you could do in a student project and you are unlikely to be able to do more than make tentative suggestions about the adequacy of an established theory. It is unlikely that you will be able to suggest alternative theories.

Criticisms of the quantitative approach

The quantitative approach is criticised on a number of grounds, however. First, non-positivists (as we suggested in Chapter 2) argue that it makes no sense to talk about *causes* in the social world in the same sense as in the natural world. It is not just a matter of it being difficult to establish social causes. People are reflective, conscious beings so they are able to change the way they behave and are not governed by causal laws. Therefore it is incorrect to look for explanations of social phenomena.

Second, the falsificationist approach assumes that theory can be changed on the basis of observation that refutes it. People opposed to falsificationism argue that this can only lead to minor changes, a sort of fine-tuning of the theory. However, if the theory is *fundamentally* flawed it will never be thrown out in its entirety by this approach. Why? Because the theory determines what empirical evidence is collected and what hypotheses are tested. To change a theory fundamentally involves a complete shift to an entirely different perspective, or *paradigm*, as Thomas Kuhn (1962) called it. This is like lateral thinking. Falsificationism does not allow lateral thinking because it is preoccupied with tinkering with existing theory.

This leads to the third broad objection, that the quantitative approach to sociology, like all falsificationist approaches, ignores the *theory laden nature of observation* (Chalmers, 1978). In short, this view suggests that observations or 'facts' do not exist in their own right but only make sense in terms of the theoretical context in which they are located. 'The Earth is the centre of the solar system' is not an incorrect 'fact' because we are able to observe that the Earth travels round the sun. The statement is flawed because we have a sophisticated theory about the nature of solar systems, planetary movements, gravitational forces, and so on. Once, when such theories did not exist, it was well known that the Earth must be the centre of the solar system and the sun revolve around it.

Given that observation of 'facts' only make sense in terms of theory, then observation alone will provide no basis for fundamentally testing a theory, as the meaning of the observations is determined by the theory that they are supposed to be testing.

The social survey as a non-positivist method

Although the social survey is mainly associated with the quantitative approach it has also been used by critical researchers and phenomenologists. It is not the survey itself but the use to which it is put in the quantitative approach that makes it quantitative. Critical social researchers use the survey for collecting information, but, rather than try to establish causal factors, they use it to provide an overview of social processes and structures in the same way that 'official statistics' are used as material for dialectical analysis (see Chapter 3). Some phenomenologists, particularly interactionists, also make use of surveys, but as exploratory or initial material that needs to be analysed in more detail. Surveys, which provide aggregate statistical material, they argue, hide what social processes and phenomenologists seek to uncover what is going on 'behind the mask' of social surveys.

> A **PARADIGM** is a prevailing view of science (or a scientific discipline) that provides a framework for tackling problems. It provides guidelines to practising scientists about how they might do their work.
>
> Thomas Kuhn (1962, 1970) argued that paradigms operate on a *metaphysical* level and an *exemplary* level. At the metaphysical level a paradigm embodies a set of principles and beliefs that are rarely explicit. This metaphysical core is taken for granted by scientists.
>
> At the exemplary level the paradigm provides clear examples of how to work in a practical way.
>
> Kuhn used the notion of paradigm to argue that science did not develop as a result of rational testing of theory (as falsificationists argue) but as a result of the scientific community gradually deciding on a new paradigm. This change involves a major reconceptualisation of the discipline. The change from Newtonian mechanics to Einsteinian relativity theory represents a major paradigm shift. This shift comes about when anomalies begin piling up and the old paradigm does not appear able to deal with them. The new paradigm must be able to explain all that the old one did and be able to account for the anomalies. Not all scientists will immediately embrace the new paradigm, but eventually the new paradigm will become the accepted approach and the old paradigm and its practitioners will die out.

Longitudinal surveys

The nature of a survey is such that it provides a 'frozen image' of the time when the study was done. It does not provide a history nor does it illustrate social change. *Longitudinal surveys* are a response to this. This form of study is one in which the same subjects are studied at intervals over a period, often several years. For example, *The National Child Development Study*, a *cohort* study of 17,000 children born during the same week in March 1958, have subsequently been surveyed at 7, 14 and 21 years of age (Fogleman, 1983). Another form of longitudinal survey is the *panel* study, where a group of people is monitored over time (usually no more than a year) to assess changes in attitude, opinion or a limited range of behaviours. The panel members may be questioned several times, often with the same questions. Panel studies are often reported in the press at the time of a general election and broadcasting companies have audience panels who provide information on listening or viewing habits and opinions on programmes.

The key differences between cohort and panel studies are, first, that panel studies usually take place over a shorter period than cohort studies. Second, that panels are representative, as far as possible, of the population from which they are drawn, whereas a cohort is not necessarily a 'representative sample'. Third, panels are mostly used to monitor attitude changes over time while cohort studies are more intensive studies of the cohort themselves. Thus members who drop out of a panel study are replaced by new members with similar characteristics, whereas replacement does not normally take place in a cohort study.

Longitudinal studies are, however, very expensive and they are difficult to get funding for. Over a long period it is difficult to keep in contact with the sample and as the size of the sample reduces it is questionable whether it remains representative. An example of the problem of keeping in contact with the original sample is *The National Child Development Study* that, in 1981, 'mislaid' the names and addresses of 6,000 of their sample.

The use of continuous surveys like those carried out by the government such as the *Census*, the *General Household Survey* and the *Labour Force Survey*, or opinion polls carried out by market research organisations (see Chapter 3) provide another way by which surveys can keep a 'running record' of changes. Continuous surveys, unlike longitudinal surveys, do not reinterview the same sample or maintain a panel. However, they allow researchers to study patterns of social change over time. Continuous surveying is very expensive and requires a substantial organisation working full-time.

Summary and conclusion

In this chapter we have considered how social surveys are used to investigate social theory. We have outlined how to undertake a survey, avoiding as many pitfalls as possible. The social survey attempts to reproduce, in a social setting, the classic positivistic approach, that is, to measure 'social facts' to provide evidence for causal relationships (see Chapters 1 and 2). We have emphasised that the survey should be related to social theory.

Surveys aim ultimately to be explanatory. If they are to be explanatory they need to show the relationship between variables. This requires that you specify a clear aim for your survey, draw up hypotheses and operationalise your concepts. It is through careful operationalisation of concepts that you devise the 'right' questions to test your hypotheses.

You will need to draw up a sample and we have outlined the various sampling procedures. When undertaking a conventional social survey you should aim for a representative sample. However, this may not be possible in practice and you will have to make the best of what you can get. Be sure to comment on the adequacy of your sample in your report.

Once you have selected your sample and you have a set of clear and accurate questions you should undertake a pilot survey. This is vital because you do not want to spend a lot of time and energy collecting information that turns out to be unusable because you were not asking the right questions. You only do your main survey once so you need to get it right. You will rarely have the opportunity, time or energy to go back to your respondents. The pilot survey provides you with a way of overcoming a lot of the errors and problems that are bound to come up in a full-scale survey. For many students, a pilot survey will be all that can effectively be managed in the time available.

Always analyse the data in terms of your hypotheses. We used an example with several interrelated sub-hypotheses and have only undertaken a small fraction of the potential analysis. In your own research you will probably only want to deal with a single hypothesis and two or three sub-hypotheses.

The first thing you should do is to take your data from the schedules and questionnaires and create a data file. This helps enormously when it comes to analysing your hypotheses. Second, compile the frequency tables that you are going to use to look at your hypotheses. This involves some counting and working out percentages. We have shown that if this is all you do by way of statistical manipulation then you can make some statements about your hypotheses. It is quite feasible that this is all you will want or need to do. Third, you may want to go further and work out some averages for comparison purposes; averages are often easier to compare than whole tables. Fourth, you may want to elaborate your analysis by constructing crosstabulations to show differences between subgroups in the sample, and thus help to explain your results. For example, we compared the attitudes and knowledge of different age groups and both sexes. Inspecting the crosstabulation will provide some interesting results without having to do any more sophisticated statistical analysis. Make sure you use the correct percentages from the crosstabulation for comparison purposes.

This is as far as you are likely to want to go. However, you must remember that none of this either takes account of sampling error nor does it measure the extent of a relationship between two variables. If you want to deal with sampling error, then you have to get into the realms of confidence limits and significance tests (see Appendix 2). Similarly, measuring the extent of the relationship between two variables also involves measures of association. The aim, in Appendix 2, is to explore what these measures show, rather than explain how to work them out.

Reporting your findings is important, otherwise no one will know what you have learnt. We have suggested, in Chapter 1, how you might compile a report. Do not expect the data to be self-explanatory. You need to take the reader through your data, so do not include material that you do not comment on and explain. Make sure that what you include, and the structure of your report, relates directly to the aims of your survey. When commenting on your hypotheses make sure you do not overstate what you have found out about them; remember that statistical procedures are at best statements of probability and not of absolute proof.

Project ideas

1. To what extent, and why, do teenagers participate in sporting activities?
2. Do male and female students differ in their television viewing habits?
3. What use do people make of Neighbourhood Offices and how effective do they find the service offered?
4. What sort of people support unilateral or multilateral nuclear disarmament?
5. The extent and nature of sexual harassment at work and the effectiveness of complaints procedures.
6. The use of and attitudes towards cultural facilities in your town or city.
7. To what extent and why do students prefer coursework to examinations?
8. Use a self-report study to analyse differences in involvement in crime.
9. The extent and nature of racial harassment and abuse.
10. What factors effect the frequency and level of alcohol consumption?

Further Reading

Social surveys: Ackroyd and Hughes, 1981; Bateson, 1984; Belson, 1986; Bulmer, 1984; Hoinville *et al.*, 1978; Marsh, 1982; McNeil, 1990; Open University, 1986; Singleton *et al.*, 1988; Vaus, 1986.

Statistics: Bryman and Cramer, 1990; Clegg, 1982; Freund *et al.*, 1986; Glenberg, 1988; Gwilliam, 1988; Kapadia and Anderson, 1987; Marsh, 1988.

Topics

Poverty: Alcock, 1987; Evason, 1985; Haralambos, 1990, ch. 4; Mack and Lansey, 1985, 1991; Oppennheim, 1990; Townsend, 1979; Townsend *et al.*, 1987; Trowler, 1989, ch. 3; Walker and Walker, 1987.

Religion: Acquaviva, 1979; Berger and Luckmann, 1963; Bruce, 1990; Bynum *et al.*, 1986; Cashmore, 1979; Durkheim, 1961; Giddens, 1989, ch. 14; Glock and Stark, 1965; Haralambos, 1990, ch. 11; Mortimer, 1982; Nelson, 1986; Robertson, 1970; Turner, 1983; Weber, 1963, 1976; Wilson, 1966.

Sexuality: Brandenberg, 1988; Cant and Hemmings, 1988; Foucault, 1978; Gagnon and Simon, 1973; Giddens, 1989, ch. 6; Gough and Macnair, 1985; Hart and Richardson, 1981; Plummer, 1981; Rich, 1981; Ruse, 1988; Weeks, 1981.

CHAPTER 5
EXPERIMENTS

In this short chapter we look at the role played by experimentation in the social sciences. We look first at the standard or 'classic' approach to experimentation. Then we briefly review approximations to the classic experiment, including field experiments and ethnomethodological experiments.

The classic experiment

Experimentation is regarded as *the* method of science (Easthope, 1974; Mayntz *et al.*, 1976). It provides a way of measuring the impact that one factor has on another one. This is done, in the standard scientific experiment, by controlling all the other factors that may also have an effect.

The experiment involves testing variables under controlled circumstances. There are two types of variable, independent and dependent (see Chapter 4). The *independent* variable is presumed to cause changes in the *dependent* variable. In the experiment, the independent variable is manipulated to see what happens to the dependent variable. There are, thus, two basic requirements of an experiment. First, that the researcher is able to manipulate the independent variable. Second, that the researcher is able to control all other factors.

The laboratory experiment

The laboratory experiment in the chemical and physical sciences is the ideal type of experiment. In such settings, the researcher sets up a situation in which all theoretically likely factors are controlled and then changes one of these factors to see what effect it has on a *dependent* factor. For example, an electric circuit might be set up which includes a possible resistor (that is, something in the circuit that interferes with the flow of the electricity). The electrical supply is turned on to see whether the resistor indeed reduces the flow of electricity.

The way the experiment is set up depends on existing theory and the result is expected to confirm or elaborate the theory. In the example above, it may be assumed that the resistor will work but its level of resistance may be unknown. The design of the experiment is based on existing electromagnetic theory in order to test the resistance. In this case, of course, the researcher will not bother to control for the colour of the insulator on the wires that make up the circuit as this is irrelevant according to electromagnetic theory. The colour of the wires will not have any *causal* effect according to the theory and thus there is no need to control for them.

Thus, an experiment is set up to confirm empirically, or to elaborate, an existing theory by testing an experimental hypothesis. It is not a means of collecting data. The stages of conducting an experiment are outlined in Table 5.1.

Table 5.1 Carrying out an experiment

1. Construct an experimental hypothesis that specifies the *independent* variable, the *dependent* variable and the *relationship* between the two.
2. Decide on a suitable experimental *design*.
3. Decide on the *control* variables.
4. Work out *how* you are going to control these variables during the experiment.
5. Work out *how* to measure changes in the dependent and independent variables.
6. Apply the experimental *stimulus*.
7. *Measure* changes in the dependent variable.
8. *Analyse* the results and accept or reject

Experimental hypothesis

An experimental hypothesis is a specific statement about the relationship between two variables that can be tested by setting up a situation in which all other relevant factors are controlled. The hypothesis will be guided by theory (see page 105).

For example, the 'risky shift' phenomenon was suggested by Filby and Harvey (1988) to explain, in part, why betting-shop punters were less successful during the busiest times in the betting shop. The theory suggests that people make riskier decisions when in a group than they would when on their own. Hence, when the betting shop is at its busiest there is more scope for punters to meet and discuss betting options, leading to riskier selections.

The risky shift phenomenon could be tested experimentally using the following hypothesis:

> Punters are more likely to make selections with longer odds when making choices in a group than when making selections individually.

Experimental design

The test–stimulus–retest design

In the social sciences two types of experimental design are normally used. The first is the *test–stimulus–retest* approach. In this situation a group is tested to measure the extent of the dependent variable. An independent variable is introduced as a stimulus and then the group is retested to see whether the dependent variable has changed. A simple example would be to test a group to see what knowledge they had about the effects of drinking alcohol, to show them a film about alcohol consumption, then to retest their knowledge. The assumption is that any change in the level of knowledge is caused by the film. This, however, raises problems of control. What if other events took place between the test and the retest that effected the knowledge of the sample group? It is possible that simply testing the group in the first place is sufficient to get them thinking and thus lead to an increase in knowledge irrespective of the film.

The control group design

The second type of experimental design is to use a 'control group'. In this approach, two samples are selected, an experimental sample and a control sample. These samples should be as similar as possible to minimise the possibility of other factors affecting the result. This approach could have been applied in the experiment with the film. The experimental group could have been shown the film but not the control group. Both groups could then have been tested to assess their knowledge of the effects of alcohol.

Alexis Tan (1979) used this design in her study of the effects of beauty advertisements on perceptions of young women (see Chapter 2, Extract 2.2). If the experimental and control groups are well matched, then any difference in knowledge is presumed to be caused by the film. However, this does assume that the two groups start from the same level of knowledge.

The retest control group design

One way to take account of this assumption would be to combine the *test–stimulus–retest* design with the *control group* design. This is a common design in social science experimental research. Thus, in the example, the experimental group and the control group would be given the two tests but

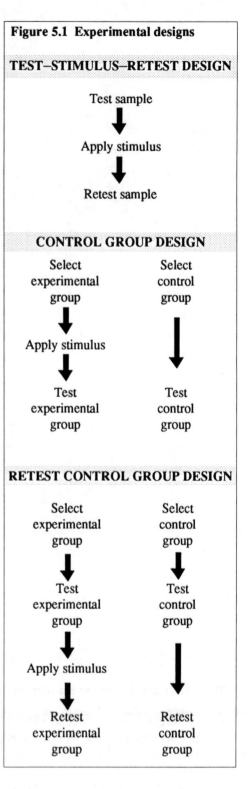

Figure 5.1 Experimental designs

TEST–STIMULUS–RETEST DESIGN

Test sample

↓

Apply stimulus

↓

Retest sample

CONTROL GROUP DESIGN

Select experimental group

↓

Apply stimulus

↓

Test experimental group

Select control group

↓

Test control group

RETEST CONTROL GROUP DESIGN

Select experimental group

↓

Test experimental group

↓

Apply stimulus

↓

Retest experimental group

Select control group

↓

Test control group

↓

Retest control group

only the experimental group would be shown the film. The difference between the first test and the retest would be compared for the two groups. If there is a larger increase in knowledge for the experimental group than for the control group then it would be assumed that the increase in knowledge was caused by the film (see Figure 5.1).

Student Activity 5.1
What experimental design would you use to test the following hypotheses:
1. **First-year students are more likely to use the library if they have an introductory talk from the librarian.**
2. **Males would be more likely to take up a career in nursing if they spent some time on work experience in a hospital.**
3. **The risky shift hypothesis (on page 140).**
REMEMBER to say which is the independent variable and which is the dependent variable. Putting your hypothesis in diagrammatic form can be a useful technique when you are trying to sort out your research design.

Control

Control is a key issue in experimentation. It is necessary to identify the control variables and then devise some way of controlling them. The control variables will be those factors that, in *theory*, are likely to change the effect that the independent variable, which is being manipulated, will have on the dependent variable. For example, an experiment to see how exposure to propaganda affected support for the Gulf War would need to take account of the gender of the respondent. Opinion polls suggested that at the outbreak of the war, a much larger proportion of men than women supported the war. Gender is thus a control variable in this case. It is often difficult to identify all the relevant control variables.

Once you have identified the control variables you need to devise some way of controlling for them. One way of doing this is, in effect, to exclude control variables. In the previous example, you can control for gender differences by making sure your experimental subjects are all the same gender. This is known as a *homogeneous* group. You may then want to test to see whether the experimental results obtained, for example, from a female group are repeated when you use a male group.

In practice, however, it is difficult to identify all the important control variables and to be able to assemble such homogeneous experimental groups.

Allocation to experimental and control groups

Allocating subjects to experimental and control groups can be done in two ways. The easiest way is '*randomisation*'. In this process a single group is allocated into two subgroups at random. The assumption is that the control variables will also be randomised. In other words, the effect of the control variables will be purely random. If the two samples show a *statistically significant* difference in the dependent variable (see Chapter 4 and Appendix 2) then it is assumed that this is due to the experimental stimulus and not the randomised control variables.

There are two major problems with this approach. First, it is not always possible to allocate a sample into two random subgroups. Second, randomisation of control variables may not be achieved if the sample groups are

---

Example answer to Student Activity 5.1, part 3

A suitable design for the 'risky shift' experiment would be to ask a sample of punters to select the winners from a race-card of six races. The sample would be divided into two groups at random. The first group to make betting selections singularly, the second group to be divided into subgroups of five individuals and asked to make their decisions as a group. Riskiness would be judged by the combined odds of the selections made by each individual or subgroup. The average odds for the two samples would be tested to see if they were significantly different.

small, and this procedure should only be used when there is an initial sample of about one hundred people.

The other way of getting a control group is by using *matched pairs*. In this procedure relevant control factors are identified. Then for every person allocated to the experimental group, a person with the same set of values of the control variable is allocated to the control group. For example, gender, age and ethnicity might be important control factors in an experiment. So, if an 18-year-old white woman was allocated to the experimental group then a matching 18-year-old white woman would also need to be allocated to the control group. There are several problems with this procedure. First, you have to decide on the important control variables. The more you have, the more difficult it will be to match people. Second, this approach is likely to be wasteful because you are unlikely to be able to match all the people in your original sample. Third, if someone drops out of one group during a test retest design, then you have to disregard the results of the matching person in the other group.

In general, it is preferable to match the control and experimental groups but also to allocate the pairs into the two groups at random. This way, control variables that you had not considered are likely to be randomly allocated.

In the risky shift experiment (example answer to Student Activity 5.1, part 3) a randomised allocation was suggested. As the 'risky shift' notion does not specify any other factors that are likely to have a bearing then it is difficult to determine other control variables for purposes of matching.

> **Student Activity 5.2**
> **Test out the risky shift phenomenon either by using the example of horse racing described above or by setting up another decision-making situation. Compare the results of those who decide alone with those who decide in groups.**
> **SUGGESTION   Look at Hughes, 1976, chapter 4, for some ideas.**

An experiment reported by Dixon *et al.* (1987) illustrates the steps in the experimental approach (see Extract 5.1).

Epistemology of the classic experiment

Experiments are used to establish *causal* relations. Readings taken during an experiment are used to confirm or deny a very precise hypothesis that has been specified in advance. Experimentation is, thus, a research *design* rather than a data collection procedure. In effect, an experiment occurs at a late stage of the research and is a practical test of a causal theory.

The researcher, by using the experiment, hopes to prove or disprove a hypothesis. Proof refers to the evidence that is collected and presented to establish a causal relationship rather than just a chance happening. The idea of proof contains the notion that there are 'objective' facts that can be verified using scientific methods borrowed from the natural sciences. Thus, the experiment is the ultimate *positivist* research design.

Survey research that adopts multivariate analysis attempts to reproduce the experimental approach. It does this not by physically controlling factors, as in the experiment, but by taking account of control variables when showing relationships between independent and dependent variables (see Appendix 2).

Although the experiment is the 'classic' positivistic approach, it has limited application in the social sciences, even for positivists. The aim of

---

Extract 5.1

EXPERIMENT ON HEALTHY SNACKS

1. The hypothesis was that students given lessons on nutritious snacks will purchase healthier snacks from the canteen.

2. The design was to use a control group to compare and measure differences in the dependent variable before and after application of a stimulus. The experimental group would have a lesson on nutritious snacks. The control group would simultaneously have a lesson on another topic. The dependent variable (that is, student consumption of nutritious snacks) would be measured before and after the lessons given to the control group and the experimental group.

3. The control variables were age, gender and course of study.

4. The experimental and control groups were selected so that they were similar in age, proportion of males to females and course of study.

5. The dependent variable was measured by asking students to indicate, on a check list, which snacks they had bought from the canteen. The researchers backed this up by also observing what the students bought. The independent variable was whether or not the student had attended the lesson on nutritious snacks.

6. The experimental group was given the lesson on nutritious snacks while the control group had a lesson on something else.

7. The types of snacks purchased after the lesson were ascertained.

8. The two groups of students are as alike as possible in all known respects and the only known difference is the attendance or non-attendance at the lectures on nutritious snacks. Thus any difference between the two groups in what snacks they chose (the dependent variable) can be assumed to be caused by the lessons on nutritious snacks (the independent variable). The results showed no significant difference between the two groups.

9. The experimenters concluded that the lesson on nutritious snacks had no effect on the selection of snacks.

Adapted from Dixon *et al.* (1987).

experiments is to allow a researcher to examine the effect that a change to one variable has upon another. In other words, to put the researcher in a position where she or he can be in control of all the variables and be able to measure and study them and their effect. The problem in the social sciences is that the researcher is unlikely either to be able to manipulate the independent variable or to control for all other relevant factors.

In practice, psychologists are more likely to use experiments than are other social scientists. Laboratory-type experiments are often used to simulate a situation to assess subjects' psychological reactions. For example, Haney *et al.* (1973) looked at the effect on individuals when they were given the role of either prisoner or guard in a simulation prison.

Reliability of the classic experiment

Reliability refers to the ability of a research instrument to measure phenomena in a consistent manner (see page 31). In some circumstances the reliability of experiments in the social sciences has been called into question because the very fact that people are taking part in an experiment can affect their behaviour. This is known as the 'Hawthorne effect' because of studies done at the Hawthorne Works (Roethlisberger and Dickson, 1939). These studies showed that people under observation do not behave normally but respond to experimental *conditions*, not the experimental *stimulus*. In the study at the Hawthorne Works, the workers increased productivity even when their work conditions had worsened. They worked harder because of what they saw as the interest shown in them by the researcher and because they though the experiment would somehow lead to better working conditions in the factory. Thus they ignored the experimental stimulus and simply went on producing more because they were in an experimental situation.

This reaction to the experimental situation undermines the measurements made. Instead of having an unreliable *measuring* device the measurements are unreliable because the *context* in which they are made keeps changing. In short, the meaning of measurements keeps changing even though the 'objective' measure is consistent. It thus questions the reliability of the outcomes of experiments involving human subjects.

Validity of the classic experiment

Theoretically, the experiment is *internally* valid (see page 32). In other words, if the idea of experimental logic is accepted, then, when all other possible factors have been controlled, changes in the dependent factor must be the result of manipulating the independent factor. The internal validity of the research can only be called into question if the design is faulty, or the means of controlling other factors is inadequate. In practice, of course, design and control are a problem, which is the main reason why experiments are not often used by sociologists. The *unreliability* of some experiments is due to the problem of controlling for the impact of the experiment itself.

Experiments are regarded as having poor *external* validity. External validity refers to the applicability of the results in different circumstances. Experimental results in the social sciences are often regarded as having very little relevance for the natural setting outside the experiment (*ecological* validity). To what extent would the experimental sample of betting-shop punters make the same decisions if they were wagering their own money in a betting shop? Would Haney's experimental prison guards still like the role if it wasn't a simulated prison? Similarly, are the effects noted as the result of an experiment long term or short term? Experiments that attempt to show the effects on subjects of televised violence have been criticised for assuming that immediate reactions are the same as long-term *effects* (see page 34).

External validity also relates to the extent to which experimental results can be generalised to a broader population (population validity). An experiment might work on a group of psychology students but does this mean that the results can be generalised to all students, or the whole population? If you are going to make claims about the population then you must conduct the experiment on a *representative* sample.

Field experiments

Not all experiments are done in laboratory-type situations. One form of experiment is called a *field experiment*. An example is a study by Piliavin, Rodin and Piliavin (1969) of 'bystander apathy' in the New York subway system. They set up a situation in which a presumed ordinary passenger got on to a train and then, as the train was going along, pretended to collapse on to the floor of the carriage. The experimenters then recorded whether the person was given help, by whom and how long it took for help to be offered. Contrary to expectations that the New York subway is one of the worst places in the world for bystander apathy, the experimenters found, in this case, that help was offered, usually within two minutes. The fact that they are involved in an experiment is not revealed to the subjects under study. This form of experiment, however, raises the fundamental issue of control. There is no way in which the field experimenter can begin to allow for all the possible control variables and this makes any causal analysis fraught with difficulty.

Ethnomethodological experiments

Ethnomethodologists have used experiments to challenge people's taken-for-granted views. Ethnomethodologists argue that people have shared assumptions and sets of taken-for-granteds that they use in making sense of the world (see page 42). To test this out, they have undertaken experiments designed to disrupt normal sets of taken-for-granteds. These experiments, which include such things as bargaining for a fixed price item in a chain store, are called *breaching* experiments as they breach shared assumptions.
The aims of the breaching experiments were to show that:

1. people have shared assumptions that allow them to interact with other people as both share the same taken-for-granted ideas;
2. these taken-for-granteds were used by people to control their world;
3. people became frustrated when the taken-for-granted rules did not work;
4. people had a different set of taken-for-granteds which they used in different situations.

This is illustrated by Garfinkel (1967), who asked his students to spend between 15 and 60 minutes acting out the role of a boarder in their home. They were instructed to be polite and circumspect, to avoid getting personal, to use formal address and to speak only when spoken to. Nine out of forty-nine of his students were unable to carry out the experiment for various reasons. The results from the other students varied. Some families reacted in astonishment, bewilderment, shock, embarrassment or anger, or demanded explanations: 'What's the matter?', 'What's gotten into you?', 'Are you sick? and so on. Normality was restored when students explained what they

Extract 5.2

CHALLENGING TAKEN-FOR-GRANTEDS

Case 1

The subject was telling the experimenter, a member of the subject's car pool, about having had a flat tyre while going to work the previous day.

Subject: I had a flat tyre.
Experimenter: What do you mean, you had a flat tyre?

The subject appeared momentarily stunned. Then she answered in a hostile way:

What do you mean, 'What do you mean?' A flat tyre is a flat tyre. That is what I meant. Nothing special. What a crazy question!

Case 2

Subject: Hi, Ray. How is your girlfriend feeling?
Experimenter: What do you mean, 'How is she feeling?' Do you mean physical or mental?
S: I mean how is she feeling? What's the matter with you? (He looked peeved.)
E: Nothing. Just explain a little clearer what do you mean?
S: Skip it. How are your Med. School applications coming?
E: What do you mean, 'How are they?'
S: You know what I mean.
E: I really don't.
S: What's the matter with you? Are you sick?

Case 3

The victim waved his hand cheerily.
Subject: How are you?
Experimenter: How am I in regard to what? My health, my finances, my school work, my peace of mind ....?
S (Red in the face and suddenly out of control): Look! I was just trying to be polite. Frankly, I don't give a damn how you are.

Case 4

My friend and I were talking about a man whose overbearing attitude annoyed us.
Subject: I'm sick of him.
Experimenter: Would you explain what is wrong with you that you are sick?
S: Are you kidding me? You know what I mean.
E: Please explain your ailment.
S (He listened to me with a puzzled look.): What came over you? We never talk this way, do we?

Adapted from Garfinkel (1967, pages 42–4).

had been doing. Most of the families were not amused and most had not found the situation instructive. After the explanation one student's sister coldly replied on behalf of her family:

> Please, no more of these experiments. We're not rats, you know. (Garfinkel, 1967, p. 49)

Garfinkel used this experiment to produce situations in which the normal rules of everyday life were changed. The students did not act as they usually did and normal interaction became very difficult. The students' families were no longer able to make sense of the situations by making use of the taken-for-granted assumptions they had previously used.

Garfinkel was also interested in the taken-for-granteds that guided conversation. As part of his 'breaching' experiments he instructed his students to start a conversation with a friend and (without saying they were involved in an experiment) to insist that the person clarify the sense of his/her 'commonplace remarks'. In other words, to breach the taken-for-granted's of everyday conversational expectations. The cases in Extract 5.2 illustrate the approach.

> **Student Activity 5.3**
> **Bearing in mind that some people may get upset and that there are ethical problems with using people without their knowledge in experiments (see below), replicate Garfinkel's conversational experiment and record your results. Did your subject(s) show similar reactions to those in the four cases in Extract 5.2?**
> **WARNING Be careful not to push the respondent too far, especially if you value the friendship. If you have any reservations about this approach do not do this activity.**

Epistemology of ethnomethodological experiments

Garfinkel (1967) was not concerned with *explanations* of social phenomena. Instead he was trying to reveal the limitations of sociology. For him, ethnomethodological experiments were less concerned with proving a *causal* connection than with revealing what we take for granted. Strictly speaking, breaching experiments are not experiments in the classic sense because they are not concerned with issues of *control* nor with *causal explanation*.

Ethnomethodologists argued that sociology starts out by presuming the nature of social interaction. Sociology ignores the process by which social interaction is made possible. What ethnomethodologists attempt to do is to analyse the way in which meanings are shared. They started by asking if people had shared meanings. The ethnomethodological experiments, by deliberately breaching taken-for-granteds, indicated that interaction was dependent on shared meanings. People made sense of the world through these shared meanings and were often unable to cope when they were removed. Sometimes, however, when one set of shared assumptions seemed useless, subjects adopted a different set to help them make sense of the situation. Garfinkel suggested that far from being 'cultural dopes', people are extremely sophisticated. The experiments showed that we are quite capable of using one set of rationalities in one situation and another set in a different situation. For example, the set of taken-for-granteds that a teenager adopts with friends in a discotheque is not the same set of taken-for-granteds that he or she adopts when in a job interview.

Thus ethnomethodological experiments are not attempting to make causal connections. They are contrived situations that are designed to challenge taken-for-granteds to see how people make sense of them. Thus, the problem of control, so central to the classical experiment, is not important. Ethnomethodologists are guided by phenomenology and are interested in meanings. Ethnomethodological experiments are a tool to explore meanings and are quite distinct from positivist experiments designed to prove causal relationships.

Ethics

All forms of experimentation raise ethical problems. It is not usually possible to tell the subjects what the point of the experiment is until it is over because prior knowledge may lead people to change their behaviour and render the experiment useless. You must then consider carefully how much you can ethically manipulate people for the sake of an experiment. Sometimes, the subjects may not even know that they are involved in an experiment. The students in the nutritious snacks experiment might have been unaware that they were part of an experiment.

Sometimes experiments cause psychological harm. For example, the experiment with the simulated prison (Haney *et al.*, 1973) came to an abrupt end when some of the individuals playing prisoners experienced severe depression and those playing the guards actively enjoyed the role.

Far more serious was a forty-year medical experiment conducted in the United States on the effects of syphillis. About 300 black males who had contracted syphillis were given a 'special' treatment. In fact they were not treated at all. The aim of the experiement was to observe the course of syphillis up to the point of death (Heller and Bruyere, 1945). Needless to say the subjects were not aware of the aims of the experiment. Even when sample members went for other treatment it was denied them. This experiment, which started in 1933 was finally stopped in 1972 .

Field experiments and ethnomethodological experiments also use unwitting subjects. These can also cause anguish and annoyance, as we have seen. Indeed Mehan and Wood (1975) argue that there is no need to do any more ethnomethodological experiments as the point has been made by Garfinkel and it would not be ethical to carry out any more.

You have to weigh the ethical considerations very carefully before setting up experiments where the subjects are being deceived into being unwitting participants.

Student Activity 5.4
In your view, are there any circumstances in which it would be ethical to undertake experiments that involved
1. **Telling subjects that they are involved in trials of a new counselling service when, in fact, it is the subjects' actions that are being monitored?**
2. **Pretending not to know something the subjects expect you to be aware of in order to provoke a reaction to your pretended ignorance?**
3. **Acting in a threatening or hostile manner towards subjects?**
4. **Getting some subjects to simulate aggressive actions towards other subjects?**
5. **Taking a child away from the care of a parent in order to observe the reactions?**

Summary and conclusion

Experimentation is a means of testing a hypothesis. It is not a data collecting method like social surveying, or observation. The researcher is not involved in collecting data from the 'real world'. Instead, a situation is set up, and the researcher notes what happens when an experimental variable is manipulated. This might be providing subjects with information to see if it changes attitudes. Or seeing if people behave differently in groups from the way they do when acting individually. Or seeing how people cope in a crisis, or when things they take for granted no longer apply. The researcher records the outcome of the experiment, much as a physical scientist might make a note of readings from a set of gauges.

Positivist 'classic' experiments are designed to test causal assumptions. The experiment is thus the *paradigm* method for positivists. Although little used by sociologists, the experiment is the model that the widely used multivariate-analysis approach attempts to recreate (see Chapter 4). To be credible, positivist experiments must ensure that other variables are controlled.

Ethnomethodological 'breaching' experiments, on the other hand, are designed to see what people take for granted. They are thus concerned with meanings, not causes. For them, the issue of control is not important.

In all forms of experimentation, though, the issue of external validity is important. The sample must be representative if the results are to be generalised (population validity). Similarly, it is necessary to ask whether the contrived setting of the experiment can be generalised to 'real life' situations (ecological validity).

Project ideas

Experimentation is little used in the social sciences and the sorts of things you can do experiments on are fairly limited. Collecting enough people together to participate in an experiment is a major problem. However, a few ideas are suggested below. It is quite likely that experimentation would be just a part of your project and you may want to consider any results that you get from an experiment in the light of data drawn from surveys or observation. It is acceptable to use more than one method to address a research aim; this is known as triangulation (see Chapter 8).

Further reading

Experimentation: Brown (1975); Dixon *et al.* (1987); Hughes (1976); Potter *et al.* (1981); Singleton *et al.* (1988), Smith (1975).

Ethnomethodological experiments: Coulter (1988); Heritage (1984); Mehan and Wood (1975); Sharrock and Anderson (1986).

1. See if males dominate mixed-gender discussions irrespective of the number of females in a group.
2. Assess whether a race awareness training programme has a positive effect in reducing racist statements and attitudes.
3. See whether people respond more readily to questionnaires that come from official agencies rather than from private individuals.
4. Examine whether an individual's tastes (for example in pop music) are effected by peer group attitudes.
5. Analyse whether people exposed to large amounts of televised violence exhibit more aggressive attitudes than those who have not been exposed.

CHAPTER 6
OBSERVATION

Introduction

Observation is a major means by which people develop their knowledge of the world they live in. Similarly, sociologists make widespread use of observation in developing their understanding of the social world. Observation studies are undertaken in nearly all areas of sociological enquiry but have been developed in particular in the sociologies of organisation, work, leisure, deviance, and education.

In our everyday activities we make widespread use of observation, but we tend to be unsystematic and very selective about what we observe. Our everyday observation tends to focus on our immediate concerns and filters out taken-for-granted background material. We tend to make use of observation to confirm our assumptions about the world around us and to reinforce our preconceptions.

When sociologists make use of observation in their study of the social world they use it to inquire *systematically* about the world they see and to develop *theories* about the social world. This is important. Sociologists undertake observation studies to see the world in a new way, not just to confirm their preconceptions. This involves 'looking hard' at all aspects of what is going on, not picking out one or two events and using them to confirm taken-for-granted views about the nature of the social world. Observation, as a methodological tool, must, therefore, be both systematic and inquisitive. Arguably, what distinguishes social scientific observation from other forms (such as journalism or 'everyday' observation) is the development and testing of theory (Hammersley and Atkinson, 1983). Sociologists adopt two broad approaches to observation, participant and non-participant.

Non-participant observation

Non-participant observation involves the researcher in getting into situations where behaviour, interactions, organisational practices and so on can be observed at first hand. Usually, the non-participant observer is visible to the subject group (although they may not know that the researcher is observing them). This type of non-participant observation might involve walking around a hospital in a white coat watching what goes on, although not pretending to be a doctor (Sudnow, 1967); hanging around football stadia watching the activities of England supporters (Williams *et al.*, 1984); or sitting in classrooms watching what happens during lessons (Lacey, 1966). Sometimes the non-participant observer may be hidden from the subjects, watching through one-way mirrors (Greenwood, 1965) or using video or recording devices to 'spy' on a group (for example, Strodtbeck, James and Hawkins (1957) hid microphones in jury rooms in the United States). Non-participant observation of this kind is a major tool in experimental studies in the social sciences (see Chapter 5).

WARNING Observation studies are very time-consuming. In this chapter we suggest some research activities that involve observation. Time constraints will mean that you are very unlikely to be able to attempt them all.

Student Activity 6.1
1. Undertake a non-participant observation study of a group of people meeting in a public place such as a shopping centre, public house, youth club or any other similar place where people meet on a casual basis. Watch them for about an hour, if possible. Should you feel uncomfortable doing the observation bring it to an immediate conclusion.
2. Note the events that take place and the ways the members of the group interact. Is the group a tight-knit group or is it a casual coming together of a number of subgroups? Are there any group leaders and in what respects do they lead? Is there any group organisation, if so, what is it? Does the group interact with any other group or person and, if so, in what way? How important is interaction with other groups or persons in the activities of the group and in the formation and organisation of the group?
3. Report your findings back to a small group of people who have also undertaken this exercise and discuss difficulties you had in recording data, deciding what events were significant, and what they meant.

Recording observational data

What data to record

When you first undertake observational research you may find that it is quite difficult to know *what* to makes notes about. How much detail do you record? Do you record all conversation? Do you describe all the actions?

If, for example, you are observing a group of three people hanging around in a shopping centre and fourth person comes up and joins them, do you simply write that 'a fourth person joined the group and was greeted by the other three and immediately joined in the conversation' or do you describe in detail what happened? You might write something like this: 'a fourth person, a black male who looked about 16, dressed in a t-shirt, jeans and trainers, confidently approached the group and greeted each in turn by slapping palms and saying "how're you doing?". The group seemed to be expecting the arrival of this fourth member, and immediately included him by asking him questions about where he had been. The conversation, which had been rather intermittent, became much more lively and animated'.

There is no easy answer to the question of how much you include. It depends on two interrelated things. First, what you are trying to find out, and second, how far your research has got. If you know exactly what you are looking for then you only have to make notes about those things you observe that are, for example, directly relevant to the hypotheses you are testing. However, the very nature of most observation research (especially participant observation as we will see in the section below) is that you are trying to find out what is relevant from the subject's point of view. So it often takes a long time before you are able to say what is relevant and what is not. The more research you have done on your subjects, the easier it is to decide what is relevant.

When you are first starting the research it is preferable to include as much detail as is feasible. For example, Elliott (1972) took the view that nothing is irrelevant when he undertook his study of the *Making of a Television Series* (see page 42). However, you cannot possibly note everything that happens and everything that is said. You have to be selective. So what do you select? You should be guided by your general research aims and broad hypotheses (see Chapter 1). The second account about the group, above, is not a comprehensive description but it does provide information about some of the broad areas of concern in Student Activity 6.1. The second account indicates the way that the fourth person became part of the group, the type of greetings that occurred (handshake, hug, nods, etc.) and the way that the fourth person integrated into the group. This is important if you are trying to determine things like group leadership, integration, tensions and so on. The first description provides you with insufficient information for any initial appreciation of how the group works, while the second one gives you some preliminary clues.

Observation studies vary enormously in length from a few months of fieldwork to several years. Typically, published participant observation studies are the result of between one and two years' fieldwork. As the study progresses the amount of detail that it is necessary to record might be reduced. For example, after watching several interactions you might simply say that 'X was dressed as usual' and only make notes on dress when a significant change in style, which might point to some form of 'leadership' via fashion-consciousness, occurred. Similarly, you might only note forms of greeting that were significantly different from normal and that might suggest the break-up of the group. However, you will not know what to omit or what is 'normal' until you have developed a substantial knowledge about the group. This will not occur until you have spent a lot of time observing, either as a non-participant or as a participant.

How to record data

Beside's the problem of what to record the observer is faced with the problem of *how* to record information. Do you write down observations as they occur? Do you remember what happens and write it down later? Or do you make notes during the observation as aids to memory and then write a full version later? Again, the answer is not straightforward and depends on the circumstances and your skill as an observer. If the subjects are aware of your presence then you may have to consider whether you should be seen writing down what is going on or even be seen making occasional notes. But it may be that, as an observer, you are in a position where it is quite feasible to record events as they occur: for example, you may be observing what goes on in a school classroom or college lecture where everyone else is writing and so it would not be seen as odd for you to do so. W.F. Whyte (1943) took on the role of secretary of the Italian Community Club as it enabled him to make observation notes during meetings. On the other hand, if you are observing social interaction in a youth club you are likely to be the only person sitting watching and writing, and people are likely to ask what you are doing. If you tell them it may well affect their behaviour. In some situations you may not be able to write down what is going on, or even make notes. Your subjects may not know you are a researcher because you are hiding the fact from them. In which case you cannot be seen to be making notes about what you are observing because it will give the game away. Even if they know that you are a researcher they may object to you making notes about what they are doing.

Usually, as you have probably already found out when doing Student Activity 6.1, you are not able to write (or tape-record) everything that happens as it occurs, or even to make quick notes about everything. Too many things happen at once, or events happen too quickly at times for you to be able to record it all as it occurs. Much more likely, you will need to remember what happens and with the help of what notes you are able to make

Supplementary Research Activity 6.1

Observe a game or sport whose rules you do not know. See if you can determine the rules by simply watching what happens. To what extent are comments by other spectators or by commentators (if you are watching on television) important in helping you make sense of the rules? If you are able to ask someone about the game as it takes place, to what extent does this help clarify the rules?

at the time, write it down later when you are alone. Thus you have to develop your memory skills. This means that you have to learn to concentrate on what is going on in detail, in particular the sequence of events. Often, you are able to remember specific events but getting them in the right order is more difficult.

With luck and skill you might be able to make brief notes as an *aide mémoire* as you observe. There may be no problem making notes openly but often you will want to avoid drawing attention to what you are doing (irrespective of whether the subjects know you are a researcher or not). Making quick notes in a pocket-sized book whilst alone (for example, whilst in the toilet), or scribbling on the back of matchboxes or bus tickets, can be invaluable aids in recalling specific details later. You might develop other tricks; for example, some researchers have reputedly learned to write notes secretly in a book in their pocket!

Writing up your observational data

It is important that you *write up* your observations in detail as soon as possible. A golden rule is 'never sleep on your observations'. Write up your data in detail before you go to bed because you will not recall things as clearly the next day, let alone days later. This requires a lot of self-discipline. It means that however late in the day your observations are concluded, and irrespective of other things you want to do, it is crucial that you sit down and write up the data. Do this before going out for the evening (especially if you are going to drink alcohol) or before going to bed. Observation research requires a substantial time commitment. Not only is it time-consuming doing the observation, writing up what you have observed can also take many hours.

Writing up observations should also be done in a systematic way. Always put a heading on the notes that says where, when and between what times the observations were made. Also note down when you wrote up the observations. Put a list of people observed at the top. You will probably use coded names to identify people because you may not know their names (if you are a non-participant) or because you will want to conceal the subject's real identities for purposes of confidentiality. It is a good idea to keep your comments on what you observe separate from the actual observations. For example, you might write the observations in black ink and your comments in red; or put comments in square brackets if typing up the observations. Where you use abbreviations, or substitute names, or use codes to refer to events or behaviour, make sure that you keep a glossary or key so that you will know what you meant when you go back to your notes later.

It is a good idea, if possible, to record your observations on a wordprocessor (making sure that you keep back-up copies). The reason for this is that it is easier to rearrange and sort your material when it comes to analysing it. (Using a wordprocessor is discussed in the analysis section, on page 177).

A short extract from Michael Filby's (1989) field notes of betting shops (Extract 6.1) shows one way of coding the data. Each day's notes were recorded on a wordprocessor document file and then a copy of the file was divided into 'event strips'. Each strip contains a heading that identifies the kind of event observed. For example, the extract from his notes for 13 April 1989 shows events relating to 'staff–customer conflict', 'work culture' 'non-work-related conversation', 'people: company staff' and 'employment recruitment and training'. All these different themes appeared in one day's notes. From an examination of the detailed data in the strips Filby was able to identify ways in which sexuality and gender were involved in the betting shop work-place. For example, a major aspect that emerges from his study is the way in which the female staff, although trained and capable of doing the more technically demanding jobs in the shop (notably settling the bets), collude with the work-place culture that sees women's role as entertaining the (predominantly) male punters and conceding to males on technical issues. The superiority of males, in this respect, is something both punters and male staff take for granted. You can see this issue emerging in the brief extract from the notes.

> **Student Activity 6.2**
> See if you can shadow someone in their job for a day. Note carefully what activities they engage in and the interactions they have with other people. See if you are able to get an idea of what the person you are shadowing takes for granted and how she or he makes sense of the work situation.
> WARNING This is a time-consuming exercise and you may not be able to attempt it.

Participant observation

Participant observation is a method of collecting empirical data that is widely used in sociological research. As the name suggests, participant observation involves the researcher in becoming part of the group or situation that is being studied. James Patrick (1973) joined a Glasgow gang; Ned Polsky (1971) played pool with poolroom hustlers; Ruth Cavendish (1982) worked for a year as an assembler on a production line; William Foote Whyte (1955) went to live in a slum area of Boston; Blanche Geer went to lectures and hung around with medical students (Becker *et al.*, 1961); Gordon Marshall (1986) spent almost a year as a barman in a licensed restaurant; and Tanya Luhrman (1989) joined a witches' coven in London.

The participant observer does not just observe and record the unusual or 'extreme' behaviour, but joins in the everyday activities of the subjects. As a member, the researcher observes social interaction and talks informally with group members. Thus, participant observation is usually taken to refer to more than just the process of observing while participating. Participant observation usually also includes the use of interviews, normally informal chats or in-depth interviews, analysis of documents such as organisational memoranda or personal documents (see Chapter 7), as well as non-participant observation.

Participant observation is a technique used by researchers in a variety of ways. Sometimes it is seen as just a descriptive tool, sometimes as a basis for testing theory. It is used for analysing patterns of social interaction (Becker *et al.*, 1961), for discovering how different cultures operate (Malinowski, 1954; Blumenthal, 1932) and as the basis for analysing the nature of social structures (Willis, 1977; Westwood, 1984). Some researchers see participant observation as a complete method in itself. Others see it as the exploratory stage for further quantitative research (Barton and Lazarsfeld, 1955) or as providing an alternative view that can be compared with data gathered in other ways, usually by more formal survey techniques (Lacey, 1966). This latter approach is known as *triangulation* and is discussed in Chapter 8.

Extract 6.1

EXAMPLE FIELDNOTES

W.B. 13.4.89
237 ** WORK CULTURE: EVENTS **

A batch of new skirts arrived, two each for everyone except Pat, who was well put out. This kept them busy for half an hour. At one point they all disappeared into the back to try on the new 'uniform'. There was discussion about sizes and weight, the cut, fitting and so on. After Dave asked if they were all right, there was general agreement that they were acceptable. I had a discussion with Tina about clothing sizes. She now fitted her 12 but she said that these firms were a law unto themselves where sizes were concerned. She modelled the new skirt, emphasising the evident new found room around the waist band.

238 ** CONVERSATION THEMES: NON WORK RELATED **

I caught the fag end of a discussion of mutual gynaecological interests between Tina, Louise and Pat as I went to show Tina my field notes following the conversation of the previous day.

> **Tina: 'You won't write this down Mike will you..**
> **Mike: 'Well I didn't really hear, I'll write down "conversation about the inner workings of the female body", will that be all right?!**
> **Tina: 'Go on then...'**

I picked up on the discussion anyway and recounted the tale of my vasectomy, Pat was interested, she was trying to get her husband to have one. But the others were interested too, ignoring the customers, as I recounted the drama of the local anaesthetic and the details of the events in the clinic. My assurances about the relative painlessness of the whole thing would not be enough to dispel the fears of Pat's husband. The discussion then became more open about birth control in general, Pat amused everyone with her account of early 60's courting antics.

239 ** PEOPLE: COMPANY STAFF **

I spent most of the afternoon chatting to Billie who was on the payout. She made an impressive entrance to the shop at about 1.00. Borrowed some money from Pat to buy a pair of shoes in the sale in *Next* for work. She introduced herself to me. I could hardly get a word in edgeways. Her chat was machine-gun-like and while she was talking to me she carried out a routine with one of the regulars, demanding that he smile.

> **'Smile then... that's better', don't spend it all at once.**
> **I'm not going away with you...'**

Billie is 30 years old and has a school-age daughter and is separated from her husband. She has worked in the business previously with WH, where she knew Lyn, for 10 years. She came back three years ago when her daughter started school. She got a job with 'the firm' simply because it was the nearest shop, having moved when she got married.

240 ** EMPLOYMENT AND RECRUITMENT ISSUES, AND TRAINING **

Billie didn't think there was much difference between the two outfits, in contrast to Lyn. The technical aspects of the job were the same and if anything she found 'the firm' a worse company to work for because it was all cloak and dagger. You didn't know where you were going to be from one moment to the next. She came back from holiday a year ago and they told her she was going to another shop. They then wanted her back here as it was a Silver Service shop. They didn't want her to work only 3 days as she had been doing. She refused to work longer. Ricky came down and said you know we don't work only three days in SS shops but he would make an exception in her case. *In relation to SS there seem to be a lot of exceptions. Though this seems to be Ricky's style, which is to get out of people what he can even if it means bending procedures occasionally.* The reasons were obvious to me, she was a very experienced cashier and as she put it "I have a bubbly personality, I'm always chatting." I picked up on this theme later when talking about the implicit skills of the job. Once she had been brought back she was put onto SS training tho' this is largely on-the-job DIY training, learning the 50 items etc....

When there were settling queries at the pay-out she always tried to work them out herself for a bit of interest. She loved settling like this without the pressure. In an emergency she once did settling for the afternoon and she found the pace difficult to keep up with and didn't like the pressure but this was only because she wasn't used to it. In fact you were supposed to know the basics of settling to be a Silver Service cashier. She noted that it was very rare that you got asked anything that you had to learn for your SS. She followed up the point made by the others that if the punters thought they had a problem they would naturally go and ask for "one of the lads to come down and sort it out". She wasn't as annoyed about this as the others but it just signified that it was a waste of time.

I asked then

> **'What do you think you are here for then?'**

She was unequivocal.

> **'For attractiveness and personality'**
> Mike: **'Because you're an attractive woman in other words?'**
> Billie: **'Oh yes...'**

241 ** WORK CULTURE: EVENTS **

At one point we were interrupted by Tina who had picked her plastic name plate up and stuck it on her forehead.

> Tina: **'Hey Billie, What's my name?'**
> Billie: **'Prat...'** Uproarious laughter.

(continued)

Extract from Michael Filby's fieldnotes used in Filby (1989).

Despite a variety of views about the nature and purposes of participant observation, most social scientists agree that it sets out to do two things. First, to allow the researcher to see the world of the subject group in its natural setting (often called *naturalistic* observation). Second, to allow the researcher to gain some sort of insight into the way that the subjects see their own world. Participant observation is thus a technique that attempts to discover subjects' meanings.

Participant observation enables the researcher to experience the natural setting at first hand through being directly involved. By being part of the group the researcher is able to appreciate the meanings that the members of the group have about the activities they are involved in and the world in which they live. The researcher, by being part of the group, is able to develop an awareness of the relationship between the actions of the subjects, their values and norms, and the constraints of organisational procedures that affect the subject group. The researcher therefore understands the meanings in the same way as the subjects themselves.

> **Student Activity 6.3**
> Undertake a similar study to that in Student Activity 6.1, but this time join the group (become a participant observer) and see if you are able to provide a better understanding of the group interaction and the meanings of the events for the members of the group.
> NOTE The comments on recording data as a non-participant observer also apply to the participant observation situation. (Only attempt this activity if you are comfortable about becoming a member of the group. You might prefer to study a group of which you are already a member. You will also find that this is a time-consuming activity.)

So, participant observation is generally about the researcher acquiring knowledge of social phenomena from the point of view of the subjects. Instead of imposing concepts, frames of reference and values *on* an understanding of the social group, the researcher acquires these *from* the subject group. For example, Blanche Geer (1964) noted in *First Days in the Field*, that most of the preconceptions participant observers start their research with are overturned very quickly once in the field. Referring to her study of medical students, she noted that during the planning stage she was bored with the thought of studying undergraduates (see Extract 6.2).

> **Student Activity 6.4**
> Re-examine the observations you made for Student Activity 6.3. What preconceptions did you have about the group and the way it was organised? To what extent did your initial observation lead you to reconsider those preconceptions?

Roles

The kind of role played by the participant observer within a group is of crucial importance in this process of acquiring knowledge. The role played will affect the sort of observations the researcher is able to make and the sort of interpretations that follow.

When undertaking participant observation the researcher must decide on an overall strategy. There are a number of possible field roles that a researcher can choose.

Extract 6.2

CHANGING PERCEPTIONS

They looked painfully young to me. I considered their concerns childish and unformed. I could not imagine becoming interested in their daily affairs – in classes, study, dating, and bull sessions. I had memories of my own college days in which I appeared as a child: overemotional, limited in understanding, with an incomprehensible taste for milk shakes and convertibles.

Remembering my attitude as I began to sort out the comments in my field notes I expected to find evidence of this unfavorable adult bias toward adolescents. But on the third day in the field I am already taking the students' side and taking the statements they make seriously.

Adapted from Geer (1964).

Complete participant

The researcher may be a *complete* participant, living in, and fully occupied in the activities of the observed group, as William Whyte (1943) did in his classic study of a predominantly Italian slum area of Boston. Whyte moved into the area, became a lodger in an Italian home, learnt Italian and became a member of one of the street gangs. This reflects the classic approach of anthropologists such as Malinowski (1922) who advocated direct observation fieldwork as the basis for the study of different cultures. Most complete observers perhaps do not go to quite such lengths. Sallie Westwood (1984) took a job in a factory to do her study of the lives of women factory workers and also became involved in the social life of the women, including spending time with some of the women in their homes. Similarly, Miklos Harastzi (1977), a poet in Hungary, went to work in the Red Star Tractor Factory following his various arrests for political activity and wrote an account of his experiences as a worker in a socialist state.

There are also cases of people who are already complete participants becoming observing researchers. Holdaway (1983) was a policeman before he became a social researcher. The 'Chicago School' of the 1920s and 1930s made use of this technique when graduate students from ethnic minorities were encouraged to be observers of their own communities (Harvey, 1987).

Complete participation allows the researcher to gain a clear and detailed idea of the way the group lives or the organisation operates. However, complete participation may result in the researcher uncritically developing the point of view of the subject group. In the extreme case the researcher may become a full-time member of the group and give up being a researcher (Vidich, 1955). Filby (1989) suggests that this can happen on an occasional basis. For example, he helped out in the betting shop on Grand National day and was so preoccupied with doing things right on this very busy day that he had no time to be an observer. Similarly, Pryce (1979, p. 293) noted that some of his interactions were so absorbing that he found it difficult to steer questions in the direction of his research interests. Elliott (1972, p. 174) too found that there came a stage during his research 'Known in the literature as "going native", in which I began to recognize beliefs and actions so clearly that it was hard to imagine how they could be different'.

Partial participant

Alternatively, the researcher may be a *partial* participant. The researcher participates in some of the activities of the subject group but not all, or participates on a part-time basis. Ned Polsky (1971), for example, in his study of hustlers, spent many hours observing what they did in poolrooms but did not observe his subjects in any other setting.

Associate member

A third alternative is for the researcher to be *associated* with the subject group. This occurs when for physical reasons the researcher cannot be a direct member of the group; for example, an adult researching juveniles. Here the researcher has to adopt a field role that enables direct participation of some sort as an associate of the subject group. Howard Parker (1974), for example, hung around with a group of kids who, among other things, stole car radios from parked vehicles. He was a residential community-youth worker at a country holiday centre for Liverpool 'street kids'. Although much older (22 compared to 16 for the kids) he did not look that much different. He became established as an 'OK outsider', that is 'boozy, suitably dressed and ungroomed, playing football well enough to survive and badly enough to be funny, 'knowing the score' about theft behaviour and sexual exploits'. Once accepted locally by a few of the boys he was able to hang around with any combinations of a wider network whenever he had the time. There were intensive periods when he spent all his waking hours with the boys and other times when he spent some weekends or evenings. Similarly, Paul Willis (1977) was clearly not one of the 'lads' but was able to hang around with them both in and out of school in order to observe their life-style and the way their anti-school culture developed.

Researchers in field roles should be aware of their actions and consider the possible effects these actions may have on the field under investigation and on the findings.

Unobtrusive research

Participant observers, as we have suggested, usually want to observe their subjects in their natural setting and so, as far as possible, try to avoid contaminating the research setting by being obtrusive. Being obvious about recording data can affect the research situation. If, for example, you are seen writing notes every time someone does something or you constantly produce a tape-recorder every time a conversation starts up, or are seen to be constantly mumbling into an electronic memo machine, then your subjects are going to stop acting naturally and are likely to avoid you.

Obtrusive research

However, not all observation research is unobtrusive. Phillip Elliott (1972) openly recorded notes in his television study because he did not trust his memory and to give him something to do despite some initial suspicion among the programme producers he was observing. Similarly, Yiannis Gabriel (1988) comments that he kept copious notes of the informal chats he had with people as they went about their work in the catering industry. These were made overtly and he recalls that he was often teased: 'Dear me, what I wouldn't give to know what goes on in those blue books of yours', and 'Just make sure you don't leave those blue books with all that's in them lying around. I wouldn't like them to know what I'm telling you'. Obtrusive recording of data was turned to good use by Michael Filby (1989) in his study of betting shop staff.

> I periodically wrote short notes in a field notebook, having explained the purpose of this. This became something of a motif. In the first shop I had the unintentional habit of forgetting where I had left it prompting ritual searches and cries of 'don't forget your notebook'. Occasionally I was asked what I was writing down but these staff never attempted to read it. The female staff in the second shop conversely needed only half an opportunity, and in consequence I tended to keep a firmer hold. Here, however, a standard call became, 'write this down Mike' or 'don't write this down Mike!'. At first I was irrationally proprietorial about my notes and on one occasion snapped at one of the workers who looked at them. We both expressed some guilt, apologised and so on. The next day I brought in some typed up notes and shared them with this and other female staff. While assuaging some of my guilt it also provided further material as we discussed some of the ideas I was developing. Towards the end of the stint another staff member decided she would write some notes on me, which, with encouragement, she completed and handed over. There were some important lessons about sharing and about subjects as theorists to be learned from these incidents.

Student Activity 6.5
Review the observation activities you have undertaken so far and assess the extent to which you have been obtrusive or unobtrusive in the way you recorded the data. Do you think that your data recording practices had any effect on the people you were observing? If so, how did it affect them?

In the main, to affect the naturalistic setting as little as possible, observation researchers are unobtrusive. This does not just apply to the way data is recorded but also to the roles that are played. A key issue is whether or not the researcher should keep the research activity secret (covert) or be open (overt) about the nature of the research.

Open or secret observation

All observers, participant and non-participant, have to decide whether to let the subjects of their observation know they are being watched. If you let the subjects know you are observing them then they may object and it may prove difficult or impossible to carry on doing the research. Even if the subjects are happy that you continue observing, they may be self-conscious and restrained in what they do when you are around. On the other hand, if you observe secretly, the subjects will not know they are the subject of observation and so will not be inhibited. However, you may have to go to great lengths to keep your observation secret.

In general, *open* observation research allows for a less stressful role than secret observation (Holdaway, 1983). Laud Humphreys (1970), a secret observer who adopted a role as look-out for gay men, was part of a group attacked by youths in a public toilet and was also arrested by the police. The open researcher is more likely to be able to ask naive questions (especially at the beginning of the research) than the participant observer who is secretly researching the group. A secret observer runs the risk of being discovered and the research coming to a premature conclusion. In the extreme case, discovery can result in actual or potential physical harm for the researcher. James Patrick (1973, p. 135) was forced to quit his secretive research of a Glasgow gang when he refused to carry a weapon and failed to turn up for a gang battle. Although protected by the gang leader, another member of the gang, who had been arrested and was serving a short sentence, intended vengeance against Patrick for his non-appearance and repeatedly threatened to 'rip his jaw'. As Patrick put it, 'my days in the gang were numbered'.

Secret observation is preferred by some participant observers because, they argue, it reduces the impact of the researcher on the group. The researcher is just another member of the group and the subjects carry on as before. Although keeping up the pretence may be difficult, it is no more difficult than negotiating to do the research in the first place and then trying to play down one's researcher role. In some cases, they argue, secret participant observation is the only viable alternative. Sometimes you have to be secretive because there is no way that certain groups will ever allow you to do the research if they know what you are doing, for example, extreme right-wing political organisations (Fielding, 1981) or religious cults (Festinger, Rieken and Schachter, 1956). In other cases, a secret approach may be considered necessary to discover what is really going on, such as studying the police at work (Holdaway, 1983). However, open observation research has taken place in both these areas. Barker (1984) was invited to study a religious cult and Grimshaw and Jefferson (1987) undertook an open, non-participant study of policework.

Other participant observers argue that secret research should always be avoided, and the researcher should not attempt to 'be one of them' (Polsky, 1971). Apart from the stress, potential danger and possible premature conclusion, secret participant observation is far too restrictive. To undertake research secretly you have to adopt a particular role within a group and this can often be a limited one with specific expectations and with little flexibility. Secret observers are, in effect, assigned a role, unlike open researchers who can develop their own, less rigid, role. The open role allows researchers to be involved in more aspects of the group activity without any expectation that they should undertake any particular tasks. This can be very important when it comes to issues of what the researcher is and is not prepared to do. If the observer is operating a secret role there will be group expectations about what she or he does that may be very difficult to get out of. The open researcher can make it clear from the outset what kinds of things she or he wants to hear about or witness, and it is important to do so. Polsky (1971) reports a social worker involved with criminals who did not make his position clear and who was manoeuvred into a situation where he had to dispose of murder weapons.

Open participant observation is thus likely to result in a more *flexible* role. This allows greater freedom of enquiry for the researcher than does secret participant observation. The subject group will not assume that the researcher is aware of group taken-for-granteds and will tolerate, at least for a while, what they see as naive or simplistic questions. However, even open participant observers are recommended to 'keep your eyes open and your mouth closed' (Polsky, 1971) because you will find 'answers to questions you never thought to ask' (Whyte, 1955).

Furthermore, if you are a participant long enough, especially if you are unobtrusive, the other members of the group will either *forget* you are a researcher or will be so used to you that they will soon overcome any inhibitions they may have. You will cease to be a threat and they will drop any 'front' that they may have constructed as a reaction to your initial presence. Anne Campbell (1984, pp. 2–3) adopted an open approach for these reasons in her study of New York female gang members.

> In [secret] participant observation, the researcher becomes part of the group by concealing her true purpose, which places her in the position of acting as a human recorder, dispassionate and removed.... Worse still, the researcher often overidentifies with the group; she assumes that her interpretation of events is the same as that of the members, and this can be a dangerous assumption when entering a subculture whose members do not share the same ethnic, educational and political background. I never attempted to disguise my identity or purpose and so was able to ask openly for explanations of ambiguous events and to query inconsistencies in accounts. Practically, I also could use a tape recorder rather than having to rely on field notes alone.
>
> The most obvious danger with this approach, however, is that members can lie to you. In remaining with a group for a period of time it is quite difficult for either researcher or subject to sustain false impressions: it is hard to maintain a systematic deceit or an alien persona for six months and members of the gang or community are apt to give the game away. But there were, I do not doubt, facts that were hidden from me. Often accounts of criminal activities were oddly inconsistent over time: I suspect that on occasion members feared they had said too much and made attempt to cover themselves. More often, girls talked freely about incriminating matters if, upon request, I did not use the tape recorder.

Extract 6.3

JOINING THE GANG

I was dressed in a midnight-blue suit, with a twelve-inch middle vent, three-inch flaps over the side pockets and a light blue hand-kerchief with a white polka dot (to match my tie) in the top pocket. My hair, which I had allowed to grow long, was newly washed and combed into a parting just to the left of centre. My nails I had cut down as far as possible, leaving them ragged and dirty. I approached the gang of boys standing out-side the pub and Tim, my contact, came forward to meet me, his cheeks red with embarrassment.

'Hello, sur, Ah never thoat ye wid come.

Fortunately, the others had not heard the slip which almost ruined all my preparations.

I had not planned to join a juvenile gang; I had been invited. For two years I had been working in one of Scotland's approved schools during my college vacations. I had met Tim, who had been committed to the school and we quickly became friends. During one conversation with a group of boys in a lunch-break at the school I was criticising people who got into trouble while on leave. Tim asked me what I knew about boys on leave and how they spent their time. The honest answer was nothing at all. At this point the signal for the end of lunch-break was given and, as the boys walked over to their 'line', Tim sidled up to me and asked me to come out with him and see for myself.

Adapted from Patrick (1973, p. 13).

Table 6.1 Participant observation roles

	Complete	Partial	Associate
Open obtrusive non-neutral	1	2	3
Open obtrusive neutral	4	5	6
Open unobtrusive non-neutral	7	8	9
Open unobtrusive neutral	10	11	12
Secret non-neutral	13	14	15
Secret neutral	16	17	18

In short, open participant observation is preferred because neither the subjects nor the researcher can keep an act going for very long without considerable effort and enormous stress.

Student Activity 6.6
Would you say that Anne Campbell conducted her study of New York gang girls in an obtrusive manner? If so, in what ways?

Complete secret observation is probably best avoided if you intend to use participant observation in your research project. Quite often, researchers adopt a *partially open* approach. The true purpose of the research may only be half known to the group. Researchers sometimes only tell the members of the group that they are writing a book or article about the area.

Sometimes the real activities of the researcher may only be known to a sub-set of the subject group (usually including group leaders). Whyte, for example, told Doc, the leader of the gang, that he was 'writing a book about street corner life', Doc then vouched for Whyte with the rest of the gang. Such an approach can lead to problems when the research is published. Doc was upset and felt betrayed by the way that the activities of the gang were reported in *Street Corner Society*.

A neutral role

A researcher cannot be present in a social setting without playing some part in it, whether as a secret or open observer. Most participant observation researchers argue that it is important to adopt as neutral a role as possible to avoid directly affecting group activities. This view suggests that the re-searcher should avoid being involved in determining group decisions, either directly or indirectly, and should not play any leadership role. Whyte, for example, was concerned when Doc, the leader of the gang, indicated that he had always acted on impulse until Whyte joined them. Now Doc tended to think what Whyte would do in the circumstances before suggesting a plan of action to the other gang members. Although not making the decisions, Whyte's presence clearly had an indirect impact on what happened through his unintended influence on the group leader. Other researchers are less concerned about playing a neutral role.

Sallie Westwood (1984) was a packer in a factory and as such had a flexible and uninfluential job. However, on occasion during social events she became annoyed by the constant sexism and made her position clear. To some extent this rubbed off on to the other women and affected their reactions to sexist activity. Westwood did not see this as a problem of 'contamination'.

Thus participant observers must decide on the degree of their participa-tion, whether to be open or secret, whether they can afford to be obtrusive or to be unobtrusive, and what role they are going to play.

Thus there are eighteen possible participant observation roles (see Table 6.1). For example, Ned Polsky's (1971) study of hustlers falls into category 11, while Whyte's (1955) *Street Corner Society* falls into category 7. Paul Willis's (1977) study of 'the lads' falls into category 12 (see page 170), Laud Humphreys' (1970) role as look-out for gay men is category 18 and James Patrick's (1973) observation of a Glasgow gang is in category 17.

Student Activity 6.7
Review the participant observation studies of which you are aware and see if you can identify which field role has been adopted in each. With other members of your class or lecture group see how many of the possible types above occur in practice. Which are the most popular?

So far, in order to give some focus to the general principles of observation research, we have tended to focus on studies of small-group interaction. However, as we suggested in the Introduction, observation studies are not confined to small-group analysis. Observation can also be used as a technique to analyse large groups, such as crowds at a sporting event or demonstration. Furthermore, it is also a technique widely used in the analysis of organisations and institutions (such as schools, hospitals and factories) and has also been applied to wider studies of social structures (such as the relationship between the education system and the world of work).

> **Student Activity 6.8**
> **Undertake a participant or non-participant observation study of an organisation to which you have access, such as a work-place, voluntary organisation, sports or social club. To what extent does the organisation operate in practice in a way that differs from the organisation's more formal rules, aims and customs?**
> **NOTE This observation activity is, once again, likely to be very time-consuming.**

Access

Doing participant observation research clearly requires becoming part of a social situation. This can be quite a difficult and fraught part of the whole operation. The degree of difficulty depends on the type of role adopted, particularly whether it is secret or open, and the kind of group or organisation being researched. If access is to be successful and the observation role, covert or overt, is to be maintained then the researcher must have a good 'cover story'. If this is not the complete truth, then the researcher must devise something that will make him or her acceptable to the group, but also one that can be sustained should close questioning about it occur.

There is no simple formula for gaining access to a group for purposes of participant observation. Sometimes access involves a long period of research, consultation and persuasion to find a suitable research setting, to make contacts and to become accepted. Some researchers are able to take advantage of existing organisational contacts, social situations or skills to negotiate access. Howard Becker (1963) used his musical skills and Ned Polsky (1971) his billiard playing skills in order to make contacts and become part of the social group they wanted to study.

Sometimes, however, the research setting almost falls into the researcher's lap. Barker (1984) was invited to do research into the 'Moonies' and Patrick (1973) starts *A Glasgow Gang Observed* with an account of how he joined the gang (see Extract 6.3 on page 159). On the other hand, Robin Page (1971), a civil servant concerned about the welfare system, made a conscious decision to become a dosser in order to find out why so many people live in abject poverty. He began his homeless career without any idea of what the problems might be in becoming a dosser (see Extract 6.4).

Patrick became a participant observer as a result of an invitation while Page decided to become a dosser and then luckily came across a group he was able to join. As both were covert observers they clearly had to develop things 'by ear' once the first contacts were made. The sometimes fortuitous and unforeseen events associated with access may not always be a good thing. It may lead to the research being determined by the way that initial contact is made and developed rather than by any concerns to undertake systematic research. Martyn Hammersley and Paul Atkinson (1983), for example, raise

---

Extract 6.4

BECOMING A DOWN-AND-OUT

My experience as a down-and-out started in May 1971, when I was deposited by friends on the Brighton Road in Croydon. Apart from the clothes I stood up in, a pair of dirty jeans, a shirt with a frayed collar, a thin pullover and a donkey jacket, I had a small bag containing a spare shirt, jeans, jumper and socks, all very tattered; a rain hat and small cycle cape, an old sleeping bag and a water container. I had just 20p in my pocket. With four days stubble on my chin I looked scruffy, and felt scruffier, and already respectable middle-class women out shopping were giving me disapproving sidelong glances as I passed them. However, the strange affinity that seems to bind down-and-outs together was quick to show itself, for as I passed a bus shelter containing two long-coated, red-faced cider drinkers, they smiled friendly alcoholic smiles at me, which seemed to indicate that I was already accepted as one of their own kind....

At Brighton, I made for the beach which was to become my home. Down on the pebbles midway between the two piers was a group of dossers about twenty strong, mostly young, some genuinely down-and-out, while others were hippies. I was accepted as one of the group straight away with no problems. One long-haired youth, wearing red corduroy trousers and a combat jacket asked me if I was 'dossing' and invited me to make myself at home.

Adapted from Page (1971, pp. 9–12).

Extract 6.5

GETTING AN INTRODUCTION

Getting an initial introduction or two is not nearly so difficult as it might seem. Among students whom I have had perform the experiment of asking their relatives and friends to see if any could provide an introduction to a career criminal, fully a third reported that they could get such introductions.... Moreover, once your research interests are publicly known you get volunteer offers of this sort. From students, faculty, and others, I have had more offers of introductions to career criminals – in and out of organised crime – than I could begin to follow up. And that is hardly anything compared to the introductions obtainable via criminal lawyers and crime reporters (to say nothing of law enforcement personnel).

Be that as it may, there are times when you don't have an introduction to a particular scene you want to study, and you must start 'cold'. In such a situation it is easier, usually, to get acquainted first with criminals at their play rather than at their work. Exactly where this is depends on your individual play interests.... I, of course, find it best to start out in the local poolroom. But if you can drink most people under the table, are a convivial barroom companion, etc., then you should start out in a tavern. If you know horses, start out at a horse parlour. If you know cards, ask around about a good poker game. If you know fighters, start out at the local fight gym.

Adapted from Polsky (1971).

the question of whether or not Elliot Liebow (1967), in his study *Tally's Corner*, should have surrendered himself so thoroughly to the chance meeting with Tally and its subsequent consequences that his initial plans to carry out a number of small comparative studies was abandoned. Liebow reports that the lines of his fieldwork were 'laid out without my being aware of it' (Liebow, 1967, p. 237).

Sometimes the researcher wants to set up the research from the outset as an observation study of certain situations and this requires negotiation with certain key individuals, or gatekeepers. Colin Lacey (1970), for example, in his study of a secondary school, had to obtain permission from the chief education officer and the headmaster. Similarly, Michael Little (1990) in his study *Young Men in Prison*, needed Home Office permission. Sallie Westwood (1984, p. 2) used a local contact to set up a meeting with the management of 'Stitch Co.' and 'for some reason, the idea of an anthropologist studying the culture of the shopfloor by hanging around the coffee bar, lurking in the lunch canteen and sharing a few "risque" jokes, appealed to management who saw my immersion as a baptism of fire'. Whyte's study of street corner life was only possible after he met Doc who vouched for him with the rest of the gang. Even Patrick's secret involvement with the Glasgow gang was made possible with the connivance of Tim, the gang leader. Polsky (1971), as we have seen, argues that research on deviant groups should be open. The use of gatekeepers is thus central to gaining access (see Extract 6.5). Polsky argues that you need to make an initial contact and *snowball* the sample (see page 120).

Student Activity 6.9
To what extent is Polsky's account (Extract 6.5), which is based on experiences in the USA in the 1960s, realistic and feasible here and now? Ask your friends and relatives to see if they know any career criminals. Do not attempt to follow up any of these. Comment, also, on the gender assumptions that Polsky makes.

Sometimes, however, access is denied. Barbara Rogers (1988, p. viii) wanted to study men-only clubs and organisations such as freemasons, rotary clubs, private boys schools, elite men's clubs, the upper tiers of the armed forces and the Church of England as well male-dominated pubs and sports clubs. As a woman this was not easy.

It is a daunting task to investigate where no woman is allowed to go: many of these organisations are very poorly documented for such important institutions in our society, and several of them rejected straightforward approaches from me. It therefore became essential to use men informants and investigators alike...to open up the different worlds of men-only to female scrutiny.

Rogers thus combined her own observations, where she could gain access, with those of male investigators who worked for her and the comments of informants who were members of the organisations she was investigating.

Continuing negotiation of access

It is important to remember that access is not a one-off event. The researcher is constantly negotiating and renegotiating access. New people come into the research situation all the time and the researcher's role and activities have to be constantly reiterated. Indeed, as the research progresses the researcher will also probably want to redefine the research role to obtain a wider range of material. This, as we have said, is more difficult for secret than open researchers. Michael Filby's (1989, pp. 21–2) access to the betting shops was gained through previous research contacts with a major bookmaking company and the project was negotiated in terms of a case study of the nature of work in a service industry.

> The broad intentions of the study were shared with all the participants in varying levels of detail. 'Access' was a continuing process of negotiation. I had to re-explain my presence and interests as subjects entered the scene. While the last person is as important as the first, it is difficult to be equally conscientious. The staff helped out somewhat in explaining their understanding to others but this is apt to create unintended impressions. Nevertheless, Bridget, a member of the first shop, invented a line which I then gratefully used ... that 'Mike is doing a study on what it's really like working in a betting shop'.

Negotiating access and data collection are not distinct aspects of the research process, they overlap, and the process of negotiating access can provide valuable information about the nature of the social setting being observed. For example, the openness with which a person may describe criminal activities shows the matter-of-fact way that the deviant 'career' is seen. Howard Newby (1977), in his study of farm workers, noted that having to go through the farmer in order to contact the workers was in itself important evidence that clearly indicated how significant the employer was in the lives of the farm workers.

Deviance

You will probably have noticed that many of the participant observation studies referred to above are concerned with social deviance. Of course, not all participant observation studies are about deviance, nor do all studies of deviance use participant observation (see, for example, the section on religion and delinquency in Chapter 4 and the section on crime in Chapter 3). None the less, deviance provides a good example of the relationship between participant observation method and social theory. There is no single definition of deviance, but it usually includes behaviour which is illegal, 'abnormal' or bizarre. What counts as deviance thus varies over time and from place to place. There are several competing theories of deviance and these will be outlined below.

Student Activity 6.10
See if you can come up with a definition of deviance. We suggest you work in pairs, where possible.

Positivist theories of deviance

Positivist theories of deviance all attempt to identify the *causes* of deviance. They include *biological* and *psychological* theories, as well as *social* theories. Biological and psychological theories attempt to link deviance to physical characteristics, genetic make-up, or defective socialisation. These approaches are deterministic. Crime and deviancy are seen to be *caused* by genetic inheritance or inadequate socialisation of the individual.

A similar individualistic approach can be found amongst positivist *control* theorists who see deviance as the result of such things as lack of parental

BIOLOGICAL THEORIES OF DEVIANCE attempt to relate deviance to biological features. Cesare Lombroso (1911) examined people detained in prisons and asylums and concluded that physiological features such the size and shape of the skull, ear size, and the presence of extra toes and fingers could be related to crime and deviance. This approach saw criminality as the result of a person's *criminal nature* rather than as the result of a *rational* act (Garafolo, 1914). More recently, Glueck and Glueck (1956) argued that stocky, muscular boys were more likely to engage in delinquent behaviour.

These biological theories drew on a rather crude reading of Darwinian evolutionary theory. They suggested that not all humans had evolved at the same rate. Criminals, distinguished by their less evolved physiological features, were at the bottom of the evolutionary human hierarchy.

When applied to women, these theories assume that female deviants differ biologically from what is 'normal' for women. Lambroso and Ferrero (1895), mixing up biological traits with gender roles, showed that female deviants lacked what they regarded as the natural attributes of women: reserve, docility and sexual apathy. Recent research has linked deviance to chromosome abnormalities among girls (Gibbens, 1971; Kaplan, 1971). Cowie *et al.* (1968) account for the lower rate of delinquency among girls by suggesting that they are less genetically liable to anti-social acts. Girls require a more extreme push from the environment (such as poor homes) to overcome their relative immunity to delinquency.

SOCIAL ECOLOGICAL THEORY OF DEVIANCE can be found in the work of many of the Chicago sociologists of the 1920s and 1930s. They suggest that deviant activity is associated with the evolving nature of human habitation, notably cities. Social change occurs far faster than social institutions or structures can keep up with and thus communities always exhibit some degree of *social disorganisation* (Thomas, 1966). The Chicago social ecologists showed that cities grew through a serious of *concentric zones*, which changed over time (Park, Burgess and McKenzie, 1925). Deviance, such as suicide (Cavan 1928), schizophrenia (Faris and Dunham, 1939; Dunham, 1941), and juvenile delinquency (Shaw and Mckay, 1931) varied across zones and was higher in *zones of transition*, where social disorganisation was greatest.

PSYCHOLOGICAL THEORIES OF DEVIANCE see deviance in terms of either genetically-based predispositions or inadequate socialisation. Some *psychological* theories attempted to link biology with psychology in explaining deviant behaviour. On the basis of a sample of nine inmates of a high security mental hospital Price (1966) argued that the presence of an extra Y chromosome in men is likely to predispose them to criminal violence. (A conclusion challenged by Hunter (1966), Sarbin and Miller (1970), and Taylor, Walton and Young (1973)). Similarly, sexual 'deviation' has been linked to an 'imbalance' of male and female hormones that effect a child before birth and supposedly predispose it towards homosexuality (Raboch and Sipova, 1974; Dorner, 1974). Hans Eysenck (1970) has argued that heredity is a 'very strong predisposing factor' in the committing of crimes. He thinks personality characteristics such as extroversion are genetically based. On the basis of a study of prisoners he concluded that there is a strong link between extroversion and deviant behaviour. (A conclusion challenged by Hoghughi and Forrest, 1970.)

Other psychological theories link psychology to *socialisation* (see page 50) and, rather than see the mental abnormality that leads to deviant acts as being inherited, argue that deviant activity is the result of inadequate or defective learning. The subject is 'under-socialised' or 'maladjusted' and turns to crime and deviance. In particular, deviants are seen as suffering from *maternal deprivation* during their early years (Bowlby, 1946). This view has been extensively reassessed (see, for example, Morgan (1975) and Rutter (1981))

Psychological theories have also been used to explain female deviance. They see women as neurotic, irrational and emotive and attempt to link deviant activity to these sexist presuppositions. Eysenck (1970), for example, compared married and unmarried mothers, arguing that the latter are likely to be more promiscuous and therefore deviant. He showed that unmarried mothers were more likely to be extroverted, emotional and neurotic than married mothers, and thus, according to his theory, more likely to be deviant. Konopka (1966) continues the tradition of Thomas (1923) and similarly confuses biological sex with socially constructed gendered roles, claiming that female delinquency is essentially a problem of maladjustment that occurs when sanctions controlling the activities of women are removed.

control (Hirschi and Stark, 1969; Wilson, 1980). A variant of this suggests that deviance occurs when benefits outweigh costs. This approach concentrates on *situations* as causes of individual deviant acts. For example, people will commit crimes if a suitable situation arises and they think they can get away with it (Cornish and Clarke, 1986; Laycock, 1984).

Positivist *social* theories of deviance draw on both social *ecology* and *functionalism*. They see deviance as the result of social conditions rather than any inherent individual factors.

Social ecology
Social ecological theories link deviance to the changing nature of urban environments. The development of cities is equated with natural growth and different areas of the city will, at different times, experience change and instability. It is in these areas that deviance is more likely to occur.

Functionalist theories of deviance
Functionalist theories assume that crime and deviance are part of all societies. Functionalist theories of deviance are influenced by Durkheim's work, particularly his notion of *anomie* (see page 11). There are several variants of functionalist theories of deviance, including strain theory and subcultural theory.

Strain theory
Robert Merton (1938) applied the notion of anomie to deviance and developed a particular form of functionalist theory that has come to be called *strain* theory. Merton argued that people had aspirations but these were social rather than individual in origin. He argued that deviance occurred when socially acceptable means cannot be used to achieve socially acceptable 'goals'. No matter how hard someone on a supermarket check-out works he or she will never achieve a high level of material wealth. Deviance was thus a result of the *strain* on the system. He argued that the myth of the 'American Dream', that anyone can achieve material wealth and power, is not matched by the structure of opportunity in America. Thus people adopt different strategies to achieve their goals, some of which are deviant. Thus strain theory sees deviance as a *rational* act on the part of the individual in the face of circumstances.

Subcultural theories of deviance
Merton's functionalist analysis has been developed by *subcultural* theorists. Some social environments, or subcultures, lead to illegal or deviant activities, others do not. According to Edwin Sutherland (1939), individuals become criminal because of associations with carriers of criminal norms. Deviancy is thus a function of what he called *differential association*. Criminal behaviour is learnt through peer groups.

However, this presumes that the subculture strives for dominant goals and adopts illegitimate means to achieve them. Other researchers have suggested that this is not the case (Cohen, 1955; Cloward and Ohlin, 1960). For example, working-class delinquent gangs do not attempt to achieve commonly-held goals. Rather, gangs set up completely different sets of goals *outside* the dominant, middle-class, culture.

> Young people's self feelings depend very largely upon how they are judged by others.... The standards by which they are judged are those current among middle-class people.... These standards include such

Extract 6.6

MIDDLE-CLASS GANGS

The field observations are based on the experiences of a participant observer who spent two weeks amongst several groups of deviant and non-deviant middle-class youths in a suburb of Los Angeles. The middle-class youngsters were located through lists of "hangouts" provided by local police, school authorities, and probation officers. The observer "hung around" these places and when asked who he was, which was seldom, explained that he was a writer doing a series of articles on teenagers. The youngsters talked freely in front of and to the observer, and after a short time included him in many of their activities, such as house and beach parties, drag races, car club meetings, bull sessions, and bowling. Altogether, about eighty youngsters ranging in age between fifteen and eighteen were observed. All were Caucasian, most in high school, Protestant, and in appearance and manner readily distinguishable from the lower-class boys and girls who occasionally mixed with them.

Impressions, activities and conversations were recorded by the observer in a daily journal, and roughly classified into the following categories: values and peer interactions, deviant activities, and group organisation. These field observations treat as data the meanings assigned to and explanations given for activities as well as the behaviour itself. It should be kept in mind that these comments are observations, not findings.

The deviant behaviour of the group observed varied greatly in seriousness. The more serious deviant activities, such as theft and narcotic use, seemed to involve the least number of people at one time. The less serious infractions were incidental to other activities such as spontaneous drag racing, drinking and sexual activity.

Many boys spoke of frequent and regular stealing, often from employers. Ready access rather than need or desire seemed to determine the choice of stolen objects. These items were seldom traded or converted into cash. Great pride was evidenced in the cleverness with which the thefts were executed and a good performance seemed more important than the acquisition of goods. Several boys boasted about never having been caught although they had been engaging in this activity for years. The stolen goods were by no means small, inexpensive, or easily portable, but included such items as tyres, car radios and television sets. Great care was taken to ensure that stolen goods were not missed. Thefts were timed to coincide with events such as inventories and the filling of orders. This phenomenon appears to be very similar to 'white collar crime' and raises questions about the generalisability of theories of delinquency causation. It may well be that the 'white collar delinquent' engages in as many anti-social activities as do lower-class youngsters but a combination of factors, particularly the form of delinquency, interact to prevent these activities from coming to the attention of the authorities, or if apprehended, prevent the middle-class youngster from being officially handled and recorded.

A local probation officer provided several examples of the middle-class group's anti-social activities which *do* come to the attention of the authorities. For example, a car full of boys drove slowly down a main shopping street spraying the well-dressed shoppers with the contents of a fire extinguisher. Another incident involved a group of boys who stole an old car and took it to a vacant lot and while one boy drove around in circles, the others threw stones at it, until it was nothing but a battered corpse.

There is a mischievous, often amusing overtone to all these incidents; they are not the kind likely to be thought to be malicious or violent. Rather they are spontaneous and gratuitous, proving nothing but providing 'kicks'. This behaviour is not the kind that is likely to seriously alarm parents or police and has none of the grim overtones usually associated, correctly or not, with the behaviour of lower-class gangs. In general, the deviant activities of these youngsters was non-violent and personal aggression rare. The anti-social activities observed among these groups rarely took the form of open defiance of authority; manipulation rather than rebellion appeared to be the preferred technique for handling trouble with authorities.

Adapted and abridged from Myerhoff and Myerhoff, 1964, p. 330–3.

criteria as verbal fluency, academic intelligence, high levels of aspiration, drives for achievement, the ability to delay gratification.... Young people of different origins and backgrounds tend to be judged by the same standards.... However, they are not all equally well equipped for success in this status game. One way that lower class children can deal with this problem is to repudiate and withdraw from the game, to refuse to recognize the rules as having any application to them, and to set up new games with their own rules or criteria of status – rules by which they *can* perform satisfactorily. It is not, however, quite that simple. The dominant value system is also, to a degree, *their* value system.... Therefore, they not only reject the dominant value system, but do so with a vengeance. They 'stand it on its head'; they exalt its opposition; they engage in malicious, spiteful, 'ornery' behavior of all sorts to demonstrate not only to others, but to themselves as well, their contempt for the game they have rejected (Cohen, 1966, pp. 65–6)

Delinquency is thus not explained by anomie but by *status frustration*. Middle-class ideas of material possessions and the legitimate means to strive for them are explicitly rejected. Instead, working-class delinquent gangs value aggression, thrills and immediate gratification. So, gang behaviour, while unacceptable to the community at large, is acceptable and *rational* to gang members. Gangs use illegitimate means to achieve their own defined status ends and deviant activity is learned via interaction with peer groups.

Other studies have raised doubts about the notion of oppositional cultures (Short and Strodtbeck, 1967; Matza, 1961, 1964, 1969) and status frustration (Shanley, 1966; Aggleton, 1987a) by showing similar practices among middle-class delinquent groups. Howard and Barbara Myerhoff (1964) studied middle class 'gangs' using direct observational techniques (see Extract 6.6).

Student Activity 6.11
1. **Comment on the adequacy of the fieldwork reported in Extract 6.6.**
2. **Do the reported observations suggest that middle-class 'gangs' undertake the same activities as working-class gangs?**
3. **Do these observations support the strain theory of deviance?**
4. **Do the observations support the theory that delinquent subcultures develop oppositional cultures?**
5. **Does the extract call into question the idea that delinquent groups exhibit status frustration?**

Phenomenological theories of deviance

An alternative approach to deviance is concerned with the *social processes* by which certain behaviour comes to be seen as deviant, rather than with the causes of deviance. There are two broad strands to this approach, one based on interactionism and the other a phenomenological critique of interactionism. These theories see deviance as a *relative* concept, varying from place to place and time to time. They therefore focus on what deviancy *means* in certain settings.

Interactionist theories of deviance
Interactionist approaches to deviance see the definition of deviance as problematic. They argue that there is no 'objective' definition of deviance. Deviance is the result of a social *process* of definition. Thus, interactionists look at the social process and the consequences. They focus on the perspective both of those who define deviance and those who are defined as deviant. They ask such question as:

- What are the circumstances under which a person gets set apart and considered deviant?
- How is a person cast into that social role?
- What actions do others take on the basis of the definition of the person as deviant?
- How does the person react to being defined as deviant? How is the deviant role adopted?
- What changes in group membership result?
- To what extent does the deviant's self-perception change?

The perception of deviance becomes the problem (not the qualities of the deviant or the character of the deviant acts). Deviance is thus seen as a *process of interaction* between deviants and non-deviants.

Edwin Lemert (1971) argued that the key to understanding juvenile delinquency was in the motivation and activities of those who were responsible for reacting to delinquency rather than the motives and actions of the delinquents themselves.

Furthermore, the definition often *produces* the deviant acts. Rather than positivist approaches that assume that social control arises out of the existence of deviance, Lemert argued that social control lead to deviance.

INTERACTIONISM originally set out to establish the causes of social phenomena. However, these *traditional* interactionists argued that it was necessary to take into account people's attitudes as well as social values. People developed their attitudes through interaction with other people. The life history of a person was important evidence in understanding how they developed their attitudes.

Interactionism was influential in the development of a science of sociology in the United States between 1910 and 1930. W. I. Thomas's notion of the *definition of the situation* (see page 40) was an important element of interactionism. It suggests that people make sense of their circumstances by defining the world and their situation in it.

Early interactionism attempted to provide causal explanations based on empirical evidence. They were concerned with the issue of social control and sought social laws to explain social phenomena which could then be used to ensure social control.

People define the situation in which they find themselves in terms of their *attitudes* and prevailing social *values* and then act accordingly. So attitudes and values both effect social action.

Interactionists thought that causal explanations had to take account of attitudes as well as social facts and values. Thus they had a similar approach to Max Weber.

The term interactionism has been applied more loosely (see page 8) and incorporates any approach that focuses on the specific details of social processes, particularly face-to-face and small-group interaction. It thus sometimes includes the various different approaches to *symbolic interactionism* (see page 183) and *ethnomethodology* (see page 158). These later developments are less concerned than traditional interactionism with broad social process and causal explanations.

Having been defined as deviant, a person will go on to play the expected deviant role (Lees, 1986).

The notion of the social construction of deviant identity has become developed in *labelling theory*.

Labelling theory

Labelling theory is the clearest exposition of the interactionist approach to deviance. Labelling theorists argue that deviant acts are those that are *labelled* as deviant. What is defined as a deviant act varies according to the following factors: time, person, place and reaction to it. (For example, on page 78, we noted how similar actions by football supporters and Oxbridge students are labelled differently.) Thus, labelling theory opposed the consensus view of *strain* theorists. Deviance is not violation of generally agreed norms but rather the result of *social reaction* to particular types of activity, which are not inherently deviant.

Labelling theory thus looked at reactions to acts, rather than the motives and the acts themselves. It focuses attention on the sorts of social situations and encounters through which behaviour is defined as deviant. It thus reconstructed the study of deviance in terms of *definitions* not *motivations*. In so doing, labelling theorists were the first to approach social reaction to deviant behaviour as *variable*. Becker (1963), for example, was interested in how acts such as marijuana smoking come to be labelled deviant. Different official agencies had quite different views as to the harmful nature of marijuana smoking but the view that the drug was dangerous became the dominant one. Using the drug then became illegal.

Becker relates this process to the labelling of users as deviants and examines how the deviant person acts once labelled. There is, he argued, a process of interaction between definers and defined that leads to a deviant *career*.

Deviant career

Deviance can thus be seen in terms of *careers* that are a meaningful and rational response to social reactions. Thus deviance is not seen as impulsive but as the result of the deviant passing through a number of stages (see Extract 6.7). The deviant career thus involves a process of *learning* which is mirrored in a process of *becoming* a deviant.

> **Student Activity 6.12.**
> 1. **Outline the stages or career structure of any other deviant activity of your choice. For example, Peter Marsh *et al.* (1978) analysed football 'hooliganism' as a career structure, David Pittman (1977) described the stages of becoming a male prostitute, James Driscoll (1977) identified the career of male-to-female transsexuals and Martin Weinberg (1966, 1970) explored the career of a nudist.**
> 2. **Comment on the adequacy and suitability of the labelling approach in the light of your review.**

Phenomenological critiques of interactionism

A number of sociologists working broadly within the interactionist approach began to raise question about some of the assumptions of interactionism, particularly as it related to deviant activity. They developed a more profound phenomenological critique which demanded that sociologists closely review the preconceptions and taken-for-granteds that they were bringing to the study of the social world. For example, interactionists talked about 'role',

---

Extract 6.7

BECOMING DEVIANT

Becoming a marijuana user involves three things. First, learning the *technique* of smoking marijuana so as to get high. Second, learning to *perceive* the effects of marijuana use. Third, learning to *enjoy* the effects. Marijuana-produced sensations are not automatically or necessarily pleasurable. The taste for such experience is a socially acquired one. The user feels dizzy, thirsty, misjudges time and distances.

The use of marijuana is controlled. The act is illegal, which makes access to the drug difficult The career of the marijuana user may be divided into three stages, each representing a distinct shift in his or her relation to the social controls of the larger society and to those of the subculture in which marijuana is used. The first stage is represented by the *beginner*, the person smoking marijuana for the first time; the second, by the *occasional user*, whose use is sporadic and dependent on chance factors; and the third, by the *regular user*, for whom use becomes a systematic, usually daily, routine.

Adapted from Becker, 1963, pp. 46–61.

'deviance' and 'process' but did not examine their own taken-for-granted assumptions about what these concepts involved. Aaron Cicourel (1973a) suggested that roles were a sociological invention and that people did not order their world in terms of the roles they played. Similarly, Phillipson and Roche (1974) suggested that 'deviant' was a category devised by sociologists and not one that people made use of in their everyday activities.

For phenomenologists, the relationships between deviants and social controllers are themselves important influences that shape and transform deviant phenomena. For example, Cicourel's (1968) study of the negotiation of juvenile justice examined how the actions of the police, probation officers and courts influenced whether or not a person is prosecuted through the courts (see Extract 6.8).

> **Student Activity 6.13**
> **How does Cicourel's approach (Extract 6.8) differ from Becker's (Extract 6.7)?**

This phenomenological approach is concerned not only with how events are constructed as deviant but also with the ways in which the sociologist comes to an understanding of the phenomenon. As Cicourel says, 'a central focus of my research was the way in which I came to know and describe what I perceived to be the social organization of juvenile justice'. Thus the phenomenological approach requires that the researcher reflect on her or his own conceptualisation of the social processes. Cicourel emphasises the importance of making the *researcher's* interests an important feature of the research.

Phenomenologists, for example, have reassessed Durkheim's analysis of suicide by asking not what are the *causes* of suicide but how some deaths get *categorised* as suicide and others do not (see Example Answer 3.22, in Chapter 3).

Moral panic and deviancy amplification

A development of the interactionist social reaction approach that begins to link deviance within a wider analysis can be found in the notion of *moral panic*. Phil Cohen (1973) developed Lemert's view that control agencies actually caused deviance by suggesting that overreaction to particular deviant phenomena by police, courts and the media constitute moral panics. An event, such as a clash between Mods and Rockers on a Brighton beach, an act of misconduct by a group of football spectators that is recorded by television cameras, or a joyride in a stolen car that ends in tragedy, becomes the focus for moral outrage. The media develop the events into 'stories' and ask questions about the adequacy of controls on youth, the state of the game of football, better security on cars, and so on. The authorities are encouraged to take 'firm' action and the police and courts tend to overreact. More publicity ensues, copy-cat events take place and gang fights, 'hooliganism' or 'twoccing' (taking cars without the owners' consent) become 'epidemics'. The moral panic has resulted in *deviancy amplification*, because the agencies designed to control deviance have actually created and amplified it. The media and the law enforcement authorities isolate subgroups and provides them with an *identity* (dirty, violent, foul-mouthed, drunken and so on). The participants adopt the media-generated identity, expect to be treated in certain ways and behave accordingly. As one travelling Tottenham Hotspur supporter put it at the height of the clamp-down on football crowds, 'We're all hooligans now' (Harvey, Little and Turner, 1982).

Student Activity 6.14
1. Can you think of a current or recent moral panic?
2. How have the press, police and courts characterised it?
3. To what extent is there public moral outrage about the panic?

Critical theories of deviance

Critical theories of deviance attempt to locate their analysis in a wider social, historical and structural setting. They relate deviance to the different forms of oppression (class, race, gender and sexuality) in capitalist society.

Class-based analyses of deviance

Class analyses are dominated by Marxist sociologists. However, not all critical class analyses purport to be Marxist. For example, Owen Gill's (1977, p. ix) study of *Luke Street* 'started as an attempt to understand the lifestyle of a group of boys who regularly came into contact with police and courts' and ended as a study of 'housing policy, policing and urban stereotyping in an attempt to understand the production of the behaviour that comes to be officially registered as delinquent'. The study combined three sociological approaches: social ecological, subcultural and social reaction (or interactionist). Gill set this in an historical context and, taking his cue from C. Wright Mills (1971), attempts 'to understand how wider social arrangements affect the lives of individuals'. He states that he has tried to:

> go beyond a description of the illegal act and the immediate contexts in which it occurs. I have attempted to recognise the conflict, imagery and disharmony of our urban society and to see how such conflict, imagery and disharmony are organised so that at the everyday and local level delinquency becomes a possibility. (Gill, 1977, p. 182)

Marxist theories of deviance

Marxist analyses focus on the ways in which class oppression is related to deviance. There are a wide variety of Marxist interpretations. They all emphasise the importance of undertaking a *materialist* analysis, seeing crime as part of wider social processes, and locating it within an historical context. The approach should be *dialectical*, people are both influenced by the social context and also influence it (see Chapter 2).

Deviant activity, such as crime, arises because of the social conditions in which people live. This does not excuse it, however, despite the romantic interpretations of some idealist *pseudo-Marxists* that criminal and deviant acts are expressions of opposition to capitalism.

Traditional Marxist approach to deviance

The so-called *traditional Marxist* approach focuses on law creation and control of deviancy. They see the law and the control of deviancy as part of the ideological and repressive *superstructure* (see page 15). Rather than see the law as the result of consensus, as Durkheim did, they see the law as the will of the powerful. Society is dominated by those who control the *means of production* (see page 10). They want to retain their control and thus their wealth and power. The ruling class employ *ideology* and *repression* to ensure the maintenance and reproduction of the economic system. Dominant *ideology* (see page 15) reflects the values of the powerful. Perspectives on

The **PSEUDO-MARXIST VIEW OF DEVIANCE** sees deviant behaviour as the activities which the ruling class define as wrong, immoral or illegal. Deviants are normal people whom the ruling class perceive as being a threat to their power and stability, that is, a threat to capitalism. Deviant acts are thus a conscious act of rebellion against the capitalist system. This approach makes use of a mixture of social control and labelling theory to suggest that the ruling class use deviant labelling as a means of establishing conformity and keeping dissent under control. The implication is that deviants deny dominant ideology and values and are striking a blow for freedom.

CORPORATE CRIME Box (1983) argues that corporate 'crime' is far more extensive and far more damaging than individual crime. Most of this 'crime', such as using harmful chemicals in food, the production of dangerous goods for profit, and overcharging are not even regarded as illegal. Box argues that corporate crime is not the unintended result of the pursuit of profit but the inevitable outcome of the ruthless pursuit of profit that leads to indifference about the harm that corporations cause.

Corporations are rarely prosecuted for their crimes. Indifference on matters of health and safety (Hagen, 1988), dishonest advertising, insider trading and so on are treated 'sympathetically' and leniently through intermediary agencies such as the Health and Safety Executive, the Factory Inspectorate and the Advertising Standards Authority and rarely result in police investigation and criminal legal proceedings. The fraud squad is discouraged from involvement in financial crime in the City of London, which is expected to police itself. Even when legal proceedings follow the judge is likely to take a lenient view. For example, the case of Geoffrey Collier, who was convicted of illicit trading in shares. He was given a fine and a one-year suspended sentence because he had lost his membership of the Stock Exchange and his £250,000 job. The judge, Mr Justice Farquaharson, was lenient because Collier had an 'uncertain financial future'. It is unlikely that a burglar with a far more uncertain financial future would be treated so leniently. Indeed, in the United States a stockbroker involved in illegal trading worth $20 million was fined and given a suspended sentence by a judge who, the day the case was tried, sent an unemployed black shipping clerk to prison for a year for stealing a television set (see Napes, 1970).

Some American Marxists explicitly analyse business corruption as organised crime with links to political processes. Chambliss (1978) used participant observation to show that leading members of Seattle's ruling class were behind organised crime in the city. He got his evidence by hanging around in bars and card schools for several years. He argued, on the basis of his substantial evidence, that crime is not a 'by-product of an otherwise effectively working political economy, it is a main product of that economy'. Furthermore, crime networks are inevitable in capitalist society.

deviance and consensus on crime are rooted in dominant ideology. Laws are thus reflections of dominant ideology. They *legitimate* the dominant view through direct control (see page 14).

> A simple example of this is the strict controls on picketing and striking which have been introduced in the last few years. The argument is based on the assumption that strikes are somehow 'bad for the country'. It is the '*national interest*' which is threatened by strikers, rather than the *interests of the employers*. The result is that the law is used to help the employers break the strike. (Moore, 1988, p. 69)

Not all laws simply favour the 'ruling class', but the system of control embodied in the courts, police and army is biased in their favour. The result is that the powerless, rather than the powerful, are subject to the rigours of the law. It is the working class, ethnic minorities and young people who are more likely to be arrested and convicted. A burglar who steals property faces imprisonment. An employer, whose employees suffer serious illness, injury or death because they are required to use dangerous chemicals or inadequately safeguarded machinery, is liable to no more than a fine. 'Working-class crime' or 'street crime' (such as burglary, car theft, 'mugging', group violence) has a high profile. Policing policies are biased towards this kind of crime and this is reflected in official statistics (see Chapter 3). 'White collar crime' and *corporate crime* is underrepresented (Box, 1983; Geis and Stottland, 1980; Hopkins, 1980).

Street crime

Marxists have been particularly concerned with street crime. Conventional approaches to street crime see it as something that the lower classes or less powerful are involved in and so look for explanations in terms of characteristics of these groups. Marxists see street crime not as a by-product of capitalism but *endemic* to it (that is, street crime has always been and will always be part of capitalist society) (Platt, 1978). Official agencies underrepresent street crime because most of it does not get reported (see Chapter 3). Furthermore, street crime is not cross-class or cross-racial; there is no redistribution of wealth going on. Quite the contrary, it is mainly poor whites stealing from other poor whites, poor blacks from other poor blacks, and so on.

In *Policing The Crisis*, Stuart Hall *et al.* (1978) developed an extensive study of street crime. They looked at the *moral panic* around mugging in the 1970s and locate it in terms of changes in class and ethnic relationships in Britain. They related the moral panic to broader political and ideological issues. Social reaction is linked to theories of the state and ideology. Hall *et al.* developed a theory of the relationship between law and order and struggles within the state as a response to economic changes. They argued that Britain could no longer rely on economic prosperity. Britain's economic decline, relative to the rest of Europe, had become apparent. Added to that, Britain no longer had an empire to exploit and so future prosperity could only be built on the back of the working class. This required *hegemonic* consensus (see page 14).

Hall *et al.* argued that the state had run into a *crisis of hegemony*, that is, the state was no longer credible because it was unable to rely on consensus support in a clearly divided and embittered class society. To deflect attention from its own shortcomings and to hide the crisis the state took up the 'war against crime'. The focus on crime was an attempt to 'manage consensus' to re-establish the legitimacy of the state.

Extract 6.9

HOW WORKING-CLASS KIDS GET WORKING-CLASS JOBS

In *Learning to Labour*, a study of how working-class kids get working-class jobs, Willis (1977) attempts to dig beneath the surface of what was seen at the time as a developing crisis in education evident in pupil misbehaviour in schools. Willis was not so much concerned with the 'misbehaviour' as such but rather set out to look at the transition from school to work of non-academic working-class boys. The primary aim of his research was to cast light upon the 'surprising' process whereby, in a liberal democratic society, where there is no obvious physical coercion, some people are self-directed towards socially undesirable, poorly rewarded, intrinsically meaningless manual work. He sets out not by asking what occurs in the classroom, but by asking what happens at school that leads some boys into low-status manual jobs?

Willis used ethnography because of its 'sensitivity to meanings and values'. Willis focused on a group of twelve non-academic, white, working-class 'lads' in their penultimate year of schooling. The subjects formed a friendship network, and were in the same year at a single-sex, working-class secondary modern school in the heart of a working-class estate in 'Hammertown' (in the West Midlands). They were intensively studied during their last two years of schooling, via participant and non-participant observation in classrooms; around other parts of the school; and in leisure activities. Willis attended, as a class member, not teacher, some of all the different classes that the group went to, including careers classes. This direct observation was supported by 'regular recorded group discussion; informal interviews and diaries'. After they left school, Willis undertook short periods of participant observation of each of the twelve in their workplace by actually working alongside them.

His ethnographic work reveals that there is a counter-culture among some working-class 'lads' which denies the expectations, values and social control that make up the 'educational paradigm'. The lads are suspicious and distrustful of schooling; see it as failing their own aspirations; as irrelevant; and they actively ridicule the schooling process. As Joey said:

> That's it, we've developed certain ways of talking, certain ways of acting, and we developed disregards for Pakis, Jamaicans and all different... for all the scrubs and the fucking ear'oles and all that. We're getting to know it now, like we're getting to know all the cracks, like, how to get out of lessons and things, and we know where to have a crafty smoke. You can come over here to the youth wing and do summat, and all your friends are here, you know, it's sort of what's there, what's always going to be there for the next year, like, and you know you have to come to school

today, if you're feeling bad, your mate'll soon cheer you up like, 'cos you couldn't go ten minutes in this school, without having a laff at something or other.

In this way, Willis provides detailed accounts of the elements of the oppositional culture. On the basis of interviews with parents and the research in the factories, this oppositional culture is then contextualised as part of a more general working-class culture. It is shown specifically to have profound similarities with shop-floor culture. Willis argues that through this the boys develop a positive image of labour power.

Willis adopts a 'critical ethnographic' approach. His material is based on extensive ethnographic enquiry, but rather than simply report his observations in terms of the sets of meanings that operate within the group, he is concerned only with the ethnographic detail inasmuch as it provides indicators at the local level of the more general *structural* questions which frame his enquiry.

Willis argues that the counter-school culture is limited in its 'penetration' of capitalism. It only partially cuts through the (middle-class or dominant) ideological notions embodied in schooling. It is limited by the contradictions and divisions within the working-class culture on which it draws. Notably, the demeaning of mental labour, the sexism and the racism in working-class culture.

The ethnographic data indicated that the lads preferred manual labour and affirmed themselves through it; thus they played into the hands of capitalism, which needs manual labour. However, capitalism does not directly generate this preference; it comes from within *patriarchal* working-class culture.

The male counter-school culture promotes and celebrates its own sexism. The lads exploit young females and have hypocritical expectations and attitudes towards them. The sexism of the wider working-class culture, evident in the division of labour at work and home and its associated power relations, provides the model for the counter-school culture. It is the gender superiority enshrined in working-class culture that enables the 'lads' to accept their disadvantage as manual rather than mental labourers.

Similarly, racial division serves to further divide the working class, both materially and ideologically. It provides a heavily exploited 'underclass' which is itself partially or indirectly exploited by the working class and which provides a basis for simplistic assertions about the superiority of self among the white working class.

Thus, Willis argues, it is their own culture which most effectively prepares some working-class lads for manual labour.

Adapted from Harvey (1990, pp. 66–72), Quote from Willis (1977, p. 23).

A moral panic was set up by the police, courts and media around street crime. This acted as a focus for reasserting hegemonic consensus. The crime had been around for many years, but was given a new importance with the importing of the American term 'mugging'. The particular focus on 'mugging' reflected a tension and hostility between the police and black communities that was grounded in racism. Allowing free reign to racist assumptions about street crime further encouraged consensus.

Cultural Marxism

Cultural Marxist theories of crime and deviance attempt to relate the structural analysis of traditional Marxism to the motives and actions of the deviants. Cultural Marxists see deviance in terms of distinct sets of cultural values. However, unlike functionalist subcultural theorists, they locate cultural values within a wider structure of oppression. For example, Paul Willis (1977) undertook a participant observation study of delinquent

CULTURAL MARXIST APPROACHES TO CRIME AND DEVIANCE developed from the work of Taylor, Walton and Young (1973, 1975). In two books in the early 1970s they argued for a fully Marxist approach that provided a structural and historical analysis of deviance but also took into account the role of the acting deviant.

Cultural approaches include what has been called *Marxist subculture theory* (Cohen, 1972) and *Marxist youth culture theory* (Brake, 1980; Hebdidge, 1979; Robins and Cohen, 1978). Much of this has grown out of work done at the Centre for Contemporary Cultural Studies (CCCS), sometimes called the 'Birmingham School'. (CCCS, 1978; Clarke *et al.*, 1979; Hall and Jefferson, 1976; Hall *et al.*, 1980; Women's Study Group CCCS, 1978).

misbehaviour in schools (see Extract 6.9).

Student Activity 6.15
1. **What techniques does Willis use (in Extract 6.9) to explore misbehaviour in school?**
2. **What are the characteristics of the anti-school culture?**
3. **How does Willis relate the anti-school culture to working-class culture?**
4. **Why is the critique of capitalism, embodied in the anti-school culture, limited?**

Willis concluded that the working-class kids' subculture reflected the wider working-class culture. That, in rebelling, the kids were showing contempt for middle-class values, knowing full well they were destined for dead-end working-class jobs anyway. The critique of bourgeois culture was, however, limited. It was not the basis for a concerted working-class attack on the dominant ideology as it was internally divisive (being both sexist and racist). In the end, the rebellion was simply playing into the hands of capitalism, which needed a supply of unskilled labour. The 'lads' were effectively colluding in their own dead-end careers.

In common with all critical approaches, the Cultural Marxist approach sets deviance in a broader context. For Willis, the issue of school misbehaviour was thus not one about control in the classroom but a broader structural issue about how working-class kids ended up with working-class jobs.

Left realism

A development of Marxist approaches to crime and deviancy can be found in what has been called 'the new criminology of left realism' (Moore, 1988, p. 86). It is regarded as controversial by many Marxists. It is set out in the work of Lea and Young (1984). In essence, it accepts that the high rate of crime among the working class is not just a result of police harassment, inadequate official statistics on crime and a legal system biased against the powerless, but reflects *real* high rates of crime. There are a lot of different subcultures and these provide sets of values that provide a *legitimation* for deviant acts (see p. 144). The subcultures are related to broader cultural values. The subcultures and the values they encompass are constantly remade by each generation.

Crime and deviance is the result of *relative deprivation* (see Chapter 4). For example, young people do not steal because they are poor but because they feel relatively deprived.

> They are frustrated and bitter because of the disparity between their high expectations and the reality of what they can actually obtain, given the levels of unemployment and the low-wage jobs on offer. (Moore, 1988, p. 88)

These unemployed youths are *marginalised*, they play little part in the economic system and are not represented in the political system. This marginalisation was even more acute for black groups. The only option that marginalised groups have is direct demonstrations and 'rioting'.

Student Activity 6.16
1. **From a Marxist view, what would you say are the limitations of the left realist position?**
2. **How does the left realist position differ from functionalist approaches?**

Feminist theories of deviance

Feminist theories explore sexist assumptions about deviance. They examine both the sexist assumptions of the wider society that understates female deviance and the sexists assumptions of sociologists of deviance who marginalise the role of females.

Feminists argue that analyses of deviance have rendered women *invisible* in a number of ways. First, statistics on crime and deviance are biased towards recording the activities of males. Official crime statistics, for example, suggest that men are five times more likely to commit crimes than are females but this ignores the process by which crimes come to be recorded (see Chapter 3). These statistics also ignore, or grossly understate, the extent to which women are victims of crime, particularly of rape and domestic violence (see Chapters 2 and 3).

Second, male domination of sociology has resulted in male assumptions applied to the subject and a focus on areas of male concern (Oakley, 1974). In the study of deviance this has meant a specific interest in street crime, gambling, drug users, and other male-dominated subcultures.

> **VARIETY OF FEMINIST THEORIES**
> It has been suggested that feminist theories of deviance all tend to be anti-positivist, opposed to stereotyping of women, and see deviance in terms of patriarchal oppression. However, feminist researchers of deviance adopt a variety of theories and there is some concern that they tend towards non-critical 'male theories' of deviance (Heidensohn, 1985). Player (1989), for example, found that *anomie* was the most satisfactory framework for explaining female burglary (see Downes and Rock, 1988).

Extract 6.10

FEMALE STREET GANGS

In 1979 I came to New York City to study the role of girls in New York street gangs. The slim quantity of work on female delinquency generally and on gang girls especially fell into two categories, each of which conspired to keep the real nature of such girls' lives effectively hidden. Many were one-off studies relating some index of social or psychological pathology such as measures of family disruption or degree of deviation from sex-role stereotypes with gang involvement. The other available data was from social workers whose clear intention was to solve the gang problem rather than account for its form and its impact on female members. I wanted to observe and interact with girl gang members and to represent their own views of the situation. The literature abounds with rich accounts of the lives of street corner men and street corner gangs, but women appear at second hand and only through the reports of male speakers. I wanted to redress the balance and to hear girls speak for themselves.

In order to represent female members as whole people with their own biographies and attitudes and relationships to the community I selected three gangs. I spent six months with each gang and in each focused on an individual girl.... I let the girls talk for themselves in Chapters three, four, and five. It is, after all, their story and it seems fitting that it should be told in their words. The girls may not agree with my interpretation of their position and the final chapter must be my responsibility, not theirs....

Girls have been part of gang life for over a hundred years, from social clubs through years of prohibition and corruption to the 'bopping' gangs of the 1950s and through the civil disorders and the women's movement of the 1970s. Social scientists are now more sensitive to relationships of girls with other girls, and the small amount of available research reflects a growing concern with girls beyond their sexual relationships. As they assume a more three-dimensional representation, girls appear increasingly as sisters in the gang instead of molls. But it cannot be said that their roles have altered substantially. They exist as an annex to the male gang, and the range of possibilities open to them is dictated and controlled by the boys. Within the gang, there are still 'good girls' and 'bad girls',

tomboys and fallen women. Girls are told how to dress, are allowed to fight, and are encouraged to be good mothers and faithful wives. Their principal source of suffering and joy is their men. And though the girls may occasionally defy them, often argue with them, and sometimes patronise them, the men remain indisputably in control.

Many social commentators might wish to find that this state of affairs has been washed away since the 1970s. Some criminologists believe that the increase in female crime is the direct result of the liberation of women. Some radical criminologists hoped to see a new revolutionary awareness springing from oppressed women and where better to look than at women in urban ghettos? Social control theorists maintain that crime results from the failure of individual ties to mainstream values, and who would be a better candidate for such alienation than urban minority women who have so little to gain by commitment to conformity?

These expectations were unrealistic. The gang is not a counter-culture but a microcosm of American society, a distorted mirror image in which power, possessions, rank, and role remain major issues but are found within a subcultural life of poverty and crime. Gangs do not represent a revolutionary vanguard rejecting the norms and values of a capitalist society that has exploited them. When gang members talk of politics they talk of the American Dream, of pride in their country, of High School Equivalency Diplomas. They want better welfare and health benefits, they want more jobs, but they don't want revolution. Gangs exist not in an anomic vacuum where sex roles are forgotten and anything goes, but in a subculture deeply embedded within the value system of Western capitalism. Girl members as women want to be American, to be free, to be beautiful, to be loved. These girls subscribe to the new woman's dream, the new agenda: No more suffering or poverty. No more lonely, forced 'independence', living alone on welfare in a shabby apartment. First, a good husband; strong but not violent, faithful but manly. Second, well-dressed children. Third, a beautiful suburban apartment. Later for the revolution.

Adapted from Campbell, pp. 1–3 and 266–7.

This has resulted in theories of crime that reproduce sexist *stereotypes* (see page 52) of women (Smart, 1977; Heidensohn, 1985). Feminists argue that existing theories of crime and deviance are dominated by *patriarchy* (see page 25) and fail to take account of sexual divisions in society. Worse, much of the non-feminist theorising about deviance falls back on *biological* and *psychological* theories of female deviance (see pages 162–3).

Feminists have also challenged *myths* about the nature of women's involvement in deviant activities. Anne Campbell (1981, 1984, 1986) has shown that females do play roles in street gangs and do get involved in fights (see Extract 6.10). Welsh (1981) has shown that female delinquents are motivated by a search for excitement in the same way as males and Player (1989) that female adolescents do get involved in such activities as burglary. However, there is still far less direct observation research on female deviants than there is on males.

Student Activity 6.17
1. **What sort of studies does Campbell criticise (in Extract 6.10)?**
2. **What approach does Campbell adopt and why?**
3. **What does she conclude?**
4. **Does this account reassert Merton's theory of deviant subcultures?**
5. **What, would you say, makes this a critical account?**

Unlike psychological and biological theories that fail to separate biological sex from socially constructed gender roles, modern feminist analysis of deviance make a clear distinct between sex and gender. They examine how the gendered roles of women have a bearing on female deviance. The focus has been on four interrelated aspects: female socialisation, social control of women, differential social reaction and reduced opportunity for women to commit crime.

Males and females are *socialised* from infancy in different ways (see pages 50–1). This leads to adoption of different values and, it is argued, females tend to be less aggressive, which accounts for their lower involvement in more violent forms of crime. Women are more likely to be convicted of shoplifting and prostitution, which reflects conventional gender roles.

Within a patriarchal structure women are subject to tighter *control* than men. They are controlled both through their role in the family context and by restricted activity in public. Tighter control means less possibility to deviate. Indeed, what is regarded as deviant behaviour is related to sexual inequality. What is 'normal male' behaviour (such as drinking in pubs, having more than one sexual partner and so on) become proscribed for women. Researchers, however, have disputed the view that reduced control of women associated with 'female emancipation' has led to more female crime (Box, 1983; Heidensohn, 1985).

Similarly, recent research has investigated *social reaction* and questioned the myth that women are treated more leniently than men. Lighter sentences passed on women and the higher probability of women being cautioned rather than prosecuted are not due to male 'chivalry' but relate to the crimes committed by women and the number of previous convictions (Fisher and Mawby, 1982; Farrington and Morris, 1983; Landau and Nathan, 1983). On the contrary, women are doubly punished when their crime breaking also transgresses their social role (Nagel, 1980; Carlen, 1983; Heidensohn, 1985; Eaton, 1986). Women involved in murder and social security frauds tend to get harsher sentences than men (Russon, 1984; Hoggarth, 1991) and girls are more likely than boys to be taken into protective custody for sexual

ANTI-RACIST APPROACHES TO DEVIANCE situate deviance within a process of racial oppression. Like feminists, anti-racists want to reveal the real relation of ethnic minorities to deviance, including the extent to which ethnic minorities are victims of racist crime (see Chapter 3). They also explode myths about the relationship between race and crime (Gilroy, 1982; Hall *et al.*, 1978, which is an anti-racist as well as a Marxist analysis). Space precludes further development of this here.

misdemeanours and truancy (Casburn, 1979; Frankel, 1979; Rowett and Vaughn, 1981). Women who are divorced or separated or who are from 'deviant' backgrounds are more likely to receive severe sentences (Farrington and Morris, 1983).

The socialisation and control of women lead to fewer *opportunities* for women to engage in deviant activities. Girls tend to be more likely to be confined to home than boys (McRobbie and Garber, 1976) and thus less likely to be involved in street crime or deviant subcultures. Women are often isolated as housewives (Hobson, 1978) and have less opportunity to commit white-collar or corporate crime.

Student Activity 6.18
Read Extract 6.11. It is an account of car theft and 'joyriding' on a Newcastle housing estate, compiled from television and newspaper reports.
1. **Which theory or theories of deviance does this account appear to support?**
2. **How would you undertake a participant observation study to assess any of the theories that might account for 'twoccing'? (a) Suggest how you might gain access. (b) Outline the nature of the role you might adopt. (c) Indicate the kinds of things you would be looking for to assess the theory.**

Ethics

Ethics are a problem in any research situation but participant observation is frequently highlighted as a particularly problematic area. This is mainly because of the potential for 'spying' which some people regard as, at best, an invasion of privacy and, at worst, a totally immoral act. To mislead people by pretending to be genuinely interested in their prophecy of the end of the world (Festinger, Rieken and Schachter, 1956), to be a voyeur in a criminal underworld (Taylor, 1984), or to use police contacts to obtain home addresses of gay men through the vehicle registration computer (Humphreys, 1970) are regarded by some people as ethically unacceptable activities. There is no easy answer to this issue of 'spying'.

Writing up and publishing the results of participant observation studies can also be seen as an ethical issue. Some researchers argue that it is unethical to betray confidence by publishing an account unacceptable to the subjects, as Whyte (1943) inadvertently did in *Street Corner Society*. Howard Parker (1974, p. 224) commented on this issue when reporting his study of a Liverpool 'gang'.

> The major problem in 'writing up' is an ethical one, however. The fieldwork data basically fell into three categories: that which I felt could definitely be published, that which could definitely not be published and that which I was unsure about. The third category was eventually broken up and distributed into the yes/no compartments through consultation with those involved and colleagues. Becker has pointed out in reviewing studies of this nature that publication will almost inevitably 'make somebody angry'. This is probably true; my main concern is that no harm comes to The Boys. Thus what I have published is related to my knowledge of what Authority already knows about. The nature of The Boys' delinquency discussed is already well known to Authority. The analysis blows no whistles but rather tries to explain what happens when whistles are blown.

Extract 6.11

TWOCCING

Car theft is the fastest growing offence in Britain and accounts for 25% of all recorded crime. One car is stolen every minute and 40% are never recovered or are written off. In the last eight years there has been a sixfold increase in insurance claims, from £85.6 million in 1982 to £432 million in 1990.

In the Newcastle area there were 30,771 cases of car crime in 1990; 28,000 vehicles had been stolen in the Newcastle area in the 12 months up to September 1991. On the Meadow Well estate, to the east of Newcastle city centre, twoccing (taking cars without the owners' consent) has become a well-established pastime. Stolen high-performance cars are driven at speed round the estate while crowds look on at the free entertainment. The exhibitions of bravado are even videotaped. The favourite targets for twoccers are Sierra Cosworths, along with 'hot hatches' such as Astra GTEs. Once the 'joyriders' have finished they douse the car with petrol and set it alight. A flare is set off to indicate that the evidence has been destroyed.

Mark Dodds, a former twoccer, who admits to having stolen over 200 cars, told *World in Action* that:

> kids think I'm a good car thief because I get the high powered cars ... the more high powered car you get the better you look in front of your mates at the time.

Jeff Briggs, of Gateshead Social Services, has spent three years interviewing twoccers for his PhD and reckons that the twoccers feel little sense of wrongdoing. The car is a glamourous escape from a bleak existence. 'The motor car means so much for these kids... It embodies status and prestige. It projects sex. Not all of them are villains. They see the motor car as the unobtainable symbol of success.'

> When you're getting a car you don't realise whose car it is. You go out to get the car. So that's what you do. You don't care whose it is. You just get it. (Billy, a teenager)

A survey of young 14 to 17-year-old car thieves revealed that nearly 70% of offenders would 'race off or encourage a chase' if approached by police, according to James Gow of Barnardo's. Indeed, the chase is often the main motivation in stealing the car in the first place. Over 60% of Gow's sample had been involved in accidents.

The joyriders are local heroes, their reputation rises every time the police ignore a challenge. The youths interpret police reluctance to enter into a chase as a 'loss of bottle' on the part of the officer, or as the police being out-manoeuvred. This raises their own self-esteem.

There have been fatalities of innocent bystanders with an estimated 80 people killed and 900 injured nationally as the result of police chases in the last four years.

On 6 September 1991, Colin Atkins and Dale Robson were killed when the Renault Turbo they had stolen crashed into a lamppost in Wallsend, Tyne and Wear, and caught fire whilst being chased at high speed by the police. Rumours spread that the car had been rammed by the police and forced to crash. Graffiti appeared saying 'Police are murderers. Dale 'n' Colin we won't let them get away with it'.

> People used the scanners [short-wave radio monitors] to pick up police messages. We know what happened. (Sean, a teenager)

Colin and Dale were minor heroes, or at least achievers, in the eyes of some of the young people on the estate. Their deaths triggered a night of riots (9 September 1991), with copy-cat riots in other parts of the city that also coincided with disturbances in Cardiff and Wareham. This was not the first time Meadow Well had seen civil disturbances; there were 3 nights of rioting on the estate in September 1969 following the arrest of two youths involved in a brawl.

The police lost control as 200–400 youths lured police into a network of roads by setting fire to shops. Power and telephone lines were cut and barricades built out of debris, cars and chain-sawed trees. The targets of the fire-bombers included a Coalite Depot at North Shields docks. Shops on the estate were looted and set on fire including the fish and chip shop of 33-year-old Ahsak Ahmed, who admitted that he would be leaving the estate as his home had been completely destroyed.

Adults on Meadow Well, while condemning the violence, appeal for understanding.

> These kids leave school to a hopeless future. They kick out at anything. They see a car parked and they think: 'God, this person's got everything. Now it's my turn.' And they take it and go thieving. I believe that there's nothing worse than losing hope, and that's what's happened to them. The whole problem here is the poverty. We need help. (Molly Woodhouse, aged 74).

A relative of one of the boys killed on the 6 September, while not condoning the stealing, understood the actions of the boys in stealing the car.

> What have the kids got these days - its just got to be based on unemployment. They can't afford all the fancy gear that kids are wearing these days. They've got to turn to crime, I think.

A young female noted that car theft and crime were related and that there was a distinction between joyriding and serious car crime.

> The papers and telly called them joyriders, but joyriders are kids of 11 who can't see over the wheel. Ram-raiding's what goes on round here. The cars aren't taken for fun, they're to earn money, which you can't get anyway else. Maybe £28 on some YTS scheme, but who wants that.

Ram-raiding, known on the Meadow Well as 'late night shopping' involves the use of a stolen car as a battering ram to smash into shops. One 'ram raider', an unconvicted veteran of over 20 raids was asked if he thought of the shop owner whose property he was stealing. His reply to *World In Action* was:

> No. He should have it securely locked up. Its so easy for lads to steal it. Some haven't even got gates on the front.... It takes about 10 seconds to get into the average car. Just with a screwdriver or pair of scissors. I think its going to get worse because there are no jobs. There are people who have just got to have cash, you know.

Inevitably, the despairing approval of crime lead to conflicts with the police and the reawakening of old antagonisms. The CID are seen as regular provokers by the youths. The officers are alleged to flick V-signs and jeer at the youths and to stop and intimidate people living on the estate.

As long ago as the 1981 Census, Meadow Well was highlighted as the worst 'problem' area in the North East. Every pupil at the estate's primary school receives grants for clothing. Meadow Well has a pay-in-and-borrow Credit Union, a sure sign of long-term poverty. It has high unemployment, officially estimated at 86%.

The self-help groups have been squatters in their premises since May when community-charge capping ended the £90,000 council grant. This withdrawal of funds was typical of the fate of enterprises in Meadow Well.

> Anything organised here doesn't get a hand, doesn't get a chance. We're just scum you know. I can tell you, I'm sick of hearing that word scum, but that's what they call you if you come from Meadow Well. (Sean, teenager)

Sources: *World in Action*; *Observer* (8.9.91); *Guardian* (11.9.91); *BBC News*.

Student Activity 6.19
Although Campbell lets the young women in her study speak for themselves (see Extract 6.10), does she avoid responsibility over the ethical issue by writing a concluding interpretation with which the subjects might not agree?

The problematic nature of ethical issues makes it difficult to suggest hard-and-fast rules for conducting participant observation. However, it is advisable always to present your research using pseudonyms and, as far as possible, make it difficult for individuals to be identified, especially if the research is likely to harm them in any way. You might want to report only what the subjects agree to but, while salving your conscience, this can be disastrous if they censor your material of its significance. You simply find yourself in another dilemma: abandon all the hard work, or 'publish and be damned'.

To familiarise yourself with ethical issues you should try to read the ethical guidelines provided by the British Sociological Association. These are summarised on page 4. None the less, as a researcher you must do what you think is ethically sound. At the very least, though, it is important that you ask yourself 'whose side are you on?' and 'who is the research for?' and give yourself honest answers before getting too involved in the research. Owen Gill (1977, p. 196) puts this forcefully in referring to his own work in a 'delinquent area'.

> The sociologist's responsibility to his subjects is a continuous one and does not stop once he returns to the sheltered employment of the university to write about his findings. In planning a study, in conducting it and in writing it the sociologist should have his subjects looking over his shoulder. He has responsibility neither consciously nor unconsciously to contribute to the stereotypes which afflict relatively powerless groups in society.

Ethnography

Observation, particularly participant observation, is often used in a style of research called *ethnography*. The term was a term originally used to mean the study (that is , description) of the institutions and customs in small, well-defined communities in societies with little technological advance. The term now has a wider meaning and is generally used to refer to the detailed study of small groups of people (for example, in factories, classrooms, hospitals, 'deviant' subcultures) within a complex society. It covers the kind of research topic that was more popularly known as 'qualitative sociology' during the 1960s and 1970s.

Ethnography, as a style of research, uses a wide range of methods of data collection, including in-depth interviewing, life histories and personal document analysis (see Chapter 7), as well as non-participant and participant observation.

Participant observation is, however, frequently regarded as the main method of ethnographic research. For some researchers there is no difference between participant observation and ethnography because they see participant observation as including in-depth interviews and document analysis. However, most people see a difference between the two because ethnography does not necessarily have to include a *participant* observation element; it can be done exclusively through non-participant observation and unstructured interviews.

The central features of ethnographic research are, first, that the researcher attempts *naturalistic* enquiry. Second, that the researcher attempts to get the *subject's point of view*. Third, that the researcher is *reflexive*.

Naturalistic research

Naturalistic research refers to methods of social enquiry that attempt to grasp the 'natural' processes of social action and interaction. The aim is to collect information from social settings without creating artificial situations (such as an interview or an experiment) and with the minimum of disruption by the researcher.

It is argued that the naturalistic approach (using observation or unstructured, in-depth interviews) places the researcher in a better position to *interpret* or *understand* social actions in their own context. It thus improves *ecological validity* (see page 32).

Some researchers argue that the naturalistic setting alone is not enough. The research is only naturalistic when it sets out to discover the subject's point of view.

The subject's point of view

Ethnographic research sets out to see the world from the point of view of the subject. Rather than impose their own views on the research situation, ethnographers attempt to achieve an understanding of what the social processes and actions mean for the people involved in them. This may result in descriptions of actions and an interpretation of what they mean for the actors. Or it may involve a much fuller attempt to understand the social world of the subjects and the place that the actions or social processes have within it.

Reflexivity

Most ethnographers argue that it is important for researchers to develop a critical attitude towards their research practices, theoretical models and presuppositions. This is known as reflexivity.

It is impossible to begin observational research without any *preconceptions* but the reflexive researcher will make an effort to confront those preconceptions and see what effect they have had on the research process. Field notes should be examined to see if the preconceptions are confronted. Extract 6.2, from Blanche Geer (see page 154), is an example of how this is done.

Reflexivity also requires that researchers assess the contaminating effect of their presence and their research techniques on the nature and extent of the data collected. Crudely put, researchers must consider to what extent respondents were telling them what they wanted to hear or were acting in a manner to impress the researcher. Researchers must ask whether or not their presence inhibited respondents. Did the method of data collection, or even the format in which it was stored, restrict the kind of data being collected, and so on?

Furthermore, ethnographic reflexivity requires that researchers critically reflect upon the theoretical structures they have drawn out of their ethnographic analysis. Researchers are expected to reconceptualise their evidence in terms of other possible models. They are expected to think laterally. Ethnographers should not just fit details into a preformed theoretical scheme

PRECONCEPTIONS refers both to the specific views that a researcher may have about the subject before starting the research, and his or her general knowledge, attitudes, beliefs, values and prejudices.

but should try to see if alternative theoretical schemes provide the basis for a better understanding of the data. Do the observations reveal different meanings when viewed in a different way?

Dealing with ethnographic data

Ethnographic research invariably leads to the collection of an enormous amount of detailed accounts, quotes, examples, anecdotes and so on. The production of a finished ethnographic report requires a selection from this detail. The choice of material is guided by the theoretical framework (or angle) that has emerged during the study.

A major problem that observation researchers face is how to deal with the vast amount of material. How can the data be sorted, coded, organised, and ultimately reported? There is often so much material that the researcher is overwhelmed by it and does not know where to begin or what sense it all makes. Even if the researcher has a clear idea of what the data is pointing to he or she may not know how to organise it to present it to its best advantage.

Probably the best way is the so-called 'pile building' approach. This involves a number of stages. This is much easier and cheaper to do if you have used a wordprocessor to write up observations. Stage one is to copy all the data. Leave the top copy alone and only use it only for reference purposes.

Stage two involves reading the data 'vertically'. That is, field notes are read chronologically from start to finish. They may be read a number of times so that the researcher has a good idea of what is in the notes. You may reread the whole thing as a block or break it up by reading about each individual or subgroup in the study in turn. Whichever way you do it, make sure that you are familiar with the contents of the field notes before you go on to the next stage.

Stage three involves identifying major themes that seem to recur throughout the data and have a bearing on the theoretical concerns.

Stage four involves going through the data and dividing each day's field notes into sections that deal with the particular themes. On each segment, note the original time and place of the observation, its precise location in the top copy of the recorded observations, the people involved, the sort of activity going on, and the theme or themes that occur in the extract. Where an extract involves more than one theme then you will need to copy the section so that you have a separate version of the section for each of the themes.

Stage five is to read the data 'horizontally' by themes. To do this, some ethnographers literally cut up their material and arrange it, according to themes, in piles (on the floor). This is why the approach is called 'pile building'. The process can equally well be done electronically using a wordprocessor (as we saw with Michael Filby's field notes (Extract 6.1, page 153)). There are also specialist programs available on personal computers for sorting and analysing qualitative field notes.

Stage six involves assessing whether the 'horizontal' reading by theme makes sense. When reading through each theme pile does it provide a cohesive account (like chapters in a book) or does it appear to be incomplete? Is there any interrelationship between the themes? Is such interrelationship consistent? Do other themes, that you had not noticed originally, appear to be emerging when you read the data horizontally?

Stage seven involves identifying additional themes, or removing or

QUALITATIVE ANALYSIS SOFT-WARE There are several software packages for IBM and Apple Macintosh personal computers specially designed to help qualitative researchers analyse their data. They work by breaking field notes into separate chunks and labelling them with a code (similar to Filby's field notes, see Extract 6.1 on page 153). These code labels can be cross-referenced. The computer is able to select and print out all the chunks with the same code without disturbing the original data. It does the 'pile-building' for you once you have labelled each chunk electronically. The selected data is printed with labels to indicate where it came from in the original field notes (that is, it contextualises the selected chunks). Using these programs allows you to work with the qualitative data in the same way as you would when working by hand. However, they are quicker and more convenient, especially if you do a lot of rearranging of your initial organising scheme. The programs are flexible and the scheme for organising the data can be developed as you go along. The *Ethnograph*, *Qualpro*, *Text Analysis Package* and *Textbase Alpha* are packages available for the IBM and compatibles. *HyperQual* based on *HyperCard* is available for the Apple Mac.

I don't think that's what they mean by horizontal reading.

collapsing the first selection of themes until another, more useful and revealing set of themes emerges. The data is then re-read in terms of the new themes. Another set of piles is built by cutting up a second copy into sections on the basis of the new themes and these are read.

Stage eight involves asking whether the new system of themes works better than the previous one. If so, it might be the basis of the analysis and report, or it might be necessary to derive yet another set of themes because the current one is still not quite right. It might be that the first breakdown into themes was better than the second one, so you go back to the previous version.

Finally, the report is organised around the themes that have been identified and the most revealing and clear examples from amongst the separate theme piles are used to illustrate the report. Make sure that you do not overload the report with examples. Inevitably, there will be examples that you would like to include but cannot because they simply repeat other examples.

> **Student Activity 6.20**
> **Extract 6.12 and Extract 6.13 are summary accounts of two partici-
> pant observation studies of restaurants. The language, style and
> concepts of the original are retained. Read the two reviews and
> compare the way they approach participant observation research. In
> particular, what theories do they use and in what context do they set
> the activities?**

Approaches to ethnography

The two studies show how observation-based ethnographic research can be done from very different perspectives. Broadly speaking, there are three approaches to ethnography: conventional, phenomenological and critical.

Conventional approach to ethnography

William Whyte's study (Extract 6.12) is an example of the 'conventional' approach to participant observation. Although dating from 1949, it should not be assumed that the approach is no longer used. Indeed, the conventional approach has been very resilient and is still widely adopted.

The conventional approach to ethnography sees participant observation as fraught with dangers in terms of it being a 'scientific' method, but one that can be extremely revealing if approached systematically. The procedure is as follows.

First, to describe the situation that is the subject of the study (what people do, what the purpose of the organisation is and how people relate to one another, and so on), as Whyte does when describing the fast-food restaurant.

Second, make some initial statements about the social processes observed (often based on crude counts). Whyte notes the relationships that occur along the chain of communication between customer and cook. He highlights the tensions that occur when low-status workers initiate actions for higher-status workers.

Third, suggest some initial hypotheses or generalisations based on the observation; that is, proceed inductively, proposing hypotheses based on the data. Whyte hypothesises that 'minimizing *direct* contact between lower and higher status workers minimizes tension'.

Fourth, test out these initial propositions by looking for negative cases. If

Extract 6.12

FAST-FOOD RESTAURANTS

We undertook a 14-month study of restaurants. We aimed to find out what sort of structure a restaurant is and what human problems are found in it. Both symbolic interactionism and structural functionalism are used to provide a broad theoretical framework for the analysis.

A restaurant is a combination production and service unit and the three-way link between producers (cooks, etc.), service staff (waitresses, etc.) and customers lead to complex human problems of interaction and of co-ordinating action. These problems get more difficult as the restaurant gets bigger. In a large restaurant there tend to be four groups: the customers, the table servers (waitresses and waiters), the pantry workers (who co-ordinate the cooking and the serving by taking customers' orders from waitresses, passing them on to the cooks, and handing the cooked meals to the waitresses to serve), and the cooks or chefs. In addition, there are various levels of supervisor to make sure the whole operation works smoothly, to the satisfaction of the customer.

The unique issue for the restaurant is that of linking the line of authority with relations that arise along the flow of work that is initiated by the customer when an order for a meal is placed. The formal structure of the work-place does not *determine* the pattern of human relations in an organisation but it does provide certain limits that shape that pattern. That is, to analyse the human problems it is necessary to outline its structure in terms of length of hierarchy, divisions into departments and flow of work.

The whole system of interactions that characterise the flow of work (customer–waitress, waitress–pantry worker; pantry worker–cook, etc.) constitute relationships that are all interdependent parts of a social system. Thus the emotional tension experienced by waitresses is readily transmitted, link by link, all the way to the kitchen. In order to deal effectively with the interdependent parts it is necessary to discover the *pattern* of relations existing at a given time and to observe changes within that pattern over time. This is done by watching how changes in one part work through and effect changes in other parts of the system.

Quantitative analysis can be used, for example, who originates action for whom and how often? In a large and busy restaurant a waitress may take orders from fifty to one hundred customers a day (and perhaps several times for each meal) in addition to the orders (much less frequent) she receives from her supervisor. When we add to this the problem of adjusting to service pantry workers, bartenders and perhaps checkers, we can readily see the possibilities of emotional tension – and, in our study, we did see a number of girls break down and cry under the strain.

The observation suggested to us that emotional tension could be related directly to this quantitative measure and it was noted that waitresses who did not get stressed were ones who initiated actions, getting customers, pantry staff, other waitresses and supervisors to fit into their work patterns rather than the other way round. But a quantitative analysis is not sufficient in itself.

However, we cannot be content simply with quantitative descriptions of interaction. We need to know why A responds to B but not C. We observe that individuals respond to certain symbols in interaction. Status and sex are symbols that affect interaction. The approach can be illustrated by analysing the hypothesis that relations among individuals along the flow of work run more smoothly when those of higher status (usually men) are in a position to originate activities for those of lower status (usually women) in the organisation and, conversely, that frictions will be observed more often when lower-status individuals seek to originate for those of higher status.

However, this is only part of a potential *explanatory* theory and by no means a complete explanation of the friction observed.

In our society most men grow up to be comfortable in a relationship in which they originate for women and to be uneasy, if not more disturbed, when the originations go in the opposite direction. It is therefore a matter of some consequence how the sexes are distributed along the flow of work.

In restaurant A, waitresses gave their orders orally to pantry girls. In restaurant B, waitresses wrote out slips which they placed on spindles on top of a warming compartment which separated them from the countermen. While we observed frictions arising between waitresses and pantry girls, such a relationship can at least be maintained with relative stability. On the other hand, it is difficult to prevent blowups between countermen and waitresses when the girls call their orders in.

The system in restaurant B seemed to work well because it cut down direct interaction between countermen and waitresses. One experienced counterman told us that the barrier was the reason why he liked his current job better than any previous one. He described earlier experiences in other restaurants where there had been no such barrier and let us know that 'to be left out in the open where all the girls could call their orders was an ordeal to which no man should be subjected. In such places', he said, 'there was constant wrangling'.

Most restaurants consciously or unconsciously interpose certain barriers to cut down waitress origination of action for countermen. There are a variety of ways of meeting the problem but they all seem to involve this principle of social insulation. Where there is no physical barrier, there can be trouble unless the men who are on the receiving end of the orders work out their own system of getting out from under.

Overall, analysing the symbolic element should always be seen in terms of the effect of symbols upon interaction. Symbols are *incentives* or *inhibitors* to interaction with specific people in certain social situations. Thus, to put it in practical terms, the manager of an organisation will find it useful to know both the pattern of interaction which will bring about harmonious relations and also how to use symbols to achieve that pattern.

Adapted from Whyte (1949). William Foote Whyte, Margaret Chandler, Edith Lentz and John Schaefer studied twelve restaurants in and around Chicago in the late 1940s.

Extract 6.13

DIXIE'S PLACE

I Undertook participant observation research into the labour process in a large licensed restaurant, Dixie's Place, in Central Scotland. The observation took nine months spread over a period of two years during the late 1970s. The thirty or so employees of the small business were found to work hard, under difficult circumstances and for relatively low wages. Yet they displayed high job satisfaction. Although the consequences of the processes connecting their own and their employer's class situations were transparent, and the processes themselves commonsensically understood, there was little or no employee dissatisfaction.

Most sociological studies of restaurants or bars tend to focus on patrons and are little more than a redescription of the minutiae of casual social encounters (Hayner, 1936; Roebuck and Spray, 1967; Byrne, 1978) or functionalist classification of establishments (Gottlieb, 1957; Maclomson, 1973) or a mixture of the two (Cavan, 1966; Jackson, 1972; LeMasters, 1975). Analysis of restaurants in terms of a work-place culture embracing both customer and staff is dominated by Whyte (1946, 1948, 1949). Although useful in imaginatively addressing the problems of fraught interaction when low-status staff put demands on high-status staff, the main weakness of Whyte's approach is the failure to address systematically the relationship between worker and customer.

Dixie's Place was a very profitable establishment, the more so for the owner because of the various fiddles he indulged in. The staff knew about them, were encouraged to collude in such activities and were rewarded for their collusion. The only people from whom the informal economy of the restaurant was hidden were the various tax officials who checked the books and accounts. Dixie had an extravagant life-style that was very apparent to his employees.

The employees were expected to be flexible and to help with other work as required. Full-time staff were paid for an official working week of forty-two hours but we never worked less than fifty-five and often much more, with no additional overtime payment. Not one of the forty or so weeks of my own employment came even close to the official forty-two hours. Dixie knew I was a sociologist (as did his staff) but it was simply his manner to use me as he used the others. The staff were paid low wages, about half the national average, and were expected to work very hard indeed. Yet despite this, and the occasional abuse from an unpredictable employer, there was remarkably little discontent amongst the employees. Although there was alternative employment available at better money hardly anyone left the restaurant to seek work elsewhere. When questioned, all the staff declared themselves not only to be 'satisfied' with their jobs but actually enjoyed being at Dixie's.

> Aye, well, it's a good shop to be in really. You get a rare laugh sometimes. And Dixie's a great bloke. Disnae hang around, checkin' up on ye a' day, ken whit ah mean?
> Your yer ain gaffer, that's what I like about it. Ye can get on wi' whit yer doin at yer ain speed. And there's a' kinds of perks too.

The quiescence among the work-force could partly be explained by their involvement in an informal workplace economy from which employees felt they benefited substantially. This went hand-in-hand with Dixie's paternalism. The symbolic significance of the gifts he offered from time to time and the involvement in the informal economy far outweighed their material value. However, the staff perceived these gifts as significant perks and all mentioned them as part of the attraction of being at Dixie's. Similarly, they all thought the fiddles to be a normal part of the bar business but did not talk of them as compensating low wages.

I became increasingly convinced that neither Dixie's paternalism nor the pilfering were sufficient alone to explain the staff's satisfaction in a blatantly exploitative situation. More subtle, cultural processes were at work. The employees viewed their work within the tavern environment in a way quite differently from outsiders looking in. The everyday language of the staff did not include references to work, instead the employees talked of 'going in to Dixie's' or 'having a dinner-dance tonight'. It was as if, despite their economic dependence on employment at the restaurant, the staff had commonsensically come to think that being at Dixie's was something other than work. Incredulous as it seems it was as if they did not really think they were working for their paypacket.

For many of the women who had had a lifetime of male-dominated society, the job was an extension of the housework tasks they performed at home and they accepted that 'only doing waitressing' was a job for 'pin money'. For these employees the symbolic boundary between work and non-work was thus very weak. Dixie also further undermined this symbolic difference by encouraging all his staff to be convivial with the patrons and to join in their leisure activities when the pressures of work permitted. This collapsing of the boundaries between work and leisure was further enabled by the presence of friends or even workmates among the clientele. On top of this there was no formal clocking on or off procedures and the ritual free drink and subsequent bout of drinking at the end of the evening created another grey area where we were at work but not working. Thus work and play became merged.

In summary, Dixie's Place offers a compelling illustration of capitalist hegemony. Dixie worked his employees hard, transparently extracted a profit from their labours, yet they neither grudged him his riches nor attempted to change their circumstances. Indeed, they identified closely with the capitalist enterprise. The physical proximity of employee and client, thus of work and leisure, leads to a work-place culture with a shared belief that bar work is different from 'real work' undertaken, for example, in a factory. The licensed restaurant employee comes to see the job as neither work nor leisure but as a whole way of life. To analyse it in terms of the extraction of surplus value would be to mystify it to the participants themselves. For them, their own exploitation was only what Dixie deserved and besides they were not doing real work anyway. Thus bourgeois ideology had become proletarian reality!

Adapted from Marshall (1986).

One possible answer to Student Activity 6.20

Apart from the blatant sexism to be found in Whyte's account (he not only refers disparagingly to women as 'girls' but also takes for granted that males have higher status in the workplace than women) the most striking difference between the two extracts above is the way they deal with the people involved. For Whyte they are links in a chain of interaction from customer to waitress to pantry staff to cook. For Marshall, they are individuals who make sense of their job in terms of meanings derived from their Scottish working-class background.

Although Whyte uses observation in his study, he adopts a positivistic approach. He adopts theoretical frameworks that reflect positivistic concerns in their focus on *explaining* interactive processes and looking for *causes* of friction and tension.

Whyte was also concerned with the 'scientific' nature of his work. He excused the non-representative nature of his sample of restaurants. He acknowledged that, although making comparisons between two similar restaurants, this did not fit the scientific ideal. The ideal requires everything else to be held constant except, in this case, differences in sex (the control variable). Whyte acknowledges that to analyse interaction solely in terms of sex and status is limited; there are other symbols that affect the nature of interaction such as tone of voice, facial gestures, body language and so on. The research reported needs to be extended to take account of the whole field of symbols in face-to-face interaction.

Marshall on the other hand is aware of the problems of generalising from a single case and admits that the findings from an isolated case-study are not representative even of restaurants or taverns let alone small businesses or service industries in general. However, he suggests that some issues do arise from the case study that are likely to be important to the service industry sector. In particular, productivity is likely to be increased, not by people constantly doing more-or-less the same job (as is usual in factories) but by emphasising flexibility. That is, employment should be based on adaptability to different tasks rather than a contracted amount of time at work.

Unlike Whyte, Marshall looked at the way in which the people working at Dixie's Place construct meaning out of their work experience and how they make sense of a situation in which they work very long hours for little pay. Rather than a concern with causes, Marshall attempts to understand the *contradiction* between the workers' satisfaction and their blatant exploitation. He does this by analysing the subject's meanings in terms of broader *cultural* issues that reflect wider issues of capitalist exploitation.

In this respect Marshall considers culture, where Whyte focuses on system. Marshall thus tries to understand the subjects' point of view rather than attempts positivist explanation. Marshall is concerned with culturally generated meanings, not the mechanisms for interactive harmony. Marshall challenges traditional theories and approaches to restaurant work by adopting a cultural Marxist perspective (see page 171). Whyte, despite his own insights, imports functionalist and traditional interactionist theories into his research (see pages 86 and 167).

Now that you have read this example answer make a note of the points we have *not* mentioned.

---

negative cases arise then modify or discard the propositions. Whyte examined situations in different restaurants to see whether his hypothesis was confirmed.

Fifth, gradually build up a model of the social organisation or the group interactive processes based on the propositions that survive the scrutiny of empirical data. Whyte did not suggest that he had tested a theory but that he was building up a model that described lines of communication in fast-food restaurants and helped explain the nature of friction within a service industry.

Thus this approach works by suggesting a model and then refining it by systematically seeking out instances that falsify aspects of the model. If it cannot be shown to be incorrect then it is taken as the best version of the model available. Gradually, by empirically falsifying the incorrect suppositions, a 'truer' model of what is happening should emerge (Becker, 1958; Becker and Geer, 1957, 1960). This approach is known as *falsificationism* and is an approach widely adopted in practice by positivists (see page 134).

However, despite the systematic development of a model in this way, the conventional approach does acknowledge that participant observation is not as 'objective' or 'reliable' as the social survey in establishing proof or providing explanations.

The conventional approach, then, does not set out to discover and interpret meanings as phenomenologists might. Rather, it tests hypotheses about the nature of social interaction or organisational structures. Meanings are not of concern in themselves, but only as supplementary material for explaining why, for example, some social interaction is accomplished smoothly while other interaction is fraught. Whyte's (1949) study is a good example of this.

The conventional approach uses existing theoretical concepts and propositions to guide the analysis through a systematic collection, classification and reporting of 'facts'. Conventional ethnography is thus characterised by detailed empirical description to reveal social processes rather than broad causal generalisations. Whyte, you will recall, was reluctant to make any broad causal generalisations although clearly pointing to factors that he thought caused friction within the restaurant's flow of work.

If participant observation is used, then the conventional approach suggests that it is crucial for the participant observer to maintain a balanced perspective. It emphasises detachment and highlights the importance of the researchers' reflexive accounts of their field role. Recent developments of the conventional approach have taken up the issue of reflexivity as central, and argue that the researcher can never actually be neutral. Indeed, the reverse is true: all researchers are participants in some form or another and therefore the reflexive activity is crucial. Researchers should take account of their impact on the research situation and ensure that they communicate this clearly in any report (Hammersley and Atkinson, 1983; Hammersley, 1990).

Phenomenological perspective on ethnography

Since the mid-1960s there has been growing interest in the development of sociological enquiry into the subjective aspects of everyday life and common-sense understandings. It is essentially an interpretive approach and is primarily concerned with meanings. This approach has come to be called phenomenological ethnography.

> The phenomenologist views human behavior – what people say and do – as a product of how people interpret the world. The task of the phenomenologist ... is to capture this process of interpretation. To do this requires what Weber called Verstehen, empathetic understanding or an ability to reproduce in one's own mind the feelings, motives, and thoughts behind the actions of others. To grasp the meanings of a person's behavior, the phenomenologist attempts to see things from that person's point of view. (Bogdan and Taylor, 1975, pp. 13–14)

So phenomenological ethnography not only attempts detailed descriptions of social processes but also aims to get insights into what people think they are doing and why they are doing it. The researcher is required to become acquainted with meanings the actions have for the members of the group. In one way or another, the researcher is expected to access members' own self-accounting. This process of accessing members meanings may be by coexisting with the group, that is, participating in one way or another and gradually assimilating their perspective, or it might be 'short-circuited' to some extent, by asking questions (see Chapter 7).

Phenomenological ethnography encompasses the work of *ethnomethodologists* (see page 42) and some symbolic interactionists, particularly those who adopt Herbert Blumer's (1969) view of symbolic exchanges:

1. Human beings act towards things on the basis of meanings that the things have for them.
2. These meanings are a product of social interaction in human society .
3. These meanings are modified and handled through an interpretive process that is used by each person in dealing with the things she or he encounters.

This view of *symbolic interaction* sees people in a constant process of interpretation and definition as they move from one situation to another. A situation has meaning only through people's interpretations and definitions of it. Their actions, in turn, stem from this meaning. It is the process of interpretation that turns an intention into an action. People define situations in different ways and act accordingly. It is possible, through communication, for a shared perspective to emerge.

Ethnomethodology is concerned with taken-for-granted aspects of the social world. It examines the routine, practical activities of everyday life to show how people make sense of them (see, for example, the ethno-methodological studies of the media in Chapter 2). It examines the processes by which we make the world 'accountable' to ourselves.

Ethnomethodology goes beyond Blumerian symbolic interaction. It investigates not only the impact on interaction of the meanings that things have for people but also how are those meanings generated in the first place. In particular, how meanings are related to common sense.

Ethnomethodologists presume that meanings are not clear, rather they see meanings as ambiguous and problematic for people in specific situations. Ethnomethodologists examine the ways in which people apply abstract rules and common-sense understandings in situations so as to make actions appear routine, explicable and unambiguous. Thus ethnomethodologists argue that meanings are not self-evident; rather, they are practical accomplishments by members of a society.

We saw in Chapter 3 that phenomenologists objected to official statistics because they said more about the taken-for-granteds involved in the compiling of statistics than they did about the phenomena supposedly described. Atkinson's (1978) work on suicide was an example. Douglas (1967, 1971) has also studied, from an ethnomethodologist's view, how coroners designate deaths as suicides. This requires the use of common-sense understandings by coroners to establish intention on the part of the victim. Coroners put together certain clues and come up with a 'suicide for all practical purposes'.

The task for ethnomethodologists, then, is to bracket or suspend their common-sense assumptions to study how common sense is used in everyday life, (for example, Garfinkel's (1967) experiments, see pages 144–6). Through an examination of common sense the ethnomethodologists hope to understand how people 'go about the task of seeing, describing, and explaining order in the world in which they live' (Bogdan and Taylor, 1975, p. 17). As a result, ethnomethodologists tend to inspect minutely social processes to reveal subjects' taken-for-granted assumptions about the social world. In practice they tend to use non-participant observation to do this.

Critical ethnography

Critical ethnography also focuses on meanings. However, it attempts to locate these within a broader setting. It sees meanings as cultural or structural. Meanings do not exist in isolation but relate to the cultures or social structures in which people live and operate. What is important for critical ethnography, then, is that the probing of the subject's meanings is not the end of the story. The group or organisation does not operate in a vacuum but is affected by all sorts of aspects of the society it is in. For example, the way that male pantry staff react to waitresses should not be seen simply as a function of the status hierarchy within the restaurant industry. For the critical ethnographer this is a reflection of wider patriarchal oppression of women by men (see page 25). Simply to excuse it, as Whyte does, by

---

SYMBOLIC INTERACTIONISM is the study of the relationship between self and society that focuses on the symbolic processes of communication between participants. There are several varieties of symbolic interactionism with different approaches to empirical research and different epistemological presuppositions.

Symbolic interactionism derives from the earlier interactionist approach of the 'Chicago School'. This took two forms. The first, inspired by W. I. Thomas, was based on the philosophical tradition of James and Cooley among others. It attempted to relate attitudes to values in a fairly 'scientific' manner and was similar to Weber's approach which linked meanings and causes (see page 141). This approach has been developed in conventional ethnography in the work of people such as Howard Becker. The second approach drew on G. H. Mead's theories of the self and was supposedly the basis of Herbert Blumer's development of symbolic interactionism which was more concerned with meanings than with causes. This approach has been further developed in the work of Ervin Goffman and the ethnomethodologists and can be seen in the development of phenomenological ethnography.

An alternative tradition of symbolic interactionism also flourished at Iowa University and this tends to be more overtly positivistic. It is not widely used or referred to these days.

NOTE Sometimes 'critical ethnography' is used to mean any form of reflexive ethnography.

suggesting that men feel uncomfortable in situations where women originate actions, is to miss the point. The broader context relates to the power that men exercise over women within a social structure that legitimates male domination.

In short, meanings are not just derived from within the group but are dependent upon broader social issues and processes that affect the interpretive process. The situating of meanings is done, not just to make sense of them, but to show how social structures and existing sets of power relationships shape the meanings. Further, it is also about assessing how meanings are developed in order to legitimate organisational practices or oppressive structures. Critical ethnography has been used, for example, by Marxists, feminists and radical black researchers in their analysis of economic, gender and racial oppression.

Critical ethnography attempts to develop an understanding by locating detailed observational enquiry directly into a critical analysis of social structures. As Willis (1977) did in his study of what takes place in school that results in some pupils ending up in dead-end manual jobs (see Extract 6.9, page 170). Critical ethnography usually starts by examining the social structure rather than taking it for granted. The ethnographic enquiry provides detailed data that helps to assess the structural analysis. However, this is not done by testing a hypothesis with a view to falsifying a theory (as a falsificationist might). There is a two-way development of understanding. The ethnographic material is used to re-examine the structural relationship and, at the same time, the structural analysis will help to make sense of the ethnographic data.

For example, Marshall (Extract 6.13) addressed the work situation of low-paid service workers in the catering industry as one of blatant exploitation. Rather than simply reproducing a *surplus-value* explanation (see page 72) he wanted to examine the 'reality' of the work-place from the point of view of the employees. His observation showed that the workers were not dissatisfied nor were they resentful at being exploited. A Marxist analysis would suggest that, among other things, workers in a capitalist economy are *alienated* because of the *division of labour* (see page 10) that fragments the work process and undermines any creativity on the part of the worker. The workers are not only exploited but also find the work unfulfilling. They do not get any satisfaction from their work but are forced into it as a means of satisfying other needs. As soon as there is no compulsion to do the work it is 'avoided like the plague' (Marx, 1963, p. 124). Alienation refers not just to the unrewarding nature of the work but also to the capitalist setting where workers have no control over their labour. Thus a Marxist analysis does not seem to apply from the point of view of the workers in Marshall's study.

However, Marshall did not simply abandon the Marxist analysis (as a falsificationist might have) but attempted to discover if there was another way to account for the apparent contradiction between exploitation and satisfaction. One solution could have revolved around the 'informal economy', that is, that the low pay was compensated for by the 'perks' and 'fiddles' that the paternalistic owner condoned. However, the extent of the 'perks' was insufficient to compensate for poor pay.

Marshall examined the work-place *culture* and found, as he examined it more closely, that it effectively denied the 'work' component of the employment. Work and leisure became merged into each other. Furthermore, the workers did not feel alienated because they felt in control of their labour. They were also not restricted to a single job. Everybody was

---

ALIENATION occurs when people are unable to relate to the world in which they live. As a philosophical concept alienation referred to the estrangement of people from themselves. It was brought into sociological analysis by Karl Marx and used in the sense of the worker being alienated from capitalist society; in particular, as being alienated from the products of his or her own labour. Marx saw creative, productive labour as the essence of human activity.

Capitalism involves the labourer selling his or her labour to the capitalist for a wage. The capitalist owns the product of the worker's labour. Labourers, under capitalism, are alienated in four ways. First, workers do not own the product of their labour nor have any control over its fate. Second, the actual work of production is undertaken in alien and unsatisfying settings (for example, factories). Third, workers are alienated from themselves because they are deprived of the essential creativity through having to produce goods for others in alien circumstances. Fourth, workers are alienated from other workers because labour has become a commodity and people relate to each other in terms of the product of their labour rather than as individuals.

expected to help out anywhere in the restaurant as and when the need arose.

Marshall thus developed the exploitation theory by looking at the *super-structural* relationships embodied in the work-place culture. Capitalism had triumphed in turning exploitation into a readily accepted way of life by blurring the edges between work and leisure for the employees in the restaurant. It had created the illusion that their flexibility, which greatly benefited the owner, gave them control over their work situation.

The role of the *critical* ethnographer is thus to keep alert to *structural* factors while probing *meanings*. This is aided by identifying *contradictions* and *ideology*. Contradictions can be seen in the difference between what people say and do, on the one hand, and their actual circumstances on the other. Ideology is reflected in the way stereotypes, myths, or dominant conceptualisations guide or *legitimate* respondents' actions and meanings (see page 14). By focusing on contradictions and the way ideology is used to make oppressive situations appear acceptable, critical ethnography is able to relate ethnographic material to wider structural processes. For example, Marshall showed how the workers at Dixie's Place convinced themselves that they were not being exploited because they were not really working.

> **Student Activity 6.21**
> Look at *any* ethnographic study of work-place activity such as *Working Lives in Catering* by Yiannis Gabriel (1988), *All Day Everyday* by Sallie Westwood (1984), *Women On the Line* by Ruth Cavendish (1982), *Working For Ford* by Huw Beynon (1973). Show clearly how the ethnographic work is undertaken. Outline which approach to ethnography is adopted in the study.

Objectivity and subjectivity

Observation studies are often seen, by positivists, as 'subjective' compared to the 'objectivity' of quantitative techniques. Participant observation, in particular, is singled out as a 'subjective method'. This notion of the subjectivity of observation studies arises for several reasons.

First, data derived from naturalistic observation is seen as being more *personal* and more idiosyncratic than answers to questions on a schedule. Yet observation that takes place in a conventional experimental setting is rarely questioned. There is an assumption that naturalistic observation gives too much leeway to the researcher to be subjective in selecting what to report. An experiment, on the other hand, is set up so that particular effects are being looked for from the outset (see Chapter 5). This predetermination of what to look for is reproduced in the use of interview schedules or questionnaires.

Second, naturalistic observation, it is argued, relies heavily on the ability of the researcher to get to see what is going on and thus the *role* being played by the researcher effects what is observed.

Third, if observation studies are concerned with subjects' *meanings* then the data of the study is itself subjective. There is no way of objectively measuring meanings and indeed there is no way that researchers can even be sure that they have grasped someone else's meanings. This means that the results of the observation are dependent entirely on the observer's interpretation and there is no possibility that the information can be reinterpreted by another researcher. Secondary data analysis (see Chapter 3) is thus virtually impossible with observational data.

Non-positivists are not convinced by these arguments. Sallie Westwood

(1984) in her study of female factory workers, for example, set out to grasp a specific 'cultural space' and this required immersion in the life of the shop floor. Participant observation was, for her, the only technique that allows the researcher to inhabit and record such a cultural space as a factory shop floor. Westwood aimed to illuminate the 'lived experiences' of women workers who come together to generate and sustain a specific feminine working-class culture. This required that she be involved as a participant so as to unravel the world of symbols and meanings that made up the culture.

Such a view makes the positivist objections irrelevant. First, the participant observer is no more selective than the experimenter or social surveyor. The experimenter and social surveyor are selective in what they are going to look for *before* the data collection takes place. The participant observer is less selective, has fewer rigid preconceptions, and tends to look at a much wider array of 'facts' in order to filter out what is significant in the development of a theory *during* the data collection. The observer thus allows the data to *inform* the development of theory rather simply test a predetermined theory.

Second, the idea that social facts can be *measured* objectively is disputed (as we saw in Chapter 2). The non-positivist view suggests that no method can provide the researcher with 'objective facts'. Facts do not exist in isolation. The words a respondent utters, or the actions a subject is observed to make have no existence on their own but only 'make sense' in relation to other utterances and actions. Someone waving at a group of people may be waving goodbye but it might also be an act of defiance or recklessness (for example, a member of a gang from one neighbourhood who is drawing attention to herself in the territory of another gang) or an acknowledgement of adulation (for example, a film star waving at a film première).

Furthermore, the meanings that actions and utterances have for the researcher is also not self-evident. Data only have meaning when they are interpreted. The meaning of an event or piece of evidence depends on theory. This may be the everyday 'theory' of unreflective common sense or it may be a reflective attempt to develop a social theory. For example, two groups of football supporters may confront each other in a side street outside a football ground after a match. For the supporters, this is a sign of their commitment to their team; for the media, this might be seen as another mindless brawl between 'football hooligans'; for the police, a potential problem of public order; for the home owners in the area, it is a nuisance; for a sociologist, it might be an incidence of working-class group machismo; for a psychologist, an example of territorial conflict; and for a magistrate, a wanton disregard of the law. In other words, what a particular event or piece of data means to the interpreter of the data is not self-evident in the data itself. It depends upon a theoretical framework within which it is located. It makes sense in different ways to different people who approach the 'fact' from different perspectives.

Reliability and validity

It is often argued that observation studies are not *reliable* because there is no consistent way of measuring the data. For example, what is observed depends on the degree and type of involvement of the researcher. As we have seen, the role adopted by the researcher is crucial. In the main, participant observers are unable to make their procedures explicit and there is no way of replicating a study to check the reliability of its findings.

The apparent unreliability of observation studies, particularly participant observation, is, however, seen as a 'red herring' by non-positivists. The positivistic view of reliability is one-sided. It relates to the ability of the data collection tool to measure *predefined* social phenomena (see Chapter 2). The point of *naturalistic* observation research, non-positivists argue, is that it is not interested in making *measures* of 'variables' but is concerned with grasping social *processes* or cultural *meanings*.

In addition, social surveyors are no more 'reliable' in what they do than observers. Just because they provide a questionnaire so that the study can be replicated does not mean that the method is reliable. As we saw in Chapter 4, it is difficult, if not impossible, to check the reliability of a questionnaire. Furthermore, providing a schedule or questionnaire does not mean that the researcher has made *explicit* the procedures used. Surveyors rarely, if ever, provide a rationale as to why they asked the particular questions. Nor do they provide the criteria by which the particular questions on the questionnaire were selected in preference to other feasible alternative questions.

More to the point, non-positivists argue that it is the *validity* of the data rather than its reliability that is important. It might be that the positivist's research tool consistently and reliability measures the variables but if what is being measured is invalid then whole process is rather pointless (see Chapter 2). For example, intelligence tests are reliable measures of intelligence *quotients* but whether this has anything to do with intelligence is debatable. It has been argued that IQ is an invalid measure of intelligence because it is biased towards middle-class, white educational skills. The data from participant observation, it is argued by people such as Westwood, is more valid than other forms of data collection whether or not it is more (or less) reliable.

> **Student activity 6.22**
> **Working in pairs, undertake a short piece of participant observation (similar to Student Activities 6.3 or 6.8) with both of you participating or observing the same group or organisation. Compare your observations and account for any differences in conclusions that you come to. Do the results of this activity lead you to regard participant observation as unreliable? If so, in what ways? What do you feel is the consequence or importance of any unreliability you might have noted?**

Summary and conclusion

Observation is a major means by which sociologists develop an understanding of the social world. Observation can be undertaken as a participant or as a non-participant; either way, observational research is undertaken in a systematic way. Observation is not a means of reinforcing preconceptions. Rather, observation should challenge what is taken for granted as well as providing data on previously unrecorded aspects of the social world. Observation is demanding because it requires the researcher to make contacts and to be in a position to observe social activities. Such activities need to be recorded in detail, and this leads to large amounts of material being collected, with consequent problems of analysis.

The role adopted by observers, particularly participant observers, can be crucial in determining the type and extent of data that you can collect and

Further Reading

Observation techniques: Burgess, 1984; Friedrichs, 1975; McCall and Simmons, 1969; Rose, 1982; Spradley, 1980.

Ethnography: Burgess, 1982; Denzin, 1970; Filstead, 1970; Hammersley and Atkinson, 1983.

Symbolic interactionism: Blumer, 1969; Charon, 1979; Couch *et al.*, 1986; Manis and Meltzer, 1978; Meltzer *et al.*, 1975; Rock, 1979; Williams, 1986.

Ethnomethodology: Benson and Hughes, 1983; Cicourel, 1964, 1976; Coulter, 1988; Douglas, 1970, 1971; Garfinkel, 1967; Heritage, 1984; Mehan and Wood, 1975; Rogers, 1983; Sharrock and Anderson, 1986; Turner, 1974.

Topics

Deviance: Aggleton, 1987; Becker, 1963; Box, 1983; Brake and Hale, 1992; Campbell, 1981, 1984; Chambliss, 1978; Cohen, 1971, 1973; Downes and Rock, 1988; Fitzgerald, 1985; Hall *et al.*, 1978; Heidensohn, 1985; Lea and Young, 1984; Luhrman, 1989; Matza, 1964; Parker, 1974; Patrick, 1973; Pfohl, 1986; Polsky, 1971; Smart, 1977; Suchar, 1978; Taylor, 1983; Taylor *et al.*, 1973, 1975; Williams *et al.*, 1984.

Work: Beynon, 1973; Cavendish, 1982; Gabriel, 1988; Hacker, 1989; Haraszti, 1977; Marshall, 1986; Watson, 1987; Westwood, 1984; Wood, 1991.

BEWARE Observation research has a great deal of appeal, particularly to new researchers. Participant observation, in particular, offers an exciting way to do research areas that are both unusual and interesting. However, it is important not to develop a romantic view of observation research. It is very hard work, time-consuming and requires a lot of self-discipline. It should not be seen as the easy option. As it takes so long to do and requires such a high degree of commitment it is not necessarily the most appropriate research technique to adopt for projects.

---

report. You also need to consider issues of privacy, ethics and, ultimately, personal danger, if you intend to do participant observation.

Participant observation tends to be regarded as an unreliable and subjective method as it relies on unrepeatable research situations in which the data collection is very much reliant on the researcher's perceptions of what is significant. Participant observers argue that this is in effect no different from other research situations and, indeed, participant observation is more flexible and more responsive to the concepts of the research subjects than any other form of research.

It is important for participant observers to be reflexive, that is, reflect upon the impact they have had on the research setting.

Although observation research is at the heart of ethnography, this does not mean that all observational research adopts the same approach. Ethnography has been undertaken from a variety of epistemological perspectives. Interactionist and functionalist approaches to ethnographic work are underpinned by positivism, while some symbolic interactionist and ethnomethodological approaches are guided by phenomenology. Critical approaches to ethnography (such as feminism and Marxism) locate the detailed analysis of social processes in a broader social context. The ethnographic material is thus used to develop the understanding of the operation of oppressive social structures (such as patriarchy, capitalism, racism and so on).

Project ideas

If you intend to use participant observation it is important that you already have *access* to your research area. Access can take a long time and you rarely have sufficient time in a school or college project to make new contacts as well as do the research. The project ideas below are thus suggestions that you might think about developing *if* you already have access to the appropriate group or organisation.

You should be careful about what, where and when you choose to observe. Make sure that you discuss any potential observation study with your tutor. Do not attempt participant observation that will put you in an uncomfortable situation. In general, it is advisable to avoid long-term secret participant observation.

1. An analysis of the sexism or racism in a factory or office.
2. A study of busking as a career.
3. The use of language in a magistrate's court.
4. A class analysis of horse-race goers.
5. A study of auction room culture and how people make sense of the auction process and their participation in it.
6. The status differences on a hospital ward and the nature of the interaction between doctors and nurses.
7. The nature of sexism within biker subculture.
8. An analysis of the extent to which the activities of football supporters are affected by working-class machismo.
9. A study of courting behaviour in a disco or bhangra.
10. An analysis of the extent to which workers in fast-food establishments see the job as meaningless and exploitative.

CHAPTER 7
PERSONAL DATA

Introduction

Personal data is another important source of data for sociological enquiry. Personal data covers a variety of types of information. It includes personal documents such as letters and diaries, accounts of experiences including life histories and autobiographies, as well as detailed discussions ranging from unstructured conversations through in-depth interviews to counselling and diagnostic interviews.

After some comments on the use of personal documents and life history we will look in some detail at how to undertake an in-depth interview as this is an important technique for securing personal data.

There is considerable difference of opinion about the usefulness of personal data. Some positivists regard it as unreliable and unverifiable and tend to avoid it. Many phenomenologists see it as very important in understanding the way that people make sense of the social world. Critical researchers, particularly feminists, find personal data invaluable in revealing the processes by which women are oppressed.

Personal documents

Personal documents reveal information about what people feel about their lives or other information about themselves. Researchers can use personal documents as a way to generate hypotheses or to study parts of people's lives, events or situations where it is not possible to study them directly.

Sociologists have made use of personal documents since the start of sociological research. For example, William I. Thomas and Florian Znaniecki (1918–20) used personal documents amongst other material in their study *The Polish Peasant in Europe and America*. They made use of autobiographies, letters, newspaper articles, accounts of court proceedings and records from social agencies.

Letters

The letters sent between Poland and America were a major source of information. The researchers knew that there was extensive correspondence between the two countries and so placed advertisements in newspapers offering cash for each letter produced. It was relatively easy for the authors to acquire the letters in America but these represented only one side of the exchange. To overcome this Znaniecki went to Poland to get letters from the Polish peasants and managed to leave Poland with a suitcase full of them despite the outbreak of the First World War. The letters were used to show how traditional family solidarity was maintained or altered as family members moved to the United States (see Extract 7.1).

Student Activity 7.1
1. **In what ways does the letter (Extract 7.1) show that the writer continues to adhere to traditional norms?**
2. **Do you think that her desire to keep her forthcoming marriage a secret indicates a shift from tradition?**

Using letters as the basis of research does raise some problems. First, common to all document analysis, is the fact that the letters are not written specifically for research purposes. For example, in the *Polish Peasant* study Thomas and Znaniecki were interested in the process of assimilation of Polish peasants into American urban life. Not surprisingly, correspondence between family members in Poland and the United States did not necessarily address this issue in any consistent way. Nor were Thomas and Znaniecki always able to obtain complete sets of correspondence between family members. Thus the data was fragmentary and incomplete.

Second, letters are very personal documents and the owners may object to them being used for the purposes of research. Thomas and Znaniecki encouraged people to provide letters by offering a cash incentive. This may have led to a biased sample. Only certain people would give up letters in such circumstances and they would be likely to be selective about which letters they parted with. A cash incentive would perhaps not be sufficient to induce some people to give up certain types of letter, for example, love letters or letters that talk about the recipient in a derogatory fashion because

---

Extract 7.1

LETTER TO A POLISH PEASANT FAMILY

We have here a case of familial attitudes quite untouched by emigration. The writer seems to represent as perfectly as possible the *ideal* of a peasant girl according to the traditional norms. There is scarcely anything in her behaviour that could be blamed from the traditional standpoint, but hardly any tendency to go beyond this traditional standpoint.

Brooklyn, N.Y., October 14th, 1911
My Dear Family: In the first words 'Praised be Jesus Christus.'...
And now, dear parents, I inform you that I am in good health, thanks to God, which I wish you also with my truest heart. And now I am on duty [a maidservant] and I do well, I have fine food, only I must work from 6 o'clock in the morning to 10 o' clock at night and I have $13 a month. And now, dear parents, I implore you don't grieve about me, thinking that I am without money.... And you thought, dear parents that I sent my last money away [to Aunt Karololska to repay a loan for the tickets to the United States]. But you know yourselves that I cannot remain without a cent, because I am in the world. I almost laughed about your sorrow. As it is I have spent more than 50 roubles on myself for the coming winter, and nevertheless I am not so beautifully dressed as all the others. Only I regret to spend money, I prefer to put it away rather than to buy luxurious dresses, like Olcia Kubaczowna who buys herself a new dress every week and doesn't look at money and doesn't think what can happen. She thinks only how to dress and says she doesn't need to think about anything more.

But I am not of the same opinion; I think about my home. I have brothers and sisters and I intend to help them all come to America....

And now, dear parents, you may hope that I will send you for Christmas 10 roubles. I would not send them but, thanks to God, I have some, and I have work, so every month money comes to me....

And now, dear parents, I will write you that I have an opportunity to be married. I have fine boy, because uncle and auntie [Kubacz] have known him for 3 years. He is good, not a drunkard, he does not swear as others often do... I do not know whether I shall marry this year or not – just as you advise me, my parents. ... I beg you so very much, let nobody learn that I am going to be married and that I have a young man.... I beg you, let nobody know that I wrote this letter. Say only 'She wrote nothing; all's well,' and let that be all. Don't say anything about this matter. And when I send the photograph, hide it also, please, so that nobody may see it.

And now I have nothing more to write, and I bow to you, dear family, and I wish you every good. May God grant that this letter finds you in good health, and I ask you for a quick answer.

Aleksandra Rembienska.

And I request you, dear parents, send letters with stamps, because I have great difficulties. A letter with a stamp arrives sooner.

Adapted from Thomas and Znaniecki [1918–20] (1958), pp. 775–8.

they perhaps had not been sending enough money back home. A further complication arose in Thomas and Znaniecki's study. Not all the Polish peasants in the villages in Poland could write. Thus some letters would have been written by the village scribe. That there was an intervening person (the scribe) may have affected the content of the letters.

Diaries

Diaries are sometimes used to keep a record of the everyday activities of individuals in a particular social setting. A useful picture of an individual's life can be built up by asking the person to keep a record of what they do at various times of the day, month, year and so on. The diary is often used as a supplement to other research methods. Grabrucker (1988) kept a diary about the development of her daughter. At the end of each day she wrote a precise account of everything that had happened. She noted what she had said and done and what had been passed onto Anneli (her daughter) and her male and female friends. In this study of *socialisation* (see page 50), Grabrucker wanted to contest the myth, which even some feminists were beginning to believe, that 'boys will be boys and girls will be girls' due to innate differences. The entries were thus made in order to assess the extent to which these trivial and frequently insignificant events play a part in gender role *stereotyping* (see pages 37 and 51). Extract 7.2 shows how Grabrucker's diary records the way her daughter was learning her gender role.

By using a diary Grabrucker concluded that the upbringing of girls is varied and experimental. Girls are confronted with two 'worlds' prescribed for the sexes and are expected to feel at home in both. For example, comments at home may make it clear to the girl that aggression is not acceptable in women, yet she is expected to stand up for herself just like a boy. The author concludes that it is now the time to start a new gender approach to boys. Only when both sexes, from childhood on, are engaged in a continual process of change is there any hope for a future of real equality between males and females.

Another example of using a diary is 'Project Sigma' (Coxon, 1988) funded by the Medical Research Council and the Department of Health. The project was a three-year longitudinal national study of the sexual and social behaviour of gay and bisexual men to examine changes in sexual lifestyles under the impact of AIDS and HIV positivity. The need for this study arose because very little information exists about the detail of gay sexual behaviour. Yet good estimates are needed if theories and models that explain and predict transmission of HIV are to be accurate. Using the usual survey method would not be appropriate here, since most people would not participate truthfully. The researchers used a variety of methods, extensive interviews, ethnographic research and a day-to-day sexual diary as the main tool.

Most people, gay and heterosexual, cannot provide a reliable detailed account of sexual behaviour further back than a fortnight (Coxon, 1988). As one of the main factors in becoming HIV antibody positive is engaging in 'high risk' behaviour with a lot of partners it becomes clear that a reliable source of information on sexual activity is needed. The information in the diary is used to find out the number of partners and other information that cannot be obtained any other way. By using the diary, people were persuaded to detail their sexual activity.

Extract 7.2

SOCIALISING ANNELI

3 May 1983 (21 months)

Grandma is visiting us and is playing with Anneli. Some soft toys have been wrapped up and are being rocked to sleep. Grandma shows Anneli how to do it and she copies eagerly. Grandma would never have done this with a boy.

She's brought Anneli a present of a little shopping basket just like mummy's, which I let her use when we go shopping, when it occurs to me that by doing so I'm identifying her with me and again defining her in terms of myself and my own activities. Of course, this isn't the first time. How often have I passed on the idea of being 'just like mummy' in my daily activities as a housewife?

The sense of just being like mummy, handed on in the daily intimacy between mother and daughter, stays with us all our lives.

From Grabrucker, 1988, p. 35.

Student Activity 7.2
Keep a diary for a week of the programmes you watch on television and note how often and in what ways people from different ethnic groups are represented in various types of programme. What do you conclude from your findings? Discuss your results with other people who have also kept a similar diary. Did you have similar observations? Explain any differences that occurred in your entries.

Both Grabrucker's and Coxon's studies involved keeping a diary for research purposes. Grabrucker kept her diary with a view to challenging the myth of innate sex differences and Coxon encouraged a sample of people to keep a diary of sexual activity. Researchers can also make use of diaries that are written for personal reasons and not intended as a research tool. Such personal diaries can provide useful research material but like letters and other personal documents the content might be quite fragmentary and incomplete for research purposes. For example, Lee Harvey (1987) used the private journal of William Ogburn in his study of the Chicago 'School' of Sociology. This journal, which was stored in the archive of the Regenstein Library at the University of Chicago, was restricted to public view for twenty-five years after the death of William Ogburn. It was used in the research to explore how Ogburn related to other members of the Chicago 'School'. Very little of the journal spoke about this central issue and mentions of it were interspersed with lengthy accounts of holidays, social events, political reflections and so on.

Finally, researchers can also make use of diaries that are kept by politicians with a view to publication, such as *The Diaries of a Cabinet Minister* (Crossman, 1975–7) or *Against the Tide* (Benn, 1989). These are particularly useful when looking at the processes of political decision-making as there has been very little social research into the area. However, such published diaries must be approached critically because of their party-political bias.

Autobiographies

Autobiographies are an obvious source of personal data. However, autobiographies are not usually produced for purposes of sociological research. None the less, they may be useful sources of sociological data as they allow the researcher to form a picture of a person's whole life from birth to death, rather than focusing on one out-of-context aspect of a person's life.

Autobiographies tend to be of three sorts. First, accounts of the lives of famous people, such as actors or pop stars. While these provide some data of sociological interest about the popular music world or Hollywood, they tend to be written to provide interesting anecdotes designed to amuse or intrigue the reader. Second, the reflections of 'the powerful'. These are accounts of politicians, army generals, civil service chiefs and so on. Like published diaries (discussed above), they show how important decisions are taken and provide insights into the processes of power. Often, though, they are constrained by secrecy legislation and tend to be of historical rather than contemporary interest. Third, the life experiences of 'ordinary people'. Often, these provide the most important source of sociological data. For example, Ellen Kuzwayo's (1985) autobiographical account of how it feels to be a black woman in South Africa is not just an account of her own life but draws on the unrecorded history of a whole people. While not entirely 'typical', such accounts provide an indication of what, for example, the everyday experience of life is like in a black South African township.

Similar kinds of autobiographical material can be found in recent accounts by women about aspects of their lives. For example, Una Padel and Prue Stevenson's (1988) *Insiders* consists of the accounts, by eleven women, of what life is really like inside women's prisons in Britain. The accounts also deal with the women's lives before imprisonment, putting the meaning of their time in prison into a personal context and the devastating after-effects of imprisonment. Awa Thiam's (1986) *Black Women Speak Out* contains the accounts of Black African women living in French-speaking countries of the Ivory Coast, Guinea, Mali and Senegal and the English-speaking states of Ghana and Nigeria. They are the voices of powerless women subject to institutionalised polygamy, forced marriages and the onerous burden of unpaid agricultural and domestic labour. The usually silenced women tell of their daily lives, their problems and their actual relationships to men. Similarly, Ingela Bendt and James Downing's (1982) *We Shall Return* gives voice to Palestinian women who have lived through the 1948 expulsion from Palestine following the establishment of the state of Israel and the Palestinian revolution of 1965, which turned them from refugees into revolutionaries. The women's account documents the impact of these events on their lives.

Life histories

Life history is the account, by a single individual, of his or her life experiences. Life histories are usually accounts that are produced especially for sociological research. Life history was an approach popular in the early development of sociology, particularly at the University of Chicago (Shaw, 1930, 1931; Sutherland, 1937) but it also experienced a mini-revival in the 1970s (Chambliss, 1972; Probyn, 1977). Thomas and Znaniecki (1918–20) included a very detailed life history in *The Polish Peasant* that provides a vivid picture of what it was like to migrate from Poland to the USA. Thomas and Znaniecki argued that:

> personal life-records, as complete as possible, constitute the perfect type of sociological material, and that if social science has to use other material at all it is only because of the practical difficulty of obtaining at the moment a sufficient number of such records to cover the totality of sociological problems, and of the enormous amount of work demanded for an adequate analysis of all the personal materials necessary to characterize the life of a social group. (Thomas and Znaniecki, 1918, vol. 3, p. 1)

A sociological life history is usually intended to explore the significant events that affected the subject's life. The intention is usually to assess the way in which social processes were interpreted by the subject and determined the course of their life. Thomas and Znaniecki, for example, set out to show how social values effect the attitudes of individuals. They thus focused on significant events identified by the subjects and investigated how these affected behaviour and perceptions.

An individual may be asked to write their life history. For example, Clifford Shaw (1930), in his classic study *The Jack Roller: A Delinquent Boy's Own Story*, asked his informant, Stanley, to construct his own life story, including all the crucial events in his life. In order to help Stanley with his life history Shaw read the account and pointed out the areas that required further detail.

Sometimes the life history may be told to the researcher and then reconstructed into a written account. For example, Rachel Barton (who did

NOTE The life history tended to decline after the early 1930s because it did not lend itself to variable analysis which became increasingly emphasised in sociology. Nor could life history be readily deployed to prove or disprove hypotheses.

However, in the 1960s the approach began to experience a revival that can be linked to the development of sociological subdisciplines such as the family, education and poverty and the growing influence of phenomenological perspectives within them. Again, life history was seen as a valuable research technique which could provide a view of history often unrecorded by documents which placed ordinary people 'centre stage'.

not set out to do social research) was doing voluntary work and met a young Indian woman called 'Sita'. Barton was teaching English to 'Sita' and to encourage her to speak more fluently asked her about her childhood in India.

> In the course of a year or more she gradually revealed the story of her brief life. I was deeply moved by her experiences and the way she expressed her thoughts and feelings, and started to write down what she told me. Through her touching and tragic story I entered to some extent that world which I thought closed to me. Eventually, with Sita's agreement I pieced together the events of her life to make this book. It is true to her own viewpoint and I have tried as far as possible to keep it in her own words.
> (Barton, 1987, Introduction)

When a researcher sets out to collect a life history, it is more likely to be through a series of detailed ethnographic interviews (see page 196) in which the respondent is encouraged to relate the events and experiences that are most important to them (Parker and Allerton, 1962). Some researchers have used a variety of research techniques when compiling a life history, including archive research, participant observation and longitudinal study. Whatever method is employed it is essential that informants have the opportunity to express what they perceive as significant factors in their lives, using their classifications and their own interpretive framework.

Evidence supporting the use of life history material is well documented by Becker (1986), who suggests that it offers great potential in two respects. First, life history materials provide a vivid feeling for what it means to be a certain kind of person in particular contexts. This can give us an insight into the subject's everyday life and work and an understanding of his or her subjective assessments of institutional processes and structures. Becker argues, further, that life history data can be used to test sociological concepts and in evaluating existing theories. The examination of general theories in the light of ethnographic accounts can highlight the limitations of the theories and generate new theoretical questions.

Nevertheless, the use of life history inevitably raises questions about the reliability, typicality and representativeness of data gathered. This has led some researchers to question the extent to which such materials can assist sociological understanding. Clearly, a life history only represents a culture to the degree that the individual it portrays has been involved in experiences common to other individuals who make up that culture. However, as Becker has argued, every story plays its part in building a picture of the social life of the time, place and group under investigation. Moreover, the significance of life history data is, like any other data, dependent on the methodological and theoretical analysis undertaken.

Mandelbaum (1982), while advocating the use of life history techniques, criticises what he sees as the lack of theoretical development in this area. He illustrates this point by reference to the extensive life history data recorded by Oscar Lewis in the 1960s, which he suggests is almost exclusively descriptive and includes little in the way of analysis. Mandelbaum argues that life history material is usually extensive and thus must be channelled in some way in order to aid analysis. Mandelbaum suggests that there are several ways that life history data can be organised other than as a chronological account.

First, note the key *dimensions* of a person's life as a way of generating categories for understanding the main forces influencing that person. Key dimensions include the biological, cultural, social and psychological areas of a person's life.

Second, identify the principal *turning points* in a person's life, such as starting work, marriage, retirement and the conditions of life between them.

Third, note the person's principal means of *adaptation* to life's inconsistencies. This directs attention to both the changes and continuities in the subject's life.

> **Student Activity 7.3**
> Carry out an interview with someone over retirement age. Find out what you can about their changing perceptions and experiences of the family throughout their lives. Where applicable, compare your results with those obtained by others on your course. Ensure you relate your results to a suitable theory of the family.
> SUGGESTION You may want to read about how to do an ethnographic interview below (see page 201) before setting out to do this activity. Or you may want to try this activity and then compare what you did with what is suggested in the discussion on ethnographic interviewing below.

Robert Burgess (1982) suggests that further work may be required in this area if we are fully to assess the usefulness of life histories. Nevertheless, they can give us an alternative view of the past, focusing as they do on the experiences of 'ordinary' people, rather than on those of the more frequently catalogued 'rich and famous'.

The family

Personal data is often used in the study of the family. The analysis of personal documents above and the discussion of in-depth interviews below draw on sociological studies of the family. It is appropriate to outline theories of the family, at this point, to provide a broader context within which to locate the research mentioned in this chapter.

Positivist approaches to the family

By far the most influential positivist approach to the family is to be found in the work of the *functionalists* (see page 82).

Functionalist theories of the family

Functionalists see the family as a basic unit of social structure. Indeed, functionalists have maintained that society, as we know it, is dependent upon the continuation of the traditional family. They argue that the family serves some basic functions that are vital to the social system. Talcott Parsons, for example, claims that the family has two basic and irreducible functions: first, the primary socialisation of children (discussed in more detail on page 50) and, second, the stabilisation of adult personalities. The latter refers to the role the family supposedly plays in countering the psychological stresses of everyday life that potentially make the adult personality unstable. Stabilisation comes from the mutual emotional support that a married couple give each other and from the role of being a parent. Through the socialisation process the parents can regress to childhood through play with their children and thus remove tensions.

The family, however, is only functional if members within it play their allocated roles. Parsons and Bales (1955) argue that women play an 'expres-

THE UNIVERSAL FAMILY Much intellectual effort has been invested in asking whether the family is universal. Murdock (1949) claims that the family performs four basic functions in all societies: sexual, reproductive, economic and educational. The 'traditional' Western notion of the family consists of an adult of each sex, with a child or children, living together as an economic unit. Not all families in Western societies have this make-up in practice, although it is still regarded as the norm. In other societies this idea of the family neither existed in practice nor was it the norm. The Israeli kibbutz (Spiro, 1965; Bettelheim, 1971), the matrilineal Nayar society (Gough, 1959) and the matriarchal 'families' of the West Indies and Central America (Gonzales, 1970) are well documented examples of societies without the conventional family unit. In the end, however, the definition of the family can be adapted to include such examples. What is important, however, is that social rules on mating, sexuality, child-rearing and gender relations are culturally specific and not universal (Gittins, 1985).

The interesting question is: Why would anyone want to claim that the family was universal? Was it an attempt to show that sociology had a universal concept, that the diversity of human culture could be reduced to a universal family form? In that way sociology could be said to have a fundamental element upon which a science could be built (in the same way that chemists use atoms and molecules to explain chemical reactions). Or was the claim of the universality of the family simply a way of legitimating the continuation of the family in the West at a time when it is increasingly coming under attack from critics who see it as an antiquated and oppressive institution?

sive' role in the family: they are kind, affectionate, cheerful, sensitive and obedient. Men play an 'instrumental' role: they are aggressive leaders, creative and original. The male is the breadwinner and the female's fundamental status 'is that of her husband's wife, the mother of his children' (Parsons, 1954, p. 224). The subordinate position of women in capitalist societies, Parsons claims, is functionally necessary to maintain family solidarity. Family solidarity is itself necessary to maintain the class structure. The maintenance of the class structure is necessary to ensure that the social structure remains as it is. In short, this is a circular argument that insists that women play a subordinate role so that the system that keeps them subordinate can continue.

Parsons tends to assume that the family plays a positive functional role. Other functionalists have called this into question and examined the dysfunctions of the family as well (Bell and Vogel, 1968). Overall, however, functionalists argue that the family is functional for its members and for society.

Phenomenological approaches to the family

Phenomenological approaches are concerned with meanings. What does it mean to an adult to be a parent? What are the differences and potential conflicts between men and women in the way they interpret their roles? How do children see the family as they wait to make their way in the wide world (Berger and Berger, 1976)? How do parents account for their children's behaviour? How do divorcees account for the failure of marriage and family life? In short, phenomenology asks how people make sense of the family situation and the roles they play within the family.

For example, Voysey (1975) studied the meanings of parents within families with a severely handicapped child. Rather than see themselves as 'coping well' in an abnormal situation, such parents adopted notions of 'normal' family life and saw what they were doing as what any normal parent would do under the circumstances. Similarly, Backett (1982) examined how mothers and fathers came to terms with, and explained, their different inputs into the parenting process.

The phenomenological approach, in attempting to explore the meanings people have in relation to the family, concentrates on the actual processes of everyday life. Phenomenologists look in detail at the conversations and actions that take place in the family setting. They focus on the ordinary, everyday activity of being a spouse or parent. Phenomenological studies tend to be microscopic rather than concerned with issues about the relationship between the family and social structure.

Critical approaches to the family

Critical approaches see the family as integrally related to social structure. The family operates as a mechanism of oppression within capitalist or patriarchal society. As we saw in Chapter 1, Marxists and feminists have differed about the relative importance of capitalism and patriarchy in oppressing women. This debate relates directly to the theory of the family.

Marxist view of the family
Marxists see the family as an evolving (rather than a static) institution that changes as society changes. For Engels (1884), the family is linked to the

development of classes, property and the state. He argued that the monogamous nuclear family became the dominant form of family relationship in Western society as the notion of private property became dominant. Private property was protected by the state through the legal system. The protection of the ownership of the *means of production* (see page 10) was essential to the reproduction of capitalism. Private property was owned by males and inherited by males. To ensure that there was a legitimate line of inheritance, men needed to control women. The monogamous family provided an efficient way of ensuring this. Just to make sure, the father was awarded all property rights within the family, including property rights over his wife and children. So, for Engels, and subsequent Marxists, the family was the result of class conflict which ensured that economic wealth remained with the capitalists (Sayers *et al.*, 1984).

In addition, the unpaid labour performed by women is a further source of *surplus value* for the owners of the means of production (see page 72). The production undertaken in the home, usually by the women and children, is paid for by the wage earner. This is, in effect, a tax on the wage earner for rearing a cheap labour supply for the capitalists (Glazer-Malbin and Waehrer, 1972).

This obligation on workers also makes it difficult for them to withdraw their labour when the family is dependent on the wage earner's income. So the family acts as a stabilising force, ensuring the continued exploitation of the worker. The family also absorbs the aggression and frustration of the worker in a capitalist society and instead of anger and resentment being turned against the capitalist employers it is often direct inwards on to the family. The Parsonian notion of the role of the family in stabilising adult personalities through mutual emotional support is transformed into one in which the family absorbs the legitimate resentment that the worker has towards the capitalist. The family thus insulates the capitalist from direct action by workers (Rowbotham 1973; Bernard, 1976).

Thus, the family was an important institution for maintaining patterns of inequality between the classes and between men and women. To change the family requires fundamental changes to society.

Feminist analysis of the family

This was all very well, but many feminists, socialist as well as radical, have pointed out that the arrangement was also convenient for men. Not just for capitalists but for all men. Women provide labour within the family for men.

Feminism sees relations and divisions within the family as well as its role in capitalist society. In short, the family is the principle location within which *patriarchy* operates (see page 25). Socialist feminists have argued that Engels was incorrect to assume that women's entry into social production would transform relations between the sexes. This would only change if there was a transformation of the sexual divisions within the family as well as outside in society (Maconachie, 1984).

For radical feminists, the patriarchal division is far more important than the role of the family in sustaining capitalism (Evans, 1982; Delphy, 1985). Indeed, some feminists argue that the Marxist analysis reduces the sexual division of labour to class divisions in production and private property. This is convenient for men as it conceals the extent of the exploitation of women within the family unit (see page 215).

Ethnographic interviews

Much personal data is collected as a result of spending time talking to people. This may range from casual *conversations* through to a series of systematic and detailed *in-depth* interviews. For convenience we will refer to these different ways of collecting personal data as *ethnographic interviews*.

Ethnographic interviews are different from the formal scheduled interviews discussed in Chapter 4. Ethnographic interviews, unlike scheduled interviews, do not ask all respondents the same questions in the same predetermined order. Indeed, there may be no formal set of questions at all. Scheduled interviews are designed to seek out information relating to categories that the researcher has decided are important. Ethnographic interviews attempt to gain access to the point of view and frame of reference of the informants themselves. Thus the primary aim of the ethnographic interviewer is to uncover the meanings that informants construct about aspects of their social world. In this respect they have more in common with participant observers than with survey interviewers (see Chapter 6).

Ethnographic interviewing encourages informants to talk in their terms and gradually probes their meanings and frames of reference. Initially, the researcher attempts to understand the informant's terminology and perspectives through their context in responses. Over time, the concepts and relationships that appear to be most important in the way subjects construct meaning can be elaborated by asking respondents to explain what they mean in more detail.

In-depth interviews

In-depth interviews (sometimes called 'depth interviews') are used for two purposes. First they represent the *formal* approach to ethnographic interviewing (unlike the *informal* conversation). Second, they are used as *exploratory* interviews, usually as a prelude to scheduled interviewing (see page 217). When used as an ethnographic method, in-depth interviews involve the researcher in trying to go deeply into some aspect of the informant's feelings, motives, attitudes, experiences or life history. Interviewers may have an idea of things they want respondents to talk about but must be flexible and allow respondents to talk about things that are important to them.

In-depth interviews may be unstructured, semi-structured or structured (see Figure 7.1). Unstructured in-depth interviews are sometimes called 'open-ended' interviews and are rather like one-sided conversations. The interviewer has no predetermined set of questions. The respondent is encouraged to talk about particular areas that are of interest to the interviewer. These may be very general, or even quite vague at the outset. The interviewer lets the respondent talk and responds to what is said to keep the interview going. The aim of this kind of ethnographic interviewing is to allow respondents to talk about what they see as important. Often, unstructured in-depth interviews are used along with participant observation (see Extract 7.3)

A semi-structured in-depth interview is usually one in which the interviewer has a checklist of topic areas or questions. The intention is still to get the informants to talk in their terms, hence questions tend not to be too specific allowing for a range of possible responses, but it is a more focused

---

TERMINOLOGY Ethnographic interview is a term most often used to refer to a face-to-face interview or conversation rather than to over-heard conversations which take place in a participant observation or non-participant observation context. Ethnographic interviewing does not normally refer to bits of dialogue that result from the researcher's participation in a social setting (see Chapter 6).

However, some commentators include the interviewing undertaken by a participant observer in the category of ethnographic interviews.

Other commentators suggest a very narrow definition of ethnographic interview that excludes informal conversations. They see the ethnographic interview as a formal process in which the interviewer makes clear the purpose of the interview and gets the informant's agreement to the recording of the exchange.

Extract 7.3

STUDENT TYPES

Teachers draw on their common-sense knowledge about different 'types' of student in dealing with deviant activity in classrooms. The interviewer referred back to an incident observed in the classroom.

I: Just after this there were some other girls making a noise, you looked up because I think you heard some people chattering, but you didn't say anything.

T: Well, I do that frequently and that's enough, if I just stare at them they know, I don't need to speak. With an easy type of girl, not the ones who are less disciplined - they will defy you sometimes and keep on talking and I would have spoken in that case. I can't remember which two they were but I only needed to look.

I: Wouldn't a look have been sufficient for those two girls at the back who you told to stop giggling?

T: I doubt it, they like to attract attention.

Adapted from Hargreaves, Hester and Mellor, 1975, p. 232.

interview than the more general and wide-ranging unstructured interview. If, during the semi-structured interview, the respondent moves from one area to another without being asked a question by the interviewer, then the interviewer checks this off without asking the specific question on the check list. The questions are not asked in any given order, rather they are asked in a way that develops the conversation. The questions are designed to get the respondent talking about specific areas that the interviewer wants to know about. So there is no requirement that the questions have to be asked in any fixed order or that the same wording has to be used for each respondent. The interviewer has to use initiative in ensuring that the topic list is covered in a way that best suits each case (see Extract 7.4).

Structured in-depth interviews (or focused interviews (Merton *et al.*, 1956) are like scheduled interviews (see Chapter 4). The interviewer has a list of specific questions. There are, however, three main differences with scheduled interviews. First, structured in-depth interviews do not have pre-coded answers. The questions are framed as 'open' questions that encourage the respondent to talk at some length about the specific area of interest. This was the approach used by Cynthia Cockburn (1985) in her study of men and women working with new computer technology, see Extract 7.5.

Second, unlike the scheduled interview, where all the respondents have the same basic set of questions, the structured in-depth interview is often customised for each respondent. Unlike social surveys, ethnographic interviewing is not used to collect responses to specific questions that can be compared across the whole sample.

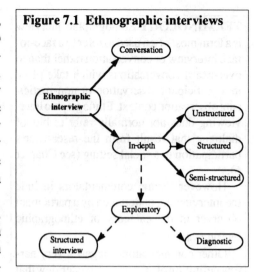

Figure 7.1 Ethnographic interviews

Extract 7.4

URBAN WORKING-CLASS SCHOOLS

The study aimed to gain an understanding of the social and pedagogic situation of some contemporary teachers of the urban working class. As has already been shown, these teachers have historically been the strategic agents of social and symbolic control. The aim was to show how the social world of the urban working-class school related both to characteristics of teachers' immediate work situation and to their position in relation to ideological formation.

The head teachers of the ten co-operating schools were asked to identify 'outstanding' teachers. The interpretation of the category was left entirely to the head teachers. This provided insights as to how teachers were defined by their occupational superiors. It also provided a sample of teachers who would represent the epitome of what was taken to be 'good' in inner-city education.

Seventy teachers agreed to participate in the project. Semi-structured interviews were conducted with these teachers, each interview lasting on average for one and a half hours. In an attempt to minimise the imposition of research categories upon members of a particular social world, the co-operative nature of the enquiry was stressed and the teachers were asked to introduce issues which seemed to them to represent real concerns in an urban school, and were generally invited to take a critical attitude to any of the questions.

The interviews were, in most cases, tape-recorded and completed transcripts were returned to the teachers in order to provide a further opportunity for them to reflect upon what they had said during the course of the interview and to invite them to make positive suggestions for the focus of the enquiry. By these means it was hoped that some notion of the authenticity of the teachers' accounts could be established.

All this activity generated a considerable number of 'accounts' of various aspects of contemporary inner-city schools and education. The problem of how these accounts might be interpreted now had to be faced. Interpretation was based on the following principles and procedures.

1. Theoretical saturation
Assuming that teachers 'theorise' about their social world the 'accounts' were read closely and repeatedly so as to obtain an empathetic entry into the teachers' social world. The aim was to become 'saturated' with the teacher's theoretical perspective.

2. Central meanings and categories
It was hoped that the initial theoretical saturation would help in grasping the meanings and categories used by the teachers. The research was clearly not an exercise in phenomenological analysis, since the categories of the researcher remained important. However, there was an attempt to be phenomenologically sensitive to the teachers' central meanings and categories. These were taken to be the things they talked about most in the interview.

3. Ideological articulation
The analysis of teachers' central meanings and categories were related to an ideal-type ideological positions. Some teachers provided accounts that were ideologically consistent. Others were much more varied and revealed uncertainty and changes in consciousness. Initially, teachers were classified in terms of their overall ideology, but subsequent analysis addressed how they related to a number of major issues.

Adapted from Grace (1978) pp. 109–15.

Extract 7.5

USING A CHECKLIST

A series of visits was made to each of the 11 organisations involved in the study. I observed people at work and gained familiarity with the technologies in use. In addition to informal contacts during these periods of observation, I carried out 196 interviews (113 with men and 83 with women). These people varied widely by occupation, status, age and training and included some informants in the industries, professions or trade unions concerned but outside the immediate case study settings.

Basic checklists of questions were devised for each occupational or situational group of informants and working schedules constructed by reference to these for each interview or group of interviews. The interviews were thus formal and structured, but they were open-ended and discursive. Some were as short as 20 minutes, others as long as three hours. Most were carried out in a private room within the work situation, by agreement with employers. Most were tape-recorded and transcribed.

Adapted from Cockburn, 1985, p. 4.

Third, because the responses are seen as 'subjective accounts' rather than 'objective answers' there is no requirement that the structured in-depth interviewer should use the exact wording of the question or the exact sequence of questions.

The extent to which structured and semi-structured in-depth interviews develop the frame of reference of the informant depends on the way the interviewer probes for information. If all data obtained is in response to predetermined questions, then, as with structured interviews, the data is unlikely to go beyond the researcher's own categories. However, if probes are more flexible and responsive to the informants' comments, they can draw out the informant's meanings, eliciting data that categorises experience in the informant's own terms.

Sequence

Using an interview or conversation to try to uncover the point of view of the respondent usually requires that the researcher talks to the respondent more than once. Often, ethnographic interviewing consists of a series of interviews. This may be a series of conversations and unstructured in-depth interviews, or an ever more specific set of interviews ranging from conversations through unstructured in-depth interviews to a semi-structured or structured in-depth interview.

Often, second and subsequent interviews are likely to be more focused than preliminary interviews. Researchers approach follow-up interviews with more knowledge of the person and with a clearer understanding of what they want to know and the direction the research should take. Discussion on particular themes may be stimulated by referring to comments or ideas that arose during the first interview. With the benefit of preliminary interviews the interviewer will be able to interject questions where information is ambiguous or unclear and even politely stop and redirect informants if they are pursuing an area irrelevant to the research.

It might be necessary to increase the directiveness of questions steadily throughout a final interview, to ensure that the informant's conceptions are clarified and all major areas of interest are addressed. At the end of the interview you may wish to ask direct questions about your original research ideas. The informant's responses may provide an interesting comparison to the data obtained by less direct questioning.

Doing in-depth interviews

It is important that you undertake background research and identify some preliminary aims before undertaking in-depth interviews.

Student Activity 7.4
1. **Draw up a research aim for an in-depth interview project in an area that interests you (we discussed research aims in detail in Chapter 4, page 102).**
2. **Outline the 'background' to the research.**
SUGGESTION If you do not have a particular area in mind design a research aim that relates to the family as this will be the topic we will use in the example answer.

Successful interviews rely in part on the skill of the interviewers. They must ask questions that will elicit relevant data without imposing their own categories on their interviewees. They should know when to speak, when to listen and when to take a passive rather than an assertive role. An interviewer must also express interest in the other person in a non-judgemental way, regardless of what he or she is saying.

Even the most experienced interviewers rarely achieve the perfect interview. Interview skills can be developed through an understanding of the procedures involved and practice of the various techniques. Below, we outline the process of setting up and undertaking an in-depth interview.

Locating respondents

In general, in-depth interviewing involves a much smaller sample of informants than survey interviewing. Elizabeth Bott (1971) interviewed twenty married couples, while Hannah Gavron's study included a sample of ninety-six women. Life histories, as we have seen, involve only one subject. The research undertaken as part of your coursework will also necessitate a very small sample. Under such circumstances it is clearly not possible to locate a representative or 'typical' sample from which generalisations can be made. However, as the ethnographic approach seeks to discover the range of meanings constructed by people themselves, even a sample of one can be seen to contribute to this discovery.

Gavron located a suitable sample of mothers, with at least one child under the age of five, from the lists of General Practitioners and from the Housebound Wives Register. For project work, however, it may be possible to locate suitable informants by using your network of friends, relatives and work colleagues, who may know someone who is suitable. You should not however select an informant who is well known to you. Over-familiarity can make it very difficult to gain basic information that may be important to your research, but of which your informant feels you should already be aware. There is also a tendency to slip out of the 'researcher' and 'informant' roles into more familiar roles such as 'friend' or 'sister'. This limits the possibility of progressing beyond friendly conversation and reduces the learning experience.

Before approaching potential informants and requesting their participation, you should consider and plan the account you will give of yourself and your research. Often a straightforward approach is best; telling them about the project you are undertaking, the number and anticipated duration of interviews and the general topic area to be covered.

> **Student Activity 7.5**
> **Referring to the aim you drew up in Student Activity 7.4:**
> 1. **Decide on a realistic number of informants to interview for a student project, the type of people you want (age, sex, etc.) and possible ways of locating them.**
> 2. **Plan an introduction to yourself and your project that you would use when first contacting informants.**

Sometimes it requires a lot of work to establish the right conditions for in-depth interviews. For example, in his study of *Young Men In Prison*, Mike Little (1990, p. 27) had to make it clear to both inmates and prison staff that he was independent.

Example answer to Student Activity 7.4

AIM

The research aims to:

1. discover the importance and value that subjects place on the family;
2. find out the ways they experience familiar relationships and arrangements;
3. gain some understanding of their perceptions of marriage and the family in their future lives.

BACKGROUND

Until recently, sociological theories of the family tended to emphasise the nuclear family structure (Goode, 1963). However, 13% of all families have a single parent (Family Policy Studies Centre, 1985). The multicultural nature of British society has resulted in a diversity of family types.

Southern Asians include communities from India, Pakistan and Bangladesh who currently number just over a million in Britain, over half of whom were born locally. The traditional pattern of family membership consisted of a husband and wife, their sons and grandsons, along with their wives and unmarried daughters (Ballard, 1982). Only sons remained family members all their lives, with daughters becoming part of their husband's family on marriage. All relationships in the traditional family structure were hierarchical whether between the sexes or by age. Nevertheless, this was constructed around an ideology of co-operative harmony with each family member being regarded as having a distinct but complementary role to play.

Men were head of the household, controlling family finances and negotiating major family decisions. Women were subordinate and restricted.

The disparity between men and women is exemplified through the importance placed on 'honour' and 'shame'. To sustain the honour of males in the family, the wives, sisters and daughters must be seen to behave with modesty, secluding themselves from the world of men. Thus a family's honour was influenced not only by the wealth it possessed, but also by the extent to which it conformed to ideal norms of behaviour. Honour could be most effectively advanced by arranging prestigious marriages for the family's *daughters* and outdoing rivals in the first exchanges they involve.

The traditional system of arranged marriage involved an agreement or alliance between two families, rather than two individuals. Thus the concept of courtship or romantic 'love' was not considered important, indeed the couple do not need to know one another before this marriage. Parents are seen to have a moral obligation to find suitable partners for their children, and ultimately their children have an obligation to accept their parents' choice. However, the process of arranging a marriage generally involves protracted discussions in which the boy receives 'proposals' as well as the girl (Ross, 1961). In this sense, the girl may have more freedom to select her husband than in the system of so called 'free marriage', in which women supposedly have to wait to be chosen.

A love marriage is based in the mythology of an everlasting emotional bond tying 2 people together. No such emotion binds together partners of a prospective arranged marriage, they are both emotionally free to reject a marriage which does not suit them for other reasons. (Liddle and Joshi, 1986, p. 209)

Of course, this description of family organisation is an 'ideal type' and not all Asian families conform to it.

Although traditional Asian family organisation and practices have been systematically under attack in Britain they have not disappeared. The attack on the Asian family is not only by the state, through the workings of immigration legislation, but also in ideological ways (Parmar, 1982). The media and welfare administrators characterise Asian families as 'pathological', a problem requiring a solution (Parmar, 1981). From this perspective, family unity can be seen to provide support in a hostile, racist cultural environment.

While the wholesale assimilation to British cultural patterns predicted by some has not occurred, there have nevertheless been changes in family organisation, and many South Asians in Britain live in conjugal households containing only a single married couple and their children. However, Westwood and Bhachu (1988) argue that this does not mean that the importance of wider family ties have diminished. Families tend to remain in close proximity and have regular and frequent contact with one another. Even widely dispersed relatives will travel great distances to attend family events. Thus family links endure, providing economic and material assistance as well as emotional support.

A common assumption among British commentators has been that the customs and traditions of Asian families would be undermined by their British-born children. They are exposed to and participate in two very different, and in some respects contradictory, cultural worlds. At home, parents expect co-operation, respect and familiar loyalty; at school individual achievement and self-determination are presented as an appropriate foundation for personal action. While it has been suggested that the 'personal freedom' of the dominant British culture would inevitably seem more attractive than the restrictions of traditional family obligations, ethnographic accounts have begun to reveal a different picture (Ballard, 1982; Brah, 1979; Crishna, 1975).

Based on data gained from in-depth interviews with Asian teenagers, Ballard (1982, p. 196) found that in dealing with contradictory realms of experience they are evolving their own distinctive life styles. They present themselves in public 'in a very "English" way, but will choose to organise their domestic and personal lives on the basis of a strong continuity with the established values of the communities into which they were born'. Thus, while adopting a modified version of their parents' life-style, their behaviour often remains distinct from that of their English peers.

This example answer is based on research undertaken by Anne Devany in 1990 that explores the ways in which the family and marriage are viewed by young Asian women in Britain.

For the younger inmate, the prison officer is likely to be an integral part of his life and there is nothing to be gained by siding with one group or another. Clearly, the quality of information will suffer if the inmates view the researcher as part of the prison organisation, so great care is required to establish an independent role in which the prisoner can have confidence.

In most situations, then, it is important that you provide an account of your research that is believable to the respondents and one in which they can have confidence. If respondents feel that you are indifferent to their interests then they are unlikely to give you the information you want, if they agree to participate at all. However, there are times when the specific aim of the research is *not* revealed to the subjects.

Hiding the purpose of the interview

When doing in-depth interviews the intention of the enquiry may never be made clear to the informant because the researcher may feel that direct mention of the topic would bias or distort the information given in the interview. For example, as part of the Open University's *Research Methods* course (DE304) students were expected to carry out in-depth interviews to explore attitudes to class. Rather than ask about class directly, the interviewers sought views on life and work experiences and analysed the extent to which these were class-related. As the aim of the research was to see to what extent people saw their lives in class terms, it would have distorted results if the researcher had *introduced* the project as research into attitudes about class.

Similarly, the specific focus of the research may not be mentioned to the respondents because the researcher only has a vague idea, initially, of what is being looked for. For example, in her study of conjugal relationships, Elizabeth Bott (1971) conducted an average of thirteen in-depth interviews with each of the twenty families. Bott was interested in the relationship between wives and husbands. She began with only vague and imprecise conceptions but, from ideas that developed during her interviews, she gradually focused on the relationship between spouses' social networks and the nature of their conjugal roles. She concluded that spouses with a 'close-knit' social network, generally consisting of same-sex friends and relations, are more likely to have segregated conjugal roles than those who have a more 'loose-knit' network. There was no way, at the outset, Bott could have told her respondents that the study was about the relationships between their conjugal roles and their social networks.

Constructing an interview guide

Although the primary aim of this type of interviewing is to get the informant talking about life in their terms, the researcher does not take a completely passive role. During the early stages of the interview, and when breaks in conversation occur, the interviewer must be prepared to stimulate talk by asking suitable questions. Furthermore, not all information is relevant and it may be necessary to guide the informant towards some things and away from others. This is particularly important when undertaking small-scale projects with limited interviewing time.

To prepare for this the interviewer may first draw up a list of possible topic areas to be covered and then devise several suitable questions on each of the areas identified. These questions must be the kind that open up a topic, rather

---

Example answer to Student Activity 7.5

To make the project manageable, it was decided to interview four young women, aged between 18 and 21 years, all studying for their A levels at a college of further education. Within the Asian population of Britain, there are a great many different cultural and religious groups. Clearly a sample size of four could not hope to represent all of these groups and instead the Sikh community became the focus of the study.

Four students known to the researcher were approached. They were selected in part because they projected both 'traditional' and 'Westernised' images. They were told about the project being undertaken, that the general topic area would be the family and the number and anticipated duration of the interviews. All four students agreed to participate in the study.

Interviews were to take place in a comfortable and quiet room within the college. As the aim was to get the subjects talking freely about their families, it was felt that the college, rather than their home, might prove less inhibiting.

than elicit a one-word response. They must also be carefully worded to allow informants free expression of their ideas and feelings. Questions should not lead respondents to talk about things that fit the researcher's preconceptions.

It is usual to conduct more than one interview with an informant when undertaking in-depth work. For example, when Ann Oakley interviewed women about their experiences of maternity she conducted four interviews with each of the women, lasting an average of 2.36 hours each (Oakley, 1979b). The nature of your interview guide will depend therefore on the number of interviews you intend to carry out. If you are conducting more than one interview, your first guide is likely to relate to basic life history data such as family, educational and occupational background.

> **Student Activity 7.6**
> **Prepare a preliminary in-depth interview guide for the research you have outlined in Student Activities 7.4 and 7.5.**
> **1 Decide on a list of main topics.**
> **2. Devise three or four questions on each of these topics, angled in ways you feel will stimulate talk and produce data relevant to the project.**

It is not intended that such a guide should be rigidly followed when conducting an interview. Rather, it should provide relevant prompts for interviewers to use at their discretion in drawing out the informant's ideas. It is unlikely that information will be elicited in neat, chronological order, but preparing a guide may help the interviewer ensure that no important areas are omitted. While it may not be possible during the interview to cover all the topics included in a guide, other more promising areas may arise.

The interview guide developed for second or subsequent interviews will be shaped by the data already collected. Areas which appear worthwhile in the first interview will need to be followed up, and more sharply focused questions might be needed to produce relevant data. Any deficiencies of the first interview can also be made good by devising questions to clarify incomplete or confusing information (see Extract 7.6). Again, it must be stressed that interviewers must avoid imposing their terms of reference on interviewees. Where possible, second interview guides should incorporate the categories the informants have used themselves.

Interviewing

The setting

The interview should take place in an environment conducive to fostering the informality required of in-depth work. Often this will be the informant's home. Sometimes, however, the work-place is preferable. Sometimes, the researcher has very little choice about the setting and you have to make the best of what is available. Mike Little (1990, p. 27), interviewing in prison, recalled that an unused room or cell is 'not ideal and is often difficult to negotiate'.

The interviewer's initial aim is to develop a relaxed, friendly atmosphere in which the informant will talk freely. However, interviews generally begin with feelings of apprehension. The interview is an unfamiliar situation and the informant will not know what to expect or how to behave.

Interviewers usually begin by introducing themselves and their research and then asking the interviewee simple and straightforward questions. For example, many people find their family background easy to talk about and whatever the research topic this may provide a useful starting point. At the

---

Example in-depth interview guide for Student Activity 7.6

Subjects:
  Young Asian women

Topic areas :
  family history
  parents
  siblings
  wider kin
  education and work
  leisure
  the future

PRELIMINARY INTERVIEW – SAMPLE QUESTIONS

Family background (parents, siblings and wider kin)

What sort of man is your father?
What does your mother do during the day?
How do you get on with your parent(s)?
Do you have any memories of your childhood?
What sort of relationship do you have with brothers/sisters?
When do you see other family members?

Leisure

What do you do in your free-time?/ With whom?
Do you go out often?/With whom?
Is this the same for your brothers?

Education, work and the future

What do you like about college?
What would you be doing if not studying?
What do you want to do when you leave college?
Is this what your parents want you to do?/Same for your brothers?
What do you think you will be doing in 10 years' time?

beginning of her interviews with young Asian women, Anne Devany asked about their family composition and history. While all the interviewees appeared nervous or apprehensive initially, they appeared to relax very quickly and seemed happy to talk at length about their families.

Rapport

To establish a friendly conversational atmosphere it is sometimes helpful if the interviewer includes occasional supportive remarks, such as 'I know what you mean' or 'Yes, my parents were like that too', or simply nod or smile encouragingly. You will find that while some people talk at length after only a couple of questions, others need rather more encouragement. To develop a rapport with an informant and encourage talk, it is often useful to incorporate questions that ask them to describe places, people, events or activities. If, for example, you were investigating the culture of homemakers, you might ask a general descriptive question such as:

What would you do on a typical weekday?

Or you could ask a question that deals with a smaller unit of experience:

Describe all the work you did in the kitchen yesterday.

If the person seems to find great difficulty answering your questions, conversation can sometimes be stimulated by the interviewer making a contribution based on their experiences. However, this may influence the informant and should therefore be approached with caution. It may be better to ask an informant about the experiences they have had in a particular setting:

What were family holidays in a caravan like?

Respondents may also be presented with hypothetical or scenario questions, which describe a situation and ask them what they would do.

Finally, it is useful in clarifying or developing ideas to pick out an event or issue already identified by the informant and ask them for an example:

You say you like a night out with your friends occasionally. What did you do last time you went out?

Probing

Although researchers aim to make in-depth interviews as relaxed and conversational as possible, in-depth interviews and friendly conversations differ in several important ways (Spradley, 1979). First, when talking to a friend we tend to take turns speaking, and the participation rate for each of us is fairly equal. Interaction is less balanced during an in-depth interview, as the researcher's contribution should be kept to a minimum. One way to encourage the informant to continue elaborating a point, besides affirmative nods, is to avoid rushing in with the next question. Leave a gap of several seconds after the informant answers (count to ten in your head) before asking the next question. This gives them time to reflect on what they have just said and often they provide additional material that develops their answer or explains ambiguities or apparent contradictions. When you first start interviewing you will be disinclined to leave a gap and are likely to rush in with the next question because you are nervous or feel that the informant will think you do not know what to ask next. This is a natural reaction but try to take time, even if a few seconds' pause does feel like an eternity to you.

Second, friendly conversations also differ from in-depth interviews in that they tend to avoid repetition. During an interview a subject relevant to the

---

Extract 7.6

FOLLOW-UP INTERVIEW GUIDE

Subjects: Young Asian women

MARRIAGE

1. You said in the first interview that you would definitely have an arranged marriage. Can you explain exactly what this involves?
2. Who will you live with? How do you feel about this?
3. Would you expect to continue your career?
4. You said your sister is worried about finding a marriage partner because of her divorce. Can you explain why?
5. Would a man face the same difficulties?

FAMILY

6. How would you describe your relationship with your parents?
7. Who are you most likely to confide in if you have worries or problems?
8. Do you behave any differently at college than you would at home?
9. Would you ever go out with a boy without your parents consent?
10. Is it the same for your brothers?

FUTURE / CHANGE

11. How do you think you would bring up your children?
12. Do you think your generation is different from your parents? How?
13. Will you continue your career after marriage?

research objectives may be returned to a number of times.

Third, everyday conversations are characterised by taken-for-granted ideas of what each participant knows (Garfinkel, 1967). Therefore (as we saw in Chapter 5) much is left unsaid. One of the aims of in-depth interviewing is to get these taken-for-granteds expanded. This is done by showing interest in detail, by admitting ignorance of things that appear obvious to the respondent, or by simply by waiting and gently probing at later points in the conversation or in subsequent interviews (see Extract 7.7).

So, to get the informant's meanings, the in-depth interviewer has to be alert to the underlying nuances and seek out the taken-for-granteds of the informant. Thus in-depth interviewers must develop the ability to 'think on their feet' to keep probe questions in their head while conducting an interview that appears to be like an interested conversation.

Student Activity 7.7
As practice, conduct a fifteen-minute interview with a classmate or colleague. Find out what they thought were the most significant events in their childhood.

Extract 7.7

DISTORTING THE TRUTH

In day-to-day interaction with each other we move swiftly and easily from one subject to another. However, there are difficulties for the researcher, who must encourage the free flow of speech, yet keep hold of any questions that arise. For example, the following extract about a youngster's first burglary throws up a number of questions which might fruitfully be pursued:

> I was wagging school, and we had about 15p. And we wanted these pies from the bakery, they were about 40p and 50p. So we didn't know what to do to get them or anything, but we saw a house and I said, 'Shall we have a go?' and he says, 'Yeh'. So I says, 'Go and knock at the door and see if anybody's in'. So he went to the door and nobody was in. So these three kids went round the back and I was keeping watch. And they smashed a window, I heard this window smash, and I was waiting about five minutes, but it seemed like an hour. So I went round and got into the house and started searching after that. Robbed £90 out of a glass. And I just started doing more after that.

During the interview the researcher must reflect upon and pursue at least another nine and possibly many more items, all of which are worthy of further discussion. These are: wagging school; the importance of the discrepancy between the cost of pies and the money the boys had; why it was that particular house they 'saw', the inconsistency of the numbers involved; the apparent passivity of his contribution; the time dimension (it seemed like an hour); what they were searching for; the distribution and use of the £90; and the subsequent burglaries.

The question of validity is more thorny. How can the researcher be sure that respondents are not distorting the truth, telling outright lies or exaggerating a point? This problem is accentuated when there is a limited amount of time allocated to fieldwork and the number of interviews is restricted. Moreover, distortions in participants' accounts have been a particular problem for this study, as the young prisoners' ability to distort the truth is one of the central theoretical propositions being explored. If it is accepted that young prisoners actively deceive, is it possible to rely upon evidence generated by interviews?

First, what qualitative interviews lose in terms of accuracy is usually balanced by the insights gained into the lifestyle and culture of the interviewee (Hammersley and Atkinson, 1983). Second, an interviewer well versed in the subject matter will not easily be deceived. The plausibility of the account can be checked during the interview, old ground can be re-turned, information constantly checked. Follow-up interviews can clarify problems. In addition to these strategies, a further subsample of inmates were re-interviewed in groups of five. The relationship between information released in group and individual interviews is most important. The groups act as a check upon the information volunteered by individuals and questions to a prisoner repeated in the presence of a group of inmates can reveal inconsistency. Gold (1966) used a similar technique when he checked the validity of subjects' accounts with their friends. The nature and quality of the contradictions are the key to this study as they tell us which aspects of behaviour can be exaggerated or lied about and the ability of inmates to relay confusing messages about their behaviour. Care was therefore taken to monitor but not to discourage distortion in participants' accounts.

Adapted from Little, 1990, pp. 27–9.

Recording interview data

Ideally, interview data should be recorded verbatim (word for word) as any summary involves a degree of interpretation. A verbatim record is usually made using a tape-recorder, but this can present certain difficulties. Some people may be reluctant to speak if they know they are being recorded, they may feel unable to relax or afraid to reveal personal or sensitive information. When using a tape-recorder it is advisable to keep it out of the line of vision of the informant, who should be reassured that it serves only as a note-taking device. In practice, tape-recorders rarely present any real problem, informants usually forgetting about them even when they can see them. Nevertheless, if the use of a tape-recorder does prevent the development of rapport between interviewer and interviewee, it must be abandoned.

Unless you are an expert at shorthand you should not attempt to write everything down. It is far better to make a *condensed* account of the interview, writing down key words, phrases and sentences that will enable you to recall items of information later. As soon as possible after the interview you should write up and expand these notes, filling in details and recalling things not recorded on the spot. It is advisable to make condensed notes during every interview, even while tape-recording. This can provide you with ideas to pursue during the interview and may prove helpful when attempting to analyse the tape and extract relevant information from it later. Sometimes, the circumstances of the interview make it difficult to make notes. For example, a study of football supporters which employed semi-structured in-depth interviews with fans at matches used only tape-recorders because the physical situation of standing and talking to people in a crowd while holding a tape-recorder made it difficult to write condensed notes as well (Harvey, Little and Turner, 1982). Similarly, there may be circumstances where respondents are distracted if you are continually making notes whilst they are talking.

Student Activity 7.8
Using the interview guide you drew up in Student Activity 7.6, undertake several in-depth interviews with different people. Record the interviews in any way that is suitable to the situation. If you make notes during the interview, write them up as soon as possible after the interview is concluded. Similarly, if possible, transcribe tape-recordings while the interview is still fresh in your memory.

All methods of recording interview data pose difficulties and it is necessary to weigh up the advantages and disadvantages of the different approaches in relation to a specific research objective and a particular informant. It will be necessary to practice your data recording techniques before attempting to use them in a real interview. You may also find after conducting a first interview that they need some adaptation.

Follow-up interviews
Follow-up interviews allow you to get a more detailed appreciation of the respondent's point of view. They do two things. First, they allow you to probe for more detail and clarification. It is not always apparent during the interview that some detail is hazy, or that contradictory statements have been made. The follow-up interview allows you to check and expand on points. Second, once you have become familiar with the content of the preliminary

TRANSCRIBING INTERVIEWS It is advisable, provided you have time, to transcribe taped interviews, that is, produce a complete transcript of everything that is said in the interview. Transcripts of interviews are much more flexible to refer to and easier to analyse than tape-recordings. When it comes to analysing the data you need to relate statements made at one point of the interview to statements made at another time, as well as relating experiences of one respondent with those of another. This is much easier if you have the data in a visible form that you can easily reproduce and move around (as we shall see later in the discussion of analysis).

We strongly recommend that you transcribe interviews on to a word-processor, if possible, as it makes it easier to store, copy, cross-reference and manipulate text without having to photocopy documents, re-write things and so on (see Chapter 6, page 177).

Transcribing taped interviews is preferable to making an edited transcript. There is a danger, especially with early interviews, that if you simply make an edited transcript you may leave out important data because you are noting only those things that fit your preconceptions. The problem with transcribing the whole interview is time. If you have an hour-long interview it will take an accomplished typist about four hours to transcribe it. It may take up to six hours if you have no previous experience of transcription.

interview you may become aware of aspects of the respondent's point of view that you had missed or thought irrelevant. Your own preconceptions during the first interview might have blinded you to things that are important parts of the respondent's world. When you have conducted several first interviews you can look at themes that recur and develop ideas for follow-up interviews. So, after you have carried out your preliminary interview you should fully familiarise yourself with the data obtained. Read and reread your notes and listen to your tapes several times. If you have transcribed the tapes, read the transcriptions. You will need to reconsider your original ideas and relate them to the data obtained. In this way, themes may begin to take shape and a framework for your second interview guide should develop.

Devany found that there was not enough time between the preliminary and follow-up interviews for her to transcribe the tapes. She listened to the preliminary interview tapes several times, along with the expanded notes she had written up. She made a note of areas that appeared important to the research aims and which required further probing or clarification.

Several themes emerged which related to the women's understanding of marriage and the family. The concept of gender (perhaps predictably) appeared to be dominant in their thinking, and a lot of comments related to controls placed upon them as females. The theme of 'change' also recurred, with references to such things as negotiated marriage, conjugal households and increasing independence. Yet this appeared, from initial interview data, to be 'change' within a framework that upholds the importance of family unity and loyalty, rather than one that rejects it.

From these notes Devany constructed follow-up interview guides including questions to develop these emerging themes more fully and to fill in any gaps in the data. As it would only be possible to carry out one more interview with each of the subjects it was necessary to introduce a considerable degree of structure to follow-up interviews. As each of the subjects had provided different information during preliminary interviews, a slightly different guide was devised for each.

The second interviews follow the same general procedure and recording techniques as the first. However, the second guide will have more specific questions than the first and the second interview is likely to be more focused than the first. You should also make use of follow-up interviews to test out theoretical issues that are raised by the study.

Student Activity 7.9
Following the preliminary interviews in Student Activity 7.8 under-
take follow-up interviews where possible. Use an amended interview
guide and do as many follow-up interviews as you think are necessary
or you are able to in the time available. You might want to do several
follow-ups with a few people rather than aim to do one follow-up with
all the people who agreed to a preliminary interview. Record the
interviews in any way that is suitable in the situation.

Analysing interview data

It is important that throughout the research process you continue to clarify and develop the main themes and issues you wish to investigate. Nevertheless, having collected the data you may feel overwhelmed by it, and doubtful of your ability to analyse it.

The first task is to familiarise yourself fully with your material, reading through your expanded notes, transcribed taped-recordings or edited accounts. Listen to your tape-recordings again. Get to know your data (see Extract 7.4). As we saw in Chapter 6, analysing ethnographic material requires a systematic approach. After reading thorough your data vertically (that is, chronologically from start to finish) you should be able to identify major themes. If you have undertaken a series of follow-up interviews, rather than one-off interviews, you will already have started to identify these themes when constructing follow-up interview guides. Do not assume that the themes you identify early on in the research are necessarily the 'best' ones for analysing the data.

As you read your data certain themes will begin to emerge and you can copy your data and rearrange it into sections (or piles) dealing with these themes. You can then read the data 'horizontally' by theme. If, on reading, they prove inconsistent or illogical it will be necessary to break down your data into alternative themes until a suitable format is achieved. The 'cut and paste' process of pile building and horizontal reading is explored in detail in Chapter 6 (see page 178).

> **Student Activity 7.10**
> 1. **Analyse the interview data you collected in Student Activities 7.8 and 7.9.**
> 2. **Write a report that clearly shows how your data relates to the aims of your research. Use quotes from your respondents to illustrate your account.**
> 3. **Relate your research to appropriate sociological theory.**

Accuracy, reliability and validity

In-depth interview data is the result of an interviewer gradually getting a respondent to provide detailed accounts of actions, attitudes, feelings, beliefs, relationships, perceptions and so on. Inevitably there are problems of accuracy, reliability and validity (see pages 31 and 32). It is a problem establishing the *accuracy* of what someone tells you. In the prisoner's account of his first burglary (in Extract 7.7), Mike Little noted the apparent inconsistency in the numbers of people involved. It would be possible, as he intended, to ask further about this to establish the accuracy of the account. However, circumstances may preclude the possibility of following up every detail in a lengthy account. You have to decide whether the accuracy of an account is important or whether it is more important to have an insight into the respondent's perception. One of Little's main theoretical propositions concerned young prisoners' ability to distort the truth, so while accuracy was important, it was not pursued to the detriment of understanding the way the respondents constructed reality.

The *reliability* of in-depth interviews, like participant observation, is sometimes called into question. The flexible nature of the enquiry and the difficulty of a repeat study makes it impossible to assess the reliability of the method. The issue of *validity* also arises, but in ways quite different from scheduled interviewing. With social surveys the major issue is whether the *operationalised* concept, as embodied in the schedule of questions, represents the *theoretical* concepts the researcher is interested in. With ethnographic interviewing, the researcher is trying to uncover the concepts that the respondents make use of in their understanding of their world. The problem, then, is how the researcher knows that her or his understanding of key

Example answer to Student Activity 7.10

The women in the sample were all born in Britain but had parents born in India. All the women interviewed lived in conjugal households with parents, brothers and sisters. However in support of Westwood and Bhachu's (1988) analysis, the wider family remained important to them. Most had other family living close by and they would regularly visit, or be visited by, family members further afield. When talking about the close family, subjects often included relatives outside the nuclear group.

The women's understanding of patriarchal and hierarchical structures within the family were revealed. All the informants clearly felt that their behaviour was more strictly controlled than that of male peers. This was linked by the informants to the idea of family honour. Females whose behaviour challenged traditional norms and values were seen to bring dishonour to themselves and to their families:

> Nita: There are times when I've thought that it would be nice to go on a date with a boy (laughs).... it's a type of experience really. But, being the person I am and being brought up by my parents .... I wouldn't do that to them. It's to do with respect. It would reflect badly on them as well as me.

As all the women in the study placed a high value on close relationships with their parents, not bringing shame on them clearly acts as a powerful controlling device. Yet they all point out that for boys the situation is very different. They can go out, drink alcohol and have girlfriends without bringing shame or dishonour on either themselves or their family.

The extent to which female family members are restricted was related to family links with the local Asian community. The more closely knit the community the greater the pressures on the family to conform to traditional modes of behaviour:

> Rani: When we were in Wales there weren't many other Asian families... most of our friends were British. What I have noticed is that parents in Wales are less dominant and less strict with their children. Here they just follow each other's families... his family do it, so the others have to do it. It's a real problem.
> Binny: They justify keeping you in by saying 'the neighbours will talk... It gets me mad'!

The influence of their religion was also seen to play a role in keeping women in their place. This was not however seen as intrinsic to the religion itself, but as a distortion of it that is entirely 'man-made':

> Binny: My sister and I are against the religion because it's so sexist. It never used to be.... at first men were not allowed to cut their hair or eat meat, same as women. But men have taken over the religion and use it for themselves.

All the informants referred to the traditional system of arranged marriage as a further means of ensuring girls' conformity. They commented on the use, or threat, of an early arranged marriage as a means of controlling women's behaviour. Yet the women did not necessarily see arranged marriage as being oppressive. They saw their future marriage as a duty to their parents, who would arrange it. However, this did not mean that they would not be consulted about prospec-

tive husbands. The women interviewed saw arranged marriage as a process of negotiation between two families and the two individuals concerned. If anyone was unhappy about the arrangement, then negotiations could be abandoned:

> Jags: We say: 'I love my parents and so have a duty to get married'. My marriage will be arranged by my parents but I will have some choice. I'll see to that (laughs). Some girls are forced into marriage, for them, it's a problem, but if you have 'good' parents it's fine. They only want you to be happy. A man will be suggested to my parents, and they will look into his background. If he seems suitable, and I agree, a meeting will be arranged between his family and mine and he and I will have the chance to meet. If all goes well, a further meeting will be arranged, and so on. But if we don't seem suited, that will be the end of it. It's just a different way of doing it. It was the same for my parents but they only had one meeting and my mother was only 14 when she got married.

The women therefore did not reject the traditional pattern of arranged marriage, but expected a have greater say in the process than had been experienced by their parents. Furthermore, they expressed some scepticism about 'love marriages':

> Rani: People criticise our way, you know, but what about a lot of English marriages? You get two people, think they're in love, she gets pregnant and so they get married. And *then* they find they're not suited. You only have to look at the number of divorces.

The women in this study supported Trivedi's (1984) assertion that arranged marriages are qualitatively different from those of the past and that some women do support the practice. They are nevertheless aware that it takes place in a patriarchal framework that helps to maintain their oppression:

> Rani: ... say, for example, a girl was engaged and the marriage was arranged, then suddenly the boy's side break it off. That's it! People would say: 'Why have they had to call it off? Was the girl a virgin? Was she too liberal?' They can't say sorry about the break-up. It's the same as if you get divorced. They say: 'I'm not marrying her...' Even if she's done nothing wrong at all. It's always the woman who is to blame.

The interviewees saw themselves as oppressed as women and showed some insight into the mechanisms they saw as perpetuating this inequality. In stark contrast to stereotypes that portray Asian women as passive conformists, their comments were critical and challenging.

The stereotyped images of Asian families have been used by the state to justify racist and sexist immigration legislation. Parmar (1981) points out that the British government argued that they banned the entry of male fiances to protect Asian women against the 'archaic practice' of arranged marriages. For the women in this study, born and educated in Britain, the cultural form remains important and influential in their lives and they felt no need of such 'protection'. They wanted greater control over their destinies, but they saw this change already occurring. Not because of government intervention, but through the growing confidence and assertiveness of Asian women themselves.

This example is based on Devany's interviews with young Asian women, conducted in 1990.

concepts is the same as the respondent's.

Student Activity 7.11
Compare and comment on the strategies adopted by Gerald Grace
(Extract 7.4) and Michael Little (Extract 7.7) to ensure the accuracy
and validity of their in-depth interviews.

Reflexivity

There are thus a number of questions that the in-depth interviewer needs to reflect upon. How much of the information gathered derives from the informants and how much is the result of the researcher's own preconceptions and interpretation? To what extent has the information gathered been distorted by what the researcher has said or done? To what extent have informants provided the data that they think the interviewer wants? It has been shown that responses to in-depth interviews are affected by the expectations and attitudes of the interviewer (Hyman, 1954). It is therefore important, as we suggested in Chapter 6, for ethnographic researchers to be *reflexive* (see page 177). This means that they should adopt a critical attitude towards their research, reflecting on the impact they have had on the research context and thus the data gained. When understanding in-depth interviews it is therefore important to consider the extent to which your presence, by disrupting the natural context, influenced your informant's responses. Were you able to set respondents at their ease? Did you manage to create a relaxed atmosphere and develop a rapport with your subject? Were informants given the scope to develop their ideas, or were they constrained by badly-worded questions that 'led' them to certain responses?

Barney Glaser and Anselm Strauss (1967) also suggest that you should be careful about using key informants. While they can be useful in some situations, they can distort your data without you realising it. If someone is particularly forthcoming or appears to be especially knowledgeable it is tempting to see him or her as a key informant and to make considerable use of the data provided. In certain circumstances this is perfectly acceptable. If, on the other hand, you are trying to get a broad or 'representative' view of a sample of people (as Mike Little was in his study of young prison inmates) then you need to avoid key informants, or at least be reflexive about the extent to which they have influenced your understanding of the social world you are researching.

Reflexivity will be aided, as we saw in Chapter 6, if you keep an ongoing journal or research diary in which you record your involvement in the research, decisions you make and your reflections on the research situation and the research process.

In-depth interviews as an ethnographic method

Ethnographic interviews share with participant observation the desire to access informants' perspectives on life. This raises the question of whether or not in-depth interviews are as good as participant observation in attempting to understand subjects' perceptions.

In-depth interviews compared to participant observation

In-depth interviewing provides a medium through which informants can talk about aspects of their social world in a way that is directed by their interests and perceptions. Hence, in-depth interviewers do not begin with a set of rigid pre-formulated questions but aim to explore the world of the informant and categorise experience in their terms. As an interview progresses the researcher will attempt to get beyond 'surface' articulations and draw out the taken-for-granteds of the social world of the subject.

However, the extent to which in-depth interviews can achieve the aims of participant observation is limited. First, in-depth interviewers are unlikely to have the same extent of exposure to the social world of the informant as participant observers. They will not be able to spend as much time with individual respondents nor will they have the same variety of data collection experiences. Unlike participant observers, in-depth interviewers are restricted to the verbal statements of the informant and have no opportunity to match them with observed behaviour.

Second, in-depth interviewing involves a disruption of the natural context in which the subject usually operates. Wherever the interview takes place, even when located in the interviewee's own home, the process of interviewing inevitably introduces a self-conscious element to the proceedings. The strangeness or artificiality of the situation may produce responses quite different from those occurring in a more naturalistic setting. Informants may, for example, try to give researchers answers they feel are impressive or show them in a favourable light.

Third, in-depth interviewing in unable to investigate directly the interactive links between subjects in the way participant observation can. As in-depth interviews rely on the input of individuals, they can only make inferences about the nature of informants' social interactions.

Conversely, in-depth interviewing may provide a means of understanding a social setting that avoids some of the pitfalls of participant observation. It may provide a means for a more extensive and wide-ranging analysis than participant observation, which is limited in terms of the number of social interactions observable. In-depth interviewing may also provide a basis for a more detached enquiry. There is rather less likelihood of the researcher becoming over-involved than could be the case with participant observation. The in-depth interviewer is not forced into playing a role, and may concentrate on probing information, and be able to do so in a more open way than could a participant observer (especially one carrying out a covert study). Finally, the recording of information is often easier in an in-depth interview, where a tape-recorder can be employed, than in the more turbulent participant observation situation.

None the less, in-depth interviewing will, despite its flexibility, necessarily involve the researcher in a process that inhibits the *naturalistic* perspective (see page 177). In practice, there are limits to the duration of interviews and the number of follow-ups that can be done. Thus even the most skilled in-depth interviewer will just have fragments of a much larger puzzle. In-depth interviewing is very much dependent upon the verbal articulations of co-operating subjects and these represent retrospective 'snapshots' rather than a continuous engagement with subjects, as in participant observation.

In-depth interviewing can thus be seen as a surrogate for participant observation although lacking in intensity. In-depth interviewing tends to be a more extensive, rather than intensive, methodological device for understanding subjects' meanings. This does not mean that we should abandon the use of in-depth interviews for obtaining ethnographic data. On the contrary, for small-scale ethnographic research projects where the researcher faces financial constraints and time limitations, the in-depth interview is a more suitable technique than participant observation. In-depth interviews can yield a rich variety of material, but the researcher must nevertheless be aware of its potential limitations.

Approaches to ethnography

In Chapter 6 we identified three broad approaches to ethnography: traditional, phenomenological and critical. In-depth interviews have been used in each of these approaches. Irving Zola's (1966) study of illness within Italian and Irish communities in an American city is a *traditional* ethnographic study using in-depth interviews. The study shows how the labelling and definition of a bodily state as a symptom of a disease is a social process as well as a medical one.

Recent uses of in-depth interviews in ethnographic research have tended towards *phenomenological* ethnography (see page 183). Lynda Measor and Peter Woods (1984) were interested in how 12-year-old children experienced the move to senior school. Similarly, the labelling theory approach of David Hargreaves *et al.* (1975) to the study of classroom deviance draws on interactionism, ethnomethodology and the phenomenology of Alfred Schutz. Their phenomenological ethnographic study explores the nature of classroom rules and how they become a taken-for-granted feature of classrooms and thus the basis for judging deviant activity. Mike Little (1990), also attempts to show how informal as well as formal rules of behaviour operate within prisons. His study focused on how rules of behaviour are central to the way young people interpret their lifestyle (see Extract 7.7).

Gerald Grace (1978) adopted a more *critical* approach to ethnography, locating his analysis of teachers in urban working-class schools in a broader socio-historical and theoretical framework (Extract 7.4). In particular, he looked at how 'outstanding' teachers acted as agents of social control. Cynthia Cockburn (1983) used in-depth interviews to explore how male print workers (called compositors) reacted to their changed job status with the arrival of new computerised technology (Extract 7.5). She adopted a critical ethnographic approach in her feminist analysis. She set the data derived from the interviews in a broader historical and structural context by outlining the history of the printing trade and the way in which male craft workers had established themselves among the working-class elite. The history showed that the industry was one of constant struggle for control between employers and workers. It also showed that men had consistently attempted to exclude women from the industry. The coming of new computerised technology undermined the skills that established the men's elite position. Not only were they losing the battle for control with the capitalists, but the skills required for the new technology could no longer be used as an excuse to exclude women. In short, the compositors had to change completely their view of the work process and gender relations. The study was thus not just about changes in the print industry but about the making and remaking of men.

Feminist research and the dialogic interview

So far we have suggested that the in-depth interview is a device used by researchers to get respondents talking in a way that reveals their understanding of the world. The researcher or interviewer gradually probes and explores the respondent's meanings and collects the information. We pointed out that in-depth interviews represent the formal approach to ethnographic interviewing. Although they are friendly and conversational they are one-sided. The interviewer records answers with minimal comment while encouraging the informant with affirmative signs. The respondent provides the data and the interviewer records it without giving anything back.

Some critical ethnographers object to this one-sided approach because it is exploitative. It embodies a power relationship of researcher and *subject* that they regard as unacceptable. This critique has been most fully developed in feminist analyses of the standard interview relationship. Ann Oakley (1981, p. 38) argues that the one-sided interview involves a *'male paradigm'* of enquiry. This male paradigm is embodied in the taken-for-granted traditional view of the 'scientific method'. The male paradigm sees detachment, objectivity, hierarchy and 'science' as more important than people's personal concerns. Oakley argues that the 'male paradigm' owes much more to 'a masculine social and sociological vantage point than a feminine one'.

In terms of research procedures, the 'male paradigm' is encapsulated in the paradox of the 'perfect interview'. Conventional wisdom demands that the interview should be a data-collecting device that works one way (interviewee to interviewer). The interviewer is in control and the interviewee is socialised into the role of information provider (Moser and Kalton, 1971; Galtung, 1967). The interview should be conducted dispassionately so that 'objective' data can be collected. The success of the interview is seen to depend on a good rapport in which the interviewee is manipulated in a kindly and sympathetic way to provide the desired information.

Rapport, then, is not about an interrelationship between interviewer and interviewee, but about the interviewee accepting the interviewers' research goals and actively helping to provide the relevant information. The interviewer must, however, avoid 'over-rapport' as this might jeopardise the 'objectivity' of the process. Thus a balancing act is required. Oakley argues that this is not possible because the relationship of interviewer and subject cannot lead to complete rapport.

Oakley (1981, p. 41) suggests that the 'irreconcilable contradictions at the heart of the textbook paradigm' are exposed when matched against her own experiences. When carrying out research into women's experiences of pregnancy and childbirth, Oakley (1979b) found that interviewees frequently asked her questions relating to their 'maternity'. She argues that to have remained detached and non-committal would have undermined the development of rapport. She also became 'involved' with her interviewees, helping with domestic tasks where appropriate and enjoying hospitality ranging from tea or coffee to a meal (Oakley 1979b). Indeed, four years after the final interview used in her study, she was still in touch with a third of her sample and four had become close friends.

Oakley argues that at root, the male paradigm is characterised by its denial of the *personal*. Emotions and feelings are treated with scorn, subjectivity is derided. According to the traditional 'male' scientistic framework, personal aspects are not accepted as part of 'objective' knowledge. However, femi-

THE PUBLIC AND THE PRIVATE

Feminists assert that the personal realm is a legitimate concern of science. They argue that mainstream sociology focuses on the public sphere of male concerns. Feminist contributions to sociology through the 1970s challenged many of the assumptions made about the private sphere. Feminist studies of motherhood, housework and domestic violence have shattered the view that the family is a harmonious unit of complementary roles determined by biological functions. On the contrary, they have shown how the family embodies exploitative relationships.

In the 1980s, the emphasis was on shifting the private sphere out of the realm of the family and into a more prominent place within sociology as a whole. This also meant changing the emphasis in analysing the family. Traditionally, the family is seen as a supporting institution related to broad social structures, either as providing a useful function (functionalism) or as providing support to capitalism (Marxism). Feminist argued that the personal goes beyond the private realm; indeed, that the 'personal is political'. What takes place within the family is merely the most obvious reflection of a fundamental social division. Patriarchy defines male and female spheres in a way that oppresses women.

Supplementary Research Activity 7.1

Ann Oakley has challenged the view that household tasks are increasingly shared by husband and wife. Carry out a survey of domestic labour (see Chapter 4). Find out which domestic tasks are largely performed by women, which by men, and which are fairly equally shared. Do your findings support Oakley's position? To what extent to you think that any differences are due to the use of a scheduled rather than an in-depth approach.

nists have argued that the personal must be seen as a serious area of research if the male stranglehold on knowledge is to be challenged (Stanley and Wise, 1983; Gamarnikow *et al.*, 1983).

In taking the personal more seriously, the researcher must challenge the exploitative power relationships between researcher and researched. In an interview context the hierarchical relationship must be substituted by a two-way exchange of equals. Thus the alternative model proposed is one in which a real dialogue takes place. Interviewers must invest their personal identity in relationships with respondents. This technique, which involves interviewer and interviewee taking an equal share in the exchange of information, is called *dialogic interviewing*.

Dialogic interviews are distinct from casual conversations because they remain formal. Potential informants will be made aware of the research objectives and consulted about participating. Adequate preparations must also be made to ensure the effective recording of data. Yet the approach involves a radical reappraisal of the conventional view of interviews as one-way data-gathering tools.

Proponents of this model argue that far more insight is gained by entering a genuine two-way dialogue. Insights are gained, not only into the subjects' perspectives, but also into those of the interviewer. Oakley argues that, furthermore, the mutually beneficial exchange incorporates a political process of mutual reflection on the nature of the oppressive structures in which both interviewer and interviewee operate. This is similar to critical feminist participant observation, for example, Sallie Westwood's (1984) *All Day Everyday* in which she regarded her role in challenging sexism as legitimate (see page 159).

While the development of this approach is generally associated with feminist analyses, other researchers have supported their call for a radical change in interviewing practices. Mishler (1986), for example, argues for dialogic interviewing rather than what he terms the mainstream 'stimulus–response' model and Woods (1986) argues that interviews ought to be democratic, two-way processes.

Student Activity 7.12
1. **Carry out a fifteen-minute dialogic interview with a classmate or colleague about their childhood.**
2. **Compare your results with the information you collected in Student Activity 7.7.**
3. **To what extent do you think that differences in the type of material you collected are the result of (a) your increased experience as an interviewer; (b) the use of a dialogic interview?**

Critics of the standard interview approach nevertheless acknowledge the value of an in-depth, rather than a structured approach. Oakley (1974) argues that in-depth interviews gain far more insight into interviewee's concerns than standardised interviews that use single-item indicators. She noted, for example, that in a reply to a single question: 'Do you like housework?' middle-class women were far more likely to give a negative answer than the working-class sample. On probing, however, Oakley's interviews undermine the view that dissatisfaction with housework is a middle-class phenomenon. She found the attitudes of working-class women to the different tasks that make up housework were very similar to those of the middle-class group. Dissatisfaction in both groups was closely associated with a perceived drop in status from paid work to unpaid housework, especially where

Extract 7.8

SEMI-STRUCTURED PILOT

The main function of any questionnaire or schedule is to translate the research objectives into specific questions and to assist the interviewer in motivating the respondent to communicate the required information. The aim of the survey was to build up a picture of the lives of the housewives in the study. In order to translate this into a series of questions, a pilot was undertaken. The subject was broken down into nine areas or topics (similar to Bott, 1971):

1. The home.
2. General background of wife.
3. General background of husband.
4. The marriage.
5. The children.
6. Organisation of family life.
7. Leisure.
8. Social contacts.
9. Work.

The interview was quite unstructured, these 'topics' being the only guide to the information needed. Every attempt was made to let the interview develop naturally, allowing the respondent to flit from one subject to another as often happens in ordinary conversation. On the basis of material from fifteen interviews conducted in this way, the schedule was drawn up. Between 7 and 20 specific questions were devised for each of the areas. For example, *Organisation of family life* included the following questions:

1. Do you know your husband's wage?
2. How do you divide it?
   a. you take it all and husband keeps pocket money;
   b. husband gives you an allowance;
   c. you share it?
3. Who makes the financial decisions?
4. If you wanted a washing machine, would you:
   a. ask your husband to buy it?
   b. save for it yourself?
   c. save for it jointly?

Whereas in the pilot study the interview had been as unstructured as possible, this was not entirely true of the actual interviews for the research itself. The schedule contained a series of questions for which answers had to be obtained. However, as in the pilot interview, each interview was allowed to develop naturally and if a respondent answered questions before they were asked this was recorded in the appropriate part of the schedule.

Adapted from Gavron (1966) pp. 152–61.

the paid employment was enjoyed.

Oakley suggests that this apparent contradiction is illustrative of a 'methodological moral': that simple questions produce simple answers.

Exploratory in-depth interviews

In-depth interviews are a technique of data collection usually associated with ethnographic enquiry. However, as we suggested earlier, they can also be used with standard social surveys (see Figure 7.1 on page 200). In-depth interviews have been used as the *exploratory* stage of social surveys. For example, in their studies of American soldiers during the Second World War, Sam Stouffer *et al.* (1949) used in-depth and group interviews as a way of exploring the issues that affected soldiers' morale. A formal scheduled interview, used on a large sample, was devised on the basis of the data collected from these exploratory interviews.

In a similar way, Hanah Gavron (1966) made use of semi-structured interviews in the 'pilot' stage of her study of housewives. During these pilot interviews she simply employed a checklist of topics (which she referred to as unstructured interviewing). These were later developed into a detailed schedule for the main sample of interviews (see Extract 7.8).

In the main, in-depth interviews area used as part of an ethnographic approach. However, they are sometimes used as exploratory interviews to determine the content of a structured interview schedule.

Summary and conclusion

Personal data provides a wealth of material that can be of use to sociologists. There is a wide range of sources of personal data, but not much of it is generated specifically with a sociological enquiry in mind. Letters, personal diaries and autobiographies are not normally produced as part of a research technique. They must then be treated in the same way as any other document source. You must put these sources of personal information in context. You must also be prepared to discard a lot of personal data of this sort that becomes available. As it is not produced with a social enquiry in mind, interesting as it is, much of the content will be incidental to your research aim.

When dealing with personal data you must approach it systematically. The techniques you use will depend on what you are trying to find out. It might be that you are looking for clues about how attitudes alter in changed social circumstances, as Thomas and Znaniecki were when they examined the letters written between Polish peasants in America and Europe. You may want to apply more rigorous approaches to personal data, such as Mandelbaum (1982) suggested, for autobiographical or life history accounts. You might want to make use of content analysis or semiological analysis of personal documents. We have not considered these in detail here as they are covered in Chapter 2.

Personal data that is generated as a result of research activity, such as guided life histories or in-depth interviews, also need to be treated with caution. In particular, researchers should be wary of exaggeration, be careful of the distortion that may arise from relying on a few 'key respondents' and be reflexive about their own impact on the respondents.

None the less, personal data can provide useful research material, and in-depth interviews, in particular, are widely used for social research purposes. Indeed, if you are considering doing ethnography as part of your project, in-depth interviews are more manageable than participant observation.

Project ideas

Research using personal data, like participant observation research, tends to result in large amounts of data which can be difficult and time-consuming to organise and analyse. It is important therefore, when undertaking a research project, not to be over-ambitious and to keep your sample size small. For example, if you are using in-depth interviews for your project you will probably only have time to interview five or six subjects.

Although our main examples have been drawn from the sociology of the family and institutions (education and prisons) there are many other areas in which personal data are useful. A few possibilities are suggested below.

1. Explore the effect physical disability has on an individual's work experiences.
2. Undertake a life history study of a retired industrial worker to assess the impact of labour relations on family life.
3. Compare the way unemployment is experienced by people in their teens, with the way people over fifty experience it.
4. Undertake a life history of someone who migrated to Britain as a child.
5. Interview teachers to see the ways they categorise pupils.
6. Carry out a life history account of a trade union official or a political or pressure group campaigner to find out how her or his political involvement developed.
7. Interview the members of a band or group to examine what music means to them.
8. Explore the workings of the legal system from the experiences of a police officer or a young offender.
9. Look at the changing role of women either by interviewing women from different generations of the same family or by undertaking a single life history.
10. Explore what it is like to experience racial prejudice using in-depth interviews, life histories or other personal data.

Further Reading

Ethnographic interviewing: Burgess, 1984; Gordon, 1980; Hammersley and Atkinson, 1983; Open University, 1979.

Personal documents: Webb *et al*, 1966.

Feminist research: Acker, Barry and Essereld, 1983; Gamarnikow *et al.*, 1983; Roberts, 1981.

Topics

Family Anderson, 1980; Anwar 1979; Barrett and McIntosh, 1982; Fagin and Little 1984; Gittins, 1985; Morgan, 1985; Prescod-Roberts and Steele 1980; Rapoport, Fogarty and Rapoport 1982; Segal, 1983; Sharpe, 1984; Sherman and Wood, 1982, chs. 7–9; Stopes-Roe and Cochrane 1985; Wilson, 1985.

Schooling: Corrigan, 1979; Grace, 1978; Hargreaves, 1967; Hargreaves *et al.*, 1975; Lacey, 1970; Measor and Woods, 1984; Willis, 1977.

CHAPTER 8
CONCLUSION

Doing Sociology has emphasised the interrelationship between theory, method and epistemology. Three major epistemological approaches have been identified and used throughout the book: the positivist, the phenomenological and the critical.

Within each of these we have considered a variety of perspectives, such as functionalism, sociobiology, interactionism, Marxism and feminism. Specific theories, such as labelling theory, reception theory and dual labour market theory have been linked to substantive areas of sociological concern such as deviance, the mass media and unemployment.

Doing Sociology is organised around chapters that explore different techniques of data collection and analysis. Each chapter links the methods to both theory and epistemology, using substantive examples to illustrate how research relates to the development of sociological ideas.

We began, in Chapter 2, by showing how analysis of the mass media has been approached. There are several different theoretical perspectives about the way the mass media is produced and received. Researchers have adopted a variety of epistemological perspectives when dealing with the media and made use of a wide range of methods of data collection.

In Chapter 3 we looked at how researchers can make use of secondary statistical data that has already been compiled by social researchers or through government administrative procedures. In Chapters 4 to 7 we looked in more detail at the main approaches to data collection used by social researchers: social surveys, experiments, observation and personal data.

Not all research data, however, is collected using such formal procedures. Researchers have also made use of opportunistic measures, often referred to as non-reactive measures.

Non-reactive measures

Non-reactive measures refer to measures where there is no interaction between the researcher and the population under study. For example, analysing how changing social conditions within a work-place affect workers' behaviour can be examined by looking at the company's records of absenteeism, sickness and the amount of output, instead of interviewing the employees or becoming a participant observer in the work-place. The compilation of administrative records by government officials is a form of non-reactive measurement (see Chapter 3).

Non-reactive measures are wide-ranging and include all data that can be used by the alert researcher. These non-reactive measures are often called *unobtrusive measures* (Webb *et al.*, 1966) because the data is created without any intrusion by the researcher. The researcher seeks out the data *after* they have occurred.

Unobtrusive measures provide clues to social processes, and collecting them is similar to detective work. Unobtrusive measures are extremely diverse and often ingenious. For example, Sawyer (1961) studied the contents of people's dustbins and counted the number of empty liquor bottles as a way of estimating the extent of liquor sales in an American city (Sawyer 1961).

Unobtrusive measures can also be used to measure populations that are no longer here to be studied. For example, reading farewell notes left in cases of suicide. Clearly, it is not possible to interview the subject once he or she becomes part of the population of suicides. The researcher has to wait until a population defines itself operationally; in this case, by committing suicide. The researcher can then use the farewell note along with biographical material and interviews with the relatives. Similarly, historians have, for example, studied suits of armour as indicators of the height and weight of medieval knights. Dave Harker (1980) uses songs as historical evidence. He takes songs from the north-west of England that deal with the theme of the industrialisation of the cotton industry as indicators of class-consciousness. He also uses songs about coal-mining over the last 200 years to represent the long-term point of view of workers in the industry.

Recent research on betting shops used betting slips as an unobtrusive measure (Filby and Harvey, 1988, 1989). This was part of a detailed longitudinal study of betting activity of punters and the effect on betting activity of changes in the law that allowed for more comfort in betting shops and broadcasting of racing. All betting slips are timed and the analysis of 9635 betting slips from a single week's racing in June 1984 showed, for example, that the timing of the bet was related to the likelihood of the bet having a winning element (see Table 8.1). Winning bets involved a pay out to the punter (which may or may not exceed the total value of the bet depending on how many horses or dogs the punter selected) and are known as 'returned bets'. The percentage of returned bets was at its lowest when racing was at its most frequent, that is, in the period between 2 and 5 p.m.. This is also the time when most bets are placed. The researchers concluded:

> One possible explanation is that afternoon, hardcore punters are more prone to 'all or nothing' single win and forecast bets without 'saver' elements. The type of bet then is an important factor. However, it is also the case that the period from 2–4 o'clock offers the maximum amount of betting opportunities in the shop, a situation explicitly intended to encourage re-betting, and punters are therefore possibly prone to decision-making overload.... It is more likely, that through overload, punters will lose at a more rapid rate (Filby and Harvey, 1988, p. 167).

Some sociologists make use of unobtrusive measures because they avoid the *effects* caused by researchers being in the field. Thus the researcher can examine documents, language and physical locations without apparently affecting the normal behaviour of their subjects. However, it would be incorrect to assume that unobtrusive measures are thus 'objective' measures of behaviour. Despite attempts to avoid reactive error, unobtrusive measures can be reactive in some situations. Take, for instance, the first example about rates of absenteeism. There is the possibility that, during the research, employees may find out what is going on and thus adjust their rates of absenteeism.

Similarly, unobtrusive measures are prone to *operational subjectivity* by the researchers. For example, in the betting shop research (Filby and Harvey, 1988), betting slips were marked as to whether or not they were passed by 'regular punters'. This involved an operational definition of a regular punter

Table 8.1 Percentage of returned betting slips, by time

Time period	% returned slips	Number of slips
10 to 11.59	27.1	1109
12 to 12.59	31.5	969
1 to 1.59	30.8	1160
2 to 2.59	19.8	1808
3 to 3.59	19.7	2004
4 to 4.59	22.2	1970
after 5.00	36.7	613

Adapted from Filby and Harvey (1988).

but it was left to the betting shop cashiers to make a subjective decision as to whether the punter fell into the 'regular' category, because slips had to be marked at the time the bet was placed. Furthermore, at busy times, it is likely that the cashiers were so rushed that they forgot to mark some of the bets placed by regulars.

Unobtrusive measures, like any other secondary source, are not self-evidently objective. As we saw in Chapter 3, using existing data can be a problem because they are not designed or structured in a way that suits the sociological research. Unobtrusive measures, like available statistical data, need to be *interpreted*. Harker (1980), for example, had to decide whether the popular songs about coal-mining were truly those of the workers or whether they were handed down by middle-class intellectuals.

Similarly, some unobtrusive measures are only available at *infrequent* intervals or may occur more-or-less randomly. In which case the researcher is likely to come across them almost by accident and it raises issues of how *representative* they are. You also have to make decisions about how inclusive are the unobtrusive measures you are using. For example, looking in the rubbish bins of a sample of business people to see how many liquor bottles they disposed of in a period of time would be a reasonable indicator of household consumption if people threw away the bottles when they emptied them. However, if bottles were recycled through bottle-banks or stored for wine-making then the number thrown away might be very misleading. In the end you have to be clear exactly what your unobtrusive measure is actually measuring and be reflective about its value. In the betting shop research, for example, the statistical results were based on the betting slips, not on punters. There was no way of being able to check how many slips each individual punter passed.

Student Activity 8.1
What unobtrusive measures could you use to find out:
1. **Which newspapers are most popular in the area where you live? How would this measure compare with information gathered through a survey or observation? Which would be the easiest and cheapest to do?**
2. **Which exhibits in your local museum or art gallery are the most popular? (Make sure you take into account the location of tea rooms and toilets.)**

There are *ethical* issues involved with using unobtrusive measures. For example, is it ethical to be snooping in people's dustbins to find out how much liquor they drink? Is it ethical to read farewell notes in cases of suicide and to use incidents of suicide to find a sample of relatives to interview? As with all research, the ethics involved in using unobtrusive measures have to be considered (see Chapter 1).

In practice, unobtrusive measures tend to be used with other data collection techniques. Few of these measures on their own are adequate for providing reliable data. However, they can be an important source for confirming data from other research such as participant observation, in-depth interviews and so on.

Irrespective of whether unobtrusive measures are used, sociologists often use more than one data collection method in a single research study. You are not required to use a single method. Some researchers argue that using more than one method of data collection increases the reliability of the research. This is known as triangulation.

Triangulation

All research methods have advantages, disadvantages and limitations. Research methods are not neutral in how they represent the world. Some researchers have therefore used more than one approach as a means of dealing with this problem in a study. This process is called triangulation. Triangulation can apply to both methods and theory.

Methods triangulation

Methods triangulation refers to three different sorts of situation:

1. One researcher using two or more research techniques: or
2. Two or more researchers using the same research technique; or
3. Two or more researchers using two or more research techniques.

For example, Colin Lacey (1970) used both observation and scheduled interviews in his education research. He first undertook qualitative case studies to arrive at a model and then used quantitative analysis on a bigger sample to try to verify his qualitative model. Similarly, Bosk (1979) used a variety of techniques in his study of surgeons in a teaching hospital (see Extract 8.1).

> **Student Activity 8.2**
> **Read Extract 8.1.**
> 1. **What methods of data collection does Bosk use?**
> 2. **What sort of gaps in his observational data do the other techniques fill?**
> 3. **What type of interviewing does he adopt?**
> 4. **He argues that the use of several methods makes his inferences valid. Do you agree?**
> 5. **What might you do in his situation when conclusions from one source of data are not confirmed by another source of data?**

Community studies provide an example of triangulation where two or more researchers use the same technique. A team of researchers undertake participant observation of the community from different points of view. They adopt different roles in the community, which provides them with more than one perspective on the research situation. An example of this is Davis, Gardner and Gardner's (1941) classic American study of the relationships between blacks and whites in an old southern city. Four researchers, a black husband and wife and a white husband and wife, lived in the city for almost two years. They had very different views of the community due to their different roles and positions. Triangulation came about through the collection and comparison of their different perceptions of the community.

Similarly, in *Power, Persistence and Change: A Second Study of Banbury* (Stacey *et al.*, 1975) Eric Batstone, Anne Murcott and Colin Bell all moved to Banbury for the duration of the two-year fieldwork and bought houses there. They were participant observers in the town and also carried out in-depth interviews with key informants as well as a social survey of a sample of 1,449 residents.

It is argued that using teams of researchers provides a check on peoples' views, perceptions and interpretations of the same situation and thus overcomes the 'subjectivity' of the research process. This is a particularly

---

Extract 8.1

TRIANGULATION

Not all the questions I set for myself could be appropriately answered by the data collected by participant observation alone. Among the questions I was interested in was the following: How consequential are negative sanctions to an individual's career path? To get at this question, I had to ask: How do attending physicians construct an evaluation of a house officer's competence from observations of the house officer's day-to-day task performance? I used two sources of data to supplement my field data: (1) I perused the written evaluations of house staff by attending surgeons as contained in personnel files and (2) I attended the faculty meetings of the Department of Surgery at which the decision to retain or terminate junior house staff in the training programme is made.

Once fieldwork was completed, I interviewed those attending physicians and house staff with whom I worked most closely. The interviews served two purposes. First, they served as a check on the validity of my data. Many of my interpretations were rephrased as questions for comment. In this way, I could match my assessments against those of actors in the scene; and I could fill in those spots where my observational material was thin. Second, the interviews allowed me to see my observations in a larger context. For example, house staff were asked to compare their performance on different services. This provided me with a fuller picture of their activity and their reaction to it than I could gather from my field observations. Two different interview schedules were constructed: one for house staff and one for attending physicians. These schedules serve as guides rather than formal instruments. All interviews were kept as conversational as possible. Interviews lasted between forty-five minutes and one and a half hours. For attending physicians the focus of the interview was on how they decided if a subordinate [house staff] was good or bad and what they considered to be unforgivable errors. Of house staff, I asked what they thought their superordinate's [attending physicians] performance expectations were, what they considered to be unforgivable errors, and what they considered the major difficulties in becoming a surgeon.

This triangulated approach to data gathering gives me confidence in the validity of the inferences which I have drawn. Often conclusions reached about performance from one data source are confirmed by another.

Adapted from Bosk (1979) pp. 15–16.

popular view concerning participant observation. We saw in Chapter 6 that participant observation is often seen as 'rather subjective' and it is assumed that having several people involved overcomes the problem of idiosyncratic individual interpretations. This, however, does not mean that the consensus view is any more 'correct' or objective. As we have already suggested, no method is intrinsically objective.

Theoretical triangulation

Theoretical triangulation involves looking at the research situation from different theoretical perspectives. For example, a study of juvenile gangs might adopt both a functionalist and an interactionist perspective. The assumption is that by applying more than one theoretical approach, a better understanding might evolve. Theoretical triangulation may be more formalised, the research design may set out to test a number of competing theories. For example, Singer (1971) used three different theories in his research on why first-born children were more adult-oriented than later-born children. He devised a research strategy to test each of the competing theories.

Advantages and disadvantages of triangulation

Triangulation is often assumed to be beneficial in any research situation. The benefits include:

1. The ability to cross-check perceptions when a team of researchers is used.
2. Cross-checking research findings by using more than one data collection method.
3. Checking out different theories using the same set of data.

However, there are also some problems with the method. First, there is the problem of available *resources*. Using more than one method can be time-consuming and expensive. It may involve employing both interviewers and observers.

Adopting theoretical triangulation can be less resource-demanding although it may lead to the researcher needing to undertake more research to validate or assess the theoretical perspectives.

Second, using a team of people can create tensions in terms of decision-making, sharing of work and supervision. Colin Bell (1977, pp. 54–5) reflecting on the Banbury study, recounts the problem of teamwork, particularly the friction that occurred over the use of the interview survey.

> The survey itself was a lot of work, cost a lot of money (it was the biggest item on the budget after our salaries) and was very time-consuming. And as the bitter recriminations later showed, it was extraordinarily difficult to do well.... In the summer of 1968 Anne Murcott and Eric Batstone went to Swansea and I went to Colchester. By that time we had all had more than enough both of each other and of Banbury.

Third, when using triangulation there is a tendency to adopt the '*safe view*' in an attempt to reach agreement. Thus potentially critical research material can be overlooked or left out altogether.

Fourth, triangulation raises *epistemological* problems. For example, combining data that has been collected via participant observation with social survey results can be difficult. The observation may have been phenomenological, looking for subjects' meanings while the survey results may have involved a positivistic search for causes. Often the two methods do not balance and one approach overrides the other. Lacey (1970), as we noted, used his quantitative data to *verify* what he had learned through observation.

The question remains: What do you do in a case where the observations and the survey data suggest very different interpretations? Do you decide that the survey material is more 'objective' and use that? Do you admit to having contradictory evidence and say that you do not know what your data tells you? The answer is to make it clear, from the outset, what your underlying presuppositions are. In the last resort, it is these presuppositions that will guide you in dealing with contradictory types of evidence. You should not be swayed by the data collection method but should consider the evidence in light of your underlying perspectives and the aim of your research.

Case studies

An area in which multiple methods of data collection are used is case study research. Case study normally refers to a detailed examination of a single 'case'. Usually, such a 'case' is an organisation, such as a factory, a hospital, a police force or a community. Westwood (1984) did her research in a single factory in 'Needletown', Grimshaw and Jefferson (1987) used a single police force in their research, Rex and Moore (1967) used Sparkbrook as a case study of community relations, and Elliott used the television series *The Nature of Prejudice* as a case study of the way in which television programmes are produced.

Sometimes researchers undertake more than one case study, for purposes of comparison. For example, Sudnow (1967) undertook a case study of a private and a public hospital in the United States.

Case study often involve interviews, observation and document analysis to collect detailed information on the particular case. For example, Colin Lacey (1970) used observation and interviews in *Hightown Grammar,* and Yiannis Gabriel (1988) used a combination of introductory chats, scheduled interviews and observation in his study of catering organisations. Sometimes, however, a single approach is adopted. Sudnow, for example, just used non-participant observation in his ethnomethodological study of death and dying in American hospitals.

The term 'case study' is used ambiguously in the sociological literature. Case studies often refer to the study of groups of people in an organisation and it is the organisation that is said to constitute the case study. However, community studies are also sometimes called case studies. Then it is the community, be it a village, town or district of a large city, which is the case under study. Examples of community studies are Blythe's (1972) study of the village of *Akenfield* and Blumenthal's (1932) study of a small American town, the two studies of Middletown (Lynd and Lynd, 1929, 1937) and of Banbury (Stacey, 1960; Stacey *et al.*, 1975) and Zorbaugh's (1929) study of *The Gold Coast and the Slum* districts of Chicago.

Some people also argue that participant observation, for example, in a gang or a poolhall, constitutes a case study. Gordon Marshall (1986) referred to his participant observation study of a licensed restaurant as a case study. Similarly, it has been suggested that life history is a form of case study because it is a detailed analysis of a single case. Compilations of life histories or life experiences, as in 'women speak out' (Moraga and Anzaldua, 1981; Bryan *et al.*, 1985; Padel and Stevenson, 1988; Osler, 1989), can also be seen as case studies of sexist or racist oppression.

When carrying out a case study it is advisable to carry out a *pilot* study first, as you would when doing a questionnaire or scheduled interview. For example, use a subgroup within the organisation to test what you intend to do to see if there are any problems with your proposed method. If you intended to get respondents to use a diary to record their leisure activities then the pilot would show up any design faults with the diary and give some idea of how reliably the respondents had completed it.

Relating case studies to the wider context

Case studies are not necessarily inward-looking. They are designed to provide detailed information about a specific area but this may be to see a group in the context of a wider setting. David Sibley (1981), for example, in his study of travellers/gypsies looks at their needs and their relationship with the wider society. In his study he draws on his own experiences of traveller/gypsy communities and makes use of two case studies, one in Hull, and the other in Sheffield. The reason for choosing these two areas for the case studies was that the author had considerable experience of travellers in Hull, and Sheffield's treatment of gypsies had been prominent in the regional and national press.

He used these two case studies as a basis for finding out about gypsy culture in Britain, how the wider society reacts to certain aspects of their culture and how the combination of the built environment, the local administration and the attitudes of local people affected the travellers.

He deliberately made use of the case study method because this provided a check on making bald statements about national and international traits of gypsies derived from scattered and sparse information. In other words, he wanted detailed material to put flesh on the bones of the fragmentary notions that he had come across. His studies were not designed with a view to generalising his research. He was aware that, regarding travellers' adaptation to the city, the data collected from one urban area may only reflect one of several possible political responses to gypsy communities.

Conventionally, it is assumed that generalisations cannot be made from case studies as they are 'one-off' studies. However, some researchers use case studies to test hypotheses. They do it by developing what are called *critical case studies* (sometimes also called *theoretical* case studies). These are case studies that are selected so they are as favourable as possible to confirming a hypothesis. The case study selected is then examined and if it does *not* support the hypothesis then it is taken as refuting the theory that underlies the hypothesis.

> The **EMBOURGEOISEMENT THESIS** argued that capitalism, in the second half of the twentieth century, had led to a break-down in the division between working class and middle class. In particular, highly paid workers in factories characterised by new technology no longer exhibited working-class tendencies or attitudes. Instead, they were adopting middle-class attitudes and values, had become like the bourgeoisie, and no longer identified with the working class. Such well-paid workers, it was argued, had become *embourgeoised*.

For example, John Goldthorpe *et al.* (1969) used a critical case study to examine the *embourgeoisement thesis*. To test this out Goldthorpe *et al.* selected an area of the country that as far as possible showed all the characteristics of the new embourgeoised worker. They chose Luton and studied workers living there who worked in three factories that paid high wages and were characterised by new technology. The case study was thus selected so that it was as favourable as possible to the embourgeoisement thesis. They selected a sample of workers, carried out two formal interviews with them (one at work and one at home) and observed the work situation. What they showed was that the workers did *not* exhibit middle-class tendencies. The embourgeoisement thesis did not hold up. If it did not apply in Luton where the circumstances were favourable they argued, it was unlikely to apply anywhere.

Similarly, in studying the way the police worked, Grimshaw and Jefferson (1986) selected what they called a *theoretical* case study. They were interested in developing a theory about the interrelationship between the law, the work situation and the public, based on actual policing practices. Reflecting Goldthorpe and Lockwood's critical case study, Grimshaw and Jefferson deliberately chose a police force that covered a large urban area hit badly by economic recession and with mixed ethnic groups. In such a situation the tension between law, work and community were at a maximum. They used non-participant observation and document analysis and showed that by focusing on the legal process the police were able to put their work concerns before the concerns of the community. This result, they argued, provided a theoretical interpretation of police work that had *general* implications for changes in policy relating to the police force in Britain.

Student Activity 8.3
Undertake a case study to investigate whether gender roles are different if both partners work full time. You could do this by using extended in-depth interviews (see Chapter 7) with 4 to 6 couples. Provide your results in a research report discussing your findings and the problems that arise from the method.

We would like to finish the book with some comments about the role of project work. We briefly review the distinction between method and methodology, argue that doing sociology is an effective way of learning about the subject, provide a more detailed overview of the research process and offer some suggestions about how you can get the best out of your sociological project.

Learning by doing

We said at the beginning that this book was called *Doing Sociology* because we felt that the best way to learn about sociology was by doing it. Changes in syllabuses and teaching methods have provided more and more opportunities for students to participate in active project work. This book sets out to help you undertake small-scale projects by outlining the research process, exploring techniques, providing activities and suggesting project areas.

More than this, though, we have emphasised how methodology is at the hub of sociology, combining theory, method and epistemology. Methodology is the point at which empirical data, theory and underlying presuppositions come together. Suppose that you wanted to do research on domestic violence. A *method* approach would be to decide that you wanted to do a questionnaire, or in-depth interviews or observation, or whatever. But why do you choose one method rather than another? Methodology is about the whole research process; it does not see 'methods' as isolated from the aims, theories and presuppositions of the researcher. A *methodological* approach starts by asking: Why research domestic violence? What are the aims of the study? What is the context in which the research is located? What presumptions does the researcher have about the nature of sociological knowledge? For example, is the intention to discover the causes of domestic violence? Or is it to find out what domestic violence means to the people involved? Or is it to examine how the structures of power make domestic violence an 'acceptable' part of patriarchal oppression?

In short, a methodological approach starts with 'What do I already know? 'What are the gaps in this knowledge?' 'What do I want to find out?' 'What sort of empirical data can I hope to get?' Only then does it ask 'What are the

NOTE We have avoided categorising sociological research as either qualitative or quantitative because this sets up a false dichotomy. Sociologists tend to pair up what they see as opposite types of methods or approaches. Techniques are seen as being either quantitative or qualitative; macro or micro; explanatory or interpretive; positivist or phenomenological. These dichotomies are also applied to social theorists. This leads to an implied relationship between social theory and research technique. This results in a list of 'quantitative' methods that are portrayed as macro, explanatory and positivistic and another list of 'qualitative' methods that are seen as micro, interpretive and phenomenological.

Such an approach is intended to produce a simple classificatory system of opposites that enables methods, theories and epistemological presuppositions to be grouped together. This leads to a false division. The published work of practising sociologists tends to get forced into one or other camp, while practitioners feel that they have to adopt either the qualitative/phenomenological or quantitative/positivist approach at the expense of the other. At worst, researchers choose between the two approaches on the basis of how good they are at doing statistics.

This approach is unsatisfactory because it confuses method and methodology and tends to see epistemology as either being positivist or phenomenological. There is, as we have seen, a whole tradition of sociology that embraces Marxism, elements of feminism, black perspectives and structuralism, but which is distinct from both positivism and phenomenology (Benton, 1977; Harvey, 1990). This alternative tradition we refer to as the *critical*. We do not claim that this three-way split is in any way definitive. Some people are unhappy that feminism should be linked to Marxism, for example. What we have suggested, however, is not that they are necessarily the same but that much feminism reflects much Marxism in analysing the structures of oppression and attempting to reveal what is going on behind the ideological screen. There are various other ways that underlying presuppositions can be identified (see Johnson *et al.*, 1984 for an alternative).

The dichotomy of positivist and phenomenological is entirely inadequate because it does not exhaust the alternatives and it leads to unfortunate implications about the relationship between method, theory and methodology.

best ways of collecting such data?' A methodological approach is one that is led by the concerns of the researcher, both in terms of the substantive area of enquiry (for example, domestic violence) and in terms of the way that the researcher sees the social world. It is not a 'method-led' approach.

So methodology is not just about data collection practices; it also involves the way that sociological knowledge is developed. There is an interrelation between: the techniques used; the hypotheses being investigated; the general theory that shapes the enquiry; the overall perspective within which it is located; and the underlying presuppositions about the nature of knowledge that is being produced.

Doing sociology is thus not just about collecting data in isolation; it is about constructing a research problem, relating data to theory, and exploring the presuppositions about the nature of the sociological knowledge that results. Doing sociology thus provides a direct and accessible way of making sense of social theory and philosophy in relation to particular areas of social enquiry. In short, doing sociology brings social theory to life.

Practicality and feasibility

We have talked about a wide range of techniques and approaches and have even suggested that it is possible to combine techniques and compare theories in some circumstances. However, we should insist that the first requirement of any project is practicality. You need to be able to complete the project you set yourself and so it is important to specify a research problem that you are likely to be able to do in the time available.

Clearly, what you can do depends on experience, resources and facilities, as well as time. We have assumed, in the main, that you are unlikely to have much longer than six months to do a project. We also expect that your resources are limited and that, in the last resort, you will be writing up an individual project. We have also suggested throughout that one facility you should try to make use of is information technology. We appreciate that getting access to computer hardware or the right sort of software may be a problem and so we have described techniques in terms of what you can do by hand. However, we have also pointed out, where appropriate, the speed and labour-saving benefits that come from using information technology during all stages of the research process.

Devising research that can be completed requires planning. This, in turn, means background reading and the clarification of the issues that the research problem raises. In the end, there is no substitute for experience when it comes to working out the feasibility of a research project, so do not be disappointed if your teacher or lecturer suggests a more limited research proposal than you envisage. You can learn far more from completing a small-scale project successfully than you can from floundering about and failing to complete a large-scale one.

This book is meant to be a guide to doing projects as well as a general review of methodology, so we would be very glad to hear how useful it has been to you in doing your project work. Let us know where it helped and where it didn't.

Project work

Doing sociology, as you will have discovered by now, is hard work, but active project work is an enjoyable and accessible way of getting to grips with sociology. More and more, the teaching of sociology is making use of

active project work. This means that you, as students, have to take some
initiative in the learning process. Doing a project is a time-consuming
activity. It is therefore important to select a research area that is of interest
to you and that are going to enjoy as well as one that is going to help you
develop your sociological skills.

Once you have decided on your research area (suppose, for example, you
want to do some research on violence,) you will need to focus on one, or
possibly two, aspects of violence so as to make your research manageable.
You might, for example, focus on domestic violence, or 'football hooligans',
or 'lager louts', or whatever. You might want to make a comparison of two
aspects; for example, to compare the violence associated with 'football
hooligans' and 'lager louts'. Before going much further in devising your
project you need to see what has already been written about the broad area
of the research and what research has been done on the particular aspects you
are focusing on. So if you were intending to research football supporter
violence you would need to find out about general theories of violence and
read whatever research you could find on 'football hooligans'.

At this stage you should be beginning to work out your *research problem*.
It is crucial to work out a manageable research problem to guide you through
your research. This often takes the form of a hypothesis and appropriate sub-
hypotheses. Setting out a hypothesis does not necessarily commit you to
testing the hypotheses in any formal quantitative way. Making a hypothesis
plain does, however, clarify the focus of your research activity. Working out
your research problem requires that you get the following three things clear.

Aim and approach

First, what the aim of the project is. If, for example, your research is on
football spectator violence then you need to decide whether you are interested in the causes of the violence, or whether you want to see how those
involved in it make sense of the 'hooligan' activities, or whether football-
related violence reflects broader forms of class culture, or whatever. In
devising the aim you therefore need to make it clear whether you are adopting
a positivistic analysis of *causes*, a phenomenological examination of *meanings* , or a critical analysis of wider social and historical *structures*.

Theory

Second, having read some of the available research, you need to develop a
theoretical perspective as a starting point. You need to spell out what theory
or theories you are going to use in your research. You may want to use a single
theory and apply it to a specific research situation or, perhaps less likely, you
may want to use your empirical material to compare the effectiveness of
several competing theories. You might decide, for example, that you find the
'working-class machismo' theory of 'football hooliganism' (Williams *et al.*,
1984) the most convincing. You may then want to use that in your research
on the role of females in football supporter violence. On the other hand, you
may want to compare the machismo theory with the 'ritual violence' theory
(Marsh *et al.*, 1978) by seeing which theory seems best to fit the behaviour
of a particular set of football supporters. A third option might be to use a
single theory, such as working-class machismo, as a basis for comparing the
activities of 'football hooligans' and 'lager louts'. The research will either
suggest that a particular theory works well, needs modifying, or does not
work at all in relation to the empirical material.

**EXTENDING YOUR THEORETICAL
KNOWLEDGE** In this book we have
illustrated research techniques by drawing
on a wide variety of areas of sociology such
as health, poverty, gender, the family, work
and leisure, sexuality and so on. We have
pointed to various theoretical issues to show
you how to link theory to method. However, we make no claim to provide an
exhaustive account of theoretical debates
and so you should also consult some of the
texts suggested for further reading at the
end of each chapter.

Techniques and method

Third, you have to work out how you are going to tackle the research problem. If you want to test the machismo theory as an explanation of the causes of 'football hooliganism' then how are you going to test this out? Where are you going to get your data from? Will you do a survey of football supporters? Although surveys are often regarded as the best tool for making generalisable causal statements, is it appropriate as a method of finding the causes of deviant activity? Will you perhaps instead watch police videos taken in and around football grounds? While this might show you what happens, and even how on occasion football hooliganism is orchestrated, will it tell you why it happens? So, will you perhaps talk to 'hooligans' to see what motivates them? If so, will this help you to determine the causes of hooliganism, or have you moved towards understanding hooliganism from the subject's point of view?

Clearly, then, your aim and presuppositions, the theories you are going to use and the methods you are going to adopt, are interrelated. When devising your research problem you need to balance all three in order to plan a manageable project.

The technique you adopt should emerge from the research problem. You should not decide on a technique and then apply it to a research problem. Okely (1983), for example, undertook a study of travellers/gypsies. She was told by her employers to use a questionnaire to generate 'objective' quantitative data. She had misgivings and sure enough found that the answers to such an instrument were so inconsistent that the approach had to be scrapped in favour of observation. Similarly, Benson (1981) found that any attempt to adopt a survey in her study of interracial families in Brixton was impossible given the suspicion, especially among blacks, of the motives and intentions of white researchers. Nor, worse still, should you decide on a technique and then work out a research problem that will be suitable for the technique. Tailoring the problem to fit the method is definitely a case of putting the cart before the horse (Mills, 1971).

While we used specific examples to illustrate different methods you should note that the methods are not restricted to specific areas of enquiry nor are specific areas only researched using the methods we have used. What technique you use depends on the *research problem* you set yourself; it is not determined by the broad area of sociology that you are researching.

Student Activity 8.4
Below are several possible research areas. Select one and devise a research problem. Indicate clearly the aim, the hypotheses, the presuppositions, the theory or theories, and the method you are going to use to tackle your research problem. State why you think the particular techniques you intend to use will be most appropriate.

- **Voting behaviour**
- **Glue sniffing**
- **Factory work**
- **Poverty in Britain**
- **Divorce**
- **Environmental protection**
- **Media presentation of industrial disputes**
- **Experience of unemployment**
- **Sexual experiences of adolescents**
- **Leisure activities**
- **Television viewing habits**
- **Alcohol and tobacco usage.**

SAFETY AND ETHICS Make sure that you are comfortable with the research techniques that you adopt. Do not undertake the collection of empirical data in ways that may lead you to situations that are personally dangerous, or that you will feel to be morally difficult to contend with. You should also always consider the ethical implications of your data collection procedure (see Chapter 1).

In Chapter 1 we provided a brief overview of the three stages of research: planning, field work and report writing. Extract 8.2 expands this and provides more detail on what is involved at each stage. It is an idealised view of the research process and would require far more time and resources than you are likely to have at your disposal. Nevertheless, it is important that you have some idea of the complete process and you may find yourself pleasantly surprised by how much of the ideal approach you have done in your project.

You should not think of the stages in Extract 8.2 as a completely inflexible compartmentalisation of the research process. The three broad parts of the process overlap, and the ordering of the elements within each part will vary, depending on the nature of your particular research. For example, you will come across other background material throughout your research and you should not ignore it just because it does not come to light during the first stage. Similarly, you will probably start to analyse your data during the data collection period. But what you should avoid doing is changing the whole balance of the project. Do not be tempted to cut down the planning and write-up time in order to collect more data. If anything, reduce the data-collection time to give yourself more time for analysis and presentation.

Referencing, footnoting and language

When writing the report use a standard form for referencing. We recommend the Harvard referencing system. It is the method used in this book. It requires that you record references in the way we suggested in Chapter 1. The Harvard system provides a simple and systematic way of referencing other work. It avoids footnotes and thus overcomes the problem of having to change footnote numbers every time a new reference is added. The Harvard system does away with the use of *'op. cit.'* and *'ibid.'* which are so common in footnote referencing but which make it much more difficult to find a reference. Harvard referencing makes it much easier for the reader to find your reference because the system is simple. Whenever you refer to a publication just write in the author's name and the date of publication. At the end of the report list all the references in alphabetical order of author, using the referencing style as shown in Extract 1.2. on page 5.

Avoid footnotes as far as possible. Use them only for material that you feel is necessary for some readers but which you do not want to include in the main text because most readers will be aware of it. You will not often have such material and if you can write a report without footnotes, so much the better.

It is also important that you do not use sexist or racist language or stereotypes in your report. The British Sociological Association provides *Guidelines on Anti-Sexist Language* (see Extract 8.3). Margrit Eichler (1988) argues that the research should have been designed in a non-sexist way from the outset. This involves avoiding seeing the world in male terms, making sure that you do not generalise references to males to the whole population, making sure you take account of gender, and applying the same standards of analysis to both men and women (Harvey, 1990).

Writing the report

Your research project is only as good as your report. Perhaps that is overstating things a little. You might have learned a lot about sociology and the research process in particular through your project work. However, nobody will know how much you have learned or what you have found out

Extract 8.2

STAGES OF A RESEARCH PROJECT

Planning stage

This involves deciding what to research, planning what to do, finding out what other research has been done, preparing data collection instruments, and sorting out a sample. At this stage you need to do the following:

1. Set out the *aims* of the research.
2. Outline why you want to do the research.
3. State how it relates to current social processes and practices.
4. Review work that has been done in the same area. Note what techniques are used, what theories are applied and what presuppositions the authors have.
5. Outline what the central concepts are that you are interested in.
6. Consider what sort of social phenomena or events are going to relate to these central concepts.
7. Draw up a specific hypothesis that you are going to investigate (that is, a single statement that is the focus of your data collection. For example, 'working-class children derive less benefit from formal education than middle-class children').
8. Draw up some sub-hypotheses that break down the main hypothesis into manageable, interrelated sections. (Examples of sub-hypotheses might be that 'working-class children obtain fewer GCSEs than middle-class children' and 'working-class children are less encouraged to continue in education than middle-class children'.)
9. Decide on the method you are going to use.
10. Design (and pre-pilot) any appropriate data collection instruments (for example, questionnaire or survey schedule). Identify secondary sources, or elements of the mass media that you are going to investigate, and so on.
11. Sort out your technical aids, make sure you have tape-recorders or video machines that work and a pile of tapes and batteries. Get familiar with the appropriate information technology at this stage. Don't leave it until you write up before learning how to use a wordprocessor. Make sure that you have tried out any statistical package on test data or pre-pilot data to make sure you know how it works. Don't leave it until the data analysis stage to learn how to use the software.
12. Decide on your sample. Get together a sampling frame where possible, or decide on quotas. If you are using snowball sampling make your first contacts. Ensure that you have access to your sample, including any official clearance.

Data collection

This is when you carry out your interviews, make your observations, get respondents to fill in questionnaires or write diaries, video-tape television programmes that you are going to analyse, collect the newspapers whose content you are investigating, or seek out secondary statistical data. At this stage you need to do the following:

1. Try out any data collection instrument (for example, pilot your questionnaire).
2. Do a preliminary analysis of the initial data to see if it is going to provide you with the material you need to assess your hypotheses.
3. Amend the data collection instruments.
4. Consider problems that you are having locating your sample.

5. Assess whether the intended kind and size of sample is going to be viable. Make adjustments as necessary to fit into your time period.
6. Decide whether the approach you are adopting is going to be sufficient or whether it will be necessary to supplement what you are doing. (For example, you may decide that questionnaires are not giving you enough in-depth information and that you need to do some in-depth interviewing as well.) Make any changes to the data collection process.
7. Ensure that, as far as possible, you collect all the data you intended. Follow up non-respondents; build up snowball samples, spend time observing the different groups you have identified and so on.
8. Transfer data from interview schedules or questionnaires into data files (that is, code up data) for quantitative analysis; transcribe tape recorded interviews; make sure observation field notes are properly recorded and referenced.

Analysis and report writing

This is the point at which you make sense of all the work you have been doing and it is your opportunity to share with others what you have found out.

At this stage you need to do the following:

1. Become familiar with the data. Read qualitative material (field notes, diaries, interview transcripts, and so on). View video-tapes, read newspapers or magazines if you are analysing the media. Look through questionnaires and schedules to see what kind of answers you got, and so on.
2. Analyse the data. Undertake statistical analysis of quantitative data or ethnographic analysis of qualitative data.
3. Use the data to come to some initial tentative conclusions about your hypotheses.
4. Work out a central argument or 'angle' for your research report.
5. Continue to analyse the data to refine this central argument, relating the argument and the data to the aims and hypotheses.
6. Write the first draft of the research report. This first draft will tend to include everything and be rather long. It is likely to be rather more descriptive than analytic. This is normal because you will be making sense of what you have found out as you write your initial draft. In many senses you will be feeling your way. Treat the first draft as a discussion document and get other people to read and comment on it. Use whatever opportunity you have to make a verbal presentation of your research in a small discussion group as this helps to sharpen the focus of the work.
7. On the basis of discussions, comments and your own reflection on the first draft, produce the second draft of the report. This should refine the first version, cutting out repetition, making the report more analytic (that is, more focused on the aims of the research) and more structured. Again, you should get people to read and comment on this before producing the final product.
8. Produce the final version of the report. This should be the finished typed, error-free, well-presented version incorporating changes from the second draft.
9. Go on holiday.

if you do not produce a report. In the end, your project will be judged on the report you produce. So make it interesting and readable. A readable report is one with a 'plot'. You should tell a story to the reader. That does not mean that you should make it up. It means that you should not expect the reader to do the work of making sense of your data. What you are telling the reader should be straightforward to follow, convincing and interesting.

A readable report is one that has a central theme or 'angle'. The report should take the reader through the aims, objectives, method, data and conclusions in the same way that you would expect if you were reading an article or book. There should be a reasoned argument and the data should

---

Extract 8.3

SEXIST LANGUAGE

The British Sociological Association has a clear policy against the use of anti-sexist language. It has issued guidelines to assist its members in avoiding sexist language by sensitizing people to some of the forms it takes and suggesting anti-sexist alternatives. The BSA suggest that teachers and students as well as authors may find the guidelines helpful.

'He/Man' Language
Do not use 'man' to mean humanity in general. Similarly, where reference to *both* sexes is intended do not use the word man or other masculine equivalents. For example:

Sexist	Anti-sexist
man/mankind	person, people, human beings
mankind	men and women, humanity, humankind
the man in the street	people in general
layman	lay person
man-made	synthetic, artificial, manufactured
the rights of man	peoples'/citizens' rights, the rights of the individual
chairman	chairperson, chair
foreman	supervisor
manpower	workforce, staff, labour power
craftsman/men	craftsperson/people
manning	staffing, working, running
to a man	everyone, unanimously, without exception
man hours	work hours
the working man	workers, working people
one man show	one person show
forefathers	ancestors
founding fathers	founders
old masters	classic art/artists
masterful	domineering, very skilful
master copy	top copy, original
Dear Sirs	Dear Madam/Sir
Yours fraternally	Best wishes
policeman/fireman	police officer/fire fighter
businessmen	business people
waitress	server
male nurse	nurse

It is important, as the last three examples show, to avoid assuming that jobs are gender specific. Not all people who serve at tables in restaurants are waitresses. Not all nurses are female. Not all police officers are police*men*, not all fire fighters are fire*men*, nor are all business people business*men*. Managers may be male or female, so don't write things like 'managers and their wives'. Women managers do not have wives.

You should also avoid using 'he', 'his' and 'him' when you are referring to people who could be of either sex. *Both* masculine and feminine pronouns can be used where appropriate: 'he or she', 'her or him', and so on. (You can write 'he/she', or 's/he' or 'her/him', 'his/her', and so on, if you prefer although this is not always acceptable style.)

Extensive use of 'she or he', etc. does tend to be rather clumsy and there are other strategies you could adopt.

1. The use of the plural. For example:

   Sexist
   Each respondent was asked whether *he* wished to participate in the survey.
   Anti-sexist
   The respondents were asked whether *they* wished to participate in the survey.

2. The omission of third person pronouns altogether. For example:

   Sexist
   The child should be given ample time to familiarise *himself* with the test material.
   Anti-sexist
   Ample time should be given for the child to become familiar with the test material.

'Ladies', 'Girls' and Women
The words 'boys' and 'gentlemen' are rarely used to refer to men in written work or speech. It is patronising and offensive, as well as inaccurate, to use the term 'girls' to refer to adult women. This term should only be applied to female children. Similarly, teenage girls should not be referred to as 'young girls'. The term 'ladies' also has patronising overtones and should be avoided. Adult females should be referred to as women.

Heterosexism
The above guidelines are intended to help 'make women visible' in our work. In the face of growing homophobia, the BSA asks its members to consider the extent to which their work is heterosexist. For example, in discussions about two-earner households avoid assuming that the partnership consists of a man and a woman. In discussions about young women and sexuality, is it assumed that becoming 'sexually active' means becoming sexually active with men? Sociology is concerned with social realities in the world and we have a responsibility to reflect on and change heterosexist assumptions.

Adapted from *BSA Guidelines on Anti-sexist Language.*

relate to the argument. Do not simply pile in table after table, diagram after diagram, quote after quote without any comment or any attempt to relate them to the aims of the survey. If you do that then the report will be boring. More importantly, remember that data does *not* speak for itself. We saw this in Chapter 2 when we interpreted the same table in several different ways according to the theoretical perspective adopted by the interpreter.

Start with the aims and the context of the research. Refer early on to your aims and hypotheses (where appropriate) and use these to structure your report. Outline what your 'angle' is and use it as a theme running through the report to give the exploration of the data a focus. In the example in Chapter 4, the 'angle' was the 'moral panic' surrounding gays and lesbians towards the end of the 1980s. The specific issue of AIDS and the political initiative of the Conservative Government in undermining Labour local authorities was linked to the broader context of right-wing moralism and family values.

Report your data in a systematic way. If, for example, you are undertaking a statistical analysis of answers to a questionnaire, relate the data to your hypotheses. Examine each hypothesis in turn and use the data to confirm or deny the hypothesis. Be careful about being too assertive; you need to check that your results are statistically significant and that you have taken account of other factors that might have an effect before you can start talking about having 'proved' anything. Indeed, the best you can say is that your survey results make your hypotheses 'highly likely' or 'highly unlikely'. When using data to illustrate your hypotheses or to draw conclusions do so in a way that fits in with the main theme of the report. Do not put a table or chart in without explaining what it means. The text of your report should still make sense even if you take the data out. You should not rely on the reader making sense of your tables and diagrams for you.

When compiling a report you have to be selective about what empirical data to include. If your data is quantitative it is very tempting to include every percentage, frequency table, crosstabulation, diagram and chart that you have taken the trouble to work out or to draw. Similarly, if you have collected qualitative data it is tempting to report large chunks of interviews or to pile in all the interesting quotes. You must resist this. If your data do not add anything to your discussion, then there is no point in including them. You only need one or two examples to make a point. If you put too many quotes or statistics in a report the effect is counter-productive because they make the report less readable.

Similarly, when reporting quantitative data, avoid presenting all the statistics in the same format. Sometimes you only need the key figures from a frequency table and these can be included in the text. Sometimes you want the whole table so as to make the point more forcefully or because it is easier to make comparisons. Sometimes a shorter version of the table will do, or you may think that a bar chart or histogram makes the point better. You may want to include complete crosstabulations, but sometimes reporting a single cell percentage will do the job for you. Page after page of charts, frequency tables or crosstabulations are guaranteed to put the reader off.

We suggest that you structure your report in a way similar to the outline given in Table 8.2. You may not have much to say on some of these areas. You may not have been able to find much on the academic context if you are looking at a very unusual area. You may not feel you are in any position to make recommendations and you may think that combining summary and conclusions gives a better report. Table 8.2 is simply a guide and should not be used inflexibly.

You should avoid using the 'Findings' section to list page after page of data, graphs, tables or quotations with no link to the aims and objectives of the research. Some people do this and then hope a brief summary will provide a general picture and make sense of it for the reader. This frequently-used approach is bad practice. Discuss the data as you introduce it and make sure that you do so in relation to your aims. Ensure the discussion relates to your basic argument or 'angle'. The summary, which is optional, should simply pull out the main elements from the report as a whole.

We hope you have found this book useful in doing your project. We have suggested activities designed to help you get to grips with different approaches. We have also emphasised the link between theory and data. A *methodological* approach allows you to make those links and provides you with an appreciation of the kinds of knowledge different research approaches lead to. In the end, doing sociology is about relating sociological theory to the real world. This book has been about how you might do that and, as a result, bring sociology to life.

Further Reading

Unobtrusive measures: Webb *et al.* (1966).

Personal document analysis: Burgess (1982)

Triangulation: Burgess (1982); Denzin (1970); Smith, (1975).

Case study: Dixon *et al.* (1987); Yin (1984).

Table 8.2 Suggested structure for a sociological project report

Aims:	What you set out to find out.
Social context:	What aroused your interest and what the background to the study is.
Academic context:	What other work has been done in the area and how this relates to your aims.
Operationalisation:	Where appropriate, how you operationalised the concepts referred to in your aims.
Hypotheses:	What your specific hypotheses and sub-hypotheses are.
Method:	What approach you decided to adopt and why.
Techniques:	How you collected the information and the problems you encountered.
Findings:	If you undertook survey research, what you found out about each hypothesis. Or, if you did an ethnographic study, what themes emerged from your data? Relate these to your aims.
Sociological relevance:	How your findings relate to other sociological research and theory.
Summary:	What, overall, your research has shown.
Recommendations:	What recommendations, if any, you can make based on your research.
Conclusion:	What, if any, the implications are of your research for theory, practice and methodology.

APPENDIX 1   DATA FILE

```
001 2 2 1 2 1 1 1 1 9 9 9 1 9 9 1 9 1 2 1 6 1 6 0 9 0 9 1 1 1 2 2 2 2 17 17 02 01
002 1 1 1 2 1 1 2 2 1 9 9 1 1 1 1 1 2 18 21 18 18 1 1 1 2 1 2 2 18 14 03 01
003 2 1 2 1 1 2 1 2 1 9 9 9 1 1 9 1 9 1 1 21 21 16 16 2 1 1 1 1 1 2 18 14 03 01
004 2 1 2 2 2 1 2 1 1 9 9 9 2 2 1 2 2 2 18 18 09 09 2 9 9 2 1 1 2 18 14 03 01
005 2 1 2 1 2 1 1 2 1 1 9 1 1 9 1 9 1 1 18 18 09 09 1 9 1 9 2 1 2 18 19 01 01
006 2 1 2 1 2 1 9 1 1 9 1 1 9 1 1 1 16 16 16 16 2 2 2 2 1 2 18 19 03 01
007 1 1 1 2 2 2 2 2 9 9 9 1 1 1 2 1 2 18 21 18 18 2 1 1 2 1 2 2 19 19 03 01
008 1 1 2 2 1 1 2 1 2 1 9 9 9 1 1 1 1 1 2 16 21 16 16 2 2 2 9 1 2 18 24 03 01
009 1 1 2 1 1 1 2 1 1 1 1 1 1 2 1 2 1 9 21 21 09 09 2 2 2 2 1 2 22 02 29 03 01
010 2 1 2 1 2 1 1 2 9 1 9 1 1 1 2 1 1 21 25 09 09 1 9 9 2 9 2 2 16 19 03 01
011 2 1 2 1 2 2 1 2 1 1 9 9 9 9 9 1 9 9 1 18 18 18 22 2 2 1 16 15 03 01
012 2 1 2 1 2 1 2 1 2 1 9 9 9 9 1 1 1 1 1 16 16 09 09 1 1 1 2 2 2 16 19 03 01
013 9 1 2 1 2 2 2 9 1 9 1 9 1 1 1 2 1 1 16 16 78 78 2 1 1 2 1 2 2 16 19 03 01
014 2 9 1 9 9 2 1 9 9 9 9 1 1 1 1 2 1 1 16 16 09 09 1 2 2 2 1 1 1 16 19 03 01
015 2 1 1 1 2 2 2 1 9 9 9 1 1 1 1 1 1 1 2 1 21 21 16 16 1 1 1 2 2 2 2 17 11 03 01
016 1 1 2 2 2 1 1 1 9 9 9 1 1 1 1 1 1 2 21 21 16 16 2 2 2 1 1 2 17 14 03 01
017 1 1 1 1 9 2 1 1 1 1 1 1 9 1 9 1 1 1 16 16 16 16 1 1 1 2 2 2 17 13 03 01
018 2 1 2 1 2 2 2 1 9 9 9 1 1 1 1 2 1 2 16 16 09 09 9 9 1 1 2 2 2 17 19 03 01
019 1 1 1 2 1 2 1 1 1 9 9 9 1 9 9 9 9 2 09 21 16 16 1 1 1 2 1 2 2 17 14 03 01
020 2 1 2 2 9 1 1 1 9 9 9 1 9 9 1 9 1 9 1 2 21 21 09 09 2 1 1 2 2 2 17 14 03 01
021 1 1 1 1 2 2 2 1 1 9 1 1 1 1 1 1 6 21 09 09 1 1 1 2 2 2 1 17 14 03 01
022 2 1 1 2 2 2 2 1 9 9 9 1 2 1 2 1 2 2 1 21 09 09 1 1 2 2 2 2 17 14 03 01
023 2 1 9 2 1 2 2 2 9 9 9 1 1 1 1 1 1 2 1 21 16 25 1 2 1 2 1 2 17 14 03 01
024 2 1 1 9 2 2 1 2 9 9 9 1 9 9 9 9 1 2 18 21 16 16 2 2 1 2 9 2 2 17 14 03 01
025 2 1 1 2 2 1 1 1 1 9 9 9 1 1 1 1 1 1 1 21 21 18 18 1 2 1 2 1 2 2 17 11 03 01
026 2 1 2 1 2 1 1 1 9 9 9 9 9 1 9 1 9 2 09 21 09 09 2 1 2 1 2 2 17 15 03 01
027 2 1 1 1 2 2 1 2 9 9 1 1 9 9 9 9 2 09 09 16 16 1 2 1 2 9 2 2 17 20 03 01
028 2 1 2 1 2 2 2 1 9 9 9 1 1 1 1 1 2 1 21 09 09 1 1 2 2 2 2 17 13 09 01
029 2 1 1 2 2 2 2 2 9 1 1 1 9 9 9 9 1 2 1 21 14 15 2 2 1 1 1 2 1 17 14 03 01
030 2 1 2 2 2 1 2 9 9 1 1 9 9 1 9 9 2 18 18 21 21 2 2 2 2 1 1 1 17 17 02 01
031 9 1 9 1 2 2 2 9 9 9 9 1 1 1 9 9 9 1 21 21 16 16 9 9 9 2 1 9 9 17 13 03 01
032 2 1 2 9 2 9 2 1 9 9 9 1 1 1 1 1 1 2 1 21 09 09 1 1 1 2 2 2 2 17 13 03 01
033 2 1 2 1 2 2 9 9 1 1 1 1 1 1 1 1 1 2 16 16 09 09 2 1 1 2 2 2 2 17 14 03 01
034 1 1 1 2 2 2 2 1 1 9 1 1 1 1 1 2 1 1 21 21 18 18 2 1 1 1 1 1 1 18 14 03 01
035 2 1 1 2 2 2 1 2 1 9 9 9 9 9 9 9 1 1 16 21 16 14 2 2 1 2 1 2 2 18 19 01 01
036 2 1 1 2 1 2 1 2 1 9 9 9 9 9 9 1 2 1 21 16 99 1 2 1 2 2 2 18 14 03 01
037 2 1 1 1 2 2 1 1 1 1 1 2 1 1 1 09 21 16 21 1 1 2 1 2 1 18 19 03 01
038 1 1 1 2 2 2 2 1 1 1 1 1 1 1 1 1 2 18 18 17 17 2 1 1 2 2 2 18 19 03 01
039 1 1 2 1 1 2 1 2 1 9 9 9 1 9 9 9 1 21 21 09 09 1 1 1 1 1 1 1 18 14 03 01
040 2 1 2 1 1 1 2 1 1 9 9 1 9 9 1 9 1 2 16 21 16 16 2 2 2 2 2 2 2 18 11 03 01
041 2 1 1 2 2 2 2 1 9 9 9 1 2 1 2 1 2 2 21 21 21 21 2 1 2 1 2 2 18 13 03 01
042 2 1 2 1 2 1 1 1 9 9 9 9 1 2 1 2 1 1 18 18 80 80 2 1 2 2 1 2 2 18 15 03 01
043 2 1 2 2 1 1 9 9 9 1 1 1 1 1 1 1 1 2 1 21 09 09 1 1 1 2 2 2 2 18 13 09 01
044 2 1 1 2 2 2 2 1 9 9 9 1 1 1 1 1 1 1 21 21 09 09 1 1 1 2 2 2 2 18 11 03 01
045 2 1 1 2 2 2 2 1 9 9 9 1 9 9 9 9 1 2 1 21 21 18 18 2 2 2 2 1 1 18 19 03 01
046 2 1 1 1 2 1 1 1 9 9 9 1 1 1 1 1 2 1 21 21 16 16 2 1 1 1 2 1 1 18 19 03 01
047 2 1 1 2 1 1 9 9 9 1 2 1 2 1 2 1 1 21 21 09 09 1 1 2 2 2 2 18 11 03 01
048 2 1 2 2 2 1 9 9 9 1 1 2 2 1 1 09 09 98 98 1 1 1 2 2 2 2 18 15 03 01
049 2 1 1 2 2 2 2 1 9 9 9 1 2 1 2 1 1 2 18 18 11 1 1 2 2 2 2 18 19 03 01
050 2 1 1 1 1 2 1 1 9 9 1 1 1 1 9 1 2 16 16 18 18 2 2 2 2 1 2 2 18 14 03 01
051 2 1 1 2 1 2 2 1 9 9 9 1 2 1 2 1 2 25 21 18 18 2 1 1 2 2 2 1 18 14 03 01
052 2 1 1 2 2 2 1 9 9 9 1 2 1 2 1 1 2 16 21 18 18 1 1 2 2 99 1 19 14 03 01
053 2 1 2 2 2 2 2 1 9 9 9 1 1 2 1 2 16 21 16 21 2 2 2 2 1 1 19 19 03 01
054 2 1 2 2 2 2 2 2 9 9 9 1 1 1 1 1 2 09 21 80 98 1 1 1 2 2 2 19 19 03 01
055 2 1 2 2 2 1 2 2 1 9 9 1 1 9 1 9 1 1 21 21 09 09 2 1 1 2 2 1 1 19 14 03 01
056 2 1 2 1 2 1 2 2 1 1 1 1 1 2 2 1 1 1 21 21 17 17 2 1 1 2 2 2 2 19 19 03 01
057 2 1 2 1 2 1 1 1 1 1 1 1 2 1 1 1 1 16 21 09 09 2 2 2 2 2 2 2 19 14 03 01
058 1 1 2 1 2 2 1 9 1 9 9 1 9 1 1 9 1 1 18 18 10 99 2 1 1 1 1 1 19 19 03 01
059 2 1 1 1 1 2 2 2 1 9 9 9 1 1 1 1 2 09 21 12 12 1 1 1 2 2 20 13 03 01
060 1 1 1 1 1 2 1 1 1 9 9 9 1 1 1 1 9 1 18 18 09 09 1 1 1 2 1 2 2 18 17 02 02
061 1 1 1 1 1 2 1 1 1 9 1 9 1 1 1 1 1 1 2 16 16 09 09 1 1 1 9 1 2 2 18 17 02 02
062 1 1 2 2 1 1 1 1 1 1 9 1 1 1 1 1 2 2 21 21 16 16 2 2 2 2 1 1 1 18 11 03 02
063 1 1 1 2 1 1 1 9 9 9 1 1 1 1 1 2 1 2 18 18 21 21 2 1 2 9 11 18 17 02 02
064 1 1 1 2 1 1 2 2 9 1 9 1 1 1 2 1 2 18 18 20 20 2 1 1 2 1 2 1 19 15 03 02
065 2 1 1 2 2 2 2 1 9 9 9 1 1 2 1 1 2 2 21 21 21 21 2 1 1 1 1 2 1 19 17 02 02
066 2 1 1 2 2 1 2 1 1 9 1 9 9 9 1 9 1 2 16 16 16 16 2 2 2 1 1 1 1 19 19 03 02
067 1 1 2 1 2 2 2 2 1 9 9 9 1 1 1 2 1 2 21 21 18 18 2 2 2 1 9 9 9 20 15 01 02
068 1 1 2 1 1 1 1 9 9 9 9 1 1 1 1 1 1 9 09 09 09 09 2 9 9 9 1 9 9 17 21 03 02
069 2 1 2 2 2 2 2 1 9 9 9 1 1 1 1 1 1 2 21 21 21 21 2 2 2 2 1 2 2 17 25 09 02
070 2 1 1 1 2 1 2 1 9 9 9 9 1 1 1 1 2 1 2 16 21 18 18 2 1 1 9 9 2 2 17 25 03 02
071 1 1 1 1 2 1 2 1 1 9 1 1 9 9 1 9 1 2 09 21 21 21 2 2 2 1 1 2 2 17 25 03 02
072 1 1 1 1 2 1 1 1 1 1 1 1 1 1 1 1 1 2 16 16 16 16 1 1 1 2 1 2 2 17 24 03 02
073 2 1 9 2 2 2 1 2 9 1 9 9 9 1 1 1 1 2 09 21 09 09 2 1 1 2 1 2 2 19 18 29 01 02
074 2 1 1 1 1 1 1 1 1 1 1 1 9 1 9 1 2 1 21 21 21 21 1 2 1 2 1 2 2 18 23 03 02
075 1 1 2 1 1 2 2 1 1 9 9 9 9 2 2 1 2 1 2 18 21 16 16 2 2 2 2 1 2 2 18 29 03 02
076 2 1 9 2 1 1 2 1 2 1 1 9 9 1 1 1 1 2 1 2 2 1 21 09 09 2 2 2 9 9 9 18 25 09 02
```

```
077 2 1 2 2 1 1 2 1 2 1 1 9 9 1 1 1 1 1 9 1 1 21 21 18 18 2 1 1 2 2 9 9 18 27 02 02
078 1 1 2 2 2 2 2 1 9 9 9 1 1 1 1 2 2 2 09 21 21 21 21 2 1 1 2 1 1 1 18 23 01 02
079 2 1 1 2 1 1 1 1 9 9 9 1 1 2 1 1 1 2 2 21 21 18 18 2 1 1 2 1 1 1 18 29 03 02
080 1 1 2 2 2 9 2 1 1 9 1 1 1 1 1 2 1 2 25 25 09 09 2 1 1 2 2 2 1 18 24 03 02
081 1 1 2 2 1 2 2 2 1 9 9 9 1 1 1 1 1 2 09 21 16 16 2 1 1 1 1 1 1 18 25 03 02
082 1 1 1 2 1 1 1 1 1 9 9 9 1 1 1 1 2 1 09 21 16 16 2 1 1 1 9 2 2 18 22 03 02
083 1 1 2 2 1 1 2 1 9 9 9 1 2 1 2 1 2 2 21 21 21 21 2 1 1 2 1 9 9 18 24 03 02
084 2 1 1 1 2 2 2 9 1 1 9 1 9 9 9 2 9 9 16 21 16 16 2 2 2 1 9 9 9 18 24 03 02
085 2 1 2 2 1 1 1 1 9 9 9 1 1 9 1 9 1 1 09 09 09 09 1 1 1 2 1 2 2 19 27 02 02
086 2 1 2 2 9 2 1 9 1 1 1 2 1 1 09 09 09 09 1 1 2 2 2 2 19 27 02 02
087 2 1 1 2 1 1 1 1 1 1 1 1 1 1 1 1 2 21 21 21 21 2 1 2 1 2 2 19 24 03 02
088 2 1 2 2 2 2 1 1 9 9 9 1 1 1 1 1 1 25 21 16 16 2 2 2 1 1 2 2 19 23 03 02
089 1 1 2 2 2 2 1 9 9 9 1 9 9 1 9 9 2 16 21 18 18 2 1 1 2 1 9 9 20 27 02 02
090 1 1 1 2 1 1 2 1 2 1 9 9 9 1 1 1 1 2 21 21 21 2 1 8 1 8 19 19 12 22 16 13 03 02
091 1 1 2 1 1 1 1 1 1 1 1 2 1 2 18 18 19 19 1 2 2 2 1 18 02 02
092 2 1 1 1 2 2 1 9 9 9 9 1 9 19 11 18 18 21 20 1 1 1 2 2 2 2 18 80 02 02
093 2 1 2 1 2 1 2 1 9 9 9 1 1 1 1 1 1 18 18 20 20 2 1 1 2 2 2 2 18 17 02 02
094 2 1 1 2 1 2 2 2 1 9 9 1 1 2 1 2 1 2 09 21 09 09 2 1 1 2 1 2 2 17 23 01 02
095 2 1 9 2 2 1 2 1 9 1 1 1 2 2 1 2 1 2 18 18 18 18 2 1 1 1 1 1 17 22 02 02
096 2 1 2 1 2 1 1 1 1 1 1 1 1 2 1 8 18 18 18 18 1 1 1 2 1 2 2 17 17 02 02
097 1 1 1 2 1 2 1 2 1 9 1 1 9 1 9 9 9 1 09 21 98 98 1 99 19 92 2 18 12 03 02
098 1 1 2 2 1 2 1 1 1 1 1 1 1 1 1 2 09 21 09 09 2 2 2 1 1 1 1 18 19 03 02
099 2 1 2 1 1 2 2 2 1 1 1 1 9 1 9 1 1 18 18 16 16 1 1 1 2 2 2 2 18 18 03 02
100 2 1 2 1 2 2 2 2 1 9 9 9 9 1 9 9 9 9 1 18 18 25 25 2 1 2 2 2 2 18 18 02 02
101 2 1 2 1 2 1 1 1 9 9 9 1 1 1 2 18 18 18 18 1 1 1 2 1 1 16 27 02 02
102 2 1 1 2 2 1 1 1 1 1 1 1 1 1 2 18 18 20 20 2 1 1 2 1 1 1 16 28 02 02
103 2 1 2 2 1 1 1 1 9 9 1 9 9 9 9 1 1 2 1 21 21 21 21 1 1 1 2 2 2 2 16 27 02 02
104 2 1 1 2 2 2 2 1 9 9 9 1 1 1 1 1 2 18 18 21 21 2 1 1 2 2 2 2 16 27 02 02
105 2 1 2 1 2 1 2 1 9 9 1 1 9 9 2 18 18 18 18 9 1 1 1 2 1 2 2 16 22 02 02
106 2 1 1 1 2 2 2 2 9 9 9 1 1 1 1 1 9 2 1 09 21 09 09 2 1 1 2 2 2 2 16 23 01 02
107 2 1 1 1 2 2 1 1 1 1 1 1 1 9 16 16 09 09 1 1 1 2 1 2 2 17 25 01 02
108 1 1 2 2 1 1 2 1 1 9 9 1 9 19 1 9 1 2 21 21 21 21 2 1 1 2 1 2 2 17 27 02 02
109 2 1 2 2 2 2 1 1 9 9 1 2 2 1 2 2 2 18 18 20 20 2 1 1 2 1 2 2 17 22 02 02
110 1 1 2 2 1 1 2 1 2 1 9 9 9 1 1 1 2 1 2 09 21 16 16 2 2 2 1 1 1 1 17 28 02 02
111 2 1 2 2 1 1 2 1 2 1 9 1 9 1 2 1 2 1 2 18 18 18 18 2 2 2 2 1 1 1 17 22 02 02
112 2 1 2 1 1 2 1 2 1 2 1 9 9 1 1 1 2 1 21 21 21 21 2 1 1 1 1 1 1 18 28 02 02
113 2 1 1 1 1 9 1 1 9 9 9 1 9 1 9 9 1 1 21 21 09 09 1 1 1 2 1 1 1 18 23 01 02
114 1 1 2 1 1 1 2 1 1 9 9 1 9 9 1 9 9 2 21 21 18 18 2 2 2 1 1 1 1 18 28 02 02
115 2 1 2 2 2 2 1 2 1 1 9 9 9 1 1 1 1 1 1 21 21 09 09 1 1 2 1 1 1 1 18 24 03 02
116 1 1 2 2 2 1 2 1 2 1 9 9 9 1 9 9 9 1 2 21 21 20 20 1 1 1 2 1 1 1 16 22 03 03
117 2 1 2 2 2 2 2 1 1 9 9 9 1 1 1 1 2 1 1 21 21 16 16 1 1 2 1 2 2 16 23 03 03
118 2 1 2 2 2 2 2 9 9 9 1 1 1 1 1 1 2 16 16 18 18 2 1 1 2 1 2 2 17 24 03 03
119 2 1 2 9 9 2 1 9 1 1 1 1 1 9 1 1 16 16 16 16 16 1 1 1 2 1 2 2 17 24 03 03
120 2 1 2 2 2 2 1 2 1 1 9 9 9 1 1 1 1 2 2 21 21 18 18 2 2 2 2 1 2 2 17 23 03 03
121 1 1 2 2 2 1 1 2 1 2 1 9 9 9 1 1 1 1 2 16 21 16 16 2 2 2 1 1 2 1 17 29 03 03
122 2 1 2 1 2 1 1 9 1 1 9 2 2 1 2 1 16 16 18 18 2 2 2 1 1 2 2 17 24 03 03
123 2 1 1 2 1 2 1 2 1 1 1 9 9 1 1 9 1 1 09 09 09 09 1 1 1 2 1 2 2 18 24 03 03
124 1 1 1 1 2 1 1 2 2 1 9 9 9 1 9 9 1 9 1 2 16 21 18 18 2 2 2 1 2 2 2 18 23 03 03
125 2 1 2 2 2 1 1 9 9 9 1 1 9 1 9 9 2 18 18 18 18 18 1 1 1 2 1 2 2 18 24 03 03
126 2 1 9 2 2 2 1 9 9 9 9 1 1 1 1 1 2 16 16 18 20 2 1 1 2 1 2 2 18 23 03 03
127 2 1 2 2 2 1 2 1 1 9 9 9 1 1 1 1 1 2 16 16 18 18 2 1 2 1 2 1 1 18 24 03 03
128 1 1 2 1 2 1 1 9 1 9 1 1 1 1 1 1 2 21 21 20 20 2 2 2 1 1 1 1 18 29 03 03
129 2 1 2 2 1 2 1 1 9 1 9 1 1 1 1 1 1 1 09 09 09 09 1 1 1 2 1 2 2 18 23 03 03
130 2 1 1 2 2 2 1 9 9 9 1 1 1 9 9 1 09 09 09 09 1 1 1 2 1 2 2 18 25 03 03
131 2 1 1 2 2 9 1 9 9 9 1 1 1 2 1 6 16 16 18 18 2 2 2 2 2 2 2 18 24 03 03
132 2 1 1 2 1 2 1 1 9 1 1 9 1 1 1 1 1 2 16 16 21 21 1 1 2 2 2 2 18 24 03 03
133 2 1 1 2 2 2 9 9 9 1 1 1 1 1 1 1 2 18 18 21 21 2 1 1 1 2 2 2 18 25 03 03
134 1 1 1 2 2 2 1 9 1 9 1 1 1 1 2 2 2 1 21 21 21 21 2 1 1 2 1 1 1 19 24 03 03
135 2 1 2 2 2 2 1 2 1 1 1 1 2 1 1 1 2 21 21 35 30 2 1 1 2 1 2 1 19 23 03 03
136 1 1 1 2 2 1 1 1 9 9 1 1 1 1 1 1 2 18 21 21 21 21 2 1 1 1 1 1 2 2 19 29 03 03
137 2 1 2 1 2 1 2 1 1 1 1 1 2 1 2 1 1 21 21 16 16 2 9 9 1 2 2 2 20 25 03 03
138 1 1 2 1 2 1 1 9 9 9 1 1 1 1 1 9 2 1 16 16 21 21 1 1 1 1 1 1 1 20 21 03 03
139 2 1 9 2 1 1 1 1 1 9 1 1 1 1 1 2 21 21 21 21 2 1 1 1 1 2 2 20 24 03 03
140 1 1 1 2 2 2 2 1 9 9 1 1 1 1 1 1 2 09 21 18 18 2 1 1 9 22 20 29 03 03
141 1 1 1 1 1 1 2 2 9 9 9 1 2 1 2 1 2 2 21 21 21 21 2 1 2 1 1 1 1 20 24 03 03
142 1 1 1 1 2 2 1 1 1 1 1 1 1 1 1 2 18 21 21 21 2 1 1 1 1 2 2 20 29 03 03
143 2 1 1 2 2 2 1 9 9 9 1 9 1 9 1 2 2 1 09 09 21 21 09 09 2 1 9 9 20 29 03 03
144 2 1 1 2 2 9 9 9 9 1 1 1 2 1 6 16 09 09 1 1 1 1 1 2 16 14 03 03
145 2 1 9 9 9 9 9 2 1 9 9 9 1 1 1 2 1 1 09 21 18 30 2 2 1 2 1 2 2 17 19 01 03
146 2 1 2 2 2 2 1 2 9 9 9 1 1 1 1 1 1 2 21 21 50 60 2 2 2 2 1 2 2 17 19 01 03
147 1 1 9 2 2 2 1 2 9 9 9 1 1 9 1 9 1 1 1 1 1 6 21 21 21 21 1 1 1 9 9 18 12 03 03
148 1 1 2 2 1 2 1 9 9 9 1 1 9 9 9 9 1 2 16 21 09 16 2 9 2 1 2 2 19 13 03 03
149 1 1 2 1 2 1 1 9 9 1 9 9 1 1 9 1 1 2 21 21 18 18 1 2 1 2 2 19 19 09 03 03
150 1 1 9 1 1 2 2 1 1 9 2 2 2 1 1 2 18 21 21 21 21 2 1 1 2 1 2 2 20 19 03 03
151 2 1 1 2 2 9 1 1 9 1 9 1 1 1 1 1 2 21 21 21 21 2 1 1 1 1 1 1 22 18 25 03 03
```

235

APPENDIX 2 DATA ANALYSIS

In this appendix we explore data analysis techniques in a little more detail, concentrating on what data analysis is about rather than on statistical computations. You are advised to consult the statistics texts referred to in the further reading suggestions in Chapter 4 if you want to develop your statistical expertise. More and more students use data analysis packages on computers, so it is important to understand what you can do and what the statistics show rather than how to compute advanced statistics.

We will link the discussion to the sample survey discussed in Chapter 4. The hypotheses are in Example Answer 4.6. The questionnaire is Extract 4.3. The coding frame is Extract 4.7. The data set is in Appendix 1.

Testing hypothesis 1

To test hypothesis 1 (the population are hostile to gays and lesbians) we need data on peoples' attitudes as to whether homosexuality should be legal (variable 23 (V23)); on what they think the consenting age for adults should be (V21 and V22); on attitudes to gay and lesbian families (V28 and V29); and views on public homosexual affectionate acts (V24 and V25).

Frequency tables

Frequency tables provide a count of the number in the sample who fall into each *value* of the *variable*. They can also be drawn up to show the appropriate percentages (see Chapter 4). Table A2.1 is the frequency table for V23 'Should homosexuality be made illegal?'.

From Table A2.1 we can see that 30.8% of those who answered the question think that homosexuality should be made illegal .

Table A2.2 shows what people think should be the consenting age for men (V22). This suggests that the sample do not support the sub-hypothesis (1b). Of those who answered the question, 67.6% think the age of consent for gays should be under 21 and only 9.0% think it should be over 21. Indeed, these results make our sample appear to be more progressive than Members of Parliament (MPs) as only 43.6% of a sample of MPs favoured a reduction in the age of consent (see Chapter 4, example answer to Student Activity 4.4).

However, the values in Table A2.2 range from 12 to 98. The six high ages of 60 or more, suggest that the respondents are opposed to homosexuality, and this may well be the case for most of the 40 missing values. Thus there are 30.6% of the sample who have given no answer or a very high one. This is virtually the same percentage as think homosexuality should be illegal.

So, in this case, a more reasonable estimate of percentage who favoured a lower age limit would be one based on the *entire sample*, whether they answered the question or not. From Table A2.3 we can see that 75 (49.7%) of the whole sample of 151 indicated that the age limit should be reduced. This is similar to the proportion for MPs (43.6%) who think the age limit should be reduced.

Note there are no value labels for Table A2.2 as the values themselves refer to ages in years, except the value 9 which is the code for missing values.

Table A2.1 V23 *Should homosexuality be illegal?*

Value label	Value	Frequency	Percent age	Valid percentage
Yes	1	44	29.1	30.8
No	2	99	65.6	69.2
Missing	9	8	100.0	
Total		151	100.0	100.0

Valid cases 143   Missing cases 8

Table A2.2 V22 *What should the consenting age be for men?*

Value	Frequency	Percentage	Valid percentage	Cumulative percentage
12	1	0.7	0.9	0.9
14	2	0.7	0.9	1.8
15	1	0.7	0.9	2.7
16	28	18.5	25.2	27.9
17	2	1.3	1.8	29.7
18	33	21.9	29.7	59.5
19	1	0.7	0.9	60.4
20	8	5.3	7.2	67.6
21	26	17.2	23.4	91.0
25	2	1.3	1.8	92.8
30	2	1.3	1.8	94.6
60	1	0.7	0.9	95.5
78	1	0.7	0.9	96.4
80	1	0.7	0.9	97.3
98	3	2.0	2.7	100.0
Missing	40	26.5		
Total	151	100.0	100.0	

Valid cases 111   Missing cases 40

Table A2.3 V22 *What should the consenting age be for men?*

Value	Frequency	Percentage	Valid percentage	Cumulative percentage
Under 21	75	49.7	67.6	67.6
21	26	17.2	23.4	91.0
Over 21	10	6.6	9.0	100.0
Missing	40	26.5		
Total	151	100.0	100.0	

Valid cases 111   Missing cases 40

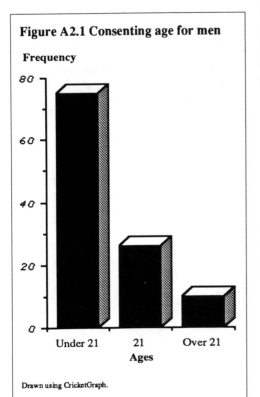

Figure A2.1 Consenting age for men

Frequency

Drawn using CricketGraph.

NOTE Apple Macintosh and IBM-PC compatible versions of the datafile and SPSS-PC+ 'include file' program to generate tables and crosstabulations are available, on floppy disk, from Lee Harvey (see details on page 268).

There is also a *cumulative percentage* column in this table. The cumulative percentage adds up the valid percentages as you go down the table. In the example, 0.9% think the consenting age should be 12, 1.8% think it should be 14 or less, 2.7% think it should be 15 or less, and so on. Thus 59.5% of the valid responses think it should be 18 or less.

Table A2.3 is a representation of Table A2.2 with various categories combined so as to make the data easier to grasp.

Graphical representation

Frequency tables can also be presented in diagrammatic form (as we saw in Chapter 3). You might feel that a bar chart, histogram or pie chart would represent the data in a more accessible or easily understood way than the frequency table. If so, include diagrams in your report rather than just use tables, although make sure you give them a title and label them properly. The choice is yours and you should do whatever makes the report most readable. It is, however, inadvisable to present all your data in the same diagrammatic way. A report full of pie charts, however colourful they may be, is just as boring as one that has endless frequency tables. Figure A2.1, produced using a graphics pack, is the histogram for the data in Table A2.3, and it shows at a glance what are the popular ages of consent.

> **Student Activity A2.1**
> **Compile the frequency table for the age of consent for women (V21) and draw a histogram to represent the table.**
> **SUGGESTION Use a computerised graphics pack if you have access to one.**

It is important, however, to note that there is no point in including tables or diagrams without analysing what they mean and showing how they relate to your hypotheses. Do not fill your report up with tables and diagrams and hope that somehow they speak for themselves. Without some commentary they are a waste of space.

Averages

We can work out the *average* age of consent that the sample thinks appropriate for gays. Sometimes data is best summarised as an average, especially for comparison purposes. For example, we might be interested in working out the average age of consent for males (V22, see Table A2.1) and comparing it with the average for females (V21).

At this point, if you are not confident with numbers, you might be thinking that this definitely looks like bad news. Working out averages, like all the other calculations in this appendix, is not as hard as it might seem. All you have to do is to follow the stages. They are quite simple and you certainly do not have to be a mathematician. Of course, you may have a computer that will work out any average you want in a fraction of a second and save you time and effort. What is important is not working out the average but knowing what it means when you have got it.

The 'average' for a variable is a single figure that is representative of all the values of the variable. It is some sort of middle figure. More accurately, 'averages' are known as *measures of central tendency*. There are several different 'averages' or measures of central tendency that you could use.

Mode

The simplest one is the *mode*. This is the value for a variable that occurs most often. From Table A2.1 we can see that '18 years old' is the age that more people choose than any other. (The 39 people whose answer is missing are excluded and we have a sample of 112.)

Median

The *median* is the value that lies in the middle of the distribution when all the values are put in rank order. The easiest way to locate the median is to look down the *cumulative percentage* column and locate which value corresponds to 50% (half way). In Table A2.1, 33% of the sample think the age should be 17 or less and 65.2% think it should be 18 or less. So the middle (that is, 50%) value will be 18. (Some people attempt to work out what the exact value is in years and months assuming that the 18-year-olds are spread evenly throughout the year, but this is usually unnecessary.)

Arithmetic mean

The *arithmetic mean* (which is often called *the* average) is the total of all the values of a variable divided by the number in the sample. We have 112 values for V21 so we need to compute the total of the 112 ages. We do it as in Table A2.4. The result is an arithmetic mean of 22.198 years.

The arithmetic mean gives a much larger value of the average than either the mode or the median. Which average is the best? The answer to that depends in the first instance on the *level of measurement* or scale of the data. This relates to the type of data that is being 'averaged'. Broadly speaking, social research data is either nominal, ordinal or interval.

Levels of measurement

Where data can only be grouped into broad categories of agreement such as 'yes' or 'no', or into religious categories such as 'Christian', 'Muslim', 'Sikh' or 'Atheist', then we have *nominal* data. People are put into *named categories* but there is no sense in which these categories can be put in any order. This is the lowest level of data.

Where the categories can be put in some sort of *order* then the data is said to be *ordinal*. Questions where people rank their preferences are examples of ordinal data, as are answers to questions where the choices range from 'strongly agree' through 'agree' and 'disagree' to 'strongly disagree'. Ordinal data is said to be of a higher level than nominal data.

Where the categories are ordered and the gap between the categories is of equal size then the data is said to be *interval* scale. The usual units of measurement such as miles, litres, kilograms and minutes are all interval, as are incomes measured in numbers of dollars or pounds. Interval scale data is of a higher level than ordinal data.

Table A2.4. Calculation of the mean age for V22 *What should the consenting age be for men?*

Value x	Frequency f	Frequency * Value fx
12	1	12
14	1	14
15	1	15
16	28	448
17	2	34
18	33	594
19	1	19
20	8	160
21	26	546
25	2	50
30	2	60
60	1	60
78	1	78
80	1	80
98	3	294
	Total fx	2464

* multiplied by

Sample size = total frequency = 111

The arithmetic mean thus equals the total number of years (Total fx) divided by the sample size, i.e.,

$$2464 \div 111 = 22.198$$

or

$$22.2 \text{ (to one decimal place).}$$

Student Activity A2.2
What scale of data are variables V1, V9, V30, V31 and V34 in the example survey?

In deciding the best average you need to take account of the scale of the data. You need *interval* scale data to work out the *arithmetic mean,* as the actual size of each value is important.

You need at least *ordinal* scale data to work out the *median* because you need to put data in rank order. You cannot work out the median religion, for example, as there is no way they can be ranked in order.

The *mode* can be computed for *nominal* or higher-level data. If you can put things in categories you can work out which category has the most in it. So you could work out the modal religion for a sample of people.

The example data in Table A2.2 is interval scale as it measures age in years. So we can use any of the three measures meaningfully. As it is high-level data, the first preference is the arithmetic mean because it takes account of all the values. However, we might want to think about the median in this case because the mean is being made artificially high by the half-dozen very high ages. They have tended to drag the value of the mean upwards because they are so disproportionately large. The median, on the other hand, simply regards these large values as 'above the middle' and disregards their actual size. So where an interval scale data distribution is skewed to one side then it is worth considering using the median as a better indication of average than the mean.

We would not normally take the mode in this circumstance as it does not take into account the other values at all. It is more or less by chance that it happened to be the same as the median in this case and it could easily have been '16' or even '21'. The mode is really only of any use with interval scale data when the distribution has a single peak, as in Table A2.3; unlike Table A2.2 where there are three separate peaks.

Student Activity A2.3
Compute the arithmetic mean, median and mode for the age of consent for women (V21) and compare them with those for men (V22).

Summing up hypothesis 1

Hypothesis 1, which posits hostility towards gays and lesbians, has three parts. First, that homosexuality should be illegal. We have seen that there are twice as many people who think homosexuality should be legal as those who think it should be made illegal.

Second, that the age limit for consenting adults should be raised. We have seen that half the entire sample thought that the age limit for consenting gays and lesbians should be reduced. The median age suggested by the sample was 18 for both gays and lesbians.

The third item was acceptance of gay and lesbian families. The majority of the sample were opposed to gays (74.6%) and lesbians (69.6%) raising children in a family situation. You can check these figures for yourself from the data file in Appendix 1.

Respondents were invited to make general comments at the end of the questionnaire and some took the opportunity to explain the reasons for their answer to this question. Where appropriate, you should make use of any relevant comments provided by respondents if it helps in the elaboration of your analysis, as in this case, and include them in your report. The main reasons given for not agreeing to gay couples raising children were that the child would grow up to see homosexuality as normal and would not have the benefit of a conventional, heterosexual family upbringing. Some people commented that having gay parents would lead to the child growing up to be gay because that would be the only relationship of which the child would be aware. In these comments there was an implicit assumption that socialisation which promoted positive images of homosexuality was undesirable. This clearly reflects the dominant heterosexist ideology and the reassertion of family values.

The first two items suggest that the sampled population is more tolerant than hostile towards gays and lesbians. However, that tolerance is tempered by the views of the sample on gay and lesbian relationships as suitable family environments. While homosexuality is broadly viewed with a degree of tolerance it is still seen as a deviation from the heterosexist norm.

Student Activity A2.4
What proportion of people think that gays and lesbians should restrict affectionate acts to the privacy of their own home? Given this additional information, what would be your initial assessment of hypothesis 1?

We have assessed hypothesis 1 on the basis of frequency tables, making use of percentages and averages.

Our conclusions have been presented as initial assessments rather than definitive proof or disproof. There are two reasons for this lack of expressed certainty. First, we have only looked at the overall frequencies for each variable and have not considered *other factors* that might affect the results. Second, the results relate to the *sample* and we have to be careful about generalising about the population from which the sample was drawn because of the problems of sample bias and sampling error.

Crosstabulation

Frequency tables are a useful start when analysing data but they only provide a descriptive summary of the answers to the questions. They do not provide explanations. For example, we know how many people had heard of Clause 28 (Table 4.4, on page 128) but the frequency table does not tell us anything about those who had, and those who had not, heard of the clause.

An important analytic technique in sociology is the use of *crosstabulation*. It allows data to be broken down. Instead of having a table for the entire sample, it allows you to break down the frequency table to take account of a related variable. For example, as part of the analysis of hypothesis 3 we want to find out whether knowing about Clause 28 is related to the age of the respondent. So we construct the crosstabulation of the answer to question 1 (V1) by age (V30).

We have done this in Table A2.5. As there were not many sixteen or twenty-year-olds in the sample we have combined the sixteen and seventeen-year-olds into one group (value 1), left the eighteen-year-olds to make up the second group (value 2) and put the nineteen and twenty-year-olds together to form a third group (value 3).

Each 'cell' of the table has three figures in it. The top one is the actual

Table A2.5 Crosstabulation: V1 *Had you previously heard of Clause 28?* **by V30** *Age in years*

Count Row % Col %	V30			Row Total
	16 or 17 (1)	18 (2)	19 or 20 (3)	
V1				
Yes (1)	12 24.0 22.2	23 46.0 36.5	15 30.0 46.9	50 33.6%
No (2)	42 42.4 77.8	40 40.4 63.5	17 17.2 53.1	99 66.4%
Column Total	54 36.2%	63 42.3%	32 21.5%	149 100%

number of people that fall into that category, the *count*. For example, 23 eighteen-year-olds had heard of Clause 28. The second figure in each cell is the *row percentage*, that is, the percentage of the total for the row that falls into the cell. So the 23 eighteen-year-olds that had heard of Clause 28 made up 46% of total of 50 people who had heard of Clause 28. The third figure is the *column percentage*; this is the percentage of the total for the column that falls into the cell. So again, the 23 eighteen-year-olds who had heard of the clause constituted 36.5% of the total sample of 63 eighteen-year-olds.

If you are constructing crosstabulations by hand the easiest way of doing this is as follows. Make a grid with large squares. You need as many squares across the page as there are values of the first variable and as many squares down the page as there are values of the second variable. Leave room for labels on the rows and columns. Draw another separate box and mark it 'missing values'. You now need to look at both the columns that represent the variables to be crosstabulated. Go down the two columns row by row and put a mark in the appropriate square of the grid for each row. If a row has missing values in either column put a mark in the missing value box. At the end you should have as many marks as you have rows in the data file. Now count up the number of marks in each box. This is the 'count' for each cell in a crosstabulation. This is a slow, time-consuming and boring activity to do by hand and a computer program that does this for you makes life much easier.

Student Activity A2.5
Look at Table A2.5.
1. **How many people are there in the sample? Why do you think this is less than the total sample of 151?**
2. **What percentage of the sample were over over the age of eighteen?**
3. **What percentage of over eighteen-year-olds had not heard of the clause?**
4. **How many people in total said they had not heard of the clause? What percentage of the valid sample is this?**
5. **What percentage of people aged eighteen had heard of the clause?**
6. **What percentage of those who had heard of the clause were eighteen?**
7. **Is there any relationship between age and awareness of the clause?**

There were 23 eighteen-year-olds who said they had heard of Clause 28. It is important to note that the percentage of people who had heard of the clause who were eighteen (the row percentage = 46%) is *not* the same as the percentage of eighteen-year-olds who had heard of the clause (the column percentage = 36.5%). This is not a trick of the data. The two figures represent very different things.

The *row* per cent in this case says that, of all the people in the sample who had heard of the clause, 46% were eighteen years old. Compare this to the percentage of people who had heard of the clause who were under eighteen years old (24%) and the percentage of those who had heard of the clause who were over eighteen years old (30%).

The *column* per cent says that 36.5% of eighteen-year-olds had heard of the clause. Compare this to 22.2% of under-eighteens who had heard of the clause and 46.9% of over-eighteens who had. If we take the *row percentages* it appears that the eighteen-year-old group is more informed about the clause than any other group. Yet if we take the *column percentages* it is the over-eighteen group that has the highest percentage of people who had heard of the clause. How can we explain this and which figure do we use?

The reason the eighteen-year-old group has the highest *row percentage* of 'yes' responses is because there are more eighteen-year-olds in the sample. In fact, there are twice as many eighteen-year-olds as over-eighteens. So it is not surprising that there are more of them in the 'Yes' row. To use the row percentages and claim that the eighteen-year-olds are more likely to have heard of the clause is misleading, as the higher percentage simply reflects a larger sample of eighteen-year-olds.

The correct comparison is the *column percentage*, as this takes into account the different sample sizes for each age group. We can then conclude that the older the respondent the more likely they are to have heard of the clause.

It is not always the case that the column percentage is the correct one for comparison purposes. The decision whether to use the row or column percentage depends on which variable is the *independent* variable and which is the *idependent*. The dependent variable is the one that may be effected by the independent variable. In the example, the age is independent and the knowledge of the clause is dependent. After all, knowing about Clause 28 may be dependent on how old the respondent is, that is, the older the respondent the more likely she or he is to have come across the clause. There is no possibility that the respondent's age is dependent upon knowing about the clause! The percentage you then use for comparison is the percentage for the independent variable. If the independent variable is the column variable then you use the column percentage, as in Table A2.5. If the independent variable is the row variable then you use the row percentage.

We can see from this crosstabulation, if we take the column percentages, that more than twice as many older students had heard of the clause than younger ones. This suggests that there is a relationship between age and awareness of the clause. We can say that it seems as though the two variables are *associated*.

Student Activity A2.6
1. Construct a crosstabulation for the answer to question 1 (V1) by sex of the respondent (V31). Is there a larger percentage of women than men who have heard of the clause?
2. Construct the crosstabulation to find out whether more men than women agree with Clause 28. What conclusions can you draw about hypothesis 3?
3. Construct other suitable crosstabulations to analyse hypotheses 4 and 5.

For most students, this will be about as far as you will want or need to go in analysing survey data (especially if you do not have anything approaching random samples).

Measures of dispersion

Sometimes you want to know more than just the average of the data; you also want to know how spread out it is. For example, the data in Table A2.2 covers a wide range of years which we have no idea about just from the average. We can also measure how spread out the data is. Measures that do this are called measures of *dispersion*. There are two commonly-used ones: the range and the standard deviation.

Example answer to Student Activity A2.6, part 3

In this example answer we will just consider the first part of hypothesis 4 and leave you to anlayse the rest. The hypothesis suggests that hostility towards gays and lesbians and support of government and media campaigns will be reduced if the respondent has friends or family members who are gay or lesbian.

An initial indicator of hostility is whether the respondent thinks homosexuality should be illegal. Table A2.6 shows that only 8.3% of those people who have gay acquaintances support the illegalising of homosexuality while 38.1% of those who do not have gay acquaintances support illegalisation.

Table A2.6 Crosstabulation: V23 *Should homosexuality be illegal?* **by V26** *Are any of your friends or family gay or lesbian?*

Count Row % Col %	V26		Row Total
	Yes (1)	No (2)	
V23			
Yes (1)	3	40	43
	7.0	93.0	30.5%
	22.2	36.5	
No (2)	33	65	98
	33.7	66.3	69.5%
	91.7	61.9	
Column Total	36	105	149
	25.5%	74.5%	100%

The impact on attitude of having gay acquaintances is, however, more marked for females than males, as we can see from the three-way crosstabulation. Table A2.7 (which is just for the males in the sample) shows that amongst males with gay acquaintances 20% thought homosexuality should be illegal.

Table A2.8 (which is just for the females in the sample) shows that 0% of females with gay acquaintances thought homosexuality should be illegal (the cell is empty).

Dividing crosstabulations in this way is known as *multivariate analysis* because you are considering more than two variables at once; in this case V23, V26 and V31. Sex (V31) is known as the *control variable* in the example, because V23 is crosstabulated with V26 controlling for V31.

Thus we can say that attitudes about making homosexuality illegal are effected by whether or not the respondent has gay acquaintances (Table A2.6). However, it is a factor that has more effect on women than men (Tables A2.7 and A2.8).

We could also check the data for example, to see whether it is a factor that effects older, rather than younger respondents. How would you do this?

Table A2.7 Crosstabulation: V23 *Should homosexuality be illegal?* **by V26** *Are any of your friends or family gay or lesbian?* **Controlling for V31** *Sex = Male*

Count Row % Col %	V26		Row Total
	Yes (1)	No (2)	
V23			
Yes (1)	3	28	43
	9.7	91.3	40.8%
	20.0	45.9	
No (2)	12	33	98
	26.7	73.3	59.2%
	80.0	54.1	
Column Total	15	61	76
	19.7%	80.3%	100%

Table A2.8 Crosstabulation: V23 *Should homosexuality be illegal?* **by V26** *Are any of your friends or family gay or lesbian?* **Controlling for V31** *Sex = Female*

Count Row % Col %	V26		Row Total
	Yes (1)	No (2)	
V23			
Yes (1)	0	12	12
	0.0	100.0	18.5%
	0.0	27.3	
No (2)	21	32	53
	39.6	60.4	81.5%
	100.0	72.7	
Column Total	21	44	65
	32.3	67.7%	100%

The range

The range is the difference between the highest and lowest value for a variable. When the data is interval the range can be expressed as a single number. The range for the ages in Table A2.2 is $98 - 12 = 86$ years. We can also talk about a range of ordinal values from 'strongly agree to strongly disagree'. It is not really meaningful to talk about the range of nominal categories, such as 'Design and Printing' to 'Catering and Tourism' (V34 in the survey) as this provides us with no way of knowing that 'Government and Sociology' students are included in the 'range'.

Standard deviation

The *standard deviation* is the most useful measure of dispersion for a number of reasons, not all of which are initially apparent. Its most obvious advantage is that it takes into account all the data in a distribution, as does the arithmetic mean. The standard deviation is a measure of the dispersion around the arithmetic mean and thus you require *interval* scale date before you can calculate it. Like the arithmetic mean, the standard deviation is distorted by highly *skewed* data.

The standard deviation is, at first glance, a peculiar measure. It is the square root of the *variance*. The variance is defined as the *mean of the squared deviation of each value of the variable from the mean of the variable*. That sounds like gibberish and if you have not come across it before you are probably wondering whether it is us or you who have gone mad. Bear with it while we explain what it involves in practice.

1. Work out the arithmetic mean of the values in the sample.

2. Work out the difference between the mean and the value for each value in the sample (that is, subtract the mean from each separate value in the sample).

3. Square all the differences (the minus differences all become positive).

4. Add up all the differences. (This gives you the total of the squared differences.)

5. Divide the total by the sample size. (This gives you the mean of the differences from the mean = the variance.)

6. Take the square root of the answer (this is the standard deviation).

This appears to be rather complicated just to measure the spread of a distribution, and conceptually it is a bit cumbersome. However, it is a measure that takes account of the values in a frequency table, unlike the range which is only concerned with the extremes. In addition it is an important measure of dispersion when it comes to making generalisations from samples of interval scale data.

The following formula provides a short cut for working out the variance from a frequency table:

variance $= $ (total fx^2)/n $-$ (Mean of x)^2

where x is a value of the variable,
$/ = \div$,
n = sample size,
f = frequency.
Mean of x = total fx/n.

Table A2.9 Calculation of standard deviation

Value x	Frequency f	Frequency * Value fx	Frequency * Value squared fx*x
12	1	12	144
14	1	14	196
15	1	15	225
16	28	448	7168
17	2	34	578
18	33	594	10692
19	1	19	361
20	8	160	3200
21	26	546	11466
25	2	50	1250
30	2	60	1800
60	1	60	3600
78	1	78	6084
80	1	80	6400
98	3	294	28812
Totals		2464	81976

Total fx = 2464.
Total fx^2 = 81976.
Sample size = n = 111.

So (total fx^2)/n = 81976 $\div$ 111 = 738.5225

Mean of x = total fx/n = 2464 $\div$ 111 = 22.198

(Mean of x)^2 = 21.198^2 = 492.7512

So variance = 738.5225 $-$ 492.7512 = 245.7713

Standard deviation is square root of 245.7718

Standard deviation = 15.677

Before you decide that you have seen quite enough formulas and this one is beyond a joke, don't give up because this is actually much less complicated than it seems.

Using the data in Table A2.2 this works as shown in Table A2.9. The standard deviation for the data in Table A2.2 is 15.677 years. Loosely translated this means that the values deviate from the arithmetic mean by an average of 15.677 years.

At this point you are probably thinking 'So what?' While it is easy to grasp the idea and point of an average it is not so easy to grasp the idea of the standard deviation or the point of it. Having calculated a standard deviation of 15.677 years you probably have no idea whether that is a large or small standard deviation. And you are probably wondering why bother to go to all that effort to work it out anyway? Let's deal with the understanding of the measure first. The standard deviation measures the *variation around the mean*. In other words, the smaller the standard deviation the more concentrated the data is around the mean. If the standard deviation were small, say two years, then this would mean that most people in the sample would agree that the age of consent should be within a narrow range either side of the mean. In the example the standard deviation is very large (15.677) because we have a number of very high values that makes the variation much larger on average.

So why is it important to know this? Because it is important when generalising the sample results to the population. If the *sample* varies a lot then we are less able to be precise about the average of the *population* from which the sample was taken. We deal with this in more detail below.

Student Activity A2.7
Compute the standard deviation and range for the age of consent for women (V21) and compare them with those for men (V22).

Generalising from samples

The analysis of survey data that we have undertaken so far has not attempted to make generalisations to wider populations from which the samples were taken. You must remember, however, that you are dealing with a sample, not a population, and what you have said about your data refers to the *sample*. Even representative samples are not identical replicas of the population but are liable to variation due to *sampling error*. The bigger the sampling error the less accurate your sample will be in estimating values for the population. If your sample is not a representative sample (see Chapter 4) then it will be *biased* as well.

So making statements about wider populations must be done with care. You must be aware of both bias and sampling error when generalising about populations from samples.

There are a set of statistical procedures that allow you to make accurate estimates of the impact of sampling error on random samples. These are called *confidence limits* and *significance tests* and are discussed below.

The other thing that you should be aware of is that when you spot a *relationship* between two variables you are not, as yet, in a position to say anything about how *strong* that relationship is. Measuring the *degree* of a relationship or an association can also be done statistically. This is also considered below.

Dealing with sampling error

Generalising from a sample raises the issue of sampling error. For example, the *sample* shows a majority 'against' making homosexuality illegal (see Table A2.1 on page 236). Does this mean that the sampled *population* is also against illegalisation? We cannot jump to conclusions because we are dealing with a sample and we have to take account of the fact that the sample will not be an exact replica of the population that it was drawn from even if it was an unbiased sample taken at random.

The variation in a sample that comes about from taking unbiased random samples is called *sampling error* and all samples have it. This is a nuisance but there is nothing that can be done to get rid of sampling error completely; it is part and parcel of sampling. The good thing about sampling error is that we can estimate the extent of it.

This makes sampling error very different from *bias* in samples. Bias, which arises when some members of the population do not have a chance of being in the sample, cannot be measured, and generalisations cannot really be made from highly biased samples.

If we assume the sample in our example survey was an unbiased random sample, we may have selected a random sample who were particularly tolerant of homosexuality. On the other hand, the sample may be particularly hostile to gays and lesbians. Or it may accurately reflect the population of 16–20-year-old college students in Birmingham. The problem is that we do not know which because we only have the information from the sample to go on. So what do we do?

Confidence limits

What we can do is to work out the *confidence limits*. What they give us is an upper and lower limit within which the *population* percentage will fall. For example, 30.8% of the *sample* thought homosexuality should be illegal. This might be an overstatement or an understatement. Using probability theory, the details of which we will not go into here, you can work out what the likely range would be for the *population* of people in favour of making homosexuality illegal.

This is how you do it. Once again the sums are not difficult (especially if you have a calculator).

1. Convert the percentage of the sample in favour (30.8%) into a decimal (0.308).

2. Work out what is known as the *standard error* of the *proportion* (that is, the standard deviation of the sampling error) using this formula:

standard error $= \sqrt{(p(1-p))/n}$

where   p = sample proportion (in favour)   = 0.308
and   n = sample size   = 143
So:

$$\text{Standard error} = \sqrt{(.308)(.692)/143}$$
$$= \sqrt{.213136/143}$$
$$= \sqrt{0.00149}$$
$$= 0.0386$$

3. Use this to find the confidence limits. The usual ones in social science are the *95% confidence limits* which are the limits around the sample

percentage that have a 95% chance of containing the population percentage. They are found from:

Upper limit: sample percentage + 1.96 (standard error)
Lower limit: sample percentage – 1.96 (standard error)

In the example we get:

Upper limit $0.308 + 1.96(0.0386) = 0.308 + .07566 = .38366$
Lower limit $0.308 – 1.96(0.0386) = 0.308 – .07566 = .23234$

4. Convert these limits back to percentages and we have a 95% condidence limit of:

23.2% to 38.4% (to one decimal place).

5. This means that there is a 95% probability that the population proportion lies between these two percentages. The population value could therefore be as high as 38.4% or as low as 23.2% given our sample. This does presuppose that the sample is an unbiased random sample of the population.

We can now be more confident than before in relation to hypothesis 1a and say that (assuming a random sample) a majority of the *population* from which the sample was taken does not support making homosexuality illegal because, at most, only 38.4% are in favour.

Student Activity A2.8
Calculate the confidence limits for the population proportion in favour of Clause 28. On the basis of this is there a majority in favour or against the clause?

Once again you should note that most computer statistics packages will work out confidence limits for you and what is important is that you know what they mean. Samples contain sampling error and confidence limits take account of sampling error. Confidence limits are a range of values, derived from the sample, within which the *population* value is likely to fall. This allows you to be more confident in making statements about the population on the basis of a sample.

In the same way that a proportion will be subject to sampling error, so will an arithmetic mean. For example, the sample mean age of consent for gays was 22.198 years. The population mean age will similarly lie between confidence limits. The equivalent formula for 95% confidence limits for a sample mean are:

Upper limit: sample mean + 1.96 (standard error)
Lower limit: sample mean – 1.96 (standard error)

Where the standard error for the *mean* = $s/\sqrt{(n-1)}$

and s = sample standard deviation
and n = sample size

In the example the standard deviation is 15.677 and the sample size was 111 (see Table A2.9). So:

Standard error $= 15.677/\sqrt{(111-1)}$
$= 15.677/\sqrt{110}$
$= 15.677/10.488$
$= 1.495$

Thus, the 95% confidence limits are:

Upper limit: 22.198 + 1.96 (1.495) = 22.198 + 2.93 = 25.128
Lower limit: 22.198 − 1.96 (1.495) = 22.198 − 2.93 = 19.268

So this means that the given the very large variation in the sample the arithmetic mean age of consent for gays for the *population* from which the sample was taken could be as low as 19.268 or as high as 25.128.

Student Activity A2.9
Calculate the 95% confidence limits for the age of consent for lesbians. Does the result suggest that the average age of consent for lesbians is lower than for gays?

Statistical significance

Table A2.5 indicates that older people in the sample are more likely to know about Clause 28 than younger people. This looks to be quite marked, with twice the percentage of over-eighteens as under-eighteens having heard of the clause. But once again we are dealing with a sample and need to consider sampling error.

In our example, we can see a difference in knowledge about Clause 28 for each age group. What is the probability that such a difference could be the result of taking a random sample from a population where in fact all the three age groups have the same knowledge about Clause 28?

We can work this out by using a *statistical significance test*. A significance test operates in the same sort of way as confidence limits. It tells us what the probability is that any observed difference within a sample could be the result of *sampling error*.

All significance tests examine a *null hypothesis*. A null hypothesis is simply a statement which says that there is *no difference* between two samples (or sub-samples) or that there is no relation between two variables. The significance test then works out the probability that this null hypothesis is true.

We decide on a cut-off point called the *significance level*. In the social sciences this is usually 5% (0.05) (which is equivalent to 95% confidence limits). If the probability that results from the test is less than 5% then we *reject* the null hypothesis. This means that we reject the idea that the difference is due to sampling error. In other words, if the test probability is *less* than 0.05 then the difference in the *sample* reflects a difference in the *population*.

A widely used significance test for crosstabulated data is the *chi-square test*. It is applicable to all size tables and is fairly easy to work out and understand (although it is not the best test in all the circumstances where it is used). We do not intend to go through how to work out chi-square statistics as this is beyond the scope of the book. But you ought to know how to interpret a chi-square result. The chi-square test operates by comparing the actual frequencies in the different cells of the table with the frequencies that you would expect if the null hypothesis were true.

So let us take Table A2.5 as an example. The null hypothesis in this case would be that *age makes no difference to knowledge about Clause 28*. What this would mean in practice is that we would expect the same percentage of 'No' answers for each age group. There are very nearly twice as many 'No' answers overall as 'Yes' answers, so we would expect twice as many of each age group to say 'No' rather than 'Yes' if the null hypothesis that there was no difference was true.

There is a *Data Analysis Resource Pack* floppy disk available from Lee Harvey which expands on the statistical analysis in this chapter. See page 269.

So our *expected frequencies* for Table A2.5 would thus be approximately:

	Up to 18	18	Over 18
Yes	18	21	11
No	36	42	21
Totals	54	63	32

(In practice, to calculate chi-square you need to work out the expected frequencies *exactly*.)

The observed and expected frequencies are then compared, via a chi-square test procedure which is explained in most statistics textbooks. The result is a value for chi-square. This can then be converted into the probability of the differences in the sample being the result of sampling error. You use a set of tables to do the conversion if you are working it out by hand. If the statistic is worked out using a computer program a probability will usually be provided for you. In our example, the calculated chi-square was 5.90 and this gives a *probability* (or *significance value*) of 0.052.

What does that tell us? It tells us that there is only a 5.2% chance that the observed sample came from a population in which there was *no difference* between age groups. This means, conversely, that there was a 94.8% chance that the differences in the sample reflect real differences in the population. Is this good enough? The answer to that depends on convention. In the social sciences, as we have said, it is conventional to take 5% as the cut off point for all significance tests. If there is *less than* a 5% chance that the observed difference in the sample is due to sampling error then the difference is said to be statistically *significantly* different. This means that you can generalise the difference in the sample to the population from which the sample is taken.

In our example, it means that although the sample shows a difference, this is *not significant* because probability is just *over* 5%. So it is possible that the differences in the sample are caused by random sampling error at the conventional 5% significance level.

Student Activity A2.10
Look at Table A2.10. Do males and females have significantly different views as to whether homosexuality should be part of sex education in schools?

You should note that there are a large number of significance tests that suit different situations. We cannot give a full account here of all the possibilities. What we have concentrated on is the meaning of significance tests and how to make sense of the statistics that you might come across, either in books or generated by computer programs.

To sum up, in general a statistical significance test will give you a value for the statistic and a probability (or significance value) which you may have to look up. If the significance value is *less than 0.05* (5%) then the *sample difference is significant* at the 5% significance level, that is, the *null hypothesis is rejected* and the differences in the sample are *not due to random sampling error* but represent a *real difference in the population*.

So significance tests and confidence limits are statistical procedures we use in order to make generalisations about the population from a random sample. They provide us with the grounds for making claims about the population. A statistically significant result means that the observed difference or relationship within a sample is due to a difference or relationship in the population from which the sample was taken.

Table A2.10 Crosstabulation: V7 *Is homosexuality promoted by being part of sex education?* by V31 *Sex*

Count Row % Col %	V31 Male (1)	V31 Female (2)	Row Total
V7			
Yes	34	22	56
(1)	60.7	39.3	37.8%
	43.6	31.4	
No	44	48	92
(2)	47.8	52.2	62.2%
	56.4	68.6	
Column	78	70	148
Total	52.7%	47.3%	100%

Chi-Square	D.F.	Signif.
1.83146	1	.1760

You must remember that statistical significance tells you nothing more than that an observed difference or relationship is unlikely to have been caused by random sampling error. It tells you nothing about the size of any difference or about the degree of any relationship.

Association

Measuring the degree of a relationship between two variables is done by using *measures of association*. They provide a measure of the extent to which two variables are interrelated. Imagine driving a car. The harder you press down on the accelerator the faster the car goes. Variable A (pressing the accelerator) is directly related to variable B (speed of the car). The measure of association between A and B in this example will be approximately 100 per cent. On the other hand, the speed of the car will not be affected in the slightest by pressing on the horn, however hard you press. So variable B (speed of the car) will be unrelated to variable C (pressing the horn). The measure of association, in this case between B and C, will be zero. Conventionally, all statistical measures of association generate a value (called a *coefficient*) between 0 and 1. A coefficient of 0 means that there is no observed association at all and a coefficient of 1 means that the two variables are perfectly related, that is, that changes in the independent variable are perfectly matched by changes in the dependent variable. In practice, in the social world, the degree of association is somewhere between 0 and 1.

For example, we could work out the relationship between hostility towards gays and age of respondent to see if hostility decreases as the respondent gets older. This would be another way of assessing the part of hypothesis 4 which suggests that age affects attitudes.

There are two ways of doing this. The first is to calculate the measure of association called the *correlation* coefficient. (Its full name is Pearson's Product Moment Correlation Coefficient, but it is more usually known just as *the* correlation coefficient and is represented, for no obvious reason, by the letter 'r'.) The correlation coefficient can only be used if both variables are *interval* scale. Age is clearly interval. But what about hostility to gays? We have a number of different aspects of hostility. We can compute a *hostility score* by counting the number of hostile responses that occur for the following questions:

Do you think homosexuality should be made illegal? (That is, score 1 if V23 is 'yes'.)
Do you think acts of an affectionate nature between homosexuals should be confined to their own home? (That is, score 1 if V25 is 'yes'.)
Do you agree with two gay men rearing children in a family situation? (That is, score 1 if V28 is 'no'.)
Do you think the age of consent should be raised? (That is, score 1 if V22 is greater than 20.)

The score for each respondent thus ranges between 0 (non-hostile) to 4 (very hostile). This can be treated as interval scale data, although you should note that the questions might not be regarded as of equal weight. This new hostility score we will call V35.

It is thus possible to calculate the correlation coefficient of hostility score and age. We will not go into the mechanics of how you calculate the coefficient as most statistical programs will work it out for you and nearly

Table A2.11 Crosstabulation: V35 *Anti-gay Hostility Score* by V30 *Age*

Count Row % Col %	V30			Row Total
	16 or 17 (1)	18 (2)	19 or 20 (3)	
V35				
0	2	5	1	8
	25.0	62.5	12.5	8.1
	5.6	11.9	4.8	
1	9	12	5	26
	34.6	46.2	19.2	26.3
	25.0	28.6	23.8	
2	10	14	11	35
	28.6	40.0	31.4	35.4
	27.8	33.3	52.4	
3	14	9	3	26
	53.8	34.6	11.5	26.3
	38.9	21.4	14.3	
4	1	2	1	4
	25.0	50.0	25.0	4.0
	2.8	4.8	4.8	
Column Total	36	42	21	99
	36.4%	42.4%	21.2%	100%

Chi-Square	D.F.	Significance
7.76994	8	.4563

Cells with EF<5 = 6 of 15 (40%)

Lambda symmetric 0.0744
Lambda with V35 dependent 0.0625
Lambda with V30 dependent 0.0877

Pearson's Product Moment Correlation Coefficient is a measure that depends on the standard deviation. What it actually measures is the extent to which the variance of the two variables coincides. To be specific, the correlation coefficient is the co-variation of the the two variables divided by the average of the deviation of the two variables separately.

Table A2.12 Crosstabulation: V35 *Anti-gay Hostility Score* **by V31** *Sex*

Count Row % Col %	V31 Male (1)	Female (2)	Row Total
V35			
0	3	5	8
	37.5	62.5	8.1
	5.9	10.4	
1	12	14	26
	46.2	53.8	26.3
	23.5	29.2	
2	16	19	35
	45.7	54.3	35.4
	31.4	39.6	
3	17	9	26
	65.4	34.6	26.3
	33.3	18.8	
4	3	1	4
	75.0	25.0	4.0
	5.9	2.1	
Column	36	42	99
Total	36.4%	42.4%	100%

Chi-Square	D.F.	Significance
4.28555	4	.3687

Cells with EF<5 = 4 of 10 (40%)

Lambda symmetric 0.0714
Lambda with V35 dependent 0.0156
Lambda with V30 dependent 0.1458

all statistics textbooks show you how to do it. What it involves is comparing each person's age with their hostility score and seeing to what extent changes in age are reflected in changes in score. If all the young people had a high score and all the old people had a low score then we would have a high degree of association between age and hostility score and the correlation coefficient would be near to 1. (In fact it would be near to −1 as the relationship is inverse, that is, like braking in a car: the harder you push the brake the slower the car goes.) If, on the other hand, some young people and some old people had high scores and similarly some young people and some old people had low scores then there would not be much association at all and the score would be near to zero.

The correlation coefficient for age (V30) and hostility score (V35) is −0.0633.

You can check this for yourselves from the datafile. It can be done easily and quickly by computer but will take ages if you do it by hand.

What does this figure tell us? The minus indicates that as the respondents get older the level of hostility decreases. But the actual size of the coefficient is very small, only .0633, which means that there is very little association at all between age and hostility.

Student Activity A2.11
1. **Using a computer work out the correlation coefficient for hostility score for lesbians and age (V30).**
2. **Compare the results for lesbians with the one shown above for gays.**
3. **Similarly, work out the correlation coefficient of hostility score and sex of respondent (V31) for gays and for lesbians and compare the results.**
NOTE If you are doing this activity you will need to compute two new variables for each person in the sample, hostility score for gays (V35) and hostility score for lesbians (V36). This will be time consuming by hand but can be performed very quickly using a computer program. The SPSSPC+ program and data can be obtained from the authors, details on page 269.

An alternative way of measuring the relationship between age and hostility score would be to construct a crosstabulation of hostility score and age and work out the degree of association within the crosstabulated table. There are a number of different measures of association for crosstabulated data. A useful one is a coefficient called *lambda* which can be used for any scale of data. It is fairly easy to compute and is provided as one of the SPSS options with crosstabulations.

Table A2.11 is a typical crosstabulation for age and hostility score that you would get from a computer program. In this case it has the value of chi-square and lambda at the bottom. We will explain how to read the additional statistical data and what they mean.

First, *chi-square*. The calculated value is 7.76994. This in itself tells you very little, because chi-square gets bigger the larger the table, irrespective of whether or not there is any statistical significance.

The column marked D.F. stands for 'degrees of freedom' and in this case there are eight. The degrees of freedom are vital when converting a chi-square result into a significance value and you would need to know them if you were looking up the chi-square in a set of tables. In this case it is additional information that you do not really need as the computer has worked out the significance level for you (that is, 0.4563).

You will recall that a significance value of 0.4563 means that there is a 45.63% chance that the difference in the sample (that is, in hostility scores for each age group) is likely to be the result of sampling error. This is far higher than the conventional 5% cut off point. Therefore we have to admit the possibility that any differences in the sample are the result of random sampling error.

The last piece of information about the chi-square is the 'number of cells with expected frequency less than 5'. In this case it is 6 out of 15 cells, which is 40%. It is conventional to treat chi-square values with great caution if the percentage of cells with 'expected frequency less than 5' is more than 20%. In this case we would therefore suggest that the chi-square statistic is unreliable because of the large proportion of low expected frequencies.

Second, *lambda*. Lambda is a measure of association that can be used for any scale of data. There are three values for lambda in the example. The first has age (V30) dependent = 0.08772. The second has hostility score (V35) dependent = 0.06250. The third is a 'symmetric' value, which is the average of the other two = 0.07438. The value we want is the one where hostility score (V35) is dependent, that is, 0.0625.

What does this tell us? It tells us that there is very little association at all between age and hostility score.

Note that the lambda value was 0.06250 and the Pearson Correlation Coefficient worked out earlier was −0.0633. They are not the same, and are unlikely to be, as they are computed in different ways. They are, however, quite close and you would expect them to be approximately the same size, given that they are measuring association between the same two variables. Remember that you can use the lambda coefficient when you have ordinal data but you need interval data for the Pearson Product Moment Correlation Coefficient.

Student Activity A2.12
Table A2.12 shows the crosstabulation of anti-gay hostility score (V35) by sex of respondent (V31) with chi-square and lambda statistics.
1. Is there a statistically significant difference in hostility scores for men and women?
2. Is association between anti-gay hostility and sex greater than between anti-gay hostility and age? Comment on your results in terms of hypothesis 4.
3. Table A2.13 is the crosstabulation for legalisation of homosexuality (V23) and gay acquaintances (V26). Does the value of the chi-square statistic suggest that having gay acquaintances effects views on illegalising homosexuality?
4. Tables A2.14 and A2.15 show the crosstabulation for illegalisation and gay acquaintances divided into two, one for male respondents and one for female respondents. Compare the two crosstabulations to see if sex of respondent effects the relationship noted in Item 3, above.
SUGGESTION If you have a computer with a statistics package it would be a good idea to construct your own crosstabulations from the data file in Appendix 1 and compute chi-squared statistics. You can then compare your results with our tables. You can do this by hand but it will take you a long time.

Table A2.13   Crosstabulation: V23 *Should homosexuality be illegal? by V26 Are any of your friends or family gay or lesbian?*

Count Row % Col %	V26		Row Total
	Yes (1)	No (2)	
V31			
Yes (1)	3	40	43
	7.0	93.0	30.5%
	8.3	38.1	
No (2)	33	65	98
	33.7	66.3	69.5%
	91.7	68.6	
Column Total	36 25.5%	105 74.5%	141 100%

Chi-square	*D.F.*	*Significance*
9.84	1	0.002

Cells with E.F.<5 None

Table A2.14   Crosstabulation: V23 *Should homosexuality be illegal? by V26 Are any of your friends or family gay or lesbian? controlling for V31 Sex = male*

Count Row % Col %	V26		Row Total
	Yes (1)	No (2)	
V31			
Yes (1)	3	28	31
	9.7	90.3	40.8%
	20.0	45.9	
No (2)	12	33	98
	26.7	73.3	59.2%
	80.0	54.1	
Column Total	15 19.7%	61 80.3%	76 100%

Chi-square	*D.F.*	*Significance*
2.36	1	0.125

Cells with E.F.<5 None

Table A2.15 Crosstabulation: V23 *Should homosexuality be illegal?* by V26 *Are any of your friends or family gay or lesbian?* controlling for V31 *Sex = female*

Count Row % Col %	V26 Yes (1)	No (2)	Row Total
V31			
Yes (1)	0 0.0 0.0	12 100.0 27.3	12 18.5%
No (2)	21 39.6 100.0	32 60.4 72.7	53 81.5
Column Total	21 32.3%	44 67.7%	65 100%

Chi-square	D.F.	Significance
5.33	1	0.021

Cells with E.F.<5   1 of 4 (25%)

Significance testing and association – an example translated

To sum up and review the above brief outline of significance testing and association we will consider a brief extract from a published survey, Extract A2.1. We will explain what the statistical references mean but will not show you how to work them out as this is beyond the scope of the book.

The percentages in Extract A2.1 are self-explanatory and show a difference in class consciousness between the two groups of workers. What does the reference to *Kendall's Tau* measure of correlation tell us? As we have seen, correlation is a statistical process that attempts to measure exactly the interrelationship between two variables, in this case between background and class consciousness. Correlation is thus a measure of association. There are many different measures of association of which Kendall's Tau is one.

The percentages show a difference between the two groups that leads us to suppose that class consciousness and background are associated. In this case the correlation is 0.41, which shows a reasonable degree of association. It is well above zero but certainly well short of a perfect relationship. Of course, in social science, very high correlations between two variables are unlikely because the social world is complex and, for example, class consciousness is likely to be the result of a number of things besides the

Example answer to Student Activity A2.12, parts 3 and 4

The crosstabulation for illegalisation (V23 and gay acquaintances (V26) for the *whole sample* shows that people with gay and lesbian acquaintances had a different view about the issue of illegalisation from those who had no gay or lesbian acquaintances. The chi-square value for this table is 9.8 with a significance value of p = 0.0017. This means that the observed difference is statistically significantly different and thus unlikely to be the result of random sampling error.

However, when taking the sex of the respondent into account we see that the difference is not significant for males (p = 0.1247) while it is significant for females (p = 0.0210). This suggests that the variation in the male group could be the result of sampling error. Thus we conclude that having gay acquaintances effects attitudes towards illegalisation of homosexuality for women but not for men.

By breaking the original crosstabulation of V23 by V26 into two tables, for males and for females, we have *controlled* for sex of respondent.

Extract A2.1

UPROOTEDNESS AND WORKING-CLASS CONSCIOUSNESS

John Leggett undertook research in the United States to see if there was any difference in class consciousness between industrial workers who grew up in industrial regions and industrial workers who had recently moved to industrial regions from the countryside. He called the first group 'the prepared' and the second group 'the uprooted'.

He used a number of questions to allocate his sample into five categories of class consciousness, from most class conscious to least class conscious. The results are shown in Table A2.16.

It was anticipated that the uprooted would express a higher degree of class consciousness than the prepared. The data support this expectation: 52% of the uprooted fall in the two most class conscious categories compared to only 22% of the prepared. At the other extreme, only 13% of the uprooted compared to 47% of the prepared fall into the least class conscious categories.

The Kendall's Tau measure of correlation is 0.41, while the difference between the uprooted and the prepared respondents is significant at the <.001 level.

Other relevant variables do not upset our findings. When one controls for ethnicity, the relationship still obtains.

Adapted from Leggett (1963).

Table A2.16 Class consciousness by background

Background	Level of class consciousness 5	4	3	2	1	Total
Uprooted	23	49	49	15	3	139
Row %	*17*	*35*	*35*	*11*	*2*	*100*
Prepared	3	18	29	35	10	95
Row %	*3*	*19*	*31*	*37*	*10*	*100*

Class consciousness: 5 = most class conscious through to 1 = least class conscious.

background of the respondent. A correlation of 0.4 between two variables would be regarded as a reasonably good association for social science data. In general, the larger the measure of association the stronger is the relationship between the variables.

What does it mean to say that the difference between the two groups is 'significant at the <.001 level'? Significance testing, as we have seen, attempts to take account of the fact that we have a sample and not the whole population. It assumes that the sample is not biased (that is, it is a random sample). However, even if it is unbiased, the sample will still have sampling error. An unbiased sample will be a good approximation to the population but it will not be perfect, that is, there will be some variation between the sample and the population. The sample might slightly overrepresent the class consciousness of the population of uprooted workers or it might slightly underrepresent it. There is no way of knowing which is the case. However, it is possible to estimate the likely degree of variation of an unbiased random sample from the population that it represents. The variation is known as *sampling error*.

The point of a statistical survey is to be able to make some generalisations about the population from which the samples were taken, and not just the sample itself. While we can say that there is some association between class consciousness and background for the sample, does this apply to the population as well? In short, we need to take account of the sampling error. In other words, we need to see if the difference for the sample is of a size that will be significant for the population, that is, whether it is bigger than the likely sampling error. This is precisely what John Leggett (1963), has done and the statement that 'the difference between the uprooted and the prepared is significant at the <.001 level' means that there is only a tiny probability (*less* than a 1 in 1000 chance) that the difference in the samples does not reflect a difference in the populations from which the samples were drawn. Or, put another way, that there is a more than 999 out of 1000 chance that there is a difference in class consciousness among the two populations.

NOTE: It is conventional to report significance tests in terms of the probability of there not being a difference, and this is usually the figure that computer programmes such as SPSS generate. So, in general, *the smaller the significance level* the *more confidence* one has that any difference in a *sample* also reflects a difference in the *population*.

REFERENCES

Abel-Smith, B. and Townsend, P., 1965, **The Poor and the Poorest: A new analysis of the Ministry of Labour's** *Family Expenditure Surveys* **of 1953–54 and 1960.** London, Bell.

Abercrombie, N., Hill, S. and Turner, B. S., eds., 1990, **Dominant Ideologies.** London, Routledge.

Acker, J., Barry, K., and Essereld, J., 1983, 'Objectivity and truth: problems in doing feminist research', **Womens Studies International Forum**, 6 (4), p. 423–35.

Ackroyd, S. and Hughes, J. A., 1981, **Data Collection in Context.** London, Longman.

Acquaviva, S. S., 1979, **The Decline of the Sacred in Industrial Society.** Oxford, Blackwell.

Adams, R. N. and Preiss, J. J., eds., 1960, **Human Organization Research: Field Relations and Techniques.** Homewood, Ill., Dorsey Press.

Adler, F and Simon, R.J., eds., 1979, **The Criminology of Deviant Women.** London, Houghton Mifflin.

Aggleton, P., 1987a, **Rebel Without a Cause?** Basingstoke, Falmer.

Aggleton, P., 1987b, **Deviance.** London, Tavistock.

Alcock, P., 1987, **Poverty and State Support.** London, Longman.

Allim, P. and Hunt, A., 1982, 'Women in Official Statistics', in Whitelegg *et al.*, 1982, **The Changing Experience of Women.** Oxford, Martin Robertson and Open University.

Althusser, L., 1971, **Lenin and Philosophy and Other Essays.** London, New Left Books.

Amir, A., 1971, **Patterns in Forcible Rape.** Chicago, University of Chicago Press.

Anderson, M., 1980, **Approach to the History of the Western Family.** London, Macmillan.

Ang, I., 1985, **Watching Dallas: Soap Opera and the Melodramatic Imagination** (Trans. Della Couling). London, Methuen.

Anthias, F., 1980, 'Women and the reserve army of labour: a critique of Veronica Beechey', **Capital and Class**, 10.

Anwar, M., 1979, **The Myth of Return: Pakistanis in Britain.** London, Heinemann.

Arcana, J., 1983, **Every Mother's Son.** London, Women's Press.

Atkinson, J., 1967, **A Handbook for Interviewers: A Manual for Government Social Survey Interviewing Staff, Describing Practice and Procedures in Interviewing** (Government Social Survey, No. M136). London, HMSO.

Atkinson, J. M., 1968, 'On the sociology of suicide', **Sociological Review**, 16, pp. 83–92.

Atkinson, J. M., 1978, **Discovering Suicide: Studies in the Social Organization of Sudden Death.** London, Macmillan.

Backett, K., 1982, **Mothers and Fathers.** London, Macmillan.

Bains, S., 1989, 'Crimes Against Women – *The Manchester Survey*', in Dunhill (ed.), 1989, **The Boys in Blue: Women's Challenge to the Police.** London, Virago.

Baker, M., 1981, **The New Racism.** London, Junction Books.

Ballard, R., 1982, 'South Asian Families', in Rapoport, Fogarty and Rapoport (eds.), 1982, **Families in Britain**, London, Routledge and Kegan Paul.

Bandura, A. and Walters, R. H., 1964, **Social Learning and Personality Development.** New York, Holt, Rinehart and Winston.

Barker, D. and Allen, S., eds., 1976, **Sexual Divisions in Society: Process and Change.** London, Tavistock.

Barker, M., 1981, **The New Racism.** London, Junction Books.

Barker, E., 1984, **The Making of a Moonie: Brainwashing or Choice?** Oxford, Blackwell.

Barrat, D., 1986, **Media Sociology.** London, Routledge.

Barrat, D. and Cole, T., 1991, **Sociology Projects: A Students' Guide.** London, Routledge.

Barrett, M. and McIntosh, M., 1982, **The Anti-Social Family.** London, Verso.

Barron, R. D. and Norris, G. M., 1976, 'Sexual divisions and the dual labour market' in Barker and Allen (eds.), 1976, **Sexual Divisions in Society: Process and Change.** London, Tavistock.

Barry, A., 1988, 'Black Mythologies: the representation of black people on British television' in Twitchin (ed.), 1990, **The Black and White Media Show**, Stoke-on-Trent, Trentham Books, pp. 83–102.

Barthes, R., 1974, **Mythologies** (Selected and translated by A. Lavers). London, Cape. (First published Paris, 1957, and in English, London, Cape, 1972).

Barton, A. H. and Lazarsfeld, P., 1955, 'Some Functions of Qualitative Analysis in Social Research', **Frankfurter Beitrage zur Soziologie**, 1, pp. 321–61. Abridged version reprinted in McCall and Simmons (eds.), 1969, **Issues in Participant Observation: A Text and Reader.** Reading, Mass., Addison-Wesley.

Barton, R., 1987, **The Scarlet Thread: An Indian Woman Speaks.** London, Virago.

Bateson, N., 1984, **Data Construction in Social Surveys.** London, Allen and Unwin.

Becker, H. S., 1958, 'Problems of Inference and Proof in Participant Observation', **American Sociological Review**, 23. Reprinted in Filstead (ed.), 1970, **Qualitative Methodology: Firsthand Involvement with the Social World**, Chicago, Markham, pp. 189 ff.

Becker, H. S., 1963, **Outsiders: Studies in the Sociology of Deviance.** New York, Free Press.

Becker, H. S., 1986, 'Introduction', in Shaw, 1930, **The Jack Roller: A Delinquent Boy's Own Story**, Chicago, University of Chicago Press (reprinted edition).

Becker, H. S. and Geer, B., 1957, 'Participant Observation and Interviewing: A Rejoinder', **Human Organization**, 16, pp. 39–40. Reprinted in Filstead (ed.), 1970, **Qualitative Methodology: Firsthand Involvement with the Social World**, Chicago, Markham, pp. 150 ff.

Becker, H. S. and Geer, B., 1960, 'Participant Observation: The Analysis of Qualitative Data.' in Adams and Preiss (eds.), 1960, **Human Organization Research: Field Relations and Techniques.** Homewood, Ill., Dorsey Press.

Becker, H. S., Geer, B., Hughes, E. C. and Strauss, A. L., 1961, **Boys in White: Student Culture in Medical School.** Chicago, University of Chicago Press.

Beechey, V., 1977, 'Some notes on female wage labour in capitalist production', **Capital and Class**, 3, pp. 45–66.

Beechey, V., 1978, 'Women and production: a critical analysis of some sociological theories of women's work' in Kuhn and Wolpe (eds.), 1978, **Feminism and Materialism: Women and Modes of Production**, London, Routledge and Kegan Paul.

Bell, C., 1977, 'Reflections on the Banbury Restudy' in Bell, and Newby (eds.), 1977, **Doing Sociological Research**, London, Allen and Unwin, pp. 47–62.

Bell, C. and Encel, S., 1978, **Inside the Whale.** Oxford, Pergamon.

Bell, C. and Newby, H., eds., 1977, **Doing Sociological Research.** London, Allen and Unwin.

Bell, J., 1989, **Doing Your Research Project: A Guide for First-time Researchers in Education and Social Science.** Milton Keynes, Open University Press.

Bell, N. W. and Vogel, E. F., eds., 1959, **A Modern Introduction to the Family**. London, Collier–Macmillan.

Bell, N. W. and Vogel, E. F., eds., 1968, **A Modern Introduction to the Family** (revised edition). New York, Free Press.

Belotti, E., 1975, **Little Girls**. London, Writer's and Reader's Publishing Co-operative.

Belson, W. A., 1986, **Validity in Survey Research**. Aldershot, Gower.

Ben-Tovim, G., Gabriel, J. G., Law, I. and Stredder, K., 1986, **The Local Politics of Race**. London, Macmillan.

Benn, T., 1989, **Against the Tide: Diaries 1973-1976**. London, Hutchinson.

Benn, T., 1990, **Conflicts of Interest: Diaries 1977-1980** (edited by Ruth Winstone). London, Hutchinson.

Bendix, R. and Lipset, S. M., eds., 1972, **Class, Status and Power** (second edition). London, Routledge and Kegan Paul.

Bendt, I. and Downing, J., 1982, **We Shall Return: Women of Palestine**. London, Zed Press.

Benhabib, S. and Cornell, D., eds., 1987, **Feminism as Critique**. Cambridge, Polity.

Benson, D. and Hughes, 1983, **The Perspective of Ethnomethodology**. London, Longman.

Benson, S., 1981, **Ambiguous Ethnicity: Interracial Families in London**. Cambridge, Cambridge University Press.

Berelson, B., 1952, **Content Analysis as a Tool of Communication Research**. Glencoe, Free Press.

Berger, J., 1972, **Ways of Seeing**. Harmondsworth, Penguin.

Berger, P. L. and Berger, B., 1976, **Sociology: A Biographical Approach**. Harmondsworth, Penguin.

Berger, P. L. and Luckmann, T., 1963, 'The sociology of religion and the sociology of knowledge', **Sociology and Social Research**, 47, pp. 417–27. Reprinted in Robertson (ed.), 1970, **The Sociological Interpretation of Religion**. Oxford, Blackwell.

Berkowitz, L., ed., 1986, **Advances in Experimental Social Psychology**. New York, Academic Press.

Bernard, J., 1976, **The Future of Marriage**. Harmondsworth, Penguin.

Bettelheim, B., 1971, **The Children of the Dream**. London, Paladin.

Beuf, F. A., 1974, 'Doctor, lawyer, household drudge', **Journal of Communication**, 25, pp. 107–31.

Beynon, H., 1973, **Working For Ford**. Harmondsworth, Penguin.

Bilton, T., 1987, **Introductory Sociology** (second edition; first published in 1981). London, Macmillan.

Blackie, D. and Taylor, I., 1987, **AIDS: The Socialist Case**. London, Socialist Workers' Party.

Blonsky, M., 1985, **On Signs: A Semiotics Reader**. Oxford, Blackwell.

Blumenthal, A. B., 1932, **Small Town Stuff**. Chicago, University of Chicago Press.

Blumer, H., 1958, 'Race prejudice as a sense of group position', **Pacific Sociological Review**, 1, no. 1, pp 3–8.

Blumer, H., 1969, **Symbolic Interactionism**. Englewood Cliffs, Prentice-Hall.

Blumler, J. and Katz, E., eds., 1974, **The Uses of Mass Communications: Current Perspectives on Gratifications Research**. Beverley Hills, Sage.

Blumler, J. and McQuail, D., 1968, **Television in Politics: Its Uses and Influence**. London, Faber and Faber.

Blythe, R., 1972, **Akenfield**. Harmondsworth, Penguin.

Bocock, R., 1986, **Hegemony**. London, Routledge.

Boden, M. A., 1978, **Piaget**. Brighton, Harvester.

Bogdan, R. and Taylor, S. J., 1975, **Introduction to Qualitative Research Methods: A Phenomenological Approach to the Social Sciences**. New York, Wiley.

Bonacich, E., 1971, 'A theory of ethnic antagonisms: the split labor market', **American Sociological Review**, 37, pp. 547–59.

Booth, 1889–97, **Life and Labour of the People of London** (9 volumes). London, Macmillan.

Bosanquet, N. and Doeringer, P. B., 1973, 'Is there a dual labour market in Great Britain?', **Economic Journal**, 83, pp. 421–35.

Bosk, C. L., 1979, **Forgive and Remember**. Chicago, University of Chicago Press.

Bott, E., 1971, **Family and Social Network** (second edition). London, Tavistock.

Bottomore, T. B., ed., 1963, **Karl Marx: Early Writings**. Harmondsworth, Penguin.

Bourne, J., 1983, 'Towards an anti-racist feminism', **Race and Class**, 25.

Bowlby, J., 1946, **Forty-four Juvenile Thieves**. London, Tindall and Cox.

Box, S., 1983, **Power, Crime and Mystification**. London, Tavistock.

Bradshaw, J., 1990, **Child Poverty and Deprivation in the U.K.** London, National Children's Bureau.

Brah, A., 1979, 'South Asian Teenagers in Southall', **New Community**.

Braham, P., Rattansi, A. and Skellington, R., eds., 1992, **Racism and Antiracism: Inequalities, Opportunities and Policies**. London, Sage/Open University Press.

Braham, P., Rhodes, E. and Pearn, M., 1981, **Discrimination and Disadvantage in Employment: The Experience of Black Workers**. London, Harper and Row/Open University Press.

Brake, M., 1980, **The Sociology of Youth Culture and Youth Subculture**. London, Routledge and Kegan Paul.

Brake, M. and Hale, C., 1992, **Public Order and Private Lives: The Politics of Law and Order**. London, Routledge.

Brandenberg, S., 1988, **What Comes Naturally**. London, The Women's Press.

British Broadcasting Corporation (BBC), 1983, **BBC Annual Report and Handbook 1984**, London, BBC.

Britten, L. and Fry, M., 1979, 'Fairness, accuracy, and the girl must always be pretty', **Spare Rib**, 86, pp. 6–8.

Broadcasting Standards Council, 1989, **A Code of Practice**. London, Broadcasting Standards Council.

Broadcasting Standards Council, 1990, **Annual Report 1989–90**. London, Broadcasting Standards Council.

Brotherston, J., 1976, 'Inequality: is it inevitable?' in Carter and Peel (eds.), 1976, **Equalities and Inequalities in Health**. London, Academic Press.

Brown, C. and Gay, P., 1985, **Racial Discrimination 17 Years After the Act**. London, Policy Studies Institute.

Brown, C., 1984, **Black and White in Britain: The Third *PSI* Survey**. London, Heinemann.

Brown, G., 1975, **Experiments in the Social Sciences**. New York, Harper and Row.

Brownmiller, S., 1976, **Against Our Will**. Harmondsworth, Penguin.

Bruce, S., 1990, **A House Divided: Protestantism, Schism, and Secularization**. London, Routledge.

Bruegel, I., 1979, 'Women as a reserve army of labour: a note on recent British experience', **Feminist Review**, 3, pp.12–23.

Bryan, B., Dadzie, S. and Scafe, S., 1985, **The Heart of the Race: Black Women's Lives in Britain**. London, Virago.

Bryant, J. and Zillman, D., eds., 1986, **Perspectives on Media Effects**. Hillsdale, N.J., Erlbaum.

Bryman, A. and Cramer, D., 1990, **Quantitative Data Analysis for Social Scientists**. London, Routledge.

Bulmer, M., ed., 1982, **Social Research Ethics: An Examination of the Merits of Covert Participant Observation**. London, Macmillan.

Bulmer, M., ed., 1984, **Sociological Research Methods: An Introduction** (second edition). London, Macmillan.

Bulmer, M., 1986, 'Race and ethnicity' in Burgess, R. G. (ed.), 1986, **Key Variables in Sociological Investigation**. London, Routledge and Kegan Paul, pp. 54–75.

Burell, E. E. *et al.*, 1986, **Statistics, Problems and Solutions**. London, Edward Arnold.

Burgess, R. G., ed., 1982, **Field Research: A Sourcebook and Field Manual**. London, Allen and Unwin.

Burgess, R. G., 1984, **In The Field: An Introduction to Field Research**. London, Allen and Unwin.

Burgess, R. G., ed., 1986, **Key Variables in Sociological Research**. London, Routledge and Kegan Paul.

Butler, M. and Paisley, W., 1980, **Women and the Mass Media**. New York, Human Sciences Press.

Bynum, C. W., Harrell, S. and Richman, P., eds., 1986, **Gender and Religion: On the Complexity of Symbols**. Boston, Beacon.

Byrne, E. M., 1983, **Women and Education**. London, Tavistock.

Byrne, N., 1978, 'Sociotemporal considerations of everyday life suggested by an empirical study of the bar milieu, **Urban Life**, 6, pp. 417–38.

Campbell, A., 1981, **Girl Delinquents**. Oxford, Blackwell.

Campbell, A., 1984, **The Girls in the Gang**. Oxford, Blackwell.

Campbell, A., 1986 'Self-report of fighting by females', **British Journal of Criminology**, 26.

Cant, B. and Hemmings, S., eds., 1988, **Radical Records: Thirty Years of Lesbian and Gay History**. London, Routledge and Kegan Paul.

Cantor, M. and Pingree, S., 1983, **The Soap Opera**. Beverley Hills, Sage.

Carby, H. V., 1982, 'White women listen! Black feminism and the boundaries of sisterhood', in Centre for Contemporary Cultural Studies (eds.), 1982, **The Empire Strikes Back: Race and Racism in 1970s Britain**. London, Hutchinson, pp. 212–35.

Carlen, P., 1983, **Women's Imprisonment**. London, Routledge and Kegan Paul

Carmichael, S. and Hamilton, C., 1969, **Black Power**. Harmondsworth, Penguin.

Caro, F. G., ed., 1972, **Readings in Evaluation Research**. New York, Sage.

Carter, C. O. and Peel, J., eds., 1976, **Equalities and Inequalities in Health**, London, Academic Press.

Carter, E., 1985, 'Property Rites', **Spare Rib**, 155, June.

Cartwright, A. and O'Brien, M., 1976, 'Social class variations in health care and in general practitioner consultations', in Stacey (ed.), **The Sociology of the NHS**, Sociological Review Monograph no. 22, University of Keele.

Casburn, M., 1979, **Girls Will Be Girls**. London.

Cashmore, E., 1979, **Rastaman: The Rastafarian Movement in England**. London, Allen and Unwin.

Cashmore, E., 1989, **United Kingdom? Class, Race and Gender Since The War**. London, Unwin Hyman.

Castles, S. and Kosack, G., 1973, **Immigrant Workers and Class Structure in Western Europe**. London, Oxford University Press.

Cathey-Calvert, C., 1983, **Sexisms of Sesame Street: Outdated Concepts in a Progressive Programme**. Pittsburg, Know Inc.

Cavan, R. S., 1928, **Suicide**. Chicago, University of Chicago Press.

Cavan, S., 1966, **Liquor License**. Chicago, Aldine.

Cavendish, R., 1982, **Women on the Line**. London, Routledge and Kegan Paul.

Centre for Contemporary Cultural Studies (CCCS), eds., 1982, **The Empire Strikes Back: Race and Racism in 1970s Britain**. London, Hutchinson.

Chafetz, J. S., 1974, **Masculine/Feminine or Human?** Illinois, F. R. Peacock.

Chalmers, A. F., 1978, **What Is This Thing Called Science?** Milton Keynes, Open University Press.

Chambliss, W., 1972, **Box Man**. New York.

Chambliss, W., 1978, **On The Take: From Petty Crooks to Presidents**. Bloomington, Indiana.

Charon, J. M., 1979, **Symbolic Interactionism**. New York, Prentice-Hall.

Chipp, S. A. and Green, J., eds., 1980, **Asian Women in Transition**. Pennsylvania State University.

Cicourel, A. V., 1964, **Method and Measurement in Sociology**. New York, Free Press.

Cicourel, A. V., 1973a, **Cognitive Sociology**. Harmondsworth, Penguin.

Cicourel, A. V., 1973b, 'Interpretative procedures and normative roles in the negotiation of status and role', in Cicourel, 1973a, **Cognitive Sociology**, pp. 11–41.

Cicourel, A. V., [1968] 1976, **The Social Organisation of Juvenile Justice**. London, Heinemann.

Clegg, F., 1982, **Simple Statistics: A Course Book for the Social Sciences**. Cambridge, Cambridge University Press.

Cloward, R. and Ohlin, L., 1960, **Delinquency and Opportunity**. New York, Free Press.

Cockburn, C., 1983, **Brothers: Male Dominance and Technological Change**. London, Pluto.

Cockburn, C., 1985, **Machinery of Dominance: Women, Men and Technical Know-How**. London, Pluto.

Cohen, A., 1955, **Delinquent Boys, The Culture of the Gang**. New York, Free Press.

Cohen, A., 1966, **Deviance and Control**. Englewood Cliffs, Prentice-Hall.

Cohen, P., 1972, 'Subcultural conflict and working class community', **Working Papers in Cultural Studies**, 2. University of Birmingham.

Cohen, P., 1988, 'The perversions of inheritance: studies in the making of multi-racist Britain', in Cohen and Bains (eds.), 1988, **Multi-racist Britain**, London, Macmillan, pp. 1–118.

Cohen, P. and Bains, eds., 1988, **Multi-racist Britain**. London, Macmillan, pp. 1–118.

Cohen, S., 1971, **Images of Deviance**. Harmondsworth, Penguin.

Cohen, S., 1973, **Folk Devils and Moral Panics**. London, Paladin.

Coleman, J., 1972, **Policy Research in Social Science**. Morristown, N. J., General Learning Press.

Comstock, G. A. and Rubinstein, E. A., eds., 1972, **Television and Social Behaviour, Volume 1, Content and Control**. Washington, DC, Government Printing Office.

Cook, S., 1990a, 'Out of the shadow of the gallows', **Guardian**, 6th March 1990.

Cook, S., 1990b, '44% of MPs favour easing of law for gays', **Guardian**, 6th March 1990.

Cornish, D. and Clarke, R., 1986, **The Reasoning Criminal**. New York.

Corrigan, P., 1979, **Schooling the Smash Street Kids**. London, Macmillan.

Couch, C. J., Saxton, S. L. and Katovich, M. A., eds., 1986, **Studies in Symbolic Interaction: Supplement 2, 1986 (parts A and B) – The Iowa School**. London, JAI Press.

Coulter, J., ed., 1988, **Ethnomethodological Sociology**. Gloucester, Edward Elgar.

Coward, R., 1984, **Female Desire**. London, Paladin.

Cowie, J., Cowie, B. and Slater, E., 1968, **Delinquency in Girls**. London, Heinemann.

Coxon A. P. M., 1988, 'Towards a Sociology of AIDS', **Social Studies Review**, January, pp. 84–7.

Coyle, A., 1984, **Redundant Women**. London, The Women's Press.

Crishna, S., 1975, **Girls of Asian Origin in Britain**. London, YWCA.

Crossman, R., 1975-1977, **The Diaries of a Cabinet Minister** (3 volumes). London, Hamilton.

Culler, J. 1983, **Barthes**. Glasgow, Fontana.

Dale, A., Arber, S. and Procter, M., 1988, **Doing Secondary Analysis**. London, Unwin Hyman.

Daly, M., 1979, **Gyn/Ecology**. London, Women's Press.

Daly, M., 1984, **Pure Lust**. London, Women's Press.

Davidson, E. S., Yasuna, A. and Tower, A., 1979, 'The effects of television cartoons on sex role stereotyping in young girls', **Child Development**, 50, pp. 597–600.

Davis, A., 1982, **Women, Race and Class**. London, Women's Press.

Davis, A., Gardner, B. and Gardner, M. R., 1941. **Deep South**. Chicago, University of Chicago Press.

Davis, K., 1948, **Human Society**. New York, Macmillan

Davis, K. and Moore, W. E., 1967, 'Some principles of stratification' in Bendix and Lipset (eds.), 1972, **Class, Status and Power** (second edition). London, Routledge and Kegan Paul.

Deem, R., 1978, **Women and Schooling**. London, Routledge and Kegan Paul.

Delphy, C., 1985, **Close to Home**. London, Hutchinson.

Deming, W. E., 1944, 'On errors in surveys', **American Sociological Review**, 19, pp. 359–69. Reprinted in Denzin (ed.), 1970, **Sociological Methods: A Sourcebook**, London, Butterworth, pp. 320–37.

Denzin, N., 1970, **Sociological Methods: A Sourcebook**. London, Butterworth.

Dex, S., 1979, 'Economists' theories of the economics of discrimination' **Ethnic and Racial Studies**, 2, pp. 90–108.

Dex, S., 1983, 'The second generation: West Indian female school leavers' in Phizacklea (ed.), 1983a, **One Way Ticket: Migration and Female Labour**. London, Routledge and Kegan Paul, pp. 53–72.

Dex, S., 1985, **The Sexual Division of Work: Conceptual Revolutions in the Social Sciences**. Brighton, Harvester.

Dill, B. T., 1983, 'Race, class and gender: prospects for an all-inclusive sisterhood', **Feminist Studies**, 9, pp. 131–50.

Dixon, B. R., Bouma, G. D. and Atkinson, G. B. J., 1987, **A Handbook of Social Science Research: A Comprehensive and Practical Guide for Students**. Oxford, Oxford University Press.

Docherty, D., 1990, **Violence in Television Fiction** (Broadcasting Standards Council, Annual Review 1990, Public Opinion and Broadcasting Standards, 1). London, Libbey.

Dorner, G., 1974, 'A neuroendocrine disposition for homosexuality in men', **Archives of Sexual Behaviour**, 4, pp. 1–8.

Douglas, J. D., 1967, **The Social Meanings of Suicide**. Princeton, Princeton University Press.

Douglas, J. D., ed., 1970a, **Understanding Everyday Life**. London, Routledge and Kegan Paul.

Douglas, J. D., ed., 1970b, **Deviance and Respectability**, New York, Basic Books.

Douglas, J. D., 1971, **American Social Order: Social Rules in a Pluralistic Society**. New York, Free Press.

Downes, D., 1966, **The Delinquent Solution**. London, Routledge and Kegan Paul.

Downes, D. and Rock, P., 1988, **Understanding Deviance: A Guide to the Sociology of Crime and Rule Breaking** (second edition). Oxford, Clarendon.

Doyal, L., 1979, 'A matter of life and death: medicine, health and statistics', in Irvine, Miles, and Evans, (eds.), 1979, **Demystifying Social Statistics**. London, Pluto, pp. 237–54.

Drabman, R. S. and Thomas, M. H., 1975, 'Does TV violence breed indifference?', **Journal of Communication**, 25, no. 4, pp. 86–9.

Drewnowski, J. and Scott, W., 1966, **The Level of Living Index**, Report No. 4, Research Institute of Social Development, United Nations, Geneva.

Duffield, M., 1988, **Black Radicalism and the Politics of De-industrialisation: The Hidden History of Foundry Workers**. Aldershot, Avebury.

Duncan, O. D., 1961, 'A socioeconomic index for all occupations', in Reiss (ed.), 1961, **Occupations and Social Status**. Glencoe, Free Press.

Dunham, H. W., 1941, 'The character of the interrelationship of crime and schizophrenia', Ph.D., University of Chicago.

Dunhill, C., ed., 1989, **The Boys in Blue: Women's Challenge to the Police**. London, Virago.

Durkheim, E., [1893] 1947, **The Division of Labour in Society**. New York, Free Press.

Durkheim, E., [1895] 1964, **The Rules of Sociological Method**. New York, Free Press.

Durkheim, E., [1897] 1952, **Suicide: A Study in Sociology**. London, Routledge and Kegan Paul.

Durkheim, E., [1912] 1961, **The Elementary Forms of Religious Life**. New York, Collier.

Durkin, K., 1985, 'Television and sex role acquisition 1: Content', **British Journal of Social Psychology**, 24, pp. 101–13.

Easthope, G., 1974, **History of Social Research Methods**. London, Longman.

Eaton, M., 1986, **Justice for Women?** Milton Keynes, Open University Press.

EC Commission, 1991, **Final Report on the Second European Poverty Programme**. Brussels, EC Commission, COM(91) 29 final.

Eco, U., [1979] 1981, **The Role of the Reader: Explanations in the Semiotics of Texts**. London, Hutchinson.

Edwards, R. C., Reich, M. and Gordon , D. M., eds., 1975, **Labour Market Segmentation**. Lexington, Mass., Heath.

Edwards, R., 1979, **Contested Terrain**. New York, Basic Books.

Eichler, M., 1988, **Nonsexist Research Methods: A Practical Guide**. London, Allen and Unwin.

Eisenstein, Z., ed., 1979, **Capitalist Patriarchy and the Case for Socialist Feminism**. New York, Monthly Review Press.

Elliott, P., 1972, **The Making of a Television Series**. London, Constable.

Elliott, P., Murdock G. and Schlesinger, P., 1986, '"Terrorism" and the state: a case study of the discourse of television' in Richards *et al.* (eds.), 1986, **Media, Culture and Society: A Critical Reader**, London, Sage, pp. 264–86.

Engels, F., [1884] 1972, **Origin of the Family: Private Property and the State**. New York, International Publishers.

Evans, M., ed., 1982, **The Woman Question**. London, Fontana.

Evason, E., 1985, **On the Edge: A Study of Poverty and Long Term Unemployment in Northern Ireland**. London, Child Poverty Action Group.

Eysenck, H., 1970, **Crime and Personality**. London, Paladin.

Fagin, L. and Little, M., 1984, **The Forsaken Families: The Affects of Unemployment on Family Life**. Harmondsworth, Penguin.

Family Policy Studies Centre, 1985, 'The Family Today: Continuity and Change', **Fact Sheet 1**. London, Family Policy Studies Centre.

Faris, R. E. L. and Dunham, W., 1939, **Mental Disorders in Urban Areas**. Chicago, University of Chicago Press.

Farrington, D. and Morris, A., 1983, 'Sex, sentencing and reconvictions', **British Journal of Criminology**, 23.

Festinger, L., Rieken, N. and Schachter, P., 1956, **When Prophecy Fails**. New York, Harper and Row.

Fevre, R., 1984, **Cheap Labour and Racial Discrimination**. Aldershot, Gower.

Fielding, N., 1981, **The National Front**. London, Routledge and Kegan Paul.

Fielding, N., 1982, 'Observational research on the National Front' in Bulmer (ed.), 1982, **Social Research Ethics: An Examination of the Merits of Covert Participant Observation**. London, Macmillan.

Filby, M., 1989, 'Selling the Service: A Study of Gender and Sexuality in the Retail Betting Trade'. University Of Warwick, M.A. Labour Studies.

Filby, M. and Harvey, L., 1988, 'Recreational betting: everyday activity and strategies', **Leisure Studies**, 7, pp. 159–72.

Filby, M. and Harvey, L., 1989, 'Recreational betting: individual betting profiles', **Leisure Studies**, 8, pp. 219–27.

Filstead, W. J., ed., 1970, **Qualitative Methodology: Firsthand Involvement With the Social World**. Chicago, Markham.

Fisher, C. and Mawby, R., 1982, 'Juvenile delinquency and police discretion in an inner city area', **British Journal of Criminology**, 22.

Fiske, J and Hartley, J., 1978, **Reading Television**. London, Methuen.

Fitzgerald, M., 1985, 'Crime and deviance' in Haralambos (ed.), 1985b, **Developments in Sociology: An Annual Review. Volume 1.** Ormskirk, Causeway, pp. 131–46.

Fitzgerald, M., McLennan, G. and Pawson, J., eds., 1981, **Crime and Society: Readings in History and Theory**. London, RKP.

Fogleman, K., ed., 1983, **Growing up in Great Britain: Papers from the National Child Development Study**. London, Macmillan.

Fothergill, S. and Vincent, J., 1985, **The State of the Nation**. London, Pan.

Foucault, M., 1978, **The History of Sexuality, Volume 1: An Introduction**. New York, Pantheon.

Frankel, L. S., 1979, 'Sex Discrimination in Criminal Law' in Adler and Simon (eds.), 1979, **The Criminology of Deviant Women**. London, Houghton Mifflin.

Freuh, T. and McGhee, P. E., 1975, 'Traditional sex-role development and amount of time spent watching television', **Developmental Psychology**, 11, p. 109.

Freund, J. E., and Manning-Smith, R., 1986, **Statistics: A First Course.** (4th edition). Englewood Cliffs, N. J., Prentice-Hall.

Friedrichs, J., 1975, **Participant Observation**. Saxon House.

Fryer, D. and Ullah, P., eds., 1987, **Unemployed People: Social and Psychological Perspectives**. Milton Keynes, Open University Press.

Gabriel, J. G. and Ben-Tovim, G., 1979, 'The conceptualisation of race relations in sociological theory', **Ethnic and Racial Studies**, 2, no. 2.

Gabriel, Y., 1988, **Working Lives in Catering**. London, Routledge and Kegan Paul.

Gagnon, J. H. and Simon, W., 1973, **Sexual Conduct: The Social Sources of Human Sexuality**. London, Hutchinson.

Galtung, J., 1967, **Theory and Methods of Social Research**. London, Allen and Unwin.

Gamarnikow, E., Morgan, D. H. J., Purvis, J. and Talorson, D., eds., 1983, **The Public and the Private**. London, Heinemann.

Garfinkel, H., 1967, **Studies in Ethnomethodology**. Englewood Cliffs, Prentice-Hall.

Garofolo, R., 1914, **Criminology**. New York, Little Brown.

Garrett, S., 1987, **Gender**. London, Routledge.

Gavron, H., 1966, **The Captive Wife: Conflicts of Housebound Mothers**. London, Routledge and Kegan Paul.

Geer, B., 1964, 'First days in the field', in Hammond (ed.), 1964, **Sociologists at Work**. New York, Basic Books. pp. 322–44.

Geis, G. and Stottland, E., eds., 1980, **White Collar Crime: Theory and Research**. London, Sage.

Gerbner, G., 1972, 'Violence in television drama: trends and symbolic functions' in Comstock and Rubinstein (eds.), 1972, **Television and Social Behaviour, Volume 1, Content and Control**. Washington, DC, Government Printing Office.

Gerbner, G. and Gross, L., 1976, 'Living with television: The dynamics of the cultivation process', **Journal of Communication**, 26, no. 2, pp. 173–99.

Gerbner, G., Gross, L., Morgan, M. and Signorielli, N., 1986, 'Living with television: the dynamics of the cultivation process' in Bryant and Zillman (eds.), 1986, **Perspectives on Media Effects**, Hillsdale, N.J., Erlbaum.

Giallombardo, R., ed., 1976, **Juvenile Delinquency**. New York, Wiley.

Gibbens, T. C. N., 1971, 'Female offenders', **British Journal of Hospital Medicine**, 6, pp. 279–86.

Giddens A., 1989. **Sociology**. Oxford, Polity/Blackwell.

Gill, C., 1985, **Work, Unemployment and the New Technology**. Cambridge, Polity.

Gill, O., 1977, **Luke Street: Housing Policy, Conflict and the Creation of the Delinquent Area**. London, Macmillan.

Gilroy, P., 1982, 'The myth of black criminality' **Socialist Register**, pp. 47–56.

Gilroy, P., 1987, **There Ain't No Black in the Union Jack: The Cultural Politics of Race and Nation**. London, Hutchinson.

Gittins, D., 1985, **The Family in Question**. London, Macmillan.

Glaser, B. G. and Strauss, A. L., 1967, **The Discovery of Grounded Theory**. Chicago, Aldine.

Glaser, D., 1973, **Routinizing Evaluations: Getting Feedback on Effectiveness of Crime and Delinquency Programs**. Washington, D.C, Government Printing Office.

Glasgow Media Group, 1977, **Trade Unions and The Media** (edited by P. Beharrell and G. Philo). London, Macmillan.

Glasgow Media Group, 1982, **War and Peace News**. Milton Keynes, Open University Press.

Glasgow, D., 1971, **The Black Underclass**. New York, Vintage Books.

Glazer-Malbin, N. and Waehrer, H. Y., 1972, **Woman in a Man-Made World**. Chicago, Rand McNally.

Glenberg, A. M., 1988, **Learning From Data: An Introduction to Statistical Reasoning**. London, Harcourt, Brace Jovanovich.

Glock, C. Y. and Stark, R., 1965, **Religion and Society in Tension**. Chicago, Rand McNally.

Glover, D., 1985, 'The sociology of the mass media', in Haralambos (ed.), 1985a, **Sociology: New Directions**, Ormskirk, Causeway, pp. 371–442.

Glueck, S. and Glueck, E., 1956, **Physique and Delinquency**. New York, Wiley.

Goldman, R., 1992, **Reading Ads Socially**. London, Routledge.

Goldthorpe, J. H., Lockwood, D., Bechhofer, F. and Platt, J., 1969, **The Affluent Worker in the Class Structure**. Cambridge, Cambridge University Press.

Gonzalez, N. L., 1970, 'Towards a definition of matrifocality' in Whitten and Szwed. (eds.), 1970, **Afro-American Anthropology**. New York, Free Press.

Goode, W. J., 1963, **World Revolution and Family Patterns**. London, Collier-Macmillan.

Gordon, A., 1988, **The Crisis of Unemployment**. London, Helm.

Gordon, P. and Rosenberg, D., 1989, **Daily Racism: The Press and Black People in Britain**. London, Runymede Trust.

Gordon, R. L., 1980, **Interviewing Techniques and Tactics** (third edition). Homewood, Illinois, Dorsey Press.

Gottlieb, D., 1957, 'The Neighbourhood Tavern and the Cocktail Lounge', **American Journal of Sociology**, 62, pp. 550–62.

Gough, E., 1959, 'Is the family universal? The Nayar case' in Bell and Vogel (eds.), 1959, **A Modern Introduction to the Family**, London, Collier-Macmillan.

Gough, J. and Macnair, M., 1985, **Gay Liberation in the Eighties**. London, Pluto.

Government Statisticians' Collective, 1979, 'How Official Statistics are produced: views from the inside', in Irvine, Miles, and Evans (eds.), 1979, **Demystifying Social Statistics**. London, Pluto, pp. 130–51.

Grabrucker, M., 1988, **There's a Good Girl – Gender Stereotyping in the First Three Years of Life: A Diary** (trans. Wendy Philipson). London, Women's Press.

Grace, G., 1978, **Teachers, Ideology and Control: A Study in Urban Education**. London, Routledge and Kegan Paul.

Gramsci, A., 1971, **Selections from the Prison Notebooks of Antonio Gramsci**. (Translated and edited by Q. Hoare and G. Nowell-Smith). New York, International.

Gration, G., Reilly, J. and Titford, J., 1988, **Communication and Media Studies: An Introductory Coursebook**. London, Macmillan.

Greenberg, B. S., 1981, **Life on Television: Content Analysis of US Television Drama** (in collaboration with C. K. Atkin *et al.*). Norwood, N.J., Ablex Publishing Co.

Greenwood, E., 1965, **Experimental Sociology**. New York, King's Crown Press.

Griffin, S., 1984a, **The Roaring Inside Her**. London, Women's Press.

Griffin, S., 1984b, **Woman and Nature**. London, Women's Press.

Grimshaw, R. and Jefferson, T., 1987, **Interpreting Policework: Policy and Practice in Forms of Beat Policing**. London, Allen and Unwin.

Gunter, B., 1986, **Television and Sex Role Stereotyping**. London, Libby/IBA.

Gunter, B. and McAleer, J. L., 1990, **Children and Television: The One Eyed Monster**. London, Routledge.

Gunter, B. and Wober, M., 1988, **Violence on Television: What the Viewers Think**. London, Libby/IBA.

Gwilliam, P., 1988, **Basic Statistics**. Harmondsworth, Penguin.

Hacker, S., 1989, **Pleasure, Power and Technology: Some Tales of Gender, Engineering, and the Co-operative Workplace**. London, Harper Collins.

Hagen, J., 1988, **Structural Criminology**. Cambridge, Polity.

Hakim, C., 1982, **Secondary Analysis in Social Research: A Guide to Data Sources and Methods with Examples**. London, Allen and Unwin.

Halfpenny, P., 1982, **Positivism and Sociology: Explaining Social Life**. London, Allen and Unwin.

Hall, R. E., 1985, **Ask Any Woman**. London, Falling Wall Press.

Hall, S., 1973, 'Encoding and Decoding the T.V. message', CCCS mimeo, University of Birmingham.

Hall, S. and Jefferson, T., eds., 1976, **Resistance Through Rituals**. London, Hutchinson.

Hall, S. and Scraton, P., 1981, 'Law, class and control' in Fitzgerald *et al.* (eds.), 1981, **Crime and Society: Readings in History and Theory**. London, Routledge and Kegan Paul.

Hall, S. *et al.*, 1978, **Policing the Crisis**. London, Macmillan.

Hall, S. *et al.*, eds., 1980, **Culture, Media, Language** (CCCS). London, Hutchinson.

Hammersley, M., 1990, 'What's wrong with ethnography? The myth of theoretical description', **Sociology**, 24, no. 4, pp. 597–615.

Hammersley, M. and Atkinson, P., 1983, **Ethnography: Principles in Practice**. London, Tavistock.

Hammond, P., ed., 1964, **Sociologists at Work**. New York, Basic Books.

Haney C., Banks C. and Zimbardo P., 1973, 'A study of prisoners and guards in a simulated prison', reprinted in Potter *et al.*, 1981, **Society and the Social Sciences: An Introduction**. London, Routledge and Kegan Paul/Open University.

Haralambos, M., ed., 1985a, **Sociology: New Directions**, Ormskirk, Causeway.

Haralambos, M., ed., 1985b, **Developments in Sociology: An Annual Review, Volume 1**. Ormskirk, Causeway.

Haralambos, M., ed., 1986, **Developments in Sociology: An Annual Review, Volume 2**. Ormskirk, Causeway.

Haralambos, M. (with Holborn, M.), 1990, **Sociology: Themes and Perspectives** (third edition). London, Hyman Unwin.

Harastzi, M., 1977, **A Worker in a Worker's State**. Harmondsworth, Penguin.

Hargreaves, D. H., 1967, **Social Relations in a Secondary School**. London, Routledge and Kegan Paul.

Hargreaves, D. H., Hester, S. and Mellor, F., 1975, **Deviance in Classrooms**. London, Routledge and Kegan Paul.

Harker, D., 1980, **One For the Money: Politics and Popular Song**. London, Hutchinson.

Hart, J. and Richardson, D., 1981, **The Theory and Practice of Homosexuality**. London, Routledge and Kegan Paul.

Hart, N., 1985, 'The sociology of health and medicine' in Haralambos (ed.), 1985a, **Sociology: New Directions**, Ormskirk, Causeway, pp. 519–654.

Hartmann, H., 1979, 'The unhappy marriage of Marxism and feminism', **Capital and Class**, 8.

Hartmann, P. and Husband, C., 1974, **Racism and the Mass Media: A Study of the Role of the Mass Media in the Formation of White Belief and Attitudes in Britain**. London, Davis-Poynter.

Harvey, L., 1987a, 'Factors affecting response rates to mailed questionnaires: a comprehensive review of the literature', **Journal of the Market Research Society**, 29, 3, pp. 341–53.

Harvey, L., 1987b, **Myths of the Chicago School of Sociology**. Aldershot, Gower.

Harvey, L., 1990, **Critical Social Research**. London, Hyman Unwin.

Harvey, L., Little, M. and Turner, D., 1982, 'The perceptions of fans on the British soccer terrace', Crowd Behaviour Project, Paper 2, Birmingham Polytechnic.

Harvey, L., Wells, J. and Place, A., 1990, **Sandwell Skills Audit**. Report for the Economic Development Unit of Sandwell M.B.C.

Hatchett, S. and Schuman, H., 1975, 'White respondents and race-of-interviewer effects', **Public Opinion Quarterly**, 39, pp. 523–8.

Hawkes, T., 1977, **Structuralism and Semiotics**. London, Methuen.

Hayner, N., 1936, **The Hotel**. Chapel Hill, University of North Carolina Press.

Hebdidge, D., 1979, **Subculture: The Meaning of Style**. London, Methuen.

Heck, M. C., 1980, 'The ideological dimension of media messages' in Hall *et al.* (eds.), 1980, **Culture, Media, Language**. London, Hutchinson, p. 122.

Heidensohn, F., 1985, **Women and Crime**. London, Macmillan.

Henwood, F., 1983, Employment, Unemployment and Housework. M.Sc. dissertation, University of Sussex, Service Policy Research Unit.

Henwood, F. and Miles, I., 1987, 'Unemployment and the sexual division of labour' in Fryer and Ullah (eds.) 1987, **Unemployed People**. Milton Keynes, Open University Press.

Heritage, J., 1984, **Garfinkel and Ethnomethodology**. Cambridge, Polity.

Hirsch, P. M., 1980, 'The 'scary world' of the non-viewer and other anomalies: a reanalysis of Gerber *et al.* findings on cultivation analysis, Part I', **Communication Research**, 7, no. 4, pp. 403–56.

Hirschi, T. and Stark, R., 1969, 'Hell fire and delinquency', **Social Problems**, 17, no. 2, pp. 202–13.

Hobson, D., 1978, 'Housewives: isolation as oppression', in Women's Study Group Centre for Contemporary Cultural Studies, 1978, **Women Take Issue: Aspects of Women's Subordination**. London, Hutchinson, pp. 79–95.

Hobson, D., 1982, **Crossroads: The Drama of a Soap Opera**. London, Methuen.

Hodge, R. and Kress, G., 1988, **Social Semiotics**. Cambridge, Polity.

Hodge, R. and Tripp, D., 1986, **Children and Television: A Semiotic Approach**. Cambridge, Polity/Blackwell.

Hoggarth, E., 1991, **Selections for Community Service Orders**. Aldershot, Avebury.

Hoghughi, M. and Forrest, A., 1970, 'Eysenck's theory of criminality', **British Journal of Criminology**, 10, pp. 240–54.

Hoinville, G., Jowell, R. and Associates, 1978, **Survey Research Practice**. London, Heinemann.

Holdaway, S., 1983, **Inside the British Police: A Force at Work**. Oxford, Blackwell.

Hollingshead, A. B., 1957, **The Two Factor Index of Social Position**. New Haven, Conn., Yale University Press.

Hollingshead, A. B. and Redlich, F. C., 1958, **Social Class and Mental Illness**. New York, Wiley.

Holsti, O., 1969, **Content Analysis for the Social Sciences and Humanities**. Reading, Mass., Addison-Wesley.

Home Office, 1990, **The 1988 British Crime Survey**, Home Office Research Study, 111. London, HMSO.

Hopkins, A., 1980, 'Controlling corporate deviance', **Criminology**, 18.

Hough, M. and Mayhew, P., 1983, **The British Crime Survey**, Home Office Research Study, 76. London, HMSO.

Hough, M. and Mayhew, P., 1985, **Taking Account of Crime: Key Findings from the Second British Crime Survey**. Home Office Research Study Paper, 85. London, HMSO.

Hughes, J. A., 1976, **Sociological Analysis: Methods of Discovery**. London, Nelson.

Humphreys, L., 1970, **Tearoom Trade**. London, Duckworth.

Hunter, H., 1966, 'YY chromosomes and Klinefelter's Syndrome', **The Lancet**, 30th April.

Hutter, B. and Williams, G., eds., 1981, **Controlling Women**. London, Croom Helm.

Hyman, H., 1954, **Interviewing in Social Research**. Chicago, University of Chicago Press.

Innis, R., ed., 1986, **Semiotics: An Introductory Reader**. London, Hutchinson.

Irvine, J., Miles, I. and Evans, J., eds., 1979, **Demystifying Social Statistics**. London, Pluto.

Iser, W., 1980, 'The reading process: a phenomenological approach', in Tompkins, J. P. (ed.), **Reader-Response Criticism: From Formalism to Post-structuralism**, Baltimore, Johns Hopkins University Press.

Jackson, B., 1972, **Working Class Community**. Harmondsworth, Penguin.

Jackson, P. R. and Walsh, S., 1987, 'Unemployment and the family' in Fryer and Ullah (eds.), 1987, **Unemployed People: Social and Psychological Perspectives**. Milton Keynes, Open University Press, pp. 194–216.

Jauss, H. R., 1982, **Towards an Aesthetic Reception**. Minneapolis, University of Minnesota Press.

Jensen, K. B. and Jankowski, N. W., 1991, **A Handbook of Qualitative Methodologies for Mass Communication Research**. London, Routledge.

Johnson, L., 1992, **The Modern Girl: Girlhood and Growing Up**. Buckingham, Open University Press.

Jones, C. and Mahony, P., eds., 1989, **Learning Our Lines**. London, Women's Press.

Jones, J., 1982, '"My mother was much of a woman": black women, work and the family under slavery', **Feminist Studies**, 8, pp. 235–69.

Joseph, G., 1981, 'The incompatible ménage à trois: marxism, feminism and racism', in Sargent (ed.), 1981, **Women and Revolution: The Unhappy Marriage of Marxism and Feminism**. London, Pluto Press, pp. 91–107.

Joseph, G., 1983, **Women at Work**. Oxford, Philip Allan.

Jowell, R. and Witherspoon S., eds., 1985, **British Social Attitudes: The 1985 Report**. Aldershot, Gower.Kapadia, R. and Anderson, G., 1987, **Statistics Explained: Basic Concepts and Methods**. Chichester, Ellis Horwood.

Kapadia, R. and Anderson, G., 1987, **Statistics Explained: Basic Concepts and Methods**. Chichester, Ellis Horwood.

Kaplan, A. F., 1971, 'Chromosomal abnormalities and anti-social behavior', **Journal of Genetic Psychology**, 118, pp. 281–92.

Kinsey, R., Lea, J. and Young, J., 1986, **Losing the Fight Against Crime**. Oxford, Blackwell.

Kitsuse, J. J. and Cicourel, A. V., 1963, 'A note on the uses of official statistics', **Social Problems**, 11, pp. 131–9.

Klapper, J., 1960, **The Effects of Mass Communication**. Glencoe, Free Press.

Kohn, M. L., 1959, 'Social class and parental values', **American Journal of Sociology**, 64, pp. 337–51.

Konopka, G., 1966, **The Adolescent Girl**. Englewood Cliffs, Prentice-Hall.

Krippendorf, K., 1982, **Content Analysis**. Beverley Hills, Sage.

Kuhn, A. and Wolpe, A. M., eds., 1978, **Feminism and Materialism: Women and Modes of Production**, London, Routledge and Kegan Paul.

Kuhn, T. S., 1962, **The Structure of Scientific Revolutions**. Chicago, University of Chicago Press.

Kuhn, T. S., 1970, **The Structure of Scientific Revolutions** (second edition with Appendix). Chicago, University of Chicago Press.

Kuzwayo, E., 1985, **Call Me Woman**. London, Women's Press.

Lacey, C., 1966, 'Some sociological concomitants of academic streaming in grammar school, **British Journal of Sociology**, 17, pp. 245–62.

Lacey, C., 1970, **Hightown Grammar: The School as a Social System**. Manchester, University of Manchester Press.

Ladner, J. A., 1971, **Tomorrow's Tomorrow**. Garden City, N.Y., Doubleday.

Lambert, J. R., 1970, **Crime, Police and Race Relations**. London, Institute of Race Relations/Oxford University Press.

Landau, S. and Nathan, G., 1983, 'Juveniles and the police', **British Journal of Criminology**, 23.

Lasswell, H. D., and Leites, N., 1965, **Language of Politics: Studies in Quantitative Semantics**. Cambridge, Mass., MIT Press.

Layard, R. and Nickell, S., 1986, **How to Beat Unemployment**. Oxford, Oxford University Press.

Laycock, G., 1984, **Reducing Burglary**. London.

Lazarsfeld, P. F., Berelson, B. and Gaudet, H., [1944] 1968, **The People's Choice: How the Voter Makes up His Mind in a Presidential Campaign** (third edition). New York, Columbia University Press.

Le Grand, J., 1987, 'Health and wealth', **New Society**, 16th January 1987, pp. 8–9.

Lea, J. and Young, J., 1984, **What Is to be Done About Law and Order?** Harmondsworth, Penguin.

Lee, N., 1969, **The Search for an Abortionist**. Chicago.

Lees, S., 1986, **Losing Out**. London, Hutchinson.

Leggett, J. C., 1963, 'Uprootedness and working class consciousness', **American Journal of Sociology**, 69, pp. 685–8.

LeMasters, E. E., 1975, **Blue-Collar Aristocrats**. Madison, University of Wisconsin Press.

Lemert, E., 1951, **Social Pathology**. New York, McGraw Hill.

Lemert, E., 1971, **Instead of Court**. Washington, DC, National Institute of Mental Health.

Liddle, J. and Joshi, R., 1986, **Daughters of Independence: Gender, Caste and Class in India**. London, Zed.

Liebow, E., 1967, **Tally's Corner**. London, Routledge and Kegan Paul.

Lilley, P., 1990, Commons Written Reply, 13.2.90.

Little, M., 1990, **Young Men in Prison**. Aldershot, Dartmouth.

Livingstone, S. M., 1990, **Making Sense of Television: The Psychology of Audience Interpretation**. Oxford, Pergamon.

Lombroso, C., 1911, **Crime, Its Causes and Remedies**. New York, Little Brown.

Lombroso, C. and Ferrero, W., [1895] 1959, **The Female Offender**. New York, Peter Owen.

London Rape Crisis Centre (LRCC), 1984, **Sexual Violence: The Reality for Women**. London, Women's Press.

Lopreato, J. and Lewis, L. S., eds., 1974, **Social Stratification: A Reader**. New York, Harper and Row.

Loveridge, R. and Mok, A., 1979, **Theories of Labour Market Segmentation**. The Hague, Martinus Nijhoff.

Luhrman, T. M., 1989, **Persuasions of the Witch's Craft**. Oxford, Blackwell.

Lull, J., 1990, **Inside Family Viewing: Ethnographic Research on Television Audiences**. London, Comedia.

Lynd, R. S. and Lynd H. M., 1929, **Middletown**. New York, Harcourt Brace Jovanovich.

Lynd, R. S. and Lynd H. M., 1937, **Middletown in Transition: A Study in Cultural Conflicts**. New York, Harcourt Brace Jovanovich.

MacInnes, J., 1987, **Thatcherism at Work**. Milton Keynes, Open University Press.

Macintyre, S., 1986, 'Health and illness' in Burgess (ed.), 1986, **Key Variables in Sociological Research**. London, Routledge and Kegan Paul, pp. 76–98.

Mack J. and Lansley S., 1985 'Pressure point: the crisis in management' in Ward, S. (ed.), 1985, **DHSS in Crisis: Social Security Under Pressure and Under Review**. London, Child Poverty Action Group.

Mack, J. and Lansley, S., 1984, **Poor Britain**. London, Allen and Unwin.

Mack, J. and Lansley, S., 1991, **Breadline Britain in the 1990s**. London, Allen and Unwin.

Maconachie, M., 1984, 'Engels, sexual divisions and the family', in Sayers *et al.*, eds., 1984, **Engels Revisited: New Feminist Essays**. London, Tavistock, pp. 98–112.

MacQueen, D. R., ed., 1973, **Understanding Sociology Through Research**, Reading, Mass., Addison-Wesley,

Malcolmson, R. W., 1973, **Popular Recreations in English Society, 1700–1780**. London, Hutchinson.

Malinowski, B., 1922, **Argonauts of the Western Pacific**. London, Routledge and Kegan Paul.

Malinowski, B., 1954, **Magic, Science, and Religion**. New York, Doubleday Anchor Books.

Mandelbaum, D. G., 1982, 'The Study of Life History', in Burgess (ed.), 1982, **Field Research: A Sourcebook and Field Manual**. London, Allen and Unwin.

Manis, J. G. and Meltzer, B. N., eds., 1978, **Symbolic Interaction: A Reader in Social Psychology** (third edition). Boston, Allyn and Bacon.

Marks, E. and Courtivron, I. de, eds., 1980, **New French Feminisms**. Amherst, University of Massachusetts Press.

Marmot, M. G., Adelstein, A. M. and Bulusu, L., 1984, **Immigrant Mortality in England and Wales 1970–78**. Studies on Medical and Population Subjects, No. 47. London, HMSO.

Marokvasic, M, 1983, 'Women in migration: beyond the reductionist outlook' in Phizacklea, A. (ed.), 1983a, **One Way Ticket: Migration and Female Labour**. London, Routledge and Kegan Paul, pp. 13–32.

Marsh, C., 1982, **The Survey Method: The Contribution of Surveys to Sociological Explanation**. London, Allen and Unwin.

Marsh, C., 1988, **Exploring Data: An Introduction to Data Analysis for Social Scientists**. Cambridge, Polity.

Marsh, P., Rosser, E. and Harré, R., 1978, **The Rules of Disorder**. London, Routledge and Kegan Paul.

Marshall, G., 1986, 'The workplace culture of a licensed restaurant', **Theory, Culture and Society**, 3, no. 1, pp. 33–47.

Marshall, G., Rose, D. and Newby, H., 1989, **Social Class in Modern Britain**. London, Routledge.

Marx, K., 1870, 'Letter to S. Meyer and A. Vogt, 9th April 1870' in Marx and Engels, 1962, **On Britain** (second edition), Moscow, Foreign Languages Publishing House.

Marx, K., 1963, 'Alienated labour' in Bottomore (ed.), 1963, **Karl Marx: Early Writings**. Harmondsworth, Penguin.

Marx, K. and Engels, F., [1887] 1977, **Capital: A Critique of Political Economy, Volume 1**. English Edition. London, Lawrence and Wishart.

Marx, K. and Engels, F., 1962, **On Britain** (second edition). Moscow, Foreign Languages Publishing House.

Mason, D., 1982, 'After Scarman: a note on the concept of institutional racism', **New Community**, 10, no. 1, Summer.

Matza, D., 1961, 'Subterranean traditions of youth', **Annals of the American Academy of Political and Social Science**, 338, pp. 102–18.

Matza, D., 1964, **Delinquency and Drift**. New York, Wiley.

Matza, D., 1969, **Becoming Deviant**. Englewood Cliffs, Prentice-Hall.

Mayntz, R., Holm, K. and Huebner, R., 1976, **Introduction to Empirical Sociology**. London, Harmondsworth.

McCall, G. J. and Simmons, J. L., eds., 1969, **Issues in Participant Observation: A Text and Reader**. Reading, Mass., Addison-Wesley.

McCombs, M. and Gilbert, S., 1986, 'News influence on our pictures of the world', in Bryant, J. and Zillman, D. (eds.), **Perspectives on Media Effects**, Hillsdale, N.J., Erlbaum.

McGhee, P. E. and Freuh, T., 1980, 'Television viewing and the learning of sex role stereotypes', **Sex Roles**, 2, 179–88.

McIntosh, N. and Smith, D. J., 1974, **The Extent of Racial Discrimination**, Vol. 40, Broadsheet No. 547. London, PEP.

McLellan, D., ed., 1977, **Karl Marx: Selected Writings**. Oxford, Oxford University Press.

McNeil, P., 1990, **Research Methods**. London, Routledge.

McQuail, D., 1983, **Mass Communication Theory, An Introduction**. London, Sage.

McRobbie, A. and Garber, J., 1976, 'Girls and subcultures' in Hall and Jefferson (eds.), 1976, **Resistance Through Rituals**. London, Hutchinson, pp. 209–22.

McRobbie, A. and McCabe, I., 1981, **Feminism for Girls**, London, Routledge and Kegan Paul.

McRobbie, A., 1981, 'Just Like A *Jackie* Story' in McRobbie and McCabe, 1981, **Feminism for Girls**, London, Routledge and Kegan Paul, pp. 113–29.

McRobbie, A., 1983, 'JACKIE: An ideology of adolescent femininity', in Wartella, Whitney and Windahl, (eds.), 1983, **Mass Communications Review Yearbook**, 4, Beverley Hills, Sage.

Mead, H. G., 1934, **Mind, Self and Society** (edited by C. Morris). Chicago, University of Chicago Press.

Measor, L. and Woods, P., 1984, **Changing Schools: Pupil Perspectives on Transfer to a Comprehensive**. Milton Keynes, Open University Press.

Mehan, H., and Wood, H., 1975, **The Reality of Ethnomethodology**. New York, Wiley.

Melischeck, G, Rosengren, K. E. and Stappers, J., eds., 1984, **Cultural Indicators: An International Symposium**. Vienna, Austrian Academy of Sciences.

Meltzer, B. N., Petras, J. W. and Reynolds, L. T., 1975, **Symbolic Interactionism: Genesis, Varieties and Criticism**. London, Routledge and Kegan Paul.

Merton, R., 1938, 'Social structure and anomie', **Sociological Review**, 3, pp. 672–82.

Merton, R. K., Fiske, M. and Kendall, P. L., 1956, **The Focused Interview: A Manual of Problems and Procedures**. Glencoe, Free Press.

Miles, I., 1983, **Adaptation to Unemployment?** (Occasional Paper no. 20). Falmer, Brighton: Science Policy Research Unit.

Miles, I. and Irvine, J., 1979, 'The critique of Official Statistics' in Irvine, Miles, and Evans (eds.), 1979, **Demystifying Social Statistics**. London, Pluto, pp. 113–29.

Miles, R., 1982, **Racism and Migrant Labour**. London, Routledge and Kegan Paul.

Miles, R., 1989, **Racism**. London, Routledge.

Miliband, R., [1969] 1973, **The State in Capitalist Society**. London, Quartet.

Mills, C. W., 1971, **The Sociological Imagination**. Harmondsworth, Penguin.

Minford, P., 1985, **Unemployment: Causes and Cure**. Oxford, Blackwell.

Mishler, E. G; 1986, **Research Interviewing**. Cambridge, Mass., Harvard University Press.

Mitchell, J., 1974, **Women and Psychoanalysis**. Harmondsworth, Penguin.

Molotch, H. and Lester, M., 1974, 'News as purposive behavior: on the strategic use of routine events, accidents and scandals', **American Sociological Review**, 39, pp. 101–12.

Moore, S., 1988, **Investigating Deviance**. London, Unwin Hyman.

Moore-Gilbert, B. and Seed., J., 1992, **Cultural Revolution?** London, Routledge.

Moraga, C. and Anzaldua, G., eds., 1981, **This Bridge Called My Back: Writings by Radical Women of Colour**. Watertown Mass., Persephone Press.

Morgan, D. H. J., 1985, 'The family' in Haralambos, M. (ed.), 1985b, **Developments in Sociology: An annual review**. Volume 1. Ormskirk, Causeway, pp. 89–108.

Morgan, M., 1982, 'Television and adolescents' sex role stereotypes: A longitudinal study', **Journal of Personality and Social Psychology**, 43, pp. 947–55.

Morgan, P., 1975, **Child Care: Sense and Fable**. London.

Morgan, R., 1978, **Going Too Far**. New York, Random House.

Morgan, R., 1982, **The Anatomy of Freedom**. Oxford, Martin Robertson.

Morley, D., 1980, **The 'Nationwide' Audience: Structure and Decoding**. London, British Film Institute.

Mortimer, E., 1982, **Faith and Power: The Politics of Islam**. London, Faber and Faber.

Moser, C. A. and Kalton, G., [1958] 1971, **Survey Methods in Social Investigation** (second edition). London, Heinemann.

Murdock, G. P., 1949, **Social Structure**. New York, Macmillan.

Murray, N., 1986, 'Anti-racists and other demons: the press and ideology in Thatcher's Britain', **Race and Class**, 27, no. 3. (Reprinted in Murray and Searle, 1989, **Racism and the Press in Thatcher's Britain**, Race and Class Pamphlet No. 12. Nottingham, Russell Press/Institute of Race Relations.)

Murray, N. and Searle, C., 1989, **Racism and the Press in Thatcher's Britain**. Race and Class Pamphlet No. 12. Nottingham, Russell Press/Institute of Race Relations.

Myerhoff, H. and Myerhoff, B., 1964, 'Field observations of middle class "gangs"', **Social Forces**, 42, pp. 328–36. (Reprinted in Giallombardo (ed.), 1976, **Juvenile Delinquency**. New York, Wiley; and in MacQueen (ed.), 1973, **Understanding Sociology Through Research**, Reading, Mass., Addison-Wesley, pp.246–54.)

Nagel, I., 1980, 'Sex differences in the processing of criminal defendants' in Weisberg (ed.), 1980, **Women and the Law**. New York.

Napes, G., 1970, 'Unequal justice: a growing disparity in criminal sentences troubles legal experts', **Wall Street Journal**, 9th September.

Nelson, G. K., 1986, 'Religion' in Haralambos (ed.), 1986, **Developments in Sociology: An Annual Review, Volume 2**. Ormskirk, Causeway.

Newby, H., 1977, **The Deferential Worker**. London, Allen Lane.

Newcastle upon Tyne City Council, 1980, **Redundancy in Newcastle upon Tyne: A case study**. Newcastle, Policy Studies Department.

Noelle-Neumann, E., 1974, 'The spiral of silence: a theory of public opinion', **Journal of Communication**, 24, no. 2, pp. 43–52.

Oakley, A., 1972, **Sex Gender and Society**. London, Temple Smith.

Oakley, A., 1974, **The Sociology of Housework**. Oxford, Martin Robertson.

Oakley, A., 1979a, **From Here to Maternity**. Harmondsworth, Penguin

Oakley, A., 1979b, **Becoming A Mother**. Oxford, Martin Robertson.

Oakley, A., 1981, 'Interviewing women: a contradiction in terms', in H. Roberts (ed.), 1981, **Doing Feminist Research**, London, Routledge and Kegan Paul.

Oakley, A. and Oakley, R., 1979, 'Sexism in Official Statistics', in Irvine, Miles, and Evans (eds.), 1979, **Demystifying Social Statistics**. London, Pluto, pp. 172–89.

Okely, J., 1983, **The Traveller Gypsies**. Cambridge, Cambridge University Press.

Open University, 1979, **Ethnography Project Guide**. Milton Keynes, Open University Press.

Open University, 1986, **Social Science: A Third-level Course, Research Methods in Education and Social Science** (Unit 3.2). Milton Keynes, Open University Press.

Oppenheim, C., 1990, **Poverty: The Facts**. London, Child Poverty Action Group.

Orbach, S., 1981, **Fat is a Feminist Issue**. London, Hamlyn.

Osler, A., 1989, **Speaking Out: Black Girls in Britain**. London, Virago.

Osman, T., 1985, **The Facts of Everyday Life**. London, Faber and Faber.

Padel, U. and Stevenson, P., 1988, **Insiders: Women's Experience of Prison**. London, Virago.

Page, R., 1971, **Down Among the Dossers**, London, Davis-Poynter.

Park, R. E., Burgess, E. W. and McKenzie, R. D. , 1925, **The City**. Chicago, University of Chicago Press.

Parker, H. J., 1974, **View from the Boys**. Newton Abbot, David and Charles.

Parker, T. and Allerton, R., 1962, **The Courage of His Convictions**. London, Arrow.

Parmar, P., 1981, 'Young Asian women : a critique of the pathological approach', **Multiracial Education**, 9, no. 3, pp. 19–29.

Parmar, P., 1982, 'Gender, race and class: Asian women in resistance', in Centre for Contemporary Cultural Studies (eds.), 1982, **The Empire Strikes Back: Race and Racism in 1970s Britain**. London, Hutchinson.

Parsons, T., 1951, **The Social System**. New York, Free Press.

Parsons, T., 1954, **Essays on Sociological Theory**. Glencoe, Free Press.

Parsons, T., Bales, R. F., Old, S. J., Zelditch, M. and Slater, P. E., 1955, **Family Socialisation and Interaction Process**. New York, Free Press.

Parsons, T. and Bales, R. F., 1955, **Family Socialization and Interaction Process**. New York, Free Press.

Patrick, J., 1973, **A Glasgow Gang Observed**. London, Eyre Methuen.

Patterson, S., 1963, **Dark Strangers**. London, Tavistock.

Payne, J., 1987, 'Does unemployment run in families? Some findings from the *General Household Survey*', **Sociology**, 21, pp. 199–214.

Pearce, F., 1989, **The Radical Durkheim**. London, Hyman Unwin.

Pfohl, S., 1986, **Images of Deviance and Social Control**. New York, McGraw-Hill.

Phillips, D. A., 1986, 'Natural experiments on the effects of the mass media' in Berkowitz (ed.), 1986, **Advances in Experimental Social Psychology**, New York, Academic Press.

Phillipson, M. and Roche, M., 1974, 'Phenomenology, sociology and the study of deviance', in Rock and McIntosh (eds.), 1974, **Deviance and Social Control**. London.

Phizacklea, A. , 1982, 'Migrant women and wage labour: the case of West Indian women in Britain' in West (ed.), 1982, **Work, Women and the Labour Market**. London, Routledge and Kegan Paul.

Phizacklea, A., ed., 1983a, **One Way Ticket: Migration and Female Labour**. London, Routledge and Kegan Paul.

Phizacklea, A., 1983b, 'In the front line' in Phizacklea, A. (ed.), 1983a, **One Way Ticket: Migration and Female Labour**. London, Routledge and Kegan Paul, pp. 95–112.

Phizacklea, A. and Miles, R., 1980, **Labour and Racism**. London, Routledge and Kegan Paul.

Piliavin, I. M., Rodin, J. and Piliavin, J. A., 1969, 'Good Samaritanism: an underground phenomenon?' **Journal of Personality and Social Psychology**, 13, no. 4.

Pilkington, A., 1984, **Race Relations in Britain**. Slough, UTP.

Pilkington, E., 1990, 'What goes on and off the record', **Guardian, EG**, 16th October 1990, p. 2.

Pilkington, E., 1991, 'Poverty', **Guardian, EG**, 2nd July 1991, pp. 2–3.

Pingree, S., 1983, '*The Guiding Light*' in Cantor and Pingree, 1983, **The Soap Opera**. Beverley Hills, Sage, pp. 97–112.

Piore, M. J., 1975, 'Notes for a theory of labour market stratification' in Edwards, Reich and Gordon (eds.), 1975, **Labour Market Segmentation**. Lexington, Mass., Heath.

Platt, A., 1978, '"Street Crime" – a view from the Left', **Crime and Social Justice**, 9.

Player, E., 1989, 'Women and crime in the city' in Downes, D., (ed.), **Crime and the City: Essays in Honour of John Mays**. London.

Plummer, K., ed., 1981, **The Making of the Modern Homosexual**. London, Hutchinson.

Polsky, N., [1967] 1971, **Hustlers Beats and Others**. Harmondsworth, Penguin.

Potter, D., Anderson, J., Clarke, J., Coombes, P., Hall, S., Harris, L., Holloway, C., and Walton, T., 1981, **Society and the Social Sciences: An Introduction**. London, Routledge and Kegan Paul/Open University.

Power, M., 1983, 'From home production to wage labour: women as a reserve army of labour', **Review of Radical Political Economics**, 15, pp. 71–91.

Prescod-Roberts, M. and Steele, N., 1980, **Black Women, Bringing It All Back Home**. Falling Wall Press.

Price, W., 1966, 'Criminal patients with XYY sex chromosome complement', **The Lancet**, 12th March.

Probyn, W., 1977, **Angel Face**. London.

Pryce, K., 1979, **Endless Pressure**. Harmondsworth, Penguin.

Psathas, G., ed., 1979, **Everyday Language: Studies in Ethnomethodology**. Englewood Cliffs, N. J., Prentice Hall.

Raboch, J. and Sipova, I., 1974, 'Intelligence in homosexuals, transsexuals and hypogonadotropic eunuchoids', **Journal of Sex Research**, 10, pp. 156–61.

Racial Attack Group, 1989, Draft Report. Reported in **Guardian** 27th April 1989.

Radford, J. and Russell, D. E. H., eds., 1992, **Femicide: The Politics of Woman Killing**. Buckingham, Open University Press.

Radical Statistics Health Group, 1980, **The Unofficial Guide to Health Statistics**. London, Radical Statistics.

Radical Statistics Health Group, 1987, **Facing the Figures: What Really is Happening to the National Health Service**. London, Radical Statistics.

Ramdin, R., 1987, **The Making of the Black Working Class in Britain**. Aldershot, Wildwood House.

Rapoport, R. N., Fogarty, M. and Rapoport, R., eds., 1982, **Families in Britain**, London, Routledge and Kegan Paul.

Rathwell, T. and Phillips, D., eds., 1986, **Health, Race and Ethnicity**. London, Croom Helm.

Reiss, A. J., ed., 1961, **Occupations and Social Status**. Glencoe, Free Press.

Rex, J. and Moore, R., 1967, **Race, Community and Conflict**. Oxford, Oxford University Press.

Rex, J. and Tomlinson, S., 1979, **Colonial Immigrants in a British City**. London, Routledge and Kegan Paul.

Reynolds, L. T., 1969, 'The sociology of symbolic interactionism', Ph.D., Ohio State University.

Rhind, D., ed., 1983, **A Census User's Handbook**. London, Methuen.

Rich, A., 1977, **Of Woman Born**. London, Virago.

Rich, A., 1981, **Compulsory Heterosexuality and Lesbian Existence**. London, Onlywomen Press.

Richards et al (eds.), 1986, **Media, Culture and Society: A Critical Reader**. London, Sage, pp. 264–86.

Richardson, J. and Lambert, J., 1985, 'The sociology of race', Section 1 of Haralmabos, M. (ed.), **Sociology: New Directions**. Ormskirk, Causeway, pp. 3–88.

Roberts, H., ed., 1981, **Doing Feminist Research**. London, Routledge and Kegan Paul.

Robertson, R., ed., 1970, **The Sociological Interpretation of Religion**. Oxford, Blackwell.

Robins, D. and Cohen, P., 1978, **Knuckle Sandwich**. Harmondsworth, Penguin.

Rock, P., 1979, **The Making of Symbolic Interactionism**. London, Macmillan.

Rock, P. and McIntosh, M., eds., 1974, **Deviance and Social Control**. London.

Roebuck, J. and Spray, S. L., 1967, 'The cocktail lounge: a study of heterosexual relations in a public organisation', **American Journal of Sociology**, 72, pp. 388–95.

Roethlisberger, F. J. and Dickson W. J., 1939. **Management and the Worker**. Cambridge, Mass., Harvard University Press.

Rogers, B., 1988, **Men Only**. London, Pandora.

Rogers, M. F., 1983, **Sociology, Ethnomethodology, and Experience: A Phenomenological Critique**. Cambridge, Cambridge University Press.

Rose, G., 1982, **Deciphering Sociological Research**. London, Macmillan.

Ross, A. D., 1961, **The Hindu Family in its Urban Setting**. Toronto, University of Toronto Press.

Ross, E. A., 1920, **Social Control**. New York, Macmillan.

Rowbotham, S., 1973, **Woman's Consciousness, Man's World**. Harmondsworth, Penguin.

Rowett, R. and Vaughn, P. J., 1981 'Women and Broadmoor' in Hutter and Williams (eds.), 1981, **Controlling Women**. London, Croom Helm.

Rowntree, B. S., 1901, **Poverty: A Study of Town Life**. London, Macmillan.

Rowntree, B. S., 1941 **Poverty and Progress: A Second Social Survey of York**. London, Longman.

Runnymede Trust and the Radical Statistics Group, 1980, **Britain's Black Population**. London, Heinemann.

Ruse, M., 1988, **Homosexuality**. Oxford, Blackwell.

Russon, S. A., 1984, 'Women and the law: The uses of images of femininity in the courts', Research Project, Department of Sociology, City of Birmingham Polytechnic.

Rutter, M., 1981, **Maternal Deprivation Reassessed** (second edition). Harmondsworth, Penguin.

Sanders, W. B., 1974, **The Sociologist as Detective: An Introduction to Research Methods**. New York, Praeger.

Sarbin, T. and Miller, J., 1970, 'Demonism re-visited: the XYY chromosome anomaly', **Issues in Criminology**, 5, pp. 195–207.

Sargent, L., ed., 1981, **Women and Revolution: The Unhappy Marriage of Marxism and Feminism**. London, Pluto Press.

Saunders, P., 1989, **Social Class and Stratification**. London, Routledge.

Sawyer, H. G., 1961, 'The meaning of numbers', Speech before the American Association of Advertising Agencies, cited in Webb *et al.*, 1966, **Unobtrusive Measures: Nonreactive Research in the Social Sciences**. Chicago, Rand McNally.

Sayers, J., Evans, M. and Redclift, N., eds., 1987, **Engels Revisited: New Feminist Essays**. London, Tavistock.

Schegloff, E. A., 1967. 'Identification and recognition in telephone conversation openings' in Psathas (ed.), 1979, **Everyday Language: Studies in Ethnomethodology**. Englewood Cliffs, N. J., Prentice Hall.

Schermerhorn, R., 1970, **Comparative Ethnic Relations**. New York, Random House.

Schlesinger, P., [1978] 1986, **Putting Reality Together: BBC News**. London, Constable.

Schlesinger, P., Murdock, G. and Elliott, P., 1983, **Televising Terrorism: Political Violence in Popular Culture**. London, Comedia.

Schramm, W. and Roberts, D. F., eds., 1971, **The Process and Effects of Mass Communication** (revised edition). Urbana, University of Illinois Press.

Schuman, H. and Converse, J. M., 1971, 'The effects of Black and White interviewers on Black responses, 1968', **Public Opinion Quarterly**, 35, pp. 44–68.

Scraton, P., Sim, J. and Skidmore, P., 1991, **Prisons Under Protest**. Buckingham, Open University Press.

Searle, C., 1987, 'Your daily dose: racism and the *Sun*', **Race and Class**, 29, no. 1. (Reprinted in Murray and Searle, 1989, **Racism and the Press in Thatcher's Britain**, Race and Class Pamphlet No. 12. Nottingham, Russell Press/Institute of Race Relations.)

Seccombe, W., 1974, 'The housewife and her labour under capitalism', **New Left Review**, 83.

Segal, L., ed., 1983, **What is To Be Done About the Family?** Harmondsworth, Penguin.

Segal, L., 1987, **Is the Future Female? Troubled Thoughts on Contemporary Feminism**. London, Virago.

Selvin, H. C., 1958, 'Durkheim's *Suicide* and Problems of Empirical Research', **American Journal of Sociology**, 63, pp. 607–13.

Shanley, F., 1966, 'The aggressive middle class delinquent', **Journal of Criminal Law, Criminology and Police Science**, 57, pp. 145–51.

Sharpe, S., 1984, **Double Identity : the lives of working mothers**. Harmondsworth, Penguin.

Sharrock, W. and Anderson, B., 1986, **The Ethnomethodologists**. Chichester and London, Ellis Horwood/Tavistock.

Shaw, C., 1930, **The Jack Roller**. Chicago, University of Chicago Press.

Shaw, C., 1931, **The Natural History of a Delinquent Career**. Chicago, University of Chicago Press.

Shaw, C. H. and McKay, H. D., 1931, **Social Factors in Juvenile Delinquency**. Washington, DC, National Commission on Law Observation and Enforcement.

Sherman, H. J. and Wood, J. L., 1982, **Sociology: Traditional and Radical Perspectives** (adapted for the United Kingdom by Peter Hamilton). London, Harper and Row.

Short, J. and Strodtbeck, F., 1967, **Group Processes and Gang Delinquency**. Chicago, University of Chicago Press.

Sibley, D., 1981, **Outsiders in Urban Societies**. Oxford, Blackwell.

Signorielli, N., 1984, 'The demography of the television world', in Melischeck, Rosengren and Stappers (eds.), 1984, **Cultural Indicators: An International Symposium**. Vienna, Austrian Academy of Sciences.

Silverman, H. J., ed., 1981, **Piaget, Philosophy and the Human Sciences**. Brighton, Harvester.

Sinfield, A., 1981, **What Unemployment Means**. Oxford, Martin Robertson.

Singer, E., 1971, 'Adult orientation of first and later children', **Sociometry**, 34, pp. 328–45.

Singleton, R. *et al.*, 1988, **Approaches to Social Research**. Oxford, Oxford University Press.

Sivanandan, A., 1982, **A Different Hunger: Writings on Black Resistance**. London, Pluto.

Slattery, M., 1986, **Official Statistics**. London, Tavistock.

Smart, C., 1977, **Women, Crime and Criminology**. London, Routledge and Kegan Paul.

Smart, C. and Smart, B., 1978, **Women, Sexuality and Social Control**. London, Routledge and Kegan Paul.

Smith, D., 1989, **North and South: Britain's Economic, Social and Political Divide**. Harmondsworth, Penguin.

Smith, M. W., 1975. **Strategies of Social Research: The Methodological Imagination**. Englewood Cliffs, N. J., Prentice-Hall.

Snead, J. A. and West, C., 1988, **Seeing Black: The Semiotics of Black Culture in America**. London, Macmillan.

Snedecor, G. W. and Cochran, W. G., 1989, **Statistical Methods** (eighth edition). Iowa State University Press.

Soothill, K. and Walby, S., 1991, **Sex Crime in the News**. London, Routledge.

Spender, D., 1980, **Man Made Language**. London, Routledge and Kegan Paul.

Spender, D., 1982, **Women of Ideas (and What Men Have Done to Them)**. London, Routledge and Kegan Paul.

Spender, D., 1984, **Time and Tide Wait for No Man**. London, Women's Press.

Spiro, M., 1965, **Children of the Kibbutz**. New York, Schocken.

Spradley, J. P., 1979, **The Ethnographic Interview**. New York, Holt, Rinehart and Winston.

Spradley, J. P., 1980, **Participant Observation**. New York, Holt, Rinehart and Winston.

Stacey, M., 1960, **Tradition and Change: A Study of Banbury**. Oxford, Oxford University Press.

Stacey, M. ed., 1976, **The Sociology of the NHS**, Sociological Review Monograph no. 22, University of Keele.

Stacey, M., Batstone, E., Bell, C. and Murcott, A., 1975, **Power, Persistence and Change: A Second Study of Banbury**. London, Routledge and Kegan Paul.

Stanley, L, and Wise, S., 1983, **Breaking Out: Feminist Consciousness and Feminist Research**. London, Routledge and Kegan Paul.

Stanworth, M., 1980, **Gender and Schooling: A Study of Sexual Divisions in the Classroom**. London, The Women's Research and Resources Centre.

Stern, J., 1981, 'Social mobility and the interpretation of social class mortality differences', **Journal of Social Policy**.

Stewart, D. W., 1984, **Secondary Research: Information Sources and Methods**. Beverly Hills, Sage.

Stopes-Roe, and Cochrane, 1985, 'As Others See Us', **New Society**, 1, November, 1985.

Stouffer, S. *et al.*, 1949, **The American Soldier**. (Four volumes). Princeton, Princeton University Press.

Strodtbeck, F. L., 1951, 'Husband-wife interaction over revealed differences', **American Sociological Review**, 16, pp. 468–73.

Strodtbeck, F. L., James, R. M. and Hawkins, C., 1957, 'Social status in jury deliberations', **American Sociological Review**, 22, pp. 713–19.

Suchar, C., 1978, **Social Deviance**. New York, Holt, Rinehart and Winston.

Suchman, E. A., 1967, **Evaluative Research: Principles and Practice in Public Service and Social Action Programs**. New York, Sage.

Sudman, S. and Bradburn, N. M., 1974, **Response Effects in Surveys: Review and Synthesis**. Chicago, Aldine.

Sudnow, D., 1967, **Passing On: The Social Organization of Dying**. Englewood Cliffs, Prentice-Hall.

Sulloway, F. J., 1980, **Freud, Biologist of the Mind**. Glasgow, Fontana.

Sutherland, E. H., 1937, **The Professional Thief**. Chicago, University of Chicago Press.

Sutherland, E. H., 1939, **Principles of Criminology**. Philadelphia, Lippincott.

Tabb, W. K., 1971, 'Race relations models and social change', **Social Problems**, 18, pp. 431–44.

Tan, A. S., 1979, 'TV Beauty Ads and Role Expectations of Adolescent Female Viewers', 56, **Journalism Quarterly**, pp. 283–8.

Taylor, D., 1990, 'Employment and unemployment statistics', paper for Radical Statistics Health Group, January 1990.

Taylor, I., 1983, **Law and Order: Arguments for Socialism**. London, Macmillan.

Taylor, I., Walton, P. and Young, J., 1973, **The New Criminology**. London, RKP.

Taylor, I., Walton, P. and Young, J., 1975, **Critical Criminology**. London, RKP.

Taylor, L., 1984, **In the Underworld**. Oxford, Blackwell.

Taylor, M. F., 1986, **ESRC Data Archive Catalogue**. Cambridge, Chadwyck-Healey.

Taylor, S., 1989, **Suicide**. London, Longman.

Terrence Higgins Trust, 1990, **HIV and AIDS: A Medical Briefing**. London, The Medical and Scientific Group of the Terrence Higgins Trust.

The National Lesbian and Gay Survey, 1992, **What a Lesbian Looks Like: Writings by Lesbians on their Lives and Lifestyles**. London, Routledge.

Thiam, A., [1978] 1986, **Black Sisters, Speak Out: Feminism and Oppression in Black Africa**. London, Pluto (originally published Paris, Editions Denoel).

Thomas, W. I. and Znaniecki, F., [1918–20] 1927, **The Polish Peasant in Europe and America** (second edition). New York: Alfred A Knoff (reprinted in 1958, New York, Dover).

Thomas, W. I., 1923, **The Unadjusted Girl: With Cases and Standpoint for Behavior Analysis**. Boston, Little Brown.

Thomas, W. I., 1966, **On Social Organization and Social Personality**. Chicago, University of Chicago Press.

Thompson, E. P., 1968, **The Making of the English Working Class**. Harmondsworth, Penguin.

Thompson, H., 1966, **Hell's Angels**. New York.

Thompson, K., 1986, **Beliefs and Ideologies**. London, Routledge.

Tichenor, P. J., Donohue, G. A. and Olien, C. N., 1970, 'Mass media flow and differential growth of knowledge', **Public Opinion Quarterly**, 34, pp. 159–70.

Tiger, L. and Fox, R., 1972, **The Imperial Animal**. London, Secker and Warburg.

Todd, K., Johal, I., Kane, A. and Barth, S., 1990, 'Homosexuality, AIDS and Clause 28', Birmingham Polytechnic, Sociology Research Workshop Project.

Toner, B., [1977] 1982, **The Facts of Rape**. London, Arrow Books.

Townsend, P. and Davidson, N., 1982, **Inequalities in Health: The Black Report**. Harmondsworth, Penguin.

Townsend, P., 1974, 'Poverty as relative deprivation', in Wedderburn (ed.), 1974, **Poverty, Inequality and Class Structure**, Cambridge, Cambridge University Press.

Townsend, P., 1979, **Poverty in the United Kingdom**. Harmondsworth, Penguin.

Townsend, P., 1984, **Why are the Many Poor?** Fabian Tract 500.

Townsend, P., 1991, **The Poor Are Poorer**. Bristol University, Department of Social Policy.

Townsend, P., Corrigan, P. and Kowarzik, U., 1987, **Poverty and Labour in London**. London, Low Pay Unit.

Trivedi, P, 1984, 'To deny our fullness: Asian women in the making of history', **Feminist Review**, 17, Autumn, pp. 46–8.

Trowler, P., 1988, **Investigating the Media**. London, Unwin Hyman.

Trowler, P., 1989, **Investigating Health, Welfare and Poverty**. London, Unwin Hyman.

Troyna, B., 1981, **Public Awareness of the Media: A Study of Reporting on Race**. London, Commission for Racial Equality.

Tuchman, G., 1973, 'Making news by doing work: routinizing the unexpected', **American Journal of Sociology**, 79, pp. 110–13.

Tuchman, G., 1978, 'The symbolic annihilation of women by the mass media' in Tuchman, Daniels and Benet (eds.), 1978, **Hearth and Home: Images of Women in the Mass Media**. New York, Oxford University Press.

Tuchman, G., Daniels, A. and Benet, J., eds., 1978, **Hearth and Home: Images of Women in the Mass Media**. New York, Oxford University Press.

Tumin, M. M., 1967, **Social Stratification: The Forms and Functions of Social Inequality**. Englewood-Cliffs, Prentice Hall.

Turner, B. S., 1983, **Religion and Social Theory: A Materialistic Perspective**. Atlantic Highlands, N.J., Humanities Press.

Turner, R., ed., 1974, **Ethnomethodology**. Harmondsworth, Penguin,

Twitchin, J., ed., [1988] 1990, **The Black and White Media Show**, Stoke-on-Trent, Trentham Books.

Unemployment Unit, 1989, **Creative Counting**. Unemployment Unit Publication UUB19.

Unemployment Unit, 1990, 'Table 1', **Working Brief**, March 1990.

United States Department of Health, Education and Welfare, 1976, **The Measure of Poverty**, A report to Congress as mandated by the Education Amendments of 1974.

Van Dijk, T. A., 1991, **Racism and the Press**. London, Routledge.

Vaus, D. de, 1986, **Surveys in Social Research**. London, Allen and Unwin.

Verwey, N. E., 1990, **Radio Call-ins and Covert Politics**. Aldershot, Avebury.

Vidich A.J., 1955, 'Participant observation and the collection and interpretation of data', **American Journal of Sociology**, 60, pp. 354–60.

Vogel, L., 1984, **Marxism and the Oppression of Women**. London, Pluto.

Voysey, M., 1975, **A Constant Burden**. London, Routledge and Kegan Paul.

Walby, S., Hay, A. and Soothill, K., 1983, 'The Social Construction of Rape', **Theory, Culture and Society**, 2, no. 1, p. 86.

Walker, A. and Walker, C., eds., 1987, **The Growing Divide: A Social Audit 1979–1987**. London, Child Poverty Action Group, No. 72.

Ward, D. and Kassebaum, G., 1966, **Women's Prison**. London.

Wartella, E., Whitney, D.C. and Windahl, S., eds., 1983, **Mass Communications Review Yearbook**, 4, Beverley Hills, Sage.

Webb, E. J., Campbell, D. T., Schwartz, R. D. and Sechrest, L., 1966, **Unobtrusive Measures: Nonreactive Research in the Social Sciences**. Chicago, Rand McNally.

Weber, M., [1904–5] 1976, **The Protestant Ethic and the Spirit of Capitalism**. London, Allen and Unwin.

Weber, M., [1920-1] 1963, **The Sociology of Religion**. Boston, Beacon.

Weber, M., 1947, **The Theory of Social and Economic Organisations**. New York, Oxford University Press.

Weber, M., 1969, **The Methodology of the Social Sciences**. New York, Free Press.

Wedderburn, D., ed., 1974, **Poverty, Inequality and Class Structure**. Cambridge, Cambridge University Press.

Weeks, J., 1981, **Sex, Politics and Society: The Regulation of Sex Since 1800**. London, Longman.

Weinberg, M. S., 1966, 'Becoming a nudist', **Psychiatry**, 24, February, pp. 15–24.

Weinberg, M. S., 1970, 'The nudist management of respectability' in Douglas, J. D. (ed.), 1970b, **Deviance and Respectability**, New York, Basic Books, chapter 12.

Weiner, G., 1985, **Just a Bunch of Girls**. Milton, Keynes, Open University Press.

Weis, L., 1985, **Between Two Worlds: Black Students in an Urban Community College**. Boston, Routledge and Kegan Paul.

Weisberg, D., ed., 1980, **Women and the Law**. New York.

Weiss, C., 1972, **Evaluation Research: Methods of Assessing Program Effectiveness**. Englewood Cliffs, N. J., Prentice-Hall.

Weitzman, L., 1974, **Sex Role Socialisation**. California: Mayfield Publishing Co.

Welsh, S., 1981, 'The manufacture of excitement in police–juvenile encounters', **British Journal of Criminology**, 21.

West, J., ed., 1982, **Work, Women and the Labour Market**. London, Routledge and Kegan Paul.

Westergaard, J. and Resler, H., 1976, **Class in a Capitalist Society**. Harmondsworth, Penguin.

Westwood, S., 1984, **All Day Every Day: Factory and Family in the Making of Women's Lives**. London, Pluto.

Westwood, S. and Bhachu, P., 1988, 'Images and Realities', **New Society**, 6th May.

Whale, J., 1977, **The Politics of the Media**. London, Fontana.

Whitehead, M., 1987, **The Health Divide: Inequalities in Health in the 1980s**. London, Health Education Council.

Whitelegg, E. *et al.*, 1982, **The Changing Experience of Women**. Oxford, Martin Robertson/Open University.

Whitten, N. W. and Szwed., J. F., eds., 1970, **Afro-American Anthropology**. New York, Free Press.

Whyte, W. F., 1943, **Street Corner Society**. Chicago, University of Chicago Press.

Whyte, W. F., ed., 1946, **Industry and Society**. New York, McGraw-Hill.

Whyte, W. F., 1948, **Human Relations in the Restaurant Industry**. New York, McGraw Hill.

Whyte, W. F., 1949, 'The Social Structure of the Restaurant', **American Journal of Sociology**, 54, pp. 302–10.

Whyte, W. F., 1955, **Street Corner Society** (revised edition with methodological appendix). Chicago, University of Chicago Press.

Wilkinson, R. G., 1991, 'Inequality is bad for your health', **Guardian**, 12th June 1991, p. 21.

Williams, J. A., 1964, 'Interviewer-respondent interaction: a study of bias in the information interview', **Sociometry**, 27, pp. 338–52.

Williams, J., Dunning, E. and Murphy, P., 1984, **Hooligans Abroad: The Behaviour and Control of English Fans in Continental Europe**. London, Routledge and Kegan Paul.

Williams, R., 1965, **The Long Revolution**. Harmondsworth, Penguin.

Williams, S. J., 1986, 'Appraising Goffman', **British Journal of Sociology**, 37, p. 348.

Williamson, J., 1978, **Decoding Advertisements**. London, Boyars.

Willis, P., 1977, **Learning to Labour**. Westmead, Saxon House.

Wilson, A 1978, **Finding a Voice: Asian Women in Britain**. London, Virago.

Wilson, A., 1985, **The Family**. London, Tavistock.

Wilson, B. R., 1966, **Religion in a Secular Society**. London, Watts.

Wilson, E. O., 1975, **Sociobiology**. Cambridge, Mass., Harvard University Press.

Wilson, H., 1980, 'Parental supervision: a neglected aspect of delinquency', **British Journal of Criminology**, 20.

Wimbush, E. and Talbot, M., eds., 1988, **Relative Freedoms: Women and Leisure**. Milton Keynes, Open University Press.

Winship, J., 1987, **Inside Women's Magazines**. London, Pandora.

Winter, R., 1987, **Action-Research and the Nature of Social Enquiry**. Aldershot, Avebury.

Women's Study Group Centre for Contemporary Cultural Studies, 1978, **Women Take Issue: Aspects of Women's Subordination**. London, Hutchinson.

Wood, R. C., 1991, **Working in Hotels and Catering**. London, Routledge.

Woods, P., 1986, **Inside Schools: Ethnography in Education Research**. London, Routledge and Kegan Paul.

Wright, J. D. and Rossi, P. H., 1986, **Armed and Considered Dangerous: A Survey of Felons and their Firearms**. Aldine de Gruyter.

Yin, R. K., 1984, **Case Study Research: Design and Methods**.

Yinger, M., 1981. 'Toward a theory of assimilation and dissimilation', **Ethnic and Racial Studies**, 4, no. 3.

Young, I., 1981, 'Beyond the unhappy marriage: a critique of the dual systems theory', in Sargent, L. (ed.), 1981, **Women and the Revolution**, London, Pluto, pp. 43–70.

Young, M., 1961, **The Rise of the Meritocracy**. Harmondsworth, Penguin.

Zanden, J. W. V., 1973, 'Sociological Studies of American Blacks', **Sociological Quarterly**, 14, pp. 32–52.

Zaretsky, E., 1976, **Capitalism, the Family and Personal Life**. London, Pluto.

Zola, I. K., 1966, 'Culture and symptoms – an analysis of patients' presenting complaints', **American Sociological Review**, 31, pp. 615–30.

Zorbaugh, H. W., 1929, **The Gold Coast and the Slum**. Chicago, University of Chicago Press.

The following are available from:
Lee Harvey, University of Central England in Birmingham, Perry Barr, Birmingham, B42 2SU, England.
Please allow 28 days for delivery.

DISK	Price* (inc p&p)	Quantity	Quantity x Price
DATA FILE AND SPSS PROGRAM			
The datafile in Appendix 1 is included on the disk in 2 versions: as a text file and as an SPSS system file. Also included is an SPSS 'include file' that will generate the statistics and tables with appropriate labels. (1 disk)			
PC Compatible 3.5 inch (high density: 1.44 mbyte)	£2		
PC Compatible 5.25 inch (low density: 320k)	£2		
Apple Mac disk (high density: 1.44 mbyte)	£2		
Apple Mac disk (low density: 800k)	£2		
DATA ANALYSIS RESOURCE PACK			
An explanation of various statistical analysis processes. It goes further than the material included in Chapter 4 and Appendix 2. It does attempt to keep mathematical formulae to a minimum and explains the principles in relatively simple language. For those using SPSS the explanation of the techniques is linked to the personal computer version. The pack is available in several formats. (1 disk)			
PC Compatible 3.5 inch (1.44 mbyte) WORDSTAR	£5		
PC Compatible 3.5 inch (1.44 mbyte) WORD	£5		
PC Compatible 3.5 inch (1.44 mbyte) FRAMEWORK	£5		
PC Compatible 3.5 inch (1.44 mbyte) WORDPERFECT	£5		
PC Compatible 5.25 inch (low density: 320k) WORDSTAR	£5		
PC Compatible 5.25 inch (low density: 320k) FRAMEWORK	£5		
Apple Mac disk (high density: 1.44 mbyte) MACWRITE	£5		
Apple Mac disk (high density: 1.44 mbyte) WORD	£5		
Apple Mac disk (low density: 800k) MACWRITE	£5		
Apple Mac disk (low density: 800k) WORD	£5		
DEFINITIONS			
A hypertext data base of definitions of sociological concepts. It is like an electronic dictionary. All terms defined in the dictionary are cross-referenced and you can jump from one concept to another by clicking the mouse. (2 high density : 1.44 mbyte disks)			
Only available on HyperCard for the Apple Mac (Future versions for the PC may become available)	£9		
*All prices may vary after 31 December 1993		Total	£

INDEX

Numbers in **bold** type refer to pages where concepts are explained in boxes